ANGUS CAMPBELL

PHILIP E. CONVERSE

WARREN E. MILLER

DONALD E. STOKES

Survey Research Center, University of Michigan

The University of Chicago Press
Chicago and London

THE AMERICAN VOTER

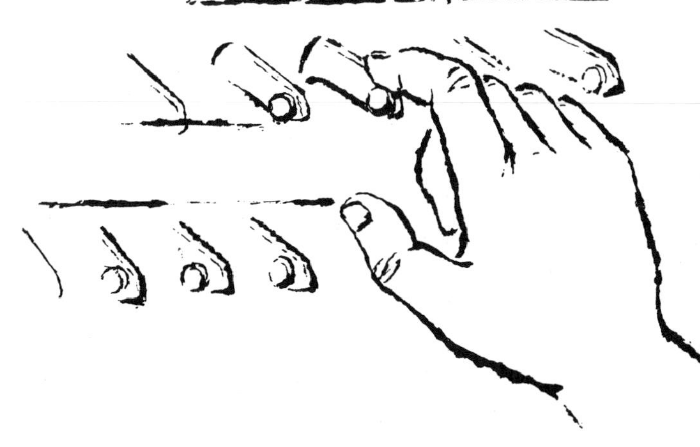

The University of Chicago Press, Chicago 60637
The University of Chicago Press, Ltd., London

University of Chicago Press edition 1976.
Midway Reprint 1980
Printed in the United States of America

ISBN: 0-226-09254-2
LCN: 76-21115

Contents

INTRODUCTORY ◇ SECTION I

Setting ◇ 1

In the contemporary world the activity of voting is rivaled only by the market as a means of reaching collective decisions from individual choices. Voting is used by parliaments and bridge clubs, by courts, consistories, and leagues of nations, and, most remarkably, it has provided the modern state with a way of connecting the actions of government with the preferences of a mass citizenry. The casting of votes as a means of decision is a practice of extraordinarily wide currency in human society, and this type of action has been of growing interest in the study of the social life of men.

Indeed, anyone who reads the literature of voting research must be impressed by its proliferation in recent years. The report of one major study lists 209 hypotheses about voting in political elections, which recent work has tended to confirm.[1] Moreover, voting has come to be of interest to widely different fields. Election studies have not by any means been pre-empted by the political scientist. The act of voting has served as a datum of great interest for the sociologist and for the social and clinical psychologist as well, and the content of voting research reflects their varied theoretical preoccupations.

Those who would add to the literature of voting have a responsibility to place their work in a broader setting. Three ways of locating our work seem to us particularly important. First, the voting behavior of a mass electorate can be seen within the context of a larger political system. The electoral process is a means of decision

[1] Bernard R. Berelson, Paul F. Lazarsfeld, and William N. McPhee, *Voting* (University of Chicago Press, Chicago, 1954, pp. 327–347). The propositions given in this work are culled only from the reports of "panel" studies utilizing the techniques of the sample survey.

that lies within a broader political order, and in research on voting it is valuable to have explicitly in view the wider political system in which the electoral process is found. Second, the empirical materials of our own work lie within a particular historical setting. The work reported here has extended through more than eight years; yet the fact that it deals with a specific historical era affects in countless ways the theoretical problems we have selected for treatment and the character of our empirical results. These effects may be better understood if certain characteristics of this historical period are kept before us. Third, this research lies within a sequence of studies on voting. Both in its methods and in its substantive concerns it has depended heavily on prior research, and an account of the development of voting research may suggest a good deal about the nature of our own studies.

Voting and the Political System

Voting behavior has been of interest to so many of the social sciences that the political importance of what is studied is sometimes lost from view. Electoral activity has been probed for what it reveals about such widely separated matters as the conditions of attitude change, the nature of group identifications, the role of personality characteristics, the effects of the mass communications media, and the ecological structure of our cities. We have no quarrel with the idea of using voting data to study any of these topics; several of them will be explored in considerable detail in later chapters. But the varied theoretical concerns of investigators of voting ought not to obscure the fact that in the modern state the electoral process is of greatest interest because of its importance in the wider political system. However much voting may tell about the psychology and sociology of human choice, it is important because of the importance of the decisions to which it leads. Electoral behavior would not have attracted the attention that it has, were it not that the collective vote decision is of great significance in many political systems. Therefore, this study of voting is also concerned with a fundamental process of political decision, and we begin by emphasizing this fact.

It would be difficult to overstate the significance of popular elections for democratic theory and practice. If politics has to do with "who gets what, when, and how," the free, competitive election has proven an essential means of insuring that the current solution of this problem enjoys the broad consent of the governed. A regime in which leaders are subject to regularized and effective control by non-leaders has been possible in the modern world only when power is granted to some and withheld from others in periodic electoral contests. No democratic state has ever been governed by direct democracy. But popular election combined with representation has greatly expanded the distribution of political power, and it has offered a creative solution to the age-old problem of transferring authority without violence.

The importance of elections in democratic government may be elaborated in terms of decision making. Conceived in these terms, the political system can be idealized as a collection of processes for the taking of decisions. We often speak of the legislative process, the judicial process, the electoral process, and so forth. Each of these processes involves a group of actors, one or more decision rules, which have at least an indirect legal or constitutional basis, and a set of effective influences to which the actors respond in reaching a decision. No one of these decision processes is independent of the rest, and some of the most interesting problems of empirical analysis in politics are posed by the interrelation of the several decision points of the political system. Decisions of the electoral process have important effects on decisions taken elsewhere in the system. What the electorate decides may determine which actors will have the power of decision, and the outcomes of past and future elections generate important influences to which these actors respond. The holders of elective or appointive office in democratic government are guided in many of their actions by a calculus of electoral effect.

The decision of who shall control the executive power of the state is of great importance in every political system. Certainly few decisions in American government rival in importance the choice of a President. In vesting the power to make this choice in a mass electorate, the American system follows a practice that is fairly rare among nations even today; and in this respect the electoral process assumes a wider importance in American government than it does in many other political systems. This question is not really one of whether the constitutional order is parliamentary or presidential. In many parliamentary nations control of the executive *is* determined, if only indirectly, by a mass electorate. It is more a question of whether the will of the electorate is manipulated or abrogated by coercive power and whether the party system presents the electorate with an effective choice. Of course, the doctrine of virtually every nation of the modern world supposes that control of the executive depends at least indirectly on popular consent. But doctrine and practice can be widely different, and examples are plentiful enough of political systems in which the electorate is deprived of an authentic choice.[2]

Although our study of voting is prompted in part by a sense of the impact of popular elections elsewhere in government, our research has focused on the electoral process itself and has not explored the relation of this process to the other decision processes of the political system. We begin with the choice of a President and look backward to the configuration of causal influences that have produced this decision rather than forward to its impact in other arenas of the political system. The theoretical scheme set forth in Chapter 2 takes the act of voting as the datum to be explained, and this assumption underlies most of the discussion in later chapters. Yet we confess to a lively interest in the place of the electoral process in the wider political system. And this interest will lead us in a final chapter to reopen the question of how decision making by the American electorate, as we have observed it, affects the process of government elsewhere in the system.

Viewing the electoral process as part of a wider political order leads to an interest not only in the effects of elections on other parts of the system but also in the effects on the electoral process of what happens elsewhere in government. The consequences of decisions taken by the President and the executive agencies, by the Congress, by the courts, and by other actors of the national government are an important part of the full set of influences to which the electorate responds in reaching its own decision. Popular attitudes on issues of public policy ought not to be treated, as they sometimes are, simply as reflections of personality factors, or group memberships, or fixed partisan loyalties. These attitudes should be studied for what they show about public response to actions taken at the decision points of government. Their causal antecedents do not lie wholly within the individual voter's psyche or within his primary group associations. They are influenced to an immense degree by the external realities of national politics and, as such, are factors that tie the electoral process to the other decision processes of American government.

In placing the subject of our work within the context of a larger

[2] Some writers, following Schumpeter, have made the free, competitive election the essential characteristic of a democratic system. For an elaboration of this view see Morris Janowitz and Dwaine Marvick, *Competitive Pressure and Democratic Consent* (*Michigan Governmental Studies No. 32,* Bureau of Government, Institute of Public Administration, The University of Michigan, Ann Arbor, Mich., 1956), especially the "criteria for competitive democracy," pp. 1–10.

political system we should be clear about two ways in which this research is restricted. First, this book is about voting behavior only as it occurs in the United States. Parallel studies in different nations might be useful in learning much more about the role of variables in the nature of the political system itself, variables which must be taken as constants when voting behavior within a single system is examined. An obvious factor of this sort is the number of major political parties that compete in the electoral process. American voting behavior is influenced in a variety of ways by the fact that it is set in a two-party system, and research within this system cannot finally establish what differences would be found if the number of major parties were greater or less than two. On occasion we shall encounter findings that provoke speculation in this comparative vein. But systematic comparison falls beyond the scope of the work reported here.

It should be clear, too, that this is a study of voting in presidential elections. Because the choice of a President has been the most important decision issuing from the electoral process, it is natural that the presidential election should attract wider interest than any other. But in focusing on this decision we do not disparage the importance of other types of elections, and neither do we imply that voting behavior in presidential elections and other national elections is essentially the same. In some respects it is, and many of the findings set forth here can be generalized to non-presidential elections. But in other respects the choice of a President differs a good deal from other decisions of the electoral process. If, for example, we compare the presidential election with the mid-term congressional election, it is plain that more of the potential electorate joins in the choice of a President than in the selection of a Congress when a President is not chosen. And there is evidence that the motivation of those who participate in both choices may differ in the two campaigns. In the presidential election the individual voter is likely to have a better-developed image of the political actors he is asked to appraise. This is particularly true of his image of the candidates themselves; perceptions of the candidates play a measurably greater role in presidential elections than they do in elections for Congress in a non-presidential year.

It is of course true that each presidential election has imbedded within it a congressional election and a host of state and local contests. As a result, a study of voting behavior in presidential elections is inescapably a study of voting in a variety of other electoral contests as well. But the choice of a President has sufficient impact on these lesser contests so that what we learn about them in a presidential year ought to be extended to other years only with caution.

The Historical Context

Our primary aim in this research is to understand the voting decisions of the national electorate in a manner that transcends some of the specific elements of historical circumstance. But anyone who works with extensive data on a social process as important as a presidential election must feel a responsibility to provide some historical description. Accordingly, much of this volume serves a descriptive as well as a theoretical purpose. We have not felt any tension between these objectives. To the contrary, one of the primary uses of theory is to improve the quality of description. In somewhat severe language, theory may be characterized as a generalized statement of the interrelationships of a set of variables. In these terms, historical description may be said to be a statement of the values assumed by these variables through time. Both characterizations leave a good deal more to be said, but they emphasize the interplay of theory and description. All too often facts are selected for descriptive reporting on an *ad hoc* and impressionistic basis. An important function of systematic theory is that it can identify variables whose values should be reported in describing some aspect of the world of experience. If a theory is accompanied by methods for connecting it to observed data, as any successful theory must be, the theory may guide the descriptive reporter to observations he would not otherwise have made.

The contribution of theory to description may be illustrated by several examples. The first comes from our findings about the political impact of identification with social class. The relationship of class identification to political attitudes and behavior is treated in our work not as a constant but as a variable that will change through time in response to changes in certain other political, social, and economic variables. As a result, we have observed this relationship not simply to show that class identifications and partisan preferences are in fact associated but rather to establish how strongly they are associated at several points in time. The variation we have found in the strength of this association is at once an important datum in the testing of hypotheses and a fact of considerable interest in the description of the presidential politics of this historical period.

A second illustration is from our theory of the psychological determinants of voting preference. Our hypothesis is that the partisan choice the individual voter makes depends in an immediate sense on the strength and direction of the elements comprising a field of psychological forces, where these elements are interpreted as attitudes toward the perceived objects of national politics. Measurements of the direction and intensity of these attitudes can be used to account for the behavior of most voters and hence to confirm our theoretical hypothesis. But these measurements may also be used to describe the set of forces that has led to a particular electoral result. The contribution of various popular attitudes to the fortunes of parties and candidates has been of very general interest to historians and journalists in their descriptive commentaries on the electoral process. By using our theory and the observations it implies we are able to describe with much greater confidence the influence of these factors on a given election outcome.

A further example is provided by adding to our theory that behavior is a resultant of psychological forces our conception of identification with party as a factor that is normally antecedent to these forces, yet susceptible at times to change by them. From this enlarged theory we have developed a descriptive classification of national elections by distinguishing among contests in which the electorate's perceptions of politics generally agree with its party loyalties, contests in which its perceptions conflict with its party loyalties without changing them, and contests in which the conflict is strong enough to produce a lasting change of party loyalties.

If theory can guide historical descriptions, the historical context of most research on human behavior places clear limitations on the development of theory. In evolving and testing his theoretical hypotheses the social scientist usually must depend on what he is permitted to observe by the progress of history. The experimental scientist often escapes this problem, at least in verifying his theoretical statements, by manipulating the variables of his theory. But the variables of large-scale social processes can rarely be manipulated in research, and the historical reality with which the social scientist must deal typically yields data that are inadequate for developing and testing a fully elaborated theory. Their inadequacy has to do partly with the problem of controlling correlated factors: when he examines the relation of two or more variables a social scientist is seldom able to remove by experimental or statistical devices the effects of all additional factors that may influence the variables of immediate interest. But the inadequacy of "natural" data has to do also with what might be called the problem of limited variation. If we return to the idea that theory consists of statements of the interrelationships of variables, it is evident that variables of great importance in human affairs may exhibit little or no change in a given historical period. As a result, the investigator whose work falls in this period may not see the significance of these variables and may fail to incorporate them in his theoretical statements. And even if he does perceive their importance, the absence of variation will prevent a proper test of hypotheses that state the relation of these factors to other variables of his theory.

The data of our research have been collected in three presidential elections, primarily by interviews with people selected by probability sampling to represent the national electorate. This collection of data spans the period from 1948 to 1956, although our interviews are much less full for the Truman-Dewey campaign than for the two Eisenhower-Stevenson elections. Of course, people are able to recall more or less accurately what they have done in the past, and this allows us to extend the historical interval to which some of our data apply. In particular, recollections of past voting behavior and even of previous identifications with the parties can lead to suggestive findings. But the capacity for accurate recall is certainly limited, and most of what we want to know about prior attitudes and behavior is simply impossible to reconstruct. In the main our data have to do with the historical interval extending from Truman's surprise victory in 1948 to the re-election of Eisenhower in 1956.

How great was the political change of these years? It seems clear that some change in the political climate occurred between the election of 1948 and that of 1952. The campaign of Harry Truman and Thomas E. Dewey belonged in many ways to the era of the New Deal. The parties chose as their candidates in 1948 the man who had been Franklin Roosevelt's running mate and who succeeded to the presidency at Roosevelt's death and the man Roosevelt had defeated in his last election campaign. The political alignments of the prewar era had remained remarkably undisturbed through the Second World War, and with the end of the war attention shifted rapidly to the circle of domestic concerns that had absorbed the nation's interest prior to the war. Undoubtedly the salience of these issues was increased by widespread industrial strife, accenting as it did the dimensions of economic interest and social class. The content of differences between the Democratic President and the Republican Congress was strongly reminiscent of issues that had divided the nation in the Roosevelt years.

It is true that the end of the war did not bring peace, and the growing tensions of the conflict with the Soviet Union prevented the nation from insulating itself from the world in the manner of a generation before. In the late 1940's the Republican Party sought to arouse public feeling about the deterioration of America's position abroad, particularly in the Far East, but it was not until the outbreak of the Korean War that the international conflict generated political effects of great importance at home. America's involvement in this unusual war, with its overtones of defeat and slight prospects of victory, created a mood of criticism toward the leadership of the Democratic Administration. In this climate a narrow segment of the population accepted the extreme accusations of the McCarthy era, and a much wider public came to view the Democratic leadership as unable to cope effectively with our problems abroad. With war in the Far East and with evidence of corruption in certain offices of the executive branch in Washington, the feeling grew that the Democratic administration deserved to be turned out of office.

The Eisenhower candidacy in 1952 seemed perfectly calculated to exploit the dissatisfactions of war and domestic corruption. Eisenhower brought hope of a solution in the Far East and of a change in Washington, and to these appeals he added his great personal popularity. In 1952 Stevenson, too, was perceived as a candidate of attractive personal qualities, and his connection with the sins of his party was thought to be slight. Yet he could hardly have been expected to leave as great an imprint on the public consciousness as did his opponent. The years from 1952 to 1956 apparently secured still further the bases of Eisenhower's electoral strength. The end of the Korean War enhanced his image as a military statesman who could assure peace. Public response to his personal qualities remained exceptionally favorable. And the force of Democratic appeals was reduced by the economic prosperity of Eisenhower's first term and the failure of his administration to disturb the basic social reforms of the New Deal.

The Eisenhower victory of 1952 extended even into the South and seemed to mark the end of an era. Yet it would be easy to overstate the extent of political change in the preceding four years. The events of these years had not swept away the appeal of the Democratic Party as the agent of economic recovery and social reform. In the election of 1952 the party's strength registered clearly in the size of its congressional vote. The Democrats restored their majorities in both houses of Congress in 1954 and two years later held this control under the pressure of Eisenhower's increased electoral majority. In the three presidential elections within the span of our research the Republican proportion of the total vote has varied by more than twelve percentage points. Yet the Republican proportion of the congressional vote in these same elections has not varied by as much as four percentage points. If the congressional vote reflects more faithfully the stable partisan loyalties of the electorate, the aggregate statistics of the period suggest that these loyalties have shifted relatively little.[3]

Despite the turnover of party control it seems likely that the stabilities of the years from 1948 to 1956 were more important than the aspects of change. Perhaps there were within this period the seeds of profound political change; we can only guess the full impact on American politics of the Supreme Court's decision in 1954 striking down segregation in the public schools. Yet we have not found in this interval what we take to be the mark of fundamental electoral change—an asymmetric shift of long-term partisan commitments by substantial numbers of people who have passed the years of early adulthood in which these allegiances usually become fixed. Though the data supporting this conclusion are reserved for a later chapter, the finding is worth mentioning here since it states an important descriptive characteristic of the period under review and since it suggests a limitation that the historical context has imposed on our research. Because these stable party attachments are of far-reaching importance in the orientation of political attitudes and behavior, voting research must seek to state the conditions under which they will change. But identifications with party have shown little variation in the historical period of our work. Neither war, nor economic distress, nor the appeal of a compelling leader has disturbed the partisan allegiance of a wide segment of the electorate. As a result, our understanding of change must remain incomplete.

The Course of Voting Research

Despite the universal interest of popular elections, systematic research on voting has appeared only in the past thirty or forty years as part of a more general movement toward empirical research in social science. To be sure, political historians and journalists have long scrutinized electoral behavior, and they have set down their thoughts about the forces influencing our national elections. But popular and historical literature on elections is often tendentious, and its conclusions frequently rest on anecdotal material or on impressionistic judgments about the circumstances that have produced gross variations in party strength between regions or states. Since presidential electors are chosen in the states and since the unit rule awards all of a state's

[3] For an evaluation of this premise in terms of survey data see Chapter 6, Table 6–1, and discussion on page 127.

electors to a single party, it has been especially tempting to "explain" the election of a President by decomposing his vote into its state components. Thus, we are told that Mr. Truman won the election of 1948 because he balanced his losses among the states carried by Roosevelt in 1944 with compensating gains among the states of the Midwest; and that Charles Evans Hughes lost the election of 1916 because he failed to carry California (and, we may observe, each of the other states or combinations of states whose electoral votes would have permitted him to defeat Woodrow Wilson).

From an examination of the vote by regions or states it is a short step to a more detailed inspection of the vote by counties, wards, or precincts. Interpretations of electoral behavior rely more and more heavily on election statistics published for divisions of this sort. The fact that voting is one of the more elaborately recorded activities in modern states has meant that an enormous body of data is supplied the investigator at public expense, and this invitation for refined analysis of voting patterns is eagerly received. In any election a set of counties, wards, or precincts will vary in the proportion of adults who vote and in the division of votes between the parties. When these variations are related to what is known about the people living within these same units, a great deal can be learned about the factors governing individual voting behavior. The worlds of scholarship and journalism have produced people who are highly skilled at this type of analysis, and they have made important contributions to what is known about political behavior.[4]

Valuable as this sort of analysis may be, it has severe disabilities. Voting choice is an act of individual human beings, and the collective decisions of a state or national electorate are formed from the choices of a great many individual people. Therefore, to unravel the decision fully it is essential that we have information about individual persons. This is obviously true if we try to assess the relation to voting choice of certain psychological and attitudinal factors. But it may also be true if we try to gage the relation to voting behavior of sociological factors that have frequently been used in the analysis of aggregate election statistics. In some cases it may not be misleading to make

[4] Published work utilizing voting statistics is not easily summarized because of the variety of its empirical interests and the relative absence of theory. Two surveys especially deserve mention: Samuel J. Eldersveld, "Theory and Method in Voting Behavior Research" (*Journal of Politics,* 13, 1951, pp. 70–87); and Seymour M. Lipset, Paul F. Lazarsfeld, Allen H. Barton, and Juan Linz, "The Psychology of Voting: An Analysis of Political Behavior" (in Gardner Lindsey, ed. *Handbook of Social Psychology,* II, Addison-Wesley Publishing Co., Cambridge, Mass., 1954, pp. 1124–1175).

inferences about individual behavior from what is known about the behavior of aggregate sets of people. But in other cases aggregate data that seem to show a good deal about the behavior of individuals will actually be ambiguous.[5]

These limitations of method tended to govern the direction in which inquiry developed. For students of aggregate voting statistics, conceptualization was restricted to the narrow range of variables available for the political units whose votes were analyzed. These variables were drawn, by and large, from census materials; they were confined to the content traditionally analyzed by the sociologist, such as race, economic status, urbanization, and ethnic background. The intentions that lay behind the vote were inaccessible; and with the exception of knowledge about previous voting patterns in the observed units, there was little of the directly political involved. Thinking was consequently forced into distinctive channels, and sociological accounts of voting behavior became prominent.

More recently social science has moved to overcome the difficulties of aggregate analysis by developing methods to yield information about individual people. Individual data about electoral behavior first began to be supplied on a large scale during the 1930's as a byproduct of the work of commercial polling agencies.[6] At last it was possible to associate a specific vote with a set of known personal characteristics, and detailed descriptions of the social composition of the national vote became available. Nevertheless, conclusions based on the efforts of these agencies tended to remain entirely sociological. In sampling public opinion the commercial pollsters typically selected their respondents by filling the quotas for groups defined by such characteristics as sex, race, and socio-economic status. As a result, when they came to predict an election outcome it was natural that they examine the voting intentions of people falling in their several quota categories and report the first careful account of the political preferences of various social groupings.

The true power of the interview survey as a tool of voting research was first demonstrated, however, not by the commercial polling agencies but by Lazarsfeld, Berelson, and Gaudet in their study of Erie County, Ohio, during the presidential election campaign of 1940.

[5] An excellent discussion of this problem appears in W. S. Robinson, "Ecological Correlations and the Behavior of Individuals" (*American Sociological Review*, XV, June, 1950, 351–357).

[6] There had, of course, been notable precursors, such as Charles E. Merriam and Harold F. Gosnell, *Non-Voting, Causes and Methods of Control* (University of Chicago Press, Chicago, 1924).

Much of the method and many of the substantive concerns of contemporary voting research first appeared in this study and in its sequel in Elmira, New York, during the campaign of 1948.[7] The 1940 study reflected the authors' belief that electoral choice could not be adequately described unless attitudes and voting intentions could be followed through the course of the campaign. Accordingly, repeated interviews were taken with a "panel" of respondents, and the analysis placed a heavy accent on the effects of the mass media, small group associates, and other stimuli on the individual during the campaign.

As a second major focus, the study examined the partisan preferences of various groupings in Erie County with particular attention to the reinforcement effect or "cross-pressures" implied by multiple memberships in groupings whose political allegiances were like or unlike. In many respects the Elmira study in 1948 continued the methods and the theoretical concerns of the 1940 research, yet it touched a wide range of additional topics. There is in the latter study a much more extended treatment of the role of interpersonal influence in unifying political opinion within the primary groups defined by the social structure of the local community. Considerable attention is given to the natural history of political issues and to their life during the campaign as elements within the individual's cognitive image of politics. And an effort is made to exploit the setting of the study in a single community by recording information about social organization and political activity within Elmira.

In one important respect the research in Erie County and Elmira is only a partial account of the behavior of the American voter. Each of these studies has examined voting behavior within a single community. The first *nationwide* study to utilize the sample survey interview-reinterview design was conducted by the National Opinion Research Center in the presidential election of 1944.[8] This study was prompted at least in part by the desire to extend beyond the bounds of a single community some of the generalizations suggested by the study of Erie

[7] The Erie County study is reported in Paul F. Lazarsfeld, Bernard R. Berelson, and Hazel Gaudet, *The People's Choice* (Duell, Sloan and Pearce, New York, 1944). The major report of the Elmira study is Bernard R. Berelson, Paul F. Lazarsfeld, and William N. McPhee, *op. cit.,* although a number of articles have drawn on the same materials.

[8] No report of this study has been published, but two manuscripts have drawn on its data: Sheldon J. Korchin, *Psychological Variables in the Behavior of Voters* (unpublished doctoral dissertation, Harvard University, 1946) and Ruth Ziff, *The Effect of the Last Three Weeks of a Presidential Campaign on the Electorate* (unpublished master's thesis, Columbia University, 1948).

County. In 1948 the Survey Research Center of the University of Michigan conducted a small interview-reinterview study with a sample drawn by probability methods to represent the national population. The scope of this study was limited; it grew largely out of a desire to utilize more fully a set of interviews the Center had taken prior to the election—interviews which promised to help explain Mr. Truman's surprise victory.[9] The materials of the study were useful in describing the timing of the electorate's decision, selected opinions on public issues, and the social composition of the vote. But these materials are also the earliest data of the program of research that has followed at the Survey Research Center; as such, they have been valuable in the establishment of a first set of measurements for the analysis of subsequent trends.

The Survey Research Center undertook a more extensive study of the Eisenhower-Stevenson election of 1952, and the interviews taken in that year comprise one major portion of the data of our research.[10] The project represented a shift in emphasis from explanation in sociological terms to the exploration of political attitudes that orient the individual voter's behavior in an immediate sense. Intensive use of unstructured questions permitted the respondent to unburden himself of the political concerns that were uppermost in his mind as Election Day approached. At a descriptive level, these materials revealed each citizen's cognitive map of the political scene as the campaigns were drawing to a close. Analytically, it was feasible to organize these spontaneous reactions into a system of attitudinal variables measuring the net partisan direction of the voter's political reactions. Taken as a system, these variables were seen to constitute a field of forces operating on the individual as he deliberates over his vote decision. Some of these forces, such as the personal attraction of a Republican candidate, might pull him toward a Republican vote, whereas resentment of the outcome of Democratic foreign policy would act in the same direction by pushing him away from a Democratic vote. On the other hand, long-standing loyalty to the Democratic party and a suspicion of Republican domestic policies would serve as pressures in the opposing direction. By measuring these forces and

[9] This study is reported in Angus Campbell and Robert L. Kahn, *The People Elect a President* (University of Michigan, Ann Arbor, Mich., Survey Research Center Series #9, 1952). Certain of its data are also utilized in Frederick Mosteller *et al., The Pre-Election Polls of 1948* (Social Science Research Council, New York, 1949).

[10] The primary report of this study is Angus Campbell, Gerald Gurin, and Warren E. Miller, *The Voter Decides* (Row, Peterson and Co., Evanston, Ill., 1954).

calculating the resultant, it was possible to arrive at an excellent prediction of the individual's vote.

This approach differed sharply from earlier sociological explanations and was intended to remedy some of the weaker aspects of these explanations. For example, the distribution of social characteristics in a population varies but slowly over a period of time. Yet crucial fluctuations in the national vote occur from election to election. Such fluctuation cannot be accounted for by independent variables which, over brief spans of time, do not vary. The attitudinal approach directed more attention to political objects of orientation, such as the candidates and issues, which do shift in the short term. It seemed clear that the key to the finer dynamics of political behavior lay in the reactions of the electorate to these changes in the political scene.

The collection of data from a third sample of the national population was undertaken by the Survey Research Center in the election of 1956. To take advantage of the possibilities of assessing change, the information gathered in 1956 follows fairly closely the data of 1952. But the strategic priorities of research have shifted a good deal. The 1952 study selected for emphasis a single class of factors that were of considerable theoretical interest and that had been neglected in prior research. The choice of these factors was not intended to disparage the importance of other variables. To the contrary, it was well understood that clarifying the relation of psychological influences to factors whose causal connection with behavior is less immediate would be a major task of future work. It is to this task, as much as any other, that this book is addressed.

Theoretical Orientation ◇ 2

From initial efforts to understand voting behavior two major currents of thought have emerged, one primarily sociological, the other more psychological in emphasis. Much work on political behavior does not, of course, hew clearly to either of these approaches. But the most intensive research efforts have tended to contribute primarily to one stream or the other. If we seek bases for a theory of political behavior at the level of the mass electorate, we find in these alternatives the most coherent beginnings.

It has been unsatisfactory, however, to leave these two approaches as independent and competing bodies of theory. They are addressed to the same reality, and conflict between them is hardly a matter of contradictory findings. Rather, they are attacking the problem at different levels, and consequently in different languages. Each approach has had its characteristic strengths and shortcomings. To the degree that these strengths are complementary, the advantages of each should be preserved in a broader framework of theory.

The construction of such a framework would solve several problems that have harassed empirical work in the social sciences. When a field of investigation is opened, small exploratory studies turn up isolated relationships between assorted variables in the area of inquiry. These relationships have a good deal of intrinsic interest and cast a welcome light upon some corner of the phenomenon being observed. Yet as such studies multiply, the flow of unrelated findings becomes more confusing than enlightening. The conceptual tools of analysis are so varied that they defy any simple ordering by the interested reader. Increasingly, the sense of the coherent accumulation of knowledge, which the empirical approach originally seemed to hold in store, is lost.

As improved methods permit a drastic expansion of hypothesis testing, pressure increases toward construction of a framework into which findings from a variety of sources may be placed. In the earliest phase of empirical effort, a concept may come into use as much because of its amenability to measurement as its relevance to the problem at hand. Theoretical contributions are small and piecemeal. But as empirical access broadens, the question becomes less what *can* be measured than what is *most strategic* to measure. A new criterion of the value of a concept may be applied: how well does it fit into a broader theoretical orientation?

The first responses to these pressures may create as many problems as they solve. A superficial approach to the consolidation of theory typically involves the restriction of explanation to one concept or a narrow set of concepts. Such "simple and sovereign" theories create "order" by simple elimination. It is true that the scientific method recommends parsimony, but this principle is most ambiguous and is subject to misuse. It is properly applied in the arbitration of conflicting interpretations, where direct test is not possible and where the opposing views require differing amounts of inference to link one datum to another. It is not intended to justify oversimplified explanations of patently complex phenomena.

If we are interested in voting behavior, it is likely that we wish to account for variation in at least two classes of events. We want to predict whether a given individual is going to vote, and which candidate he will choose. Although these are pleasantly simple dependent variables, it is clear that they represent extremely complex behavior; no single-factor theory is likely to tell us much about them. A multitude of determinants converges to produce the final behavior. A framework ample for a full-scale systematic theory must therefore be a broad one. The outlines of its structure should follow from the functions we expect systematic theory to play in the development of our knowledge.

The Functions of Theory

***Understanding* versus *prediction*.** We are concerned with prediction *per se* only as it serves to test our understanding of the sequence of events leading to the dependent behavior. It is important to recognize the demand that the goal of understanding places upon the investigator. Prediction alone simply leads one to amass factors that have been found to relate to the dependent event. For instance, insurance companies want to predict the probability of automobile accidents under varying circumstances. If someone were to discover that the length of a driver's fingers is related to the probability of accident, such a factor would be thrown into the predictive equation whether there was any *understanding* of how finger length changed accident propensity. The fact that its inclusion permitted more accurate calculation of rates would be sufficient reason for its use.

We may be able to predict accurately in the face of relatively little understanding; or again, we may understand a great deal but have only a limited capacity for prediction. In the first instance after a time our predictions may suddenly go astray, and we will be thrown back to where we started. Suppose that short fingers led to accidents because the diameter of the steering wheel was too large for ready control. Suppose further that aesthetic considerations led the manufacturers to reduce this diameter. If we had understood the original relationship, steering wheel specifications would have been coupled with finger length in our predictive theory, so that when such specification changes occurred the theory would suffer no change in predictive capacity. But if no effort has been expended to understand the circumstances intervening between short fingers and accidents, we would be likely, upon finding that finger length no longer improved our computations, to throw it out and search for replacements. Failure to arrive at an understanding of the significance of relationships makes us overlook conceptually relevant conditions that govern them.

On the other hand, we may understand thoroughly a full system of "relevant conditions" and yet be greatly limited in our predictions if this system is subject to constant intrusion of "exogenous factors." For example, the sudden illness of a presidential candidate in October could wreak havoc on the most elegant of predictive models. Of course the theorist must strive to understand the chain of events that will be touched off within the system whenever such an exogenous factor intrudes upon it. But he is not expected to include in his system the biochemical conditions that may govern the health of the candidates.

Understanding is forced to range more widely than is prediction. At the level of prediction, once we have found a variable that forecasts our chosen event, we rest content. To find another, which in turn predicts the event, or which intervenes between it and the dependent event, is superfluous. Yet for the purpose of understanding, such additional factors are invaluable, although they do not improve our prediction of the final event materially. They do enhance our grasp of the total situation and the full range of conditions that operate within it.

The problem of causality. In the first stages of inquiry, we may be satisfied with the fact of relationship, without knowing whether one term of the relationship is cause or effect, or without knowing that both are not produced by some third factor. In the ultimate phase of inquiry in certain types of subject matter, such as the physical sciences, the mathematical models that are the core of theory do not express relationships in a way that distinguishes cause from effect. But in the intermediate stages understanding seems to demand that we be able to distinguish cause from effect in our relationships.

The notion of causality, when useful, is remarkably slippery. Intuitively, we know that a time dimension is of fundamental importance to the judgment of causes. An event that occurs *after* another event cannot have caused it. But this logical dictum provides only a first step toward clarifying the concept of causality. Aristotle devoted a fair portion of his *Physics* to a discussion of the variety of ways in which the term "cause" might be understood. John Stuart Mill, in the nineteenth century, labored to specify procedures by which "true" causes might be sifted from the welter of occurrences that surround any event, but his most convincing efforts demand a degree of control by the investigator that is rare within social science. More recent evaluations of the concept of causality have disclosed many fallacies surrounding the traditional views of "laws of nature." Nonetheless, limiting the concept to refer to uniformities of sequence observed in time past, which may be expected in the absence of exogenous factors to hold in the future, remains useful to our inquiry. Unfortunately, however, reformulations of the concept give us little instruction on strategy in the approach to complex systems of events.

Let us illustrate the problems imposed by considerations of causality in the context of voting behavior with a series of case studies which, as a set, are fairly representative. We may presume that we have a complete knowledge of past events affecting these individuals. From this store of information we draw the following material.

1. *Oil worker, Texas.* Life-long Democrat but rarely voted. In 1952 heard that Stevenson wanted to give Texas oil away to all the country. Also knew that the Democratic party had been trying to push racial mixing. Did not vote in either 1952 or 1956, but was glad each time that Eisenhower won.

2. *Woman in Ohio.* Had been a Republican, but her husband was a Catholic from Boston and a strong Democrat. She did not like Truman, and admired Eisenhower. She did not know much about politics. She wanted to vote Republican in 1952 and 1956, but her husband insisted that she vote Democratic.

3. *Carpenter in Connecticut.* Was badly hit by the depression, blamed the New Deal for his problems, thought the government in Washington had gone crazy. Argued about the matter with all his friends, who were Democrats; came to feel that they were all very ignorant politically. Suffered through the Democratic administrations up to 1952, then voted triumphantly for Eisenhower. Soon decided that the Republicans were even worse, since his son was drafted into the Army. Became vitriolic about government generally. In 1956 voted Democratic.

4. *Woman, has spent life in Virginia.* Grandfather had settled there from the North after the Civil War. He had not liked Southerners, had staunchly maintained his Republican allegiances. His granddaughter is the last of the line, and the family fortunes have declined to a point of real poverty. She is disinterested in politics, but feels it is her duty to vote. She has always voted Republican. She knew little about the issues in 1956, but liked President Eisenhower. Voted Republican.

5. *Dentist, in California.* Republican by birth but came to respect President Roosevelt during period of military service in World War II. In 1948 voted Republican, disliking campaign tactics of President Truman. In 1952 was very attracted to Stevenson, did not find Eisenhower impressive. He was familiar with most of the campaign issues and favored the Democrats in most of them, particularly the foreign issues. In 1952 he voted Democratic. The first Eisenhower administration was not as bad as he expected, but he was still drawn to Stevenson and his stand on issues. He fell ill just before the 1956 election and did not vote, but was sorry he had not been able to vote Democratic.

6. *Young woman, Illinois, eligible to vote for the first time.* A typist in a business office. Her family had been Democratic, but all of the men where she worked were Republican. She liked President Eisenhower, but she did not like the men she worked for. She did not vote, but secretly hoped the Democrats would win.

7. *Wife of a brewery worker in Kansas.* She had migrated from Alabama to Kansas. Had been a Democrat, but felt that all good people in Kansas, save her husband, were Republican. Did not know much about Stevenson or Eisenhower, but felt Eisenhower was well-liked. She voted Republican in 1956.

8. *Laborer, Massachusetts.* From a Catholic family which had never been interested in politics. During the depression joined a union and became strongly Democratic. In 1952 did not like Stevenson and thought Eisenhower was a great man. Still, he felt the Democratic party was the party of the common man, and ended up not voting. In 1956 he held the same set of attitudes. He voted Democratic.

9. *Farmer, Nebraska.* Republican background. Not much interested in politics until 1946, when questions arose concerning subsidies for some of his crops. Came to like the Republican Administration in his state very much, but did not mind the Democrats in Washington. In 1954 encountered financial troubles, and policies of the Department of Agricul-

ture did not work out favorably for him, although some other farmers he knew were helped. In 1956 he voted Republican.

These brief case histories give us some idea of the problems that face us in our attempt to account for a current behavior, such as voting in 1956. The temptation is to assign to each case a cause that appeared to affect the life history at the point where the last change in partisanship occurred. The nature of the cause is fixed by the content of events at this most recent point of change. But if we deal with the matter in such simplified form, we create severe conceptual problems.

For example, we might list the following types of causes of 1956 preference for the nine cases: (1) Domestic-issue attitudes, (2) primary-group pressures, (3) personality traits of voter, (4) family political history, (5) candidate and issue attitudes, (6) family influence, (7) social pressures, (8) the depression, (9) local politics. Several characteristics of this list impress us, however. In many cases another "cause" might be given that would be equally suitable. In Case 8, for example, we might have said that membership in secondary groups like the labor union and the Catholic Church was "responsible" for 1956 political preference. In Case 9 we might have chosen family background as a cause. Even when operating with a set of facts carefully selected for relevance, there are a number of conceptual domains within which explanation can proceed for any case.

If we look at the factors across the entire list, we are impressed too by their heterogeneity. We cannot afford to build an explanatory model that treats each case as a distinctive phenomenon, with unique mechanisms at work. A systematic theory must be able to accept a set of data pertaining to any individual case and provide an ultimate prediction of behavior. The factor of family influence bulks large, over the list as a whole. Yet all nine of our cases grew up within a family circle of some sort. If we are to use the family as an explanatory tool in several instances, we must be able to deal with it in the cases where such influence looms less crucial. Similarly, Case 8 was crucially affected by the depression. Yet Case 4 experienced the depression also. Why was the political response so different?

In the face of such a variety of determining factors, we need some method of maintaining conceptual order. One such method is to restrict explanation to a set of factors of the same logical domain. If we took into account two social factors, religion and social class, we would be able to predict 1956 preference in our nine cases at a level higher than chance. Or, we might limit ourselves to political attitudes, and arrive at a somewhat more successful prediction. But either type of restriction seems to waste important information. If we deal only in current attitudes, we ignore the fact that there is a relationship between religion and voting that any full-fledged theory of political behavior must help us to understand. A major function that a structure for theory can perform, then, is to provide us with a way to use several levels of explanation without confusion. It should give us some satisfactory way of assigning a conceptual status to any variable that we wish to include in our explanatory system.

A Structure for Theory: The Funnel of Causality

The particular explanatory problem that we have chosen has certain important characteristics. We wish to account for a single behavior at a fixed point in time. But it is behavior that stems from a multitude of prior factors. We can visualize the chain of events with which we wish to deal as contained in a *funnel of causality*.

The notion of a funnel is intended merely as a metaphor that we find helpful up to a certain point. That is, like all physical analogies for complex and intangible processes, it becomes more misleading than clarifying if pressed too far. With these cautions in mind, then, let us imagine that the axis of the funnel represents a time dimension. Events are conceived to follow each other in a converging sequence of causal chains, moving from the mouth to the stem of the funnel. The funnel shape is a logical product of the explanatory task chosen. Most of the complex events in the funnel occur as a result of multiple prior causes. Each such event is, in its turn, responsible for multiple effects as well, but our focus of interest narrows as we approach the dependent behavior. We progressively eliminate those effects that do not continue to have relevance for the political act. Since we are forced to take all partial causes as relevant at any juncture, relevant effects are therefore many fewer in number than relevant causes. The result is a convergence effect.

Now let us take a cross section of the cone of the funnel at any point, erecting a plane at right angles to the axis. Let us imagine that we can measure all events and states as they stand at the moment they flow through this plane. We would expect two results. First, we would have a congeries of variables that would be, in a peculiar and limited sense, of the same "conceptual order," that is, owing to their simultaneity. Second, this array of variables should be able to predict the dependent behavior perfectly, provided that we know the necessary combining laws.[1]

[1] This proviso means that we must understand the interaction of our system of factors at all cross sections that intervene between the measurement screen and the actual behavior.

One way of maintaining conceptual clarity, therefore, is to restrict our measurements to states as they exist at one "slice of time." For example, we would not say that the 1956 preference of the woman in the previously-mentioned Case 4 was "caused" in 1860 and that of Case 3 in 1954. Instead, if we chose to make 1954 our point of measurement, we might measure the so-called "cause" of Case 3 directly, but the "cause" at a coordinate conceptual level for Case 4 would lie in a certain state as it existed in 1954—strong attachment to the Republican party, for example.

We do not wish to preserve conceptual order at the price of restriction in the scope of our theory. We want a theory that will help us assess the current political effects of remote events like the depression or the Civil War. Now the funnel is bounded at its narrow end by the event that we are trying to explain. If we are dealing with the 1956 election, then we think in terms of a funnel terminating on Election Day, 1956. If we wish instead to study the 1960 election, we think of a new funnel that narrows to a point in 1960; events and states of Election Day, 1956, now represent one cross section of time four years prior to the dependent behavior. Yet, there is no fixed boundary for the funnel earlier in time. In effect, we can range freely in time back through the funnel.

To think of a funnel in this way greatly enlarges our explanatory chore, for in the ideal case we want to take measurements that refer to states not at one cross section alone, but at a great number. Each cross section contains all the elements that will successfully predict the next, and so on, until we have arrived at the final political act. Nevertheless, in such an expanded theory, we must remain cognizant of the temporal area in the funnel to which any particular measurement refers. The "conceptual status" of each measurement of an independent variable involves, as one element, location on a time dimension.

But time alone is not sufficient as an ordering dimension. The states that must be measured at any cross section in time to permit perfect prediction would be extremely heterogeneous. Since qualitative differences in content are involved, a great number of ordering dimensions could be established. Let us take note of three important ones.

***Exogenous factors* versus *relevant conditions*.** First, any single cross section will be divisible into (1) exogenous factors and (2) relevant conditions. Exogenous factors are those eliminated from consideration by fiat at the outset. They include all those conditions that are so remote in nature from the content interest of the investigator that their inclusion in a system of variables, even if possible, would be undesirable. A potential voter who has a flat tire on the way to the polls may fail in his intention to vote. In this instance, failure to vote would be due to certain accidental circumstances. Sufficient motivation was present and effort was expended that would normally have led to the casting of a ballot. The immediate cause of non-voting involved a flat tire. Once we have located this circumstance, we do not wish to pursue the matter further, tracing out the chain of events in the funnel that led to the mishap with the tire. We shall have no difficulty agreeing that such concerns are alien to our interest.

We will be obliged to understand what happens within our system of relevant conditions when exogenous factors impinge upon it. If "accidental" obstacles such as flat tires and bad weather block the way to the polls, we would like to be able to specify how much motivation will be required to surmount obstacles of varying magnitude, as well as the general incidence of such obstacles in the election situation. At the same time, we are not obliged to construct a theory that will indicate when and where flat tires will occur, or make long-range predictions about the weather on Election Day.

This relegation of some factors to an exogenous status, even though they affect the system at a time close to the dependent behavior, stands in sharp contrast to treatment of other forms of non-voting. In many cases, for example, the immediate cause of failure to vote may be a low motivational state readily linked to general indifference toward political matters. Here we are interested in seeking determinants of apathy that lie deeper in the funnel. A flat tire may be as efficient in preventing a vote as apathy, but the causes of apathy remain within our content interest. The causes of the flat tire do not.

The distinction between exogenous factors and relevant conditions is quite relative; that which is an exogenous factor for a narrow conceptual system may become a relevant condition within the terms of a more inclusive system. Ordinarily, the boundary is dictated by the level at which units of analysis are chosen and by the subject matter of the discipline in which investigation is conducted. But there is always room for choice on the breadth of the system that is to be employed.

Hence we may imagine that an outer ring of conditions within the funnel is left unobserved as exogenous. This fact has an important implication. As long as every cross section in the funnel has some exogenous factors, our predictions will never be perfect. *How* excellent they will be depends upon the proportion of the total cross section that such factors occupy. We can presume that this proportion increases the deeper we recede in the funnel, away from the dependent behavior.

The distinction between exogenous and relevant factors, though left to the discretion of the investigator, can be maintained with clarity under all circumstances. A given factor, if measured and treated within the conceptual system applied to the phenomenon, is thereby defined as relevant. We may make some other distinctions as well, which, if less clear-cut, will be of value in thinking about the nature of events in the funnel.

Personal* versus *external conditions. For some purposes it is convenient to subdivide relevant and exogenous factors according to whether or not they enjoy a subjective reality for the individual at a given point in time. We shall call *personal conditions* those events or states within the funnel of which the individual is aware, although he need not conceptualize them as the investigator does. *External conditions* are those that warrant a place in the funnel because they are causally significant for later behavior, yet which currently lie beyond the awareness of the actor.

This distinction is most useful in a consideration of the political stimuli that can affect behavior only when perceived by the actor. Suppose, for example, that we were to trace events backward in time through the funnel conceptualized for a given election. We would soon encounter a point at which the individual is unaware of the existence of the candidate-to-be, although events that will lead to that candidate's nomination and that ultimately will exert profound influence on the individual's behavior are crystallizing rapidly. At such a point in the funnel, the conceptual status of the candidate as potential stimulus object is that of an external condition. When the individual knows who the candidate is, the conceptual status shifts to that of a personal condition.

By and large we shall consider external conditions as exogenous to our theoretical system. We want to understand the individual's response to politics by exploring the way in which he perceives the objects and events of the political world. Our approach is in the main dependent on the point of view of the actor. We assume that most events or conditions that bear directly upon behavior are perceived in some form or other by the individual prior to the determined behavior, and that much of behavior consists of reactions to these perceptions.[2]

Nonetheless, the distinction between exogenous factors and external

[2] It cannot be said that *all* behavior toward a class of objects is determined by conscious attitudes concerning those objects. The area of unconscious motivation provides many illustrative exceptions. But in general, we find it fruitful to analyze behavior as a function of the individual's own "definition of the situation."

conditions will command attention at some points. For example, we shall make use of the fact that differences in legal forms that surround the conduct of elections serve to parcel the nation into electoral subcultures. It is likely that some of these legal forms affect behavior without being reacted to as objects or even cognized. In effect, they define the limits of possible behavior; they are the external "givens" of the situation, and actors make choices within these boundaries with little sense that other "givens" are conceivable. Hence many of the legal forms, as measured and related to behavior, are external conditions; yet they are not exogenous, for we have deemed it important to include them within our current explanatory system.

Tracing the antecedents of such external conditions deeper into the funnel is the obligation of institutional analysis. Why one aspirant wins the party nomination rather than another and why one legal form was instituted in preference to another are questions beyond the scope of our inquiry. Such antecedents we therefore consider exogenous. But to recognize that conditions exist in the funnel at any point in time, which are external for the actor yet which affect current or ultimate behavior, leaves our theoretical structure open for increasingly firm liaison with institutional analysis. As these bridgeheads become established, we may deal with convergent chains of external and personal conditions, neither of which will be discarded as exogenous.

Responses toward most objects are prefaced by attitudes toward those objects, which, in a proximal sense, determine the response. Therefore, the understanding of external conditions becomes more and more important as we attempt to anticipate behavior over longer and longer intervals. When we predict at short range, few events or conditions not already personal can intervene to deflect behavior to a new course. The deeper we range into the funnel, the larger the proportion of external factors with which we must cope.

Political **versus** ***non-political conditions.***[3] Finally, conditions in the funnel may in a rough way be classified into those that are political and those that are not. If we may locate factors as central or peripheral within any cross section, according to our interest in them and their presumed importance as determinants of ultimate behavior, then conditions that are political form the core, or central artery, running longitudinally through the funnel. This central position of the political in the funnel follows quite naturally from the fact that the subject of inquiry is political. The non-political relevant conditions form a shell around this political core. What portion of non-political condi-

[3] A supplementary discussion of the rationale underlying the distinction between political and non-political conditions may be found on page 192.

tions shall also be considered relevant depends again on the scope of the investigation.

When is a specified condition political, and when is it not? In everyday thinking we readily categorize events and objects in this fashion. Various individuals, groups, public problems, and current happenings are considered to be more or less political. And the relationship of such objects to politics can be seen to change in time. A person may decide to "go into politics"; a public controversy is "made a political issue"; a group should "get out of politics."

More formally, classification can be made on either an objective or a phenomenological basis. Once again, an objective set of criteria would be most appropriate for some institutional types of analysis. A factory shutdown in Kankakee may or may not have political reverberations. An institutional approach might provide specifications of the conditions under which such a shutdown is most likely to "become political."

But whatever the objective definition of the situation, some individuals affected may link the shutdown with political objects such as parties, issues, and candidates, whereas others will not. Thus we may depend on a phenomenological definition of the degree to which an event, state, or factor is political. If the object or event is not cognized at all (an external condition), then no such determination can be made. But as soon as a condition is made personal, then determination of its political or non-political status can rest upon the individual's particular perceptions. Wherever possible, we shall treat this distinction here as it occurs phenomenologically.

We have said that at each juncture in the flow of events, effects that are not relevant for understanding the voting act are eliminated, thus creating the shape of a funnel. This fact now has a further implication; the proportion of events that are political (objectively or subjectively) increases as we take our cross sections closer and closer to the final behavior. Relevant measurements just prior to the act will be almost completely political. At a greater distance we will have to consider a larger proportion of other social and economic factors, unless we eliminate them by definition at the outset.

Process variables: communication and "political translation." Enough of the composition of the funnel has been outlined to suggest that as events approach the narrow end of the funnel, they are more completely relevant, personal, and political. Now the boundary line between the exogenous and the relevant is drawn at the discretion of the theorist. But when we use a phenomenological approach, the way in which external events become personal, and the way in which non-political events become political, depend on processes that operate within the funnel itself. The analyst does not intervene to make a citizen aware of an external condition. Nor does he point out the political implications of objects or events that the subject perceives as non-political. These are perceptual and cognitive changes that occur naturally as events unfold. Their timing and scope depend on individual conditions and hence must be predicted within the terms of the theory itself.

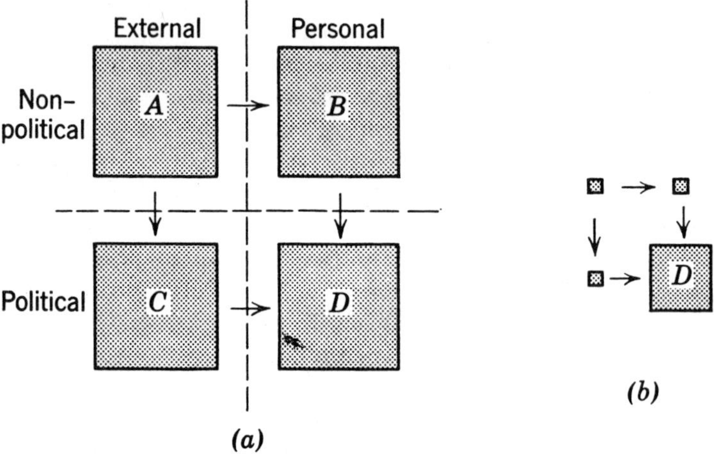

Fig. 2-1. Change in status over time of events affecting behavior. (*a*) The situation at a point in time remote from the behavior; (*b*) the situation at a point in time close to the behavior.

Figure 2-1 shows the four possible ways in which events may be categorized according to these two distinctions. An event may at some point in time be external and non-political (*A*); personal and non-political (*B*); external and political (*C*); or personal and political (*D*). The second portion of the figure provides a schematic indication of the situation just before the vote to be predicted is cast. By this point in time, personal and political elements predominate: most events and conditions that are going to affect the behavior have come into the voter's awareness and have acquired political meaning.

The mechanisms involved in these categoric changes of elements over time are critical to our understanding of events in the funnel. If the vote to be predicted is that occurring in 1956, an example of an external, non-political sequence of events (*A*) lying within the funnel at a point early in the 1940's would be the emergence of Dwight D. Eisenhower as a major military figure. As we move forward in time, the consequences of these events can proceed from *A* toward *D* by one of two routes. In this case, the normal route was $A \rightarrow B \rightarrow D$. Early in the war few voters were aware of the rise of Eisenhower or would have attributed to it any political significance. By 1945, most Americans were aware of General Eisenhower. But for very few was this a fact of even potential political significance (*B*). During the mid-1940's, awareness led to some emotional content; for most Americans in this case the affect was positive. If we were measuring a cross section in time in 1947, it is likely that we could find a relationship between affect toward General Eisenhower shown at that time, and the individual's 1956 vote, even if traditional party preference were held constant. As Eisenhower began to receive mention as a possible presidential candidate, processes leading from *B* to *D* were set in motion. The object, Eisenhower, began to take on political coloration. This was faint, until his announcement that he would run for the Republican nomination. The affect that the individual felt for Eisenhower now was placed in contact with all the political cognitions and predispositions that had been formed independently in the core area of the funnel.

The second possible route from *A* to *D* lies through *C* (Fig. 2-1). In the illustration under discussion, this route was more rare. But there were undoubtedly a number of Americans who were personally unaware of the figure of Eisenhower until the point at which he broke into their consciousness as a political candidate. In this case, Eisenhower's movement into politics was an external event.[4]

The major process by which an external event becomes personal is that of communication. That part of our theory that deals with the conditions under which an object or condition moves from a non-political area of the funnel to a political area will depend upon examination of communication vehicles such as the mass media and interpersonal communication. There are other more direct processes that can effect this transformation: loss of a job in 1930 may have turned the depression from an external to a personal event without mediation of a communication system in the normal sense. But most of the beliefs that come to affect political behavior are probably developed by way of communication processes.

A non-political event becomes political by a process we shall call *political translation.* As Fig. 2-1 suggests, political translation may

[4] Once again, we may note that determinants of movement from *A* to *C* lie in the province of institutional analysis. But, it is important to know which route has been followed. The fact that Eisenhower had been cognized for a long period of time as a non-political figure, whereas his opponent, Stevenson, was first known to most people as a Democratic candidate, must have made a critical contribution to the differences in partisan support that the two men enjoyed.

occur externally; it also may occur within the individual himself. For some people, the fact of a depression in the 1930's immediately took on political meaning, with a minimum of outside suggestion. It was perceived directly as something that the government could and should do something about. The role of the Hoover Administration was evaluated accordingly. For others, with a different set of existing perceptions regarding the potential of governmental activity, the translation was made outside, by other agents in the society. The labor unions contended that the depression was subject to governmental control; during the Hoover Administration, Democratic Party spokesmen bore down hard on the same point. Thus the fact of depression was presented to many Americans with a political meaning already attached.[5]

Strategies of Explanation

We have indicated some of the more important characteristics of the theoretical superstructure that serves as a framework to organize our thought. We could add other characteristics, and indeed as the framework begins to receive empirical content it will be important to do so. Nevertheless we have covered enough ground that we may begin to locate approaches to the study of political behavior within the structure.

It is clear that the framework proposed is an enormous one. It is perhaps better to deal with a framework challenging us to growth than with one that cramps our progress. But lest it appear that we have built too large a structure altogether, it should be pointed out that proper abstraction of concepts contributes a great economy to any explanatory venture. It is extremely difficult, in the early stages of inquiry, to arrive at concepts that are pitched at a sufficiently high level of generality. As work proceeds, the necessary abstractions begin to form out of the specificity of concrete events. The perspectives that extensive data from even three elections provide have been very helpful in this regard. This book includes a number of formulations that

[5] The fact that anti-Republican elements in 1930 were eager to communicate a particular *type* of political translation, whereas the Republicans were equally eager to forestall such translation, does not mean that all Americans accepted the *anti-Republican* direction of the translation. If the source of the communication was negative—if the individual hated labor unions or the Democrats—the thrust of the translation might be reversed. Or the political relevance of the depression might be rejected altogether. The important point is that a key process in the funnel is that by which events or conditions move, or fail to move, into the central or political core of the funnel.

are at a far more satisfactory level of generality than could have been achieved ten years ago.

Nonetheless, the magnitude of the work to be done forces us to consider carefully the strategy of explanation that is to be followed in the development of a theory of political behavior. Our theoretical superstructure immediately poses several such questions. What cross sections in time deserve our most immediate attention? What shall we exclude as exogenous factors? How far back shall we attempt to explore in the infinite regress of antecedent factors? The two major approaches to the problem, the social and the attitudinal, represent different solutions to the problem of strategy. In several key respects these solutions are diametrically opposed. By surveying the arguments for each, we can clarify the problem of strategies a good deal.

At the beginning of inquiry, the investigator finds himself in a dilemma. On one hand, practical problems of measurement, along with difficulties in maintaining conceptual clarity before functional relationships are well understood, constitute a pressure toward closure of the system within narrow bounds. On the other hand, there is pressure to "account for variance" by an expansion of the system that will reduce "noise" from alien factors. The larger the system with which the investigator can cope, the more thorough his understanding.

The field theoretical approach. The attitudinal approach, exemplified by *The Voter Decides* (1954) represents a strategy that maximizes explanatory power while dealing with a minimum number of variables. This solution to the dilemma is accomplished by concentrating on a cross section of measurements at a point close to the dependent behavior. At such a point, the funnel is narrow. It is easier to develop a set of conceptually uniform variables that will span most of the cross section.

This mode of explanation has its intellectual roots in the movement known as "field theory," fostered in the behavioral sciences by Kurt Lewin. In essence the field-theoretical approach represents a reaction against a genetic treatment of causality. This doctrine is based upon the replacement, in the nineteenth century, of Newton's "mechanical" laws by the "field laws" of Maxwell. Mechanical laws presume action at a distance; they connect two widely separated events. In field theory, however, the field at the present moment is seen as a product of the field in the immediate neighborhood at a time just past. Of course, our metaphor of the funnel of causality fails to represent adequately all of the philosophical implications of field theory and adds other conditions peculiar to our explanatory task. But the general field-theoretical argument may be considered an appeal for initial measurement at cross sections of the funnel that lie very close to the dependent event, with "historical" explanation proceeding backward in short steps.

The use of political attitudes to predict voting behavior hinges upon this proximal mode of explanation. It assumes that whatever effect distant events (being unemployed in 1933) may have on current political behavior (deciding to vote Democratic), this effect must be present and measurable in some form (suspicion of Republican domestic policy) just prior to the dependent event. If it is present in no form, then the effect cannot be considered to be a determinant of the event. Such an approach reduces the number of variables to be taken into account. For example, it might be possible to construct a genetic picture of an individual's relationship to his chosen political party. We might take into account the party affiliation of his parents, if any; events that had changed his allegiance from one party to another; the degree to which he had been committed to any particular party during his adult life; and hence arrive at a fair prediction of his current party choice and his strength of allegiance to it. This accounting presumes a knowledge of a multitude of past events, including many that were not themselves political but which had political effects. The field-theoretical alternative is to measure the individual's party identification at the current time, on the assumption that this is a perfect distillation of all events in the individual's life history that have borne upon the way in which he relates himself to a political party.

The characteristics postulated for the funnel serve to explain why this approach has such high explanatory power relative to accounts that are based on events lying at a point more remote from the dependent behavior. First, the exogenous factors that can intervene are reduced to a minimum. Second, the use of attitudes restricts measurement to relevant conditions that are already personal, so that we do not have to take into account the conditions of communication that govern the transition from external events to personal events. Finally, and perhaps most important, events are observed after they have received their political translations, so that the conditions of uncertainty that surround prediction of the voter's interpretation of events are excluded from the system.

This field-theoretical approach is well suited to the type of measurement employed in our survey studies of the American population. The interview represents a set of observations at a point in time close to the dependent behavior. Of course, an interview may tap other areas of the funnel as well. When we observe personality traits or certain socio-economic characteristics, we deal with factors that have colored political perceptions for an unknown period of time stretching into the past. Or various forms of recall may be requested, a technique that permits more or less reliable measurement referring to a past time. But the most direct and accurate measurement has to do with current states.

Maximizing explanatory power in the early stages of inquiry has certain intrinsic advantages. This statement is particularly true when the dependent variable communicates little specific information. A Republican vote may represent all manner of endorsements or aggravations. Until we can command an array of attitudes that relates highly to the vote, we can sort out these intentions only by inference. Furthermore, once such an array is at hand, it provides us with a set of empirical priorities to guide research deeper in the funnel. If the components isolated analytically "in the immediate neighborhood at a time just past" have differing capacities to predict the vote, we will do well to trace first the roots of those elements that are the strongest determinants.

On the other hand, the attitudinal approach entails some liabilities as well. Measurement close to the behavior runs the risk of including values that are determined by the event we are trying to predict—that is, the vote decision. To the degree that this occurs, some elements of a system of supposed independent variables may in fact be effects rather than causes. Careful use of the technique can keep these difficulties at a minimum; but there is little way, within the normal study design, to measure precisely the confusion that may occur concerning the causal flow in the field.

A second shortcoming of the attitudinal approach to explanation lies in its failure to span a greater distance in the funnel. If we were interested in prediction without understanding, we could hardly improve upon such a system of attitudinal variables. It is difficult to find events deeper in the funnel that account for variance independent of the system of political attitudes. Of course, this is an excellent proof of the adequacy of the screen that has been thrown across the funnel close to the behavior.

But since we are interested in the way events unfold in the longer term, we want a set of empirical relationships that carry us deeper into the funnel and move outward from events and attitudes that are expressly political. We want to explore the political core of the funnel, particularly within the chain of personal events, at a considerable distance from the current vote. But we also want to know how external events can become or fail to become personal, and where and how they are given political translation.

Alternate strategies. The social approach to explanation attempts prediction from points more remote in the funnel. This remoteness is to some degree temporal, although there has been no clear attempt to spell out how many of the social variables are to be conceptualized as causes in time past. Most variables of this order have characterized the individual for some considerable period of time, and their effects on political responses are certain to be distributed in time. Such variables are also removed in a cross-sectional sense from the political core of the funnel. They have no political significance save that which may be brought to them by the discovery of relationships between them and political behaviors.

It follows from the fact of remoteness that these concepts tend to account for much less variance than do attitudinal materials drawn closer to the behavior. We do not yet know how well a set of political attitudes measured in 1956 will predict a 1960 vote. It is likely that such a temporal span alone would substantially reduce the predictive capacity. Events left unmeasured in 1956 as external or non-political would be expected to move into the stream of the personal and the political in the four intervening years. Nonetheless, any measurement of political attitudes at a point in time remote from a dependent vote may well predict more effectively than an equivalent set of social variables, owing to the additional logical distance of the latter from the core of the funnel. Relationships that span these dimensions of "distance" in the funnel are particularly exciting, however, because they give us a glimpse into a "longer" chain of events. We are even willing to sacrifice some predictive capacity in order to span a greater distance in the funnel.

The social approach encounters other difficulties beyond the problem of lowered prediction. We have already remarked upon its inadequacy in handling important short-term fluctuations in the national vote division. Without a broader conceptual base, it suffers severe limitations in the long term as well. These problems arise from the frequent failure to explore in a systematic fashion what goes on in the funnel between two superficially disconnected terms of a relationship. A correlation between the fact of being a Negro and the casting of a Democratic ballot gives us interesting information, yet information pitched at a low level of abstraction. Generalizations of this sort tend to fall by the wayside with the passage of sufficient time, if not reformulated in more general terms. In the case of Negroes, for example, there is evidence to indicate that not more than a decade or two ago the relationship was reversed, with Negroes tending to favor the Republican Party. And it seems entirely plausible that the relationship might become reversed again in the fairly near future, without upsetting any very deep-seated "laws" of social behavior.[6]

Such laws we presume to exist, and with proper phrasing they should not only outlast reversals of voting pattern but should predict them. Yet "proper phrasing" seems to require thorough understanding of the perceptual and motivational conditions that lie between such facts as race and party choice. As we speculate about these intervening terms, we are again subject to the vagaries of prediction without understanding. We have no tools with which to anticipate the circumstances under which the Negro vote will grow more or less distinctive or what other population groups might be expected to respond in the same manner. To attain a truly firm understanding, we must systematically unravel the motives that sustain the voting pattern, as well as the many other social, psychological, and political mechanisms which mediate the relationship.

[6] Nor is the Negro a unique instance. In ensuing chapters we shall encounter other cases in which earlier sociological propositions, *as formulated,* have become period pieces in the span of a few years.

POLITICAL ATTITUDES AND THE VOTE ◇ SECTION II

Through most of this volume the arrangement of material depends on our theoretical conception, set forth in Chapter 2, of the order of factors determining electoral behavior. In unraveling the causal threads leading to the vote we begin with the immediate psychological influences on the voting act. By casting a vote the individual acts toward a political world whose objects he perceives and evaluates in some fashion; the view he has formed of the presidential candidates, of the two major parties, and of various political issues and politically involved groups has a profound influence on his behavior. In Walter Lippmann's phrase, the voter has a picture of the world of politics in his head, and the nature of this picture is a key to understanding what he does at the polls.

The *content* of popular perceptions of national politics is the focus of Chapter 3, where we examine the qualitative themes the electorate has associated with the parties and candidates during the period of our research. Because we have recorded these themes in successive elections we are able to say how the public's image of the political world has changed through time, and the description of change will be a central feature of the chapter. This kind of account raises naturally the question of how change is induced. Only a partial answer can be given, but we are able to draw some inferences about the dynamics of mass percepts by confronting the record of change in popular perceptions with what we know has happened in the wider political environment.

The significance of political perceptions for behavior depends largely on their evaluative character. The popular image of parties and candidates is not neutral, and the fact that it is colored by positive and negative feeling vests it with great motivational importance. This motivational role will concern us in the two latter chapters of the section. In Chapter 4 we treat the impact of political attitudes on the individual's partisan choice at the polls. We will see that this choice springs immediately from a matrix of psychological forces, and that by taking account of attitudes toward six discernible elements of politics we can explain quite well the individual's choice between rival parties or candidates. Moreover, we will see that the internal coherence of this system of attitude forces has a good deal of significance for other aspects of voting. In particular, by taking account of the extent of conflict in the individual's political attitudes we are able to say more surely whether his partisan choice will be made early or late and whether he will cast a straight or split-ticket ballot.

No aspect of voting is of more fundamental importance than the individual's decision whether to vote at all. In Chapter 5 we shift our attention from the partisan decision to influences on voting turnout. We will see that partisan preference and turnout are bound together by the fact that the attitude forces which influence the individual's partisan choice may influence his decision whether to vote. Yet the contribution of partisan attitude to the explanation of turnout is a limited one, and additional psychological factors are needed to account for this aspect of voting behavior. In seeking a better explanation of turnout we will focus primarily on the extent to which the individual is psychologically involved in politics. The emotional commitment that people have toward political affairs varies widely between individuals, and political involvement is of far-reaching importance for voting turnout. Chapter 5 will deal with several areas of the individual's orientation to politics, areas that reflect a common dimension of involvement yet which are in some measure distinct. The extent of a person's interest in the campaign, his concern over its outcome, his sense of political effectiveness, and his sense of citizen duty all will be seen to have a clear influence on whether he joins in the electoral process.

Although the importance of psychological involvement in politics will be a theme of several later chapters, Chapter 5 will suggest something of its significance for electoral behavior by considering the changes that have occurred over a period of time in the partisan preferences of non-voters. An extraordinary shift in the preferences of those who have failed to vote undermines a generalization that became familiar in the Democratic years of the New Deal and Fair Deal, and it foreshadows the importance of involvement in understanding the attitudes and behavior of other groups within the electorate that differ in the extent of their involvement in political affairs.

Perceptions of the Parties and Candidates ◇ 3

If we are to understand what leads the voter to his decision at the polls we must know how he sees the things to which this decision relates. In casting a vote the individual acts toward a world of politics in which he perceives the personalities, issues, and the parties and other groupings of a presidential contest. His image of these matters may seem at times exceedingly ill-formed, but his behavior makes sense subjectively in terms of the way these political objects appear to him. As a result, measuring perceptions and evaluations of the elements of politics is a first charge on our energies in the explanation of the voting act. Indeed, it would be difficult to overstate the importance of the perceptions formed by a mass electorate for the decisions it must periodically render. Hyman has written of this aspect of voting:

> Men are urged to certain ends but the political scene in which they act is perceived and given meaning. Some cognitive map accompanies their movements toward their ends.[1]

It is the cognitive map of national politics held by the American electorate that is our concern here. Plainly the map is a colored one. The elements of politics that are visible to the electorate are not simply seen; they are evaluated as well. Evaluation is the stuff of political life, and the cognitive image formed by the individual of the political world tends to be positively and negatively toned in its several parts. This mixture of cognition and evaluation, of belief and attitude, of percept and affect is so complete that we will speak of the individual's cognitive *and affective* map of politics.

[1] Herbert Hyman, *Political Socialization* (The Free Press, Glencoe, Ill., 1959), p. 18.

The Influence of Historical Reality

Voting research has tended to miss the importance of cognitive factors on the causal forces leading to behavior. When processes of perception or cognition have been treated at all, interest has centered mainly on evidence of perceptual distortion. But the point needs equally to be made that the motives of individual psychology can distort the image of real objects only within limits. Perceptions are not free-floating creations of the individual voter or of the small social groupings in which they are shared. They are tied in fundamental ways to the properties of the stimulus objects that are perceived. As these properties change, the perceptions will tend also to change. As a result, the flow of historical reality has enormous influence on the electorate's perceptions of its political environment.

The influence of historical reality is of central interest to us here. This chapter is concerned first of all with the way the changing political environment affects the public image of the parties and their candidates, the non-party groupings that are involved in the political process, and the issues of national policy. Yet percept and reality are not the same, and to gain an understanding of the way change in the external world of politics alters the popular image of political objects, we will ultimately have to consider not only the "real" properties of these objects but certain processes of individual psychology as well.

The motivational significance of these percepts is such that understanding the way a changing political environment can redraw the popular map of politics will explain a good deal of the dynamics of electoral change. This problem is so important that any extensive body of data on the changing image of politics held by the national electorate ought to be pressed hard for the insights it can yield.

Yet several characteristics of our data limit the inferences we are able to draw. Our observations have to do with the change of a relatively brief interval. The data of a single four-year period can suggest hypotheses; they can hardly supply their proof. Despite the fact that thousands of interviews are involved, our information might be said to refer to one "case"—to the effects on public attitude of a single section of historical reality. Also, our interviews in this interval were taken at two points in time, four years apart. To unravel the problem of change we would want ideally to sample the opinions of the electorate more frequently. Lastly, our data describe only the dependent variable of the causal process that is of interest. What we have measured are public cognitions and evaluations of politics and not the elements of the wider political environment that we have cast in a causal role. Of course the latter element tends to be known to us much more from other sources than is the content of public attitude. But this is not always true. And what is probably more important, we do not have data on the means by which information about the external world was carried to the electorate in this period. In particular, we know little of the political content of the mass communications media. In examining the fit between perceptions and what is perceived, we will not deal systematically with connecting mechanisms whose potential influence on the degree of fit can scarcely be doubted.

A Case Study in Change

At the beginning of the Eisenhower years our interviews with a cross section of the electorate explored the public image of Eisenhower himself, of his Democratic opponent, of the Republican and Democratic Parties, and of the groups and issues that the parties and candidates were thought to affect. These materials were duplicated by interviews with a new sample of the electorate in the campaign of 1956, at the end of Eisenhower's first term. By comparing interview responses at these two points in time we have a remarkable portrait of public feeling toward the elements of politics in this period and of changes in its content through an interval of four years.

These interviews are permeated by perceptual materials about national politics, but to evoke a free expression of public feeling that might yet be submitted to a disciplined analysis, an early portion of each interview (amounting on the average to a quarter of an hour) was devoted to free-answer questions designed to call forth the individual's view of what he saw in national politics.

The design of these questions took for granted the fact that the public's image of politics is evaluatively toned. Percept and affect are freely mixed in the view of parties and candidates held by the electorate, and the qualities attributed to these objects evoke strong evaluative feeling. What is more, the design of these questions assumed that public feeling varied along the two-valued dimension imposed on political attitudes by our party system. The property of being pro or anti, favorable or unfavorable, and so forth, is inevitably found in attitudes within a political system that is polarized by two parties. Accepting this fact, we invited those interviewed to tell us what they *liked* and *disliked* about each party and candidate.[2] We will report what they said in some detail in this chapter for the light it throws on the problem of attitude change and for the help it gives in interpreting the more severe statistical summaries of these answers that we will have to use in later chapters.

The flood of responses evoked by these questions occurred in two election campaigns separated by four years, but the historical events mirrored in the answers extend over much more than a four-year interval. Owing to the hardihood of our principal parties, partisan feeling has not in a hundred years been deflected by the disappearance of a major party. Undoubtedly some of the ideas voiced in these election campaigns were first associated with the parties in the Civil War and Reconstruction era, and others perhaps became attached to one of the parties during the great periods of foreign migration to our eastern cities or during the successive outbursts of agrarian unrest through the South and West. A voter past retirement in 1952 could have remembered the politics of free silver and the full dinner pail. And only a few years separated his coming of age from the carpet bag and the bloody shirt.

The first historical period to leave an unmistakable imprint upon these responses, however, is that of the Great Depression. Three marks of the depression experience and its political aftermath are discernible in the responses given in the first Eisenhower-Stevenson election. First of all, the Democratic Party was widely perceived in 1952 as the party of prosperity and the Republican Party as the party of depression. Great numbers of responses in that year associated the Democrats with good times, the Republicans with economic distress. Secondly, there was in 1952 a broad measure of approval for the domestic policies of the New Deal and Fair Deal. Favorable references to the domestic policies arising out of the Roosevelt and Truman administrations were quite frequent. And as a third legacy of the depression experience, there was in 1952 a strong sense of good feeling toward the Democratic Party and hostility toward the Republican Party on the basis of the groups each was thought to favor. The Democratic Party was widely perceived as the friend of lower status groups; the Republican Party in opposite terms.

We do not know to what extent these attitudes had lessened in force from the mid-Depression years. Yet it is remarkable how strongly they

2 For this purpose a standard set of eight free-answer questions was used in the pre-election interviews of 1952 and 1956. For each of the parties one question sought favorable responses and one unfavorable responses. And for each of the candidates, one question sought favorable comment and one unfavorable comment.

carried over into the 1950's despite the efforts of Republican presidential candidates in every election since 1936 to create a more liberal image of the party. With a Republican President elected at last, the events of 1952 to 1956, however, challenged several of the assumptions on which the attitudes of an earlier era had rested. In the first place, a Republican occupied the White House in these years without a serious break in the nation's good times. With the recession of 1957–1958 yet to be experienced, the influence on public attitude of the nation's high non-farm prosperity during the first Eisenhower Administration is suggested by Table 3-1. References to prosperity

TABLE 3-1. References to Prosperity and Depression

	1952[a]	1956
Pro-Democratic and Anti-Republican	974	316
Pro-Republican and Anti-Democratic	70	213
Totals	1044	529

[a] In this and subsequent tables the number of responses in 1952 has been increased by the ratio of the size of the 1956 sample to the size of the 1952 sample to make possible a direct comparison of frequencies in the two years. The effect of the adjustment is to equate frequencies whose size relative to the size of their respective samples is the same. In reading these tables it should be kept in mind that one respondent could make more than one reference; hence the number of references may be larger than the number of individuals mentioning a given subject.

and depression declined 50 per cent from 1952 to 1956. And four years of Republican good times destroyed most of a 14-1 margin the Democrats had had in the partisanship of these responses. After haunting every Republican candidate for President since 1932, memories of the Hoover Depression had receded at least temporarily as a direct force in American politics.

A second aspect of this four-year interval that might be expected to challenge the attitudes of the past was the willingness of the Eisenhower Administration to embrace most of the reforms of the New Deal. This disposition to accept and even extend the social welfare policies of the previous twenty years undoubtedly lessened an important difference the public had perceived between the parties. The extent of this change is suggested by the summary of references to social welfare policies in Table 3-2. The references to policies of this sort was reduced by a third between these election campaigns, and the proportion of responses associating the Democrats favorably or the Republicans unfavorably with any of these policies declined substantially. As a token of this shift, the Democratic advantage on social security was reduced by two-thirds from 1952 to 1956.

TABLE 3-2. References to Social Welfare Policies[a]

	1952	1956
Pro-Democratic and Anti-Republican	421	259
Pro-Republican and Anti-Democratic	96	101
Totals	517	360

[a] This tabulation is limited to domestic policies clearly in the area of social welfare. References to farm policy, civil rights legislation, etc., are not included.

The Eisenhower Administration was not equally successful, however, in dispelling the popular belief that the Republicans were the party of the great and the Democrats the party of the small. Despite the change in public attitude toward the Republican Party on matters of economic and social welfare, the years 1952 to 1956 did not lessen this aspect of the image of the parties fixed in the Depression era. A large number of responses in 1956 still approved of the Democratic Party and disapproved of the Republican Party on the basis of the groups each was felt to support, as may be seen in Table 3-3. The Democrats were still thought to help groups primarily of lower status: the common people, working people, the laboring man, Negroes, farmers, and (in 1956 only) the small businessman. The Republicans, on the other hand, were thought to help those of higher status: big businessmen, the upper class, the well-to-do. This facet of public attitude is undoubtedly strongly colored by the past; but it could

TABLE 3-3. References to Groups

	1952	1956
Pro-Democratic and Anti-Republican	1438	1659
Pro-Republican and Anti-Democratic	256	294
Totals	1694	1953

hardly have remained so pronounced in these years without some reinforcement from public response to the performance of the Republican Administration. The public may have been sensitive to the evidence of the business orientation of an administration that recruited most of its prominent officials from private industry. At least the conduct of government in these years failed to blur a feature of the public image of the parties decidedly to the disadvantage of the Republicans.

Changes in these parts of the popular view of the parties show the impact that changes in the external world can have on political attitude. It was enough that a Republican Government could hold office in good times to weaken the popular connection between the Republican Party and economic distress. Similarly, the disposition of the Eisenhower Administration to accept domestic policies that had won popular support lessened public uneasiness about the party's probable attitude toward issues of this sort. The forces underlying these changes may be more sharply defined if we consider the farm sector of the economy. The prosperity of the Eisenhower years was felt only uncertainly on the nation's farms, and the posture of the Administration toward farm problems aroused widespread opposition. As a result, the moderation of public attitude toward the economic and social welfare record of the Republican Party did not extend to matters of farm policy. References to farm policy increased markedly between 1952 and 1956 and were strongly Democratic in partisanship. Moreover, references linking the Republicans unfavorably or the Democrats favorably with the welfare of farmers as a group were much more frequent in the latter year.

Other elements of the historical setting from which the attitudes of these years evolved are apparent in the responses given in these campaigns. Events more recent than the Great Depression had received wide attention in the years preceding the 1952 election. The worldwide struggle with the Soviet Union had culminated in a limited war that was widely seen as having exposed the nation to a humiliating defeat without having gained any essential end. The years preceding the 1952 election were also marked by increasing publicity about evidences of corruption in the federal government. Each of these more contemporary sets of events left an impression clearly discernible in the responses of 1952. References to foreign policy and the Korean War were of high frequency and strongly Republican in partisanship. And great numbers of responses cited misdeeds of the Democratic Administration and the need for a change in party control of the Executive Branch.

The attitudes, too, were modified by the unfolding of events from

1952 to 1956. Several changes in the external political world are reflected in the perceptions of the parties and candidates held by the electorate. In the first place, the ending of the Korean War enhanced the impression that the Republicans were better able than the Democrats to assure peace. Mr. Eisenhower and his party were widely supported in 1952 in the belief that they might end the Korean conflict. Their success in doing so and in preventing the outbreak of hostilities

TABLE 3-4. References to War and Peace

	1952	1956
Pro-Democratic and Anti-Republican	68	15
Pro-Republican and Anti-Democratic	514	595
Totals	582	610

involving the United States elsewhere in the world added to public confidence that the cause of peace would be better served if the Republicans were continued in office. References to war and peace in 1952 were pro-Republican or anti-Democratic by a ratio greater than seven to one. By 1956 the ratio had increased five times, owing to the virtual disappearance of comments favorable to the Democrats or unfavorable to the Republicans.

Through the first Eisenhower Administration, moreover, the Republican advantage in foreign affairs came to center much more completely on questions of war and peace. The finding of fault with the Democratic handling of the early cold war conflict, particularly in eastern Europe and China, seemed to lessen with the passage of time. And there was apparently a greater sense that what a Republican Administration might be able to do in these troubled areas was not widely different from what had been done by a Democratic Administration. The trend of these responses is shown in Table 3-5.

TABLE 3-5. References to Other Foreign Issues

	1952	1956
Pro-Democratic and Anti-Republican	143	145
Pro-Republican and Anti-Democratic	567	342
Totals	710	487

It is noteworthy that the total volume of comment about war and peace and other issues of foreign affairs was small relative to the level of other sorts of responses in these years. The Second World War as well as the Korean War had intervened between the experience of the Depression and the years 1952 to 1956. Yet the number of responses reflecting the Great Depression and its political aftermath was much greater than the number referring to issues raised by these wars or any other aspect of foreign affairs. Neither conflict seems to have had a great and lasting impact on popular political attitudes. It could be argued that a foreign war has not supplied a partisan dimension on which American political attitudes have been re-oriented since the earliest years of the Republic. The conflict with the greatest consequences for our political life was fought on American soil; its most lasting effects have been felt in the region in which it produced the most far-reaching change in personal circumstance and social institutions. By comparison with the impact of the Civil War, the effect of the wars of the twentieth century seems slight indeed.

Public concern about the corruption issue subsided rapidly with the Democratic Party out of power. However strong the sense of Democratic sin four years earlier, the party's loss of power seems to

TABLE 3-6. References to Corruption and "Time for a Change" Theme

	1952	1956
Pro-Republican references to corruption	546	93
Pro-Republican references to need for a change	490	...
Pro-Democratic references to corruption	...	20
Pro-Democratic references to need for a change	...	23

have accomplished its expiation by 1956. The swift decline of comment of this sort suggests that mismanagement and corruption are not issues that are easily kept alive after a change in control of the government.

At least one aspect of our recent political history is notable for the relatively slight extent to which it influenced public attitude toward parties and candidates in these years. In view of the enormous furor over internal subversion and the conduct of Senator McCarthy, it is astonishing to discover that the issue of domestic Communism was little mentioned by the public in 1952. The third element of the slogan reminding the electorate of "Corruption, Korea, and Communism" apparently was wide of the mark. Corruption and Korea were salient partisan issues for the electorate in that year. Communism, in the sense of domestic subversion, was not. Fewer responses touched the issue of domestic Communism in 1952 than referred to such esoteric subjects as the Point Four program and foreign economic aid and Mr. Stevenson's marital problems. By 1956 the issue had virtually disappeared.

The response to the issue of Communists in government serves to remind us that a great public commotion about an issue does not necessarily make it a matter of central importance to the electorate. It may be true that despite the convulsion in the federal government over this issue and the deep interest of the attentive public, it was of slight concern to a wider audience, or it may be that a large segment of the electorate failed to connect charges made about certain executive agencies, notably the Department of State, with its diffuse image of the Democratic Party. In any event, the central partisan charge, that the Democrats had permitted Communists to infiltrate the Department of State and other agencies of the federal government, appealed so little to the public that it was scarcely mentioned to our interviewers.[3]

Of the elements of politics that had emerged relatively recently as objects of partisan feeling, none was of greater importance in these years than the presidential candidates. The fact that the great prize of American politics is won by popular endorsement of a single man means that the appearance of new candidates may alter by a good deal an existing balance of electoral strength between the parties. An inspection of popular response to the candidates in these years suggests the correctness of the Republican strategy of using a figure who had won immense public esteem outside politics to overturn a long-established Democratic majority. The content of this response tells something, too, about the changes that may occur in public reaction to the figures of presidential politics. It is likely that in any election campaign the candidates for President will be associated to some extent with issues of foreign and domestic policy and the interest of various groups within the population. Undoubtedly there is a good deal of variability in the extent to which the candidates are evaluated in these terms. If our measurements extended far enough back in time to encompass the elections of the 1930's, we might find that in 1932 Franklin Roosevelt was asso-

[3] When a further cross section of Americans was asked during the congressional campaign of 1954 whether the endorsement of a candidate by Senator McCarthy would influence its preference, the most frequent response was one of indifference; only a small minority said it would heed such an endorsement.

ciated only moderately closely with the issues raised by the economic crisis, but that by 1936 he was connected in the public mind with a very wide range of these issues and with the welfare of many groups within the population. Similarly, we might find that Roosevelt was seldom related to questions of foreign policy in 1932 and 1936, but that by 1940 or more certainly 1944 he was clearly associated with the issues arising out of the European War.

An inspection of references to matters of group interest and to domestic isues in 1952 and 1956 makes clear that response of this sort was

TABLE 3-7. References to Groups

	1952	1956
Associated with the Republican Party	563	663
Associated with the Democratic Party	855	886
Associated with Eisenhower	112	219
Associated with Stevenson	164	185
Totals	1694	1953

TABLE 3-8. References to Domestic Issues

	1952	1956
Associated with the Republican Party	1276	898
Associated with the Democratic Party	1825	1001
Associated with Eisenhower	164	322
Associated with Stevenson	162	357
Totals	3427	2578

associated more with the parties than it was with either of the candidates. A summary of these references strongly suggests that the attitudes they reflect were for the most part formed prior to the entry of Mr. Eisenhower and Mr. Stevenson into the political arena. In 1952 neither of these men was perceived in these terms to any significant degree. Although each candidate evoked somewhat more responses of this sort four years later, the numbers of responses connecting either with group interest or issues of domestic policy were still small by comparison with the volumes of comment on these matters associated with the two parties. With respect to Mr. Eisenhower, this result was due in part to a moderation in domestic controversy during his first

Administration. But it must also be an extraordinary comment on the way Mr. Eisenhower had interpreted his office. In view of the enormous responsibilities for legislative, partisan, and executive leadership that attach to the presidency, it is difficult to believe that a man could serve four years in this office and yet be associated with domestic issues to as slight a degree as an opponent who was wholly without public office in the same period.

Mr. Eisenhower was of course much more widely associated with issues of foreign affairs. Owing to his background, somewhat more than a third of all references to war and peace and to other foreign issues in 1952 were associated with Eisenhower. In 1956, with a smaller volume of total comment about foreign affairs, this fraction

TABLE 3-9. References to Foreign Issues

	1952	1956
Associated with the Republican Party	336	329
Associated with the Democratic Party	420	183
Associated with Eisenhower	546	481
Associated with Stevenson	62	58
Totals	1364	1051

was increased to nearly one half. Both major parties were frequently linked with foreign issues in the first of these elections, but with the Democratic Party's record receding in time, relatively fewer of these comments referred to the Democrats in the second campaign. In neither year did Mr. Stevenson make any marked impression on the electorate in relation to foreign affairs. In view of his great concern with foreign policy, the attention he gave to foreign issues in his campaign addresses, and his travels abroad between these elections, this fact suggests how deep may be the gulf that separates the public's view of a candidate and the image he seeks to project. Mr. Stevenson probably had had more contact with foreign affairs than most presidential candidates. Yet this contact failed to cross the threshold of public awareness.

We have already called attention to the likelihood that a new figure in national politics will be evaluated by the public partly in terms of his connection with his party. This was true of both Mr. Eisenhower and Mr. Stevenson in these years. In each campaign, references were made to the fact that a candidate was the representative of his party and bore the party symbol. And other responses referred to the association of a candidate with some element of his party, such as the Taft or Truman leadership. The extent to which Eisenhower and Stevenson were evaluated in these terms may be seen in Table 3-10. These figures make clear that the tendency to evaluate the candidates in terms of party was less pronounced in the second of these elections. Responses referring a candidate explicitly to his party were given in

TABLE 3-10. References to Candidates in Terms of Party

	1952	1956
Favorable to Eisenhower	121	57
Unfavorable to Eisenhower	220	162
Favorable to Stevenson	264	202
Unfavorable to Stevenson	360	64
Totals	965	485

the latter campaign with much less frequency than they were when these men had first emerged as presidential candidates. In the course of four years, association with party had become both less an asset and less a liability for each of them.

Although a candidate is likely to be seen partly in terms of his connection with party and with issues of public policy and matters of group interest, he will be evaluated as well in terms of personal attributes. In the presidential elections of the 1950's most references to the candidates dealt with their record and experience, their abilities, and their personal characteristics. Since General Eisenhower entered politics as an established public figure it is not surprising that his personal attributes were much more fully described in public response than were those of Governor Stevenson. In the campaign of 1952 references of this sort to Eisenhower exceeded in number references to personal qualities of Stevenson by more than sixty per cent. The figures of Table 3-11 indicate that at the end of Eisenhower's first term his personal characteristics were far better known to the public than were those of Mr. Stevenson. Nonetheless, a profound change in public attitude toward Stevenson is evident in these data. The perception of Stevenson's personal characteristics was less full in 1952 than that of Eisenhower's; but it was warmly favorable. By 1956 the response to Stevenson was much less approving. More than half the references to his personal attributes in the latter year were unfavorable.

TABLE 3-11. References to Personal Attributes of the Candidates

	1952	1956
Favorable to Eisenhower	2256	2226
Unfavorable to Eisenhower	906	854
Totals	3162	3080
Favorable to Stevenson	1416	1045
Unfavorable to Stevenson	555	1184
Totals	1971	2229

A finer analysis of response to the candidates brings to light a number of changes in their public images between the two campaigns.

TABLE 3-12. Favorable References to Eisenhower[a]

	1952	1956
Generally good man, capable, experienced	301	330
Record and experience		
Military experience	202	111
Record in Europe	250	94
Political and other experience	57	106
Qualifications and abilities		
Good leader, knows how to handle people	138	107
Good administrator	64	26
Strong, decisive	53	32
Independent	70	17
Educated	97	62
Good speaker	31	42
Personal qualities		
Integrity, ideals	271	291
Sense of duty, patriotism	70	74
Inspiring, inspires confidence	53	39
Religious	19	85
Kind, warm	11	41
Sincere	63	126
Likeable, nice personality, I like him	220	363
Good family life	26	57

[a] Since a number of minor categories have been omitted from Tables 3-12 through 3-15, the totals in these tables are somewhat smaller than the entries of Table 3-11.

The character of these changes suggests several clues to the forces shaping perceptions of the candidates in these years. A full classification of references to Eisenhower suggests that his appeal, already strongly personal in 1952, became overwhelmingly so in 1956. In the earlier campaign, Eisenhower's military experience and record in Europe were clearly remembered. By 1956 these themes had receded without the substitution of nearly as many references to his record and experience as president. Moreover, references to his skills as leader and administrator were fewer in 1956 than before. It was the response to personal qualities—to his sincerity, his integrity and sense of duty, his virtue as a family man, his religious devotion, and his sheer likeableness—that rose substantially in the second campaign. These frequencies leave the strong impression that in 1956 Eisenhower was honored not so much for his performance as President as for the quality of his person.

TABLE 3-13. Unfavorable References to Eisenhower

	1952	1956
Generally not a good man, not qualified	41	36
Record and experience		
Unsuccessful record	3	28
Inexperienced, no government experience	198	16
Part-time president	. . .	64
Qualifications and abilities		
Poor leader, can't handle people	2	14
Poor administrator	6	6
Weak, indecisive	9	13
Not independent, run by others	46	73
Poor speaker	26	13
Poor health, too old	9	386
A military man	446	63
Personal qualities		
Low integrity	12	16
Not enough humility	1	. . .
Not religious	3	1
Cold, aloof	1	1
Insincere	1	. . .
Rich, has lots of money	1	2
Not likeable, I don't like him	6	10
Poor family life	. . .	. . .

TABLE 3-14. Favorable References to Stevenson

	1952	1956
Generally good man, capable, experienced	200	190
Record and experience		
Record as governor	150	48
Experience	204	67
Qualifications and abilities		
Good leader, knows how to handle people	19	20
Good administrator	36	10
Strong, decisive	7	11
Independent	32	21
Educated	149	180
Good speaker	141	100
Personal qualities		
Integrity, ideals	111	77
Sense of duty, patriotism	25	20
Inspiring, people have confidence in him	14	4
Religious	7	2
Kind, warm	11	8
Sincere	33	33
Likeable, I like him	91	77
Good family life	9	4

The flaws in the Eisenhower image were few, and in neither campaign were they matters for which the candidate could be held entirely accountable. In 1952 a large number of references cited Eisenhower's background as a military man and his lack of experience in civil government. Presumably his induction as President and subsequent non-military bearing quieted most of these doubts, though comments on his military background were still given in 1956. Critical response in the latter year dealt primarily with the issue of his health and his capacity to be a full-time president. Other than this the only unfavorable reference of any frequency was the doubt that Eisenhower as President was wholly his own man.

The popular response to Stevenson showed a general lessening of enchantment in his second appeal to the electorate, but several details of this loss in esteem stand out. The benefit to Mr. Stevenson of having been Governor of Illinois, as measured by references to his record and experience, seems largely to have been dissipated after four years. References to his experience in public service dropped quite low in 1956, and comments about his lack of experience were made with greater frequency. Second, references to Stevenson's personal qualities, which had been substantially favorable in his first campaign, were much less so in his second. Surprisingly, Stevenson's divorce seemed more on the public's mind in the latter year. Finally, the response to Mr. Stevenson's campaign performance was much more critical in 1956 than in 1952.

TABLE 3-15. Unfavorable References to Stevenson

	1952	1956
Generally not a good man, not qualified	37	122
Record and experience		
Unsuccessful record	18	14
Inexperienced	25	72
Qualifications and abilities		
Poor leader, can't handle people	7	16
Poor administrator	2	2
Weak, indecisive	17	25
Not independent, run by others	41	14
Poor speaker, don't like his speeches, too high fallutin', jokes too much	103	261
Personal qualities		
Low integrity	34	73
Not enough humility, too self-confident	...	22
Not religious	8	11
Cold, aloof	6	11
Insincere	6	40
Undemocratic, snobbish, aristocratic	14	22
Not likeable, I don't like him	34	159
Divorced, poor family life	85	137

We cannot know from these data what part of Stevenson's loss in esteem by 1956 should be laid to the fact that he had once been defeated. In failing a second time to win the presidency Mr. Stevenson shared the experience of two other candidates in this century. It is not unreasonable to think that each of these men, as well as defeated candidates who have failed in their quest even of a second nomination, suffered a considerable loss in public favor simply because they were once defeated. In each of these cases the fact of their rejection, which is of great public salience, may have added a "normal" loss of favor to the changes in popular support arising from other factors. If we had measurements of the sort reported here for the two election campaigns of Thomas E. Dewey and the three campaigns of William Jennings Bryan we could say with greater confidence whether this is so.

The Dynamics of Mass Percepts

The materials we have reviewed disclose the elements of presidential politics, not as they were, but as the public perceived them in the Eisenhower years. Taken together, the cognitive and affective themes recorded in our interviews suggest the "sense" the electorate made of the objects it acted toward in two elections. When they are laid against what we know of the objects themselves, the images found in these interviews suggest, too, some general ideas about the factors that have shaped their content.

Generalization and the permanence of objects. The individual voter sees the several elements of national politics as more than a collection of discrete, unrelated objects. After all, they are parts of one political system and are connected in the real world by a variety of relations that are visible in some degree to the electorate. A *candidate* is the nominee of his *party;* party and candidate are oriented to the same *issues* or *groups,* and so forth. Moreover, we may assume that the individual strives to give order and coherence to his image of these objects. As a means of achieving order, the transfer of cognitive attributes and affective values from one object to another undoubtedly plays an important role. A good deal of psychological research leads us to assume that under certain conditions the properties that one political element is perceived to have will be generalized to another, or that the emotion directed toward one object will be extended to a second. The "conditions" of this transfer may be exceedingly simple—as two elements bearing the same party label—although in the intellective processes of the most sophisticated, politically involved portion of the electorate they are probably very complex.

The fact that one element of politics may color another in both a cognitive and an affective sense is of especial importance because political objects enter public awareness at different times and have greatly different degrees of permanence. The world of politics is full of novelty, yet some of its elements persist for relatively long periods. Moreover, the features of these objects that are most widely known may heighten the sense of their unchanging character. At the simplest level, the elements of politics, like so much else in the external world, are known to the individual by name, and these symbols are of considerable cognitive importance to the electorate. What is more, a good deal else about the objects of politics may be characterized by symbols, such as the terms "New Deal" or "Fair Deal," whose persistence through time may give the objects an unchanging aspect despite wide changes in their "real" properties.

The most enduring objects of the political environment are of course the Republican and Democratic Parties, and the relative permanence of our major parties has two main consequences for the dynamics of popular attitude. First, the novel objects of presidential politics may receive a marked initial coloration by reason of their association with one or the other of the parties. The frequencies of Table 3-10 show that nearly a thousand references to party were among the responses to the two new candidates for President in 1952. Second, perception and feeling that were initially associated with other objects may survive in the image of the parties after the elements from which they arose have left the political environment. It is quite probable that the attitudes from the New Deal era that were expressed in our interviews were associated at first largely with Roosevelt but became imbedded so deeply in the image of the Democratic and Republican Parties that they remained powerful ideas years after Roosevelt's death. The role of party as a carrier of attitude that arose in public response to things past may be one of profound significance. To a great extent the image of the Republican and Democratic Parties in 1952 and 1956 *was* the public's response to issues and events of the past generation, whereas popular perceptions of Eisenhower and Stevenson seemed to be fashioned of more current materials.

The threshold of awareness. A great deal of change in the electorate's map of politics can be explained in terms of what has and what has not penetrated the public consciousness.[4] In the electorate as a whole the level of attention to politics is so low that what the public is exposed to must be highly visible—even stark—if it is to have an impact on opinion. The evidential basis of this remark must await the discussion of later chapters, but its correctness is strongly implied by some of the frequencies we have examined. For example, despite

[4] It is here that information is most needed on communication variables. Awareness is partly a matter of motivation and predisposition: the individual is aware of things he wants to attend. But it is also a matter of sheer currency or visibility, as the success of modern advertising suggests. Hence, the decisions of those who control communication are partial determinants of public awareness, and more information is needed about them.

a concentration on foreign issues by Mr. Stevenson, which must have been at least as great as that of any candidate in this country, the public was largely unaware of his positions. Nor in some respects did Mr. Eisenhower fare better as President. Despite the fact that his action or inaction as Chief Executive had wide impact on the course of our affairs at home, the public connected him with issues of domestic policy only to a slight degree in 1956.

The difficulty the phenomena of politics have in crossing the threshold of public awareness makes it much more likely that a party will be known more for its deeds in office than for its words out of office. A clear example of this is provided by changes in public attitude about the economic implications of a Republican administration. Having been associated with the great economic collapse of 1929–1932, the Republican Party was unable for twenty years to dispel the notion that its return to office would jeopardize our economic well being. Despite the earnest campaign declarations of Landon, Willkie, Dewey, and Eisenhower, this theme remained strongly in perceptions of the party in the campaign of 1952. Not until economic prosperity had been experienced with a Republican in the White House did the party make substantial headway against this theme. The point is not that economic prosperity during Eisenhower's first term was any better evidence for the Republican case than what had been cited by Messrs. Landon, Willkie, and Dewey (witness the events of Eisenhower's second term). The point is rather that the evidence was visible enough that it could enter the awareness of the mass electorate and have a broad impact on perceptions of the parties.

Some implications of the low salience that most of national politics has for the electorate may seem fairly novel. For example, it is not unlikely that most new Presidents take office without their stance toward issues or groups having had much impact on popular attitude. What perceptions the public has are likely to be highly derivative carry-overs from perceptions of the President's party. In this respect the extent in 1952 of public knowledge of Eisenhower's orientation in world affairs, arising as it did out of the impact of his career as a soldier-diplomat, must have been quite unusual. It is largely *after* the President has taken office and has assumed the position of matchless visibility in American politics that his image begins to acquire the large number of issue themes we might expect. The acquisition may be dramatically sudden, as it probably was in the case of Roosevelt; or it may be slow and uneven, as it clearly was in the case of Eisenhower.

The social bases of stability. Our review of the content of public attitude shows that the duration of public response to political objects is quite variable and that although the more intense attitude tends to be the longer-lasting, some types of feeling can reach high levels in one election and scarcely be evident in the next. What accounts for the very unequal time that different percepts survive in the electorate's map of politics? We have already touched part of the answer: objects persist in the political environment for different lengths of time, as do the relations among them that may give rise to public feeling.

The stability of mass percepts depends, too, on how well they are bound into the social fabric. To make this point clear let us return to the problem of the impact on subsequent attitude of the wars in which America has been involved. We have remarked that the world wars of the twentieth century did surprisingly little to remake the partisan perceptions held by the electorate. Of course these wars had a deep impress on American thinking in a variety of ways. But they left in their wake relatively few issues that would continue to divide the electorate, and, what is most important, except perhaps for the alienation of those of German ethnicity[5] from the administration party these issues failed to coincide well with stable groupings within the population. The impact of the Civil War was very different, opening, as it did, issues of intense partisan contest, which coincided very closely with enduring regional and racial fissures in the social order. The stability of percepts arising out of the Civil War experience undoubtedly was greatly reinforced by the fact that they became enmeshed in conflict between enduring social groupings.

Additional weight is lent this view if we consider the group themes associated with the parties and candidates in the Eisenhower years. We have said that these references usually implied a status dimension: the Democratic Party was approved for championing lower status groups, the Republican Party disapproved for failing to do so or for favoring high status groups. (Of course it was also true that some of our respondents *approved* the Republican Party for taking this position or for resisting group politics altogether and disapproved the Democratic Party for appealing to groups and setting class against class.) Despite the fact that the Depression experience was more than a decade away, these attitudes were widely expressed in 1952, much more widely indeed than were those that might be traced in any way to the Second World War or even to the Korean War. What is more, although the public's perception that the Republican Party would bring bad times was seriously eroded during Eisenhower's first term,

[5] For evidence on this point see Samuel Lubell, *The Future of American Politics* (Harper and Brothers, New York, 1951), especially Chapter 7, "The Myth of Isolationism," pp. 129–157.

the group themes associated with the two parties actually increased in vitality between 1952 and 1956; if one cognitive legacy of the Roosevelt years was disappearing, another was not. Thus the vitality of these group-related percepts may be due in part to the fact that they are supported by the mechanisms that conserve social norms. Here the group may serve not only an element of politics to which parties and candidates adopt some attitude; it may also serve as a reference group whose perceived opinion reinforces the individual's own perception of what is the stance toward the group of other actors in the political environment.

To say this much is to raise the broader question of how perceptions of the political world differ between the groupings that make up the whole electorate. The measurements of this chapter have been of the composite image held by the total population, but the fact of differences between groups is clear enough. Although a survey of these differences is beyond the scope of discussion here, we may note that the stability of the partisan perceptions dividing the electorate will depend in part on the extent to which these divisions coincide with enduring social groupings.

Partisan Choice ◇ 4

The cluster of percepts and feelings that make up the popular image of the parties and candidates are ultimately of interest for their effect on what the electorate does. When the public must act toward the elements of politics, as it must every four years in choosing a President, evaluations of these subjects are of fundamental importance as guides to the electorate's choice. The popular image of politics is continuously changing, at least in its detail, with changes in the wider political environment and in the circumstances of individuals and groups within the electorate. Yet as the moment of decision arrives periodically, the image as currently formed has a profound influence on public choice.

In assessing the impact on behavior of the public's cognitive and affective map of politics we will have to describe this map in terms of *individual* attitude. However much the composite summary of the preceding chapter may reveal about mass perception, voting is in the end an act of individuals, and the motives for this act must be sought in psychological forces on individual human beings. In this chapter we will conceive the individual's evaluative orientations toward the several elements of politics as a system of partisan attitudes and examine the place of this system among the psychological forces governing behavior.

The motivational role of perceptions of the wider political environment deserves greater attention than it has received in electoral research. Since the content of these perceptions has been used chiefly to show perceptual distortion, it has been natural to regard them as having slight motivational significance independent of the predisposing factors whose creatures they are thought to be. Attitudes toward the candidates or toward issues of the campaign have sometimes been treated as rationalizations of preferences fixed by long-term party allegiances or by social characteristics such as ethnic or religious memberships, socio-economic status, and place of residence. Even if it were true that the individual's cognitive and affective map of politics is tightly determined by such influences as these, its content would still be worth exploring for what it tells us about the links connecting party loyalties or social characteristics to behavior. Learning what cognitions and evaluations of politics are implied by identification with party or by membership in one or another social grouping is a task of genuine importance, and if it can clarify or "interpret" the ambiguous statistical associations between social characteristics and voting behavior it will be worth all the attention that can be given it.

Yet it is *not* true that attitudes toward the several elements of politics are only reflections of party loyalty or group memberships or of other factors that may lead to perceptual distortion. To suppose that they are is to understate the importance of changes in the properties of what the individual sees in his environment. Changes in the external realities of politics can have effects on popular feeling within every partisan or social grouping in the electorate. The truth of this statement is easily seen if we observe that attitudes toward the objects of politics, varying through time, can explain short-term fluctuations in partisan division of the vote, whereas party loyalties and social characteristics, which are relatively inert through time, account but poorly for these shifts. Key and Munger have pressed this view using aggregate voting statistics,[1] and it can clearly be supported with survey data.

An example from our own studies is provided by the shift in the two-party division of the national vote between 1948 and 1952. The composition of the electorate by occupation, religion, ethnicity, and other social characteristics changed little between these years. The increase in Republican strength over this four-year period could *not* be explained by a rise in the proportion of the population falling within social categories voting predominantly Republican. Instead, the increment was recruited from nearly every visible social category in the nation. Similarly, if we consider the voting behavior in 1948 and 1952 of those who classified themselves in the latter year as Republicans or Democrats on a standard measure of party allegiance, the Republican proportion of the two-party vote increased in every class

[1] V. O. Key, Jr., and Frank Munger, "Social Determinism and Electoral Decision: The Case of Indiana," ed. Eugene Burdick and Arthur J. Brodbeck, *American Voting Behavior* (The Free Press, Glencoe, Ill., 1959), pp. 296 ff.

along the party scale.[2] Whatever the shade of the individual's party loyalty, the likelihood of his voting Republican was greater in 1952 than it had been four years earlier. Clearly neither social characteristics nor stable partisan attachments accounted for the general movement toward the Republican standard between these two elections. However, the movement can be explained if we accord independent motivational significance to evaluations of the elements of politics and observe that the popular image of the Republican candidate and of the issues that held public attention was much more favorable to the Republicans in 1952 than it was four years before. We attribute this shift largely to changes in these stimulus objects themselves—the substitution of Eisenhower's personality for Dewey's, the outbreak of war in the Far East, and so forth. In both years attitudes toward the candidates and issues were deeply influenced by party loyalties and group memberships. But it is the change of public attitude unrelated to predisposing factors of this sort that can best explain the general shift in voting preference from 1948 to 1952.

Psychological Forces on Behavior

However important more remote factors may be in the causation of behavior, if we limit our inquiry to their relation to the vote we miss important elements of motivation. For this reason we begin our search for causality at the psychological level and conceive of the voting act as the resultant of attitudinal forces. The effect of all factors leading to behavior is finally expressed in the direction and intensity of the forces of a psychological field, in which the individual's attitudes toward the elements of politics have a central place. The elements of national politics—the presidential candidates, questions of group interest, the issues of domestic and foreign policy, the performance of the parties in the conduct of government—are not simply perceived by the individual; they are evaluated as well. Orientations to these objects, seen by the voter as positive or negative, comprise a system of partisan attitudes that is of primary importance for the voting act. The nature of this system and its significance for behavior concern us here.

Of course these partisan attitudes do not exhaust the set of psychological forces that may affect the voting act. For most persons, the partisan decision at the polls depends largely on attitudes of this sort, and a good deal of evidence on this point will be offered here. But for other persons additional forces, such as the perceived preferences of

[2] The nature of our scale of party identification is explained in Chapter 6.

primary group associates, come to bear, as they do in the case of a wife who votes her husband's preferences either against her own inclinations or without developing perceptions of her political environment. In saying this we are not raising the question of what the antecedents of the partisan attitudes may be. In *most* cases information picked up through face-to-face contact with family, work associates, and friends will have some influence on the individual's attitudes toward the elements of presidential politics. We are speaking rather of the cases in which psychological forces other than the partisan attitudes—or even contradicting these attitudes—are of greater importance for behavior.

To assess the impact of the partisan attitudes on behavior we need to reshape the materials on perceptions of politics to measure the psychological forces acting on the individual. From our knowledge of what political objects are visible to the public and the characteristics of attitude toward these objects we have defined six dimensions of individual partisan feeling. In the elections of 1952 and 1956 the elements of politics that seemed most clearly to be objects of popular attitude were these: the personal attributes of Stevenson; the personal attributes of Eisenhower; the groups involved in politics and the questions of group interest affecting them; the issues of domestic policy; the issues of foreign policy; and the comparative record of the two parties in managing the affairs of government. We have conceived evaluative orientations toward these classes of things as six dimensions of partisan attitude. Of course not everyone articulated feeling about each; most people in our samples expressed attitudes toward less than the full set.

To locate the individual on these dimensions of attitude we have used the same sequence of free-answer questions about the parties and candidates that elicited the responses analyzed in Chapter 3. By classifying each answer according to the type of object involved we were able to allocate all the responses given by our samples in 1952 and 1956 and to construct six measures of individual partisan feeling. Although the details of these measures need not be reviewed here,[3] two of their properties should be understood. First, the measures were designed to show the partisan *direction* of an individual's attitude toward a given element of politics; that is, they were constructed to tell us whether a person's attitude was pro-Republican, neutral, or pro-Democratic. Second, the measures were designed to show the *intensity* of partisan attitude; for other than neutral feeling, they were

[3] A description of the methods used appears in Donald E. Stokes, Angus Campbell, and Warren E. Miller, "Components of Electoral Decision," *American Political Science Review,* LII (June 1958), 367–387.

fashioned to tell us how strongly pro-Republican or pro-Democratic was the affect directed toward a political object. With measures having these properties we are able to examine the influence of these psychological forces on the voting act.

The effect of these forces on voting behavior is seen first in their impact on the partisan decision. The fact that we are confronted with a *system* of attitude forces will be clear from the increase in our capacity to explain this choice as we introduce more of the forces comprising the system. But the partisan decision is by no means the sole aspect of voting that these attitudes affect, and other dimensions of the voting act show even more clearly that we are treating a system of forces. We will consider several characteristics of the vote that seem to depend on the presence or absence of conflict between the partisan attitudes. A person may form distinct but conflicting evaluations of the several elements of politics, and the consequences of this conflict for electoral behavior are of substantial importance.

Partisan Attitude and Voting Choice

That the partisan decision of the individual is profoundly affected by the psychological forces we have measured seems clear in the data of several election campaigns. To illustrate the extent of the dependence of this choice on each dimension of partisan feeling, let us examine the behavior of voters in 1956 according to the direction and intensity of their feeling toward the personal attributes of Eisenhower. The variation of behavior across this dimension of attitudes was almost as great as possible, as may be seen in Table 4-1. At the negative end of the scale, those whose image of Eisenhower was quite unfavorable voted Democratic in nearly every case. Among those whose attitude toward Eisenhower was more favorable, the Republican proportion of the vote was greater, increasing without exception as we move toward the other end of the scale. When the extreme positive end is reached, those whose image of Eisenhower was strongly favorable voted Republican in virtually every case. In the extreme differences of partisan behavior it discloses, Table 4-1 is quite representative of the associations we have found between each dimension of attitude and the individual's partisan choice.

Yet we may easily exaggerate how well public attitude toward any single element of presidential politics, such as the Republican candidate, can account for the voting act. Table 4-1 does show that the individual's evaluation, positive or negative, of one of the candidates

TABLE 4-1. Relation of Attitude toward Eisenhower to Party Division of the Vote, 1956

	Attitude toward Eisenhower								
	Unfavorable					Favorable			
	– – –	– –	–	0	+	+ +	+ + +	+ + + +	+ + + + +
Voted Democratic	94%	81%	79%	56%	31%	21%	14%	6%	2%
Voted Republican	6	19	21	44	69	79	86	94	98
	100%	100%	100%	100%	100%	100%	100%	100%	100%
Number of cases	35	73	151	275	232	216	139	99	46

could be of such strength that it would insure a vote in the same partisan direction. But only a slight fraction of the electorate had feelings toward Eisenhower that were extremely strong. The frequencies given in the bottom row of the table indicate that most of the electorate had less intense attitudes and fell in the scale categories where behavior was far less unidirectional. The extreme differences in behavior between the ends of the scale need to be coupled with the fact that most of the electorate was nearer the middle of the scale, if we are to get a correct idea of how well this dimension of attitude alone could explain the choices of individual voters in 1956.

The insufficiency of one dimension as an explanation of the voting act deserves a good deal of emphasis if we are to demonstrate the dependence of behavior on a *system* of partisan attitudes. For this reason the statistics of Table 4-1 are brought into sharper focus by Fig. 4-1. Figure 4-1*a* shows the division of the party vote across the scale of attitude toward Eisenhower; the succession of light and dark bars in this figure repeats the percentages of Table 4-1 and indicates how extreme is the difference in behavior across the scale. But to take into account the location of the electorate on this dimension of attitude, Fig. 4-1*b* shows the party vote within each scale category as a percentage of the total vote. When this is done, it is clear that both parties received the larger portion of their votes not from the extreme categories, where everyone voted much the same way, but from the more moderate categories of attitude, where sizable minorities voted in

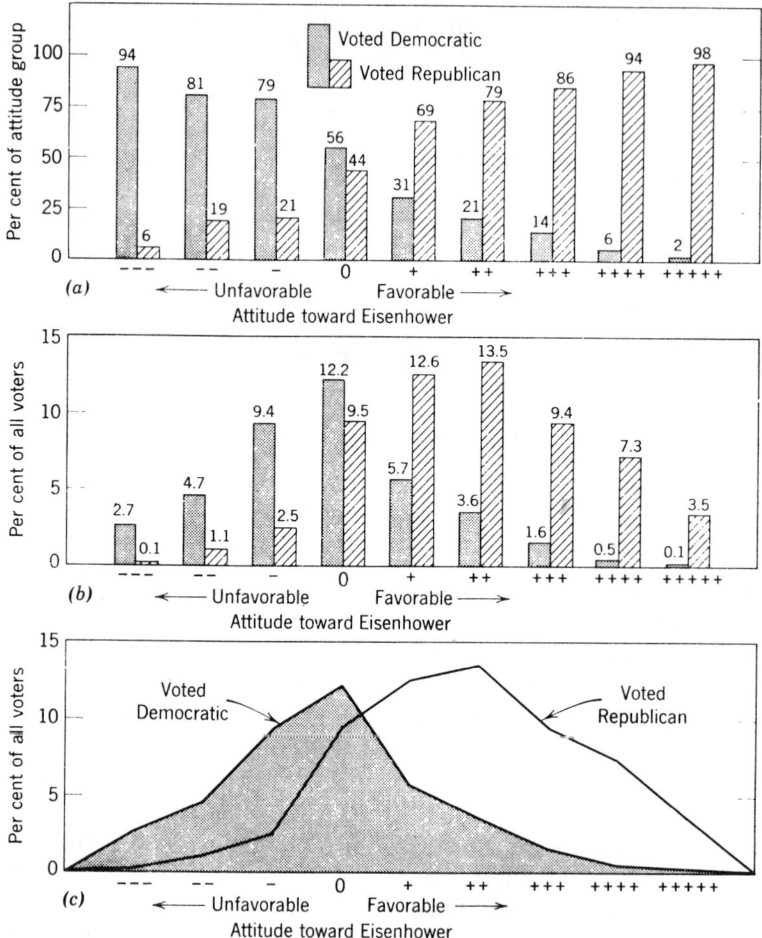

Fig. 4-1. Relation of attitude toward Eisenhower to party vote, 1956.

the opposite direction. If we consider the light bars as defining a distribution of Republican votes and the dark bars as defining a distribution of Democratic votes, the two distributions have a considerable "overlap," which we would have to regard as error in trying to predict behavior from a single dimension of attitude. The size of this error is shown more clearly in Fig. 4-1*c*, which makes explicit the overlap of the frequency curves implied by Fig. 4-1*b*. Roughly speaking, the area under *both* the Republican and Democratic curves is the error we would have confronted in 1956 in predicting behavior from attitude toward Eisenhower alone.

The increase of our power to explain the voting act by taking account of attitude toward more than a single element of politics may be shown by combining a second dimension of feeling with attitude toward Eisenhower and observing the joint effects of two psychological forces on behavior. For this purpose let us consider the joint relation to the vote in 1956 of attitude toward Eisenhower and partisan feeling related to issues of domestic policy. Table 4-2 shows the proportion

TABLE 4-2. Relation of Attitude toward Eisenhower and Attitude on Domestic Issues to Per Cent Voting Republican, 1956[a]

Attitude toward Eisenhower[b]		Attitude on Domestic Issues[b] Extent to which Attitude Favors Republicans							
		− − − −	− − −	− −	−	0	+	+ +	+ + +
Favorable	++++	...	...	...	79	97	97	100	100
	+++	...	...	63	83	85	96	100	89
	++	...	...	47	61	83	87	85	100
	+	...	18	47	64	79	83	87	...
	0	0	8	16	37	48	75	64	92
Unfavorable	−	0	0	18	6	23	67	...	...
	− −	0	8	10	11	25	40	...	...

[a] Entries give per cent voting Republican for each combination of attitude toward Eisenhower and attitude on domestic issues.

[b] Both the scale of attitude toward Eisenhower and the scale of attitude on domestic issues assumed more values than are shown in the table. In order to lessen the sampling variability associated with low frequencies, many of the extreme cells have been combined. Hence the percentages at the first and last of each row or column include cases falling in more extreme cells.

of the vote cast for the Republican candidate across these two dimensions of attitude at once. In the table the horizontal dimension is attitude on domestic issues, the vertical dimension attitude toward Eisenhower. Hence each row indicates how the behavior of individuals of the same attitude toward Eisenhower varied with the partisan direction and intensity of their attitude on domestic issues; and each column shows how the behavior of those of the same partisan feeling on domestic issues varied with their attitude toward Eisenhower. It is clear that measuring a second psychological force enhances our ability to account for the vote.[4] For example, knowledge of this second attitude makes it possible to separate the people who were neutral in their feeling toward Eisenhower—a group that divided its vote fairly evenly in 1956—into classes more nearly homogeneous in their behavior, except for those at the neutral point of both dimensions of attitude. The entries of Table 4-2 are quite representative of those we would obtain by displaying the relation to the voting act of orientations toward any two of our six elements of presidential politics.

From these specimen findings with two dimensions of attitude it requires only a change of technical procedures to consider the combined effects on the partisan decision of all six dimensions of partisan feeling.[5] Our hypothesis that the voting act depends in an immediate sense on the individual voter's evaluative orientations toward *several* objects of politics ought to be tested by an examination of the influence of all these orientations at once. When this test is made for the presidential elections of 1952 and 1956, the findings are consistent with the motivational hypothesis. In these years the individual's partisan decision could be predicted from his evaluations of the elements of national politics with a relatively slight error both in the sense of statistical estimation and of statistical discrimination.

Across the full national electorate the multiple correlation of the six dimensions of attitude with the partisan decision was greater than 0.7 both in 1952 and 1956, and the magnitude of these coefficients is the more impressive if we keep in mind that they have been depressed by errors of measurement and other factors that are not contradictory to our theoretical hypothesis. But it is the capacity of these attitudes to discriminate the actual Republican voter from the actual Democratic voter that perhaps best suggests their explanatory power. The test of our theoretical hypothesis in terms of statistical discrimination is shown in Fig. 4-2. Figure 4-2*a* gives the distribution of all major-party voters

[4] If this ability is measured in terms of a ratio of variances, we may compare a point biserial correlation of 0.52 between attitude toward Eisenhower and voting choice with a multiple correlation of 0.59 between both attitude factors and this choice. If our ability to account for behavior is measured in terms of the proportion of individuals whose vote is predicted correctly, we may compare the seventy-five per cent correctly classified on the basis of one dimension with the seventy-nine per cent correctly classified on the basis of two.

[5] Examination of the relation of the vote to *two* dimensions of attitude by inspecting multivariate frequency distributions presses the number of cases in a sample of well over a thousand persons. To examine the relation of the vote to *six* dimensions by the same method is plainly out of the question. For this reason we have fitted a statistical model to our data and have examined the relation of the voting act to the six partisan attitudes by the methods of multiple regression and of statistical discrimination.

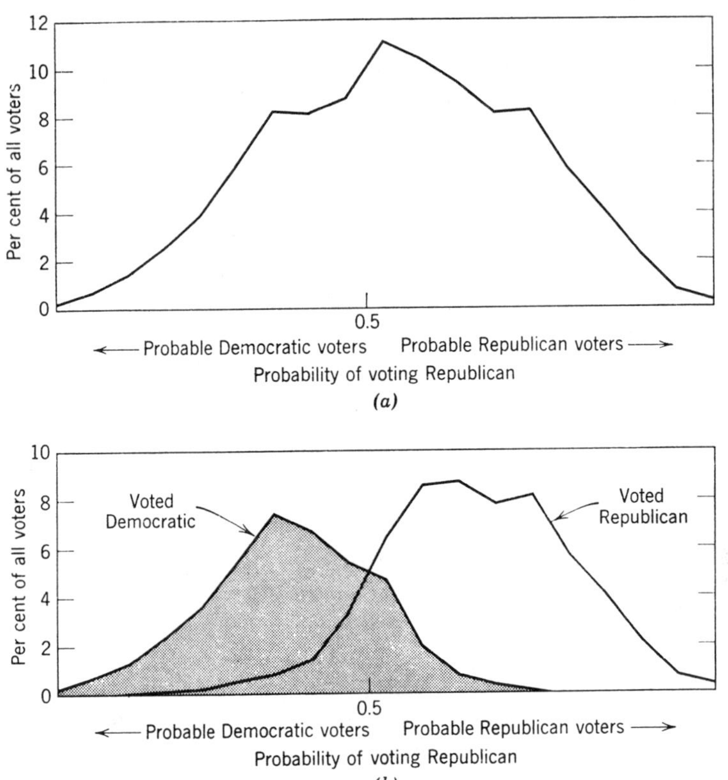

Fig. 4-2. The prediction of voting choice from all partisan attitudes, 1952 and 1956 combined. (*a*) Distribution of all respondents by probability of voting Republican; (*b*) distribution of actual Democratic and Republican voters by probability of voting Republican.

in our 1952 and 1956 sample according to the probability of their voting Republican, as we have estimated this probability from the direction and intensity of their attitudes toward the several elements of national politics.[6] Individuals toward the left of this distribution have a low probability of voting Republican (hence, a high probability of voting Democratic), those toward the right a high probability of voting Republican. To predict actual behavior from these probabilities we would select the value 0.5 as a point of discrimination and predict that

[6] The probabilities are computed by the methods of multiple linear regression by assigning a score of 0 to a Democratic vote and a score of 1 to a Republican vote and treating the equation giving the regression of voting choice on the six partisan attitudes as a linear probability function.

those with a probability less than 0.5 of voting Republican would vote Democratic and that those with a probability greater than 0.5 of voting Republican would in fact cast their votes for the Republican candidate.

The success of these predictions in the elections of 1952 and 1956 is shown in Fig. 4-2*b*, which gives separately the distributions of probability scores for *actual* Democratic and Republican voters. As in Fig. 4-1*c*, the overlap of the Democratic and Republican curves indicates the error of our predictions. But unlike the earlier figure, the overlap here is quite small relative to the total area under the two curves. The proportion of cases in which we would be in error has almost been halved.[7] Both in 1952 and 1956 the behavior of more than 85 per cent of the electorate is consistent with our theoretical hypothesis. This percentage may have sharper meaning if we observe that it is actually larger than the percentage of voters in these samples who were able before the election *to predict correctly their own behavior.* That is, the number of our respondents whose votes we are able to foretell from what we know of their partisan attitude is greater than the number who were able to foretell their own votes. Too fine an interpretation ought not to be placed on a comparison of this sort since the differences are small and our prediction is *post facto* in the sense that the discriminatory analysis requires that we already know how the people in our samples did vote. Yet the comparison is nonetheless interesting. Electoral research has invested a great deal of attention in explanatory factors that are vastly less efficient in predicting behavior than the simple device of asking a person how he intends to vote. To be sure, these explanatory factors in most cases are theoretically more interesting than the individual's own description of a latent vote decision. Yet even the best-known explanatory factors, such as combinations of social characteristics, fare poorly when their predictive power is compared with that of self-prediction. The greater success of the psychological forces we have considered here is of course chiefly due to their greater immediacy to behavior. But it is remarkable that *any* explanatory

[7] The greater predictive power of the full set of six dimensions of partisan attitude may be summarized as follows for the election of 1956:

When Prediction Is From:	Correlation of Predictors with Voting Choice	Proportion Correctly Classified
Attitude toward Eisenhower only	0.52	75%
Attitude toward Eisenhower and attitude on domestic issues	0.59	79%
All six dimensions of partisan attitude	0.71	86%

factors can be found which surpass self-prediction in their capacity to distinguish those who will actually vote Republican from those who will vote Democratic.

The components of error. The very success of the partisan attitudes in accounting for behavior leads to a consideration of the deviant case. What factors can explain the partisan choices of those for whom we were in error, particularly when behavior seems strongly to have contradicted the direction of partisan attitude? A close inspection of the interview protocols suggests several components of error, and certain of these are factors of theoretical importance in the total field of forces leading to the voting act.

As one might expect, some errors are of measurement and do not contradict our theoretical hypothesis. The slight overreport of votes for the winning candidate in the Eisenhower elections suggests that a few of our respondents have falsely reported their behavior in the post-election interview.[8] Moreover, with interviews as early as six weeks before the election, in some cases attitude change can occur between the interview and election day. For example, the frequency with which the Middle East crisis was mentioned after the 1956 election by persons we had expected to vote Democratic yet who voted Republican suggests that in some cases the Suez War moved their opinions in the Republican direction after the time of our pre-election interview. Our data suggest strongly that eleventh-hour events such as this and the offer of Eisenhower to go to Korea in 1952 could not possibly have had the great impact in the whole electorate with which they are often credited. But there is little doubt that some errors of prediction are due to attitude change induced by events after our pre-election interview.

Paralleling errors of measurement are those arising from the nature of our statistical methods. The probability model we have fitted to the interview data from a national sample assigns weights to the several partisan attitudes according to the strength of their association with the voting act across the entire electorate. But these statistical averages may distort the relative importance of the several forces in the decision of a single individual. For example, a southern respondent in 1956 had formed a favorable estimate of Eisenhower, of Republican foreign policy, and of the success of the Republican administration in cleaning up the "mess" in Washington. But he knew that Eisenhower and the Republicans were wrong on a single domestic issue—the issue of segre-

[8] However, both in 1952 and 1956 the division of the vote reported by our samples was less than 3 per cent more Republican than the true division of the votes cast, as recorded in official election statistics.

gation—and so he unhesitatingly cast his vote for a Democratic candidate he did not like. The choice of this individual did not depend less on attitudes toward the objects of national politics than did the choices of most of the persons for whom our predictions proved correct. Yet in this case the relative importance of the several attitudes departed so widely from what was usual that we were led to make a wrong prediction.

There is occasional error of another type that appears traceable to direct interpersonal influence. Not only does the individual absorb from his primary groups the attitudes that guide his behavior; he often behaves politically as a self-conscious member of these groups, and his perception of their preferences can be of great importance for his own voting act. Our interviews suggest that the dynamics of these face-to-face associations are capable of generating forces that may negate the force of the individual's own evaluations of the elements of politics. Probably this happens most often in the relations of husband and wife, but an analysis of error provides many other illustrations of this influence as well. For example, one respondent traced an abrupt reversal of his vote intention to the arrival of a brother-in-law from California; another to the pressures he felt from work associates; another to face-to-face badgering by a precinct committeeman.

Important as primary group influence may be in forming or contradicting partisan attitude, an interview survey of widely separated individuals is not well suited to its study. The small group setting of attitude and behavior is one of great significance, but estimates in survey studies of its importance for voting typically have had to depend on what respondents tell about the partisan preferences of their family, work, and friendship groups. The degree of homogeneity suggested by these reports is impressive. Among respondents in our 1952 sample who voted Republican or Democratic and who ascribed a partisan color to one or another of their primary groups, the agreement reported between own preference and that of primary group associates was very high, as shown in Table 4-3. The difficulty with figures such as these is that they cannot be checked against independent observations of the preferences of these groups. Until they can be checked, we will not be sure how much the reported agreement rests on perceptual distortion. Yet this difficulty does not lessen our qualitative sense of the importance of the small group setting of partisan attitude and the partisan choice. And it does not obscure the finding from an analysis of errors of prediction that primary group associations may in the exceptional case introduce forces in the individual's psychological field

TABLE 4-3. Relation of Reported Partisan Preference of Primary Groups to Respondent's Own Partisan Choice, 1952[a]

Respondent Voted	Spouse Voted		Family Voted[b]		Friends Voted		Work Associates Voted	
	Dem.	Rep.	Dem.	Rep.	Dem.	Rep.	Dem.	Rep.
Democratic	89%	7%	80%	8%	83%	15%	79%	24%
Republican	11	93	20	92	17	85	21	76
Totals	100%	100%	100%	100%	100%	100%	100%	100%
Number of cases[c]	337	496	75	108	355	574	271	290

[a] This tabulation is limited to persons who reported voting for a major-party candidate for President and who could attribute to the primary group in question a clear partisan preference.

[b] Asked only of unmarried respondents.

[c] Includes a small number of persons who voted for a minor-party candidate.

that are of sufficient strength to produce behavior that contradicts his evaluations of political objects.

The Effects of Attitude Conflict

In many cases attitudes toward the elements of presidential politics are well formed before the campaign opens. The associations found in the preceding chapter between changes in the external political world and popular feeling toward the elements of that world suggest that important shifts of attitude occur *between* campaigns. For example, the transformation of political mood associated with the Korean War and the "mess" in Washington almost certainly antedated the campaign of 1952, as did the origin of favorable attitudes toward Eisenhower. Nevertheless, politics is more salient to a good deal of the electorate during an election campaign, and the weeks of the presidential contest heighten the intensity of partisan attitude in most individuals. Moreover, response to the candidate who is not familiar to the public may be formed largely during the campaign and its immediate prelude.

A problem to be explained: motivational differences by time of vote decision. A description of shifts in attitude through the campaign has not been a main objective of our research. In each election year we have assessed the psychological forces acting on the individual by means of a single pre-election interview; we have not sought the repeated interviews that would be needed to measure short-term change within a single campaign. And neither have we asked our respondents to recollect these changes, owing to the uncertain nature of this type of recall information.

Yet we have asked those interviewed in each election year to tell us when it was that their vote decision crystallized.[9] The answers to this question, too, are subject to the hazards of recall, but the responses undoubtedly give a sense of the location in time of individual choices. They are summarized for the elections of 1952 and 1956 in Table 4-4.

TABLE 4-4. Reported Time of Vote Decision

	1952	1956
Knew all along how they would vote	30%	44%
Decided when Eisenhower or Stevenson became a candidate or at time of conventions	35	32
Decided after conventions, during campaign	20	11
Decided within two weeks of election	9	7
Decided on election day	2	2
Do not remember	1	1
Not ascertained	3	3
Totals	100%	100%
Number of cases	1195	1291

The entries of the table confirm the judgment that the psychological forces guiding behavior arise before the campaign opens. In each of these elections fewer than two voters in five felt they had decided in the course of the campaign proper. Apparently this proportion was somewhat less in 1956 than it had been even in 1952. In the rematch of Eisenhower and Stevenson only 20 per cent of the voters felt they had reached their decision while the campaign was in progress.

The distribution through time of individual choices tells something about the background of partisan attitude, but a more revealing finding emerges when the relation of attitudes to the voting act is examined according to the timing of the individual's partisan decision. The

[9] The question used was: "How long before the election did you decide that you were going to vote the way you did?"

remarkable pattern of differences that is found when our samples are divided according to the reported time of vote decision is shown in Fig. 4-3. Among persons indicating they knew all along how they would vote the joint relation of the several attitudes to the partisan decision was very high both in 1952 and 1956. Among those who reported deciding before or during the conventions this relation was somewhat lower. Among those who said they decided in mid-campaign, the relation was lower still. And among those who told us they decided within two weeks of the election or on election day, the relation was found to be fairly slight. In both the elections of 1952 and 1956 the proportion of the variance of voting choice explained by these psychological forces was more than seven times greater among persons who knew all along than it was among those who decided in the final days of the campaign.

The extraordinary differences of Fig. 4-3 make clear that the psychological forces we have measured influence the time at which the vote decision is made. But to interpret the nature of this effect more information is needed than is supplied by the figure. What explains the extreme variation of the relation of the partisan attitudes to behavior that appears when our samples are divided in this way? The answer lies largely in the presence or absence of conflict among the several psychological forces acting on behavior. Although the near-random

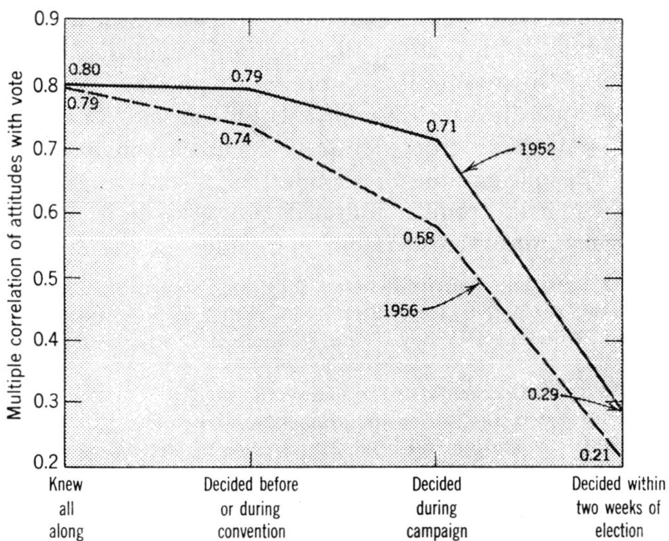

Fig. 4-3. Relation of reported time of decision to ability of partisan attitudes to explain vote.

behavior of those deciding late in the campaign is not to be explained altogether in terms of conflict, persons who reported deciding early are distinguished from those who reported deciding late primarily in the degree to which they experienced conflict in their evaluations of the several elements of national politics. In raising the question of attitude consistency, Fig. 4-3 leads to a problem that transcends in importance the explanation of the time of the individual's vote decision.

Psychological conflict and social cross-pressures. The interest of voting research in conflicting pressures goes back to the revealing study of Erie County, Ohio, by Lazarsfeld, Berelson, and Gaudet. As set forth in *The People's Choice* and as restated in *Voting* the "cross-pressures" hypothesis has been phrased much more in terms of the association of variables than in terms of the causal mechanisms that were thought to be involved.[10] The Erie County study in particular cast its net very widely in the variety of conceptual levels at which cross-pressures were examined.[11] Yet despite the range of the factors treated, there is implicit in these discussions the assumption that conflicting factors will have consequences for behavior because they are experienced as conflict within the individual's psychological field. The very term "cross-pressures" has strong connotations of this sort. And several passages imply that the common aspect of these conflicts of diverse factors is their tendency to create psychological conflict within the individual.[12]

Cross-pressures have been treated in our own work primarily in terms of attitude conflict. In focusing attention on psychological conflict we will remove the discussion of cross-pressures somewhat from the concerns out of which it arose. Conflict within the individual's psychological field may result from politically heterogeneous memberships, and we will give one example of a connection, albeit a fairly weak one, between psychological conflict and social cross-pressures. Yet conflicts of psychological forces may arise for quite different reasons than this,

[10] See Paul F. Lazarsfeld, Bernard Berelson, and Hazel Gaudet, *The People's Choice* (Duell, Sloan and Pearce, New York, 1944), p. 53, and Bernard R. Berelson, Paul F. Lazarsfeld, and William N. McPhee, *Voting* (University of Chicago Press, Chicago, 1954), pp. 128 ff.

[11] Six specific conflicts examined were those between religion and socio-economic level; between objective occupation and subjective occupational group identification; between 1936 presidential vote and 1940 presidential vote; between own preference and preference of others in family; between own preference and preference of associates; between own preference and view of the importance of business experience for presidential candidates.

[12] For example, see the discussion of why people subject to cross-pressures delay their final vote decision until late in the campaign (Lazarsfeld, Berelson, and Gaudet, *op. cit.*, pp. 60–61).

and most of our discussion will proceed without inquiring into what has led to attitudinal cross-pressures. It is the effect, rather than the cause, of conflict that is of primary interest.

In devising our measures of partisan attitude we have sought to reduce to a minimum what the investigator must infer to establish the fact of psychological conflict. The portion of our interview schedules used to assess these attitudes presents the individual with the objects of the political world and elicits responses *that the individual himself* identifies as being positive or negative, pro-Republican or pro-Democratic, and so forth. As a result, we can easily tell whether the individual's attitudes toward the several objects of his feeling are consistent in their partisan direction. Referring once more to the dimensions of attitude used illustratively in Table 4-2, we may say that the person who likes Eisenhower and also the Republican position on domestic issues is consistent in his attitudes toward these things, and so is the person who dislikes Eisenhower and Republican domestic policies. But the individual who likes Eisenhower and dislikes the Republican position or who dislikes Eisenhower but approves his party's stands may be said to experience some conflict in preparing his voting act.

We have noted before that not everyone in our samples showed clear evaluative feelings toward all six classes of objects we have considered. Indeed, most of those interviewed in 1952 and 1956 appeared to be neutral on one or more dimension either by showing a balance of feeling toward a given object or by showing no feeling toward the object at all. Because the meaning of conflict can vary a good deal according to the number of psychological forces acting on the individual, we will treat separately those having partisan feeling on two, three, four, or five dimensions. So few people had partisan feeling on all six dimensions that they are excluded from the analysis. Those who showed partisan feeling on one dimension or on none are also excluded since they could hardly be thought to experience conflict in the sense we define it here. Let us speak of the number of partisan attitudes as the individual's *attitude level*. It is clear that at the level of two, three, four, and five attitudes we can distinguish those whose feelings are fully consistent in the Democratic or Republican direction from those who exhibit some degree of conflict of partisan attitude.

The effects of attitude conflict. Let us now return to the role of partisan attitudes in fixing the time of the individual's vote decision. If we examine the relation of attitude consistency to the reported time of decision at each attitude level, a clear set of differences is found, as

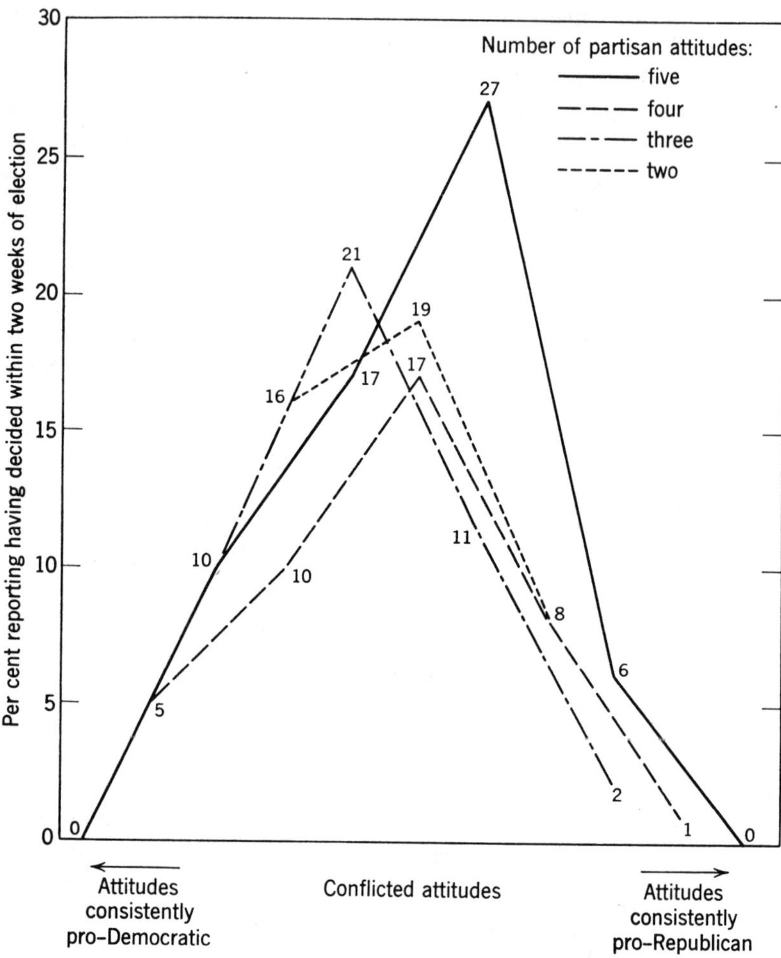

Fig. 4-4. Relation of extent of attitude consistency to reported time of vote decision, 1956.

is shown by Fig. 4-4. In the design of the figure each of the four curves is associated with a distinct level of attitude. The shape of each curve shows the differing proportions of voters deciding late in the campaign as we move from full attitude consistency in the Democratic direction through various degrees of attitude conflict to full consistency in the Republican direction. The proportion deciding late *always* is greater as the degree of attitude conflict is greater; at any attitude level, those of a given degree of attitude consistency will have a larger proportion of late deciders than any group of greater consistency, and it will have a smaller proportion of late deciders than any group showing less consistency. At the level of five attitudes, where conflict and consistency probably were subjectively most intense, those who were fully consistent reported in every case deciding before the last two weeks of the campaign; and those at this level who experienced the maximum conflict reported as often as one case in four making up their minds within two weeks of the election or on election day itself.

The data of Fig. 4-4 supply an important key for interpreting the striking differences in the power of the partisan attitudes to explain behavior that we have seen in Fig. 4-3. It is now clear that the persons in our samples who reported deciding very late were often people whose attitudes were in conflict. If the choices they eventually made agreed now with one attitude and now with another, the explanatory power of the total system should prove to be much less than it was among the more consistent individuals who decided earlier. To be sure, the extreme differences of Fig. 4-3 cannot be attributed entirely to the consistency of partisan attitude. We encounter some cases in which it is clear that causality is operating in the opposing direction. That is, the individual's field appears inconsistent, not because of conflict in any dynamic sense, but because politics is of remote interest and political perceptions are left in a disorganized state. But a substantial part of the reduction in the power of these attitudes to explain behavior among those choosing later can be laid to the fact that a deferred choice was one more likely to issue from conflicting psychological forces.

Not only does the degree of attitude consistency affect the time of the individual's vote decision; it affects other aspects of behavior as well. The person who experiences some degree of conflict tends to cast his vote for President with substantially less enthusiasm, he is much more prone to split his ticket in voting for other offices, and he is somewhat less likely to vote at all than is the person whose partisan feelings are entirely consistent. The similarity of these relationships to the relation between time of decision and the consistency of attitude can be illustrated by examining the proportion failing to vote a straight party ticket among those of different degrees of attitude conflict. From Fig. 4-5 for the election of 1956 it is clear that at every level of attitude those who experienced conflict voted a straight ticket less often than did those whose attitudes were consistent.

One other finding may be drawn from Fig. 4-5. The greater variation in the curve for those with five partisan attitudes suggests that the disposition to vote a straight ticket depends more on the degree of partisan consistency at this higher level than at lower levels. The difference at the higher level of more than 50 per cent in the proportions of conflicted and unconflicted voters voting a straight ticket records the central role of psychological conflict at this level in determining this aspect of behavior. The exaggerated peak of the curve for those with five partisan attitudes tends to confirm the validity of a classification of straight and split-ticket voters into the four categories of the

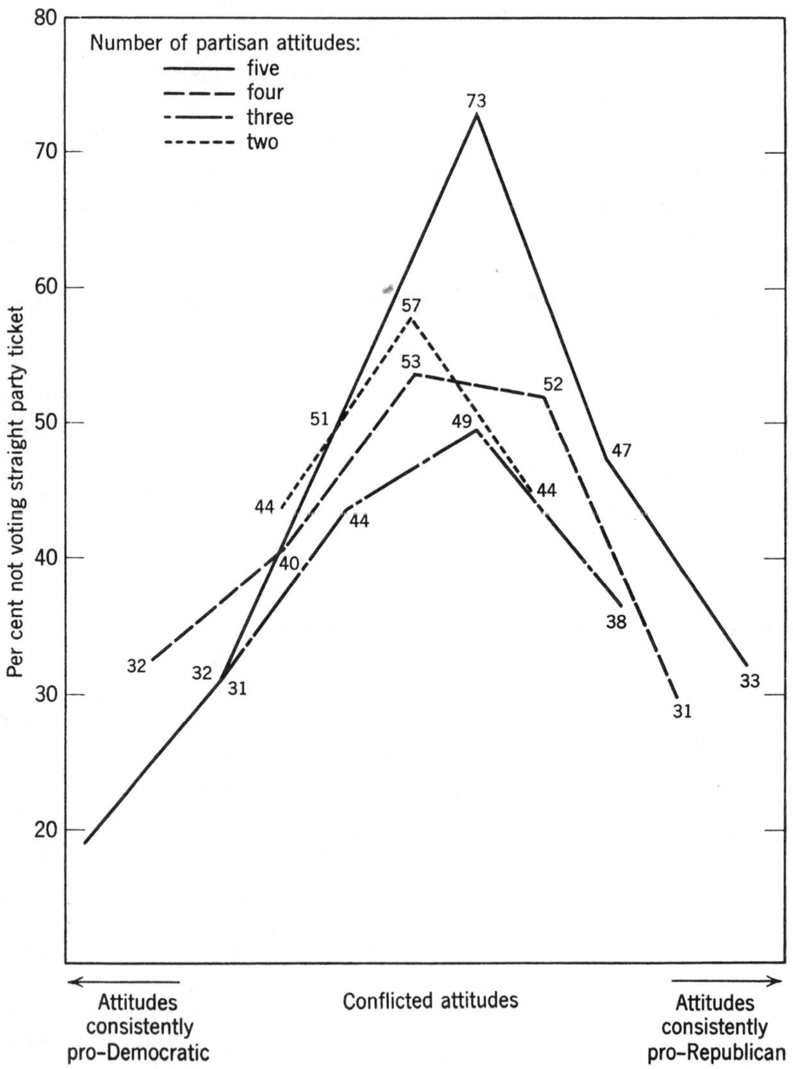

Fig. 4-5. Relation of extent of attitude consistency to degree of straight-ticket voting, 1956.

motivated straight-ticket voter, the motivated split-ticket voter, the indifferent straight-ticket voter, and the indifferent split-ticket voter.[13] Apparently those in Fig. 4-5 who are at the highest level of attitude provide relatively pure examples of the first and second types of this classificatory scheme.

If attitude conflict leaves its impress on several aspects of behavior it also influences what we will call the individual's involvement in the election. In our data from several presidential election campaigns it is clear that persons who show some degree of conflict of partisan attitude are less likely to be interested in the campaign than those whose attitudes are fully consistent, and they are less likely to care how the election turns out. These relationships must be interpreted with caution, since we would expect the strength of a person's long-term psychological involvement in politics to affect both his orientation toward a particular election and his evaluations of the elements of national politics. We assume, however, that most of the influence of this common, underlying factor is reflected in the strong relation between the number of partisan attitudes a person forms, which we have called his *level of attitude,* and his orientation to the election. The strength of this relation is seen in the entries of Table 4-5. To suggest how much the proportion not caring varies over the whole range of attitude levels, we have included in this table levels falling outside the range we have treated in Figs. 4-4 and 4-5.

TABLE 4-5. Relation of Attitude Level to Proportion Not Caring How Election Turns Out, 1956

	Level of Attitude						
			Levels Included in Figs. 4-4 and 4-5				
	None	One	Two	Three	Four	Five	Six
Proportion not caring	83%	57%	40%	36%	22%	21%	8%
Number of cases	36	60	169	286	350	274	60

If we assume that to describe separately the several levels of attitude removes most of the effect on partisan attitude of the individual's long-term involvement in politics, we may look for evidence within each attitude level that those who experience conflict tend to become indif-

[13] See Angus Campbell and Warren E. Miller, "The Motivational Basis of Straight and Split Ticket Voting," *American Political Science Review*, 51 (1957), 293–312.

ferent to the election's outcome as a means of defense against the difficult alternatives that they encounter. This evidence is given in Fig. 4-6, which shows that in the election of 1956 the proportion indifferent to the outcome was greater among those who showed some conflict than among those who did not at every attitude level. It is still possible that within a given level a person of deeper long-term involvement in politics may be more likely to form attitudes that are consistent in their partisan direction and to express concern over the election outcome. But it is difficult not to read this figure as showing that attitude conflict lessens the individual's concern over the outcome.

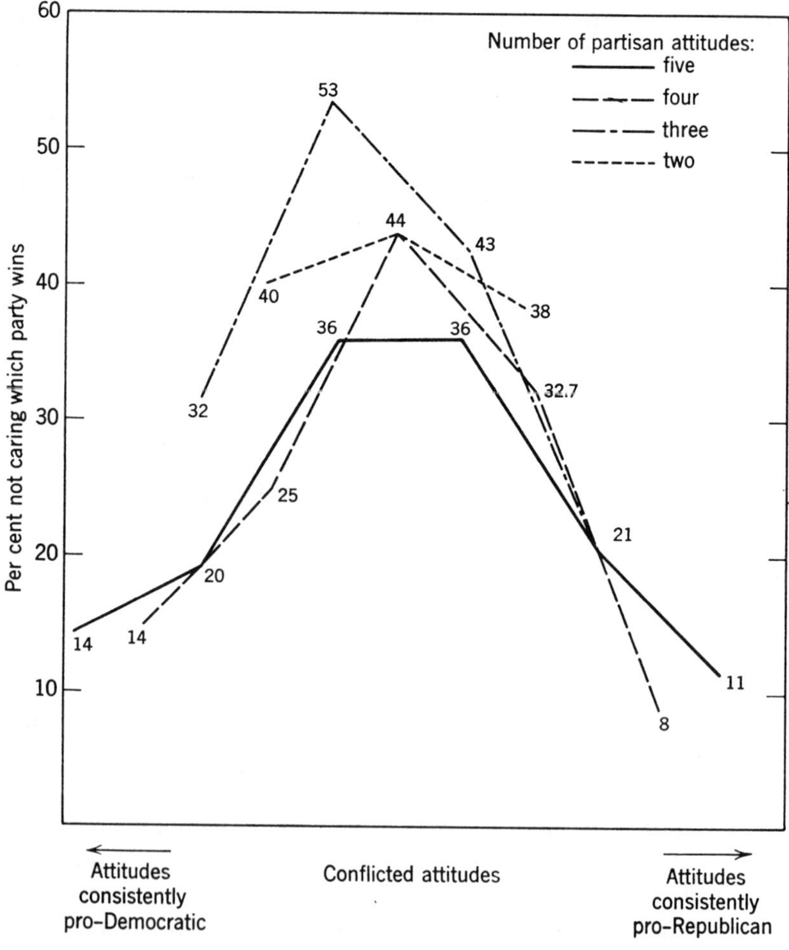

Fig. 4-6. Relation of extent of attitude consistency to degree of indifference to election outcome.

A test of social cross-pressures. Having observed the impact of attitude conflict on the voting act and on the individual's orientation to the election, we may raise the question of the relation of these findings to prior research on social cross-pressures. What evidence can be found that would tie conflict within the individual's psychological field to membership in social groupings of dissimilar political preferences? To be sure, attitudes toward the several elements of the world of politics do not constitute the total set of psychological forces acting on the individual in performing the voting act, and certain of the forces lying outside the system of partisan attitudes are those most likely to be affected by the individual's group memberships. This is specifically true of direct interpersonal influence. As a result, our measurements of the individual's evaluations of political objects may lead us to describe a type of psychological conflict that is linked less closely to politically heterogeneous memberships than are other types of conflict, such as perceptions of different partisan standards in two or more primary groups to which the individual belongs. Nevertheless, the hypothesis that social cross-pressures contribute part of the conflict we observe in the system of partisan attitudes is one deserving careful exploration. Unfortunately the size of the groups within our samples that could be used to test the hypothesis is small. Yet some evidence of the sociological roots of the psychological conflict we have measured can be found in a group suggested by the Erie County study as a clear example of social cross-pressures. Although the political homogeneity of Catholics is not nearly so great as is often supposed, Catholics do tend to perceive members of their faith as more Democratic than Republican in their political allegiance.[14] Similarly, the political differences of occupational groups are often overstated, but we may accept the fact that business and professional people are perceived as being pro-Republican, whereas blue collar workers are perceived as being generally pro-Democratic. Therefore we would presume that white-collar Catholics are subjected to cross-pressures flowing from their religious and occupational groupings. These cross-pressures should be reflected in a less consistent field of partisan attitudes.

A test of this hypothesis for the election of 1956 is given in Table 4-6, which shows the per cent of Catholics in each occupational group and at each level of attitude who experienced some degree of conflict. The differences shown here are not large and are based on fairly small occupational and religious groupings, yet they are uniformly in the direction

[14] Angus Campbell, Gerald Gurin, and Warren E. Miller, *The Voter Decides* (Row, Peterson and Co., Evanston, Ill., 1954), p. 214.

TABLE 4-6. Proportion of Catholics Showing Some Conflict of Partisan Attitude by Occupation and Level of Attitude, 1956

	Two Partisan Attitudes	Three Partisan Attitudes	Four Partisan Attitudes	Five Partisan Attitudes
Blue Collar	15%	45%	45%	74%
Business or Professional	50%	47%	59%	85%

that leads us to accept the hypothesis. At every level of attitude, those who belong to the occupational group whose political coloration tends to be the same as that of their religious group show less conflict of partisan attitude than those who belong to the occupational group whose political preference tends to be opposite to that of Catholics as a whole. The relation is only of moderate strength, but the pattern of these data seems to suggest an interesting connection between widely separated factors in the causal funnel that leads to the voting act.

Voting Turnout ◇ 5

The act of voting requires the citizen to make not a single choice but two. He must choose between rival parties or candidates. He must also decide whether to vote at all. Since a partisan decision can be effective only if it is expressed at the polls, people's decisions whether or not to vote have great influence on party fortunes. Indeed, the dramatic turns of our electoral history have been accompanied as much by wide changes in turnout as they have by shifts in relative party strength. The rising strength of the Democratic Party during the Roosevelt years probably depended heavily on new voters drawn to the polls by the Great Depression and the New Deal. And the Republican victory that brought the New Deal–Fair Deal era to an end was also marked by a great increase in turnout. In percentage terms, the change in turnout between the 1948 and 1952 elections was greater than the change in relative party strength.

Citizen participation at the polls is highly valued in American society, and every national election campaign brings its spate of exhortations to vote. Because of the high value placed on turnout, a good deal of the attention given it in popular discussion has to do with why so many people fail to vote. Despite the great public interest aroused by a presidential contest, our national elections bring less than two thirds of the adult population to the polls.[1] Of course, in any year a great many people are kept from voting by legal barriers—most commonly, in a nation of movers, by the requirements of minimum

[1] For example, the 61,522,000 people who voted for President in 1952 constituted 62.7% of the 97,574,000 people the Census Bureau estimated to be civilians of voting age on November 1 of that year. In 1956, 62,027,000 voters comprised 60.4% of an estimated 102,179,000 civilians of voting age.

residence in a state and its lesser divisions.[2] And many others are kept from voting by political or personal obstacles they could not reasonably overcome. But in each of our national elections millions of people whose way toward registering and voting is relatively clear fail to do so, and this fact has excited wide comment.

Although accounting for non-voting is important in understanding the turnout decision, we will conceive the problem of explanation too narrowly if we concentrate solely on failures to vote. The really extraordinary aspect of our presidential elections is that tens of millions of people *do* expend the energy required to reach their polling-places and register their votes. If we are to explain this type of behavior we must find the patterns of motivation that lead these people to vote, as we must find the conditions that keep others from doing so. The explanatory problem is just that of finding what it is that distinguishes the voter from the non-voter, and we will see as the discussion proceeds that the deviant voter—the person we "expect" *not* to vote yet who does—is somewhat more difficult to explain than is the person we expect to vote yet who fails to do so.

In fundamental respects our approach to the explanation of turnout and partisan choice is the same, and the theoretical considerations set forth in Chapter 2 have guided our orientation to each of these dimensions of the voting act. In particular, we assume that the decision to vote, no less than the decision to vote for a given party, rests immediately on psychological forces, although non-psychological barriers to action are more prominent among the causes of turnout than they are among the causes of partisan choice. Hence, our quest of understanding begins with an examination of motivational forces, and this chapter will describe a number of psychological influences that affect the likelihood the individual will vote. Yet we assume that the proximate causes of turnout, like the immediate determinants of partisan choice, are intervening variables that express the influence of a wide array of antecedent factors. Turnout, as much as partisan preference, can be conceived as the end variable of a causal funnel extending backward in time and outward from the individual's orientation to the world of politics.

Modes of Political Participation

For most Americans voting is the sole act of participation in politics. If a majority of the nation goes to the polls in a presidential election,

[2] A comparison of reported length of current residence with state and local residence requirements indicates that these requirements have prevented at least 3 per cent of our respondents from voting.

much less than a majority canvasses for one of the parties, contributes to campaign funds, or engages in any of the other types of behavior we associate with political activism. Table 5-1 shows for the two Eisenhower elections the proportion of the electorate that was politically active in each of four elementary ways. Whatever the implications for the future of the increase in reported contributions shown here,[3] the percentages of this table make clear that only small fractions

TABLE 5-1. Popular Participation in Politics, 1952 and 1956[a]

	1952	1956
"Do you belong to any political club or organizations?"	2%	3%
"Did you give any money or buy tickets or anything to help the campaign for one of the parties or candidates?"	4%	10%
"Did you go to any political meetings, rallies, dinners, or things like that?"	7%	7%
"Did you do any other work for one of the parties or candidates?"	3%	3%

[a] Entries are proportions of total samples answering affirmatively.

of the public are connected with a party apparatus or help with the work and expense of a campaign. Moreover, since the groups in our samples who did report engaging in these activities are widely overlapping, the percentages cannot be added together to reach an estimate of the total number who were active.

Beyond these modes of participation there are several informal, less well-defined ways in which large numbers of people become "engaged" in a presidential contest. One of the most important of these is informal political discussion. In each of the Eisenhower elections about a fourth of the electorate reported having talked to other people and having tried to persuade them to vote a given way.[4] The casual nature of this behavior should not conceal its importance either as an expression of individual motivation or as a means by which the final distribution of partisan preference in the electorate is achieved. Discus-

[3] This increase, statistically significant at a high level, undoubtedly reflects the efforts of the parties and interested non-partisan groups to broaden the base of financial contributions.

[4] The question "Did you talk to any people and try to show them why they should vote for one of the parties or candidates?" was answered "yes" in 1952 by 27% of our respondents; in 1956 by 28%.

sion of this sort is undoubtedly one of the most significant forms of political behavior by a mass public, even if it does not draw the individual directly into organized political activity.

Although it requires still less personal energy, following the campaign through the mass communications media might also be described as a type of informal participation. For some individuals, gleaning the political content of newspapers and magazines and of radio and television is a principal means of relating to politics. For others—presumably for a great majority of Americans—following the campaign in the mass media is a much more passive activity. Yet since the audiences of the media screen out vast amounts of their content, the individual plays at least a minimal role in deciding what he will and will not attend, and in this sense following an election campaign in the media may be called a form of participation.[5] In the Eisenhower elections only about one person in twenty said that the campaign had failed to reach him through any of the principal media of communication.

Since this book is concerned primarily with the act of voting itself, we will fix our attention on turnout rather than on other types of participation in politics. Yet it is well to keep in mind through the discussion that turnout is only one of several forms of political activity in which the citizen may engage. Voting can be conceived as one act located on a more extended dimension of participation that might be defined, if we were to broaden our view, to include a variety of participation forms.[6] The importance of this statement lies in the fact that many of the forces on turnout are forces on other acts of participation as well. As a result, in assessing the determinants of the voting act we are assessing factors which may underlie other modes of behavior by which the individual may participate in the political process.

In one other respect the act of voting in a given election can be interpreted as an element of a broader dimension of behavior. It is plausible to think of voting as a type of conduct that is somewhat habitual and to suppose that as the individual develops a general orientation toward politics he comes to incorporate either voting or non-voting as part of his normal behavior. Certainly we have found a pronounced association between what people tell us their past behavior

[5] See Angus Campbell, Gerald Gurin, and Warren E. Miller, "Television and the Election," *Scientific American,* 188 (May, 1953), p. 47.

[6] Although by no means all the forms of participation mentioned in these pages can be arranged naturally in a cumulative scale, a number of them can and can thus give one type of formal meaning to the idea of a more extended participation dimension.

has been and whether they vote in the elections we have studied. The strength of this relation is shown by Table 5-2 for the election of 1956.

TABLE 5-2. Relation of Regularity of Past Voting to Voting Turnout, 1956

	Proportion of Past Presidential Elections in Which Respondent Has Voted[a]			
	None	Some	Most	All
Voted in 1956	22%	54%	84%	94%
Did not vote in 1956	78	46	16	6
Totals	100%	100%	100%	100%
Number of cases	261	284	390	740

[a] The classification of respondents by the regularity of past voting turnout is based on responses to this question: "In the elections for President since you have been old enough to vote, would you say that you have voted in all of them, most of them, some of them, or none of them?"

From this viewpoint our inquiry into the determinants of voting turnout is less a search for psychological forces that determine a decision made anew in each campaign than it is a search for the attitude correlates of voting and non-voting from which these modes of behavior have emerged and by which they are presently supported. As the inquiry proceeds we will find that some of the dimensions of attitude that are most helpful in accounting for turnout appear to have the character of orientations to politics much more than they do the character of forces acting on a present decision.[7]

Measuring Voting Turnout

The measurement of turnout in our research, like the measurement of partisan choice, has depended on self-report. Soon after the elections of 1948, 1952, and 1956 we asked the individuals in our samples to tell us whether they voted and, if they did, for whom they had voted. The possibility that verbal reports may depart from actual behavior has been of interest to a number of investigators, and the problems that a departure of this sort would raise for inference from these data

[7] For a discussion of the causal relation of participation behavior and various psychological dimensions see Heinz Eulau and Peter Schneider, "Dimensions of Political Involvement," *Public Opinion Quarterly*, XX (Spring, 1956), 128–142.

are important enough that the likelihood of this error should be carefully assessed. In the case of partisan choice a test of the extent of error is to compare the division of the two-party vote within the sample with the division of the vote as recorded in official election statistics. For each of the elections we have studied, the proportions in our samples voting for the several parties agree within a few percentage points with the corresponding proportions in the population. This method does not guarantee that compensating errors of individual report are not found in our data, but it does suggest that large numbers of errors have not resulted from the desire of our respondents after the election to be counted on the winning side.

Unfortunately, a parallel test of the extent of error in reporting turnout is not easily made. If we compare the proportions of our samples that reported voting for President (74 per cent in 1952, 73 per cent in 1956) with the proportion of the civilian population of voting age that voted (63 per cent in 1952, 60 per cent in 1956) a difference of about 12 percentage points is found. Some of this difference is due to the fact that a few of our respondents have told us they voted when in fact they did not. Yet much more of the difference comes from sources quite unrelated to errors of individual report.

The most important source of this difference is the disparity between the universe we have sampled and the civilian population of voting age. The first of these populations is substantially smaller than the second because we have not sampled several groups that are almost wholly non-participants in the electoral process. Our samples regularly exclude non-citizens, the institutional population—people living in prisons, hospitals, homes for the aged, etc., the "floating" population—people with no fixed addresses, traveling salesmen, people in transit to new addresses, hoboes, etc.; and mental incompetents living in private homes. Just how large these groups were in the Eisenhower elections is not known. We are certain they did not include less than six million people, and they may well have included many millions more. It is not unreasonable to attribute to this source as much as half the difference between the proportion of our samples that has reported voting and the proportion of the civilian population of voting age that has been recorded as voting.

A second source of the difference that does not involve errors of individual report is the fact that some votes are not counted. In any election a portion of the votes cast is invalidated by election officials (or by the citizen's misuse of complicated voting machinery) and not included in the official tally of votes. Estimates of how many votes are lost in this way have run as high as 3 per cent. As a result, we may suppose that about 2 per cent of our respondents who reported voting have cast ballots that were not in fact counted.

A third source of the difference that is unrelated to errors of individual report is the greater difficulty we have in interviewing people who are less involved in politics and less likely to vote. In each election year we have not been able to reach at all some of the people we have sought to interview, and we have been unable to interview others a second time after the election. Neither of these groups is included in the sample total on which the proportion of voters is based, since a report of turnout has to be taken in a post-election interview. It is reasonable to think that these marginal groups—comprising together a little less than a fifth of all the people we might have interviewed after the election—contain a somewhat larger number of non-voters than does the group we have interviewed twice. Obviously this cannot be checked for those we failed to interview at all. But we are able to compare the voting *intentions* of those we have interviewed only before the election and those we have interviewed both before and after the election, and this comparison shows that the proportion intending to vote is 8 or 9 per cent greater among those interviewed twice than among those interviewed once. When this is coupled with the fact that voting intentions are a good predictor of actual turnout, it is clear that at least 1 per cent of the difference between sample and population proportions is attributable to the greater ease of reinterviewing voters.

The over-all difference between the sample and population proportions, amounting to about 12 per cent, may therefore be allocated roughly as follows:

Differences between population sampled and civilian population of voting age	6%
Invalidation of ballots cast	2
Higher reinterview rate among voters	1
Unexplained	3
Total	12%

We have little doubt that the small part of the difference still to be explained arises chiefly from the fact that some people have told us they voted when actually they did not. Our belief that the incidence of false reports is not higher than this is supported by the findings of studies that have checked individual reports of turnout given in survey interviews with public voting records.[8] Although their evidence is still somewhat fragmentary, these studies suggest several factors that influence the likelihood that a false report will be given.

Each of these factors inclines us to discount the importance of this sort of error in our data. To begin with, the probability of error seems to depend very clearly on the recency of the election. It is hardly surprising that people are able to recall quite well whether they voted if asked within a few weeks of the election, as our respondents were, and that the probability of their giving a false report rises with the passage of time. Secondly, the probability of error seems to depend on the quality of contact between interviewer and respondent. Understandably, error occurs least often when a person is interviewed long enough to permit the development of good rapport. Those interviewed in our research have been asked in the second of two long interviews to report whether and how they voted. Finally, the probability of error seems to depend on the size of the election turnout. The incidence of false reports is less in high-turnout, high-interest elections, in which voting is a more memorable experience. And in high-turnout elections there are fewer "usual" voters who missed voting and who are therefore under some psychological pressure to misrepresent their behavior. The findings of research that have compared self-reports with voting records cannot yield a numerical statement of the extent of false reports in our data, but the conservative nature of the estimate we have given is suggested by the study of voting in Elmira, New York, in the presidential election of 1948. In that study, a comparison of survey answers with public records verified all but 2 per cent of the individual reports of turnout.[9]

Turnout and Partisan Preference

However useful it may be to distinguish turnout and partisan choice analytically, we ought not to suppose that these dimensions of the voting act appear distinct to the individual citizen. It is natural for

[8] Several studies of this sort are discussed in Hugh J. Parry and Helen M. Crossley, "Validity of Responses to Survey Questions," *Public Opinion Quarterly*, XIV (1950), 61–80. See also Mungo Miller, "The Waukegan Study of Voter Turnout Prediction," *Public Opinion Quarterly*, XVI (Fall, 1952), 381–398. Results comparable to the American experience are reported from a study of the Swedish electorate carried out by Professor Jörgen Westerståhl and Mr. Bo Särlvik of the University of Gothenburg.

[9] Helen Dinerman, "1948 Votes in the Making—A Preview," *Public Opinion Quarterly*, XII (Winter, 1948–49), 585–598.

the individual to perceive that he votes because he wants to make his preference between parties or candidates count, or that he fails to vote because he does not have a clear preference between partisan objects that he feels are equally appealing, unappealing, or without any affective content at all. Almost certainly this perception of the motives for voting overreaches the facts: we will see that the strength of preference only partially accounts for turnout. Yet the perception catches a clear element of motivation, and the relation of turnout to the intensity of preference is the first important fact we should establish in seeking to explain why some people have voted and others have not.

The evidence for this relation is readily seen if we classify people according to the intensity of their preference, and observe what proportion has voted at each level of intensity. Data of this sort from our combined samples of 1952 and 1956 are arrayed in Fig. 5-1. The pattern seen in the figure shows that the probability that a person will vote depends on the strength of his partisan preference. Across vir-

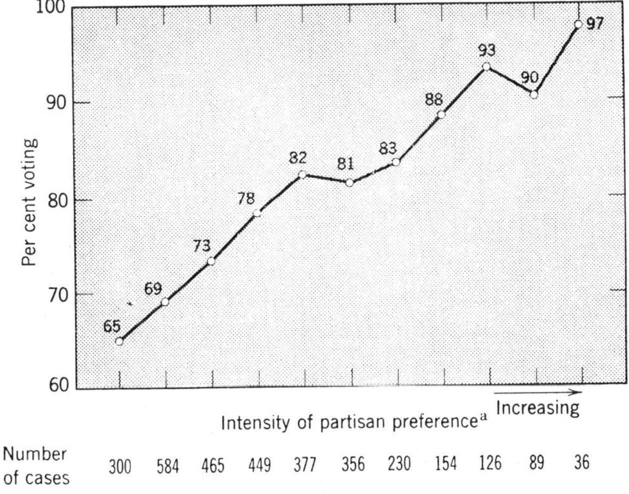

[a] Respondents in the 1952 and 1956 samples are divided according to the intensity of partisan preference by "folding" at the point of partisan neutrality the scale expressing the probability of voting Republican, where this probability is calculated from the set of partisan attitudes treated in Chapter 4. In other words, respondents are classified by the magnitude of the difference of their probability scores from the "neutral" value of this scale.

Fig. 5-1. The relation of intensity of partisan preference to voting turnout, 1952 and 1956.

tually the entire range of intensity found in these samples the greater the strength of the individual's preference, the greater the likelihood he would vote. And the rate of voting at the highest levels of intensity shows that the individual's preference virtually insures his turnout.

Intensity of preference affects not only whether the individual votes; it affects how "strongly" he votes as well. A common observation is that people go to the polls with different degrees of concern about voting. For some the act is imbued with strong positive affect, whereas for others it is much more neutrally toned. To measure these differences we have asked each person who voted how much he cared about

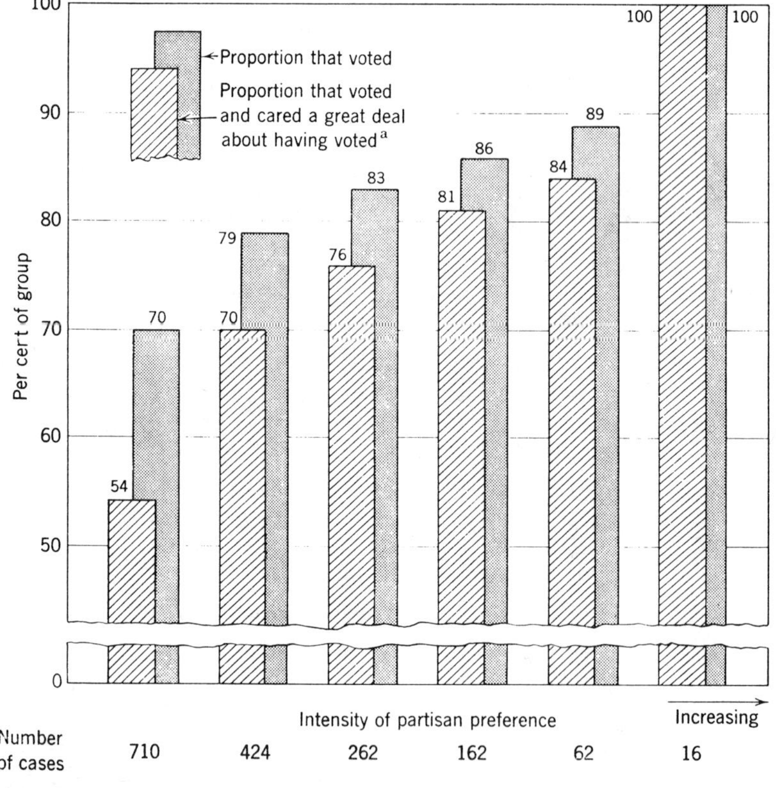

[a] Voters in the 1956 sample were classified as having cared a great deal about voting on the basis of their response to this question: "We would like to know how strongly you felt about the importance of voting in this election. Would you say you *cared a great deal whether or not you voted, cared somewhat,* or *didn't care too much this time?*"

Fig. 5-2. Relation of intensity of partisan preference to degree of voting intensity, 1956.

having voted, and we have used the answers to this question to identify people who cared a great deal and those who voted in a much more perfunctory way. As Fig. 5-2 shows for the election of 1956, the strength of voting is plainly associated with the intensity of preference. Among those of low preference intensity, the proportion of perfunctory voters is a good deal larger than it is among those whose strength of preference is high. The difference between light and dark bars in the figure is progressively less as we move from left to right.

The sketch of the influence of preference intensity that emerges from Figs. 5-1 and 5-2 is in one respect overly simple and needs to be complicated by the addition of a perceptual factor. Despite the immediacy of the impact that we would expect strength of preference to have on turnout, its motivational force seems to depend on how close the individual perceives the election to be. The interaction of these factors in the motivation of turnout is shown in Table 5-3 for

TABLE 5-3. Relation of Perceived Closeness of Election and Intensity of Partisan Preference to Voting Turnout, 1956

	Election Perceived to Be					
	One sided Intensity of Preference			*Close* Intensity of Preference		
	Weak	Medium	Strong	Weak	Medium	Strong
Voted	70%	71%	73%	71%	79%	89%
Did not vote	30	29	27	29	21	11
	100%	100%	100%	100%	100%	100%
Number of cases	130	170	88	301	360	226

the election of 1956. In this table, the levels of intensity in Fig. 5-1 are combined into three broad categories, and the proportion voting in each of these categories is given separately for those who expected the election to be one sided and those who expected it to be close. What the entries of the table have to say about the motivation of turnout is quite clear. The person who thinks the outcome of the election is a foregone conclusion is not more likely to vote if his preference is strong. But the person who thinks the outcome is in doubt is more likely to vote if the intensity of his partisan preference is high. The power of partisan choice to motivate turnout evidently is contingent on the individual feeling, at least in some diffuse way, that his vote may "count." [10] To put the matter another way, the turnout behavior of a person of weak preference is not affected by whether he thinks the election will be close. But the behavior of someone of stronger preference is affected a good deal by his perception of how close the election will be.

In several respects the relation between strength of preference and turnout that is seen in our data needs to be interpreted with a greater time perspective. In the first place, the relation found in these cross-sectional data makes it reasonable to assume that shifts in the level of turnout over time result in large part from changes in the intensity of popular feeling toward the elements of national politics. We may suppose, for example, that the unusually low turnout of 1948 was due to the slight appeal of the major-party candidates and the absence of issues arousing strong popular feeling and that the marked increase in turnout in 1952 reflected the appearance of candidates of greater appeal and the presence of issues attracting wide concern. Support is lent this hypothesis by the fact that a moderate decrease between 1952 and 1956 in the average intensity of partisan preference was accompanied by a small decrease in the proportion of the electorate going to the polls.

But what is equally important, if our measures spanned a broader interval in the life of the individual we would expect to find that the strength of his preference in prior elections has an effect on the likelihood of his voting in later elections. In showing the relation of turnout to the strength of preference in single elections, our data undoubtedly understate the full impact of preference intensity on the decision to vote. A strong commitment to one side or the other in any election tends to involve the individual psychologically more deeply in politics. As a result, the probability of his participating in subsequent elections increases, even though his preference may be substantially less strong in the later campaigns. In this sense, the influence of partisan choice on turnout transcends that shown by the data we have presented here. Yet this secondary effect plainly involves intervening factors. The effect of intensity of preference in time past

[10] The questions we have used to classify respondents according to their expectations about the election have referred to the contest *in the nation as a whole.* Because presidential electors are chosen by states and because all of a state's electors are usually awarded to a single party, we might suppose that how close a person feels the presidential candidates are running in his own state would be of greater importance. But the analysis of answers to a question referring to the presidential race within the respondent's state indicates that it is the election *as a whole* that has cognitive and motivational significance, despite the existence of the Electoral College.

must be transmitted through forces that act on the individual at the moment of his present behavior.

The need to identify additional psychological forces on the turnout decision is strongly reinforced by a realistic appraisal of how well the intensity of current preference can explain this type of behavior. The findings we have given demonstrate that in a single election someone of strong preference is more likely to vote than is someone of weaker partisan dispositions. Yet Fig. 5-1 should dispel altogether the idea that the strength of partisan choice can by itself fully explain why some people go to the polls and others do not. Indeed, the figure is as noteworthy for what it shows about the degree of independence of turnout and partisan choice as it is for what it shows about the dependence of one on the other. The inadequacy of strength of preference in accounting for turnout is perhaps most clearly seen in its failure to explain the behavior of those of minimum partisan disposition. Although the proportion voting is lowest in the group having the slightest degree of preference, nearly two-thirds even of these people were found to have cast a vote.

Turnout and Political Involvement

The partial dependence of turnout on preference is of theoretical importance in large part because it implicates everything that may influence the intensity of preference as a possible influence on the disposition to vote. The fact that one basic dimension of voting is related to the other means that any element in the array of factors leading to partisan choice may lead to turnout as well. The truth of this is recognized at least implicitly in a number of discussions that have explained the disposition to vote in terms of what may strengthen or weaken the disposition to vote a given way.[11] Furthermore, many discussions of the antecedents of partisan choice can throw light on the causes of turnout as well.

Our concern for the moment is not with the antecedents of the intensity of preference but rather with psychological influences on turnout that act apart from the effect of a disposition to vote a given way. In pressing this aspect of our research our major effort has been to relate turnout behavior to what we will call the individual's psycho-

[11] It is of central importance, for example, in the discussion of turnout appearing in Seymour M. Lipset, *et al.*, "The Psychology of Voting: An Analysis of Political Behavior," *Handbook of Social Psychology*, ed. Gardner Lindzey (Addison-Wesley Publishing Co., Cambridge, Mass., 1954), II, 1124–1175.

logical involvement in politics. We have felt that the individual develops a characteristic degree of interest and involvement in political affairs, which varies widely among individuals but which exhibits a good deal of stability for the same person through successive election campaigns. Postulating a dimension of this sort leads naturally to the hypothesis that the stronger the individual's psychological involvement the more likely he is to participate in politics by voting.

In speaking of involvement as a single dimension we do not preclude the possibility that there are distinct aspects of the individual's orientation to politics. Our belief in the reality of an important central component is strongly supported by the interrelations of the several measures of involvement we have used.[12] But we have sought to design measures that would catch several aspects of the individual's psychological involvement in politics, and we have no doubt that the variability of our several measures that cannot be explained by a common factor confirms the existence of distinct aspects of involvement. In particular, we have measured two sorts of attitudes that describe the individual's orientation to a specific election and two additional attitudes that characterize his orientation to politics and elections more generally.

Interest in the campaign. The first aspect of involvement we have sought to measure is the degree of a person's interest in the campaign. The presidential contest holds the attention of different people quite unequally, and the degree of interest has varied widely among the individuals we have interviewed in several election campaigns. The importance of this aspect of involvement for voting turnout is demonstrated by Table 5-4 with data drawn from the election of 1956. The entries of the table show that the rate of turnout among persons of high interest exceeded that among persons of low interest by nearly 30 per cent. What is more, the incidence of non-voting among the third of the electorate that is lowest in interest is appreciably greater than it is among the third that is lowest in strength of partisan prefer-

[12] When the four measures to be discussed here are treated as quantitative scales and their interrelations examined by the methods of component analysis, a principal component is found that can account for half the variance of the several measures across our 1952 and 1956 samples. The correlations of the four measures with the principal component are as follows:

	1952	1956
Interest in the campaign	0.77	0.71
Concern over the election outcome	0.68	0.59
Sense of political efficacy	0.72	0.76
Sense of citizen duty	0.63	0.72

TABLE 5-4. Relation of Degree of Interest in Campaign to Voting Turnout, 1956

	Degree of Interest in Campaign[a]		
	Not Much Interested	Somewhat Interested	Very Much Interested
Voted	58%	72%	87%
Did not vote	42	28	13
	100%	100%	100%
Number of cases	540	695	520

[a] Respondents were classified according to the degree of their interest in the campaign by using responses to the following question: "Some people don't pay much attention to the political campaigns. How about you? Would you say that you have been very much interested, somewhat interested, or not much interested in following the political campaigns so far this year?"

ence, as shown by Fig. 5-1. Our measure of interest carries us further than the measure of partisan intensity in finding the conditions of non-voting, although we still need to learn what brought to the polls more than half of those who tell us they are not much interested in the campaign.

Concern over the election outcome. A person's orientation to a specific election can be described also in terms of his concern over its outcome. Some people are deeply involved, psychologically speaking, in the electoral result, whereas others are relatively indifferent. Concern over the election result would seem intuitively to be somewhat distinct from political interest, and in our data it is by no means perfectly correlated with interest. Yet the association of the two suggests the influence of a more general involvement factor and leads us to concur in Lane's observation that "questions on 'interest' and 'concern' tend to select out the same populations and to be related to behavior in roughly the same way." [13] The relation we have found between the individual's concern over the outcome and the probability of his voting is shown in Table 5-5 (page 104) for 1956. Here again, the effect of involvement on voting turnout seems very clear.

Sense of political efficacy. Our measures of interest and of concern over the election outcome refer explicitly to the election at hand. As such, they are likely to catch important short-term fluctuations of the

[13] Robert E. Lane, *Political Life* (The Free Press, Glencoe, Ill., 1959), p. 134.

individual's political involvement. These measures may tap more enduring orientations to politics as well. The individual does not react *de novo* to each election but tends rather to respond to the stimuli of a new campaign in terms of stable attitudes and dispositions he has toward politics generally. His social environment, immediate and distant, is composed of a number of areas that compete for his emotional energy and in which he comes to have a characteristic level of emotional involvement. Politics is such an area, and most

TABLE 5-5. Relation of Degree of Concern About Election Outcome to Voting Turnout, 1956

	Degree of Concern over Election Outcome[a]			
	Don't Care At All	Don't Care Very Much	Care Somewhat	Care Very Much
Voted	52%	69%	76%	84%
Did not vote	48	31	24	16
	100%	100%	100%	100%
Number of Cases	230	367	627	459

[a] Respondents were classified according to the degree of their concern over the election outcome by using responses to the following question: "Generally speaking, would you say that you personally care a good deal which party wins the presidential election this fall, or that you don't care very much which party wins?"

adults have a relatively fixed degree of involvement in it, although their commitment to political affairs, as to work, family, religion or sports, may vary somewhat over time. This characteristic level of involvement differs widely among people. A really intense commitment to politics probably is limited in American society to a small fraction of political activists, but even in the wider electorate we find substantial differences in the extent of emotional involvement in political affairs.

An important aspect of the individual's response to politics as a general area is the degree to which this response is passive in character. To some people politics is a distant and complex realm that is beyond the power of the common citizen to affect, whereas to others the affairs of government can be understood and influenced by individual citizens. We have assessed the effectiveness the individual feels in his relation to politics by using answers to several questions probing attitudes of this sort to develop a cumulative scale, on which we could array our samples.[14] The influence this dimension of attitude has on the turnout decision is shown by Table 5-6 for the election of 1956. The rate of voting turnout was found to increase uniformly with the strength of the individual's sense of political efficacy, and more than 40 percentage points separated those whose sense was least developed from those whose sense of effectiveness was strongest.

TABLE 5-6. Relation of Sense of Political Efficacy to Voting Turnout, 1956

	Sense of Political Efficacy[a]				
	Low				High
Voted	52%	60%	75%	84%	91%
Did not vote	48	40	25	16	9
	100%	100%	100%	100%	100%
Number of cases	263	343	461	501	196

[a] Respondents were classified according to the strength of their sense of political efficacy on the basis of a cumulative scale formed from responses to four questions.

Sense of citizen duty. The final aspect of involvement we have sought to measure also transcends a single election. Wide currency in American society is given the idea that the individual has a civic responsibility to vote. When this norm becomes a part of the value system of the individual, as it has for most of our citizens, it may be regarded as a force acting directly on the turnout decision. Of course its strength is not the same for everyone, and the degree to which the individual feels an obligation to vote is an important aspect of his orientation to politics. We have measured the strength of this attitude by constructing a cumulative scale from several questions about the responsibility to vote and classifying those we have interviewed into the categories of the scale. When the proportion voting is shown for each category, as it is in Table 5-7 for the election of 1956, it is clear that the strength of a person's sense of citizen duty has a very great influence on the likelihood of his voting.

[14] For a detailed discussion of the construction of cumulative scales to measure sense of political efficacy and sense of citizen duty see Appendices A and B in Angus Campbell, Gerald Gurin, and Warren E. Miller, *The Voter Decides* (Row, Peterson and Co., Evanston, Ill., 1954), pp. 187–199.

TABLE 5-7. Relation of Sense of Citizen Duty to Voting Turnout, 1956

	Sense of Citizen Duty[a]				
	Low				High
Voted	13%	42%	52%	74%	85%
Did not vote	87	58	48	26	15
	100%	100%	100%	100%	100%
Number of cases	89	78	146	639	812

[a] Respondents were classified according to the strength of their sense of citizen duty on the basis of a cumulative scale formed from responses to four questions.

The most striking entries of Table 5-7 are those indicating that voting is rare among people whose sense of citizen duty is least strong. Since this group is small, including less than 6 per cent of the sample and less than one fifth of the non-voters, these entries ought not to suggest that we have explained why it is that people fail to vote. Yet the smallness of the group indicates that we have located a set of people at the lowest edge of involvement, and their behavior lends credence to this view. In those whose sense of citizen duty is weakest we have found a group whose motivation to participate in politics is so near zero that other forces inducing them to vote only rarely bring them to the polls.

Despite the evidence that the four aspects of political involvement we have measured share an important common component, we have considered separately their relation to turnout because each aspect contributes a distinctive element. However, we can assess how well involvement accounts for behavior only if we examine the joint relation to turnout of the four measures. In order to make entirely clear what we have *added* to our ability to account for the turnout decision by measuring these aspects of involvement, we will include strength of partisan preference among the explanatory variables so that their combined power to account for behavior may be compared directly with that of the intensity of preference alone, as shown in Fig. 5-1.

Such a comparison attests the fundamental role of involvement in motivating turnout behavior. As is seen in Fig. 5-3, the rate of turnout increases steadily with political involvement and differs by more than 75 per cent from one extreme to the other, whereas the proportions voting at the extremes of low and high intensity of preference

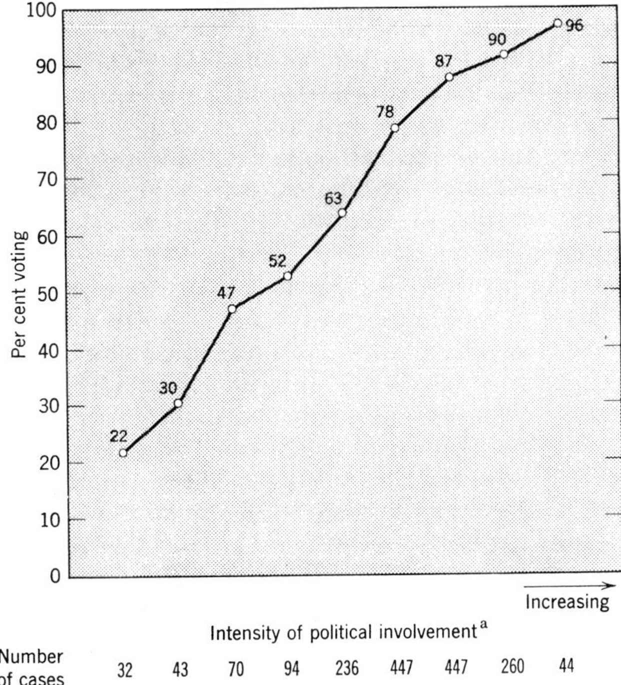

[a] Respondents in the 1956 sample are classified according to the strength of their psychological involvement in politics by partitioning into nine intervals a scale formed as a linear combination of intensity of partisan preference, interest in the campaign, concern over the election outcome, sense of citizen duty, and sense of political efficacy. The reader should note that at other places in this and later chapters one or more of the *components* of this combined scale, especially interest in the campaign and concern over the election outcome, will be used to measure political involvement.

Fig. 5-3. The relation of intensity of political involvement to voting turnout, 1956.

differed by less than half this much. The fact that persons of the highest involvement are more nearly unanimous in voting than are those of lowest involvement in not voting suggests that we are still beset more by the problem of the deviant *voter* than we are with that of the deviant *non-voter*. And the existence of any group of similar motivation whose behavior is not homogeneous invites us to push further the quest for explanation.

Divergent cases. Most of the variability in turnout that political involvement fails to explain is found in the middle categories of Fig. 5-3, where the psychological forces we have measured are neither so weak that the individual is highly unlikely to vote nor so strong that he is highly unlikely *not* to vote. In these middle categories other factors, some of them undoubtedly exogenous to our theoretical concerns, have determined whether the individual will vote. But the "error" in Fig. 5-3 that is most interesting is found at the extremes of political involvement, where we would expect to be able to predict with higher confidence whether the individual will in fact vote. The presence of error of this sort leads naturally to an intensive examination of divergent cases to learn why it is that our expectations have proven wrong.

We are better prepared, by the popular lore about voting, for error at the extreme of high involvement. Located here is the person of strong motivation who is kept from voting by personal circumstances he could not reasonably overcome, as the individual who was prevented from voting by a flat tire on his way to the polls. We doubt that this specific factor, which we would unhesitatingly declare exogenous, has had a very high incidence in American politics, but it suggests well the sort of barrier that may keep a highly motivated person from voting. An inspection of our interview protocols provides a number of such cases.

> Respondent is a 69 year old unemployed janitor with heart trouble, not working because of bad health. In answer to pre-election question on expectation of voting said "No, I have heart trouble and I can't get in crowds or get excited." In post-election interview when asked if he voted answered "No, I wanted to but I am not well and it wouldn't have been good for me."
>
> Respondent is a 48 year old cameraman in Los Angeles, widely travelled, very much interested in foreign affairs and politics generally. In pre-election interview answered the question on intention to vote by saying "Yes, definitely." In post-election interview thumbnail sketch says "Respondent's regret at not having been able to vote was very sincere." In answer to question on voting he said "I had to be at the studio at 7 o'clock in the morning and I did not get home until 10 at night so I couldn't."

Located here, too, are the individuals of strong motivation who are barred from voting by legal disabilities. Some of our respondents living in states that make no provision for absentee balloting have been away from their homes on election day. Others have changed their residences too recently to satisfy the requirements of minimum residence. Non-registration ought generally to be regarded as a legal barrier only with caution, since the failure to register may simply reflect the same motivational factors as the failure to vote. Yet in certain cases the impossibility of registering has stood as a clear barrier for those who were motivated to perform the voting act.

Respondent is a 54 year old apartment manager, has lived in California only 9 months, greatly interested in the coming election. Thumbnail sketch says "I think he'd have registered if they had been in state the required year. His wife feels terribly sorry they can't ballot this time." To post-election question about voting he answered "No, because I am not eligible."

Respondent is a 28 year old professor of economics at an eastern college, calls himself an Independent, very much involved in the election. In answer to pre-election question on voting said he was not eligible because of movement from one state to another but at later point said "I expect to go back to Jersey to vote in the presidential election at my old residence but not take part in the state or local elections because I have moved from that state." In post-election interview said no he had not voted. He had moved and was unable to vote at his new address. He had intended to vote at old address but "was talked out of it."

Deviant cases of the opposite sort, in which a person of slight motivation has voted, are less familiar in the common lore, except perhaps for what is known of party machines that have voted the dead. An analysis of interviews with people of very low motivation who have gone to the polls indicates that the most important force on their behavior is interpersonal influence, as we have found it to be in inducing deviant partisan behavior. Personal influence seems particularly important within the family group. Of the twelve voters in 1956 who had the least reason for going to the polls in terms of the psychological factors we have measured, nine were women who appeared to respond to the wishes of husbands or of other men in their immediate families.

Respondent is a 25 year old farm housewife in Iowa, described by the interviewer as perhaps the most non-informed person he has talked to. "Almost every answer was 'I don't know.' In fact in answer to the question 'Who do you think will be elected president in November?' she asked first who was running. Husband and father-in-law commented frequently during the interview." In pre-election interview when asked if she was registered she asked her husband whether or not she was qualified to vote. Said she didn't know whether she would vote or not. On reinterview said she had voted Republican. Said husband had also voted Republican but answered "I don't know" when asked if his opinions had anything to do with the way she had voted. Husband obviously better informed than respondent.

Respondent is a 29 year old jockey and truck driver, unmarried, living with widowed mother and sister. Interview was a succession of "Don't knows." Not interested in the election. Said he was registered but didn't know whether he would vote. Barely reads or writes. In pre-election interview said in answer to question about the candidates, "I don't know nothing about that. I just vote the way the guy at the corner tells me. (Why?) Because he does me favors I just vote the way he says." In post-election interview said he voted and gave the reason "Well, I had to vote for somebody. One was going to get in and I was registered Republican with this politician down the street so I did him a favor. I vote the way that guy wants me to."

The Preference of Non-Voters

If partisan preference and turnout are related by the fact that one is an influence on the other, they are brought together also by the fact that we may consider separately the partisan dispositions of the two groups defined by turnout. Of course it is the preferences of those who vote that are of primary importance in the wider political system. But the preferences of those who do not are by no means of trivial importance; indeed, in recording substantial shifts over time they prove to be of considerable theoretical interest. Let us examine the partisan preferences of non-voters, as they have been assessed over a twenty-year period.

With the rise of public opinion polls in the 1930's the first systematic evidence began to appear that non-voters—or at least people who expected not to vote—were more Democratic than the electorate as a whole. This evidence accumulated through the latter years of the New Deal and the Fair Deal until the generalization that non-voters tend to be Democrats had worked itself into the popular understanding of politics. Since it was well known that both partisan preference and voting turnout were related to social class, an explanation of the strongly Democratic color of non-voters was easily supplied.

The report of partisan preferences we obtained from a national sample interviewed after the election of 1948, the high-water mark of the Fair Deal, was consistent with this description of non-voters. Whereas the preferences reported by voters were divided very nearly evenly between the parties, the preferences reported by non-voters favored the Democrats by a margin of more than 4–1. Were it not for the fact that the Truman vote exceeded the advance expectations, the closeness of the Democratic victory in 1948 relative to earlier years would probably have been explained in terms of the lower level of turnout.

If the report taken from those who failed to vote in 1948 supported the contention that non-voters tend to be Democrats, the post-election reports of 1952 and 1956 dealt this notion severe blows.[15] In our interviews following the election of 1952 only about half of the non-voters indicating a preference said they would have voted Democratic; in our interviews following the election of 1956 little more than a quarter of the non-voters giving a preference said they would have voted Democratic. The extreme nature of this shift in the Democratic proportion over an eight-year period is shown by Table 5-8. Few statistics in all of our studies have shown so violent a change over time as this one.

TABLE 5-8. Post-Election Preference of Non-Voters, 1948 to 1956[a]

	1948	1952	1956
Would have voted Democratic	82%	52%	28%
Would have voted Republican	18	48	72
Total	100%	100%	100%
Number of cases	192	417	429

[a] Among non-voters giving a preference between major-party candidates.

What can explain so great a shift among non-voters? Over a period in which the division of preference changed by little more than ten per cent among voters it changed by more than 50 per cent among non-voters. How are we to account for the difference? Undoubtedly a number of factors have been at work, but we believe that much of the observed change can be explained by a few central ideas. The major key to understanding is supplied by what we have found to distinguish non-voters from voters: the non-voter tends to be a person of lower involvement whose emotional investment in politics and its partisan decisions is on the average much less than that of the voter. As a result, we would expect the non-voter to be less stable in his partisan inclinations than the voter and more responsive to the massive political stimuli that produce shifts of popular attitude over time.

[15] The discussion here assumes that the composition of the group of non-voters is relatively constant over time. That it is may be inferred from the fact that the primary influence on voting turnout is political involvement, which is itself relatively stable over time. That there is only moderate turnover in the group of non-voters may also be inferred from the entries of Table 5-2 above. However, a more definitive treatment of changes in preference *between* elections must await the analysis of panel data encompassing more than a single campaign.

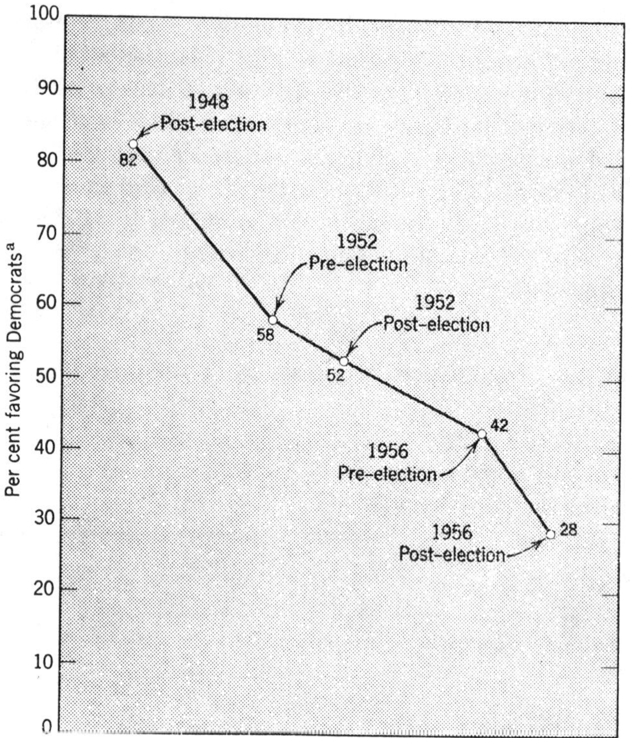

[a] Figures are percentages favoring Democrats among these expressing a preference for the Democratic or Republican candidates.

Fig. 5-4. Partisan preference of non-voters, 1948 to 1956.

And we have little doubt that for the non-voter a stimulus of great importance in this period, as in any other, was the fact of who was winning elections. For at least part of the way between his position of 1948 and his position of 1956 the non-voter was riding a psychological bandwagon.

Several kinds of evidence can be marshalled in support of this general view. First of all, if we are right in thinking that the outcomes of these elections were stimuli of relatively greater importance for the non-voter, we ought to find evidence of the fact in a comparison of the reported preferences of non-voters before and after each election. We do not have the data to make this comparison for the election of 1948, but for each of the Eisenhower elections we may examine the non-voter's report of preference in the first and second interviews of our brief panel studies spanning the elections. The division of preference among non-voters shifted in the direction of the winner in each of these years; indeed, the post-election shift toward Eisenhower in 1956 was 14 percentage points—as great as the shift of preference among voters over the entire period from 1948 to 1956. As Fig. 5-4 indicates, the change in the preference of non-voters *within* the 1952 and 1956 elections fits into a broader change *between* elections to produce the full variation observed over this period. Moreover, what we observe of the turnover of preference among non-voters in the Eisenhower elections leads us to suspect that the post-election percentage for 1948 shown in Fig. 5-4 is considerably higher than we would find the pre-election point for the same year to be, if we were able to reconstruct it from our data. We would suppose that the Truman victory had much the same effect on the preference of non-voters—although in the opposite partisan direction—as the Eisenhower victories had in each of the elections that followed.

TABLE 5-9. Relation of Degree of Political Involvement to Change in Partisan Preference of Non-Voters[a]

	1952 Election		1956 Election	
	Before	After	Before	After
Very much interested	51%	54%	43%	37%
Somewhat interested	56%	57%	40%	37%
Not much interested	63%	52%	42%	24%

[a] Entries are percentages favoring Democrats of those giving a preference.

The most telling evidence for our characterization of change, however, is obtained by further dividing non-voters according to the degree of their involvement in politics. In any election some individuals whose involvement is high and whose motivation is strong fail to vote. If we can separate these people from individuals who are weakly involved, we should have a clearer sense of the forces inducing change in preference over time. Table 5-9 makes such a separation for each of the Eisenhower elections by classifying non-voters according to the extent of their interest in the campaign. Several observations that are important for our formulation of change can be based on this table. First, it is clear for both the 1952 and 1956 elections that change in the Republican direction between the pre- and post-election interviews occurred more among the slightly involved than it did among those of greater involvement. Only the group least interested in the campaign shifted toward Eisenhower in his first victory; hence, the shift seen among non-voters as a whole rests on the fact that most non-voters are people of little involvement. Second, the fact that the Democratic percentage prior to the 1952 election was highest among those of slightest interest suggests that these people were most under the influence of past Democratic victories. Yet it is this same group that responded most strongly to the Eisenhower victories and shifted far enough that by the post-election interview of 1956 less than one fourth of their number favored the Democrats.[16]

The movement occurring at each level of involvement between the first and fourth columns of Table 5-9 suggests the action of a pendulum. The highest level has moved least (14 per cent), the middle level an intermediate amount (25 per cent), and the lowest level by far the most (39 per cent). We do not see the top of the pendulum, the level of involvement at which there is little or no movement, because we have confined our attention entirely to non-voters. (Among voters of highest involvement the proportion favoring the Democrats actually *increased* slightly over the same period of time.) Presumably the movement of the pendulum would be the more impressive if we could separate our 1948 respondents, too, according to the degree of their interest. Unfortunately, questions probing the extent of the individual's political involvement were not used in the earliest of our studies. However, among those respondents who told us they had never voted and who tended, we may suppose, to be people of less involvement, the proportion expressing a preference for the Democrats after that election was somewhat higher (86 per cent) even than the very high proportion we found among non-voters as a whole. If we accept this figure as the point of furthest movement in the Democratic direction, the bottom of the pendulum may be said to have swung 62 percentage points in the Republican direction in the next eight years.

This unbroken swing in the Republican direction dissolves the generalization that non-voters are pro-Democratic and calls attention in the most dramatic way to the importance of psychological involvement in explaining political behavior. We have treated in some detail the shifts of preference among those who fail to vote because these changes suggest the far-reaching effects on behavior of the low involvement

[16] Of course we have repeated measurements of the preferences of the same persons only within a single election and not over two or more elections. The assumption that the composition of the several involvement groups would be fairly stable over time cannot be validated with these data, and comparisons of their preferences between elections ought to be treated with caution.

that is the non-voter's primary quality. Yet voters and non-voters are by no means the only groups within the electorate that differ in the extent of their political involvement, and we shall have occasion in later chapters to examine the behavior of other groups as well for which involvement supplies a key to understanding.[17]

[17] See particularly the discussion of agrarian voting behavior in Chapter 15.

THE POLITICAL CONTEXT ◇ SECTION 

In developing the metaphor of a funnel of causality, we located events and states within either of two broad classes, political and non-political. Whether an event was one or the other depended on the meaning ascribed to it by the individual. For example, an economic fact such as the loss of a job becomes a political fact as well only when the actors involved perceive unemployment as a condition for which governments may be blamed or which governments may alleviate. The development of a perception that politics is relevant for pressures arising outside the political order is a psychological process that we have labelled "political translation." An important accompaniment is the frequent perception that the political parties differ in their stance toward these pressures.

The array of attitudes considered in the preceding section are proximal to the voting decision in more than one sense. First, we have made it clear that they must be located at a point in time close to the dependent behavior. The psychological field was assessed as it existed just prior to the election itself; in many cases the objects evaluated had not been known as much as a year in advance of the presidential campaign. But in addition, these attitudes are proximal in that the object of each attitude is already a *political* object. Some of the attitudes may have arisen in response to pressures from outside the political order. However, these non-political events and states have been given not only political meaning, but *partisan* political meaning. That is, the full process of political translation has occurred.

From this point we may seek the roots of the proximal attitudes in either of two directions, moving deeper in time past or outward from the political core of the funnel. It is common to explain voting behavior in terms of roots that are in the first instance relatively contemporary, and, in the second, largely non-political. In the traditional view, democratic elections are periodic reviews of governmental conduct. Hence roots of behavior are sought within the time interval since the preceding election. Similarly, it is recognized that political behavior is instrumental behavior. The act of voting is not an end in itself; rather, it is a choice of means toward other ends. More often than not, these ends concern facets of human experience that are at core non-political, involving problems of economic security, the disruptions of war, rights of minorities, the distribution of social status, and the like. These facts turn attention immediately to non-political sources of the vote decision.

We have chosen instead to devote our initial attention to the purely political roots of the proximal attitudes and the voting act. For we find that the individual's current choice tends to have simple and direct roots in time prior to the current era, and that this past is, in no small measure, a *political* past. We have already seen that the images of the parties most firmly imbedded in the public mind represent a variety of political eras in time past as well as reflecting the immediate partisan controversies of the preceding four years. These potent "after-images" attest to the weight of the partisan past in current partisan choice. If we were to trace the roots of behavior deep enough in time past to encounter important apolitical sources of current behavior, we would frequently be forced to search into previous generations. Initial selection of a party may often be a response to non-political pressures; but once made, partisan choice tends to be maintained long after its non-political sources have faded into oblivion. Current pressures arising outside the political order continue to affect the evaluation process, and from time to time they may contribute to a critical margin of political victory. Yet for most of the people most of the time such contemporary forces turn out to be but minor terms in the decision equation.

We shall attempt, over the ensuing chapters, to document these assertions and suggest why they are so, given the nature of our political system and the psychological makeup of the individual. The coin has two sides. We shall consider in turn why the connectives with the partisan past are so strong and, on the other hand, why the intrusion of current non-political forces is no more potent. Principal among connective mechanisms is a growing sense of identification with the party. The role of these enduring attachments in the genesis of the proximal attitudes is examined in Chapter 6. Chapter 7 inquires in some detail into the nature of these identifications as psychological phenomena, and traces their roots to more remote points in time past.

Such party loyalty, although it helps the individual to make sense out of politics, serves in a peculiar way to insulate him from non-political pressures that might otherwise push him to more frequent partisan re-evaluation. But review of this kind is infrequent as well because of the fallibility of the process of political translation. We shall consider the vicissitudes of this translation process in Chapters 8, 9, and 10. The most obvious bridges aiding the citizen to link non-political conditions with partisan evaluation are to be found in claims of the parties for support on the basis of policies toward social, economic, and other problems. Thus our attention shifts here from the political parties to the political issues. We shall progress from a discussion of the role of issues at a level of relatively specific policy demands to the role of the most general dimensions of evaluation suggested by the term "ideology."

Other more elusive forces requiring conception in purely political terms shape behavior as well. We shall complete our discussion of the political context of the voting act by considering, in Chapter 11, the rules and norms for behavior that vary by political subcommunity across the national electorate. In some instances these norms have become institutionalized in the legal regulations that circumscribe political participation from area to area; in others they remain informal matters of community sentiment, reflecting local differences in political tradition. Although both formal and informal norms generally have been overlooked in analyses of individual responses, we shall find that both have interesting effects on behavior and that their impact may be strong or weak according to the motivational system of the individual actor.

The Impact of Party Identification ◇ 6

The behavior of the American voter as presidential elector can be described initially as a response to psychological forces. The individual's attitudes toward the elements of national politics comprise a field of forces that determines his action in an immediate sense, and the field's properties account for much of the behavior we observe. In particular, the intensity of attitude helps explain why some people vote and others do not. For those who vote, the consistency of attitude reveals in part why one person casts a straight-party vote, whereas another divides his support between the parties. And most important of all, the intensity and partisan direction of attitude can account for the choice each elector will make between the rival candidates for President.

How do these forces arise? The manner in which the individual perceives and evaluates the elements of national politics may orient his behavior, but if we seek to account for the variability of these factors we confront a fresh problem of explanation. In an important sense these attitude forces are intervening variables linking behavior with a host of antecedent factors. The very success of these forces in accounting for behavior heightens the interest in locating prior factors by which the properties of individual attitude may in turn be explained. In the present chapter we consider an antecedent factor that lies still within the realm of individual psychology, and, like the proximal attitudes, is defined in political terms.

A general observation about the political behavior of Americans is that their partisan preferences show great stability between elections. Key speaks of the "standing decision" to support one party or the other, and this same phenomenon soon catches the eye of any student of electoral behavior. Its mark is readily seen in aggregate election statistics. For virtually any collection of states, counties, wards, precincts, or other political units one may care to examine, the correlation of the party division of the vote in successive elections is likely to be high. Often a change of candidates and a broad alteration in the nature of the issues disturb very little the relative partisanship of a set of electoral units, which suggests that great numbers of voters have party attachments that persist through time.

The fact that attachments of this sort are widely held is confirmed by survey data on individual people. In a survey interview most of our citizens freely classify themselves as Republicans or Democrats and indicate that these loyalties have persisted through a number of elections. Few factors are of greater importance for our national elections than the lasting attachment of tens of millions of Americans to one of the parties. These loyalties establish a basic division of electoral strength within which the competition of particular campaigns takes place. And they are an important factor in assuring the stability of the party system itself.

The Concept and Measurement of Party Identification

Only in the exceptional case does the sense of individual attachment to party reflect a formal membership or an active connection with a party apparatus. Nor does it simply denote a voting record, although the influence of party allegiance on electoral behavior is strong. Generally this tie is a psychological identification, which can persist without legal recognition or evidence of formal membership and even without a consistent record of party support. Most Americans have this sense of attachment with one party or the other. And for the individual who does, the strength and direction of party identification are facts of central importance in accounting for attitude and behavior.

In characterizing the relation of individual to party as a psychological identification we invoke a concept that has played an important if somewhat varied role in psychological theories of the relation of individual to individual or of individual to group. We use the concept here to characterize the individual's affective orientation to an important group-object in his environment. Both reference group theory and small-group studies of influence have converged upon the attracting or repelling quality of the group as the generalized dimension most critical in defining the individual-group relationship, and it is this dimension that we will call identification. In the present chapter the political party serves as the group toward which the individual may develop an identification, positive or negative, of some degree of intensity.

The importance of stable partisan loyalties has been universally recognized in electoral studies, but the manner in which they should be defined and measured has been a subject of some disagreement. In keeping with the conception of party identification as a psychological tie, these orientations have been measured in our research by asking individuals to describe their own partisan loyalties. Some studies, however, have chosen to measure stable partisan orientations in terms of an individual's past voting record or in terms of his attitude on a set of partisan issues. Thus Republican and Democratic identifiers are sometimes defined as those who vote consistently for the same party and "Independents" as those who do not. The fact that a definition of this sort serves many practical and scholarly purposes underscores the immense influence of party identification in motivating behavior. But we feel that such a definition blurs the distinction between the psychological state and its behavioral consequences. We have not measured party attachments in terms of the vote or the evaluation of partisan issues because we are interested in exploring the influence of party identification on voting behavior and its immediate determinants. When an independent measure of party identification is used it is clear that even strong party adherents at times may think and act in contradiction to their party allegiance. We could never establish the conditions under which this will occur if lasting partisan orientations are measured in terms of the behavior they are thought to affect.

Our measurement of party identification rests fundamentally on self-classification. Since 1952 we have asked repeated cross sections of the national population a sequence of questions inviting the individual to state the direction and strength of his partisan orientation.[1] The dimension presupposed by these questions appears to have psychological reality for virtually the entire electorate. The partisan self-image of all but the few individuals who disclaim any involvement in politics permits us to place each person in these samples on a continuum of

[1] The initial question was this: "Generally speaking, do you think of yourself as a Republican, a Democrat, an Independent, or what?" Those who classified themselves as Republicans or Democrats were also asked, "Would you call yourself a strong (Republican, Democrat) or a not very strong (Republican, Democrat)?" Those who classified themselves as Independents were asked this additional question: "Do you think of yourself as closer to the Republican or Democratic Party?" The concept itself was first discussed in George Belknap and Angus Campbell, "Political Party Identification and Attitudes toward Foreign Policy," *Public Opinion Quarterly*, XV (Winter, 1952), 601–623.

partisanship extending from strongly Republican to strongly Democratic. We use the word "continuum" because we suppose that party identification is not simply a dichotomy but has a wide range of intensities in each partisan direction. In practice this range has to be represented by relatively few points, but we have devised our measures to preserve as much of the true variability as possible. The sequence of questions we have asked permits those of strong Republican or Democratic allegiance to be distinguished from those of weaker identification with one of the parties. Moreover, it allows us to distinguish the Independents who lean toward one of the parties from those who think of themselves as having no partisan coloration whatever.

The measure these methods yield has served our analysis of party identification in a versatile fashion. To assess both the direction and intensity of partisan attachments it can be used to array our samples across the seven categories shown in Table 6-1, which gives the distribution of party identification in the electorate during the years from 1952 to 1958. By treating Independents as a single group we may reduce seven categories to five. By suppressing, too, the distinction between strong and weak partisans we have a three-point scale showing only the direction of partisanship. And by "folding" the measure of party identification at its central point we have a scale showing only the strength of this psychological tie to party.

In using these techniques of measurement we do not suppose that every person who describes himself as an Independent is indicating simply his lack of positive attraction to one of the parties. Some of these people undoubtedly are actually repelled by the parties or by partisanship itself and value their position as Independents. Certainly independence of party is an ideal of some currency in our society, and it seems likely that a portion of those who call themselves Independents are not merely reporting the absence of identification with one of the major parties.

Sometimes it is said that a good number of those who call themselves Independents have simply adopted a label that conceals a genuine psychological commitment to one party or the other. Accordingly, it is argued that a person's voting record gives a more accurate statement of his party attachment than does his own self-description. Our samples doubtless include some of these undercover partisans, and we have incorporated in our measure of party identification a means of distinguishing Independents who say they lean toward one of the parties from Independents who say they do not. We do not think that the problem of measurement presented by the concealed partisan is large. Rather it seems to us much less troublesome than the problems that

TABLE 6-1. The Distribution of Party Identification

	October 1952	September 1953	October 1954	April 1956	October 1956	November 1957	October 1958
Strong Republicans	13%	15%	13%	14%	15%	10%	13%
Weak Republicans	14	15	14	18	14	16	16
Independent Republicans	7	6	6	6	8	6	4
Independents	5	4	7	3	9	8	8
Independent Democrats	10	8	9	6	7	7	7
Weak Democrats	25	23	25	24	23	26	24
Strong Democrats	22	22	22	19	21	21	23
Apolitical, don't know	4	7	4	10	3	6	5
Total	100%	100%	100%	100%	100%	100%	100%
Number of cases	1614	1023	1139	1731	1772	1488	1269

TABLE 6-2. Relation of Strength of Party Identification to Partisan Regularity in Voting for President, 1956[a]

	Strong Party Identifiers	Weak Party Identifiers	Independents Leaning to Party	Independents
Voted always or mostly for same party	82%	60%	36%	16%
Voted for different parties	18	40	64	84
Total	100%	100%	100%	100%
Number of cases	546	527	189	115

[a] The question used to establish party consistency of voting was this: "Have you always voted for the same party or have you voted for different parties for President?"

follow if psychological ties to party are measured in terms of the vote.

This question can be illuminated a good deal by an examination of the consistency of party voting among those of different degrees of party identification, as is done in Table 6-2. The proportion of persons consistently supporting one party varies by more than sixty percentage points between strong party identifiers and complete Independents. For the problem of the undercover partisan, the troublesome figure in Table 6-2 is the 16 per cent of full Independents who have voted for the candidates of one party only.[2] The importance of this figure diminishes when we remember that some of these persons have voted in very few presidential elections and could have supported one party consistently because of the way their votes fell, free of the influence of a genuine party tie.

A simple test of this hypothesis is made in Table 6-3 by separating persons who have come of voting age relatively recently from those who have been of voting age for a greater number of elections. Plainly, the length of time a person has had to develop a variable voting record

[2] In this discussion we assume that the concealed partisan is less likely to distort his voting record than his description of his party attachment; that is, we assume that what the undercover partisan values is chiefly the designation "Independent." To the extent this is untrue, the analysis of voting consistency by strength of party identification fails to enhance our understanding.

TABLE 6-3. Relation of Strength of Party Identification to Partisan Regularity in Voting for President, by Age Groups, 1956

Age	Strong Party Identifiers	Weak Party Identifiers	Independents Leaning to Party	Independents
21 to 34				
Voted always or mostly for same party	91%	78%	60%	33%
Voted for different parties	9	22	40	67
Total	100%	100%	100%	100%
Number of cases	104	120	53	21
35 and above				
Voted always or mostly for same party	80%	55%	26%	11%
Voted for different parties	20	45	74	89
Total	100%	100%	100%	100%
Number of cases	440	405	136	93

influences the likelihood that he will report that he has voted for the candidates of more than one party, whatever the strength of his party identification. But among complete Independents the proportion of people thirty-five years old or older who could reasonably be called concealed party identifiers is now reduced to 11 per cent. A detailed inspection of these cases shows that a number of these individuals have voted in relatively few elections and have had little opportunity to form an inconsistent voting record. When the frequency of voting turnout is considered, the proportion of extreme Independents who have voted only for the candidates of one party is not greater than we would expect it to be by chance alone.

If Table 6-3 suggests that we will describe relatively few genuine partisans as Independents by using self-classification to measure party attachments, it also suggests some of the difficulties of trying to use voting behavior to measure psychological identifications with party. The number of votes an individual may cast in a lifetime is small. In the early years of adulthood a person has voted too few times to give a sure indication of party allegiance; and if the individual seldom goes to the polls through the middle and later years, we have no better indication of his allegiance. And for the sensitive task of indicating *change* in these psychological identifications a simple record of behavior is clearly inadequate.

The measurement of party identification in the period of our research shows how different a picture of partisan allegiance voting behavior and self-description can give. Despite the substantial Republican majorities in the elections of 1952 and 1956, the percentages of Table 6-1 make clear that the Democratic Party enjoyed a three-to-two advantage in the division of party identification within the electorate in these same years.[3] Moreover, Table 6-1 documents the stability of this division of party loyalty in a period whose electoral history might suggest widespread change. Except for the shifting size of the group of respondents refusing to be assigned any position on the party scale, there is not a single variation between successive distributions of party identification that could not be laid to sampling error.

The constancy of partisanship in the nation at large in these years implies a good deal of constancy in individual identifications with party. This implication is a loose one since the percentages of Table 6-1 show only the absence of net change in this interval of time. The similarity of these distributions may conceal a substantial volume of compensating change. To show conclusively that this is not the case we would need to have data collected through time on the party attachments of individual people. But the great stability of partisan loyalties is supported, too, by what we can learn from recall data about the personal history of party identification. We have asked successive samples of the electorate a series of questions permitting us to reconstruct whether an individual who accepts a party designation has experienced a prior change in his party identification. The responses give impressive evidence of the constancy of party allegiance.

The fact that nearly everyone in our samples could be placed on a unitary dimension of party identification and that the idea of prior movements on this dimension was immediately understood are themselves important findings about the nature of party support within the electorate. In view of the loose, federated structure of American parties it was not obvious in advance that people could respond to party in these undifferentiated terms. Apparently the positive and negative feelings that millions of individuals have toward the parties are the result of orientations of a diffuse and generalized character that have a

3 Because Republican identifiers voted with somewhat greater frequency than Democratic identifiers in these years, the Democratic edge in party allegiance was slightly less among voters.

common psychological meaning even though there may be a good deal of variation in the way party is perceived.

Party Identification and Political Attitude

The psychological function of party identification undoubtedly varies among individuals. Our interest here centers primarily on the role of party as a supplier of cues by which the individual may evaluate the elements of politics. The fact that most elements of national politics are far removed from the world of the common citizen forces the individual to depend on sources of information from which he may learn indirectly what he cannot know as a matter of direct experience. Moreover, the complexities of politics and government increase the importance of having relatively simple cues to evaluate what cannot be matters of personal knowledge.

In the competition of voices reaching the individual the political party is an opinion-forming agency of great importance. This is not to say that party leaders are able as a matter of deliberate technique to transmit an elaborate defense of their position to those in the electorate who identify with the party. To the contrary, some of the most striking instances of party influence occur with only the simplest kind of information reaching the party's mass support. For example, a party undoubtedly furnishes a powerful set of cues about a political leader just by nominating him for President. Merely associating the party symbol with his name encourages those identifying with the party to develop a more favorable image of his record and experience, his abilities, and his other personal attributes. Likewise, this association encourages supporters of the opposite party to take a less favorable view of these same personal qualities. Partisans in each camp may incorporate into their view of the candidates whatever detailed information they can, and the highly-involved may develop an elaborate and carefully-drawn portrait. But the impact of the party symbol seems to be none the less strong on those who absorb little of politics and whose image of the candidates is extremely diffuse.

Apparently party has a profound influence across the full range of political objects to which the individual voter responds. The strength of relationship between party identification and the dimensions of partisan attitude suggests that responses to each element of national politics are deeply affected by the individual's enduring party attachments. If we return to the attitude forces of Chapter 4 and examine their strength and direction across the party identification scale, a

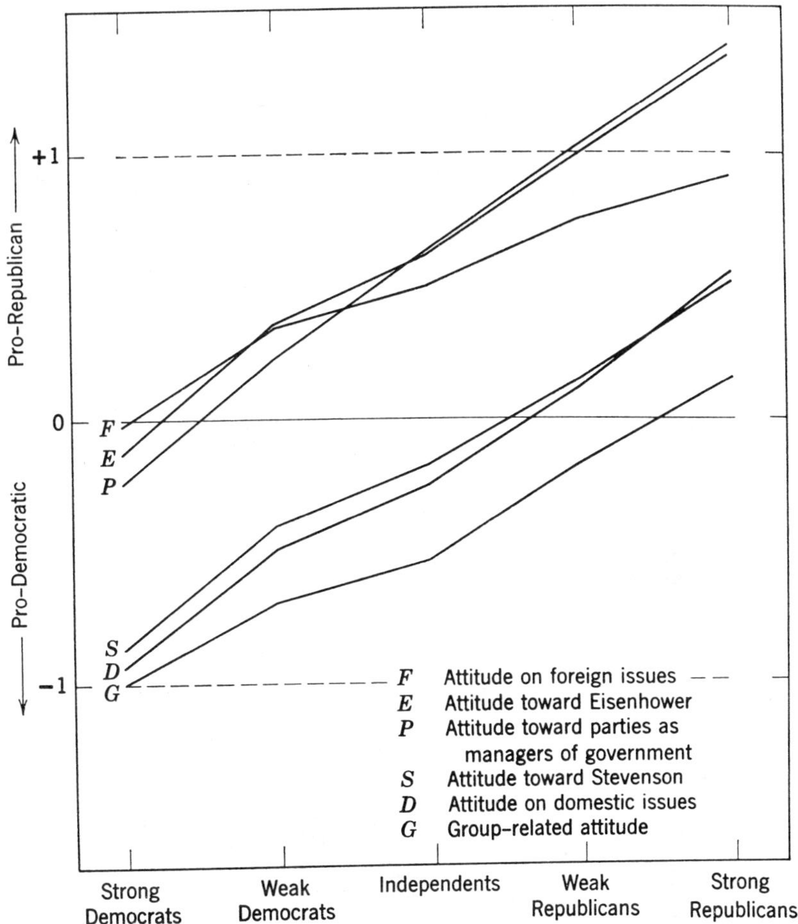

Fig. 6-1. Relation of party identification to partisan evaluations of elements of national politics, 1952.

remarkable pattern is seen. Figures 6-1 and 6-2, respectively, show this pattern as it appeared in 1952 and 1956 by displaying the mean of each attitude in each of five groups spanning the party dimension.[4] In the design of these figures the vertical dimension indicates the inten-

[4] In each case the mean of an attitude factor for a party identification group has been divided by the standard deviation of the factor for the group in order to express the mean in standard units about the zero point. The effect of this normalization is to lessen differences in the means that are attributable simply to differences in the number (rather than the relative partisanship) of references a party identification group has made to a given element of national politics.

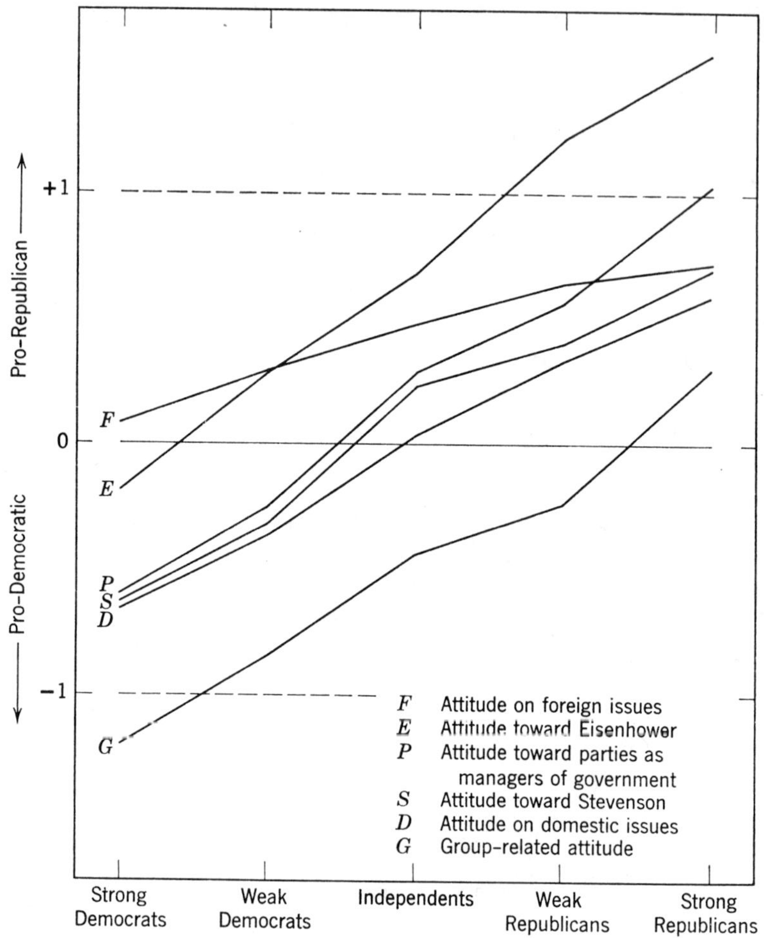

Fig. 6-2. Relation of party identification to partisan evaluations of elements of national politics, 1956.

sity and direction of attitude partisanship, the horizontal dimension the strength and direction of party identification. If we take any group along the party identification scale, it will be *more* pro-Republican in all its attitudes than the group immediately to its left and it will be *less* pro-Republican in all its attitudes than the group immediately to its right, except of course as a group may fall at the end of the party scale. The fact that without exception these attitude forces become steadily more pro-Republican as we move from the Democratic to the Republican end of the party dimension suggests the extent of the party's impact on the electorate's evaluations of the elements of politics. In both of these elections the influence of party on foreign issue attitudes seems to have been less pronounced than its influence on attitudes toward the other elements of politics. It may well be that in this period the "realities" of America's situation in the world were so clear—at least in the simple terms of which party or candidate could better preserve the peace—that there was less opportunity for partisan loyalties to form the electorate's response to the issues of foreign affairs. All the same, party identification *did* color attitudes toward foreign issues in some measure, as it colored individual feeling on every one of the dimensions of attitude we have examined.

Of course party identification cannot account for all the observed variation of political attitude. However great its impact, partisan loyalty does not by any means express the total influence of factors antecedent in a causal sense to the attitudes we have studied. Paradoxically, the very data that show the enormous influence of party allegiance on political attitude in these elections show also the limits of its explanatory power. In Figs. 6-1 and 6-2 we may note that some attitudes are more favorable than others to one of the parties *across the entire party identification scale.* For example, in each of these elections the Republicans fared better with the public on foreign issues than on domestic issues in each of the groups defined by our measure of party identification. And between the two elections this difference in attitude partisanship diminished in every one of these groups by a lessening of pro-Democratic feeling on domestic policy. These findings plainly have to be explained in terms of antecedent causal factors whose effects were independent of what is measured by our party identification scale.

Another aspect of the data from which Figs. 6-1 and 6-2 were prepared shows the limits of party identification as an explanatory factor, although this limitation cannot be seen in the figures as they are drawn. These charts describe the attitude partisanship of persons within the several party identification groups by showing averages for the groups. But each of these averages has associated with it a set of individual scores, which would lie above and below the mean values if they were shown in the figures. And this variability of individual people about the group means cannot be explained by party identification itself.[5] Later chapters of this book will touch upon several antecedent factors

[5] Part of this variation within groups may result from putting in a few discrete categories a population that really is spread out at many more points along an underlying dimension of party loyalty. The effects of grouping cannot explain the full variability within groups, since the individual scores of different groups "overlap."

that help to account for differences of political attitude which party identification cannot itself explain.

In the elections described by our data, party identification could not account for all aspects of the image formed by the public of the elements of national politics; but it gives to this image a central partisan coherence. The dimensions of attitude we have considered were bound together by the common influence of identifications with party. The extent to which this was true may be seen by examining directly the partisan coherence that is found within this system of attitudes in these years. Instead of inspecting the relation of each attitude dimension to party identification, in the manner of Figs. 6-1 and 6-2, we may assess the importance of a common partisan factor by examining the interrelationships of these attitudes themselves.

When this assessment is made, a common partisan factor is found to explain a large part of the variation of attitude. The full implication of the results of this analysis is not easily expressed in words, for reasons that the controversial history of the statistical techniques we have used may serve to make clear. But the examination of these interrelationships does yield a single partisan factor that could explain nearly half of the total variance of attitudes toward the elements of presidential politics among those who voted in the elections of 1952 and 1956.[6] Moreover, the relation of this common partisan component to each type of attitude was quite high, although as we would expect from Figs. 6-1 and 6-2, its relation to foreign issue attitude was somewhat less strong. In these results the ability of a general partisan orientation to color evaluations of current political objects seems impressive.

If party identification deeply influences the partisan character of a field of psychological forces, it also will have marked effects on the

[6] This examination was by the methods of principal component analysis due to Hotelling. See Harold Hotelling, "Analysis of a Complex of Statistical Variables into Principal Components," *Journal of Educational Psychology,* XXIV (1933), pp. 417–441, 498–520. The correlation among voters of each attitude variable with the component we interpret as a party factor is given below:

	1952	1956
Attitude toward Stevenson	0.74	0.69
Attitude toward Eisenhower	0.74	0.70
Group-related attitude	0.60	0.67
Attitude on domestic issues	0.69	0.63
Attitude on foreign issues	0.54	0.46
Attitude toward parties as managers of government	0.70	0.65

internal consistency of the field. Our conception of the role of partisan loyalties leads us to expect this result. Identification with a party raises a perceptual screen through which the individual tends to see what is favorable to his partisan orientation. The stronger the party bond, the more exaggerated the process of selection and perceptual distortion will be. Without this psychological tie, or perhaps with commitments to symbols of another kind, the Independent is less likely to develop consistent partisan attitudes.

The earlier discussion of attitude conflict is readily extended to give empirical support to this view. As in the measurement of consistency used there, we will take a person's attitudes toward the several elements of politics to be fully consistent here if each attitude that is not politically neutral has the same partisan direction. The importance of party identification for the consistency of this field of forces is quite clear if the relative incidence of attitude consistency is examined among those of different degrees of attachment to party, as it is in Table 6-4 (next page). For the four groups defined by strength of party identification the table compares the number of people who have consistent attitudes that we would "expect" to find in the group, with the number actually found. The notion of expected number is introduced here to allow for the fact that we would expect some consistency by chance and that the fewer the number of partisan attitudes a person has, the greater the likelihood he will exhibit a consistent attitude structure simply by chance. The entries of Table 6-4 show the great significance of party identification for the internal consistency of attitude. If the number of people we would expect to have consistent attitudes by chance is taken as a suitable zero, a slight tendency toward consistent partisanship is seen even among extreme Independents. But the tendency is much more marked among Independents who lean toward one of the parties and among weak party identifiers, and it is vastly greater among those who describe their party allegiance as strong.

The patterns of relationship found in cross-sectional data ought not to suggest too simple an idea of the connection between party identification and attitudes toward the elements of politics. A relation that may appear static and unidirectional in data of this sort is undoubtedly fairly complex, and several more things need to be said about it if our formulation is to do justice to psychological realities. In particular, it should be clear that the influence of party identification on attitudes toward political objects extends through time. The relationships found in the interviews of a relatively brief campaign period reflect a process of opinion formation and change that may

TABLE 6-4. Party Identification as an Influence on Partisan Consistency of Attitude, 1956[a]

	Strong Party Identifiers	Weak Party Identifiers	Independents Leaning to Party	Independents
Number expected to have consistent attitudes	107	122	47	31
Number observed to have consistent attitudes	358	259	94	43
Increase of observed over expected number	235%	112%	100%	39%
Number of cases	597	558	230	117

[a] This tabulation includes only individuals having at least two non-neutral attitudes; that is, only respondents for whom the notion of consistent or inconsistent attitude could be given meaning. For two, three, four, five, or six non-neutral attitudes the probabilities of someone having attitude consistency by chance alone are easily calculated, assuming the probability is 0.5 that a particular attitude will have a given partisan sign. The probabilities so calculated may be combined with what we know about the number of people in each of the four party identification groups who have each of the possible numbers of non-neutral attitudes. From this combination we obtain the number of people of each degree of party identification that we would expect to have consistent attitudes by chance. The difference between these expected frequencies and the actual frequencies of consistent individuals in each group seems an appropriate statistic for assessing the importance of strength of party identification as an influence on consistency of attitudes.

go back over many months or years. Hence the explanatory problem we confront is a dynamic one; we need to understand the causal priorities of a process extending through time and not just the direction of influence at a given moment. It seems likely that at the peak of a presidential campaign the causal relation of party identification to attitudes toward the things that are seen in national politics is two-directional. If the individual has formed attitudes that are consistent with his party allegiance, that allegiance will continue to support the attitudes it has shaped. But these attitudes in turn comprise an important defense of the individual's fixed partisan commitment, one that may well give service in discussions with face-to-face associates during the campaign. If the individual has developed attitudes *not* consistent with his party allegiance, that allegiance presumably will work to undo the contrary opinions. But they in turn must exert some pressure on the individual's basic partisan commitment. If this pressure is intense enough, a stable partisan identification may actually be changed. When such a change occurs in a considerable part of the electorate, as it has at rare moments of our political history, the great realignments occur that change the course of electoral politics for years to come.

Therefore, an adequate account of the relation of party identification to the attitudes we have considered must allow for the fact that attitudes of this sort, when they agree with party allegiance, help to conserve this partisan tie; and when they disagree with party allegiance, are potential agents of change in the individual's basic partisan orientation. But this does not alter our judgment that in the period of our studies the influence of party identification on attitudes toward the perceived elements of politics has been far more important than the influence of these attitudes on party identification itself. We are convinced that the relationships in our data reflect primarily the role of enduring partisan commitments in shaping attitudes toward political objects. Our conviction on this point is rooted in what we know of the relative stability and priority in time of party identification and the attitudes it may affect. We know that persons who identify with one of the parties typically have held the same partisan tie for all or almost all of their adult lives. But within their experience since coming of voting age many of the elements of politics have changed. For example, the 1952 campaign brought two new candidates to presidential politics and a set of issues arising very recently from the Korean War and the charges of corruption during the later Truman years. Yet the reactions to the personalities of Eisenhower and Stevenson, to the issues of the Far Eastern war, and to the probity of the Democratic Administration differed markedly according to the individual's party allegiance. If we are to trust the evidence on the stability of party identification, these differences must be attributed to the capacity of a general partisan orientation to color responses to particular political objects.

What is more, even the elements of politics that carry over from one election to another may be evaluated anew in later campaigns by part of the electorate. The involvement of many Americans in politics is slight enough that they may respond *de novo* to issues and personalities that have been present in earlier elections but that are salient to them only at the height of a presidential campaign. For many voters the details of the political landscape may be quite blurred until they are brought more into focus during the campaign period. The formative influence of party identification on these re-evaluations would not be essentially different from its influence on responses to newer elements of politics.

Because the influence of party identification extends through time, its workings cannot be fully disclosed by the relationships seen at a particular moment. For this reason, our statement of causal priorities is in the end an inference, but one for which the evidence is strong. If the inference is correct, the differences in attitude between those of differing partisan loyalties enlarge considerably our understanding of the configuration of forces leading to behavior. We have seen in Chapter 4 that the voting act can be explained in an immediate sense by the strength and direction and consistency of attitudes toward the political objects this act touches. We find now that an important part of the variation in the partisanship and internal coherence of these attitudes may in turn be accounted for by stable partisan identifications.

This causal paradigm requires one additional amendment. Our hypothesis that party identification influences the voting act by influencing attitudes toward the objects to which this act relates needs to be modified for the person who has only the faintest image of these objects. If someone has little perception of the candidates, of the record of the parties, of public issues or questions of group interest, his attitudes toward these things may play a less important intervening role between party identification and the vote. Presumably, among people of relatively impoverished attitude who yet have a sense of partisan loyalty, party identification has a more direct influence on behavior than it has among people with a well-elaborated view of what their choice concerns. Like the automobile buyer who knows nothing of cars except that he prefers a given make, the voter who knows simply that he is a Republican or Democrat responds directly to his stable allegiance without the mediating influence of perceptions he has formed of the objects he must choose between.

Party Identification and Electoral Choice

If some voters respond directly to a lasting sense of party identification, the behavior of most of the electorate is better explained as a response to current evaluations of what they are acting toward. We have conceived these evaluations as a field of attitude forces whose strength and direction and mutual consistency determine behavior in an immediate sense. The role of party identification seems primarily to be that of an antecedent factor that colors these attitudes as they are formed. By no means is party the only antecedent: this field of psychological forces reflects the influence of a great range of prior factors, which may at times lead the individual to form attitudes inconsistent with his stable party attachment. But the role of general partisan orientations in molding attitudes toward the elements of politics is very clear.

As a consequence of this role, party identification has a profound impact on behavior. A sense of its impact may be gained if we return to the statistical model used in Chapter 4 to express the probability that a given individual would vote in a given partisan direction. From the strength and direction of attitudes toward the various elements of politics we could order the individuals in our samples according to the probability of their voting Republican. That is, we could form an array extending from those most likely to vote Democratic to those most likely to vote Republican. Let us now make explicit the impact party identification has on behavior through its influence on attitude, by showing a separate array for each of five groups defined by our party identification scale. For each of the distributions shown in Fig. 6-3 the

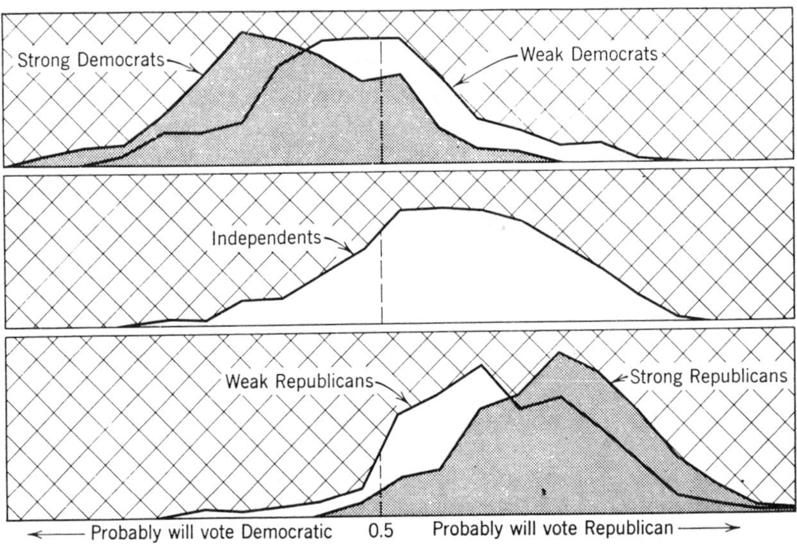

Fig. 6-3. Probable direction of vote by party identification groups, 1956.

horizontal dimension is the probability an individual will vote Republican: to the left this probability is low (that is, the likelihood the individual will vote Democratic is high) and to the right the probability that the individual will vote Republican is high.[7] The effect of party is seen at once in the changing location of the distributions along this probability dimension as we consider successively Strong Democrats, Weak Democrats, Independents, Weak Republicans, and Strong Republicans. The moving positions of these arrays show clearly the impact of party identification on the forces governing behavior.

The properties of Fig. 6-3 serve also to demonstrate once again that party allegiance is not the sole determinant of the attitudes supporting behavior. We may attribute to the influence of party identification the movement from left to right of the centers of the arrays as we proceed from Strong Democrats to Strong Republicans. But we cannot attribute to party attachments the spread of these distributions about their centers. The probabilities we have calculated vary widely within each of the party identification groups, indeed widely enough that in some cases persons identified with one party are shown to be inclined by their attitudes to vote for the opposite party. However, the extent to which attitudes toward political objects contradicted party ties was not equal for the two parties, and this is a second aspect of these data that party allegiance cannot itself explain. In the election of 1956 all five of these arrays were "biased" in the Republican direction in the sense that many fewer strong or weak Democrats than strong or weak Republicans are seen to be probable voters for the opposite party and fewer Independents are probable Democratic voters than are probable Republican voters. Evidently in this election powerful antecedent factors other than party allegiance influenced in a direction favorable to the Republican Party the psychological forces acting on behavior.

The distributions of Fig. 6-3 foreshadow the division of the presidential vote within the several party identification groups in the election of 1956. In view of the dependence of voting choice on the psychological forces we have treated, these probability arrays lead us to expect extreme differences in the division of the vote across the

[7] As stated on page 73, the probabilities are computed as a linear regression of the six attitude factors we have measured. To simplify the comparisons between party identification groups the distributions of Fig. 6-3 have been standardized by expressing the frequencies of probability values as percentages of the total number of individuals within each group. The effect of this transformation is to make the area of each of the five curves approximately the same.

party groups. And they lead us to expect, too, that the Republican Party had an advantage in this election in securing the votes of Independents and of persons identifying with the opposite party. Both these expectations are confirmed by Table 6-5. In the elections of 1952 and 1956 the Democratic percentage of the vote for President varied from 1 per cent among Strong Republicans to approximately 85 per cent among Strong Democrats. And the Republican candidate fared better than his Democratic opponent in attracting Independent votes and the votes of those identified with the opposite party, an advantage that was indispensable to each of his victories.

TABLE 6-5. Relation of Party Identification to Presidential Vote

	Strong Demo-crats	Weak Demo-crats	Inde-pendents	Weak Repub-licans	Strong Repub-licans
1952					
Republican	16%	38%	67%	94%	99%
Democratic	84	62	33	6	1
	100%	100%	100%	100%	100%
Number of cases	262	274	269	171	199
1956					
Republican	15%	37%	73%	93%	99%
Democratic	85	63	27	7	1
	100%	100%	100%	100%	100%
Number of cases	286	270	305	194	211

Differences in the motivational forces acting on voters of contrasting party loyalties lead us to expect wide differences between party groups in the division of the presidential vote. Yet the variability of the vote shown in Table 6-5 is so extreme that it naturally raises the question of whether party identification does not have a residual effect on behavior apart from its impact through the attitudes it influences so profoundly. That this residual effect is small is indicated by the fact that adding party identification to the set of attitude variables from which we have predicted behavior brings only a slight improvement in explanation in either the sense of statistical estimation or of the discrimination of actual Republican voters from actual Democratic voters.[8] The improvement that *is* found we attribute primarily to the role of party identification in motivating directly the behavior of persons who are without a well-developed image of the things to which their vote relates. For them, the connection of party identification and behavior may not be mediated by attitudes toward the political objects this behavior concerns. As a result, knowing their stable partisan loyalties improves our ability to predict behavior more than it does for individuals who have formed stronger evaluations of the things toward which the vote is directed.

The nature of this difference—and of our conception of the place of party identification in the forces leading to the vote—can be made clearer if we examine the behavior of individuals whose attitudes toward the current elements of politics contradict their sense of party identification. To enlarge the number of cases we may inspect, let us combine into the single array shown in Fig. 6-4 the probabilities of voting Republican we have calculated on the basis of attitude forces for every voter in our 1952 and 1956 samples. Near the center of this array we may define an interval of relatively slight partisan attitude

[8] Incorporating party identification in the statistical model used for prediction in Chapter 4 increases the multiple correlation with voting choice from 0.72 to 0.74 in the election of 1952 and from 0.71 to 0.73 in the election of 1956. In each year the addition of this factor raises less than 2 per cent the number of persons who could be correctly classified as Republican or Democratic voters. However, it will be clear from the argument that follows that the degree to which prediction is improved would be somewhat greater among those of relatively slight attitude formation.

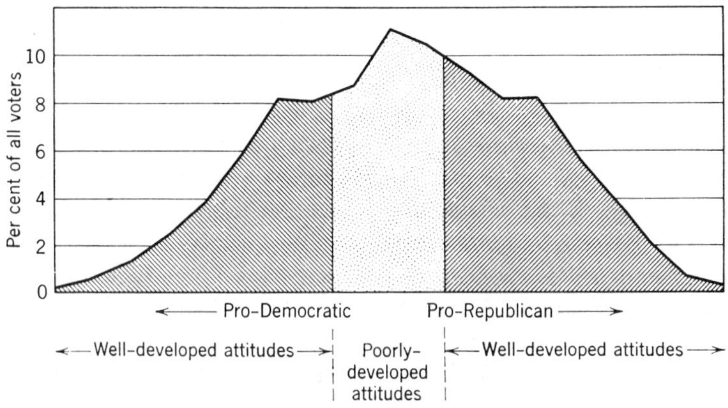

Fig. 6-4. Location of individuals with well-developed attitudes and poorly-developed attitudes within distribution of all respondents, 1952 and 1956.

formation in which lie people whose perceptions of the elements of presidential politics are either little-developed or without a clear evaluative tone. This group is represented by the lighter area in the figure. Outside this interval lie the people whose attitudes are better formed in a partisan sense and of greater motivational force. The boundaries of the interval are of course somewhat arbitrarily chosen, but if we have conceived the role of party identification correctly we ought to find that a disagreement of party allegiance and attitudes toward current political objects has very different consequences for those who lie outside this interval and for those who lie within it. In persons of strong attitude we would expect voting behavior to follow these attitudes, whatever the individual's sense of party allegiance might be. Of course, the influence of party identification on perceptions of political objects is so great that only rarely will the individual develop a set of attitude forces that conflicts with this allegiance. But when other antecedent factors lead to evaluations of the elements of politics that strongly contradict the individual's party identification, we anticipate that behavior will conform to these evaluations rather than to party allegiance. In contrast, we anticipate that when party identification is found to disagree with attitudes toward political objects formed by people whose attitudes are less numerous or motivationally weak, party allegiance will have a larger influence on behavior. Even among people of this sort evaluations of objects to which the vote relates may play an intervening role between party allegiance and behavior that is important enough to cause the individual to act against his party identification when it fails to agree with current attitude. But we would expect party allegiance to have a greater direct influence on behavior among people who have little perception of the things their behavior concerns than it has among people with a more developed or evaluatively toned view of these things.

These ideas are supported by the entries of Table 6-6, which compares the behavior of persons outside and inside our interval of limited attitude formation whose attitudes are found to disagree with their sense of party identification. Among those who have a strong evaluative image of the elements of presidential politics, behavior coincides with these evaluations in 80 per cent of the cases. The fact that party allegiance prevails in only one-fifth of these cases is the more remarkable if we keep in mind the very strong relationship of party identification to the vote across the electorate as a whole. Among those who have a less clear evaluative image of the objects of politics, behavior coincides with party identification in a much greater pro-

TABLE 6-6. Relation of Degree of Attitude Development to Direction in which Conflict of Party Identification and Partisan Evaluations Is Resolved in Voting[a]

	Those Who Have Formed Evaluations		
	That Are Well-Developed	That Are Poorly-Developed	Those Who Have Formed No Evaluations At All
Vote agrees with party identification	20%	47%	75%
Vote fails to agree with party identification	80	53	25
Total	100%	100%	100%
Number of cases	143	164	36

[a] Figures in this table are based on a combination of data from the 1952 and 1956 election samples.

portion of cases. For these people the relation of party allegiance to behavior does seem to be mediated less by evaluations of political objects, although a good half of even these persons act in accord with the evaluations they have formed, rather than in accord with their party loyalties. Table 6-6 also describes the behavior of the very small group of individuals in our samples who identify with one of the parties yet who appear on our standard measures to have no perceptions of current political objects whatever. This is the group for which we would expect the causal sequence connecting party allegiance, attitudes toward the elements of politics, and the voting act to be most severely truncated. With evaluations of political objects playing no apparent intervening role between partisan allegiance and behavior, 75 per cent of these people simply vote their party loyalties at the polls.

Party Identification and Political Involvement

Evidently no single datum can tell us more about the attitude and behavior of the individual as presidential elector than his location on a dimension of psychological identification extending between the two great parties. Yet our discussion of the impact of party identification should not close without some consideration of the relation of party allegiance to the dimension of political involvement introduced in Chapter 5. It is not accidental that the individual's general partisan orientation and the extent of his involvement in politics, either of which may influence a wide set of attitudinal and behavioral characteristics, are related to each other. Although our causal understanding of this relation is far from sure, the fact of association is clear enough: the stronger the individual's sense of attachment to one of the parties, the greater his psychological involvement in political affairs.

The association is easily missed in popular accounts of electoral behavior.[9] The ideal of the Independent citizen, attentive to politics, concerned with the course of government, who weighs the rival appeals of a campaign and reaches a judgment that is unswayed by partisan prejudice, has had such a vigorous history in the tradition of political reform—and has such a hold on civic education today—that one could easily suppose that the habitual partisan has the more limited interest and concern with politics. But if the usual image of the Independent voter is intended as more than a normative ideal, it fits poorly the characteristics of the Independents in our samples. Far from being more attentive, interested, and informed, Independents tend as a group to be somewhat less involved in politics. They have somewhat poorer knowledge of the issues, their image of the candidates is fainter, their interest in the campaign is less, their concern over the outcome is relatively slight, and their choice between competing candidates, although it is indeed made later in the campaign, seems much less to spring from discoverable evaluations of the elements of national politics.

These differences may be illustrated in terms of two of the measures of involvement used in Chapter 5. When those of strong partisan identifications are compared with those who call themselves Independents, the partisan tends both in his interest in the campaign and his concern over the outcome to be more involved than the political Independent, as Tables 6-7 and 6-8 indicate. What is more, a further division of the Independent group would show in each case that those who refused to say they were closer to one party or the other are even

[9] But it has been found by other investigators of voting behavior. See Bernard Berelson, Paul F. Lazarsfeld, and William N. McPhee, *Voting: A Study of Opinion Formation in a Presidential Campaign* (University of Chicago Press, Chicago, 1954), pp. 25–27, and Robert Agger, "Independents and Party Identifiers: Characteristics and Behavior in 1952," *American Voting Behavior,* ed. Eugene Burdick and Arthur G. Brodbeck (The Free Press, Glencoe, Ill., 1959).

less involved than other Independents. It is of course true that the percentages of Tables 6-7 and 6-8 are group proportions and that some of the Independents in our samples are highly involved. But these individuals are rare enough that the characteristics of Independents as a group are widely different from those suggested by the familiar stereotype.

TABLE 6-7. Relation of Strength of Party Identification to Interest in Campaign, 1956

	Strong Party Identifiers	Weak Party Identifiers	Independents
Very much interested	42%	23%	25%
Somewhat interested	38	42	43
Not much interested	20	35	32
Total	100%	100%	100%
Number of cases	624	651	415

TABLE 6-8. Relation of Strength of Party Identification to Concern over Outcome, 1956

	Strong Party Identifiers	Weak Party Identifiers	Independents
Care very much or care pretty much	82%	62%	51%
Don't care very much or don't care at all	18	38	49
Total	100%	100%	100%
Number of cases	609	621	395

It is by no means clear what causal interpretation should be given the association of strength of party identification and degree of political involvement found in the interviews taken at single points in time. For the moment we may suppose that a person's location on either of these fundamental dimensions will influence his location on the other. The individual who has a strong and continuing involvement in politics is more likely to develop a commitment to one or the other of the major parties. And the individual who has such a commitment is likely to have his interest and concern with politics sustained at a higher level. But we may suppose, too, that the relation of partisanship and involvement is to be explained in part by common antecedents. Discovering what it is in the individual's life experience that could account both for his party allegiance and his political involvement leads naturally to a consideration of the development of party identification.

The Development of Party Identification ◇ 7

Identification with political parties, as we have seen, is an attachment held widely through the American electorate with substantial influence on political cognitions, attitudes, and behavior. We may now turn our inquiry toward an exploration of the circumstances from which party identification itself may be thought to spring. This will carry us backward in the life experience of the individual citizen and into the political history of our society.

Origins of Party Identification

When we examine the evidence on the manner in which party attachment develops and changes during the lifetime of the individual citizen, we find a picture characterized more by stability than by change—not by rigid, immutable fixation on one party rather than the other, but by a persistent adherence and a resistance to contrary influence.

Early politicization. At the time we meet the respondents of our surveys they have reached the minimum voting age, and most of them are considerably beyond it. The only information we can obtain about their political experience in their pre-adult years depends on their recall. Hyman's review of the literature on "political socialization" brings together the available data to extend our understanding of this important stage of political growth.[1] It is apparent from his presentation that an orientation toward political affairs typically begins before the individual attains voting age and that this orienta-

[1] Herbert Hyman, *Political Socialization* (The Free Press, Glencoe, Ill., 1959).

tion strongly reflects his immediate social milieu, in particular his family.

Our own data are entirely consistent with this conclusion. The high degree of correspondence between the partisan preference of our respondents with that which they report for their parents may be taken as a rough measure of the extent to which partisanship is passed from one generation to the next.[2] This correspondence is somewhat

TABLE 7-1. Intergenerational Resemblance in Partisan Orientation, Politically Active and Inactive Homes, 1958

	One or Both Parents Were Politically Active			Neither Parent Was Politically Active		
Party Identification of Offspring	Both Parents Were Dems.	Both Parents Were Reps.	Parents Had No Consistent Partisanship	Both Parents Were Dems.	Both Parents Were Reps.	Parents Had No Consistent Partisanship
Strong Dem.	50%	5%	21%	40%	6%	20%
Weak Dem.	29	9	26	36	11	15
Independent	12	13	26	19	16	26
Weak Rep.	6	34	16	3	42	20
Strong Rep.	2	37	10	1	24	12
Apolitical	1	2	1	1	1	7
	100%	100%	100%	100%	100%	100%
Number of cases	333	194	135	308	187	199

higher among those people who report one or both of their parents as having been "actively concerned" with politics than among those whose parents were not politically active. If we make the reasonable assumption that in the "active" homes the political views of the parents were more frequently and intensely cognized by the children than in the inactive homes, we should of course expect to find these views more faithfully reproduced in these children when they reach adult years. In contrast, we find that persons from inactive homes, especially those with no clear political orientation, tend strongly toward non-partisan positions themselves. For a large proportion of the electorate the orientation toward politics expressed in our measure

[2] There are obvious weaknesses in this measure. Some of our respondents had undoubtedly carried an "inherited" party identification into early adulthood but had changed by the time we interviewed them.

of party identification has its origins in the early family years. We are not able to trace the history of these families to find an explanation of why the homes of some people were politically oriented and others were not. Such homes appear to exist in all social strata, less frequently in some than others of course.

The persistence of partisanship. The extent to which pre-adult experience shapes the individual's political future may be judged from the constancy with which most people hold to the partisan orientation they have at the time they enter the electorate. We find a number of evidences of this in our data, aside from the fact of parent-child relationship shown in Table 7-1. When we ask people to recall their first presidential vote, for example, we discover that of those who can remember their first vote for president two thirds still identify with the same party they first voted for. A majority (56 per cent) of these presidential voters have never crossed party lines; they have always supported their party's candidate.

A direct assessment of the stability with which the average citizen holds to his political orientation may be obtained from his report on whether he has ever identified himself differently than he does at present. The picture is generally one of firm but not immovable attachment (Table 7-2). The greatest mobility is found among those people whose party attachment is weakest, the strongly identified are least likely to have changed sides.

It is apparent from these various pieces of evidence that identifica-

TABLE 7-2. Stability and Change in Party Identification, 1956

	Strong Dem.	Weak Dem.	Ind. Dem.	Ind.	Ind. Rep.	Weak Rep.	Strong Rep.
Have not changed from one party to other[a]	93%	89%	69%	68%	55%	74%	85%
Were Rep., changed to Dem.	7	11	...	...	...	...	...
Were Rep., changed to Ind.	...	...	13	10	8	...	...
Were Dem., changed to Ind.	...	...	18	22	37	...	...
Were Dem., changed to Rep.	...	...	...	...	...	26	15
Number of cases	364	397	108	145	144	250	261

[a] Included here may be some people who moved from an Independent position to one of the parties. Our interview does not permit us to isolate such cases.

tion with political parties, once established, is an attachment which is not easily changed. Not all members of the electorate form strong party attachments, however, and they make up a sufficiently large proportion of the population to permit the short-term influence of political forces associated with issues and candidates to play a significant role in determining the outcome of specific elections. Even strong identifiers are not impervious to such influences and, as we shall see, occasional cataclysmic national events have had the power to produce substantial realignment in long-standing divisions of political sentiment.

Fluctuations in Party Identification

Changes in public attitudes may be classified according to the type of stimulus that produces them. We may speak of *personal forces,* which move individuals selectively without reference to the larger social categories to which they belong, or of *social forces,* which move large sections of the population more or less simultaneously. Personal forces produce changes that vary in an uncorrelated way from individual to individual and do not have a significant impact on the prevailing pattern of attitudes, even though the total proportion of people shifting their position may be sizable. Social forces influence large numbers of people in similar ways and may produce substantial realignments of the total distribution of attitudes.[3]

Changes produced by personal forces. A variety of circumstances in the life of the ordinary citizen have political significance for him as a person without having any accompanying implications for broader groups. When we examine the reports of those of our respondents who shifted parties for reasons that appear to be entirely individual, we find that their change in partisanship tended to be associated with a change in their social milieu.

> A 41-year-old minister's wife in Texas calls herself a Democrat, says there was a brief time when she was a Republican. "I was a Democrat long before I voted Republican. Then for three years we lived in another state where everyone was Republican. During that time I thought of myself as a Republican but that was just a phase. I'm voting Republican now only because of the candidate. I'd give anything in the world if Eisenhower were on the Democratic ticket."

[3] This formulation closely resembles a model for the explanation of attitude changes developed by George Katona. See his "Attitude Change: Instability of Response and Acquisition of Experience" (*"Psychological Monographs,"* Vol. 72, No. 10; Washington, D. C.: American Psychological Association, Inc., 1958).

A foreman in an Indiana foundry says he is an Independent, had been a Democrat until five or six years ago. Says he changed "when I went on the management side in business in place of being in the union."

A widow, 72 years old, says she is a Democrat but she had been a Republican. "When was it that the women started to vote? That's when I changed. My father was a Republican but my husband was a Democrat. I just went along with him."

A 29-year-old Negro, owner and manager of a music store in Connecticut, says he is now an Independent. He had been a Democrat until about a year ago. "I changed when I got away from home and went into business for myself. I've read a lot of confidential stuff and my opinions are broader. I got away from the opinions of the regular working man and saw things from a businessman's point of view."

A marriage, a new job, or a change in neighborhood may place a person under strong social pressure to conform to political values different from his own. Close personal relationships are usually associated with common political identifications in American society, and discrepancies tend to create strain, especially if the conflicting political views are strongly held. Although there are many strong-minded people who hold out despite the pressures implicit in this type of situation, others find it more congenial to accept the coloration of those persons or groups whose approval they value.

Of the 20 per cent of our respondents who say they have changed party affiliation during their lifetime only about one in six explain this change as a result of the kind of personal influence the previous quotations illustrate. Considering the high degree of mobility in American society, one might have anticipated that changes of this kind would be more numerous. The movements of large numbers of people from the farm to the city, from the city to the suburbs, from region to region, and from one employment situation to another undoubtedly result in profound differences in their manner of living. But none of these movements necessarily implies a change in one's immediate political surroundings. As we know, there are large representations of both parties at virtually all social and occupational levels and it would not be surprising for a person of either political persuasion to find himself among co-partisans in almost any new situation into which he moved. We would, in fact, expect him to seek out such associates. Only in certain special groups, such as labor union members in mass industry in Northern metropolitan centers or high income business owners and executives, do we find such strong consensus of political belief that a dissenter might find himself in a lonely position.

Changes produced by social forces. Although the changes resulting from purely personal circumstances may be expected to occur about as often in one partisan direction as the other, changes brought about by experiences shared in common are likely to be cumulative. If these experiences are sufficiently intense and sufficiently widespread, their political consequences may be profound.

Social forces create cumulative changes, but these changes need not disturb the prevailing balance of party strength. If the stimulus to which the public is subjected strikes different segments of the electorate in ways that have contrasting political implications, the resulting shifts in partisanship may change the make-up of each party's support without altering the relative proportions supporting each party. This phenomenon of *polarization,* which we will discuss at length in Chapter 13, is most prominent in the public's response to economic forces. Fluctuations in the economic climate tend to be reflected in the degree to which working-class and middle-class voters draw apart in the camps of the opposing parties. These movements may balance each other, however, so that the total effect on comparative party strength is not substantial. The impact of social forces may, also, have quite a different character, producing systematic movements from one party to the other that are not offset by movements in the opposite direction. There are two general types of public experience that appear to have this quality: those experiences associated with great national crises and, less obviously, those associated with progress through the life cycle.

The average citizen is very much less involved in politics than is often imagined. His awareness of political events is limited and his concern with ideological problems is only rudimentary. Our surveys force us to the conclusion that only an event of extraordinary intensity can arouse any significant part of the electorate to the point that its established political loyalties are shaken.

The terms, involvement, vote, and party identification have been used in this volume to denote quite different political phenomena, each having a good deal of independence of the others. It is easily possible that both involvement and vote might be considerably influenced by circumstances that would leave party identification virtually untouched. We regard 1952 as a case in point. Party identification is a durable attachment, not readily disturbed by passing events and personalities. But there have been occasions when national crises have shaken prevailing political loyalties, and two of them were so violent that they reversed the balance of party strength throughout the country.

The political upheaval associated with the Civil War imposed a regional dimension on the partisan attachments of the American electorate. The violent reaction in the East and Midwest to the passage of the Kansas-Nebraska Act in 1854 led to the creation of the Republican Party, committed to resisting the extension of the "great moral, social, and political evil" of slavery. The Free Soil movement, taken up as a major principle by the Republican Party, and the Homestead Act of 1862 created a resource of rural Republican strength throughout the Northern and Western areas. Within a short period the political contours of the nation had been drastically reshaped. The South, which in prewar years had divided its votes in proportions similar to those of the North, became the Solid South. Northern communities that had been Democratic turned Republican and remained so for decades.

The distribution of partisan attachments in the nation today, a century after the Civil War, follows the same regional lines laid down at that time. The South, despite its occasional desertions of the Democratic presidential candidate, is still the citadel of the Democratic Party, with the Republican Party offering hardly more than token opposition in large parts of the area. The Northeast, including New England and the Middle Atlantic States, which was the center of abolitionist sentiment, is now the strongest Republican area of the country. The Far West, which was both geographically and psychologically removed from the conflict in the Southern states, is at present the most Democratic region outside the South.[4]

We do not wish to suggest that these regions are still preoccupied with the issues of the Civil War. The participants in that conflict have long since passed from the scene, and slavery and secession now have only historic interest. But as Key has made clear, community patterns of party affiliation have a remarkable capacity to persist long after "the disappearance of (the) issues that created the pattern." The inheritance of the struggle between the states is unmistakably present in the distributions of partisan attachments as we find them across the country, not so sharp as it was in the 1860's certainly, but still clearly visible.

Our surveys do not of course give us any direct information on the character of the party changes that occurred a hundred years ago, although they document the regional distribution of party attachments that was laid down at that time. On the other hand, the second national crisis that reshaped the political profile of the nation took

[4] As we shall see in Chapter 16, the Far West now contains a large number of recent migrants from the South who make a significant contribution to the Democratic character of that region.

place during the lifetime of most of our respondents, and we can see directly the impact of that event in their lives.

The economic collapse that befell the nation during the administration of Herbert Hoover swept out of office a party that had dominated national politics since the election of William McKinley in 1896. The Republican Party lost the presidency in 1912 when Theodore Roosevelt split the Republican vote and in 1916 when the First World War helped keep Woodrow Wilson in office. But in 1932 the Republicans were substantially defeated in a straight party contest. Their humiliation was extended in the congressional elections of 1934 and brought to a climax in 1936 when Governor Landon won only eight votes in the Electoral College. Not until 1946 were the Republicans able to regain a majority in the Congress and not until 1952 did they again win the White House.

The scope of the reversal of the party fortunes that followed 1932 is amply documented by the election statistics. In the early years of the New Deal there was a swing to the Democratic ticket, which was felt in varying degrees throughout the country. Districts that had been Democratic became more Democratic, and many districts that had voted Republican for generations sent a Democrat to Congress. The tide then receded, and those areas that had been centers of Republican strength returned to Republican majorities. But the Republican Party did not regain the national majority that it had obviously had prior to 1932. When we ask from what levels of society the Democratic Party drew this new strength, we find from our survey data and from the aggregative election figures that the impact of the events of that period appears to have been felt most strongly by the youth, the economically underprivileged, and the minority groups.

1. *Youth.* There can be little doubt that some of the new Democrats were old Republicans. There is reason to believe, however, that a good many of these Republicans who defected into the Democratic ranks during the early years of the Roosevelt period were soon disenchanted. Some erstwhile Republicans never returned to their party, but these party-changers do not appear to have made up a very large part of the long-term Democratic increase. Our inquiries into the political histories of our respondents lead us to believe that a larger component of the gain came from young voters entering the electorate and older people who had previously failed to vote.

Our information regarding these depression period voters comes in part from our question to our respondents as to how they voted "the

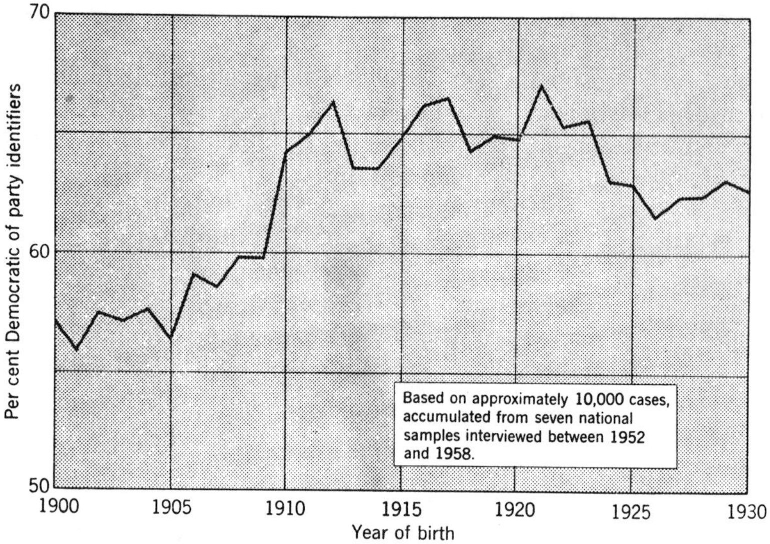

Fig. 7-1. Party identification of party identifiers born between 1900 and 1930.

first time (they) voted." When we look at the votes reported cast by those people who voted for the first time during the period from 1924 to 1940 we see a significant turn toward the Democratic Party in 1932 and the ensuing years, both among those who were just coming of age at that time and those who had failed to vote prior to that time. These new voters reacted to the political drift of the times much more violently than did the electorate as a whole (Table 7-3, page 155).

An additional demonstration of the impact of the depression on the people reaching voting age at that time is given in Fig. 7-1 above. Instead of depending on the memory of our respondents of their first vote, we have here arrayed them by age group according to the party identification they reported at the time of our interview with them. Those members of the present electorate who came of age during the 1920's have a lower proportion of Democratic identifiers than do any of the groups that entered the electorate in later years. The sharp increase in Democratic identification among those who reached their majority at the end of this decade or during the early 1930's does not represent the total shift toward the Democratic Party at that time, but it does show the proportion of that shift that has persisted over the intervening years to the present time.

The considerable discrepancy in the depression shift, as shown in Table 7-3 and Fig. 7-1, may be assumed to derive from a number of unrelated factors. It seems likely in the first place that the report of first vote is subject to a certain amount of long-distance bandwagon effect—people tending to remember themselves as having voted for the winner. The depression shift, as reported from remembered first votes, is thus probably somewhat exaggerated.

TABLE 7-3. Reported First Votes of New Voters: 1924–1940

Year in Which First Vote Was Reported	(Per Cent Democratic of Two-Party Vote) Reported First Vote of "Coming-of-Age" Voters	Reported First Vote of "Delayed" Voters	Actual Election Result
1924	29	20	35
1928	38	53	41
1932	80	93	59
1936	89	77	62
1940	69	72	55

Quite aside from such errors, however, we would not expect the residual of the shift in the 1930's still remaining in the 1950's to approximate the actual shift of votes that took place at that time. It is evident that some of these new Democratic votes were coming from young people whose background was Republican and that, given a normal amount of disillusionment with political realities, they must have found it easy to slide back into the party of their fathers. Finally, we must take account of a long-term age dimension that we find in American politics. There are apparently life-cycle changes in orientation toward politics that work to the advantage of the Republican Party. Such an influence would of course tend to reduce the Democratic majority created among those who came of age during the early years of the Depression.

Despite all these considerations the evidence seems to justify our conclusion that the Great Depression swung a heavy proportion of the young electors toward the Democratic Party and gave that party a hold on that generation, which it has never fully relinquished. We may now ask why it was that this age group seemed more susceptible to the pressures of the time than the older generations of voters. Our evidence from the 1950's leads us to believe that people in their twenties are not particularly concerned about political matters and indeed have a very poor record of voting turnout. There is little reason to believe that youth were more politically involved relative to the rest of the population in 1930 than they are today.

The political program that Mr. Roosevelt and the New Deal were offering the voters may have had a special appeal to young people. There was a certain "brave new world" character to some of the Democratic slogans of that period, an impatience with traditional ways of doing things, and a good deal of emphasis on social experimentation. It would not be surprising if the drama and excitement of the period should seem more appealing to youth than to their less impressionable and probably more thoughtful elders.

A second hypothesis, which has the virtue of some supporting evidence, would propose that the new voters are always more likely to be moved by the prevailing political tides because they have not as yet developed stable party attachments. The claim that a party has on its members tends to increase as their tenure of association with it increases. During the 1930's the new voters, having relatively limited experience with either party, were thus most susceptible to the impact of contemporary events and, having moved into the Democratic camp, were least likely to return to a previous attachment that had not had time to develop strength.

2. *Economic groups.* The appeal of the New Deal was unquestionably strongly economic in character; it had, after all, been brought into being in the midst of the greatest economic catastrophe in American history. It was criticized by its opposition for setting class against class. Mr. Roosevelt spoke about the "forgotten man" and sponsored a program of social legislation that his critics regarded as outright socialism. It is difficult to estimate how much influence all this had on the economic composition of the followings of the two parties, but it can be said with assurance that the economic and class distinctions between the two parties increased during this period. The Democratic Party appealed for the support of those groups most disadvantaged by the Depression and bluntly attacked those they chose to call "economic royalists." Such associations as had existed prior to the Depression between the less favored sections of the electorate and the Democratic Party were undoubtedly greatly enhanced.

On the basis of extensive analysis of the election returns from 1932 and 1936 Key offers these "educated guesses." "The policies of the New Deal brought in 1936 substantial new support from their beneficiaries. Metropolitan, industrial workers turned in heavy Democratic majorities. The unemployed, and those who feared they might become unemployed, voted Democratic in higher degree. Organized labor moved more solidly into the Democratic ranks."[5]

Our surveys do not go backward in time sufficiently for us to follow the political changes at the various economic levels during the depression period, but the impact of the Depression is unmistakable in the images of the parties that we find in the public mind long after that tragic decade had passed. The association of the Republican Party with economic depression was one of the strongest features of the picture the public held of that party at the time of our 1952 study. Through their twenty years out of office the Republican Party could not erase the memory that lingered in many minds of the hardships of the Depression nor rid itself of the onus of responsibility for them. Many of our respondents still interpret the politics of the Depression in highly personal terms as the following quotations illustrate:

> A sales clerk in Pittsburgh says she was a Republican until Mr. Hoover's Administration, now she is a strong Democrat. "My husband was a government employee and we got three cuts in pay under Hoover. We lost our house on account of that."
>
> A Negro tire recapper in Florida gives his reasons for disliking the Republican Party: "One thing I don't like was when Hoover was President, how I had to work and keep moving on. I remember how in Palm Beach they made me keep on moving, I couldn't get no job. I fell out with the Republicans then."
>
> An ardent Democrat in Los Angeles uses these terms: "There's nothing I like about the Republican Party. I remember I didn't get a job from 1929 to 1933. I was healthy and able to work but no job. In those days you had to have a reservation to sleep in the park."

To illustrate current differences in the party identifications of people living in the major geographical regions of the country, and at the same time to indicate the relationship of social class to partisanship, we have organized our data in Table 7-4 to show class differences within regions. Though the contrast in regions is apparent, the class component of American politics is also clearly seen. In the South, where Democratic adherence was for many years an essential feature of regional loyalty, both classes are heavily Democratic although the middle class dilutes its support of the Democratic Party somewhat by a tendency to report itself as Independent. In the North, however, the parties draw quite unevenly from the two classes. The appeal of the Democratic Party to working class people is evident in all three

[5] V. O. Key, *Politics, Parties and Pressure Groups* (4th ed. Thomas Y. Crowell Company, New York, 1958), p. 578.

TABLE 7-4. Regional and Class Differences in Party Identification, 1952 and 1956

	Northeast			Midwest			South			West		
	Work. Class	Mid'l. Class	Total	Work. Class	Mid'l. Class	Total	Work. Class	Mid'l. Class	Total	Work. Class	Mid'l. Class	Total
Strong Dem.	20%	10%	16%	22%	13%	19%	34%	29%	32%	27%	16%	23%
Weak Dem.	22	14	19	25	17	22	36	34	35	30	14	24
Ind.	27	30	28	27	25	26	13	20	16	26	25	26
Weak Rep.	16	21	18	15	19	16	9	9	9	11	18	14
Strong Rep.	15	25	19	11	26	17	8	8	8	6	27	13
	100%	100%	100%	100%	100%	100%	100%	100%	100%	100%	100%	100%
Number of cases	492	317	809	649	435	1084	531	311	842	265	145	410

northern regions. Although the political significance of class varies from one election to another, class is clearly one of the underlying dimensions of party affiliation in the United States. It does not, however, have the overriding importance that it has in the party systems of many Western European democracies, where the parties tend to be more closely identified with specific economic ideologies. There are many reasons why this is true, not the least of which is the fact that the regional dimension, which was superimposed on American politics a hundred years ago, was largely lacking in class content.

3. *Minority groups.* The impact of the Depression and the New Deal was not exclusively economic. The philosophy of the Roosevelt Administration contained a strong element of social equalitarianism, which gave it a special appeal to religious and racial minorities who had reason to feel themselves discriminated against. Catholics have had a long history of association with the Democratic Party. Key has shown that this affinity was greatly strengthened, at least in the New England states, at the time of the 1928 election when Governor Smith was the Democratic nominee.[6] The prominence of James A. Farley, Democratic National Chairman, Frank Murphy, Attorney General, and other Catholics in the New Deal entourage must have given further assurance to Catholic voters. Their support of the Democratic ticket carried on down through 1948. During the Eisenhower elections there were substantial defections among Catholics to the Republican nominee, but even at that time Catholics were more likely (5–2) to consider themselves Democrats than Republicans.

The Jewish minority comprises one of the most Democratic groups to be found in the electorate; Democratic Jews outnumber Republican Jews in the order of 4–1. This appears to be largely a consequence of the Depression and subsequent events during the Roosevelt period. During the 1920's the vote in heavily Jewish districts of the eastern metropolises ran as high as 80 per cent Republican.[7] Although vote is not the same as party identification, it can scarcely be doubted that the orientation of this group toward the two parties was substantially altered during the 1930's. We may surmise that the rise of the Nazi dictatorship in Germany and the opposition of the Roosevelt Administration to it must have played an important role in this change. Whatever the cause, the shift of Jewish allegiances to the Democratic

[6] V. O. Key, "A Theory of Critical Elections," *Journal of Politics,* XVII (1955), 3–18.

[7] Lawrence H. Fuchs, *The Political Behavior of American Jews* (The Free Press, Glencoe, Ill., 1956), p. 56. See also Oscar Handlin, *The Uprooted* (Boston, Mass.: Little Brown, 1951), 216.

Party was one of the most impressive of the several group movements in political preference during the Roosevelt period.

Prior to the 1930's, so far as we can tell from election statistics, the prevailing political preference among Negroes was Republican. This was a consequence, of course, of the Civil War and the attachment of Negroes to the party of Lincoln. During the 1930's politics took on a different signficance to the Negro tenth of the electorate. It is impossible to know whether the shift of Negro allegiances to the Democratic standard from the traditions inherited from earlier generations occurred as the reactions of individual Negroes to the personalities and events of the times or as a mass movement resulting largely from the mobilization of Negro sentiment by an articulate leadership. No doubt both of these circumstances were present. In any case, the conversion of Negroes to the Democratic Party was very substantial. During the Eisenhower period Democratically identified Negroes outnumbered Republican Negroes by a margin of 3–1.

A full assessment of the influence of the Depression and the New Deal on the partisanship of the electorate would require data from the 1920's and 1930's that are not available. Judging from what we know about party identification in the 1950's and from such insights as we can derive from the election returns of the earlier period, we can hardly doubt that the decade of the Great Depression saw a profound reorientation of political partisanship. In part this appears to have been an extension of divisions that already existed, among Catholics and low-income people, for example. In part it expressed the changing affiliation of special interest groups such as Negroes, Jews, and certain nationality groups. By the conversion of erstwhile Republicans, the activation of previously inert people and the capture of the young voters, the Democratic Party emerged from this period as the majority party. Although Mr. Eisenhower attracted a substantial number of Democrats to his support, he did not succeed in altering basically the pattern of party commitments which existed when he took office.

We turn now to a class of changes in party identification that does not depend on the dramatic impact of national catastrophes but on the gradual and commonplace changes in life situations that occur as one grows older. The fact that the successive phases of the life cycle are associated with a certain degree of common experience for most members of our society means that we may expect to find systematic changes in attitudes and behavior associated with changes in age. Such age-related changes are clearly present in the political orientation of the American electorate.

Intensity of identification. The steady increase in strong party attachments that we find as we move through the successive age levels in Table 7-5 demonstrates the presence of age-related influences that are obviously not random. Young people, just entering the electorate, are more likely than any of the older age groups to call themselves Independents. This proportion drops among people in their late twenties and thirties and is accompanied by a proportionate increase in the number of strong identifiers. The older half of the electorate are clearly more likely to show a strong party attachment, with the most extreme position of all held by those people over 65 years old, a group that now constitutes approximately one twelfth of our adult population.

Whenever we encounter relationships of this sort involving age, we are forced to choose between two competing interpretations. First, age may mark an historical epoch in which the person has matured or undergone some special variety of experience that has left an imprint on his attitudes and behaviors. Or, alternately, age may serve as an index of the length of time that the individual has lived in a specified state or engaged in a specified behavior. With regard to strength of party identification, the historical interpretation of our data would suggest that partisan feeling was more intense several decades ago than now. If older persons have more intense party loyalties than younger, it is a reflection of the politics of an earlier American period. Furthermore, if this were true, then the nature of the relationship between strength of party identification and age would depend on the period when the observations were taken: in another era, young people might be more dedicated to a party than old.

The second interpretation presumes instead that older people will always feel stronger bonds with a political party than will newer members of the electorate. To the extent that we can perform a critical test with our data, it is this hypothesis which finds support. Such a test is difficult, since most people remain identified with the same party throughout their life. For these individuals, the length of time of attachment to the party cannot be distinguished from the historical period in which they matured. But a few people report having shifted their allegiance from one party to the other during adulthood. A person 60 years of age in 1956 who was converted to the Democratic Party during the Depression has thought of himself as a Democrat for only twenty years, whereas others of his own generation who have never changed parties have been party identifiers for a period of forty years or more. Among such "changers," then, duration of party attachment is no longer synonymous with age or era of maturation. We may

TABLE 7-5. Relation of Age to Party Identification[a]

Party Identification	Age 21–24	25–29	30–34	35–39	40–44	45–49	50–54	55–59	60–64	65–69	70–75	Over 75
Strong Dem.	16%	20%	21%	21%	24%	22%	25%	23%	23%	26%	28%	25%
Weak Dem.	32	29	29	31	29	24	23	22	21	18	17	17
Independent	31	26	24	23	22	23	19	20	19	15	14	16
Weak Rep.	13	18	16	15	15	16	17	16	18	19	16	16
Strong Rep.	8	7	10	10	10	15	16	19	19	22	25	26
	100%	100%	100%	100%	100%	100%	100%	100%	100%	100%	100%	100%
Proportion of Strong Identifiers	24%	27%	31%	31%	34%	37%	41%	42%	42%	48%	53%	51%
Number of cases	552	1038	1201	1221	1081	977	915	741	677	473	354	297

[a] These data are combined from seven national samples interviewed by the Survey Research Center between 1952 and 1957.

ask whether the 60-year-old whose length of attachment is only twenty years has a strength of identification more like those of his own era or like other lifetime members who are substantially younger.

The results are rather striking (Table 7-6). Duration of attachment among changers is quite strongly related to strength of party identification, whether or not age is controlled. But if we control duration of attachment and examine the relationship between age and strength of party identification, we find that it is actually reversed,

TABLE 7-6. Relation of Age to Strength of Party Identification, by Duration of Party Identification

	Duration of Identification with Current Party							
	0–3 Years		4–7 Years		8–15 Years		16–39 Years	
Strength of Party Identification	44 or under	45 or over	44 or under	45 or over	44 or under	45 or over	54 or under	55 or over
Strong	22%	19%	28%	20%	27%	26%	50%	35%
Weak	54	48	40	47	52	47	37	33
Independent	24	33	32	33	21	29	13	32
	100%	100%	100%	100%	100%	100%	100%	100%
Number of cases	76	27	57	40	48	38	52	51

becoming slightly but significantly negative. Once length of membership is held constant, identification is stronger among the young than among the old.[8]

This pattern of relationships fits very well a more general thesis that group identification is a function of the proportion of a person's life he has been associated with the group. The longer a person thinks of himself as belonging to a party, the stronger his sense of loyalty to it will become. This means also that as time passes, stress of increasing severity must be required to induce him to shift his allegiance to the opposing party, or even to cast a vote "away" from his party. Moreover, if he is in fact driven from one party to the other by critical

[8] The multiple correlation (Pearson) of age and duration of party identification with strength of party identification is 0.24. The partial correlation between duration of identification and identification with age controlled is 0.19. The partial correlation between age and party identification, with duration of identification controlled, is −0.09.

events during his adult life, the rate at which his identification with the new party will develop will be less rapid the more advanced his age, just as an older man migrating to a new country will learn its customs less rapidly than a younger person.

We may now consider the way in which identification with political parties develops over the lifetime of the individual elector. Most people learn the party labels and something of what they mean during the early years when they are living with their parents. As young adults they are not overly interested in politics, they are indifferent voters, and they do not typically regard themselves as strongly attached to the political parties. As the young adult passes through the early egocentric years, however, the salience that political matters have in his life gradually increases. This happens for a variety of reasons. He is, for one thing, drawn into close association with social groups of one kind or another, some of which may have strong political orientations. He becomes aware of their political interests and he absorbs their interests as his own. It is also likely that as he becomes a more fully integrated community member he becomes more aware of the immediate implications for him of political decisions.

In addition, since political affairs become more familiar to a person as he matures, they seem less distant and unrealistic. He may become personally acquainted with someone who is actively involved in political matters or have some other experience that puts him in personal contact with some representative or agency of government. His image of politics is likely to become less impersonal and more readily responded to. The number of people who become politically active themselves, either as candidates or as party workers of one kind or another, is very small, but a much larger number of people acquire a certain familiarity with political goings on, and it seems likely that this fact is associated with an increasing identification of oneself with the party symbols.

Finally, for some people politics and parties may take on reality only as the result of some personal or national crisis. For example, many apparently inert people were stimulated to vote for the first time during the early years of the Great Depression. The Korean War appears to have activated several million people who had sat out the previous elections. On a more personal basis a business failure, a bad crop year, the loss of a job, or an encounter with the law may create a need for action and a sharpening of interest in what can be accomplished through political channels. Crises of large or small magnitude occur repeatedly during the lifetime of the ordinary citizen and serve to keep him alive to his role in the total political process.

Once a person has acquired some embryonic party attachment, it is easy for him to discover that most events in the ambiguous world of politics redound to the credit of his chosen party. As his perception of his party's virtue gains momentum in this manner, so his loyalty to it strengthens, and this fact in turn increases the probability that future events will be interpreted in a fashion that supports his partisan inclination. There are limits on the extent to which reality can be distorted to fit expectations and preferences, and exceptionally critical circumstances may induce a party identifier to cross party lines for a single election in the spirit of "time for a change." It is even possible that the flow of events may place his party in such an unfavorable position as to bring an actual change in his identification. But this is unusual; more typically party identification is not only sustained but strengthened by the passing show of political acts and actors.

It is a matter of particular interest that party identification does not decline in significance in the later years of life; on the contrary, strong party attachment is more common among people of retirement age than it is at any other period. Table 7-6 has given us reason to believe that intensity of party identification is directly related to the length of time a person has felt some degree of attachment to his party. As we move through the successive age cohorts we are consequently more and more likely to find people who have had a long unbroken experience of party identification. Older people have had more time to accumulate tenure in their party association, even those who in their earlier years moved from one party to the other. As they settle in their ultimate choice and their tenure with it grows, they become increasingly rigidly attached to it and less and less susceptible to cross-party pressures.

Partisanship of identification. It remains now to consider one further aspect of the relationship of age to political orientation. If we look back at Table 7-5, where we saw the increasing tendency toward strong party identification in successive age groups, we find an equally substantial relationship between age and the direction of partisan choice. Republican identification increases progressively from the younger to the older age groups.

This peculiarity of the distribution of party identification presents an interesting question that we cannot fully answer. Is the Republican Party gradually aging and being replaced by a party that has captured the bulk of the young people coming into the electorate? If we assume from the Republican domination of national politics in the 1896–1932 period that the majority of the electorate identified themselves as Republican during those years, we should expect to find evidences of these loyalties in the political attachments of people who came to maturity at that time. We know on the other hand that the Depression and the Roosevelt regime brought large numbers of people into the Democratic ranks partly as converts from the Republican Party and especially from those voting for the first time, and that the Democratic claim on the coming-of-age part of the electorate persisted into the Eisenhower period. If party identification is typically a life-long commitment, changed on the national scale only by major social cataclysms, it would be reasonable to conclude that the present age division in party identification is the consequence of the Depression and the New Deal and that the present Republican following must inevitably decrease as time replaces the older age groups with the younger groups in which people of Democratic commitment are more numerous.

To this explanation, however, one may oppose the hypothesis that the two parties have different appeals to people of different ages, and although the Democratic Party may have an advantage in its appeal to young people, this advantage may be gradually dissipated as these young Democrats grow older and respond differently to political stimuli. It would seem likely in a society in which one major party was widely perceived as conservative and middle-class and the other as liberal and working-class that the two parties would not be equally attractive to the older and younger members of the electorate. The two American parties do not altogether fulfill these qualifications but as we have seen earlier the public image of the parties does have an unmistakable flavor of class distinction. This undoubtedly varies in different parts of the country and in different communities, but in general the Republican Party has an air of respectability, conservatism, and social status which the Democratic Party does not fully share. If we assume that these values have an increasing appeal to older people we have the essential conditions for the creation of an age dimension in political partisanship.

If we examine in detail the reports of individual political history that we have summarized in Table 7-2 we find that there was a substantial shift of party attachments during the New Deal period, most of it toward the Democratic Party. In each of the four-year periods during the last twenty years, however, there has been additional shifting, balancing out in each case to a relatively small advantage to the Republican Party. These findings lead us to doubt the proposition that either of the major parties is likely to expire as the result of old age. The great break toward the Democratic Party at the beginning of the Depression undoubtedly split the electorate along age lines.

This split appears to have been maintained in the ensuing years by the heavy proportion of young people who declared themselves for the Democratic Party as they entered the electorate, but it has been offset by the Republican advantage in cross-party conversions among those in the older age brackets. During the 1950's these two components of the total following of the two parties appeared to balance each other very closely. Both the proportions of the electorate identifying themselves with each party and the age composition of each party's adherents remained constant throughout this period.

Public Policy and Political Preference ◇ 8

It is a basic tenet of democratic tradition that the citizen should have access to the making of public policy. But the reduction of this simple principle to a set of practical arrangements can arouse much debate. There is always room for factual questions on the access actually permitted by various systems of representation. There are pressing normative choices to be made as well. Different political philosophies advocate more or less direct access, and the theorist may appraise the process with more or less faith that the citizen will act wisely in contributing to policy decisions. Nonetheless, there is little tendency for supporters of democratic theory to argue that popular political participation should not be concerned with the making of policy.[1]

The obvious importance of public policy issues attracts both practical and academic interest to the manner in which they are resolved. Much of the work of the political analyst or the political theorist is given over to discovering why a particular course of action evolved, or to judging which of several courses of action should have been followed. Many of the grand questions of government flow from the search for the best mechanisms, ethical and procedural, to control action taken in the name of the public interest.

Just as the citizen's political behavior may be taken to affect, in one degree or another, the course of public policy, so questions of public policy may be presumed to affect the citizen's political behavior. The substance of partisan debate forms one of the most visible aspects of the political context in which voting decisions are made. For this reason we have conceived of issues as one of the major classes of

[1] Robert A. Dahl, *A Preface to Democratic Theory* (The University of Chicago Press, Chicago, 1956).

political objects, and have included issue perceptions explicitly among our six partisan attitudes. A "proper" issue position taken by the candidate or party is a major source of favorable evaluation.

Up to this point we have examined issue perceptions only as they are cast after the person has successfully translated a policy belief into a partisan motivation. However strongly a citizen may feel about an issue, his belief receives no recognition in our system of partisan attitudes, unless it has produced some positive or negative feelings toward a party or candidate. Thus references to foreign and domestic issues are included in the measurement only as they reflect credit or discredit on one of the partisan objects; where no partisan implication of this sort is drawn, the reference is not scored.

The process whereby issues are created and come to be endowed with partisan meaning over a mass electorate is as fascinating as it is complex. Party loyalty plays no small role in the formation of attitudes on specific policy matters. The identifier who sees his party take up a new issue is likely to be influenced thereby. On the other hand, if the individual has intense feelings about an issue before partisan alignments form, and his party's subsequent policy conflicts with such belief, they may act as important forces toward partisan change.

We have no adequate method for determining which of these sequences has led to an observed congruence between the individual's issue position and that of his current party. However, we do know that this congruence is less prevalent than commonly assumed; and we know that the mass electorate encounters difficulties in translating issue feelings into partisan motivations.

The Conditions of Issue-Oriented Political Behavior

The role that any specific issue may play in ultimate partisan choice is limited in several directions. Only rarely does a single policy belief comprise the sole force in the psychological field as the voting decision is made. Except in the referendum, votes are cast directly for candidates and parties. Not only do these objects represent numerous issue positions at once; they also have properties of their own independent of any issue significance. Reactions to these properties, as we have argued, token further forces on behavior.

More important for our current purposes are the circumstances under which we could not legitimately expect a specific issue to exert any force in the individual's field. We may specify at least three conditions to be fulfilled if an issue is to bear upon a person's vote decision:

1. The issue must be cognized in some form.
2. It must arouse some minimal intensity of feeling.
3. It must be accompanied by some perception that one party represents the person's own position better than do the other parties.

If an issue is to motivate a voter, he must be aware of its existence and must have an opinion about it. Although this statement is obvious, it draws our attention to the fact that many people know the existence of few if any of the major issues of policy. The teacher concerned with adult education, the member of a League of Women Voters engaged in civic education, the politician trying to drum up grass-roots support for a new campaign plank: these and others will testify that one of the greatest limitations on civic participation is imposed by sheer ignorance of the existence of major social and economic problems. From the viewpoint of social action, the problem of creating familiarity with issues is the first task; from the viewpoint of social analysis, understanding the evolution of public familiarity with issues is also a necessary beginning step.

The second condition requires that there be some sense of the importance of an issue, for involvement cannot be assumed on the basis of familiarity alone. The voter may understand that Issue X exists, but he may consider it trivial, of no concern to him and of little concern to others. Another citizen may see Issue X as a crucial question calling for immediate action. It is obvious that Issue X is thereby more likely to weigh heavily in his political evaluations. Intensity of opinions may vary widely from voter to voter, but when opinions are relatively intense we have another important indication that they will have some bearing on the voter's ultimate decision.

An issue may be recognized, and recognized as important, without having serious consequences for the voter's partisan preference unless the final condition is fulfilled. Intense feeling about an issue must be translated into a partisan motivation, and this process can only be completed if the individual has some sense that the parties will handle things differently. In short, he must perceive that the political system offers alternatives, and he must be able to determine which of them matches his own position most closely.

These three conditions are entirely obvious ones. Yet their simplicity should not deceive us into assuming that they are generally fulfilled across the electorate. Instead, large portions of the adult population fail to meet each succeeding condition on a wide variety of prominent issues. It is important to note, therefore, that we take these three conditions as necessary rather than sufficient conditions, if issues are to affect the vote decision. If any of these conditions is *not* met, we can hardly expect the issues involved to bear in any meaningful way upon partisan preference. On the other hand, all three conditions may be fulfilled without giving us genuine assurance that the issue has played any major role in determining the voter's choice. Those people who meet all conditions thus represent the largest number for whom the issue might have had partisan effect; for many of these, other forces may so dominate the psychological field that effects of the issue are small or trivial.

Issue Familiarity

If we wish to know how familiar an issue is to the members of an electorate, we soon find that most of the traditional cues are as likely to be misleading as they are to be enlightening. The amount of public attention paid an issue by political leaders is an unreliable index of public familiarity. Political leaders may avoid discussing an issue which they assume to be prominent but which they also assume to be a weak point in their political position. The Democratic candidates' avoidance of the corruption issue in 1952 is a case in point. In many other instances leadership attention to an issue reflects a conviction that few people are familiar with it and that constant reference to it is needed to create widespread familiarity.

In a similar fashion, it is seldom wise to rely on even the most rigorous study of the mass media for indications of the public's familiarity with any specific issue. Attention accorded an issue on the television screen or in the newspaper column may disclose useful information about the role that various people *want to assign* to the issue; but, even at best, the treatment given an issue reflects no more than another informed judgment about what the media audience is or should be interested in.

In general, public officials and people involved in public relations tend to overestimate the impact that contemporary issues have on the public. They find it difficult to believe that the reams of newspaper copy and the hours of television and radio time could be ignored by any normal person within the reach of those media. The fact seems to be, however, that the human perceptorium is highly selective, and unless it happens to be tuned to a particular wavelength, the message transmitted over that wavelength will be received only as noise. Increasing its amplitude does not always make the message more intelligible, nor does it impel the listener to pay closer attention rather than flicking the "off" switch. Like the homeostatic mechanisms that control the range of variation in body temperature, blood sugar, blood pressure and the like, this perceptual screening seems to protect the individual citizen from too strenuous an overload of incoming information. Some individuals have a much greater capacity than others of course, but it may be assumed that all of the content of politics encounters some resistance at the point of reception.

An example of public indifference to an issue that was given heavy emphasis by political leaders is provided by the role of the Taft-Hartley Act in the 1948 election. Following the rather swift and firm action of the Eightieth Congress in replacing the Wagner Act of the New Deal with the Taft-Hartley Act, the Democratic Party chose the latter act as a major point of attack in the 1948 campaign. Despite the prominence given to the problems of strikes, labor unrest, and labor legislation in the postwar period, and despite the fairly direct clash of the major parties over amendment and repeal of the Taft-Hartley Act, a full third of the public indicated in November of 1948 that they had not heard of the Taft-Hartley Act. An additional third did not have an opinion on this issue. Almost seven out of every ten adult Amcricans saw thc curtain fall on the presidential election of 1948 without knowing whether Taft-Hartley was the name of a hero or a villain.

Components of familiarity with an issue. To gather better information about public familiarity with issues of politics, a set of questions on public policy was posed for a cross section of the 1956 electorate. The questions were deliberately presented in such a manner as to yield an indication of the variation in public familiarity with these issues.[2] The presentation of each policy item was prefaced with the direct suggestion that it was quite proper for the person to respond by telling us that he (or she) did not happen to have an opinion on the question.

We cannot be sure that every person willing to voice an opinion had given the issue much prior consideration. And it is likely that upon occasion persons in conflict over or indifferent to an issue might decline an opinion. But there was good reason to believe that any such variations in the screening process were minimal, and remained

[2] It is necessary to maintain a sharp distinction between the data referred to in this discussion and the issue-related data concerning political attitudes described in Section II. Consequently, we shall refer to these public policy questions as "specific" issues even though they include some broad questions of policy.

largely constant from issue question to issue question. Therefore, relative differences in the proportion of people having an opinion on various issues may be taken to reflect differences in familiarity with the issues.

Our 1956 data illustrate the extent of variation in public familiarity with issues. About one fourth of the national population claimed familiarity with fewer than one out of every two issues presented to them. At the other extreme we find almost a third who claimed enough familiarity with the issues to give us statements of attitudes on at least 14 out of 16 issues posed for them. If these items were typical of all political issues, a more extensive listing would not have greatly changed our estimates of issue familiarity. It is likely, though, that our list included most of the better-known issues and could have been extended only by adding items familiar to fewer and fewer persons. If this is true, the previously given estimates may overstate the average level of familiarity with specific issues in 1956.

For many purposes of political analysis it is useful to introduce a further criterion in a discussion of public familiarity with issues. As we have implied, it is possible—indeed, quite likely—that some persons hold opinions that are of relatively little significance for them, even though the opinions may be on important topics. A person sensitive to the importance of appearing well informed may collect opinions as avidly as small boys collect butterflies. But the possession of an opinion about governmental policy is of greatest interest to us when the person holding the opinion can and does relate it to a pertinent part of the political system.

Therefore it was important to ascertain whether the person had any notion of what the federal government was doing with respect to the policy in question. If a person goes on record in favor of leaving electric power production to private industry, but has no idea what the Administration is doing about the question, we may deduce that his opinion is not based on substantial familiarity with the subject. He has an opinion but knows so little about the topic as to deprive the opinion of significance for his subsequent political behavior.

The person's accuracy in evaluating the performance of the government is not pertinent here. "Knowing what the Administration has been doing" about insuring medical care in the early 1950's may have consisted of condemning the Administration because the opinion holder had concluded that the creation of a Department of Health, Education, and Welfare meant support for socialized medicine. Even though this view of governmental action would not have fit the usual interpretation of the actual situation, such individual perception may have existed and may have been the link between attitudinal opposition to the policy and a vote for the Democrats. Familiarity thus is intended to refer only to the existence of an opinion that is given some sort of political meaning by its possessor; it is not confined to the existence of "accurate" opinions that are "correctly" related to the "reality" of the political world.

Use of both criteria of familiarity over a variety of issues leads to the results summarized in Table 8-1. On the average, about one respondent out of every three failed to survive these two hurdles for

TABLE 8-1. Public Familiarity with Selected Issues, 1956

Issue	No Opinion	Hold Opinion But Do Not Know What Gov't Is Doing	Hold Opinion Know What Gov't Is Doing	Total
Foreign Policy				
Give aid to neutral countries	28%	19	53	100%
Send soldiers abroad	20%	13	67	100%
Economic aid to foreign countries	17%	16	67	100%
Act tough toward Russia, China	20%	11	69	100%
Avoid foreign involvement	14%	15	71	100%
Friendliness toward other nations	12%	10	78	100%
Domestic Policy				
Firing of suspected Communists	16%	39	45	100%
Leave electricity, housing to private industry	30%	19	51	100%
Segregation of schools	12%	34	54	100%
Influence of big business in government	28%	18	54	100%
Influence of unions in government	25%	20	55	100%
Insure medical care	12%	29	59	100%
Cutting taxes	19%	18	63	100%
Government guarantee of jobs	10%	23	67	100%
Racial equality in jobs and housing	14%	19	67	100%
Government aid to education	10%	23	67	100%

any issue. There is some variation according to the nature of the issue. When the item involves some general posture that this nation might adopt, such as "being friendly with the other countries of the world," there appears to be more likelihood of an opinion being expressed and some perception of what the government is doing. Where an item deals with more specific programs such as aid to neutrals, however, fewer perceptions emerge. It is clear that the level of specificity is not the only determinant of familiarity: relatively specific programs of social welfare that have been under debate for some time appear more familiar to the public. But it seems that the specificity with which the issue is formulated does play some role in responses, and this fact provides some warning about the relative nature of the results, as well as a substantive indication of the sorts of objects toward which the public can respond most freely.

The development of issue familiarity. The existence of an opinion on an issue depends on both cognitive and affective factors. In the first case, the person who fails to cognize the basic components involved in a policy question will not have any great familiarity with the question as a political issue.

One of the functions of education is to acquaint a person with a wide range of information about social, psychological, economic, and political problems. A person with little or no education (where education includes both formal and informal gathering of knowledge) will not have opinions on many issues simply because he is not aware of the existence of the issue. If we use the number of years of formal schooling as a measure of the extent of a person's education, we can readily test this conclusion. As Table 8-2 shows, there is a direct relationship between increasing years of schooling and increasing familiarity with our selection of issues.

TABLE 8-2. Relation of Education to Familiarity with Issues, 1956

Familiarity with Issues	From No Formal Schooling to Completion of 8 Grades	High School, Some or Completion	College, Some or Degree
High	21%	31%	50%
Medium	37	47	44
Low	42	22	6
	100%	100%	100%
Number of cases	543	890	331

Sheer awareness of a problem is, of course, not enough to bring an opinion into being. An attitude takes shape as cognitions become related in some manner to values held by the person. Unless various states of affairs associated with an issue are evaluated as good or bad, desirable or undesirable, a person will not express an opinion about the issue. Thus if he sees neither good nor bad in the vigorous enforcement of fair employment practices he may show no feeling about the matter, even though he may have more than enough information to classify as "aware" of the issue.

The Intensity of Issue Opinion

The second important component of issue involvement that may lead to issue-oriented political behavior is, then, the extent to which the issue arouses intense feelings. In the context of elections, an issue that creates only mild sentiments of support and opposition is not a politically important issue, regardless of its actual importance to the national welfare. This is not to say that most important policy decisions of the nation have been made only after violent and widespread popular political argument; it is simply that the policy questions on which the voters' tempers flare seem to be the policies that create the drama of popular politics and provide the analyst with a vantage point for viewing mass political behavior.

Intensity is an important property as far as the opinion holder is concerned, and it is useful to understand the conditions associated with intense opinions on policy questions. At first glance it might seem difficult to disentangle the properties of familiarity and intensity. After all, how can an issue become a prominent part of the election scene without exciting relatively deep disagreement? We do find that the most familiar issues are also the issues that evoke most strong feeling. For example, the question of federal aid to construction programs in the public schools was one of the most familiar of all issues about which we inquired. It was also an issue that aroused many persons to the expression of extreme, strongly held opinions. The question of providing aid for countries "even if they are not as much against communism as we are" is found near the other end of both distributions—relatively few persons were familiar with this issue, and their opinions were the least intense.

Nevertheless, it is clear that familiarity is not synonymous with intensity. Even our restricted selection of public issues contains examples of a distinct lack of congruence between these properties. The question of the role of the federal government in electric power production and housing construction provoked almost as large a proportion of extreme opinions as did the education question, but it was familiar to many fewer persons. Both questions were the object of intense opinions, but one question was known to two thirds of the population, whereas the other was familiar to little more than half of the people.

Only one of our issues displayed the fourth logical combination of properties. The item advocating "economic help to the poorer countries of the world even if they can't pay for it" was widely known but was the object of only mild expression of opinion. Although almost seven out of every ten persons showed some familiarity with the issue, less than half of them expressed strong or intense opinions.

Variation in intensity. The factors associated with variations in intensity of opinions are in part the same factors that lead to familiarity. A most parsimonious statement of the difference between the two is that the analysis of intensity rests on *quantitative* rather than *qualitative* variations. In defining familiarity we may reduce the term to a question of whether a person possesses or does not possess a given quality of response to an issue. That is, we are interested in the presence or absence of two qualities that comprise familiarity: awareness of the issue and awareness of the political relevance of the issue. In defining intensity we work within the context of familiarity: among persons who are familiar with an issue, what variation can be observed in a quantitative measure of intensity, extremity, or strength of opinion? It should be remembered that we have specified two essential components of familiarity, one cognitive and the other evaluative. It is the latter that is most clearly subject to variation in intensity.

If a great many persons possess values that are thought to be relevant to a widely recognized problem, the result will be a familiar issue. If the values involved are all very important to their possessors, the opinions may be very intense opinions; if the values are not at all important to most persons, the opinions may be mild. For a given problem of government, intensity of opinion will depend on the importance of the values involved.

And yet this is not the whole story. The factor governing the intensity of a person's opinions is really not merely the absolute importance of values but the discrepancy in importance between values that will be realized and values that will be thwarted under alternative resolutions of the policy question. In the simple case, enactment of policy may result in goal achievement for a person; failure to enact will result in the alternative failure to achieve. The importance of the value that is enhanced by achievement or denied by non-achievement will determine the intensity of opinion.

The more common case, however, may well involve conflict and competition among goals. If policy A is pursued, goal X is achieved but goal Y is denied; if the policy is not pursued, Y will be achieved and not X. If the goals are equally important, the opinion on policy A may be extremely mild, really a matter of indifference. But if goal Y is much more highly valued than goal X, the opinion will be one of opposition to policy A. The intensity of the opposition will depend on *how much more important* Y is than X; that is, it will depend on the discrepancy in importance of the values which are in conflict. Questions of governmental policy frequently pose such dilemmas. The individual may desire to keep taxes at a low level; yet he may feel as well that if the government does not provide certain services, important needs will go unfilled. The intensity of his attitude may depend, then, upon the degree to which one of these values surpasses the other in importance.

A second major source of variation in intensity springs from the fact that some people find an issue more relevant for their values than do others holding the same values. Two people may be equally eager to keep taxes down, and equally desirous of a new governmental service. Yet one sees new governmental expenditure as coming from his own pocket in a very direct sense; for the other, the route between budget needs and own taxes is much more remote. Hence, values about low taxes in the second case are much less likely to become geared into the evaluation of the issue, leaving room for more intense advocacy of the new governmental service. Other things equal, then:

1. Persons for whom a value is more important will be more likely to express intense opinions than will persons for whom the same value is less important.
2. Persons who perceive issues to be more relevant for their values will be more likely to express intense opinions.

The manner in which values caught by an issue lead to more intense opinions may be readily illustrated by responses to our issue items. A striking example is provided by White and Negro attitudes on the question of the government "helping Negroes get jobs and housing." Of course the division of opinion on this issue between the racial groups conforms to our expectations. Whereas White respondents gave strong support to the policy of governmental aid to Negroes, the Negroes themselves were virtually unanimous in their approval. However, our interest here lies not in the division of opinion but in the relative frequency of strong statements of policy position as opposed to milder expressions of feeling.[3] Although the White members of the population lined up 66 to 34, intense to moderate, on the question, Negroes divided 94 to 6. This differential undoubtedly reflects the greater importance to Negroes of the values involved. Completely comparable differences between opinions of White and Negro citizens were found both in the South and in the non-Southern states.

A second example illustrates both generalizations that we have advanced to explain intensity of policy opinions. Here the policy question is that of federal intervention in the program of school integration. In the first place, we can again compare Negroes and Whites as was done on the FEPC and Housing question; in the second place we can compare the attitudes of Whites in the North, where integration as a policy question (if not as a practical matter) has been quite uniformly settled, with the attitudes of the Southern Whites for whom the policy threatens still-predominant values and norms of behavior.

The first test comparing Negroes and Whites corroborates our findings on the earlier race-related question. Negro responses were more intense than those from White respondents by a substantial margin. The second test is almost equally well supported. Northern Whites who supported or opposed federal action on school integration divided with 74 per cent expressing strong opinions and 26 per cent expressing more moderate opinions. Southern Whites divided their comparable responses 87 to 13.

Thus within parts of the population selected so as to isolate peculiar values, we find evidence of heightened intensity of opinion on issues relevant to those values; and persons experiencing threat to values of a type held generally in the population likewise register an intensification of issue feeling. It is at these pressure points that issues are most likely to have a bearing on the direction of political behavior.

The Perception of Party Differences on Issues

Even when the individual has some feeling invested in an issue position, we assume that the issue will have no meaningful bearing on partisan choice unless the person can discriminate between the policies of the two parties in the matter. When the individual sees the parties

[3] This measurement of intensity differs radically from that employed in the analysis of political attitudes in Chapters 3–5. There, intensity referred to the repetition of references to an issue; here, intensity refers to the weakness or strength of a single reference to the issue.

to be in conflict on an issue that concerns him, there is usually little further problem in his deducing which party policy is most congruent with his own view. But it is only as these links are completed that the way is paved for partisan motivation on an issue base.

Only 40 to 60 per cent *of the "informed" segment* of the population (that is, the part that holds an opinion on an issue) perceive party differences and hence can locate one or the other party as closer to "own" position. There is considerable variation in this figure from issue to issue, just as there was with issue familiarity itself. Some of the long-standing issues of the New and Fair Deal period show two out of every three informed persons perceiving party differences; on most of the foreign policy issues fewer than one out of every two persons think the parties differ appreciably. In either case, the discrepancy between those who hold attitudes and those who can relate the content of these attitudes to differences in party position is substantial. The lesson seems clear that even when "political" attitudes are held, there is no guarantee that *partisan* implications are drawn.

What underlies this failure to perceive party differences on policies of concern to the individual? Its roots are to be found in circumstances of the external world as well as in limitations of the individual. In the first case, policy differences between the parties on one or another issue might be invisible even to the expert observer. There are as many possible criteria of party policy as there are spokesmen, factions, and legislative or executive behaviors by party members, and in the heterogeneous American parties, these several indicators may give contradictory accounts. Even where a basic thrust in party policy *can* be discerned, we know that at some times on some issues there is greater cleavage between the parties than at other times or on other issues. Thus the stimuli to be discriminated are themselves more or less ambiguous. Where distinctions between the parties are academic, it would not be surprising if few people did succeed in a discrimination, however intense popular feelings on the issue might be. Nor can we always assume that people failing to perceive differences are less well informed than those who do, although this may be the general rule; they may simply be more "up to date" in their images of parties whose policies are indeed converging.

There is reason to believe that policy differences between the parties in both domestic and foreign affairs were narrower in 1956 than they had been in some time. In the early postwar period there had been persistent and acrimonious debate between Republicans and Democrats on many of the issues included in our battery of questions. However, the moderate positions adopted by the first Eisenhower Administration and control of Congress by more conservative elements of the Democratic Party reduced the display of sharp party differences on many policy points in the quadrennium before the 1956 election. The considerable failure to perceive party differences in 1956 might be traceable to these circumstances.

It cannot be denied that actual ambiguities in the positions of the parties must have some effect on views of party differentiation. But we feel that a large measure of the observed failure to perceive party differences by people holding opinions on an issue can be traced to the same personal limitations that keep many others from recognizing the issue at all. Knowledge of party position is an item of information, just as is knowledge of the initial issue. In many ways it is more subtle and more complex information. If a fair portion of the electorate fails to have standing cognitions of the issue, it is not surprising that a further portion has not absorbed the additional information concerning the parties.

Some 15 to 30 per cent of the people who held opinions but failed to perceive party differences indicated in so many words that they did not know the parties' stands. Admission of ignorance is embarrassing, and when an interview item poses two or three simple alternatives, there is reason to believe that respondents tend to gamble on a choice rather than confess lack of knowledge. Hence any frequency of "don't know" responses may be taken as an underestimate of the true numbers who in fact have no perceptions. The proportion of frank "don't know" answers to the question on perceptions of party differences among opinion holders is itself a token that failure to perceive differences can in many cases be traced to lack of information rather than actual perceptions that the parties hold the same position.

We take it as significant also that party differences are most clearly recognized on the policy controversies of the New Deal era. Issues of this type were the focus of bitter debate for twenty years or more prior to the 1956 election, and over most of this period the cleavage between the parties appeared broad. Although some small portion of the electorate is continually sensitive to party stands even on transient and discrete policy issues, it may take controversy of such breadth, depth, and duration to create a sense of party policy differences across as much as one third or one half of the adult population.[4]

[4] Perception of differences in matters of specific policy is, of course, distinct from the formation of more global party images of the type discussed in Chapter 3. Subsequent chapters in this section should help to make clear why these broader images are of but limited use to the individual in deducing more specific policy stands of the parties.

In general, people pay much less attention to political events and issues than is commonly realized. For this reason we have proceeded with painfully small steps in assessing the issue perceptions abroad in the public. The three conditions for issue-oriented political behavior laid out at the beginning of the chapter may seem rather obvious. Yet they assume considerable importance as we see the large numbers of people within the electorate who are excluded by each condition on our several issues. Table 8-3 permits a summary glance

TABLE 8-3. Perception of Partisan Implications of Own Issue Beliefs

Issue	Proportion of Respondents Who Perceive Party Differences on Issue, Having Fulfilled Prior Conditions
Foreign Policy	
Act tough toward Russia and China	36%
U.S. international involvement ("Stay Home")	32%
Friendliness toward other nations	32%
Economic aid to foreign countries	23%
Send soldiers abroad	22%
Give aid to neutral countries	18%
Domestic Policy	
Influence of big business in government	35%
Influence of unions in government	31%
Government guarantee of jobs	31%
Segregation of schools	31%
Cutting taxes	30%
Racial equality in jobs and housing	28%
Aid to education	27%
Insure medical care	24%
Firing of suspected communists	23%
Leave electricity and housing to private industry	22%

at the proportions of our sample who survive all three conditions—the expression of an opinion, the perception of what the government is doing, and the perception of relevant differences in party policy—on each issue. As we have observed, even these survivors need not be materially affected in their partisan choice by their issue beliefs; instead, they represent no more than a maximum pool within which the specified issues might have conceivable effect. It seems, then, that the sequence of events that must intervene before bitter partisan controversy dramatized in the press becomes significant for the political response of the man-in-the-street is both lengthy and fallible. Many people fail to appreciate that an issue exists, others are insufficiently involved to pay attention to recognized issues, and still others fail to make connections between issue positions and party policy.

Consensus on Issue Positions of the Parties

If our findings suggest only a modest articulation between party policy and voter response, they raise questions as well concerning the issue significance that may be ascribed to national elections, at least at the level of the relatively specific policy matters under consideration here. Other aspects of the data serve to underscore these doubts. When we analyze further the party differences perceived on each issue by the quartile of the population that makes any discrimination at all, we find that there is only a limited degree of consensus as to which party advocates which policy. Thus we find some proponents of government activity in matters of health insurance who feel the Republican Party best represents their position, and some who feel the Democrats are closest to this view. Others who fear government intervention similarly include people of opposite partisan perceptions.

At this point our argument departs from the problem of individual motivations. If the person sees a party supporting his issue beliefs in a given area, it is fair to assume that this perception has motivational significance however inaccurate others might judge the perception to be. Nevertheless, if we wish to assess the policy significance of a popular vote decision it is clear that the existence of mutually contradictory views as to the direction of policy differences between the parties would be a critical datum.

Where there is a babel of perceptions about party positions on a prominent issue, the significance of the public mandate becomes inscrutable. This fact would be true even if all other sources of ambiguity, such as narrow margins of victory and high competition of issues for voter attention, were removed from consideration. We can imagine, for example, a hypothetical case in which a single issue motivates the march to the polls, and one party wins an overwhelming landslide of votes. If there was no prior consensus among the voters as to the respective party positions, there can be no clear issue outcome: the victorious party may have drawn support equally from both opinion camps.

We find clear evidence of some consensus about party position only for those issues that concern the familiar New Deal-Fair Deal controversies. Questions having to do with governmental underwriting of medical costs, aid to education, guaranteed employment, control of big business and labor unions, and federal housing and electric power production all revealed tendencies to link the Democratic Party with the New Deal position. On the other hand, questions having to do with desegregation, protection of Negro rights in jobs and housing, and dismissal of government workers accused of being Communists revealed no consistent party image. Similarly, there was no sign of consensus about party position on any of the items covering aspects of foreign policy.

Although agreement on party alignments on New Deal controversies was substantial, it was in no sense complete. Where it was strongest—on the item concerning private control of electric power and housing—about 75 per cent accepted the view that the Republicans were the advocates of laissez faire. Since 50 per cent would mark the lowest possible ebb of consensus and 100 per cent its maximum, we see that there was substantial contradiction in perceptions even here. For one or two other issues in the New Deal grouping that we have cited, the majority view was held by as few as 65 per cent.

There are several factors that might lead to such a confused state of affairs among the people who feel best informed on each of these issues. One possibility has to do with the local base of the national political parties. If the image of national politics were an expanded version of local politics it would not be unreasonable to expect diversity among localities to produce an incoherent picture of a national party. In Virginia in 1957 it may have been clear to some voters that the Republican Party and the Republican candidates offered the better alternative for the foes of racial segregation; in Michigan in the same year it may have been equally clear to other voters that the Democratic Party offered the better vehicle for fighting segregation. In some farm states in 1956 the Republican Party appeared as the defender of the small farmer; in others the Democratic Party succeeded in establishing prior claim to support from this quarter. However clear party positions might be locally or regionally, differences in these positions from place to place would create a national picture of limited consensus on party policy.

The question is not whether local party differences exist; they clearly do, although the more local the party leadership, the less likely that it will address itself to most of the issues discussed. Instead, we must ask in what degree policy characteristics of more local or regional parties are perceived by the public. Any relevant data that we can bring to bear on the problem suggest that the national party is most central in the formation of public images. It is reasonable that this should be so. The mass media tend to give much more attention to political developments at the national level. The absorption of political information from these media is not great under any circumstance, and we would expect news given secondary attention to have very little impact at all. With an occasional exception due to the political distinctiveness of the South, we find little suggestion in our data that national consensus on party positions is materially lowered by local party differences.

Another reasonable source of confusion over party alignments lies in the heterogeneity of policy position within the national party leadership. Where there are conflicting pronouncements and behaviors from visible figures associated with a party, either of two patterns may ensue. The alert citizen may take note of the contradictory cues and become confused as to the likely direction of party policy. The person whose attention to political matters is more sporadic may focus on one set of pronouncements, whereas his equally casual neighbor may absorb a different set of cues. Hence consensus on party position is undermined.

It is likely that party identification also plays an important role in reducing consensus over the issue alignments of the parties. The individual who has a sense of loyalty to a party will feel most comfortable to be in agreement with the party's position on matters perceived to be of some importance. This fact has several consequences, for there are at least three important ways in which the individual's issue position and the perceived position of the party may come to coincide.

The first case comes about when the parties succeed in their role as purveyors of policy alternatives. The involved citizen with an opinion on broad questions of policy makes a choice of party that will best fulfill his own belief. Inasmuch as any complex election situation is likely to involve a variety of issue controversies at once, it could not be assumed that such a person would agree with all party policy; still, this sequence of events would lead us to expect congruence between rank-and-file opinion and leadership policy on the central issues of the day. Furthermore, we would expect a fair amount of shifting in partisan preferences from election to election, for such central issues change over time and should lead to party realignments among individuals. We have failed, however, to find much congruence between opinions of members and party leaders, and we have seen as well that partisan allegiances are formed early and tend to endure over the life span. Hence it is hard to imagine that this sequence of events is common.

Congruence between individual opinion and party policy may develop in a second way. The party attempts to draw new support and maintain the old by its advocacy of various policy positions. When the identified member is aware of these positions, he is likely to espouse the goals urged by his party leadership. To the degree that the party is the source of political attitude formation, there would be congruence in issue position between party and individual. There should also be consensus among adherents of both parties as to respective party positions on such issues.

It is our impression that the second pattern of events occurs much more often than the first. Nonetheless, it is not extremely prevalent either. Like the first instance, the pattern presumes issue involvement on the part of the individual. It presumes as well a capacity to discriminate between the policy stands of the parties. It would lead to high congruence between leadership policy and the issue opinion of the rank and file. And, like the first pattern, it would produce substantial consensus between supporters of each party as to their respective policy positions. Yet we have found the incidence of these circumstances to be low. There seem to be widespread ignorance and indifference over many matters of policy. And even when opinions are held, many persons are not motivated to discover or are unable to sort out the relevant positions adopted by the parties.

Under these conditions it is likely that a third pattern of events is actually the predominant one. It follows from our prior discussions that the strong partisan who lacks any real information permitting him to locate either party on a question of policy may find it relatively easy to presume that his chosen party is closer to his own belief regarding that policy than is the opposition. The fact that only a minority of the population seems concerned as to party position on any specific issue indicates that much of the opinion formation that goes on in the electorate occurs independent of party cues. This is likely to mean that people who identify as Democrats will arrive at much the same distribution of opinions as those who identify as Republicans. Hence if adherents of opposing views within each party presume that the party reflects their own beliefs, the parties appear to be all things to all people. We would find little congruence between member opinion and leadership policy, and little consensus on where the parties do stand, a picture that fits the data well. In a sense the fact of party loyalties actually serves to *reduce* consensus about party position.

At this level, then, we are forced to conclude that articulation between party program, party member opinion, and individual political decision is weak indeed. Naturally the subject is not exhausted by this analysis. It may well be argued that we have imposed a view of issues and policies that is unrealistically specific. Significant differences do exist in the public images of the parties. The public may well have broader perceptions of the policy roles that the parties are prepared to play, and articulation between issue concerns and partisanship may be clearer at this level.

It seems significant, for example, that almost twice as many people were able to fulfill all three of our conditions on foreign policy items that had to do with broad postures of the government toward other nations (acting "tough," being "friendly," or minding its own business) than were able to react to more specific programs concerning foreign aid and military assistance (Table 8-3). Similarly, although we found no consensus as to party position on these matters of foreign policy, when we ask which party the person believes will do a better job of keeping the country out of war, a much larger proportion perceives party differences, with a sizable majority of members of both parties naming the Republican Party as better able to preserve the peace.

It is important for our understanding of the political system that we attain some grasp of the level at which issue concerns affect mass participation in politics. If most of the policy items discussed in this chapter are so specific in character that only a small portion of the electorate can respond meaningfully to them, this is in itself an important fact.

Attitude Structure and the Problem of Ideology ◇ 9

The widespread lack of familiarity with prominent issues of public policy, along with confusion on party position that remains even among individuals familiar with an issue, attests to the frailties of the political translation process. The fact that a policy question is subjected to intense partisan debate between elections does not assure us that at the next election the public will respond to the substance of the argument.

This insensitivity to policy controversies seems particularly significant when laid against our data concerning the stability of party identification over time. For the flow of policy questions on which the parties take up opposing positions is, potentially, a prime source of change in partisan preference from election to election. Indeed, much democratic theory presumes that as new problems arise the citizen will arrive at fresh evaluations of the alternatives of policy. However, if the political relevance or, more especially, the partisan relevance of "new" problems is seen but darkly or not at all, it is less surprising that party allegiances gain momentum over time and are rarely derailed by pressures arising outside the political order.

We may plumb the matter still further and come to grips with unresolved facets of the problem. For example, the data presented up to this point do not exclude the possibility that different individuals are strongly influenced by matters of public policy within restricted areas but are largely uninformed in areas beyond this focus of concern. If half of the electorate paid attention to foreign affairs but ignored domestic policy debates, and the other half restricted its interest in the opposite fashion, issues might play a large role in the partisan preference of individuals despite aggregate evidence of large-scale apathy and misinformation on any single issue. In fact, no such neat division of labor exists, at least in any extreme form. Familiarity with issues is unevenly distributed among the electorate. People familiar with one issue are much more likely to be familiar with others, even though content may vary widely. Nonetheless, this question reminds us that our analysis remains incomplete until we have paid closer attention to the patterns of attitudes held by individuals, as opposed to our analysis of a sequence of discrete issues in the preceding chapter.

It also might be argued that although the man-in-the-street may have only a loose idea of what is going on in terms of specific policy, he has a firm sense of the global policy differences between the parties, and relates them with equal firmness to highly generalized values of his own. A hypothesis of this sort could be fitted nicely with findings concerning the stability of party identification over time. Leaders of each party are continually forced to take positions, and from time to time these specific decisions fail to square well with the broader philosophy that normally characterizes the party. But policy as it may be formulated in the most general dimensions of ideology seems fairly stable for a party or tandem of parties throughout long political eras. Parties of the "left" and "right" do not trade positions from election to election. Assuming stability in parallel values in individuals, it would follow that partisan preferences would be pursued for long periods of time.

This suggestion, like the preceding, directs our attention to the clusters or "structures" of attitudes involving political issues. We shall scan our data for evidence of this attitude structure, first at the level of the specific policy matters considered in the preceding chapter and subsequently at a more abstract level of generalized political value. Since our several modes of procedure reflect some widely held presumptions as to what "attitude structure" is, it is important to make these notions clear at the outset.

"Attitude Structures" and Ideology

We speak of an "attitude structure" when two or more beliefs or opinions held by an individual are in some way or another functionally related. As a simple example, we might encounter a person who is opposed to government activity in the area of low-cost housing. If we question him further as to his attitudes toward government ownership of utilities, he might oppose intervention here as well, and go on to say that in general he dislikes the idea of government intrusion in economic areas where private industry has traditionally held sway. In such a case, we would feel that we had struck upon a cluster of attitudes that were functionally related, inasmuch as there seems to be interdependence between each opinion. If this individual were to be persuaded that government intervention was generally desirable, we would expect attitudes toward both the housing problem and the utilities problem to change accordingly.

We may imagine a number of types of functional relationship binding attitudes together. There is, for example, a means-end relationship that often emerges clearly in attitude structures. A government activity thus may be favored because it is seen as a stepping stone to some broader goal. Or attitudes may be functionally related if they operate in the service of a similar need. There may be a sharply aggressive cast to all of an individual's foreign policy opinions that would lead us to suspect that out-group objects like foreign peoples and nations were targets for release of hostility.

One property of an attitude that is useful to recognize has to do with the specificity of the object that is evaluated. Affect may be aroused by objects as specific as a clause in a House bill or as general as the abstraction "freedom." Attitude structures are often thought of as hierarchies in which more specific attitudes interact with attitudes toward the more general class of objects in which the specific object is seen to belong. In some cases it may be conceptually desirable to divide the layers of this belief hierarchy quite finely. For example, reactions to a new bill appropriating money for public housing may be linked with certain underlying attitudes toward government activity in the area of housing more generally. These attitudes in turn may be conditioned by still more generalized attitudes toward the proper role of government in questions of private enterprise and social welfare. Beliefs at this level may show meaningful congruence with basic values concerning the intrinsic desirability of change in the scope of governmental responsibilities. And, finally, such values might have root in tendencies toward conservatism and innovation so general as to be aspects of personality, coloring the individual's response to change of any type, political or otherwise.

This conception includes other forms of functional relationship as special cases. Thus the appropriations bill is favored as a specific means toward a more generalized goal. And it has been suggested among students of attitudes that a traffic between the specific and the general is basic in questions of attitude development and attitude change. However useful this view, it is at best an extremely simple model of the evaluative process. Any complex object may be located in a variety of general classes at the same time, and the values engaged may be in conflict. Furthermore, in the practical situation, evaluations may be strongly affected by extraneous concerns. A legislator stiffly opposed to government activities in a specific economic area may react warmly to a proposition of this nature that would provide spectacular benefits for his constituents.

At the very best, judgment on the presence or absence of a functional relationship between two or more attitudes demands some degree of inference on the part of the investigator. In most attitude studies, functional relationships are presumed to exist where it is found that knowledge of a person's belief on one issue helps to predict his belief on some other issue. It is important to recognize that an individual may hold attitudes that appear congruent from the point of view of the analyst when there is in fact no functional contact between them. A person who decries government activity in housing construction and at the same time opposes government ownership of utilities may be evaluating the two proposals in quite independent terms. He may react negatively to government housing developments because of their attendant policies against racial discrimination. He may on the other hand reject the idea of government utilities because of a perception that these efforts aid people in other regions at the expense of his own. If neither issue was evaluated on the basis of the common thread of government activity in areas traditionally reserved for private enterprise, new experiences might change one attitude without affecting the other.

Although any specific person may show such congruence of opinions "accidentally," it is generally supposed that correlations between attitudes that are visible in aggregates are reliable evidence of some structuring of the attitudes on the part of individual members. At an operational level, there are several methods of determining whether or not such underlying dimensions exist. We may ask simply whether there is a correlation between positions held by individuals on each of two issues across an aggregate. This procedure may be extended to analyze relationships between large numbers of issues. Or, where a number of items are involved, we may seek evidence of a unitary underlying dimension of attitude through the Guttman "scale" criteria. In effect, this technique depends on the notion that some specific opinions in a content domain are more extreme (more "difficult" to accept) than others. If the individual takes (for example) a liberal viewpoint on a very radical proposition, the presence of scalar relationships in the Guttman sense tells us that he will tend to take a liberal position with items on which a larger number of people accept the liberal alternative. Where these "scale" criteria are met, individuals may be located at various points on the underlying attitude dimension, which produces the scale according to the extremity of the alternatives that they will accept.

Whereas there is reasonable consensus about techniques for determining whether attitude structures are present or absent, there is no clear method for determining the "true" character of the underlying dimension in *content* terms. In many cases, the nature of the common thread seems unequivocal by simple inspection of the items involved. Yet some element of conjecture remains. It is a matter of great concern that we analyze these shared elements accurately, since other predictions and extrapolations may stand or fall according to the adequacy of our judgment. If we find, for example, that people who endorse governmental activity in housing tend also to endorse governmental control of utilities, what common factor leads to this structure? Is it a basic belief in the extension of governmental control over economic areas once monopolized by private enterprise? If so, to what end? Does it represent a liberal ideology and receptiveness to social planning? Or is it simply a perception that the individual will gain economically from either arrangement?

One objective check of some merit on these interpretations would be a direct measurement of the generalized, "master" attitude presumed to bind these responses together. This approach is not always easy, for some suspected general orientations are hard to formulate in simple question form. But in the previous illustration we might be able to ask directly whether or not the individual was concerned about the growth of government activities in the economic sector. If there were no relationship between responses to more global items and reactions to the specific items, we might feel obliged to revise our view of the character of the underlying dimension.

Ideology. An "ideology" may be seen as a particularly elaborate, close-woven, and far-ranging structure of attitudes. By origin and usage its connotations are primarily political, although the scope of the structure is such that we expect an ideology to encompass content outside the political order as narrowly defined—social and economic relationships, and even matters of religion, education, and the like. For the ideologically-inclined reader, the practice of conceptualizing economic events like unemployment as being at base "nonpolitical" may seem odd, for an ideology is an ideology in no small measure because it connects various facets of social, political, and economic experience. An ideology is a highly differentiated attitude structure, but its parts are organized in a coherent fashion. In terms of our metaphor of "political translation" it provides a table of equivalences between events within the political order and those in other sectors of endeavor. For the person who possesses a full-blown ideology, then, political translation has been accomplished for a wide range of events.

Two characteristics of ideology are of major concern to us here. First, any cognitive structure that subsumes content of wide scope and diversity must be capped by concepts of a high order of abstraction. An ideology, once its affective components are set aside, shares some of the characteristics of any taxonomic system. Perceived events and states are given meaning because they may be coded into classes. The wider the range of objects so classified, the more remote and general the concept that is necessary to capture their similarity. Secondly, if ideology supplies a manageable number of ordering dimensions that permit the person to make sense of a broad range of events, the political analyst is delighted to capitalize upon this fact. The attitudes that might conceivably be important in taking the political pulse of a nation are extremely diverse. To deal with political events parsimoniously the analyst is thrown back on those basic ordering dimensions that appear to lend generalized patterns of meaning to political motivations.

Perhaps no abstraction of this genre has been used more frequently in the past century for political analysis than the concept of a liberal-conservative continuum—the "right" and the "left" of a political spectrum.[1] The generality of this dimension makes it a powerful summary tool. Above the flux of specific domestic issues lie a number of broad controversies regarding the appropriate posture of the national government toward other sectors of the social order, such as the development of resources, industry, and trade; the church; the privileged and the underprivileged; relatively local political bodies; and

[1] In recent literature, note for example Richard Hofstadter, "The Pseudo-Conservative Revolt," *The New American Right,* ed. Daniel Bell (Criterion Books, New York, 1955); or Louis Hartz, *The Liberal Tradition in America* (Harcourt, Brace and Company, New York, 1955). Also, recent efforts to synthesize findings based on a wide range of studies underscore the importance attributed to this dimension in empirical investigation. See Herbert Hyman, *Political Socialization* (The Free Press, Glencoe, Ill., 1959); or Seymour Lipset *et al.,* "The Psychology of Voting: An Analysis of Political Behavior," *Handbook of Social Psychology,* ed. Gardner Lindzey (Addison-Wesley Publishing Company, Cambridge, Mass., 1954). Lipset has criticized the dependence of voting studies upon this dimension in his essay "Political Sociology," *Sociology Today,* ed. Robert K. Merton, Leonard Broom, Leonard S. Cottrell, Jr. (Basic Books, Inc., New York, 1959).

the world community. Differences between liberal and conservative tend to focus upon the degree to which the government should assume interest, responsibility, and control over these sectors of endeavor.

At the same time, the very generality of the "left-right" distinction creates a number of pitfalls. The fact of a liberal or conservative position does not in itself describe an attitude toward the extent of government activity within a given area. A viewpoint that is liberal in one time or place may be conservative in another. In the modern era, advocacy of greater government control over the economic order is typically a liberal position; in late eighteenth century Europe, however, after an epoch of close government control, the new and radical doctrine was one of "laissez faire." Similarly, at any point in time the liberal may favor much government intervention in one area and little in another. In twentieth century France the separation of church and state remains a basic plea of the same "left" that calls for more extensive government intervention in economic affairs.

Thus while the liberal-conservative controversy centers on the extent of government activity, the nature of the advocacy that is called liberal or conservative comes to depend, within the immediate context, upon what is and what is hoped for. The viewpoint termed conservative may thereby become that which is reluctant to disturb the existing order of relationships, whether they be laissez faire or interventionist. The liberal viewpoint sees room for improvement in the product of social and political process through change in these relationships.

The widespread use of a liberal-conservative distinction in political analysis leads us to focus attention upon it rather heavily in this and the following chapter. We shall first consider the evidence for structures of attitudes emerging from our items of relatively specific public policy. Then we shall attempt to improve our grasp of the meaning that may reasonably be attributed to these structures, by assessing their status as "ideology."

Attitude Structures in Issues of Public Policy

Analysis of the ten domestic issues and six foreign policy items explored in 1956 yields one set of opinions within each area that forms a satisfactory Guttman scale.[2] Five domestic issues contributed to

[2] Scales mentioned over the course of this chapter in connection with the Guttman technique meet the criteria described in Angus Campbell, Gerald Gurin, and Warren E. Miller, *The Voter Decides* (Row, Peterson and Co., Evanston, Ill., 1954), pp. 187–189.

one scale, including the items on aid to education, medical care, employment guarantees, FEPC and Negro housing, and public versus private production of electricity and housing. In primary content these items all have to do with the desirability of governmental action in areas of social welfare. Therefore, although we intend to inquire further into the meaning of this structure, we shall label this the "social welfare" structure.

Similarly, four of the six foreign policy items showed relationships of a sort that qualified the set as a second attitude structure. The content shared across these issues and relatively absent in the two excluded items concerned the desirable degree of United States' intervention in international affairs. At one extreme were persons who thought our government should not be concerned with problems in other parts of the world, should not give economic aid to poor countries, should not maintain overseas military installations to fight Communism, and should not offer aid to the so-called neutral nations. At the other end of the continuum were persons favoring American activity in all of these spheres.

There undoubtedly were other issues in 1956 which, had we attempted to measure them, could have qualified as parts of either the social welfare or the foreign structure. Neither of these sets of issues should be considered as more than a selection from the opinions that might be shaped by the same underlying attitude. On the other hand, the fact that the other attitudes that we had measured within each broad policy area failed to fit the major structures located gives us a sense of the boundaries for each structure, and hence sets limitations on their meaning. From this viewpoint the data evince a rather slight degree of structure in the attitudes of the mass electorate.

This fact is particularly clear as we survey the domestic issues that fail to qualify as part of the social welfare structure. On the basis of *a priori* assumptions commonly made, several if not all of the five items empirically excluded might be thought appropriate parts of this issue structure. Why should attitudes toward the role of big business in government lie outside an organization of attitudes concerning government activity in sectors of the economy once restricted to private business? Why do we fail to find the stereotyped picture of a national partisan division on questions of tax levels and governmental social welfare activity reflected in a general organization of opinions?

An examination of the correlates of particular issue positions provides some explanation for these discontinuities and increases our understanding of the reasons why the existing structure shows its coherence. The opinions on the taxation proposition are instructive from this point of view. One might expect that interest in tax reduction would be greatest among people of high income. However, our data make it clear that even among persons of equal education or with similar occupations, it is the high income people who are relatively *more* willing to pay taxes than have the government postpone doing things that need to be done. It is the low-income group that demands a tax reduction even at the expense of such postponement.[3]

Although this finding runs counter to political folklore, it is unreasonable only if we are unwilling to doubt some of the long-standing assumptions about ideological structure on these matters. It is not hard to imagine that willingness to pay taxes is dependent upon ability to pay, and that the present tax structure does not result in a perfectly progressive incidence of tax burden. Under these circumstances we need not be surprised that a man whose family must live on less than $4,000 a year is more often unconditionally in favor of tax reduction than is the householder whose family has $6,000 or more to spend each year.

Furthermore, although traditionally the Republican Party argues for balanced budgets and tax reductions, rank-and-file Democrats in 1956 were somewhat more likely to favor cutting taxes than were their Republican counterparts. Thus tax reduction was favored, more often than not, by low-income persons and Democrats. This relationship runs at cross purposes to the correlates of the social welfare structure, where we find the more "normal" tendency prevailing—low income persons and Democrats welcoming heightened government activity in social welfare areas with high income persons and Republicans more likely to be opposed. These cross-currents give us some understanding of the failure of the tax question to fit the social welfare structure.

It is important to recognize the degree to which our "normal" or *a priori* expectations in these matters are conditioned by sophisticated views of the parts that make up a coherent political ideology. Locked in this perspective, we may wonder at the low-income person who wants to see government services extended, yet favors postponement of important government activity in order to reduce taxes. However, both responses may spring from the same motivation—a simple desire for improvement of one's economic lot. As long as the structure of political attitudes is loose and specific evaluations have little cognitive contact, potential contradictions will not be confronted.

[3] Each of the conclusions presented here has been tested and sustained with controls on possible confounding "third factors." That is, the tendency for lower-income people to favor tax reduction more than those of higher income remains when differences in education, occupation, party allegiance, and the like are controlled.

The data concerning the tax question illustrate another related point. The fact that an issue reaction fails to fit into a larger organization of attitude that seems appropriate for it, does not mean that the response is random or in any other sense "uncaused." The problem is rather that the structure imposed on the situation by the analyst turns out in such instances to be inadequate. It may be that the sources of responses to an issue are so diverse from individual to individual that all sense of patterning across an aggregate is lost. More often, as in the tax question, clear roots may exist that the analyst ignores because they have no place in his preconceptions concerning "logical" or traditional ideological positions. His organizing dimensions simply depart from the modes of organization abroad in the general population.

The interrelationship of foreign and domestic policy structures. Across our sample as a whole in 1956 there was no relationship between scale positions of individuals on the domestic and foreign attitudinal dimensions. An interventionist position in foreign affairs was as likely to be taken by a domestic conservative as by a domestic liberal, and the relative isolationist was as likely to favor social welfare activities in Washington as he was to oppose them. Whether this seems surprising depends once again on our preconceptions. Certainly the content involved in the two structures is, on its face, disparate. It is true as well that many tightly organized and far-reaching ideologies become rather ambiguous as to the desirable courses of action outside national borders. But in terms of elite behavior and party programs there has been some reason to associate parties of the "right" in domestic affairs with nationalism in foreign questions, as opposed to the frequent humanitarian internationalism of "leftist" parties.

It is because this type of alignment was quite visible in the primary positions espoused by the two American parties in the era prior to the Eisenhower period that we might reasonably expect to find a similar pattern of opinion in the public. After the first Roosevelt years and through the Truman Administrations, the Democratic Party gave legislative support to programs involving government activity both in social welfare areas and abroad. Yet it is difficult to find evidence for this configuration of attitudes in the general electorate of 1956, and we are forced to conclude once again that the typical American lacks a clearly patterned ideology of such breadth. He may feel strongly about a variety of individual issues, but there are severe limitations on our ability to predict his position in one issue area from his position in another.

Now that we have assessed some of the outer limits of structure visible in the electorate, it becomes important to focus more careful attention on the two major structures that are apparent. What is the nature of the commonality that underlies each of these structures? What political significance may be attributed to them? We may increase our understanding of these attitude patterns by analyzing some of their more important correlates.

The Significance of Attitude Structures on Policy Issues

Foreign policy. Not only do the differences in activism-withdrawal fail to correlate with placement on the social welfare dimension; they fail as well to show a correlation with political partisanship in 1956. People who tended to give internationalist responses to the four foreign policy items were no more likely to express identification with the Democratic Party than with the Republican Party (Table 9-1). This finding, when laid against other aspects of our data, is of great interest.

TABLE 9-1. Relation of Party Identification to Attitudes on Foreign Policy, 1956

	Party Identification				
Internationalism	Strong Democrat	Weak Democrat	Independent	Weak Republican	Strong Republican
High	54%	58%	56%	55%	57%
Medium	26	23	24	32	27
Low	20	19	20	13	16
	100%	100%	100%	100%	100%

First, the absence of correlation between foreign policy position and partisanship seems to be of much the same cloth as the general confusion that we encountered in the preceding chapter as to the foreign policy alignments of the major parties. However, it appears to clash with other findings that we have presented. We noted in Chapter 3, for example, that in the Eisenhower elections the partisan balance of foreign policy concerns was of considerable benefit to the Republican cause. The Democratic candidate was virtually excluded from comment by persons concerned over foreign affairs, and the thrust of their remarks about the Republican Party and Mr. Eisenhower was almost unanimously supportive. Similarly, there are clear patterns in the responses to a broad question concerning which party is best trusted to keep the country out of war. A considerable majority chose the Republican Party. And it seems that but for party loyalties, this perception would have been more nearly unanimous: most of the minority who continued to maintain that the Democratic Party was more capable in avoiding war were Democratic partisans.

Thus we can hardly say that foreign policy concerns failed to effect partisan choice in 1956, or even that partisan perceptions were so diffuse and contradictory in that year as to make the nature of the foreign policy mandate inscrutable. Rather, we must resolve the apparent contradiction by examining more closely the types of response that produce a sense of clear partisan pattern, as opposed to those that produce instead a sense of confusion in perceived partisan implications.

Partisan patterns on foreign concerns developed most clearly in 1956 where the issues were formulated at the simple and global level of getting into war or staying out of it. Such patterns faded out when the issue grounds were shifted to the more specific *means* of attaining the goal. People had feelings about the desirability of American engagement abroad that lent consistency and a sense of structure to their responses on items of this nature. But the "bridge" perceptions were lacking that would meaningfully link activist or withdrawal feelings to one of the parties. Hence the broad public mandate in 1956 could be taken to express, among many other things, a fear of getting into war, and an appreciation of the political agents thought best capable of avoiding war. But there was no visible mandate concerning the choice between intervention and isolation as a means toward peace. The victorious party drew no greater support from people of either policy persuasion.

The 1956 findings on this score contrast with those of 1952. In the earlier study, foreign policy questions involving the activism-withdrawal dimension showed Republicans tending to choose isolationist alternatives, whereas Democrats were more likely to be internationalist in outlook.[4] This difference may well spring from changes in party position between 1952 and 1956. Before 1952, the Republican Party, represented largely by its Congressional leaders, had tended to oppose the active internationalism of the Democratic Party. In 1953 and thereafter, when the focus for the Republican Party shifted to the White House, the general adherence of the Eisenhower Administration to the internationalist policies of its predecessors served to minimize party differences in foreign affairs. We may be encountering here an

[4] Campbell, Gurin, and Miller, *op. cit.*, pp. 118 ff.

indication of the role played by the parties in lending structure to mass political opinion.

The withdrawal-activism dimension of foreign policy attitudes did show some association with other dispositions toward politics, a fact that helps to round out our understanding of these opinions. Generally, internationalists were more likely to be politically informed and involved than were those favoring withdrawal from international commitments. The internationalist was more aware of differences in the policy commitments of the two major parties. He was also more likely to be interested in and familiar with a more extensive range of the policy questions that we probed than was his isolationist counterpart. And he was more likely to perceive a partisan coloration in the political tendencies of major social groupings, such as the oft noted Democratic inclination of lower-class levels and the more Republican bias of higher-status levels.

The internationalist, too, tends to register a stronger sense of political efficacy than does the isolationist. People advocating withdrawal from foreign engagements are, by their own assessment, less effective participants in politics; the internationalist feels that he is in control of his political world and that it is responsive to his desires and acts. For the isolationist, it seems reasonable that a pattern of withdrawal and avoidance is one way of coping with a body of complex relationships that he has difficulty understanding, just as he tends to give up on domestic politics as too complicated to follow. Of course there are more sophisticated rationales that have and may continue to support an isolationist belief structure. But it is not difficult to understand that an argument for cutting the nation free of its many foreign commitments as a road to peace would have appeal for persons of this disposition.[5]

The involvement and sense of effectiveness that characterize the internationalists undoubtedly have further political implications. In terms of the actual 1956 election, the mandate of the public on the activism-withdrawal question was rendered unclear by confusion over party lines. However, the rallying of more informed, involved, and active citizens to the internationalist position suggests that this persuasion is likely to be pressed more diligently outside of the immediate

[5] Although it is the more educated citizens who are, by and large, more involved and informed, there is little evidence that broader education itself creates more willingness to have the United States assume a range of international responsibilities. With involvement controlled, there is no systematic variation in position on the withdrawal-activism continuum as a function of education. With education controlled, however, there remains a visible relationship between activism-withdrawal and involvement.

election situation than a census or unweighted poll of the national constituency would lead us to expect.

Domestic policy. The items involved in the domestic issue structure reflect the social welfare controversies of the New Deal-Fair Deal era. They are, by and large, the questions that revealed the clearest consensus as to party differences in the preceding chapter. Therefore it is not surprising that although foreign attitudes had lost their partisan element in 1956, position in the domestic issue structure remained clearly associated with partisan preference. Persons who favored social welfare activity by the federal government were likely to be identified with the Democratic Party. They perceived the Democratic Party to be closer than the Republican Party to their own position on other issues, and their voluntary references to domestic issues, within the system of proximal attitudes, were highly favorable to the Democratic cause or critical of the Republican.

We also get a clearer picture here of the role of the parties in developing attitude structures in members of the electorate. In the process of determining whether a set of responses meets scale criteria, we identify some persons as "non-scalar types" whose attitudes are not so organized as to indicate comparable structures. We find that there is a relationship between the expression of a "scalar" pattern of attitudes on the social welfare items and the nature of the person's party identification. Persons strongly identified with a party were least likely to exhibit non-scalar attitudes; persons weakly identified were somewhat more likely to do so; and persons who classified themselves as Independents closer to one party or the other were, in turn, most likely to be classified as non-scalar on the domestic issue scale (Table 9-2). No

TABLE 9-2. Relation of Party Identification to Scalar and Non-Scalar Patterns of Domestic Issue Opinions, 1956

	Party Identification						
Number of Non-Scalar Opinions	Strong Democrat	Weak Democrat	Independent Democrat	Independent	Independent Republican	Weak Republican	Strong Republican
0	71%	60%	59%	67%	65%	72%	76%
1	25	34	32	30	33	22	22
2	4	6	9	3	2	6	2
	100%	100%	100%	100%	100%	100%	100%

relationship of this sort appears in connection with the foreign issue dimension, a fact that fits well with our previous discussion. Thus the parties appear to have served two important functions in the case of the domestic welfare attitudes. They not only have indicated a basic posture for their followers to assume; but they have also provided the party follower with cues that facilitate the structuring of his opinions.

The structure of opinions built around the problem of social welfare activity is of intense interest to us for reasons that go beyond its unique partisan implications, however. For this structure is one which has clearest relevance for traditional discussions of the "left" and the "right" in political ideology. Advocacy of increased government activity in matters of social welfare and increased government control in economic production have been the most characteristic "liberal" positions in the recent era, and the positions most vigorously contested by conservative leadership. Although we can hardly gainsay the significance of these core dimensions of modern ideology in the decision making of political elites, how important may we presume them to be at the level of mass political behavior?

Our conception of the ideology as a massive bridge that brings perceptions of a variety of non-political events into contact with cognitions of political objects is not in itself an unorthodox view. The ideology is a medium of political translation *par excellence;* the possessor of ideology can readily ascribe political meaning to events and states within the social, economic, or even religious orders of experience. However, evidence as to the great momentum of long-standing party loyalties and the vicissitudes of the political translation process where specific policy matters are concerned have moved us toward the tentative conclusion that events outside the political order impinge only feebly upon the evolution of partisan decisions at the mass level. It would seem to follow that ideology of a sort that binds a broad range of human experience to dynamic evaluations of politics cannot be thought to be widespread in the American population.

This is, however, argument by indirection, and we can now confront the matter directly. We have isolated an attitude structure capturing the core ideological controversies of our epoch. The structure exists empirically, and, moreover, it shows relationships of substantial magnitude with partisan preference in the direction that would be predicted by notions of ideology. That is, people sort themselves into patterns of response that are coherent in terms of a liberal-conservative dimension; and people who choose liberal alternatives tend to identify with the more liberal, or "leftist" Democratic Party, whereas people choosing conservative alternatives tend more often to express loyalty to the conservative, "rightist" Republican Party. Furthermore, we find that people of lower status predominate both among those who rank as "liberal" in their social welfare attitudes and among the adherents of the "liberal" party. Citizens in higher strata tend to prefer the "conservative" alternatives to such questions, and give primary support to the conservative party.

It is this triangle of relationships, replicated in dozens of empirical studies, which has provided continuing assurance to sophisticated observers that their notions of social and political process are sound. Individuals who already enjoy high prestige under the *status quo* should not, on the basis of self-interest, wish to have existing arrangements tampered with: in short, they should be conservative in orientation. But individuals who are not faring well under existing arrangements should be "liberal" or "radical" advocates of change in social and political institutions.

Since this standard pattern of relationships has loomed so large in recent thought concerning political behavior, we must analyze the role of ideology most painstakingly. Obviously, the facts presented by these relationships cannot soberly be questioned; and without further conceptual embellishment, they communicate important data concerning the operation of the political system. However, it is common to leap from these bare facts to the conclusion that traditional ideological structures are important parts of the armory of attitudes generally used in political evaluation. For some predictions the social and political outcome is the same whether or not this assumption is warranted. In other cases, however, our expectations may be sorely betrayed if we are not more cautious in our view of ideology at a mass level. It is our contention that this assumption is frequently overdrawn. We shall attempt to demonstrate a number of other facts, equally real, which are inexplicable once this assumption is made. And we shall consider how the basic triangle of relationships laid out above can be generated with very little in the way of full-blown "ideology" in the motives and values of the actors involved.

First it is important to distinguish between behavior impelled by self-interest in a primitive and short-sighted sense, and the operation of self-interest within a structure of attitudes that might reasonably be labeled an "ideology." This discrimination may seem difficult, since it is customary to assume that perceived interest is the primary criterion whereby the individual locates an appropriate ideology. Thus ideology and self-interest become tightly linked in our minds.

We have no quarrel with the view that ideological position is largely determined by self-interest. But we do maintain that it matters whether self-interest proceeds in a simple and naked sense, or has indeed become imbedded in some broader ideological structure. We have suggested, for example, that the possession of ideology equips the individual to perceive the connectedness of many superficially diverse events and relate them to one another coherently. One important implication of such understanding is that the person is sensitized to the existence of "roundabout" routes that, despite a superficial detour, will better secure ultimate gratification.

Political action is, in itself, a roundabout route to the fulfillment of most forms of self-interest. From the point of view of a frontier farmer harassed by price cuts and discrimination in freight rates, the formation of a political organization to send a representative to a distant parliamentary body is a less clear means of remedying evils than burning the grain elevator. Even where it is perceived that the path to a goal is through politics, usually a variety of more and less direct paths are available. Frequently shorter paths are less effectual than the longer. One function of ideology is to maintain the perspective of time and roundabout routes that permit the most effective long-range political evaluations.

The question of taxes provides an excellent case in point. For obvious reasons, immediate self-interest rebels against the payment of taxes. And with all other things equal, it is the rational course to advocate lighter rather than heavier tax loads. But within a progressive tax system, reduction of taxes and elimination of government services is not presumed to be in the self-interest of lower-status segments of the population. The whole ideological rationale for increased government activity—the core of our social welfare attitude structure—collapses if this interpretation of self-interest is more often than not, correct. Thus we arrive at a juncture where the demands of ideology run counter to the demands of short-term self-interest. For if simple self-interest rules, lower-status people should desire tax reduction, and we should find that the motivation to get taxes reduced "at all costs" increases simply as a function of financial need. These are, of course, precisely the findings presented previously.

We may survey our domestic policy items more generally from this new vantage point. The responses that come to form a coherent "social welfare" structure lending credence to ideological assumptions are at the same time questions in which the path of self-interest for a lower-status person is quite clear, and they are scarcely more obscure for the individual of higher status. Several of the other items that might be comfortably located in a broad liberal or conservative ideology do not turn out to fit this key structure. In a rough way, we may distinguish two types. First, there are those in which some other dimension than the economic appears primary, or in which the number of steps necessary to link a policy choice to self-interest is multiplied and hence less clear. For a person who fears unemployment, a question concerning government guarantees of employment can be directly related to self-interest. But a question about the role of business in government can only be related to self-interest if one has an understanding of business interests and the advantages conferred by political power. The items of this type show little or no relationship with items in the social welfare structure. The second type, in which there is an actual conflict posed for lower-status persons between immediate financial interest and longer-range, indirect gains, is represented only by the tax item. And in this case alone the visible relationship with items of the social welfare scale runs in a direction perfectly contrary to our ideological expectations.

In sum, then, the pattern of responses to our domestic issues is best understood if we discard our notions of ideology and think rather in terms of primitive self-interest.[6] Of course, the basic triangle of relationships between status, issue "liberalism," and party is no more difficult to account for in these terms than it is when more full-fledged ideology is assumed. Indeed, the fact that these relationships are never overwhelming in magnitude is probably a good deal *more* comprehensible once we have scaled our assumptions down in this fashion. For the possibility of widespread confusion about political means and ends among the least informed seems easier to countenance if we recognize that the level of sophistication about such matters is generally rather low.

There are other points at which we may pit ideological expectations against simpler notions of self-interest. The fact that no mean pro-

[6] Lipset has pointed out that although lower-status groups favor "liberal" policies on matters of social welfare legislation, they tend at the same time to take anti-liberal or intolerant positions on matters involving treatment of deviants or ethnic minorities. These empirical facts have contributed to Lipset's sense of dissatisfaction with common assumptions concerning the configuration of beliefs treated generically as "liberalism." He argues for a distinction between "economic" and "non-economic liberalism." See Seymour Martin Lipset, "Democracy and Working-Class Authoritarianism," *American Sociological Review,* XXIV (August, 1959). We are most sympathetic with this critique. However, the data concerning opinions on taxes suggest that even the connotations of the term "economic liberalism" may be unrealistically broad. If these attitudes have internal coherence, they are expressions of self-interest, not "liberal ideologies."

portion of lower-status people are Republican and high-status people are Democratic has always occasioned a good deal of comment. Whether we deal in terms of ideology or simpler interest concepts, these people are out of step, for they appear to espouse a political instrument counter to their interest. What forces permit them to maintain this apparent disequilibrium? Perhaps the most familiar explanation is an ideological one. For strongly ingrained ideology is one of the few motivating forces that can be seen to induce a person to act in terms of interest other than his own. The stereotype built up to account for the low-status Republican involves an origin in the tradition-bound individualism of rural America. He has had little contact with urban ideologies. He believes in the free enterprise system despite the fact that his station in the system is low. His hopes are pinned to the dream of individual mobility; schemes for collective action or government "dole" are offensive to his values of rugged individualism. Even the difficulty of his economic lot fails to overcome his deep-seated resistance to innovations that might change the basic contours of American life.

Ideology may similarly be seen as the cement that binds certain higher-status persons to the liberal party. Here two types of mechanisms receive attention. The person who has achieved status from modest beginnings may maintain his old ideology because of the deep impressions that past experiences of social inequity have made upon him. The aristocrat by birth, on the other hand, may be motivated to liberal ideals by what is essentially *noblesse oblige*. He himself has not known want and is not likely to. But he is sensitive to the fact that his position is an accident of birth and he is moved by the knowledge that others are forced to live under unnecessarily oppressive conditions. Warm and humanitarian, he wishes to invest his energies in their behalf.

There is no doubt that within mid-century America many persons fitting these descriptions could be located. In the higher-status group where individuals have greater visibility, for example, we could rapidly name a host of Democratic personages who in one degree or another resemble these types. But the question remains whether persons meeting such specifications loom at all large among the low-status Republicans and high-status Democrats to be found in a cross-section of the electorate. It is our contention that they do not, but represent instead a deviant few who have attracted attention because of the pleasing manner in which they fill ideological preconceptions.

Several pieces of data may be brought to bear on the question. Figure 9-1 shows for example that low-status Republicans fall rather close to the radical extreme of the social welfare scale.[7] Their attitudes are not greatly different from those held by Democrats of equivalent status. With these findings in hand we are not likely to be impressed by the argument that these low-status people are kept within Republican ranks by their exceptionally conservative political ideologies.

Figure 9-1 suggests that the relationship between partisanship and social welfare attitudes noted previously is slightly stronger among persons of higher education levels. In the degree that higher-status Democrats depart from the attitudes of higher-status Republicans there is an indication that ideology of the sort postulated may be playing some role. However, this role appears weak at best. We would not be convinced, for example, that the higher-status liberal maintains his unusual position by any striking commitment to liberal causes. Higher-status Democrats are very substantially more conservative in their attitudes than either low-status Democrats *or* low-status Republicans. Differences in attitude attributable to party, although statistically significant, are thoroughly eclipsed by those differences correlated with status.[8]

If the ideological explanation fails to account for the low-status Republican and the high-status Democrat, what interpretation may be substituted? Figure 9-1 (page 208) suggests again that we consider the problem in two parts. The strong attitude-status correlation that appears within each party grouping is now adequately accounted for in simple self-interest terms. The question then remains why people of low or high status with appropriate social welfare attitudes identify themselves with the "wrong" party. We must remember that a variety of other factors influence partisan choice. The importance of this fact increases as we scale down our assumptions about the role of ideological concerns in decisions by the broad electorate. For the sophisticated observer, the ramifications of some of these core domestic policy decisions are so broad that dimensions of attitude relating to them deserve heavy weight in any political choice. But in the degree that the public lacks this ideological superstructure, the significance accorded such policy matters must be somewhat less. Consequently, other factors independent of these concerns, such as candidate attractiveness or long-standing party loyalty, increase in relative importance.

[7] For reasons that will be apparent in the subsequent text, we use education as the criterion of status in this figure. However, other status criteria produce similar. patterns.

[8] Although this is clear even on the basis of Fig. 9-1, the use of a single status criterion understates the full significance of the status dimension in predicting social welfare attitudes. For example, income as a second criterion makes a considerable independent contribution to the prediction of attitudes.

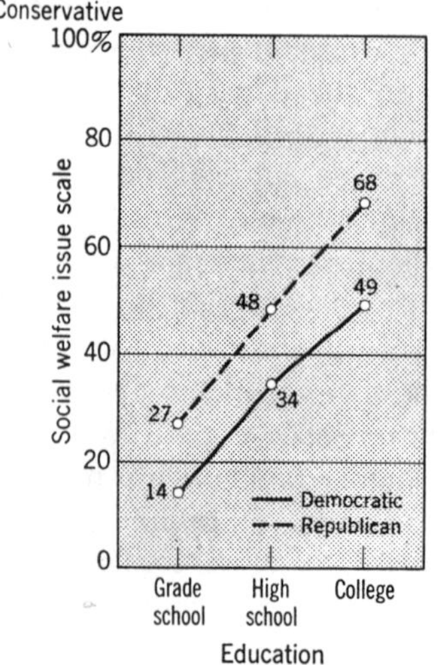

Fig. 9-1. Relation of education to social welfare attitudes, by party.

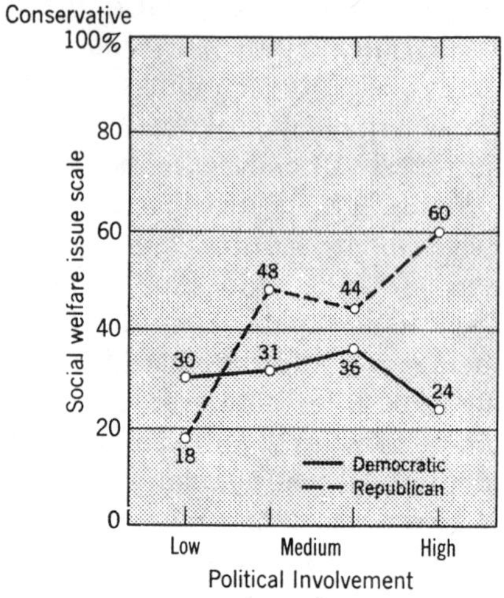

Fig. 9-2. Relation of political involvement to social welfare attitudes, by party.

Furthermore, although people presented with certain policy alternatives can do a reasonable job of selecting responses that appear to further their self-interest, this fact is in itself no guarantee that they have ever sorted out how the parties stand on the matter. If the person has never been motivated to follow political affairs closely, we can well imagine that he may feel a bond with a party and may be able to discern self-interest in a set of policy propositions without having established a link between the party and its policy position.

This possibility is supported by Fig. 9-2 above, which shows that partisan differences on social welfare attitudes are indeed dependent on political involvement. Differences between adherents of the two parties are sharpest among the most highly involved; where involvement is low, there is no significant variation in social welfare attitude by party. Thus we conclude that one important factor in the choice of a party that is "wrong" in view of the individual's social welfare attitudes and status location is simple indifference and the lack of information thereby implied.

Generally, then, closer examination of some of the connections that have been assumed to exist on the basis of the original triangle of status, attitude, and party relationship reveals a variety of gaps. Although from time to time we catch glints of possible ideology operating, by and large the pattern of relationships that are statistically significant is explicable only in terms of a much more modest self-interest assumption. And even the simple self-interest assumption produces partisan relationships only where there is some degree of formal education and involvement in politics.

Ideology as a Posture toward Change

Thus far we have examined the role of ideology in terms of self-interest and content themes peculiar to our immediate era. Notions about ideological structure are often extended to include generalized responses toward change. In this vein, whatever the content of ideological controversy, the liberal seeks amelioration through innovation; the conservative hesitates to court the unknown. This theme is easily wedded to the self-interest theme: people who have attained comfort and privilege are not eager to see the *status quo* disturbed and may oppose change on a broad front, whereas those who have fared less well have little to lose and much to gain by change. But this theme is also seen as an independent source of conservative or liberal ideology. It is often suggested, for example, that older people are more likely to be Republican because apprehension about change increases with age, and this apprehension becomes translated into conservative political attitudes and increased probability of support for the conservative party. Similarly, people living in remote and rural areas are often presumed to be tradition-bound in a manner that gives a strong conservative cast to their political ideologies.

Therefore, although we have come to doubt that attitude organization of the scope implied by the term "ideology" underlies the sparse lines of structure that we have isolated in public opinion, a generalized sense of affect toward potential change may contribute to responses on domestic issue policies. This hypothetical predisposition need not be any attribute that the actor himself could recognize in his own thinking. If we present situations in which traditional values are questioned and gage the individual's reaction, we may be able to sort people into those who are relatively more or less receptive to the prospect of change, whether or not the individuals involved might be able to articulate their general feelings about change.

However, when scales designed to measure "resistance to change," "traditionalism," or some related variable are applied to cross-section populations, we immediately encounter patterns that are, from the point of view of ideological expectations, rather anomalous. People in lower social strata register as substantially more conservative than do people of higher status. Thus the same portion of the population that the investigator decides to classify as "liberal" or "radical" in the light of its response to questions of public policy appears least receptive to change in a generic sense.

If we are willing to set our political preconceptions aside, this finding is as eminently reasonable as is the finding that policy matters are reacted to in terms of simple self-interest. We readily associate traditionalism and apprehension about the possibility of change with people for whom education and life horizons have been most restricted. Our sense of discontinuity arises, then, because of the sophisticated political concepts that we bring to bear on the matter. Endorsement of government activity in medical insurance is, *ipso facto,* an endorsement of substantial change in governmental responsibilities, change of great ideological significance. If we apply close logic to the situation, there is a basic contradiction in subscribing to such signal change on one hand, while wishing on the other that "things would not change so much."

But this logic depends upon a great deal of knowledge, which most respondents fail to share with the analyst. The person who has little or no grasp of traditional governmental roles is not likely to shy away from the social welfare proposition because it will strain the fabric of familiar political forms. Even where the fact of change is made clear, it can hardly be of paramount concern to the person who has no sense of its implications. If change signifies becoming "better off" in a simple and concrete sense, it is not likely to be refused. Evaluations can be formulated at this level without imputing further trappings of ideology.

McClosky has devised a scale of conservatism that we have applied to our national sample.[9] Although constructed directly from writings on conservatism by political philosophers, the items are not expressly political. The nature of change toward which attitudes are measured covers a broad variety of forms of innovation. The correlates that this measure of resistance to change reveals within our national sample are familiar. We find, for example, an inverse relationship between status (particularly as measured by education) and resistance to change.[10] There is, furthermore, a substantial tendency for conserva-

[9] Herbert McClosky, "Conservatism and Personality," *American Political Science Review,* LII (March, 1958), 27–45.

[10] The McClosky measure of conservatism is subject to a severe problem of response set, which is itself correlated with social status. A fairly adequate method of removing this artifact has been developed from independent sources within our materials. All findings presented here concerning this measure remain after the response set is controlled.

tism to increase with age, as we might expect on common sense grounds. McClosky has also demonstrated a network of empirical relationships between this measure and other deeper "personality" dimensions.[11] But of the relationships that emerge when conservatism is laid against more specific political attitudes, McClosky writes:

> The correlation (s) between them tend, however, to be fairly low, suggesting that for the present, at least, many Americans divide in their party preferences, their support of candidates, their economic views, their stands on public issues, or their political self-identifications without reference to their beliefs in liberalism or conservatism. The latter have influence, of course, especially among some of the more articulate groups; for the general population, however, political divisions of the sort named appear to be more affected by group membership factors than by personality.[12]

These findings are clearly corroborated by our data on a national sample. If a "positive" relationship is one that fits ideological assumptions, we find that conservatism shows a patchwork of negative, positive, and indeterminate relationships with various of the social welfare and domestic items. As we might expect, one large positive correlation emerges in connection with the tax question. However, this result matches ideological predictions for reasons that are entirely spurious. Only one of the five attitudes included in the social welfare structure (public versus private production of electricity and housing) shows a positive correlation; two of the five (employment guarantees and medical care) show negative correlations of a magnitude surpassing any of the positive relationships, including that involved in the tax question.[13]

Similarly, the absence of direct relationships between conservatism and partisanship fit McClosky's description. Even with Southern respondents excluded there is no significant correlation between conservatism and party identification. In short, if we focus upon the total range of individuals represented in the national electorate, we find almost no correlation between a general disposition that we would expect to be of prime political relevance and variation in issue attitudes or partisanship. However, we may locate subgroups in the population for which sophisticated expectations do receive some support. These islands of support become highly instructive in assessing the reasons for discontinuity elsewhere. For example, McClosky,

[11] *Ibid.*

[12] *Ibid.*, pp. 44–45.

[13] It is possible that with sufficiently stringent controls exerted on status location more positive relationships between conservatism and issue attitude would emerge. Unfortunately, as the conservatism scale was applied to only a subset of our respondents, we lack sufficient cases to press the matter further.

before applying his scale to a cross-section population, used it with leaders of both political parties. He found that it discriminated at a very satisfactory level between Republican and Democratic elites.[14] Now we can surmise that such party leadership must have differed radically from a "normal" population in a number of ways. First, such people certainly would rank as highly involved in politics. Second, we would suppose them to have a very abnormal command of political events and recent party history. Third, it is likely that they were disproportionately people of high education, for whom conceptual abstractions of the sort used in ideological thinking are relatively common coin.

These traits that distinguish political party elites are traits shared with the several "spectator" elites—journalistic and academic—who tend to apply concepts such as the liberal-conservative continuum to analyses of political motivations and events. The fact that theoretical expectations are borne out within party elites attests once again to the value of such concepts for the understanding of behavior in these circles. But party activists of this type represent such a tiny fraction of the electorate that they are too few to permit analysis even in a relatively large national sample. These data lead to the same conclusion as our preceding analyses: as we depart from the extreme combinations of involvement, background, and education, represented by such elites, the significance of familiar ideological frames of reference drops off rapidly. It is not hard to see why the sophisticated observer is readily misled in his analytic constructions. He recognizes of course that individuals differ in the partisan or issue content of their political beliefs, for he sees these differences contested in the daily drama of politics at an elite level. But he falls prey to the assumption that the same basic frames of reference are shared by all citizens who take any interest in politics whatever.

We have suggested in Chapter 7 that most citizens tend to locate themselves in a political party at an early point in their adult life, and that this identification typically then gains strength throughout life. The party that wins favor appears to depend predominantly upon social transmission from the family or early reference groups. The critical initial decision appears to be taken most frequently under strong social influence early in life, when involvement in politics is at low ebb, and, presumably, political information is most scanty as well. Thus if involvement and background are preconditions for the establishment of meaningful links between basic values and party preference, then we must suppose that in the bulk of cases, the individual is

[14] *Ibid.*

committed to a party at a time when he is least likely to have the wherewithal to bring ideological considerations of this sort into play. Thereafter, the self-reinforcing aspects of a psychological identification progressively reduce the probability of change in partisan allegiance. If the crucial identifications were postponed until the individual had observed the parties for some time with the modest but more active involvement and fuller information of the middle-aged adult, we would expect that ultimate partisanship would show more convincing relationships with underlying values of this sort. Or if the psychological potency of party identification were weaker later in life, so that existing partisanship dictated less thoroughly the interpretation of political events, we might also expect more rearrangement of partisanship to achieve better fit with underlying values. In the absence of these conditions the impression of discontinuity between such values and partisanship remains almost complete.

If our analysis is correct, however, we would expect to find some further islands of evidence for this type of political value structure within even a national sample. For there are individuals in the population who have thrown over initial party allegiance later in life. If involvement and information increase with age and are preconditions for the organization of political behavior in a manner congruent with underlying values, then we would predict that the small fraction of the electorate that has shifted party identification later in life would show more visible signs of such organization than we find among nonchangers. These deductions apply to "late" changers only when the motivation for change is not as superficially social as we have presumed much initial party identification to be. Among the total number of our respondents who report that they have changed party identification at one time or another, some 15 to 20 per cent indicate that the reason for change was primarily social.[15] If we remove these people from consideration, we find that persons who have changed party identification on "political" grounds divide as shown in Table 9-3 (page 214) with regard to the liberal-conservative dimension.

As we move from liberal to conservative elements among changers, the flow from party to party comes to favor the Republican Party more and more. This relationship is not overwhelming in strength; it is apparent that a substantial amount of change occurs in the direction opposite to our sophisticated expectations. Yet the relationship between conservatism and current Republican Party identification is

15 The most frequent response of this sort comes from the wife who reports that the "main thing that made (her) change" was marriage to a person of opposing partisan allegiance.

TABLE 9-3. Relation of Liberalism-Conservatism to Change in Party Identification

	McClosky Scale		
Change in Party Identification	Liberal	Medium	Conservative
Were Democratic, became Republican	58%	69%	81%
Were Republican, became Democratic	42	31	19
	100%	100%	100%
Number of cases	31	26	16

higher among this small portion of the population than it is within any other subgroup of comparable size that seemed plausible to consider. It is substantially higher here, for example, than among the total group of college-educated people within our sample.

As hypothesized, then, change in party identification later in life contributes some small relationship between conservatism and political partisanship that would not otherwise have existed in a national sample. Changers are too few to press the matter further with great confidence. But we do find that in absolute terms (subject to sampling error), the relationship between conservatism and current party identification is visibly higher among persons who changed party after 35 years of age than it is among people who changed earlier in life.[16] Finally, although our cases remain few, there seems to be no relationship between direction of party change and conservatism among those individuals who report change of party as a result of social influence.

Generally, whether we approach ideology in terms of attitudes on policy issues or in terms of broad postures toward change, our data appear to tell very much the same story. The closer the individual stands to the sophisticated observer in education and political involvement, the more likely it is that the observer's analytic constructs will bear fruit.

The findings concerning change of party identification add a further dimension to the discussion. If partisan attachments tend to represent lifelong commitments for the vast majority of the public, it is not

[16] If we reduce the measure of conservatism to a dichotomy in the manner that maximizes balance of cases, we find that among people changing party before 35 (Number of cases, 25), the proportion of more conservative individuals becoming Republican is only 7 per cent greater than the same proportion within the more liberal group. Within the older changers (Number of cases, 30), however, the comparable difference is 20 per cent.

surprising that ideological concerns seem trivial in attempting to account for the mainstream of political behavior. On the other hand, if we are interested primarily in understanding political change, we may be willing to ignore sixty to eighty per cent of the population entirely, focusing upon the minority that appear to contribute to the tides of partisan victory and defeat. It is at the point of political change, then, that attitude structures partaking of ideology might loom more important.

The effects apparent in Table 9-3 are not in themselves of a magnitude to assure us that this role is very great. We must remember that less than ten per cent of the population reported some past change in party identification linked to events outside the primary-group milieu. Even within this narrow subgroup, conservatism failed to account for a very large portion of the variance in the direction of partisan change. Furthermore, the changes in party identification juxtaposed in Table 9-3 are scattered through several decades of political history and do not all pertain to any partisan shift observable in a shorter period.

Nevertheless, the table is suggestive. And it does not purport to cover all partisan change that may occur from election to election, but only the portion which involves actual realignment of party loyalties. We have made it clear that under certain circumstances a person may vote against his preferred party for a time without shifting his party loyalty. Although the type of change captured in the table is probably the more significant, other more transient forms of change might be attributable to ideological perceptions, and need to be taken into account as well.

We may comment further on the problem of partisan change over time by undertaking another approach to the analysis of ideology. We have suggested that the types of attitude structure presumed in ideological accounts of political behavior are not very prevalent in the American electorate. Though we could never expect great precision in this matter, it would be convenient to have a firmer sense of how prevalent they are. Further analysis in this direction might also improve our understanding of the various modes of conceptual organization that are brought to bear on matters of policy controversy, *in lieu of* full-blown ideology. Some estimate of the relative incidence of these modes of concept formation would not only help to corroborate suspicions expressed in this chapter; we might also inquire as to whether any greater potential for partisan change may be associated with some of these modes than with others, and thereby throw more light on the issue meaning of political change.

The Formation of Issue Concepts and Partisan Change ◇ 10

The popularity of the conservative-liberal distinction has been particularly notable in analyses of partisan change from election to election. If a liberal party wins an unusually strong popular vote, we are frequently informed that the public mandate is for a shift toward the left in governmental policy; if the party of the right gains new support, the public has become "cautious" or conservative about further political change. When the parties are loose coalitions of conservative and liberal wings, the meaning of the election outcome may be pursued at the level of legislative seats. Which wing within each of the parties showed the higher mortality rate in the balloting?

Any election may elicit diverse explanations, for change can hinge upon several crucial terms in the equation. If the Democratic Party is buried under a landslide of Republican votes, it may be argued that the electorate has become more conservative, that the Democratic Party has pushed too far to the left, that the Republican Party has moved in to capture votes of the "center," or any combination of the three. Other ingenious analyses incorporate still further plausible variables. The staunch partisan, finding that his party has lost strength in an election, may resist the conclusion that the public is departing from his ideological position, and claim instead that his party, by compromising its principles to win votes of the center, has left a large body of its more extreme clientele too disgruntled to participate in the election.

Despite their differences, all these accounts depend on similar assumptions concerning the frames of reference used by the electorate to assess political events. Such accounts presume that some significant portion of the electorate is (1) sensitive to its own policy mood in terms of a left-right continuum; and (2) is sensitive as well to the shifting policy positions of both parties on the same continuum. The notion of the continuum is as crucial as the content here. The assumption is not simply that people consider one party to be "left" and the other "right" in a dichotomous sense. Instead, there is presumed to be some perception of distance separating the parties, and this distance can be discriminated as greater or lesser at differing points in time. Often it is presumed as well that people also have a sense of the distance of either party from a neutral point, a "middle of the road."

In view of the data we have presented these assumptions strain our credulity; yet, we cannot reject them out of hand. We have found some evidence to suggest that for a fraction of the American population these assumptions may be realistic. And the changes in the partisan vote division that attract these ideological descriptions rarely exceed a magnitude of ten per cent of the active electorate. Thus it is conceivable that a balance of power may be held by a small minority of ideologues who are sensitive to shifts of the parties along a left-right continuum. Whether this view is valid is critical to an understanding of the issue meaning of partisan change.

If the liberal-conservative notion is not common, as we have maintained, the question remains as to what frames of reference for ordering issue concerns *do* enjoy more widespread use. Certainly the process of political evaluation is carried on by most citizens, and this process leads to more or less predictable organization of behavior. Furthermore, there are broad currents to this behavior, as observed in the mass, which lend themselves admirably to treatment in the ideological terms discussed above. The great exodus of voters from the conservative party during the dire economic stress of the 1930's in this country is an excellent case in point. Since the migration was toward a party more receptive to change in the existing structure of political, social, and economic relationships, this trend has been taken to reflect the rejection of the old order by an exercised populace. More recently, the increasing electoral success of the Republican Party has been taken to signify a return to the middle of the road, a "revolt of the moderates" after a sharp detour to the left.

If ideology in a sophisticated sense is not widespread in the population, there must be surrogates for ideology that bring large aggregates to act *as though* propelled by ideological concerns. It is important to understand the character of these surrogates not only to satisfy intellectual curiosity, but also because the fact that they are surrogates rather than full-blown ideology may from time to time lead to crucial differences in behavior.

The Formation of Political Concepts at a Mass Level

Smith, Bruner, and White, in their volume *Opinions and Personality,* report an intensive analysis of the political attitudes of ten relatively well-informed and intelligent subjects. Nine of the ten, on the basis of their performance in a standardized test, ranked within the top 10 per cent of the national population in intellectual capacity. Of the tenth, the authors write:

> Many of the verbal coins used in the exchange of opinions were unfamiliar to him, so that we had to learn his views without relying on such standard pieces as "Socialism," "Liberalism," "veto" and "isolationism." . . . At a concrete level he functioned effectively, showing good common sense and practical judgment. It was in the realm of abstraction that his limitations were most marked. . . . He never read books, rarely listened to the radio, and did little more than scan such newspapers and magazines as came his way. Both his information and his opinions were arrived at almost wholly through channels of conversation.[1]

Now "Sam Hodder," as this anonymous subject is called, was not a person of meager intelligence. He was *well above the average* in basic intellectual capacity, standing in the top twenty per cent of a cross-section population. But limited to a grade school education and subsequent life as a factory employee, events had not conspired to foster those habits of abstract concept formation taken for granted in intellectual strata of the society. Despite substantial innate capacity, then, even Sam Hodder did not in practice measure up to the expectations of political concept formation that often seem assumed for the bulk of the electorate.

Politically, Sam Hodder seems an average sort. He is not without opinions on public issues that have caught his attention. To be sure, there are numerous "prominent" political debates of which he is unaware, and his issue opinions have not sprung from any differentiated view of history, of government, or of social process. But he has undoubtedly arrived at an abiding preference for one of the major parties and implements this preference with fair regularity at the polls. In fact, he may have been one contributor to the mass shift of the

[1] M. Brewster Smith, Jerome S. Bruner, and Robert W. White, *Opinions and Personality* (John Wiley and Sons, New York, 1956), p. 196.

American public to the party of the "left" under the burden of events of the 1930's. What makes Sam Hodder tick politically?

The description provided by Smith, Bruner, and White is rather truncated, in part because Sam Hodder was not the most rewarding subject they examined, and in part because they were restricting their attention to attitudes toward Russia rather than partisan political behavior. Enough background is given, however, to make us feel that we have met Sam Hodder many times in our own free-answer protocols from a national population. We know that he is a union member, and "had taken a part, though not a prominent one" in the original union organization of the plant. Nonetheless, his union participation is described as "casual," and he is "little interested in long-range plans for social betterment."[2]

We would imagine that if we asked Sam Hodder what he liked and disliked about the major parties, his predominant opinion would be that he liked the Democratic Party because "it is the party of the working man." If his political world was largely undifferentiated, he might have few perceptions beyond this. If there were further differentiation, he would perhaps indicate that the Republican Party had shown him it was actively against labor or the worker, or actively for big business, management, or one of the "natural" antagonists of the working man. He might be able, also, to document his impressions by reference to specific events or policy debates: the role of the parties in the Depression, or the championing of legislation such as Taft-Hartley or social security. His view of partisan politics might be more or less differentiated, but his evaluations would revolve around the perception that one of the parties took special pains to look after the day-to-day interests of a significant grouping in the population with which he identified.

This is not ideology in a programmatic sense. There is little comprehension here of the basic problems that lead to the need for political protection; nor is there, as we have said, any interest in "long-range plans" that would aim at resolution of these problems. In fact, there is little that requires abstract thinking at all: the most significant elements of this sort implied are the quasi-abstractions "group" and "interest." As the authors note, "because of his concrete thinking he could not [attribute evil to] an abstract construct such as the economic order." He is concerned with politics to the degree that he feels that political change might rob him and others like him of their jobs or of concrete benefits involving wages, working conditions, and the like. He has no conception of the modes whereby political power secures

[2] *Ibid.*, pp. 196–198.

or protects interests—these are the concerns of group leadership, whether that leadership be of union or of party. Having perceived some correlation between group success and the emergence of concrete benefits, he is willing to put his faith in any leadership that has shown enough interest in his group to figure out what must be done to maintain its welfare. He partakes of ideology by endorsing a leadership that has ideology. He engages, so to speak, in an "ideology by proxy."

This is not to say that Sam Hodder could never be jarred loose from these loyalties. Quite to the contrary, we must suppose that he remains a perceiving, evaluating individual with a healthy capacity for suspicion. If he were to suffer economic distress under circumstances in which the union appeared impotent or indifferent, or if the party stopped doing things that he felt made his lot a better one, he would undoubtedly cast about for new loyalties, new leadership.

But the difference between ideology and "ideology by proxy" is more than academic. For at points of political change the concepts employed by Sam Hodder in his evaluations make for critical differences in attitude and behavior. Let us suppose that union and party are committed to long-range economic, political, and social change toward the general end of improving the lot of many Sam Hodders; that is, we will suppose that union and party are, in ideological terms, "of the left." Now suppose that over a period of time union and party leadership swing back toward the center or even come to collude with the right, although by one mechanism or another the day-to-day security of Sam's economic position is maintained. If Sam were ideologically inclined he might become disturbed and disillusioned at the forsaking of broader goals. Sensitive to ideological matters, he would behave as the analyst would presume: the changed relationship between his own position and that of the group on an underlying ideological continuum would change the values that the group held for him. He might participate in moves to change the leadership, or he might seek more promising agents further to the left.

Without such frames of reference he has little reason even to be aware that change has occurred. As long as concrete experience within his perceived world goes on as usual, his loyalties will proceed as usual also. To the degree that these loyalties color his interpretation of events, they may even proceed despite some "objective" contradiction in events. Or if the fact of change in goals should actually be brought to Sam's attention, he would lack any independent reference points from which to evaluate the matter. Leadership programs have helped him in the past. If leadership ideas have changed, it is probably for good reason; the people at the top are in a better position to know what must be done than he is. He will always be able to judge what are, for him, the "results." Hence under certain circumstances the total flavor of political events may come to depend on the level at which the many "followers" like Sam Hodder have been in the habit of conceptualizing their relevant experience.

Favorable or unfavorable reactions to the political parties or candidates often consist of beliefs that they are agents that will aid or ignore this or that grouping in the population. In some of our protocols these perceptions are connected tightly with other comments more clearly ideological in character. But often it is apparent under probing by the interviewer that the respondent does not fit these notions of group benefit into any broader or more abstract frame of reference. They are, of course, self-sufficient without it: there is nothing logically incomplete in the belief that a leader or party is sensitive to problems unique to a social grouping.

However simple these conceptions of politics may appear, there are many people in the American electorate whose modes of conceptualizing the political world and its social or economic consequences are a good deal less complex still and who appear even more remote from the type of thinking presumed by "ideology." In a diffuse way "times are good" or "times are bad"—there is war or peace, depression or prosperity. If some pattern can be perceived linking the nature of the times with a particular party in power, this pattern may come to be considered a causal sequence. Once again, however, after such perceptions have been volunteered, further probing usually seems to indicate that most political issue content has thereby been exhausted.

There are many citizens whose issue perceptions are even more impoverished. Some of these people are staunch adherents of one of the political parties, although they freely admit it is simply a matter of family tradition and they personally have no idea what the parties "stand for." Others ignore the parties despite direct questioning, and focus their political evaluations upon the personal characteristics of the current candidates themselves—their sincerity, their religious beliefs, their family life, their "popularity." And, finally, there are those who lack the interest or background to differentiate successfully between either the candidates or the parties.

It seems important to estimate the incidence of these various modes of conceptualizing issue controversy in a cross section of the adult population. Unfortunately, there are no simple yardsticks to measure the sophistication of a person's conceptualization. We cannot quantify the character of a person's political conceptions even in the loose manner with which we measure the intensity of attitudes. We are interested in the presence or absence of certain abstractions that have to do with ideology; but we are also interested in the degree to which the individual's political world is differentiated and, most important, in the nature of the degree of "connectedness" between the elements that are successfully discriminated. In short, we are interested in the structure of thought that the individual applies to politics; and this interest forces us to deal in typologies and qualitative differences.

Toward this end we attempted to assign our 1956 respondents to various "levels" of conceptualization on the basis of their discursive responses in evaluating the good and bad points of the two parties and the two candidates, as described in Chapter 4.[3] Despite the inevitable crudities of the categories employed, these levels seemed to provide a clear ordering in terms of conceptual sophistication. The expected ordering turned out to receive striking confirmation in other characteristics of the occupants at successive levels. And the classification system was sufficiently clear to insure satisfactory inter-rater reliability.[4]

The nature of the categories used has been foreshadowed above. A fairly flexible view of ideology was taken as a point of departure, and lower levels involved an increasing remoteness in content and in level of conceptualization from this "ideal." Each respondent was assigned to the highest level warranted by any portion of his commentary. Although some finer differentiations were employed in the actual coding process, we shall focus most of our attention upon four major levels.

The first of these (to be denoted Level A) embraces all respondents whose evaluations of the candidates and the parties have any suggestion of the abstract conception one would associate with ideology. We did not wish to be bound to familiar content in assessing this level of issue conceptualization. However, it rapidly became apparent that virtually all high-order abstractions used were familiar from current political commentary. This seems to mean simply that insights as to basic new ordering dimensions are not likely to be forthcoming in a restricted sample of the population. Even our most sophisticated respondents were no more than alert consumers of the refined content of the political culture. They might express original viewpoints, but they were totally dependent on the standard abstractions for their

[3] The interviewer is instructed to probe extensively for further content on each of the eight questions comprising the sequence. This instruction is generally successful enough that this portion of the interview schedule absorbs on the average ten to fifteen minutes of time near the beginning of the questionnaire.

[4] Eighty-two per cent of 211 respondents independently classified by different coders were assigned to the same one of our broad levels. Only 3 per cent were discrepancies beyond an adjacent level.

basic conceptual tools. We did encounter one or two respondents who might be suspected of seeking unfamiliar dimensions of high abstraction. These people were included in Level A. Otherwise, persons placed here talked in terms of the liberal-conservative continuum, or one of the narrower domains of abstract content involved in current ideological controversy: trends in the relationship between federal power and local autonomy, the fate of individual incentive under government "dole," and the like.

The second grouping (Level B) was reserved for persons whose issue comment revolved around fairly concrete and short-term group interest, or what we have already described in some detail as "ideology by proxy." In the next category (Level C) were persons engrossed in simplistic associations between the "goodness" and "badness" of the times and the identity of the party in power, or who appeared to have exhausted their view of the situation with mention of some rather isolated and specific issue. The final level (Level D) thereby contains individuals who evaluated the political objects without recourse to issues that might fairly be related to debates over domestic public policy. Excluded as true issue content, for example, were observations concerning mudslinging, charges of graft, comments on the personal attributes of the candidates, or references to their age, health, or past experience. It should also be kept in mind that our concern is with public policy relevant to *domestic* social and economic problems. Although foreign policy matters may, by some criteria, be intimately related to domestic policy questions, they are not treated in this discussion. Their exclusion rests in part on the previously described absence of relationship between domestic and foreign policy issue concerns among the general public, in part on the absence of any analytic relationship that could be postulated apart from the specific content of particular ideologies, and in part on the need for maximizing simplicity in our explication of this innovation in political analysis.

Although our central focus was upon the abstract concepts implied in the commentary, attention was also paid to the degree of differentiation and the "connectedness" of the ideas in which critical issue perceptions were imbedded. Since variation at this point was wide enough to justify internal distinctions within some of the gross levels, it is important to illustrate how the presence or absence of "normal" connections between ideas is communicated by the protocols. For example, a storekeeper in upstate New York responded in the following manner to questioning about the parties:

I'd like to ask you what you think are the good and bad points about the two parties. Is there anything in particular that you like about the Democratic Party?

I don't know much about the Democratic Party so I cannot answer one way or the other.

Is there anything in particular that you don't like about the Democratic Party?

The only thing I associate the Democratic Party with is that it seems to be the party that is in power during a war.

Is there anything in particular that you like about the Republican Party?

I think that the Republican Party has handled the foreign situation —that is, the cold war—with success, and it is always associated in my mind with peace and prosperity.

Is there anything in particular that you don't like about the Republican Party?

Nothing that I can think of.

Here the simple links in the respondent's mind between party and non-political states (war, peace, prosperity) are extremely clear. In general, we are willing to assume that absence of commentary means absence of linkage that would draw other elements into association with political objects. In some cases, however, the response includes several elements that the individual cannot seem to link in the normal fashion. For example, a woman in Indianapolis, having indicated at the outset that she did not know much about "any of this" and was "not a good one to talk to," upon further questioning as to reactions toward the Democratic Party, responded:

> Well, I've heard people—a lot of them say they're more for the working man. And I noticed all big union leaders are for them. But I don't know and don't understand just how they're for the working man. Like I told you, I honestly don't know much.

In this case, the individual has absorbed enough political content to realize that certain links are imputed often between party and a segment of the population, but is unable to bring meaning to the association. Similarly, a farm laborer in California included the following remarks in his response to the party questions:

> I don't think it makes much difference to poor people—*any* of their parties don't do nothin' for us. I got hurt and I still had to go to the Welfare to get my bills paid—the *party* don't pay you. Poor people don't get nothin' from bein' interested in politics.

Here the ingredients are present for a response fitting Level B: the speaker perceives in thoroughly concrete terms the interests of a grouping in the population with which he identifies. But his immediate experience has failed to suggest to him the possible links between political power and the existence or conduct of the welfare agency. However completely these links may be taken for granted among the sophisticated, perceptions of this sort force us to reflect on the subtlety and intangibility of such relationships. For the person whose perceptions are bound to his concrete, day-to-day experience, they are far from self-evident.

We were eager to avoid a number of potential pitfalls in a classification procedure of this order. We did not wish the assignment to be influenced by the partisan implication of the concepts employed. To the degree that the two parties tend to stress different ideological vocabularies, we desired to give each party vocabulary equal recognition. Similarly, the respondent who dislikes a party because it caters to the interests of special groups is employing concepts at the same level as the person who expresses gratitude for this interest, and should therefore receive the same classification. In short, we were not interested in the partisan product of the evaluation process, but rather in the character of the concepts that were playing a role in that process.

Secondly, we did not wish to confuse enthusiasm for quality of conception. A person who felt very strongly about a particular evaluation was not to be rated more highly than a person who used the same concepts for an offhand evaluation. To be sure, we would expect the individual who is intensely interested in politics to have arrived at different organizing concepts than the person who pays little attention to political events. But we need not think that a sense of pleasure or displeasure about a candidate or party that is fuzzy in focus and vague in source is intrinsically weak in its motivational significance for the individual. Particularly if the person lacks the capacity to organize what might seem more "telling" evaluative structures, these vague premonitions can be emotionally consuming. Consider the following interview:

> *I'd like to ask you what you think are the good and bad points about the two parties. Is there anything in particular that you like about the Democratic Party?*
>
> No, there's nothing I've got against them. I feel that Eisenhower ought to have a show. He's done a lot in his first four years and he should have a chance at another four years. He's pulled us out of the war and kept us out of war these last four years. I think he's done wonders myself! Of course there's his health but I think he'll pull out of that all right. Give him good thoughts! (*Give him good thoughts?*) Yes. (*Pray for him?*) Sure. I liked him when he came in the first time. I like the looks of his face.

Is there anything in particular that you don't like about the Democratic Party?

No, I've got nothing against them, only I believe in giving Eisenhower a show for what he's done. Let him finish one! The only thing I've got against them is they'll just have to start where Eisenhower started from. We aren't going to be any better off.

Is there anything in particular that you like about the Republican Party?

Nothing in particular, no. (*Anything in general?*) Well, I've always been a Republican, and my husband was, too.

Is there anything in particular that you don't like about the Republican Party?

No!

Now I'd like to ask you about the good and bad points of the two candidates for President. Is there anything in particular about Stevenson that might make you want to vote for him?

No—I have got nothing against him or nothing for him as far as that goes. He might make a good man and all that. But he'll just have to start again and all that. But the way things are in such a mess I think Eisenhower should continue.

Is there anything in particular about Stevenson that might make you want to vote against him?

No, I don't know anything about the man.

Is there anything in particular about Eisenhower that might make you want to vote for him?

Well, I just like him for what he's done. (*Anything in particular in mind?*) Well, he's pulled us out of the war. I can't just say what other things he's done.

Is there anything in particular about Eisenhower that might make you want to vote against him?

No.

There was no lack of intensity in this Michigan woman's admiration for the Eisenhower Administration. Only one "issue" theme—the termination of the Korean War—can be mustered to illustrate the "wonders" accomplished, yet there is an obvious fervor in the evaluation that might not be matched even where much fuller documentation of good works is available to the individual. It is likely that the traditional Republican partisanship mentioned had predisposed this respondent to evaluate the Republican candidate positively, and perceptions of good works could arise from such a base even though the individual knew little or nothing of what the incumbent had actually done or "stood for." If this woman could not proceed beyond the war issue in supporting her impressions, however, we should not leap to the conclusion that she had never recognized and evaluated other specific positions taken by the Administration. We lack evidence to make a judgment either way.

The crucial fact for our purposes is that these specific details, if they were ever apprehended, readily escape her. They have not been captured on any preserving framework of generalized notions concerning what is politically desirable. They have not become lodged as illustrations of a broader direction in which the Administration is heading. They were discrete perceptions without meaning, save as proof of the benevolence of party or candidate; and, otherwise isolated, they have rapidly faded beyond recall. The residue is a real and potent "glow" felt toward the relevant objects, but it is the result of an evaluation process rather remote from that of the "ideologue." Motivation may be high at any level of conceptualization, and we tried to honor this fact in our classification.

Differences in Political Concept-Formation: Illustrations from a Cross-Section Sample

Level A, ideology and near-ideology. We shall consider two categories of respondents distinguished within Level A. The first was reserved for persons whose comments imply the kinds of conception of politics assumed by ideological interpretations of political behavior and political change. We shall refer to these individuals as "ideologues." The second category within Level A includes people who employ concepts of some ideological flavor but who, for one reason or another, do not apply them in a manner that seems to qualify them as "ideologues."

Some people clearly perceived a fundamental liberal-conservative continuum on which various of the political objects might be located and along which these objects might shift relative positions over time. Although we were more interested in the fact of this conception than in the manner in which the individual related himself to it, in most cases such respondents clearly located themselves at one or another point on the continuum and evaluated the parties or factions within parties from this position. These ideologues are not, from a sophisticated point of view, exceptional observers. Their commentary is neither profound, stimulating, nor creative. But they have absorbed some of the ideological abstractions of our day, and are able to put them to use in their political evaluations. In brief, they are the persons who fulfill most clearly the assumptions about political perceptions discussed at the beginning of the chapter.

It should not be inferred that mastery of the terms "liberal" or "conservative" was necessary for inclusion in this upper "ideologue" grouping of Level A. The category was open to respondents who might deal in rather unorthodox modes of organization, although only a case or two of this variety was recruited.[5] Similarly, some respondents who appeared unaware of the sophisticated terms banked their evaluations of the parties on perceptions that the Democrats "rushed into things too fast" or were willing to "work on problems right when they came up, not hanging back like the Republicans." Comments of this sort, although very rare, cut so directly to the heart of the liberal-conservative distinction that there was no question of their classification in the upper grouping of Level A. These are clearly people whose conceptions are subsumed in the descriptions of the "liberal" or "conservative" temper of the public mind.

The first interview drawn from this upper category within Level A is somewhat unusual in the degree of content pertaining to state politics, but otherwise is quite representative of the responses that received this classification. The respondent is a woman residing in the suburbs of Chicago.

> (*Like about Democrats?*)[6] No. (*Is there anything at all you like about the Democratic Party?*) No, nothing at all.
>
> (*Dislike about Democrats?*) From being raised in a notoriously Republican section—a small town downstate—there were things I didn't like. There was family influence that way. (*What in particular was there you didn't like about the Democratic Party?*) Well, the Democratic Party tends to favor socialized medicine—and I'm being influenced in that because I came from a doctor's family.
>
> (*Like about Republicans?*) Well, I think they're more middle-of-the-road—more conservative. (*How do you mean, "conservative"?*) They are not so subject to radical change. (*Is there anything else in particular that you like about the Republican Party?*) Oh, I like their foreign policy—and the segregation business, that's a middle-of-the-road policy. You can't push it too fast. You can instigate things, but you have to let

[5] A Kentucky woman who seemed to be struggling to express an ordering dimension rather distinct from the liberal-conservative continuum is commenting unfavorably about the Democratic Party:

> They are being more Europeanized. It's too much a party. The party does it instead of the voters. The party rather than their goal is important.

Or, of the Republicans:

> They do not seem to be so much a party. They seem to be working for a common goal for each party—working together as individuals, instead of as a party.

[6] The initial questions having to do with the parties and candidates are the same throughout. From this point on, we shall abbreviate them in this fashion, although further probing that was introduced under each "root" question will continue to be reproduced in full.

them take their course slowly. *(Is there anything else?)* I don't like Mr. Hodge. *(Is there anything else?)* The labor unions telling workers how to vote—they know which side their bread is buttered on so they have to vote the way they are told to!

(Dislike about Republicans?) Mr. Hodge! *(Is there anything else?)* I can't think of anything.[7]

This respondent operates with a fairly clear sense of the liberal-conservative distinction and uses it to locate both the major parties and the more specific policy positions espoused. The second interview drawn to represent this category is somewhat weaker. The following remarks, transcribed from a woman in a small Ohio city, serve to illustrate the marginal inclusions in this category:

(Like about Democrats?) Well, that depends on what you are thinking of—historically or here lately. I think they are supposed to be more interested in the small businessman and low tariffs. *(Is there anything in particular that you like about the Democratic Party?)* Nothing except it being a more liberal party, and I think of the Republicans as being more conservative and interested in big business.

(Dislike about Democrats?) I think extravagance, primarily. *(Is there anything else?)* Nothing that occurs to me offhand.

(Like about Republicans?) Well, I never thought so. I have been a Republican the last several years because of the personalities involved, I guess.

(Dislike about Republicans?) This again is traditional—just that they give too much support to big business and monopoly concerns. *(Any other things you don't like about the Republican Party?)* No.

In this case the concept of the liberal-conservative continuum appears to be relatively peripheral. The respondent feels that evaluations based on concepts of this order favor the Democratic Party, but by her own account the "personalities" have in recent years loomed larger in her voting decisions. However, these concepts *are* present, and although not impressively developed, are used in a manner that implies that the respondent is sensitive to changes over time in the location of political objects on the underlying continuum. Hence in order to be lenient, she was assigned a position in the upper category of Level A.

It is striking, then, that responses of only 2½ per cent of our cross-section sample warranted inclusion in this top category. Since people placed here are much more likely to take a fuller role in politics than

[7] In order to preserve space, we shall omit reproduction of responses to the questions regarding the candidates, save where such responses add integrally to our understanding of the manner in which the respondent evaluates politics.

are persons lower on the scale, they bulk somewhat larger in the active electorate. But these ideologues still represent no more than 3½ per cent of our actual voters in 1956. In view of the fact that the partisan division of the national vote for federal office often shifts by as much as five or ten per cent within the biennial or quadrennial period, it is clear that this group alone could account for only a tiny portion of such short-term change, either by switching party or by staying at home.

There is, however, a more substantial group of respondents who have some claim to ideological perception. We have segregated them from the upper layer of ideologues because we are somewhat less confident that they fulfill the assumptions that we are examining. These people displaying "near-ideology" consist of three general types.

The first type is most similar to the full "ideologue." Frequently these people employ the liberal-conservative distinction, but their use of these concepts has little of the dynamic or highly relativistic quality found in the ideologue. "Liberalism" or "conservatism" is a status attribute of a party: there is less sense here of a continuum embracing many shadings of position, with objects shifting inward toward the center or outward toward extremes over time. Others give no explicit recognition to the liberal-conservative distinction, but employ organizing concepts of a sufficiently high order of abstraction to cut some swath through areas of ideological controversy. One interview drawn to exemplify this type of "near-ideology" comes from a man in southern Ohio:

> (*Like about Democrats?*) Yes, I like their platform. (*What is that?*) They're more inclined to help the working class of people, and that is the majority in our country. And I like the idea of stopping the hydrogen bomb tests. It would make for more friendly feelings toward other countries, and they would be more friendly to us. I think the Democratic Party wants peace as much as the Republican Party.
>
> (*Dislike about Democrats?*) Yeah, there's a lot of things. One thing is they're too much for federal control of utilities. (*Is there anything else you don't like about the Democratic Party?*) Well, it seems they don't always run the best men there are for their offices. (*For example?*) There's several I could mention that don't have the best reputation in the world.
>
> (*Like about Republicans?*) Well, they play up to individual rights, which is good. That's good—it makes a person feel more independent.
>
> (*Dislike about Republicans?*) They believe in big industry, utilities, etc. (*Anything else you don't like?*) They've passed a lot of labor bills I don't approve of.

This respondent does not introduce the liberal-conservative distinction explicitly. His opening comment about Democratic interest in the working class is of the group-interest type that will form the broad criterion for Level B. But he also includes commentary about the problem of federal control over utilities and the value of individual rights. Both of these observations involve abstractions common to the ideological disputes of our era. The respondent's own position concerning the role of government toward utilities is left rather unclear: he resents tendencies of the Democrats toward federal control, yet appears to dislike the Republican position as well. Here as elsewhere, however, we restrict our attention to the nature of the concepts employed rather than become involved in judgments of the coherence of ideological positions.

The other interview drawn to represent this group comes from a man in upstate New York.

> (*Like about Democrats?*) Well, I like their liberalness over the years. They certainly have passed beneficial legislation like social security and unemployment insurance, which the average man needs today.
>
> (*Dislike about the Democrats?*) The Communists linked to Roosevelt and Truman. Corruption. Tax scandals. I don't like any of those things.
>
> (*Like about Republicans?*) I also like the conservative element in the Republican Party. (*Anything else?*) No.
>
> (*Dislike about Republicans?*) No, not at present.

The subject here may suffer some confusion about the full meaning of "liberal" and "conservative," since he seems to find both to be pleasing attributes. However, he does pair these characteristics off, and he brings appropriate specifics to one of these terms. Another 2 per cent of our sample was considered to be of this type. These people constituted about 2½ per cent of our 1956 voters. Up to this point, then, we have accounted for about 4½ per cent of the total sample, and for slightly less than 6 per cent of our voters.

A second type of interview considered "near-ideology" included persons who used one or another of the labels common to ideological discussion, but in a context rather bare of supporting perceptions, so that we must take it on faith that the term had the normal connotations for the user. Generally the flavor of the context is not one to cast great doubt on the appropriateness of the meaning, but the lack of supporting material usually indicates that other simpler concepts are equally or more prominent in the individual's thinking about politics. The New York man quoted previously illustrated his generalized perception of Democratic "liberalness" with specific instances of liberal legislation. Such mustering of appropriate evidence is one of the characteristics distinguishing the first type of near-ideology from the second. The respondent drawn to exemplify the second type is a man from Texas:

> (*Like about Democrats?*) (After a long delay.) I think the Democrats are more concerned with all the people. (*How do you mean?*) They put out more liberal legislation for all the people.
>
> (*Dislike about Democrats?*) They have a sordid history over the past 20 years, though no worse than the Republican Administrations. (*How do you mean?*) Oh, things like deep freezes and corruption in government.
>
> (*Like about Republicans?*) No!
>
> (*Dislike about Republicans?*) Oh, they're more for a moneyed group.

Here the bulk of the content follows the lines of group benefit concepts that are generally classified at a lower level. Nevertheless, the term "liberal" is employed in a context of some reasonable meaning, and it is possible that fuller probing would have developed a more explicit indication of more abstract ideological conceptions.

Lest it seem odd that we approached our interviews with caution when ideological labels appeared with little surrounding evidence that the term was understood, we should point out that in some cases it is clear that the respondent is aware of the term without appearing to understand its normal meaning. For example, a college graduate, when asked what she meant in styling herself as a "liberalist," replied that she liked *both* of the parties. In other instances, words with a common political meaning were employed in a more colloquial manner. "Liberal" sometimes meant merely "generous," as was the case with the farmer who felt the Democrats were liberal with price supports whereas Republicans were "stingier." Similarly, it became clear that "radical" could mean "outspoken," when applied to Harry Truman's method of dressing down his adversaries in campaign speeches. Finally, there were some few cases—less than half of one per cent—in which it seemed obvious that "Communistic" and "Socialistic" had little meaning for the respondent beyond the punch of a political "swear-word." Respondents who used such ideological terms, but in such non-ideological manner, were not included in the second type of "near-ideology" unless further qualifying comment was present.

The second type of near-ideology adds another 3½ per cent of the sample to Level A, and another 5 per cent of our total of 1956 voters. Thus it is the largest group so far considered, although we have only accounted for about 8 per cent of the sample up to this point.

The final type of interview classified as near-ideology within Level A was in one sense the inverse of the preceding type. Persons were classified here who had highly differentiated images relevant to one or another ideological content domain, yet failed to introduce the generalized concepts that are normally used to summarize and order these perceptions in sophisticated debate. Whereas respondents of the preceding type had absorbed labels but had difficulty bringing appropriate specific information to them, individuals here were laden with information but showed no tendency to distill such detail to a higher level of abstraction.

In some of these cases, it was conceivable that the failure to indicate an awareness of more generalized organizing dimensions was accidental. Nevertheless, we find among these people, as well as those of the preceding type, an increasing tendency to depend upon party and group concepts as organizing focuses for issue content, rather than ideological positions. Thus responses of these types are already merging with the concept usages of individuals in Level B.

The interview drawn to represent this final type of near-ideology was contributed by a man in southern California:

> (*Like about Democrats?*) The Democratic Party is more for higher social security. They're more for old age pensions and better working conditions for the working man. They want a higher standard of living for all people, not just a few. The promises that are made by the Democrats are kept if at all possible. The facts are told to the American people.
>
> (*Dislike about Democrats?*) It seems to me they could handle their campaign better. (*How do you mean?*) Well, for instance, they could do a little better job of selling to the public. They should try and quiet Truman down so he will not pull a boner as in the Democratic convention. (*Do you have any other dislikes for the Democratic Party?*) No.
>
> (*Like about Republicans?*) Not one thing! (*In general, is there anything that you like about the Republican Party?*) No!
>
> (*Dislike about Republicans?*) I dislike everything about the Republican Party. (*Could you explain what you mean?*) I was growing up at the time of the Hoover Administration. What a time I had, too. There was barely enough to eat. I don't think the Republicans wanted that, but they did nothing to stop it. Not until Roosevelt came along and made things start to happen. Now the Republican Party still stands for big business, at the expense of the farmer and the working man. Promises made are not kept—ask the poor farmer, if no one else.

Over the course of these remarks there are points at which summary constructs familiar in ideological discussion would be highly appropriate. However, the recital of specific measures supported by the Democrats is not generalized to such a level of abstraction. Instead, the "standard of living" is used to sum up the direction of party policy, and this matter is treated as a benefit linked to a group, albeit a large group, within the population. Similarly, a perception of Republican passivity in the face of the Depression is vividly contrasted in the subject's mind with initiatives taken by Roosevelt. Yet this is not seen as a special case of a general posture toward change. Rather, it is left as a concrete vignette, developed once again into a proposition about group interest.

We did not feel that any of the types of response discussed here as "near-ideology" provided satisfactory support for assumptions concerning ideological perceptions. We include them as part of Level A, however, for it is possible that some among them would, in other settings, so amplify their observations as to merit "ideologue" classification.

If the reader has been struck by this generosity of assignment, he should hold this fact in mind as we measure our progress across the electorate. For despite our attempts at generous estimates, we find that with all of the ideologues and near-ideologues of Level A cumulated we have only covered about 12 per cent of all subjects interviewed, and 15 per cent of our 1956 voters. In other words, about 85 per cent of the 1956 electorate brought simpler conceptual tools to bear on their issue concerns.

Level B, group benefits. In the last interviews to be cited from Level A, we noted an increasing tendency to evaluate the political objects in terms of their response to interests of visible groupings in the population. Such perceptions are the dominant themes characterizing Level B, and constitute what we have described earlier as "ideology by proxy."

Such relationships between political object and group can be appreciated at a simple and concrete level. A party or candidate is sympathetic with or hostile to the group. Some perspective into the future is presupposed, inasmuch as the subject expects the orientation of party or candidate toward the group to endure, thereby assuring a continued protection and flow of benefits. But this perspective is foreshortened. As with Sam Hodder, there is little comprehension of "long-range plans for social betterment," or of basic philosophies rooted in postures toward change or abstract conceptions of social and economic structure of causation. The party or candidate is simply endorsed as being "for" a group with which the subject is identified or as being above the selfish demands of groups within the population. Exactly *how* the candidate or party might see fit to implement or avoid group interests is a moot point, left unrelated to broader ideological concerns. But the party or candidate is "located" in some affective relationship toward a group or groups, and the individual metes out trust on this basis.

As was the case with Level A, several types might be distinguished within Level B. One major content distinction had to do with the degree to which perceptions of group interest were elaborated. Some respondents tended to perceive politics in terms of a competition of these group interests, with the political parties arraying themselves in favor of one group and in opposition to another. However, many respondents did not develop the discussion of group benefit beyond the context of a single group, nor did they express a feeling that the party or candidate not seen as favorable was actively pursuing a threatening policy, either by ignoring or seeking to harm the group, or by supporting another group seen as a natural antagonist. Individuals who perceived a conflict of group interests in the political arena seemed to give more sophisticated interviews than those whose perceptions were bound up in the sympathy that one of the parties or candidates might be expected to show toward a single group. In terms of numbers, Level B was fairly evenly split between these two types.

In addition to this content distinction, there was a considerable range in the quality of response within both types. For example, some of the people who paired the parties with opposing interest groups could bring little further content to the matter under probing. That the Democrats were for the working man and the Republicans for business often seemed no more than slogans. Frequently the respondent would indicate in so many words that he or she had little personal knowledge about it: this was simply what somebody in the family who knew something about politics had always said. For analytic purposes, these rather shallow versions of the group benefit theme were separated from the normal run of responses of this sort.

People having relatively substantial perceptions of a competition of group interests make up the first category of any size that we have encountered. Fourteen per cent of our sample received this classification. Although the perception of group interest provides a tangible criterion for inclusion at this level, the reader is urged to compare the illustrative interviews drawn randomly from this group with those of the higher level in terms of the more general grasp of politics that is represented. The first illustrative responses come from an Iowa man:

> (*Like about Democrats?*) I don't know of anything. (*Is there anything you like about the Democratic Party?*) No, I wouldn't say there is.
>
> (*Dislike about Democrats?*) I don't particularly agree how they have passed out the money and increased the taxes.

(Like about Republicans?) I think they try to run the country without running in debt and keep us out of wars. *(Anything else that you like about the Republican Party?)* No.

(Dislike about Republicans?) They are more for big business. *(Anything else?)* No. *(What do you mean by "big business"?)* Well, the little man gets crowded out. They cater to the big men.

(Now I'd like to ask you about the good and bad points of the two candidates for President. Is there anything in particular about Stevenson that might make you want to vote for him?) No, I don't believe so.

(Is there anything in particular about Stevenson that might make you want to vote against him?) No, not as a man.

(Is there anything in particular about Eisenhower that might make you want to vote for him?) He has been a good leader all of his life. *(Anything else?)* No.

(Is there anything in particular about Eisenhower that might make you want to vote against him?) The only thing is whether or not his health would permit him to finish his term.

The second illustration of category B-I comes from an Ohio farm woman.

(Like about Democrats?) I think they have always helped the farmers. To tell you the truth, I don't see how any farmer could vote for Mr. Eisenhower. *(Is there anything else you like about the Democratic Party?)* We have always had good times under their Administration. They are more for the working class of people. Any farmer would be a fool to vote for Eisenhower.

(Dislike about Democrats?) No, I can't say there is.

(Like about Republicans?) No.

(Dislike about Republicans?) About everything. *(What are you thinking of?)* They promise so much but they don't do anything. *(Anything else?)* I think the Republicans favor the richer folks. I never did think much of the Republicans for putting into office a military man.

(Like about Stevenson?) I think he is a *very smart* man. *(Is there anything else?)* I think he will do what he says, will help the farmer. We will have higher prices. *(Anything else?)* No.

(Dislike about Stevenson?) No. But I have this against Stevenson, but I wouldn't vote against him. In the Illinois National Guards he had Negroes and Whites together. They ate and slept together. I don't like that. I think Negroes should have their own place. I don't see why they would want to mix.

(Like about Eisenhower?) No.

(Dislike about Eisenhower?) Yes. He favors Wall Street. I don't think he is physically able, and he will step aside and that Richard Nixon will be president. *(Anything else?)* To tell the truth, I never thought he knew enough about politics to be a President. He is a military man. He takes too many vacations and I don't see how he can do the job.

One theme that appears here, the attention to specific "promises," deserves special comments, for it symbolizes several of the basic differences in modes of thought that we encounter as we move downward through these levels of conceptualization. In the upper ranges, particularly among the full ideologues, references to promises made or broken are almost non-existent. But as we depart from the upper level, references of this sort increase in frequency to the point at which they become almost the center of any attention paid to content with policy implication.[8]

The political "promise," in the form retained by the respondent, has characteristics that contrast sharply with the sorts of concerns associated with ideology. Promises are campaign pledges to bring about a certain product or state, such as more jobs, peace, or higher farm prices. Promises arise *de novo* with each campaign; they have minimal roots in either a party tradition or a long-range program. The time perspective they imply is foreshortened in the future as well as the past, for they create expectations of immediate results. Finally, they are formulated in a manner which ignores the many factors, independent of man or party, that are certain in the short term to help or hinder the emergence of the end-state promised. The tendency to focus upon these pledges as the issue core of politics seems to token narrow time perspectives, concrete modes of thought, and a tremendously oversimplified view of causality in social, economic, and political process.[9]

With the interview involving perceptions of conflicting group interest added to those of Level A, we have now accounted for about one quarter of our sample and slightly less than one third of the voters. Another 17 per cent of the respondents talked of benefits accruing to a single group through the aid of a single party. The first interview drawn to illustrate this type comes from a man in Texas:

> (*Like about Democrats?*) Well, I don't know. I've just always before

[8] This is not true within Level D, of course, for subjects were classified here only if there was no reference to the sort of issue material made concrete in the campaign promise.

[9] The fact that promises are evaluated and digested in a form as simple if not simpler than that in which they are introduced does not mean that they are accepted at face value. A substantial portion of the people who are oriented to politics in these terms are extremely cynical about the probability of fulfillment of this or that specific pledge. The important point is that as often as not the cynicism reflects less doubt that the candidate will be able to fulfill the promise than doubt that he will take the trouble once in office. Hence the view of causality implied is the same. Once again, we are concerned here with the conceptual tools employed in the evaluation process, rather than the outcome of the evaluation.

been a Democrat. My daddy before me always was. (*Can you name any good things that you like about the party?*) Well, no, I guess not.

(*Dislike about Democrats?*) I don't know of anything.

(*Like about Republicans?*) No.

(*Dislike about Republicans?*) Well, I just don't believe they are for the common people. (*Anything else that you don't like about the Republican Party?*) No, I don't think so.

(*Like about Stevenson?*) No, ma'am.

(*Dislike about Stevenson?*) Well, I wouldn't know hardly how to put that. I just don't hardly think he's the man for President.

(*Like about Eisenhower?*) Well, his past is all. (*Is there anything else that might make you want to vote for him?*) No.

(*Dislike about Eisenhower?*) Nothing but the right man in the Democratic Party.

A woman in South Carolina responds:

(*Like about Democrats?*) They're more interested in small businessmen and farms. (*Can you tell me any more about that?*) No, but I've always heard this.

(*Dislike about Democrats?*) The race problem. (Its stand on the race problem.)

(*Like about Republicans?*) No.

(*Dislike about Republicans?*) Race problem.

(*Like about Stevenson?*) No.

(*Dislike about Stevenson?*) He's divorced.

(*Like about Eisenhower?*) I don't know of anything in particular but in general he's a good man.

(*Dislike about Eisenhower?*) His health. (Respondent is a nurse.)

These interviews, chosen randomly from among the more capable responses falling in Level B, serve to represent the conflict-of-interest and the single-group interest responses. As we have suggested, some interviews of rather low calibre with group-benefit mentions were separated to form a lower category within Level B. By and large, the quality of responses here is close to what we shall later encounter in Level C, despite the group references. These poorer interviews of Level B, making up another 11 per cent of the sample include responses similar to that of a New York City woman:

(*Like about Democrats?*) Well, my father is a Democrat and I'm one by inheritance sort of. I know nothing about politics but I like the Democratic Party because I know they are more for the poorer people.

(*Dislike about Democrats?*) Nope.

(Like about Republicans?) No, there isn't.

(Dislike about Republicans?) Yes. They are out to help the rich people.

(Like about Stevenson?) I heard him talk on TV, and he is a wonderful talker. I believe what he says and I think he will make a good President. I think he is capable and honest and I like him.

(Dislike about Stevenson?) No.

(Like about Eisenhower?) He is a fine man. A good military man, though, not a good President.

(Dislike about Eisenhower?) Yes, he was not a good President because he relied too much on his helpers. They led him. He didn't lead them.

Many of the poorer responses involving the interest of a single group referred to the plight of the farmers in 1956. As one might expect, a fair proportion of these came from farmers themselves.[10] However, some of the people who felt that one of the parties was working in the interest of the farmer were of urban background, such as this wife of a machinist in Louisville, Kentucky:

(Like about Democrats?) That's Stevenson, ain't it? *(Yes, that's his party.)* No, I don't know anything about Stevenson, but I do like the party. *(What is it that you like about the Democratic Party?)* There's always been more Democrats running for President than there has been for the other party, and they've got in more. *(Is there anything else you like about the Democratic Party?)* No.

(Dislike about Democrats?) I don't know anything about the Democratic Party. (Respondent was thinking so awfully hard and getting nowhere at all.) Well, for one thing, they were hard on the farmers. (I explained that we were talking about the Democratic Party and repeated the question.) No, I always liked it until Truman was in. He said he was going to do things for the farmers and he backed out.

(Like about Republicans?) That's Stevenson, ain't it? I get them mixed up. *(No, that's Eisenhower's party.)* Well, one thing, I heard he lowered taxes. *(Is there anything else you like about the Republican Party?)* And he's a good man—I hope he gets in this time.

(Dislike about Republicans?) No, I can't think of anything.

(Like about Stevenson?) No, I just don't like Stevenson.

(Dislike about Stevenson?) No, there's no faults. I just don't like him.

(Like about Eisenhower?) I don't know of any.

(Dislike about Eisenhower?) No, I don't have anything against Ike.

10 Generally, it became apparent that the calibre of the farm responses was quite low, even relative to other single-group interest interviews. This matter will receive more extended discussion in our consideration of the political behavior of farmers in Chapter 15.

As we complete our survey of the range of interviews included in Level B, it seems undeniable that we have moved to levels of conceptualization remote from those presumed by ideological interpretations of political behavior. Yet Levels A and B taken together account for little more than half of the total sample, and for only some sixty per cent of the 1956 respondents who voted.

Level C, the "goodness" and "badness" of the times. The third level coincides closely with the third quartile of our sample. In some ways interviews classified here are most effectively defined in negative terms. On the one hand, these responses do not include perceptions of group interest, and they lack as well any sense of a structure of concepts that might be conceived to border on ideology. On the other hand, these interviews escape classification in Level D by virtue of some reference, however nebulous or fragmentary, to a subject of controversy over public policy.

The issue content of this sort tends to be sparse within each interview and heterogeneous from interview to interview. Nonetheless, it is subject to some characterization. The most prevalent type of response provides the denotation for this level. We have presented samples of simple associations that may be made between the nature of the times—war or peace, recession or prosperity—and the incumbent administration. These responses probably fall closer to what is usually meant by ideology when they deal with prosperity than they do when they deal with war. But even when the substance is economic, the reasoning process underlying seems extremely remote from anything that might be considered ideological. Typically, there is a perception of the economic state of the immediate family, which is an index of the "goodness" or "badness" of the times. The possibility that what happens to some may not happen to others in the same way seems too differentiated a view of society or politics to have much role in the evaluation process. And, of course, once the nature of the times is assessed, the leap to party culpability is simple and direct.

Although the perception of a state of war is less readily based on concrete personal experience and is in fact affecting the total society, the remarks about war are particularly striking in terms of the view of causality implied. Often it appears that war is seen entirely as a matter of party choice or the personal whim of the President. The epitome of such perceptions was supplied by the woman sufficiently angry at Eisenhower to have switched her vote away from him in 1956. He had stopped the war as he had promised he would do, but he didn't do it just as soon as he got in office, and hence lives were needlessly sacrificed.

A second prominent type of response assigned to Level C involved the concrete detail that had issue relevance but appeared to stand as an isolated structure, an island of cognition in a sea of darkness. A prototype is the elderly woman economically dependent on her social security checks, who associates this aid appreciatively with the Democratic Party. Beyond this single policy item, however, she professes to know nothing whatever about politics, and is unable under probing to supply further content. Thus while Level C includes vague generalities about the times, it includes as well these isolated and specific issue perceptions. On occasion, a more informed respondent of this sort might produce a minor shower of specific observations. Thus there might be a rapid cataloguing of items such as Stevenson's promise to halt nuclear bomb testing; a perceived position on school segregation; promises to lower taxes. Whenever such details were internally elaborated, or linked one to another as illustrations of a broader policy posture, the interview was classed as "near-ideology." Only when neither characteristic was present was an interview with more than one issue reference placed in Level C. But such cases of multiple reference are rare in any event; the great bulk of responses in Level C involve a single issue reference which could not be elaborated.

Level C houses the extremes of the global, nebulous mood and the isolated specific perception. It was assumed on *a priori* grounds that such concept formation represented less sophistication than did perceptions of group interest, which involve minimally a discrimination of a group or groups in the society and group goals for which political power is relevant. Neither the global sense of the "goodness" or "badness" of the times, nor the limitation of cognitions to isolated policy measures seemed to indicate conceptualization of equal breadth or differentiation.

Several characteristics not used as criteria for assignment had great incidence in these Level C interviews. We have already pointed to the focus that emerges here on promises made or broken. There is a vastly increased tendency as well for the respondent to plead great ignorance of anything political. Now and again there is some apparent element of modesty underlying this confession; in the great majority of the cases, however, it is easy to see what the individual means. Although more than two thirds of the people in Level C voted in 1956, there is a pervasive recognition of inadequate information among these respondents.

Furthermore, there seems to be an increasingly moral cast to evaluations at this level. Irritation and concern over matters of graft and campaign "mudslinging" are given frequent vent. Such observations are not absent from responses at higher levels; but in Levels C and D they come to form the main thrust of the individual's perceptions with monotonous regularity. As one might expect, the strong partisan often tends to lay charges of mudslinging entirely on the ledger of the opposition. Sometimes indignation is lodged in a definitive statement that the opposing party or candidate has said "things"—often the person cannot specify further under probing—that have been "proved false." But such allegations do not begin to exhaust the references to mudslinging. An impressive proportion of individuals at these lower levels roundly condemns both parties for "running each other down so." These people seem genuinely depressed by any cross-party criticism of policy and platform. When a person has just watched or listened to some of the campaign speeches, these reactions often remain much more salient than the content of the criticism itself.

Let us present some sample interviews from Level C. While we limit ourselves to four illustrations, these illustrations stand for about one quarter of our interviews. Hence responses of this sort outnumber all those of Level A by more than 2 to 1, and they outnumber responses of the top ideological category by a ratio approaching 10 to 1. The first interview drawn is that of a Philadelphia woman:

> (*Like about Democrats?*) This is a very hard ground—a lot of promises were made that weren't kept. (*What ones do you mean?*) It confuses the public and it confuses me. A person don't know who to vote for. All the same, both parties are guilty in some instances of breaking campaign promises.
>
> (*Dislike about Democrats?*) No.
>
> (*Like about Republicans?*) No particular thing as long as they do good for the people.
>
> (*Dislike about Republicans?*) Just what I said before. (Respondent very vague, difficult to pin down to a particular question.) More should be done for human beings, for the good of the people. Those who take responsibility should worry about all the people of the world. We had bloodshed and we don't want it any more.
>
> (*Like about Stevenson?*) I think he's a very smart man as far as he's concerned. (*Anything else?*) I think he's very ambitious.
>
> (*Dislike about Stevenson?*) No.
>
> (*Like about Eisenhower?*) The only reason that I would want to vote for him is that he is a former Army man and saw the horrors of war and therefore would want to keep the peace. That's the main concern in the world today.
>
> (*Dislike about Eisenhower?*) No.

The second interview comes from a white woman in North Carolina:

(Like about Democrats?) They's a lot of nice Democrats. They's not too much difference in the parties.

(Dislike about Democrats?) Nothing in particular. Politics is something I don't study on much.

(Like about Republicans?) Seems like they helped a lot to stop the war.

(Dislike about Republicans?) The only thing is they's a lot of Republicans seems like they can be bought over—seems like they say they're Republicans, but they'll vote Democratic for money.

(Like about Stevenson?) I don't know much about the man. Our radio's tore up and I ain't heard any news lately.

(Dislike about Stevenson?) I don't know much about the man. I don't know what to say.

(Like about Eisenhower?) Seems like he's done pretty well this time, but I don't know. We could of had a better President than he is, I guess.

(Dislike about Eisenhower?) Well, no. I don't know whether I'll even vote or not. Sometimes I say I don't never intend to vote again.

The third interview comes from a woman in New York City:

(Like about Democrats?) What was in all the papers last week. Stevenson will see to it that they stop testing the bomb and I'm in favor of that. I don't want them to explode any more of those bombs. *(Is there anything that you like about the Democratic Party?)* I don't know anything about the party, really. I just want them to stop testing the bomb.

(Dislike about Democrats?) I don't know much about the parties. *(Is there anything you don't like about the Democratic Party?)* No—I don't know much about the whole thing.

(Like about Republicans?) My husband's job is better. (Laughed.) *(How do you mean?)* Well, his investments in stocks are up. They go up when the Republicans are in. My husband is a furrier and when people get money they buy furs.

(Dislike about Republicans?) No. *(Is there anything at all you don't like about the Republican Party?)* No—I don't know that much about the parties.

(Like about Stevenson?) As I mentioned before, he's saying stop testing the bomb because it can cause so much damage. My husband says that's such a minor point, but I don't think so.

(Dislike about Stevenson?) Nothing, nothing at all.

(Like about Eisenhower?) No, nothing in particular. *(Is there anything at all?)* No.

(Dislike about Eisenhower?) That he might die and Nixon would be President and I don't care for Nixon. He might not have his four-year term. There's a lot said about the other sickness that he had—not the heart attack.

The final interview comes once again from a woman in Louisville:[11]

> *(Like about Democrats?)* Well, I really don't know enough about politics to speak. I never did have no dealings with it. I thought politics was more for men anyway. *(Well, is there anything you like about the Democratic Party?)* I like the good wages my husband makes. *(It is the Republicans who are in now.)* I know, and it's sort of begun to tighten up since the Republicans got in. *(Is there anything else you like about the Democratic Party?)* No.
>
> *(Dislike about Democrats?)* No, I couldn't think of a thing.
>
> *(Like about Republicans?)* Well, truthfully, the Republican Party just doesn't interest me at all. *(There isn't anything you like about it?)* No—I just am not particularly interested in either one.
>
> *(Dislike about Republicans?)* I just don't know. It's immaterial to me about the Republican Party. I never thought enough about them to get interested in them.
>
> *(Like about Stevenson?)* Well, I'll tell you, I haven't read enough about either one of the candidates to know anything about them at all. *(Is there anything about Stevenson that might make you want to vote for him?)* None other than that he's a Democrat.
>
> *(Dislike about Stevenson?)* No.
>
> *(Like about Eisenhower?)* No.
>
> *(Dislike about Eisenhower?)* Well, just that he's a Republican.

Level D, absence of issue content. The remaining quarter of the sample failed to comment upon any issues of political debate in their responses to the unstructured questions. While vote turnout is relatively low within this group, these people still account for 17 per cent of our voters in 1956, and hence by themselves outnumber our ideologues in the active electorate by a 5–1 ratio.

To the degree that occupants of Level D have perceptions of the parties at all, they are bound up in moralistic themes like mudslinging and chicanery. More often the parties are poorly discriminated, and comment is devoted almost entirely to the personal characteristics of the candidates—their popularity, their sincerity, their religious practice, or home life.

Although we have encountered occasional bizarre conceptions in the previous interviews, these are more intrusive in Level D responses. Sometimes these oddities betray rather unorthodox conceptions of

[11] Since all four interviews drawn to represent Level C turned out to be from women, it is worth noting that whereas women are more numerous at the lower levels than men, these categories are in no sense devoid of men. About 42 per cent of the people in Level C are male, a figure not many percentage points from the sex ratio in the total adult population.

fundamental aspects of American political process. A few respondents, for example, confess to little understanding of what is going on but have a feeling that "it's a critical time, all right." An occasional individual appears to fear that the nation may emerge from the campaign without any president at all. "I don't know much about either of them, but just so long as one of them wins it will be all right."

In other cases there are factual inaccuracies that often have come to loom large in the respondent's thinking. One man was pleased with Eisenhower because he was the first American President who had ever gone to church. Another man appeared deeply angered because he had heard a speech in which Stevenson pronounced that there was no God. A woman who reported that she had become entranced by the Republican convention on television and had watched every minute of it came away without visible issue content but some perplexity at the fact that Nixon had received the vice-presidential nomination. "He's a foreigner, isn't he?" she asked the interviewer.

Initially our interest in the upper ranges of response was such that we planned no differentiation of types within Level D. It became apparent in the classification process that three broad types were emerging clearly. The first group consisted of party-oriented people. These were persons whose only conscious connection to the political process seemed to lie in a potent sense of membership within a party. They tended by and large to pay little attention to the candidates, and their presence in Level D indicates that they were unable to suggest how their party differed in its stands from the opposing party. Frequently, under probing from an interviewer who presumed that such a deep sense of loyalty must be supported by more specific perceptions, the subject would confess that he had never stopped to think of what it was that he liked about the party. Often these party people were simply accepting a family tradition. Often, too, particularly in the South, the subject resorted to religion as a metaphor to explain the attachment. A California woman observed, "most of us are what we were raised, and especially in church and in politics." Likewise, a Texas man commented "I was just raised a Democrat and I guess no matter what I'll always be a Democrat. It's like being born to a religion and just always staying in it."

The second type stood in sharp contrast in its preoccupations. These people had little information about or patience with the parties. The prevailing theme was "parties don't make any difference. It's the man who counts." Once again, the fact of location in Level D signifies that there were no issue implications in the subsequent perceptions of the candidates. These perceptions had to do almost exclusively with comparisons of looks, sincerity, popularity, religious practice, and family life.

The third type comprises the individuals who were unable to say anything about politics at all, save to explain why they found it difficult to pay any attention to it. This set of respondents was not, however, completely inactive politically, as about one quarter of them, for one reason or another, managed to vote in 1956.

The party or candidate types in Level D are not unique in the sample from the point of view of basic partisan motivations. In numerous interviews at higher levels it seems patent that issue perceptions are no more than garnish for a deep sense of partisanship, and throughout the sample generally, party loyalty exerts a substantial influence on perceptions of more specific events. Similarly, there are individuals at higher levels who disavow interest in parties and claim to attend primarily to the candidates. But at higher levels there are large numbers of respondents who could not be classified clearly in either camp. In Level D, where all else is shorn away, these primitive modes of approach to politics become most clearly differentiated, and seem to be of great analytic significance.

Since Level D comprised one quarter of the sample it was feasible to return to the interviews and subdivide respondents into these types. The distribution that emerged within Level D was as follows:

	Proportion of Level D
Simple Party Orientation	1/5
Simple Candidate Orientation	2/5
No Political Perceptions	1/5
Unclassified (mixed types)	1/5

Let us turn to samples of these major types. A white man from North Carolina was the first of a pair drawn from the party-oriented individuals in Level D.

(*Like about Democrats?*) No, Ma'am, not that I know of.

(*Dislike about Democrats?*) No, Ma'am, but I've always been a Democrat just like my daddy.

(*Like about Republicans?*) No.

(*Dislike about Republicans?*) No.

(*Like about Stevenson?*) No'm.

(*Dislike about Stevenson?*) No, Ma'am.

(*Like about Eisenhower?*) Not as I know of.

(*Dislike about Eisenhower?*) No, Ma'am.

A California woman was drawn from the same category:

(*Like about Democrats?*) I'm a Democrat. (*Is there anything you like about the Democratic Party?*) I don't know.

(*Dislike about Democrats?*) I'm a Democrat, that's all I know. My husband's dead now—he was a Democrat. (*Is there anything you don't like about the party?*) I don't know.

(*Like about Republicans?*) I don't know.

(*Dislike about Republicans?*) I don't know.

(*Like about Stevenson?*) Stevenson is a good Democrat. (*Is there anything else about him that might make you want to vote for him?*) No, nothing.

(*Dislike about Stevenson?*) I don't know. (*Is there anything about him that might make you want to vote against him?*) No.

(*Like about Eisenhower?*) I don't know. (*Is there anything about Eisenhower that might make you want to vote for him?*) I don't know.

(*Dislike about Eisenhower?*) I don't know. (*Is there anything about him that might make you want to vote against him?*) No.

A woman from the state of Washington provides the first illustration of the candidate-oriented response.

(*Like about Democrats?*) I vote for who I think is the best man. The last two elections have been mudslinging, and the Democrats are responsible for this. (*Is there anything good about the Democratic Party?*) They're just as good as the Republicans.

(*Dislike about Democrats?*) Mudslinging (see above).

(*Like about Republicans?*) They've just had the best man for the last two elections, that's all I can say.

(*Dislike about Republicans?*) I don't know that there is right at the present. I couldn't see the Republican Party when Roosevelt was in. Now I can.

(*Like about Stevenson?*) No.

(*Dislike about Stevenson?*) I just wouldn't vote for him, period. (*Is there anything about him that makes you want to vote against him?*) I just like Eisenhower better.

(*Like about Eisenhower?*) Everything, as far as I'm concerned.

(*Can you mention anything?*) No, I don't think so.

(*Dislike about Eisenhower?*) I wouldn't vote against him at the very present anyway.

A Texas woman serves as a second example:

(*Like about Democrats?*) No, I don't know anything about political parties. I'm not interested in them at all.

(*Dislike about Democrats?*) No, nothing.

(*Like about Republicans?*) No, I don't know about the *party*. I like Ike.

(*Dislike about Republicans?*) No, nothing I can put my finger on.

(*Like about Stevenson?*) Right now I can't think of anything I like well enough to vote for him.

(*Dislike about Stevenson?*) No, I just have my choice and it is not Stevenson. It is Ike.

(*Like about Eisenhower?*) I just like him, the way things have gone. (*How do you mean?*) That's really all I know.

(*Dislike about Eisenhower?*) No.

The final illustration of the candidate type within Level D comes from a Massachusetts man.

(*Like about Democrats?*) I haven't heard too much. I don't get any great likes or dislikes.

(*Dislike about Democrats?*) I hate the darned backbiting.

(*Like about Republicans?*) No.

(*Dislike about Republicans?*) No.

(*Like about Stevenson?*) No, I don't like him at all.

(*Dislike about Stevenson?*) I have no use for Stevenson whatsoever. I had enough of him at the last election. I don't like the cut-throat business—condemn another man and then shake hands with him five minutes later.

(*Like about Eisenhower?*) As a man I like Eisenhower better. Not particularly for the job of President, but he is not so apt to cut your throat.

(*Dislike about Eisenhower?*) No.

The interviews that had virtually nothing to say may be rapidly disposed of. The first illustration drawn came from a woman in California, who was unable to respond to any of the free-answer questions. The interviewer notes:

> The respondent explained that she works 11 hours a day (night shift) in a cannery, cares for her large family, and had no time left to read newspapers and keep up with politics. She was only being polite when she consented to the interview.

The second interview from this group came from a Missouri woman:

(*Like about Democrats?*) No—I don't know as there is.

(*Dislike about Democrats?*) No.

(*Like about Republicans?*) No, it's the same way I am about the other party.

(*Dislike about Republicans?*) No. Parties are all about the same to me.

(*Like about Stevenson?*) No, I don't think so.

(*Dislike about Stevenson?*) No.

(*Like about Eisenhower?*) I really don't care which man is best or otherwise. I don't know about either one of the men enough to give an opinion.

(*Dislike about Eisenhower?*) No.

We have now accounted for our total sample. This profile of an electorate is not calculated to increase our confidence in interpretations of elections that presume widespread ideological concerns in the adult population. To be sure, we have been able to assess only those aspects of political conceptualization that are revealed in conscious verbal materials. It might be argued for example that poorly educated people would have difficulty expressing a sense of apprehension at aggressive leadership of the "left," at a time when no need is felt for aggressive action. Such ineffable sentiment might, for the inarticulate, come to focus on reactions to personal attributes of the candidate. This is a possibility, yet one which we are not inclined to credit highly. If there were strong links between elements of the "deeper self" and reactions to ideological position that do bypass conscious concept for-

TABLE 10-1. Summary of the Distribution of the Total Sample and of 1956 Voters in Levels of Conceptualization

	Proportion of Total Sample	Proportion of Voters
A. Ideology		
I. Ideology	2½%	3½%
II. Near-ideology	9	12
B. Group Benefits		
I. Perception of conflict	14	16
Single-group interest	17	18
II. Shallow group benefit responses	11	11
C. Nature of the times	24	23
D. No issue content		
I. Party orientation	4	3½
II. Candidate orientation	9	7
III. No content	5	3
IV. Unclassified	4½	4
	100%	100%

mation and evaluation, we might have expected a stronger association between our measurement of conservatism and partisan decisions. Many of the people who reacted with dismay to the possibility of change suggested by the scale items undoubtedly failed to think of themselves, at a conscious level, as "conservative," if for no other reason than the fact the concept is not part of their cognitive tool chest.

But the fact remains that both the structured approach and the analysis of free answers lead to precisely the same conclusions: the concepts important to ideological analysis are useful only for that small segment of the population that is equipped to approach political decisions at a rarefied level.

Correlates of differences in conceptualization. The background factors that permit decision making at this level are the same suggested by earlier analyses with the conservatism measure. First, it has probably become obvious from the sample interviews that the character of an individual's conceptualization of politics depends heavily upon his education. Table 10-2 summarizes this relationship.

Since we feel that our judgment of levels of conceptualization captures a sophistication about political content dependent in some measure on a more general capacity to cope with the abstract, it is likely that education leads to differences in political concept formation by a number of routes. The education process is one in which individuals are constantly selected for passage to higher levels on the basis

TABLE 10-2. Relation of Education to Levels of Conceptualization, 1956

	Education		
	Grade School	High School	College
A. Ideology			
I. Ideology	0%	2%	10%
II. Near-ideology	5	8	22
B. Group Benefits			
I. Normal group response	27	36	30
II. Shallow group response	13	13	8
C. Nature of the times	29	25	20
D. No issue content			
I, II. Party, candidate	15	13	9
III. No content	11	3	1
	100%	100%	100%
Number of cases	514	856	315

of existing intellectual capacities. Furthermore, it is the purpose of education to develop these capacities, so that a person who moves to higher levels is likely to employ different modes of thought in evaluating objects than someone of equal initial capacity whose education was abbreviated. And, finally, the education process itself is responsible for the propagation of a good deal of the content that makes for political sophistication. The individual who fails to encounter this content is prey to some of the dire misconceptions that emerge among our respondents. And these misconceptions are hardly trivial in understanding the direction of political behavior. A person who expends energy in concern over whether or not at least one of the presidential candidates will be elected may be in a poor position to pay much attention to a "normal" evaluation of their relative merits.

Education is an obvious and prosaic variable, but we believe that differences in education have fundamental implications for political behavior that have been examined insufficiently. Certainly Table 10-2 may give pause to the investigator who hopes to arrive at a general understanding of the mainsprings of political behavior from research conducted entirely upon college students in social science classes. Hypotheses that seem reasonable to the sophisticated analyst and which are borne out on sophisticated subjects may have no relevance whatsoever for nine tenths of the population forming the mainstream of an electorate.

Yet education is not the sole source of differences in conceptualization. There are important motivational components as well. Generally, motivation to attend to political stimuli and to participate in the political process increases steadily with increasing education. Thus political sophistication is higher among the better-educated of Table 10-2 in part because they are more highly motivated to "keep up with politics." Yet the factor of involvement is a potent determinant of level of conceptualization in its own right, *independent of differences in education.* In Table 10-3 we may compare the different levels of conceptualization which appear within categories of involvement and education.

Sufficient involvement in politics may act as a fair surrogate for education in providing more efficient modes of organizing political perceptions. Few people whose formal education is limited to a grade school level reach Level A, and none of them is classified in the top rank of ideologues. But a small group, distinguished by an involvement more extreme than that registered by any college or high school group, manages to attain classification in the categories styled as "near-ideology." We presume that it is only through such intense interest

TABLE 10-3. Relation of Political Involvement and Education to Level of Conceptualization, 1956

Level of Conceptualization	Grade School			High School			College		
	Involvement[a]			Involvement			Involvement		
	Low	Medium	High	Low	Medium	High	Low	Medium	High
A. Ideology	0%	3%	16%	4%	9%	16%	20%	30%	35%
B. I. Normal group response	19	28	36	24	37	42	22	28	30
II. Shallow group response	11	15	12	13	13	11	13	7	6
C. Nature of times	25	35	22	24	24	21	25	18	21
D. No issue content	45	19	14	35	17	10	20	17	8
	100%	100%	100%	100%	100%	100%	100%	100%	100%
Number of cases	245	180	116	239	410	240	40	170	120

[a] The Involvement index is based on responses to questions concerning the respondent's interest in following the campaign and concern about its outcome.

in political events that the background is accumulated which permits classification at this level.

Yet we cannot be sure that the flow of causality runs always from involvement in politics through increased attentiveness to more sophisticated modes of evaluating political objects. It makes a good deal of sense to suppose that causality flows the other way as well. Some of the people encountered in our sample interviews indicate that they find politics downright confusing, and they are very numerous at the lower ranges. These people lack the conceptual tools that aid in making order out of chaos. The political parties provide one organizing dimension that seems accessible to persons of very impoverished political understanding. We have analyzed in great detail the pervasive role that party cues play in political evaluations of issues as well as candidates. Yet when debate over public policy rages, the individual who feels an issue should be resolved on its own merits, as well as the individual who fails to pick up party cues on the matter, is lost without some further organizing dimensions of the sort supplied conveniently by ideology or by perceptions of group implications. And it is clear that when much of politics is perceived as policy debate, inability to make sense out of the controversy must certainly dampen interest, just as low interest reduces the probability that politics will be observed enough to become comprehensible.

We feel that the problem goes a good deal beyond limitations of time and information, or even motivation, in themselves. For in our society freedom of time and access to information of a political nature have increased to an astonishing degree over the past century. And if we presume that a spark of motivation is broadly distributed in the electorate in the form of a perceived "ideal" mode of political evaluation based on a calculus of policy implications, then there must be further practical limitations on the citizen to produce the picture of the electorate presented here. We suggest that once below the higher deciles of the population, there are major barriers to understanding that disrupt the processing of even that information about public policy to which the person attends. To some degree these barriers are the product of an inadequate backlog of information. In some measure too they reflect the incapacity to handle abstractions that permit the individual to maintain an ordered view of remote events.

A fair number of our subjects even in the lower ranges are interested enough in political events to watch some portion of the nominating conventions or a campaign speech or two. Yet for a striking proportion of these people the primary fruit of such attention seems to be a reaction to the "nice way" the candidate speaks or looks, his apparent sincerity, etc. If we may assume that these are still people who value a policy criterion in political choice, then we find them in a situation where neither access to the valued information nor motivation to absorb it appears to be lacking. Yet it is information of another character that becomes absorbed in a form that remains available for later evaluations.

If we were able to analyze all content relevant to the political campaign that is dispensed through all mass media, it is likely that issue materials, in one form or another, would predominate. Certainly items like a candidate's divorce or religious practice, although sure to draw journalistic comment, would in the current era form but a tiny portion of the total volume of information concerning a presidential race. Yet in the lower ranges of conceptualization particularly, these small kernels relevant to personal life are seized upon, whereas the great bulk of the information dispensed concerning issue positions blows away like chaff. If people at this level were generally uninformed because they paid no attention to political communications, minor facets of personal life, less dominant in the news, would be the more likely to pass unnoticed. Yet this is not the case, and it is clear that somewhere in the process of communication and assimilation potent mechanisms of selection are active.

To be sure there are many citizens who, like Sam Hodder, read little and depend largely upon conversation for political information. It is not only plausible but likely that the selection process has already intervened before political information reaches these people. But the fact remains that at some prior point, selection of this order has occurred. From the total flow of information received from the mass media certain facts about the candidate have "stuck," whereas other facts, although in some sense more highly valued and certainly more heavily stressed at the source, have not.

These differences undoubtedly arise from variation in the richness of meaning that individuals bring to these different types of information. A fact like divorce is, for most people, a concrete and familiar part of social experience. It can have full meaning for the person who knows nothing whatever of politics. It is likely to be met in the consciousness with ready-made evaluations enjoying a clarity that far surpasses any bases of judgment available for the subtleties of politics, which are encountered sporadically and then only in a remote and peripheral way. Where matters of public policy are concerned, limitations upon the understanding of information that is actually attended must be added to these posed by problems of sheer access to current information.

The evaluation process is, therefore, narrowly circumscribed by limits of existing information, understanding, and the wherewithal in time and energy to increase either. It is undeniably important to improve our knowledge of the dynamics of evaluation, in cases where we may assume that certain raw materials are given. Yet it seems of equal importance to understand the consequences of initial differences in these raw materials, whether they involve cognitive capacity or background of political lore.

Our typology reflects at least two dimensions of difference between political actors. First, it depends on the appearance of certain types of content, which the individual is not likely to master unless he pays continuing attention to the flow of political developments over a period of time. Secondly, whatever the depth of a person's political involvement, there are rather basic limitations on cognitive capacities which are likely to make certain of the most sophisticated types of content remain inaccessible to the poorly endowed observer.

We presume that any cognitive limitations affecting the modes of political thinking would have a rather constant effect over time, although a rising level of education might permit a slow upgrading in the level of conceptualization. To the degree that certain types of content are at stake, however, we would expect the motivation to absorb it to vary according to the situation. As a result, we can imagine circumstances in which there would probably be some modification in the proportions of the citizenry classified within each level.

In a major depression, for example, we would expect some flow of individuals from Level D to Level C. The perception that times are bad and that there might be hope for improvement if the political leadership were changed does not seem to be a tremendously taxing notion. This is not to say that even here there are no cognitive limitations. The farm laborer whose interview we introduced might continue to have difficulty comprehending the devious route from vote to the securing of economic interest.[12] And we know that this is not an isolated case: groupings of people of low education living in dire economic straits have been unable, even under careful coaching from interested elites, to perceive politics as a possible path to amelioration.[13] Nonetheless, we presume that some proportion of people classified in Level D are placed there not because they are unable to comprehend these possibilities, but because the times do

[12] See pages 223–225.

[13] Seymour Lipset, *et al.*, "The Psychology of Voting: An Analysis of Political Behavior," *Handbook of Social Psychology*, ed. Gardner Lindzey (Addison-Wesley Publishing Company, Cambridge, Mass., 1954), II, p. 1142.

not focus their attention on the relevant political phenomena.

Similar observations might be drawn about the possibility of traffic between other levels, although we suspect that cognitive limitations come to play an increasing role as we analyze possible shifting of personnel up through the hierarchy of levels proposed. We have tried to leave the substance of ideology that merits classification in Level A sufficiently undefined that it is hard to imagine eras in which the predominant content of political debate would fail to qualify. Hence we do not feel that Level A might become seriously depopulated because extant political controversy is not in some sense "of the proper sort." But there are periods in which the heat of partisan debate slackens and becomes almost perfunctory, and the positions of the parties become relatively indistinct on basic issues. In times such as these, even the person sensitive to a range of political philosophies may not feel this knowledge to be helpful in an evaluation of current politics, and hence may fail to receive proper assignment in a level of conceptualization.

In general, then, we would expect some shifts over time in the distribution of the electorate across levels, particularly in the lower ranges and in periods of crisis. However, we would never expect this change to be of sweeping magnitude, and there is still less reason to believe that the picture of the voting public presented previously was captured at an abnormal moment. In any event, the possibility of individual movement from level to level should not obscure the fact that there must be some constancy of meaning to any partisan change undertaken by individuals who conceptualize their issue concerns in a similar manner.

Differences in Conceptualization and the Interpretation of Partisan Change

We have surveyed conceptual modes used in the American electorate in order to check assumptions that are frequently implicit in interpretations of partisan change. These accounts presume that a significant portion of the voters contributing to partisan change are responding to the current location of political objects on some "left-right" continuum. We have been unable to find evidence that any substantial portion of the electorate formulates its issue concerns in such a manner. This fact in itself raises some severe questions as to the adequacy of the assumptions. Yet there are two other aspects of the problem that demand examination as well.

First, it may be that the size of the ideologue contingent is less critical than the role that this contingent plays in time of partisan change. If propensity to partisan change were exceptionally high among the upper levels, it might still be argued that discussions of change in ideological terms are appropriate. If, however, there were greater partisan fluidity at lower levels, such interpretations would become of marginal value indeed.

Second, we know that at times partisan change involves larger portions of the population than the contingent of ideologues could conceivably account for. Furthermore, these shifts in party fortunes often follow ideological expectations very well. What issue meaning may safely be attributed to such changes? The significance of shifts in party resides ultimately in the character of events that precipitate the response. To analyze these events for the several levels will cast light upon the question of propensity for partisan change that may characterize each level. Therefore, we shall approach this problem first.

The nature of partisan change at various levels. Our data give reason to believe that we should maintain the distinction between "ideologues" and "near-ideologues" in discussing the character of partisan change within Level A. In Chapter 4 we introduced a method for determining the internal consistency of the six partisan attitudes. A structure of partisan attitudes is deemed perfectly consistent if all of the political objects discussed are evaluated favorably for the same party. Such a structure is inconsistent if, for example, the individual likes certain aspects of one party but prefers the candidate of the other. We noted that in general such partisan consistency increases with political involvement.[14] Since involvement varies markedly across levels of conceptualization, we would expect consistency to increase as we progress from lower to higher levels in our typology. By and large, this is the pattern. Perfect consistency is least frequent in Level D (94 per cent more observed cases than expected by chance) and highest in Level A (250 per cent). If, however, we separate the near-ideologues from the ideologues, we find the maximum is attained at the near-ideology level (290 per cent), whereas the frequency of perfect consistency among ideologues (141 per cent) falls well below the "average" figure for the total sample.

This characteristic of the full ideologue group fits well with some of the criteria for assignment to the category. Many people qualified for classification here because they were adept in locating political objects at various relative positions on some underlying continuum

[14] See Chapter 4, page 81.

relevant to ideology. Often the person would differentiate either or both parties into liberal or conservative wings. A party wing that the individual felt was more remote from his own position was subject to negative comment, even though the wing might be a part of his own party. Similarly, other objects associated with the preferred party were criticized if they failed to meet ideological expectations.

Evaluations of this sort are, from a partisan point of view, rather "gray." They stand in sharp contrast to the black and white partisanship of people considered to hold "near-ideology." These latter subjects are more likely than any others to see all things connected with their preferred party as good, whereas objects associated with the opposing party are disapproved. The content of the evaluations is sophisticated, but the party itself seems a prime focus for the assessment of political leaders and policies. By contrast, the focus for political evaluations in the highest category is the respondent's own ideological position. Just as Archimedes asked for "a place to stand" outside the world in order to lift it, the full ideologue has found a place to stand outside the spheres of direct party influence. He has an independent point of reference that can only be imperfectly approached by the ideologically heterogeneous American parties.

In what instances change would occur for the full ideologue, as well as the meaning that might be attributed to it, is undoubtedly well covered in the literature, for these are the people who best fit widespread assumptions about "political man." They are most sensitive to changes in the broad ideological cast of party policies, and are sensitive as well to the more haphazard changes that arise as factions of differing political beliefs vie for party control. As party policy is seen to drift toward or away from the individual's own position, his reactions to the party may change accordingly.

Persons of near-ideology are less likely to be sensitive to these nuances. For many of them, party loyalty may have primacy over any issue positions that they have espoused. The alert observer committed to a party may simply take on the more sophisticated rationales propagated by the party in its defense. Hence he emerges with a set of political evaluations that consistently favor the objects associated with his party. Where such a pattern is operative, the individual might well follow the party through a dramatic ideological realignment, although such realignments are so rare in American politics as to pose little more than an academic question.

In the earlier discussion of Sam Hodder we contrasted behavior governed by ideology with that which might be expected under conditions of political change among people of Level B, whose evaluations depend on links established between groupings in the population and the political parties. We need not repeat that discussion here. There is a good deal more to be said about the character of political change when an external reference point, the non-political group, functions to mediate between the individual member and the world of politics. This added element, however, carries us into complex considerations of the social context of political evaluation, a matter to which Chapter 12 will be devoted.

Although the conceptions of politics grouped together within Level C are too heterogeneous to permit adequate discussion, the core group at this level—people who form simple associations between the nature of the times and the party in power—are particularly interesting to consider in terms of partisan change. To the extent that people falling in Level C evaluate the current political situation free of distortion from existing party bias, their reactions are likely to be of two sorts.[15] If they perceive that times have been hard, as symbolized primarily by economic dislocation or war, they will react in a spirit of "throwing the rascals out." If they perceive that times have been relatively good, the tendency will be to adopt a "don't rock the boat" attitude.

This repertory of responses can lead to aggregate behavior, which (again under certain circumstances) may appear to be impelled by ideology. In the early years of the Great Depression it would have been hard for the staunchest Republican to perceive that things were going well. Only a belief that a political party could not be held responsible for an economic collapse of this magnitude would remain as a defense for partisanship. Yet it is a sophisticated understanding that sees lines of causality fade from sight in a welter of complex events like the economic collapse after 1929. Such understanding is not generally accessible to people who conceptualize politics in the modes representing Level C. Hence we can imagine a strong wave of Democratic support emerging in 1932 from persons operating at this level, who wished to "throw the rascals out." Such a tide, coming in the

15 It is important to keep in mind that we are focusing here upon such change in partisanship as does occur in the electorate. It is readily demonstrable that perceptions of the nature of the times are substantially affected by pre-existing party allegiances. Mishaps during the administration of national affairs by one's own party are more readily written off as accidents not traceable to party guidance, whereas mishaps under a regime of the opposing party tend to be viewed as examples of its incompetence or malevolence. Thus party loyalty exerts a tremendous force toward political stability over time throughout all of our levels. Nonetheless, partisan change does occur. It is our purpose here to come to grips with the policy meaning that partisan change may be considered to have when and to the degree that it occurs.

face of economic disaster, lent itself to interpretation as a shift to the left.

It is important to recognize how inappropriate this description may be for contributors to the tide from Level C. If perceptions do not pass beyond the attitude of throwing the rascals out, we are still left at a point rather remote from ideology. The "rascals" phrase is deliberately chosen, for it makes minimal assumptions as to the sophistication of the actor. Times are bad. Whatever else an administration may do, the individual expects it to maintain the nation on an even keel in domestic economics and foreign affairs. If difficulties of this sort accumulate, he will protest. There is no need to presume that he sees any specific way in which the administration has courted the current ills, or that he has a sense of what might have been done differently, or even that he knows what the opposition intends to do, save for its predictable promises that ills will be remedied. The salient fact is that the party in power has failed in its most basic obligations, and deserves to be turned out. Protest can be bitter without a breath of program behind it.

We can easily imagine situations, then, in which the political responses of people in Level C would confound ideological expectations. Let us suppose that the nation were to encounter a major depression during the administration of "the party of the left." The reactions of ideologically minded voters might be hard to predict without knowledge of the way in which such an event would affect the policies of both major parties. But we may suppose that the ideologue would locate the difficulty primarily as a flaw in the economic system and would "shift to the left" in the sense of demanding new approaches on the part of government to remedy matters and prevent their recurrence. Provided the two-party structure remained intact, however, we would predict unequivocally that the response at Level C would be a strong shift to the right. Of course, such a description of the change would be misleading, for it rings in the familiar ideological assumptions. But people at this level would be posed to "throw the rascals out," and would do so, short of a third party, by shifting support to the opposition, whatever its political philosophy.

The striking fact is that in such a case, although people of Level A would be moving to the left, the predominant effect would be the "shift to the right," simply because voters at Level C far outnumber citizens who appear in Level A. Thus, over the electorate as a whole, the "ideological" expectations would be directly controverted. It is in such a circumstance that it becomes important to know that "protest" responses at this level have little to do with ideology.

Voters of Level C act, then, as a rather crude and insensitive thermostat geared to the goodness and badness of the times. They fail to perceive ideological niceties, and it may require bad times of some extremity before sufficient numbers among them shift in the same partisan direction at the same time to have much striking effect on the evolution of party history. Furthermore, they are not notably discriminating in the type of events for which they may hold the party in power responsible.

Nonetheless, they contribute to a potent if gross reward-punishment system that party leadership must respect. In fact, to the degree that much ideological debate has to do with the most certain means toward a vague end state called the general weal, it is precisely this general weal that citizens of Level C pass upon from election to election. They could not be expected to understand and evaluate alternative *means* on any "rational" grounds. But they do judge the product, as it appears at the moment, and hence serve as some control mechanism. The pressure remains upon the political leader to work from that ideology which he sees as most likely to promote the general weal, or at least one which will guide the nation at a safe distance from catastrophe.

We presume that the seeming insulation of people in Level D from any issue concern in 1956 is subject to variation over time. Hence it is difficult to predict behavior within this grouping as it might emerge at such pressure points for political change as a major depression. It is probably fruitless to speculate concerning partisan change in the case of the extremely party-oriented individuals of this level. Some other persons here would probably remain psychologically aloof from the political process under any circumstance. In conditions of severe economic dislocation, the behavior of some of the candidate-oriented occupants would undoubtedly merge with that expected of Level C. To the degree that still others remained bound to evaluations based on perceptions of the personal attributes of the candidates prediction is impossible, save for the obvious prediction that the significance of partisan choice would bear little resemblance to ideological description.

Differences in propensity for partisan change. The preceding discussion provides clues about what we might expect of various types that we have isolated in terms of fluidity of partisan preference. For example, the contrast in partisan consistency of attitude between ideologue and near-ideologue would suggest that the ideologue would show greater propensity for partisan change. The near-ideologue, inasmuch as he may build a tightly-knit attitude structure on the basis of party rationales, lacks the independent platform in a self-sustaining ideology that would make him a freer critic of party policies.

At the opposite extreme of the typology we have encountered another small segment of the population that we would expect to stand like a rock against the tides of political change. The party-oriented citizens of Level D have, on the one hand, a profound commitment to one of the political parties. And on the other, they are distinctively well insulated against the assaults of new political information that might bear the impetus to partisan change. No partisanship is, in the limiting case, immutable; but individuals whose contact with politics is of this order seem to hold what is closest to an impregnable position.

Beyond these observations we may feel that there is little theoretical reason to predict continually higher rates of change within any of the conceptual levels. Our past discussion has implied that different types of events would precipitate change within different levels. War might evoke more change within Level C than among ideologues, who would be less likely to hold the party in power responsible in a simplistic fashion. On the other hand, a shift in control of a party from a conservative to a liberal wing might disturb the partisanship of the ideologues although passing unnoticed among persons of Level C. Assuming that these two types of events may occur independently, we are forced to conclude that high rates of change could characterize first one level and then another according to the situation.

Nevertheless, with situation "controlled," systematic differences in potential for partisan change might remain from level to level, owing to third factors. That is, we know that people assigned to various levels differ sharply on background characteristics such as education and political involvement. Low involvement or education might also predispose the individual to take his party allegiance lightly. Thus potential for partisan change would differ by conceptual level, although this fact would be difficult to deduce from conceptual level directly.[16]

We may therefore consider it an empirical matter as to whether partisan change has appeared more frequent within some levels of the typology. Since we cannot control the broad political situation, and since our data have reference only to the Eisenhower period, we must remember that positive findings may be bound to peculiarities of this period. However, enough ideological interpretation has been directed

[16] In a causal sense, the association between level of conceptualization and partisan stability would be "spurious," that is, owing to a common third factor. However, our purposes would be served simply by establishing the fact of association: the causal question is not crucial here.

at voting trends in this period to make even this excursion well worth our effort; and it is entirely possible that our findings have more general significance.

One approach to the question hinges on differences in strength of party identification within the several levels. Where such loyalties are intense we would expect less partisan fluidity over time than where they are weak. The mild relationship between political involvement and strength of identification suggests that party allegiance should be stronger at higher levels of conceptualization. This does turn out to be the observed pattern. Although full ideologues appear free to criticize their party, they show a degree of commitment to party as high or higher than near-ideologues or people in other levels. Generally, we find a very slight but monotonic decline in strength of party identification as we progress downward through the strata of our typology. Differences are sharp only at one point, however. People in Level D are much less strongly identified with a party than are members of higher levels. This is true even though Level D includes some traditional party-oriented people who, when isolated, show extremely strong party allegiance. With this group extracted from Level D, of course, the remainder becomes accordingly more distinctive.

The conclusion that in the Eisenhower period partisan change was most visible at the lower levels is equally supported by another quite different approach. To the degree that party identification reflects an abiding loyalty to a party and a tradition of past electoral support for it, individuals who are drawn to a partisan choice contrary to their current party allegiance would appear more susceptible to short-term change than individuals who remain within party lines. Since an insignificant handful of Republican identifiers voted for Stevenson in 1956, we focus attention here upon the substantial numbers of Democratic partisans who cast ballots for Eisenhower in 1956. We do indeed find higher rates of defection from party identification at lower levels of conceptualization (Table 10-4).

That susceptibility to partisan change of this sort is increasingly likely at the lower levels of conceptualization is not surprising in the light of data outlined in Chapter 5 concerning non-voter preferences. We noted that non-voters have shown extreme instability in their partisan choice for President since 1948, and that among non-voters, those who were relatively interested were least susceptible to forces toward partisan change. Table 10-4 suggests that the non-voters phenomenon is merely an extreme case of a pattern which marks the total electorate.

The continuity between these findings is highlighted when we recognize that turnout rates decline at the lower levels of conceptualization. This fact would of course be readily deducible from the restricted education and indifference to politics of persons classified here. Among the ideologues of Level A, 94 per cent voted in 1956.

TABLE 10-4. Relation of Defection of Democrats in 1956 to Levels of Conceptualization

	Proportion Defecting from a Democratic Identification in:	
	1956 Presidential Vote	1956 Vote and Non-voters' Preference
Level A: Ideology	18%	19%
Level B: I. Normal group	20%	24%
II. Shallow group	25%	31%
Level C: Nature of times	46%	53%
Level D: No issue content	36%	46%

The turnout rate was 78 per cent in Level B, and 69 per cent in Level C. Only 56 per cent of citizens located in Level D voted. When we survey the increasing vote defections from stable party attachments at lower levels in Table 10-4, then, it seems rather clear that these behaviors are of the same cloth as the marked instability of preference among non-voters. It appears that quite generally in this period, people who paid little attention to politics were contributing very disproportionately to partisan change. To be sure, the effects visible in the national vote totals were muted by the fact that people paying little attention to politics were also less likely to vote. But the proportion of the population that we have classified in these lower categories is large; and despite low turnout rates, people within Levels C and D still made up 40 per cent of the active 1956 electorate.

We cannot be entirely sure that the potential for partisan change is generally greater among persons whose interest in political process is slightest, reasonable hypothesis though this seems to be, since the observed effects may be a function of the immediate political period. But they do cast provocative light upon the many prominent interpretations of political change in the 1950's, which picture an electorate seeking respite from continued "leftist" pressure toward social and political change. The latter portion of the discussion has led to conclusions that complement the description of the electorate presented earlier in the chapter. People who appear to fit the assumptions underlying the "left-right" accounts are few enough that they could not physically have accounted for any substantial portion of the resurgence of the Republican Party at the presidential level in 1952 and 1956. Furthermore, the data suggest that these people were proportionally much less likely to have contributed to this partisan change than were people for whom the assumptions are a poor match indeed. It is hard not to conclude, then, that these accounts, popular though they have been, are thoroughly overdrawn.

Election Laws, Political Systems, and the Voter ◇ 11

The political world to which the voter responds is composed of more than the actors and events that mark the competition for his support. It includes as well the formal rules and informal norms that circumscribe his participation. These written and unwritten expectations that channel political behavior are no small part of what we mean when we talk of "political systems." It is commonly assumed, when international comparisons are at issue, that behavior varies in subtle ways as a result of the manner in which political life is traditionally organized. But one need only consider the electoral laws of the several states or the tenor of political activity where serious interparty competition is lacking to be convinced that the American political system, although bound together by many nationwide features, embraces a variety of political subcommunities. Each of these communities is a pervasive medium within which behavior must occur. And each leaves some characteristic impress on that behavior.

We cannot conclude our examination of the political context of the voting act without a closer recognition of these facts. Up to this point we have been primarily concerned with an interplay between remote events of national politics and individual constructions of political reality that result. Such national events may be conveyed to all corners of the nation by our media of mass communication. Yet these events are interpreted by groups of individuals in local settings—cities, counties, states and regions—and these settings differ in their characteristics as political communities. Without empirical evidence we would have little basis to predict whether the effects of these "system" factors on individual behavior would be strong or weak relative to others. But even the discovery of moderate effects could shed important light on the nature of the American political process as a whole.

The professional student of politics is mindful of the formal ground rules laid down to govern participation in the game of politics. In the early days of the nation these rules were storm centers of political debate and the point of departure for experiments in political theory and practice. In the present era, interest in the right to vote is still a live brand in the civil rights conflagration.

Those rules of the game that govern the conduct of elections (as distinct from those concerning the right of the individual to vote in elections) have received considerable scholarly attention in the relatively recent era of professional interest in political reform. Of course, it is not unusual to have electoral administration treated as a rather barren field in the otherwise fascinating terrain of politics; but the student rapidly discovers that the administration of elections is a matter of intense concern to the politician and to others directly engaged by political activity. V. O. Key suggests that many election laws "were intended for no other purpose than to insure the supremacy of the temporarily dominant political party."[1] At the same time, and perhaps viewing the same election code, the student of government or the citizen of civic virtue may decry the fact that "no other phase of public administration is so badly managed."[2] He may go on to point out that "our elections have been marked by irregularities, slipshod work, antiquated procedure, obsolete records and many varieties of downright fraud."[3] Implicit in both concerns is the assumption that election laws have some real consequences on the day of elections. In a different context, careful examination of such electoral forms as the direct primary has, in later days, disclosed the probability that many unforeseen but very important changes in party competition have resulted from the "progressive" alteration of electoral forms a few decades past.[4] Taken together, the legal limits on political participation and the rules governing the conduct of partisan politics constitute an important aspect of the individual's political environment that bears directly upon our analysis of electoral behavior.

The immediate political environment varies not only in terms of electoral codes but in terms of intangible political atmosphere as well.

[1] V. O. Key, Jr., *Politics, Parties, and Pressure Groups*, 4th ed. (Thomas Y. Crowell Co., New York, 1958), p. 672.

[2] Joseph Harris, as quoted in *ibid.*, p. 673.

[3] *Ibid.*

[4] See Austin Ranney and Willmore Kendall, *Democracy and the American Party System* (Harcourt, Brace and Co., New York, 1956), pp. 281–283, for discussion and bibliography.

At times, subtle community sentiment becomes embodied in more formal regulations, just as formal regulations act to guide the development of community sentiment. However, other aspects of the political atmosphere also mark the community. We know, for example, that the American party system is summarily described as a two-party system of politics, with the one-party South a prominent example of its deviant cases. It is also accurately described as being composed of fifty state party systems whose heterogeneity challenges if it does not defy simple classification.[5] Although analysis of the formal regulations governing the franchise provides a first level of description of political communities across the nation, any account would be incomplete without recognition of at least the gross differences in party system that occur from area to area.

If these components of voters' political environment are familiar, our treatment of them departs somewhat from customary modes of analysis. In keeping with our dual interest in political preference and political participation, we have organized electoral regulations into two mutually exclusive sets of rules, the one concerned with the regulation of *participation* and the other concerned with political *partisanship*. With one or two exceptions we will not consider the unique implications of any particular item included in either set. Instead, by considering simultaneously all regulations that relate to the partisanship of voters we will, for example, establish a range of conditions relevant to partisan behavior. We can then rank the residents of the various states according to whether the sets of electoral laws and regulations under which they live make partisan behavior easier or harder for them. At one extreme we have residents of states in which the voter's partisan allegiance might be promoted or facilitated through such devices as severe tests of party loyalty or the use of closed primaries. In these states a citizen who wishes to participate in primary elections is encouraged if not forced to maintain an alliance with one party, and the manifestation of that alliance in the general election may be further facilitated by a ballot form which promotes the casting of a straight party ticket. At the other extreme are residents of states whose election laws encourage non-partisanship or at least do not call for demonstrations of party affiliation or loyalty. In such states the most active participant is seldom if ever forced by law into the role of an avowed party supporter.

The specific items on which our summary measure of the facilitation of partisanship is based include the following: type of primary election—open, closed, or blanket; arrangement of primary ballot—separate

[5] *Ibid.*, Chapter 7.

tickets, consolidated ballot, etc.; party tests for voting in primary; existence of non-partisan primary; form of general election ballot and provision for presidential primary.

We shall treat the regulation of suffrage in a similar fashion. In general, we shall not isolate the poll tax or the literacy test and examine their correlates in political behavior. We shall consider all state regulations governing suffrage and organize them to provide an over-all measure of the formal facilitation or inhibition of political participation within a state. The regulations governing participation vary between the major regions. Consequently, in the North we base our summary measure of vote facilitation on the following: required length of United States citizenship, residence requirements in state, county, and voting district, and presence of a literacy test for voting. In the South the components of the measure include age, residence requirement in state and county, and poll tax requirement for voting.

These two sets of regulations do not constitute particularly impressive criteria. We might wish for longer rosters with greater possibility of state-to-state variation. We might also wish for criteria whose existence does not depend on the enforcement policies of local election officials, with their various interpretations of the law and of the need for rigor in its application. Finally, we might prefer a uniform set of criteria for both Northern and Southern parts of the electorate. We are limited in each instance by the objective facts of life: the rosters of criteria include all the items that are reported to exist in the respective state statute books; we have no means of assessing systematically the uniformity of enforcement; and the regional differences are empirically imposed.

The Formal Facilitation of Partisanship

We would suppose that election laws relevant to partisanship would have their greatest significance for the development of the loyalties represented in our measure of party identification. The data confirm such expectations. Although almost all segments of the population appear to respond meaningfully to questions about party loyalty, we see in Table 11-1 that the character of these allegiances varies in conjunction with laws having to do with partisanship. Voters governed by rules most likely to promote partisanship are most likely to be strong party identifiers and least likely to classify themselves as Independents. Conversely the voters in states that provide minimal

TABLE 11-1. Relation of Formal Facilitation of Partisanship to Party Identification[a]

Strength of Party Identification	Facilitation of Partisanship		
	Minimal	Moderate	Maximal
Strong	34%	37%	40%
Weak	32	39	38
None (Independent)	34	24	22
	100%	100%	100%
Number of cases[b]	502	755	718

[a] This table includes only Northern voters.

[b] The statistical significance of the research findings reported in this chapter is enhanced by virtue of replication of the findings in 1952 and 1956. The tables present the combined data from the two independent samples of the national electorate.

encouragement of partisanship are significantly more often self-classified Independents and less often strongly identified with a party.

In extending our comments on the significance of this association two important points must be made. First, although there is a relationship between extent of party identification and the election laws governing the residents of the states outside of the "Border" tier and the Solid South, there is no such relationship within the remaining fifteen states. This is probably a function of several factors. There is little variation, state to state, in these election laws across the South, so that differences between states on the measure of partisan facilitation are slight. Most Southern States are clustered at the extreme of partisan facilitation relative to electoral requirements outside that region. More important still, it is likely that the unique monopoly enjoyed by the Democratic party throughout the South alters the impact of many factors that might otherwise be associated with independence in the partisan competition for allegiance.

Secondly, we must proceed with caution in treating the causal implication of the relationship as it emerges outside the South. It is tempting to conclude that the legal structure concerning partisanship "causes" or inhibits the development of party allegiances; yet supplementary data raise questions about such an interpretation. The nature of the election laws comprising our measure of partisan facilitation is such that we would expect a person to be "forced" to a declaration or choice of party only as a part of the act of voting, and usually the act of voting in a primary election. The closed primary, the oath of party loyalty, the casting of a straight party vote and the others might be expected to have little meaning for the persistent non-voter who has seldom if ever come into contact with them. We find, however, that people who seldom if ever vote show the same substantial differences in their strength of party identification under differing state laws as do citizens who never miss an election. Hence the causal sequence from election laws to partisan attachments cannot be as simple as it may first appear.

Public sentiment in an area favoring or opposing regularized partisanship in politics might produce *both* legal provisions governing partisan elections and personal reactions to partisan commitment. Thus the norms of the political community—in this case, the state—might act as a third prior factor leading to a correlation between legal structures and individual identifications with the parties. Such an interpretation depends on the assumption that people who fail to participate in the political process in a formal sense still may share in popular sentiment concerning the desirability of partisan approaches to politics. Though we lack data, some plausible notions documented for other purposes do provide support for this assumption.

Even politically inactive persons rarely exposed to the usual political stimulation of the mass media or local campaign events may by social mechanisms have some contact with the political life of their communities. The informal "opinion leader" may serve as one such social agent. In the course of casual daily conversation the political pundit of the work group, the bridge-playing wife of a political "active," the well-informed neighbor—these and others may well convey the relevant political sentiment to a more or less passive audience. In the somewhat unique setting of a presidential election campaign, about one out of every four persons reports engaging in informal attempts to convince someone else to support a given party or candidate.

In addition to the information carried by the self-selected opinion leader, a broad variety of political information is undoubtedly transmitted in the more structured setting of the group. Many primary groups as well as secondary groups perpetuate political standards or norms and convey these to their members. In some instances this transfer may be a matter of deliberate group policy, as with the political education committees of the labor unions and the political activities of many large industrial organizations. In other instances standards may be transmitted more subtly, as in the case of religious groups, many civic and service clubs, and such broad secondary groupings as are constituted by Negroes or farmers. The group may well join the informal opinion leader in transmitting cues about political partisanship to the less involved members of the community.

In the absence of historical or longitudinal analysis, such an explanation of the causal link between election laws and the partisanship of citizens would at least satisfy the logical demands of available data. It would also suggest that election laws are significant elements of our political system and not merely the esoteric interests of election officials and manipulative politicians. And if it is a valid account, we have an interesting demonstration of the relatively localized subcultures that operate within the larger context of national politics. The regional differences between North and South provide the broadest example of such subcultures, and this example lends credence to far-reaching notions such as that expressed by V. O. Key when he suggests that "the appropriate cross-national analysis might shed light on the question of the relation between extent and nature of citizen participation and the character of political systems in the large."[6] Similarly, it helps document the contention that our national party system is built in some degree on the unique systems of each of the member states. This follows because the rather sparse legal boundaries that each state provides for the politics of its citizens are somehow associated with electoral behavior that is consonant with them.

There are other provocative aspects of these data. We find situations in which the *relationships* between party identification and other political phenomena are affected by variations in the formal facilitation of partisanship. Quite apart from differences in the level of partisanship from state to state we find that identifiers in some communities behave differently from their counterparts elsewhere. Partisans in the South provide an excellent example. Since there was no evidence that extent of partisan allegiance varied with legal encouragement of partisanship in the South, it is of special interest that the *voting behavior* of party identifiers in that region *is* related to differences in such encouragement. As Table 11-2 illustrates, the relationship between one's party identification and one's vote was visibly higher in states providing maximum facilitation of partisanship. Comparable scrutiny of the party identification-vote relationship outside the South reveals no such variation to match differences in election laws.

These findings suggest that under some conditions there may be a direct causal tie between a specific legal form, such as the electoral code, and a social behavior, such as voting. In the absence of a mean-

[6] Key, *op. cit.*, p. 638.

ingful association between the extent to which legal forms facilitate partisanship and the intensity of party identification in the South, we cannot presume that variations in those legal forms will be asso-

TABLE 11-2. Variations in the Party Identification-Vote Relationship and Differences in Formal Facilitation of Partisanship

	Proportion of Votes That Are Consistent with Party Identification	
	South	North
High Facilitation of Partisanship	78%	83%
Number of cases	217	555
Low Facilitation of Partisanship	69%	86%
Number of cases	200	566

ciated with a factor that also causes variation in individual political identifications. The attitudes of the political community apparently do not provide a common base for both legal and personal emphasis on partisanship. Instead, it appears that the formal facilitation of partisanship is of independent origin but then has its impact on political behavior through facilitation or inhibition of a party-oriented vote.

We may undertake to describe the difference between the political settings of the North and the South as a difference in the causal sequence by which component parts of the two different political systems develop. In the North there is a political sentiment in the community reflected in individual political predisposition *and* in the legal framework for political participation. The legal code may provide continuing legitimacy to the community sentiment, but it does not seem to be an independent factor in the determination of one major category of predispositions—identification with a party. The regular pattern of association between these personal and impersonal political phenomena nevertheless defines an institutional arrangement that is a part of the Northern political system. A plausible statement of the causal relationships between components of that system and individual behavior is depicted in Fig. 11-1.

A parsimonious summary of the relevant and necessary causal linkages is represented by the figure. A single antecedent (Community sentiment) is associated with a formal statement of the com-

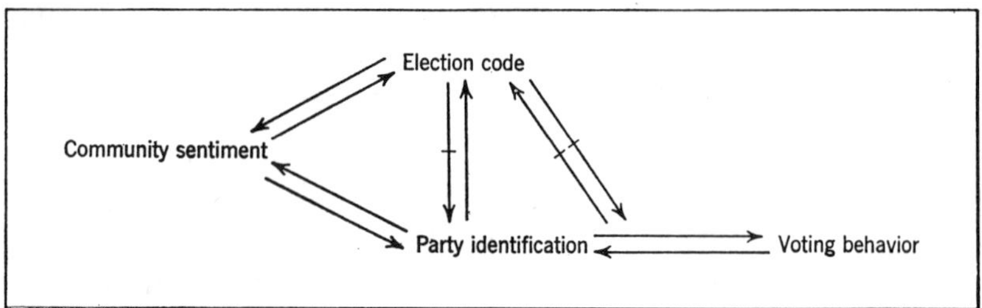

Fig. 11-1. A selected institutional form involving the vote: North.

munity's attitude toward partisan politics (the relevant portions of the Election code) *and* with the individual community member's expression of partisan loyalty (Party identification). This individual expression of partisanship is, in turn, associated with the individual's statement of partisan preference at the polls (Voting behavior). There is, however, no surplus of meaning or function in the election codes—once established they have no further discernible independent impact on the extent of individual partisanship (Party identification), and no visible influence on the subsequent relationship between party identification and the vote choice.

In Fig. 11-2 the same variables are depicted as they appear to exist in the South. Here there is no indication of an interactive relationship between the expression of partisan allegiance by the individual and the encouragement or discouragement of such partisan allegiance as offered by the legal codes governing elections. Consequently, we must posit the prior existence of two independent, if not unrelated factors (Community sentiments X and Y) to account for the independent development of individual partisan loyalties and of community codes for the conduct of partisan elections.

Moreover, there is evidence that variations in the election code *are* associated with variations in the party identification-vote relation-

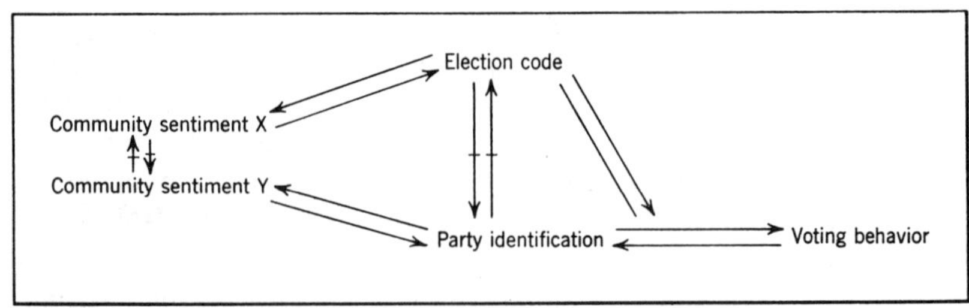

Fig. 11-2. A selected institutional form involving the vote: South.

ship. (The general party identification-vote relationship is, of course, common to both Southern and Northern political behavior.) Such a correlation could not occur if the election code and individual partisanship shared completely common origins. This is so because the sense of the correlation is that a given intensity of party loyalty is more closely associated with a compatible vote under one condition imposed by an election code than it is under a different condition imposed by a different code. There is independent variability in the election code—and that variability is reflected in the variable *behavior* of voters with similar identifications with party.

The delineation of North-South differences in the interactions of these few variables is a first step in a systematic analysis of cultural differences in political behavior. Three important ideas are illustrated by this exercise. First, the interplay of individual-level and community-level variables constitutes one significant manifestation of the nature of institutions. Institutional analysis is enhanced by the ability to specify the interrelationships that obtain between the formalized proscriptions and the informal individual behaviors that fulfill the institutional demands. Second, a given operationally defined variable may have different conceptual meanings in different cultures or subcultures, a fact revealed by attitudes and behaviors of their members. In our example, the meaning ascribed to the election code differs for the Northern and the Southern voters. Third, the systematic empirical study of interrelationships among variables may point to the necessary existence of different variables in different cultures. It is logically possible for both the election code and individual party allegiances to have a common origin in the North. Replication of the analysis in the Southern context requires one to posit the independent existence of an additional "first cause."

Ballot form and ticket splitting. There are, of course, specific institutional forms that are quite unambiguously related to voting behavior, whatever the specific nature of the political subculture. One of these, which contributed as well to our summary measure of the formal facilitation of partisanship, is the general election ballot. Any attempt to explain why the voter marks a straight or split ballot must take account of the physical characteristics of the election ballot. Disregarding the minor parties, the ballot usually consists of a series of paired choices pitting Republicans against Democrats. The voter may choose within each pair either on the basis of the personal qualities of the individual candidates, or on the basis of their party labels, or both. In over half of the states the ballot permits him to resolve the entire complicated series of decisions for all offices by the simple procedure of marking a party circle or pulling a party lever. There are a number of variations of this straight-ticket voting procedure in the other states. Some states divide the presidential vote from the rest of the ballot, some divide the ballot into presidential, congressional, and local sections, some group the candidates by office rather than by party but identify the party of each candidate.

Whatever relationships we find between the political motivations of the voters and the way they mark their ballots, the form of the ballot itself has an influence on the proportion of straight and split tickets cast. This becomes evident when we divide our sample of the national electorate into those voting in states with the single choice type of straight-ticket voting and those in which a straight ticket requires more than one mark on the ballot.

In 1956, of the Eisenhower voters in single-choice states, fifty-nine per cent voted a straight ticket; in multiple-choice states, forty-eight per cent; of the 1956 Stevenson voters in single-choice states, sixty-nine per cent voted a straight ticket; in multiple-choice states, sixty per cent. Since the distribution of party identifiers in the two types of states did not differ we conclude that the sheer ease of voting a straight ticket facilitated this type of behavior.[7] The role played by the form of the general election ballot thus provides a more specific illustration of the formal facilitation or inhibition of partisanship in political behavior.

Formal Restrictions on Voting

The second set of formal or legal factors that we shall consider includes those related to suffrage. The most significant definitions of eligibility to vote were made in times past through constitutional amendment. By comparison, the present-day legal qualifications set by each state are of small consequence. Nevertheless, in some states a combination of election codes and extra-legal practices has led to the effective disfranchisement of many citizens. The general effects of legal restrictions on voting may be studied with the aid of summary measures analogous to those described in the discussion of partisanship. The data presented in Table 11-3 indicate that here again we encounter a significant difference between the South and the rest of the nation. In the South the proportion of citizens who have never voted is clearly

[7] Angus Campbell and Warren E. Miller, "The Motivational Basis of Straight and Split Ticket Voting," *American Political Science Review*, LI (June, 1957), 293–312.

TABLE 11-3. Relation of State Restrictions on Voting to Past Frequency of Voting, by Region

Frequency of Past Voting	Laws Governing Suffrage, North: Restrictive	Laws Governing Suffrage, North: Moderate	Laws Governing Suffrage, North: Permissive	Laws Governing Suffrage, South: Restrictive	Laws Governing Suffrage, South: Moderate
Voted in all elections	52%	48%	49%	21%	30%
Voted in most elections	20	23	23	17	17
Voted in some elections	11	15	16	21	20
Have never voted	17	14	12	41	33
	100%	100%	100%	100%	100%
Number of cases	691	942	724	410	528

associated with state-imposed restrictions on voting. Moreover, among those *who have voted* in some previous presidential elections, the residents of the more restrictive states have voted less regularly in those elections for which they were eligible. Under such restrictive legislation, therefore, there are not only more citizens who never vote, but proportionately more of the persons who have voted are irregular, in-and-out voters. In the North these associations between institutional restrictions on voting and the act of voting are so small that they may be regarded as inconsequential.[8]

Here again the empirical findings are illuminated by our consideration of differences in regional political systems. With regard to institutional restrictions on voting, the reaction of Southerners resembles that observed in the Northerners' concern with partisanship. The difference in regularity of voting in the South fits the concept of a community concerned about the extent of political participation. In the more restrictive states the institutional forms maintain a larger

[8] Given our measure of voting regularity and the mobility of our population, particularly outside the South, it should be noted that in any one election the proportion of eligible voters disfranchised by recent changes of residence may, for young citizens, be reflected in a part of the 5 per cent difference in persistent non-voting. It should also be kept in mind that our measures of facilitation of voting, and of partisanship, are based on the existence of regulations but do not reflect probable variations in enforcement or application by election officials.

pool of citizens who never vote, and the presumed sentiment of the political community does not stimulate the regular performance of civic duty by those who do establish their voting eligibility. In the North, on the other hand, legal forms in some states disfranchise some potential voters—but those who do vote are apparently quite unaffected by any local impediment to their appearance at the polls.

In the two-party competition of the North it is of mutual interest to members of the political community to encourage the participation of potential supporters. It is generally accepted that a wide base of political participation is good, but sentiment concerning the extent to which real commitment to a party should be encouraged varies. Although we cannot turn to survey data for insight into why this should be so, political history provides a likely answer. In numerous Northern states the end of the nineteenth century and the first third of the twentieth century saw many vigorous and successful efforts to curtail partisanship in politics. Under the banner of reform, and sanctioned by more than a few political scientists, the anti-party spirit waxed strong in the early 1900's and may be assumed to have left a large residue of antipathy to party politics.

In the one-party South, the absence of effective interparty competition has made the question of whether such competition should be facilitated or minimized irrelevant. There is, however, real concern over the actual extension of the suffrage—and where the concern is greatest both community sentiment and legal proscription combine to limit extensive and regular participation.

Restriction of suffrage in the South has in recent years been directed primarily at limiting the political activity of the Negro. However, there is remarkably little evidence on the extent to which the Negro is in fact the principal victim of restrictive Southern election practices.[9] Although we lack sufficient cases for an adequate analysis of the socio-economic differentials important in Southern voting behavior, we can nevertheless turn our attention to data that bear on the incidence of suffrage limitations in the South. Table 11-4 provides our most general description of Negro and White voting.

The high rate of persistent non-voting among Negroes is the most obvious message of the table. In comparing differences in non-voting among both Whites and Negroes we also observe evidence of considerably greater relationship between legal restrictions and non-

[9] Donald Strong, "American Government and Politics: The Poll Tax: The Case of Texas," *American Political Science Review*, XXXVIII (September, 1944), 693–709. See also Strong's *Registration of Voters in Alabama* (University of Alabama, Bureau of Public Administration, 1956).

TABLE 11-4. Relation of State Restrictions on Voting to Past Frequency of Voting, by Race (South Only)

	Negro		White	
	Law Governing Suffrage			
Frequency of Past Voting	Restrictive	Moderate	Restrictive	Moderate
Voted in all elections	3%	10%	26%	34%
Voted in most elections	0	10	22	19
Voted in some elections	12	20	24	19
Have never voted	85	60	28	28
	100%	100%	100%	100%
Number of cases	95	89	315	439
Proportion of totals	(52%)	(48%)	(42%)	(58%)

voting among Negroes. We assume that the greater impact of restrictive electoral laws on Negroes is, in part at least, a function of the relatively low motivational levels among Negroes. This does not fully explain the racial differences in voting behavior, however, as we discover when we add a third dimension to our analysis, the racial composition of county populations.

In Table 11-5 we have subdivided each of the population groups in Table 11-4, separating residents of counties with populations that are less than thirty per cent Negro from those in counties where more than thirty per cent of the people are Negroes. In this table we may note three significant facts. First, most Negroes living in heavily Negro counties do not vote—regardless of the stringency or leniency of state laws (only two per cent classify themselves as relatively consistent voters). Second, Negroes living in counties with a smaller proportion of Negroes in the population vote more often than do other Negroes living in the same states under the same laws but in counties with larger Negro populations. And third, the variability in the turnout of the Southern Negro is not fully accounted for by differences in state legislation; the racial composition of the county is also a contributing factor. Where White dominance is numerically more extreme, there is apparently less community resistance to Negro voting.

It has been suggested that Southern attempts to limit voting have

TABLE 11-5. Relation of State Restrictions on Voting to Past Frequency of Voting, by Race within Density of Negro Population (South Only)

	Per Cent Non-White in County			
	Under 30 Per Cent		*Over 30 Per Cent*	
Frequency of Past Voting	Suffrage Laws Restrictive	Suffrage Laws Moderate	Suffrage Laws Restrictive	Suffrage Laws Moderate
White				
Voted in all elections	26%	34%	27%	33%
Voted in most elections	21	17	27	28
Voted in some elections	25	20	21	15
Have never voted	28	29	25	24
	100%	100%	100%	100%
Number of cases	230	372	85	67
Proportion of totals	(38%)	(62%)	(56%)	(44%)
Negro				
Voted in all elections	(23%)[a]	16%	0%	3%
Voted in most elections	(0)	14	0	5
Voted in some elections	(38)	16	7	25
Have never voted	(39)	54	93	67
	(100%)	100%	100%	100%
Number of cases	(13)	49	82	40
Proportion of totals	(21%)	(79%)	(67%)	(33%)

[a] Figures in this column are given in parentheses because of the small number of cases.

had fully as much impact on the poor White as on the Negro. If this is true it is not generally evident among the White residents of the more heavily Negro counties. The participation of White residents of these counties is only slightly affected by variation in state laws. And the frequency of regular voting (voting in all or most elections) is not only very much higher than that of Negroes in the same districts, but it is somewhat higher than that of other Southern Whites living in counties with smaller Negro populations.

A number of major conclusions are suggested by this analysis: (1) it is the informal, extralegal barriers—not state legislation—that account for much of the variability in the turnout of the Southern Negro; (2) greatest regularity in voting among Whites is reported most often in heavily Negro counties and, in particular, in those counties where voters are not greatly hampered by state-imposed limitations on voting; and (3) the institutional pattern relating legal regulations to individual behaviors persists in all four major categories formed by combinations of race and racial composition of counties. Our earlier generalization concerning the significance of participation in the political system of the South has not been vitiated by the analysis of racial differences in voting behavior. Instead, this analysis suggests two distinct dimensions to be found in the structure of Southern politics—one centered on the position of the Negro, the other concerned with the absence of stable party competition.

In both instances the question of political participation is central. In the case of Negro voting, the local institutions outside the formal rules and regulations are clearly significant. The patterns of Negro and White voting must be understood in the context of the Southern struggle to define the role of the Negro citizen in a manner compatible with cultural norms that are not limited to the world of national presidential politics. But in all areas, even where this problem is most acute, we find the patterned reflection of a system of one-party politics.

The interplay between formal rules and individual behaviors among Negroes and Whites outside the South adds a further dimension to our understanding of the situation.[10] As Table 11-6 indicates, there are very sharp differences in the vote participation of Whites and Negroes in the North. Again, there is no apparent relationship between the formal rules and individual behavior for the 95 per cent of the population that is White. Under restrictive legislation some 75 per cent report participation in all or most elections; 72 per cent of the Northern Whites who enjoy *more permissive* electoral codes report a comparable frequency of voting. The same comparison for

10 The heavy clustering of Negroes in metropolitan areas outside the South makes it impossible to compare areas that differ sharply in proportion of non-Whites to parallel the Southern analysis. It may be noted, however, that outside the South non-White proportions never exceed 30 per cent, a figure that was the cutting point between area types in the examination of the South.

Northern Negroes, however, discloses significant differences: under restrictive legislation only 30 per cent report fairly regular voting in the past, whereas 54 per cent of the Negroes governed by more permissive laws report regular voting. The effect is not so great at the other end of the scale, where 35 per cent of those under restrictive legislation report that they have never voted as compared to 22 per cent of those under more moderate legislation.

TABLE 11-6. Relation of State Restrictions on Voting to Past Frequency of Voting, by Race (North)

	Negro		White	
Frequency of Past Voting	Suffrage Laws Restrictive	Suffrage Laws Moderate	Suffrage Laws Restrictive	Suffrage Laws Moderate
Voted in all elections	20%	23%	55%	49%
Voted in most elections	10	31	20	23
Voted in some elections	35	24	9	16
Have never voted	35	22	16	12
	100%	100%	100%	100%
Number of cases	49	62	753	1515

It would seem that insofar as the process of political disfranchisement of Negroes is concerned, the selective impact of legal codes is felt in both the North and the South, and in the South this effect is amplified by the selective application of informal extralegal sanctions. The rate of Negro participation in the Northern elections is, of course, much higher than under nominally equivalent conditions in the South. Indeed, Northern Negroes governed by the more permissive regulations participate at a higher rate than do three of the four categories of Southern Whites we have examined. Nevertheless, Negroes in the North not only participate in politics substantially less than their White neighbors but also appear to be more seriously handicapped by the legal restrictions on the franchise in their districts.[11]

[11] As mentioned briefly at the beginning of this discussion, it would be highly desirable to pursue this investigation by imposing an extensive set of controls on relevant socio-economic factors. Much of the absolute difference in Negro-White participation is undoubtedly a function of differences in education, occupational

Conditions of Institutional Effectiveness

Thus far in this chapter we have introduced a number of observations on the interrelations of institutions and political systems. Toward this end we have attempted to locate party identification in the context of relevant political institutions. We have also cited instances in which the institutional forms apparently by-pass the individual motives or attitudes usually important as intervening terms and show their effects directly in individual behavior, as in the case of the ballot form and straight-ticket voting. We are now in a position to clarify more directly the behavioral effects of the interplay between situation or context terms and the attitudes central to our analysis.

Proper juxtaposition of institution, attitude, and behavioral variables leads repeatedly to the conclusion that *formal political institutions have their greatest impact on behavior when the attitudes relevant to that behavior are least intense.* In terms of the suffrage problem, for example, this means that the magnitude of the effects of legal restrictions on voting depends on the degree to which the individual voter is motivated to vote. If his motivation is high, formal facilitation or inhibition of his behavior is relatively ineffective; if his motivation is low, his actual performance may be greatly affected by the same legal forms.

To demonstrate this proposition let us first consider the role of voting restrictions in the South as strength of motivation to vote varies (Table 11-7).[12] Among those Southerners highly motivated to vote who live under the more permissive laws regulating suffrage, 12 per cent

status, etc. The limited numbers of cases available to us prohibit the use of controls on such factors. Nevertheless, it should be noted that such controls could provide a non-legal, social explanation of the major differences we have discussed *only* under a peculiar set of circumstances. For example, interracial differences on such items as education could explain the differences in participation *only* if variation in education is coincidentally associated with variation in the legal codes of the North and only if such coincidental association holds only for Negroes. *If* poorly educated Negroes cluster in states that enforce restrictive limits on voting, and *if* poorly educated Whites *do not* cluster disproportionately in such states—then it would be possible to account for at least a part of the observed discrimination against Negroes by attributing their failure to vote to their own lack of desire to vote. Unless there is a unique coincidence of the legal form and the socio-economic characteristics for Negroes but not for Whites, we could not hope to dismiss the above conclusions as artifactual.

12 Motivation level is measured here by the range of political attitudes possessed by the voter. Involvement in all six major political attitudes indicates maximum motivation.

have never voted; under the more restrictive codes, 18 per cent. Among those who have voted, 57 per cent in the first situation have voted in every election, whereas 52 per cent of the less advantaged report a comparable record of participation.

TABLE 11-7. Individual Participation and the Facilitation of Voting, Variations Associated with Variations in Voter Motivation (South Only)

	Suffrage Laws Restrictive	Suffrage Laws Moderate	Difference in Per Cent
Motivation high			
Persistent non-voters	18%	12%	6
Proportion of voters who have never missed an election	52%	57%	5
Motivation low			
Persistent non-voters	51%	32%	19
Proportion of voters who have never missed an election	10%	23%	13

When motivation to vote is low the pattern is quite different. There is, of course, a generally lower level of past participation; less than one in five has voted in every election and almost half have never voted. The important data, however, concern the differences to be found when we compare persons residing where institutional barriers are weaker with their counterparts in restrictive states. First, the level of persistent non-voting goes up from 32 per cent to 51 per cent, an increase of 19 per cent. Among the highly motivated the comparable absolute difference was 6 per cent. Similarly, among actual *voters* with low motivation levels, 23 per cent operating under more permissive rules report never missing an election, whereas only one in ten who was confronted with the greater barriers to voting, reports never missing an election. Again, this difference of 13 per cent is to be compared to a difference of only 5 per cent among highly motivated voters. Both absolute and relative differences in participation, associated with formal facilitation and inhibition of participation, are visibly greater for citizens with low levels of motivation.

A second demonstration of the same general proposition may be observed among the nation's voters using single-choice and multiple-choice ballots in the general election. The impact of the form of the ballot on straight- and split-ticket voting varies with the motivation of the voter. In view of the fact that a high level of partisan motivation leads to straight-ticket voting, we would predict that other factors such as the ballot form will have their greatest influence on such voting in the absence of partisan motivations. This prediction holds true. For the extreme party identifiers (strong Republicans and strong Democrats), the ballot form has no discernible effect on the use of a straight ticket. Strong Republicans given multiple-choice ballots still vote a straight ticket just as frequently as do strong Republicans who can cast a party vote with a single "X" or by pulling a single party lever; the same is true of strong Democrats. Among weak identifiers, Independents, and among identifiers whose presidential vote is in conflict with their party identification, the form of the ballot plays a progressively more and more important role in facilitating or inhibiting straight-ticket voting.[13] The data may be summarized as follows:

Among strong party identifiers, a single-choice ballot increased straight-ticket voting by	0%
Among weak identifiers it increased it by	27%
Among Independents it increased it by	60%
Among weak identifiers whose vote conflicted with their identification it increased it by	60%

Again, less support from internal motivation is associated with greater influence of the institutional form on behavior.

A final illustration, involving a different political attitude, also comes from an analysis of ticket splitting. In 1956 the single-choice type of ballot appeared to hold Democratic identifiers more securely to their party's presidential nominee than did the multiple-choice ballot. In the single-choice states 91 per cent of the strong Democrats voted for Stevenson, 9 per cent for Eisenhower; in the multiple-choice states, the percentages were 86 and 14. "Weak" Democrats gave Stevenson 70 per cent of their votes in the single-choice states, 30 per cent to Eisenhower, and in the multiple-choice states they divided into groups of 64 and 36 per cent, respectively. The votes of Republican identifiers using the two types of ballots did not differ. From what we now know of Mr. Stevenson's appeal to the voters in 1956 the relevance of this finding for our present discussion is clear. The weak pro-Stevenson attitudes of Democrats allowed the ballot form to influence their voting for him. With a single-choice ballot before him, the Democrat would more often let his partisan allegiance carry the day and cast his vote for Mr. Stevenson. However, confronted with a multiple-choice ballot, the Democrat unimpressed by Stevenson would take advantage

[13] Campbell and Miller, *op. cit.*, p. 307.

of the opportunity to vote for Mr. Eisenhower. The much stronger positive appeal of Mr. Eisenhower forestalled any such defections on the part of Republicans.

In each of the situations just reviewed we have observed substantial evidence that the formal political institutions in question had their greatest impact on political behavior when the attitudes relevant to that behavior were weak. This proposition is of considerable importance both to the study of political institutions and to the study of individual attitudes and behaviors of political significance. The role of the institution, whatever the specific political system dictates that it be, is not of uniform importance to all citizens. The political involvement of some overrides or at least mitigates the influence of the institution. Programs of institutional change, whether sponsored in a spirit of civic reform or in the interest of narrower goals, are of less consequence for such citizens. The need for change is less pressing—as the highly involved citizen surmounts the formal obstacles to his personal goals—and the consequence of change will therefore be less dramatic. Alteration of those institutions that have greatest relevance for the casual or marginal voter will, on the other hand, probably have maximum impact by virtue of their pronounced influence on the relatively uninvolved participant. The easing of registration requirements, for example, might increase voting rates among the uninvolved citizens, but probably would not greatly affect the behavior of intense partisans.

The analysis of individual perceptions, values, and behaviors must also take this proposition into account. Under certain conditions lack of attention to institutional forms misses an important element in the shaping of behavior. The data suggest that the micro-analytic approach does not embrace the full range of phenomena relevant to individual behavior unless it attends to the broader variables that define the context of that behavior. And the less satisfactory the analysis of the psychological dimensions of involvement, the more important the contextual variables become. In view of the very large proportion of uninvolved, peripheral participants in politics, this is a matter of considerable importance.

Formal Institutions, Informal Environment, Motivations, and Behavior

We have now examined two quite different kinds of environmental factors. We have been concerned with the formal institutions, the legal regulations and laws related to suffrage, and the conduct of elections. In defining limits for the individual voter they variously function independently to shape the behavior of the voters or they mirror the informal environment as it is constituted by the sentiments of the voting community. Our interest in the second class of factors, the informal political milieu as defined by the sentiment of the community, was prompted by our attempts to represent the political subsystems of the North and the South; the same interest was enhanced by our analysis of racial differences in voting behavior. We may now consider the manner in which formal and informal aspects of the individual's environment interact in affecting his behavior. Generally, it appears that *informal environmental factors have the greatest direct relevance for political behavior when political motivations pertaining to that behavior are reinforced by formal institutional arrangements.*

This proposition is documented in Table 11-8, where results of the voting behavior of various categories of party identifiers may be observed under differing conditions, both formal and informal. The formal institutional arrangements are those considered earlier in connection with the facilitation and inhibition of partisanship. The informal political environment is represented by the proportion of the two-party vote cast for the Democratic presidential candidate, permitting counties (non-Southern only) to be arrayed as more or less

TABLE 11-8. Differences in the Voting Behavior of Five Sets of Party Identifiers in Relation to the Institutional Facilitation of Partisanship[a]

	Party Identification				
Facilitation of Partisanship	Strong Democrat	Weak Democrat	Independent	Weak Republican	Strong Republican
Low facilitation	−2	+6	−7	−4	−7
High facilitation	−4	+19	+20	+11	−3
Difference in Democratic margin associated with high facilitation	−2	+13	+27	+15	+4

[a] Each entry indicates the excess of the Democratic margin in the more Democratic counties over that in the more Republican counties. "+" indicates that the group in more Democratic counties cast more Democratic votes than did its counterpart in the less Democratic counties; "−" indicates that the former group actually had a smaller margin of Democratic votes (or a larger Republican margin) than did the latter group.

Democratic. Political motivations are represented by the party identifications of the individual citizen.

The specific application of our hypothesis calls for the vote division within any category of party identification to reflect the more Democratic nature of the county more sharply in the presence of partisan facilitation and less sharply in its relative absence. To measure the influence of the informal environment in the less advantageous situation—that where one's party identification is not supported by formal facilitation of partisanship—we must compare the vote division among pairs of identifiers when both pairs have the same party identification and both come from states that do *not* facilitate partisanship, but when one member of each pair is located in more heavily Democratic counties and the other in less heavily Democratic counties. To measure the impact of the county environment when it *is* reinforced by legal codes facilitating partisanship we make the same comparison of the behaviors of pairs of identifiers when both members of each pair come from states that *do* facilitate political partisanship. Finally, the ultimate test is provided by comparing the *differences* between pairs in states that do less to facilitate partisanship with the *differences* between pairs in states that do more to facilitate partisanship. The first two rows of entries in Table 11-8 present the differences from our first two sets of comparisons. The bottom row of Table 11-8 shows the results of the final comparison of differences and makes clear the variation which is associated with variations in the facilitation of partisanship.

In general, we see that the differences in the Democratic vote margin associated with greater partisan facilitation are substantially larger and reflect the partisan climate of the county vote more often than do the differences exhibited without benefit of formal facilitation of partisanship. The greatest positive influence of institutional support for community partisan sentiments is found among Independents. Table 11-8 may be read to indicate that the Democratic margin among Independents varies some 27 percentage points more where the legal code facilitates partisanship. For weak identifiers the presence of the code adds some 13 to 15 points to the "effectiveness" of the communal environment. Among strong identifiers, there is virtually no variation in voting behavior associated with the partisan sentiment of the community—either with or without the facilitation of partisanship.

We concluded earlier that under proper conditions the partisan climate of the community may influence individual behavior. We may now conclude that the proposition is more likely to be true when the attitude of the community toward partisanship provides formal support and encouragement to partisan behavior.

It would appear that the partisanship of the environment affects the voting behavior of weak party identifiers and Independents only in situations in which there is formal facilitation of political partisanship. The absence of such facilitation—earlier identified as a reflection of the sentiment of the community and a component of the political subsystem—nullifies the potential influence of the partisan coloration of the community. It is the combined interaction of formal and informal components of the system that makes them immediately or directly relevant for individual behavior. The absence of similar findings among Southern voters serves to re-emphasize the particular differences between the party systems of North and South. It adds weight to our conclusion that electoral behavior can be understood only through a comprehension of the context in which it occurs.

Finally, we have noted the failure of strong party identifiers, Democrats and Republicans alike, to fit this pattern of behavior. We saw in Table 11-8 no tendency for strong identifiers to give larger or smaller margins of support to their respective parties as they find themselves in majoritarian or minoritarian situations, regardless of the presence or absence of formal institutional facilitation of their partisanship. Although weak identifiers and Independents are apparently susceptible to informal as well as formal influences, the strong identifier appears impervious in his partisanship. This "failure" of response actually supports and broadens our earlier proposition that formal political institutions have least impact on political behavior when the attitudes relevant to that behavior are most potent. This conclusion apparently can be taken to embrace relationships involving informal environmental influences as well as the formal legal or institutional factors examined earlier.

THE SOCIAL AND ECONOMIC CONTEXT ◇ SECTION IV

As we have pushed behind the initial attitudes supporting the vote decision we have become impressed by the importance of antecedents that must be conceived in political terms. This has been as true in the treatment of short-term fluctuations in partisan division of the vote among the few as in the discussion of the great partisan stability of most persons in the electorate.

We noted in Section II, by way of example, the importance of personal attributes of the presidential candidates in creating temporary shifts in party fortunes, particularly when there is wide consensus on the attractiveness of a candidate. To account for such consensus, we may ask why people see these attributes as desirable in a President, or why this candidate rather than another was chosen. The first question has to do with perceptions of political roles, whereas the second leads rapidly out of the field of vision of the voter himself into aspects of decision making within political elites. On the other hand, to the degree that a candidate evokes a mixed response, we would want to know primarily what differences in individuals underlie such variation in feeling. Even here, however, the primary antecedent remains political. For the most potent factor differentiating responses is not economic status, social milieu, or variation in deep-seated temperament, but quite simply the political party, which more often than not has been espoused years before the candidate takes up a position as an object in the psychological field.

Thus prior party attachments form the great watershed for public reaction to current political events. With the examination of this phenomenon in Section III it was natural to ask what conditions lead to the formation of partisan allegiances *initially*. The instrumental character of the political system would suggest that if we trace a party commitment deep enough into the past, we must sooner or later encounter recognizable "beginnings," and that these beginnings are likely to involve pressures arising outside the political order as narrowly defined. True as this may be, such a tracing leads with surprising frequency to events lying years or even generations behind us, in such remote circumstances as a ravaged Georgia plantation or a job for a bewildered Boston immigrant. It is such roots of current choice that provide a strange commentary on the view of the democratic process as a periodic re-evaluation of contemporary events. Hence we have stressed, in building our metaphor of the causal funnel, the importance of a "political" core running backward in time, which more often than not provides the clearest explanation of current behavior.

It is not, however, our intention to leave the matter in such restricted form. The causal priorities assigned in the course of our argument are a judicious reflection of the total cast of the data that we have analyzed over the years. None of our ensuing observations should be construed as contesting this emphasis; many further facts will come to light that tend rather to underscore it. Yet it has been presented only as an emphasis, and not as a "simple and sovereign" principle of political behavior.

Already, as our materials have been developed, we have noted a constant if "premature" intrusion of non-political causes and intervening mechanisms in our account. We have remarked upon the widespread perceptions of group interest that appear in citizen evaluations. We have considered visible biases in individual response that appear to rest on diffuse sentiment communicated by primary groups within the political community. We have also encountered some of the reverberations touched off in the political order by grosser events—

most notably, disasters like war and depression—that envelop the society.

Over the ensuing chapters we shall approach some of the prominent social and economic elements in the causal nexus more directly. We need not restrict our attention to the role that such non-political factors play in initial party choice, for it is apparent that many of these determinants and intervening mechanisms contribute to the course of events up to the time of the act itself, even for the long-term partisan. Knowledge of social processes may add much to our understanding of the fact that party allegiances not only remain stable but grow stronger over time. In addition to intra-psychic mechanisms that act in this direction, social communication in a congenial primary group may constitute a potent extra-psychic process leading to the same end. The ambiguity of the merits of political objects and events is such that people are dependent upon "social reality" to support and justify their political opinions. When primary groups engage in political discussion and are homogeneous in basic member viewpoints, the attitudes of the individual must be continually reinforced as he sees similar opinions echoed in the social group.

Although the fact of membership in a politically alert primary group is of no help to an understanding of the partisan direction of an individual's vote, it does suggest that he is likely to hold a more stable party preference over time. By the same token, such primary-group mechanisms are of obvious import in maintaining the patterns of distinctive political behavior long associated with many sociologically defined groupings in the electorate.

We shall find it of value to distinguish between those patterns associated with self-conscious groups, such as racial or ethnic communities, and those groups that emerge from certain formal categories, such as the age cohort of people over 60 years old or such as women. Although the primary group may be influential in sustaining distinctive patterns within both polar types, other mechanisms that contribute to these patterns differ quite radically according to the nature of the grouping. In Chapter 12 we shall propose a system of variables that seems critical for the operation of group influence in the case of the self-conscious group. Location of a group as a set of values on these variables appears to increase our understanding of its political homogeneity at any point in time, and thus to cast light upon trends in the distinctiveness of such groups as voting blocs and upon conditions of member deviation from group standards related to politics. Treatment of the far more diverse mechanisms that create patterns in the opposite type of social entity—the simple sociological category—is postponed until Chapter 17.

The intervening chapters deal with social phenomena that are intermediate between these poles or with economic phenomena that we must consider in the light of their effects upon the political process. The social class provides a natural point of convergence between the social and the economic problem in politics. Its status as a self-conscious group or mere analytic category has often been debated. We shall find it useful in Chapter 13 to conceive that this status varies markedly over time in response to economic conditions, and to evaluate its political implications in these terms. Chapter 14 is devoted more directly to the economic backgrounds of political change in the current period. Recent fluctuations in the economic welfare of the nation that have not appeared to affect the broad class phenomena of Chapter 13 are examined in greater detail outside the class frame of reference. Several conceptual threads developed in the chapters on group influence, social class, and economic antecedents are drawn together in a discussion of agrarian voting in Chapter 15.

Having considered several aspects of group behavior, we turn in Chapter 16 to an analysis of change wrought in personal dispositions when the individual shifts his social and political milieu. Although primary stress is laid here upon geographic movement from one partisan climate to another, we shall also find it enlightening to consider some of the effects of analogous change resulting from individual mobility in the social hierarchy.

After treatment in Chapter 17 of behavior patterns marking sociological categories that cannot be seen as self-conscious groups, we conclude the section with a brief consideration of the role of "personality" factors in the mass decision process. Questions concerning the conceptual relationship of personality elements to the other types of factors employed—social and attitudinal—permit us to review in summary vein the conceptual status accorded to these diverse elements in the causal sequences leading to the individual vote.

Membership in Social Groupings ◇ 12

Most Americans, though not officially enrolled as members of the political parties, hold a form of psychological membership in the party that exerts great influence on their political behavior. The active membership group that forms the core of each party is small; the *psychological* group, however, is very large. Most American citizens can be classified according to their identification with one of the major parties, and the degree of this identification is an important tool for the analysis of political behavior.

Many other groupings in the nation are watched by students of politics because of the political influence they seem to wield. During each campaign we hear comment about the "Catholic vote," the "Negro vote," the "labor vote" and so on. Unlike the political parties, these groups stand at one remove from the political order. Their reason for existence is not expressly political. The labor union exists to force management to provide more liberally for the worker; the Catholic church exists for religious worship. But members of these groups appear to think and behave politically in distinctive ways. We assume that these distinctive patterns are produced, in one fashion or another, by influence from the group.

The Problem of Group Influence

The concept of a group's influencing a set of members poses some difficult logical problems. For the group is, after all, no more than a set of individuals who are its members. If we say that a group (a set of members) influences its members, we appear to be reasoning in circles. Social scientists of fifty years ago were particularly concerned with this difficulty. For a time the solution was provided by the doctrine of the "group mind," an entity above and apart from the sum of group members, which was accorded a reality of its own. If members of a group behaved differently from individuals who did not belong to the group, it was this "real," external group entity that provided the influencing force. When this position fell from respectability, many social scientists avoided the subject of group influence entirely.

But the distinctive behavior of group members was too obvious to leave unanalyzed. After a time the psychologist, Kurt Lewin, suggested a convincing resolution to the problem of the "group mind." "Groups are real," he said, "if they have real effects." Groups are real because they are *psychologically* real, and thereby affect the way in which we behave. If we hear that "the labor union" is advocating a piece of legislation, we rarely think of many individuals, characterized by certain occupations, who advocate the measure. Rather, we are likely to think of the labor union as a single entity or unit. Now and then we may think primarily of the union leadership as the agent, or even certain specific leaders. But we still tend to regard these individuals as spokesmen for the group. And this psychological shorthand has effects on our opinions and behavior. If we know that "the union" makes a political endorsement, we may well react positively or negatively to the candidate or issue, *according to whether our sympathies lie with or against the union.* The "kiss of death" of an unpopular group endorsement describes precisely this phenomenon.

Groups have influence, then, because we tend to think of them as wholes, and come to respond positively or negatively to them in that form. In this sense, even people who are not members of a group may be influenced by the position that a group takes in politics. Groups can become reference points for the formation of attitudes and decisions about behavior; we speak then of *positive* and *negative reference groups.* People who are actually members of the group are likely to have a more differentiated image of it. But there remains a sense of norms and values attributed to a generalized "group": these are the expectations concerning appropriate behavior for the "loyal" Catholic or union member. It is the group standards that are psychologically real and are responsible for influence when it occurs.

In this chapter we are concerned with the apparent political influence exerted among major, nationwide groupings such as the labor unions, Negroes, Catholics, and Jews. This is not the only level at which political influence dependent on social contact may be examined. Much influence is exerted in smaller, face-to-face "primary" groups such as families, circles of friends, and the like. In fact, there is some evidence to suggest that when primary-group influences run counter to secondary-group political standards, the more intimate contacts may more often than not carry the day.[1] Nonetheless, although many of the mechanisms of influence may be the same in both cases, the study of secondary-group effects has its own unique fruits. It is probably accurate to assume that influence ramifies through primary groups at the grass roots of the nation in a manner fairly constant for both parties. The success or failure of influence at a face-to-face level is not likely to account for the gross trends of the sort constituted by secondary-group voting. If every man managed to influence his wife to vote as he does, we would have no more than a "multiplier" effect on both sides of the political fence. In contrast, successful influence by secondary groups can cause a large-scale, unidirectional shift in the partisan division of the national vote. We are interested in understanding the conditions under which these group pressures are more or less successful.[2]

When we discussed the political parties, it seemed reasonable to speak in terms of a "psychological group," in part because the boundaries of the parties are so poorly delimited by the fact of official membership. In secondary membership groups like labor unions, these formal group boundaries are quite clear. We do not have to ask our informants whether they "consider" they belong to one or another groups; membership is a factual matter. But as we examine these groups more closely, it turns out that the concept of group identification and psychological membership remains extremely valuable. Individuals, all of whom are nominal group members, vary in *degree* of membership, in a psychological sense; and this variation provides us with an excellent tool for breaking apart a voting "bloc,"

[1] Norman Kaplan, "Reference Group Theory and Voting Behavior," (Unpublished doctor's dissertation, Columbia University, 1955). Although the homogeneity of all immediate reference groups made definitive test impossible, the author finds evidence to suggest that when norms of different reference groups conflict, the individual's primary group (family, friends) tends to become the "crucial" reference group, eclipsing the effects of co-workers and other secondary memberships.

[2] To be sure, the primary group is ubiquitous, and phenomena at this level become involved in circumstances of sweeping political change. For example, the primary group may serve as agent or medium for the propagation of standards from the secondary group, or of information about those political events that do stir broad shifts in public sentiment. As one common phase in the influence process, it deserves careful study in the political context. But it is not the sole medium for communication of such pressures toward change, and its study does not relieve the obligation to attack the actual sources of change more directly.

like the American Negro community, in order to understand the workings of influence within the secondary group.

The significance of group identification in all social groupings provides us with a foundation for a more general model of group influence in politics. In such a model, not only the labor union and the farm organization, but the political party and to some degree the social class can be located. The scheme would tell us what dimensions of the situation were important for measurement, and how these measures should be combined once they were taken. For example, a specific labor union in the 1956 presidential election would be found to have certain characteristics as a group and stand in a certain relationship to the issues of the election. Appropriate measurements based on such a scheme would allow us to anticipate the direction and degree of the influence that the union would wield in the specific situation.

In this chapter we treat membership in social groupings by sketching the outlines for a general model of this sort. The specific currents observed in the Negro vote in the 1956 election become, in this light, substance of a case study to lay against the more abstract elements called for by the scheme. Likewise, the distinctive behavior of union members toward the objects of politics becomes a special case of the broad phenomenon of group influence.

The Elements of the Model

A model for group influence should perform two distinct services:

1. Increase our understanding of deviation from group political standards by individual members. Once we have ascertained that a particular group behaves distinctively, we immediately note that there are exceptions. If the group exerts influence on its membership, and these individuals are members, how and why do they resist?

2. Increase our understanding of the waxing and waning of distinctive political behavior on the part of certain social groupings in the population. Under certain conditions, a group may show extreme homogeneity in its political disposition; then, as time passes, this homogeneity dies away. What specific conditions govern this variation in group political "strength"?

The same system of variables can handle both problems, for the problems are closely related. If we can specify the conditions under which an individual fails to be influenced by his group, then it is likely that the decline of group potency in politics will result from the extension of these conditions to an increasing proportion of the membership. The aggregate phenomenon is but the group-level extension of events at an individual level and vice versa. But it is important to recognize that explanation may proceed at either of two levels, for circumstances arise in which the distinction becomes important.

At the simplest level, there is a triangle of elements involved in the situation: (1) the individual, (2) the group, and (3) the world of political objects. This triangle suggests three different relationships among these elements: (*a*) the relationship of the individual to the group; (*b*) the relationship of the group to the political world; and (*c*) the relationship of the individual to the political world. These three relationships determine the types of variables that we take into account. A full model will call for measurements that adequately capture the important dimensions of each relationship, if we are to understand the way in which the individual will respond to politics *given the presence of a group that is real in the sense that it can exert a greater or lesser influence on his behavior.*

We have already treated in detail the variables that characterize the relationship of the individual to the political world. The perceptions and attitudes that generate political motives lie in the political core of the funnel of causality; they indicate the conclusions the individual has drawn about the world of politics at a point close to the voting act. We have thought of this manifold of attitudes as a field of forces that determines behavior. It is also congenial to think of influence exerted by a group on the individual as a force, having strength and direction as primary properties. If we suspect that an individual is subject to influence from a given group in the process of a vote decision, then the total field of forces that leads to the decision may be analyzed into a set of group-induced forces and a set of forces from other points of origin.[3]

Hence the relationship of the individual to the world of politics represents a combination of group and non-group forces. The group forces in the field are predictable as a function of two "background" terms: the relationship of the individual to the group and the relation-

[3] For the sake of simplicity, we shall refer to group-induced or "group forces" and "non-group forces" in this context. In a strict sense, the latter phrase can be a misnomer, since some of the forces in the field not attributable to the group under analysis may still lend themselves to conceptualization as arising from other groups. However, our exposition will be most clear if we restrict our attention at the outset to the single-group case.

ship of the group to the world of politics. The non-group forces are, of course, independent of either of these terms.[4] An analysis of the social origins of political motives therefore involves (1) the manner in which the two background terms interact to produce group forces; and (2) the manner in which group forces interact with other forces in the immediate field of political attitudes.

Two important implications are suggested by a logical exercise of this sort. On one hand, we must arrive at some means of sorting the group forces in which we are interested from non-group forces, within the total field that characterizes the relationship of the individual to the world of politics. Therefore we are interested in a complete analysis of relationships *a* and *b*, but we are only interested at the outset in one aspect of relationship *c*, that is, that portion which exists only by virtue of the individual's cognizance of the group.

If we pay little systematic attention to the total relationship of the individual to the political world in elaborating this portion of the model, we must not forget that these non-group forces exist. In fact, this is a first-level answer to the problem of member deviation from group political standards. Group members do not make political decisions in a psychological field limited to group forces, any more than non-members make decisions in a vacuum. The current objects of orientation in the political world are available to everybody and, if perceived, have characteristics that can be distorted only within limits. A strong set of Democratic beliefs will give a particular coloration to incoming stimuli from the external world of politics. But perception is more likely to color than create; its latitude is not infinite. If there is corruption in a Democratic administration, definitively proved and extravagantly publicized, the most ardent Democrat cannot perceptually turn it into another argument for voting Democratic. Similarly, in the group setting, a labor union might like to shield its membership from the general attractiveness of an Eisenhower candidacy. It cannot censor the image completely, nor can it convince its staunch adherents that the candidate is dishonest or mentally deficient. It must try to find the weak spots, and chip away as best it can, or strive to heighten the effect of other more favorable forces in the field. In brief, it is force against force; the same exertion of influence from the union will have less net effect when the Republican candidate has the stuff of popularity than when his image is drab.

[4] This is true by definition, but it should be remembered that at some point prior to the behavior, non-group forces interact with group-induced forces. The *resultant* of this interaction determines the state of the proximal attitudes just before the voting act, as well as the behavior itself.

Our immediate concern lies with the strength of group-generated forces. We wish to understand the conditions under which that strength varies, over time, from individual to individual and from group to group. For this task we can conceptually ignore other forces in the field, which derive from the relation of the individual to politics *group considerations aside.* But we must remember that these forces exist, and contribute to the final attitudes and behavior.

Establishing the Fact of Group Influence

The immediate problem is to find ways to estimate the strength of group forces on the individual. With other forces present in the field, it is easy to mistake their effects for the effects of group influence. In fact, we shall never be certain in any absolute sense that we have isolated the "pure" effects of group influence at either the individual or the group level. But before we proceed to lay out elements of the model in greater detail, we must have a clearer picture of the strength of those forces which the model hopes to predict. By proceeding with care, we can arrive at satisfactory working estimates.

First, it is important to think in terms of the *distinctiveness* of group behavior, rather than its absolute nature. For example, a majority of Catholics in our 1956 sample voted Republican. Traditionally, there has been a Democratic norm among Catholics. Does this finding mean that the norm has died away, or that the group now has new, pro-Republican standards? It means neither. The Catholic Republican vote moved only slightly above the 50 per cent mark, when the nation as a whole was voting 57 per cent Republican. In other words, Catholics still voted distinctively Democratic, even though this deviation to the Democratic side did not amount to a Democratic majority within the group. The group force was weak and non-group forces pushing toward a Republican vote were strong; the non-group forces were dominant enough to pull a majority of Catholics into the Republican camp, but the presence of group forces in a Democratic direction remains detectible, *relative to the behavior of non-group members.*

With vote distinctiveness as a criterion, Table 12-1 summarizes the behavior of several key secondary-membership groups with traditional Democratic voting norms, over a period of three presidential elections. Several aspects of the table are striking. First we find that there is considerable variation in *degree* of distinctiveness, from election to election and from group to group. We also find that each group

TABLE 12-1. The Distinctiveness of Voting Behavior among Several Social Groupings with Democratic Norms, 1948–1956[a]

	1948	1952	1956
Members of union households[b]	+35.8	+19.8	+18.1
Union members	. . .[c]	+24.9	+21.4
Catholics	+16.2	+12.8	+7.1
Negroes:	. . .[d]	+41.2	+24.7
Non-South	. . .[d]	+50.8	+33.1
South	. . .[d]	+17.6	−1.1
Jews	. . .[d]	+31.9	+40.8

[a] The entry in each cell represents the deviation in per cent Democratic of the two-party vote division from the comparable per cent among the residual, non-member portion of the total sample. A positive deviation indicates that the group vote was more Democratic; a negative deviation indicates that the group was more Republican than the residual non-group.

[b] Members of union households includes both union members, where interviews were conducted with the member himself, and other non-union individuals living in a household that contained a union member. In most cases, the non-member is the wife of a member.

[c] Members and non-members were not separated within our sample of union households in 1948.

[d] Due to the reduced size of the 1948 sample and the small proportion of Negroes and Jews in the parent population, insufficient cases are available for presentation.

seems to vary within a characteristic range. Catholics tend to be least distinctive throughout; the labor unions fall in a middle range. Negroes, despite a sharp drop in distinctiveness between 1952 and 1956, remain on the high side along with Jewish voters. We want a model that will serve at the group level to predict changes in distinctiveness of political behavior; but many of the elements that seem reasonable to include in such a model—the characteristics of the group as a group, and the relation of individual members to it—are not likely to vary radically in the short term. Therefore, these elements of stability are encouraging. They may be taken to reflect the underlying stability of many variables in the model.

Nevertheless, there is room for dissatisfaction with distinctiveness, cast in this form, as a working measure of influence. Social scientists have long felt a need to distinguish between two types of distinctive behavior among group members. In the first case, members come to respond distinctively because their action is informed more or less subtly by standards of conduct extant in the group. It is behavior that is group oriented and, in a strict sense, group determined. Distinctiveness of this sort warrants consideration as "group influence." The second type of distinctiveness develops from the fact that group members encounter patterns of stimuli that are somewhat distinct from those encountered by non-members. Since certain stimuli may evoke specific responses, group or no group, members may react quite independently of one another, yet so similarly that group behavior is distinctive, even though the group has not mediated the response.[5]

In secondary groupings of the type we are considering, this conceptual problem is critical, for the fact of membership in these groups locates the person in a peculiar position in social structure, which in itself ensures a distinctive pattern of life experience. For example, Negroes have been kept in the lower levels of the nation's status structure; they tend to predominate in the least desirable occupations, receive the lowest pay, are least well educated, and so on. Their high birth rate means that young people are more numerous among Negroes than among other elements in the population. In the North, they tend to reside in metropolitan areas; in the South, in small towns and rural areas. All of these distinctive characteristics have a potential effect on their reactions to politics; and this would be true *even if the group did not exist as an entity cognized by its members.* Northern Negroes as a group made a massive shift of allegiance from the Republican to the Democratic Party during the 1930's. Was this group cohesiveness in response to an Administration interested in the welfare of the Negro community, or was it simply the independent reaction of a set of individuals to economic pressures, part and parcel of the nationwide establishment of Democratic dominance at the lower status levels? In the one case, we would speak of group influence; in the other, we would turn to considerations of social class and economic deprivation.

Of course, we cannot ignore the fact that group influence is in part contingent upon the life situations of the membership. Minority status, by relegation of group members to characteristic areas of the social structure, creates the needs and dissatisfactions that are so often the foundation for group influence. But the important point remains that group influence *is* an additional element in the picture; shared

[5] Note in this regard the discussion by Angus Campbell and Homer C. Cooper, *Group Differences in Attitudes and Votes* (Survey Research Center, The University of Michigan, Ann Arbor, Mich., 1956), p. 5 ff.

membership provides a focus and direction for behavior that is lacking among non-group members who happen to be placed in the same life situation. Therefore, it is important to distinguish between the patterns of behavior that develop from the life situations of group members, without reference to the group *qua* group, and the residual distinctiveness that may be traced directly to the fact of group membership.

Hence we must contrast behaviors of group members not simply with those of the remainder of the population, but with the restricted part of that population that shares the peculiar life situations of group members. We want to isolate a *"control"* group of non-members that matches the *"test"* group of members on all important aspects of life situation save the fact of membership. If the test group has a disproportionate number of elderly people, our control group must be selected with similar age bias. If the social class composition of the test group is heavily lower status, the control group must derive from the lower-status levels as well.

The various aspects of life situation could be elaborated infinitely. Construction of such a control group presumes that we know which aspects are of real significance in the responses of the individual to politics. As empirical work proceeds our knowledge improves accordingly, but there may always be a dimension of importance that we have not yet discovered. In general, however, over a period of time we become increasingly confident that we know how to control the most important effects of life situation.

We know, for example, that the sharpest discontinuities in partisan political behavior occur between the South and the remainder of the country. Since our secondary groups are not evenly distributed between the two great political regions of the country, we must create the same balance in the control group. The differences between residence in metropolitan areas, towns, and rural districts need similar attention. Also, the stability of party identifications requires that we take account of the past residence of individuals with regard to region and to urban-rural differences. Though we shall find later that social class was not an important factor in the vote in 1956, it is still sure to influence other dimensions such as general involvement in politics. Therefore, we will control all of the major status dimensions as well: education, income, and occupation. In addition, we will control age and number of generations that the informant's family has spent in the United States. Finally, since it is our thesis that membership in certain social groupings creates additional forces on behavior, we shall take into account any overlap in personnel of our test groups. If one third of all Catholics are union members, we shall want the same union representation in the Catholic-control group.[6]

With life situation controlled in this fashion our estimate of group distinctiveness should be materially improved. Table 12-2 summarizes this new estimate for our groups in the context of the 1956 election. If we compare the figures for vote distinctiveness with those in Table 12-1, we find that much of the picture has remained the same. Catholic distinctiveness has almost disappeared, and the estimate of Jewish distinctiveness has risen slightly. But the major change has been a substantial reduction in the estimate of distinctiveness of the non-Southern Negro vote. This group remains significantly Democratic; but taking into account its extremely low status, its relative youth and its Southern origins leaves it less Democratic than might appear at first glance.[7]

With such controls, we have more nearly reduced the relationship between the individual and the world of politics to its group-relevant aspects. In effect, we have arrived at an improved estimate of the strength of group forces in the total field at the time of the voting act. The estimate is not perfect and depends on an aggregation of cases; we cannot say that any specific group member is more swayed by the

[6] This rigorous control procedure was made possible by the fact that all of our secondary groups are minorities; hence substantial case shrinkage among the set of possible non-member controls can be withstood. Precision controls were used for region, urban-rural residence, and occupation status, thereby holding constant any interaction effects between these variables. Other aspects of life situation were subjected to looser, distribution controls.

[7] The application of the Southern origin factor to Negroes represents one point at which we lack sufficient information to exercise controls prudently. Over two thirds of the adult Negroes now living outside of the South report that they grew up in the South, and a large proportion of these are young enough that their migration must have occurred during or after the Second World War. Since White migrants from the South are notably Democratic compared with the non-Southern population, their use in a control group cuts into the distinctiveness of the non-Southern Negro population. (For a more detailed discussion of these effects, see Chapter 16, "Population Movement.") It may be argued that this is an instance of "overcontrol," since Negroes in the South have not shared the Southern White tradition favoring the Democratic Party. There are several knotty conceptual problems involved here, but one crucial body of data concerning the past political preferences of the Negro in the South is simply not available in any reliable form. Within the scope of survey explorations—and this takes us back to 1948—Southern Negroes are in fact strongly Democratic in party identification, as are Southern Whites. If Southern Negroes were at one time a Republican group, as they must have been following the Civil War, some radical political change must have occurred in the interim. Unfortunately we cannot specify the period, and this fact would bear directly on the control problem. As the matter stands, the distinctiveness of the Negro group may be underestimated in Table 12-2.

TABLE 12-2. Distinctiveness of Presidential Vote among Certain Groups, with Life Situation Controlled, 1956[a]

	1956 Presidential Vote
Members of union households	+17.1
Union members	+20.4
Catholics	+2.9
Negroes:	
Non-South	+11.6
South	+15.4
Jews	+45.4

[a] The entry in each cell represents a deviation in per cent Democratic of the two-party vote within the test group from a comparable per cent computed for control groups matched with the test groups for a variety of conditions of life situation.

group than any other, although we get the clear impression that some groups exert more effective influence than others. We must now turn to other elements in the model to account for this variation in influence.

The Relationship of the Individual to the Group

The first variables to be considered must define the way in which the individual relates himself to the group. We would like to measure aspects of the individual-group relationship that are meaningful for the relationship of *any* individual to *any* group, whether or not that group ever expends effort in political affairs.

Let us think of the group as a psychological reality that exerts greater or lesser attractive force upon its members. Although all the individuals with which we deal are nominal members, some are intensely drawn to the group, some are much less interested, and, in groups where membership is involuntary, there may be some nominal members who are repelled by the groups and would prefer to be non-members. Whatever the nominal membership status of the individual, there is room for a great deal of variation in the degree of psychological membership that characterizes the relationship.

Psychological membership can in turn be divided analytically into a number of components. We might find that three individuals, all highly identified with the group, are attracted by different aspects of group membership. One takes pleasure in the companionship of other members who are friends; another finds that the group offers him a chance to engage in rewarding activities; another feels that group membership is a source of prestige. The influence the group could exert on each of these members might vary somewhat even though all showed the same general degree of identification. For our purposes, we will take a generalized strength of group identification as a concept adequate to summarize the nature of the individual-group bond. Just as party identification measures the sense of personal attachment to a political party, so a measure of group identification will indicate the closeness or "*we* feeling" that an individual senses with regard to his membership group.

We have measured group identification by asking members of various politically significant groups the following questions:

> Would you say that you feel pretty close to (e.g.) Negroes in general or that you don't feel much closer to them than you do to other kinds of people?
>
> How much interest would you say you have in how (e.g.) Negroes as a whole are getting along in this country? Do you have a good deal of interest in it, some interest, or not much interest at all?

From responses to these items an index of group identification was prepared. The first hypothesis that the model suggests is as follows: *the higher the identification of the individual with the group, the higher the probability that he will think and behave in ways which distinguish members of his group from non-members.*

Actually hypotheses much like this have found supporting evidence in other empirical work on voting behavior.[8] Therefore, we are not surprised to find that if we take all members of groups that vote distinctively Democratic, the people who are highly identified with these groups vote even more distinctively Democratic than members who are less highly identified. The least identified third voted 43 per cent Democratic, a figure not very different from the vote proportion in the population as a whole. Medium identifiers, however, voted 56 per cent Democratic; and those most highly identified with these groups voted 69 per cent Democratic. In general, then, the hypothesis receives clear support, and strength of group identification deserves a place as a variable in our model.

[8] Edward A. Suchman, and Herbert T. Menzell, "The Interplay of Demographic and Psychological Variables in the Analysis of Voting Surveys," *The Language of Social Research,* ed. Paul F. Lazarsfeld and Morris Rosenberg (The Free Press, Glencoe, Ill., 1955).

The same effect appears when we look at a range of other political behaviors and attitudes. High identifiers in these groups vote more distinctively Democratic at all levels of government; they are more frequently Democratic in their party identification. They also react differently to political issues than low identifiers. For example, labor union members in general are more likely to feel that the government should provide for full employment than are members of a control group matched with them. But among union members, the strong identifiers are even more distinctive in their views about full employment than those who identify less strongly.

Secondary groups that are not primarily political take little interest in some issues, and in these cases group members do not hold attitudes that differ significantly from those of non-member control groups nor do high identifiers differ from more peripheral members. But as a general rule, whenever a group holds distinctive beliefs about some issue, then within the group a differentiation appears between members according to the strength of their group identification.

This combination of facts argues most conclusively that we are dealing here with a true group-influence phenomenon. Influence of this sort is notoriously difficult to document, even though it is clear that it abounds in our social world. The person influenced does not like to think that his views are not entirely of his own creation, although very few views are likely to be, whether held by union member or businessman. Thus direct measurement is difficult. And we have seen that inference from unrefined statistics concerning the voting record of a particular group is vulnerable to a number of simple but cogent criticisms. But once our data have been shaped as we now see them, it is difficult to imagine an explanation of their regularities that does not in some way involve "influence" as we have defined it. These are, then, the group's "real effects."

To ascertain that influence exists is but a first step. We are also interested in assessing the relative strength of influence exerted by various groups and the conditions under which this strength increases or decreases. We find considerable variation in the degree of disparity in presidential vote between strong and weak identifiers within various groups. Table 12-3 summarizes this variation. If we compare these figures with those in Table 12-2, we find some interesting similarities in the rank ordering of the groups. Vote distinctiveness *within the group* bears some relation to distinctiveness between the group and a control group matched for life situation, as we would expect if both were taken to reflect strength of group political influence. But there are differences, also: high identifiers are more distinct in the union case and less distinct in the Negro case than Table 12-2 would lead us to expect. Most Negroes are highly identified with their group; therefore the total group is more clearly Democratic than it might appear if the proportion of high and low identifiers within the Negro group was closer to that found within the union group. But part of the discrepancy results from other factors to be added to the model shortly.

TABLE 12-3. Vote Division Within Four Test Groups, According to Strength of Group Identification, 1956[a]

	Highly Identi-fied	Weakly Identi-fied	Discrepancy
Members of union households	64	36	+28
Catholics	51	39	+11
Negroes:			
Non-South	72	63	+9
South	. . .[b]	. . .[b]	. . .[b]
Jews	83	55	+28

[a] The entries in the first two columns represent the per cent Democratic of the two-party vote division. The final column summarizes the differences between percentages in the first two, a plus indicating that high identifiers in the group voted more strongly Democratic.

[b] Southern Negro voters in the sample are too few for further subdivision.

Group identifications, summarizing the individual-group relationship with considerations of politics aside, help to answer the two primary questions with which a theory of group influence must deal. At the individual level, we may sort out a set of nominal members who are most likely to deviate from the group position under non-group forces. They are the people who do not strongly identify with the group, who are psychologically peripheral to it.

A similar proposition can be formulated at the group level. Some groups boast memberships intensely loyal to group purposes and interests. Others have trouble maintaining member identifications. We shall call a group enjoying high member identification a *cohesive group*.[9] Group cohesiveness is one determinant of the influence which a group can wield over its membership.

[9] Dorwin K. Cartwright, and Alvin Zander, *Group Dynamics: Research and Theory* (Row, Peterson and Co., Evanston, Ill., 1953), Part II, pp. 71–134.

If a group has generated distinctive political attitudes and behavior among its members, this distinctiveness will fade if group cohesiveness is destroyed. Cohesiveness itself must depend on a number of factors according to the type of group and the setting involved. Within the large and far-flung social groupings under discussion in this chapter, a prime determinant may simply be the degree to which group members feel set apart from other people by virtue of social barriers. If we set up a mean identification score as a simple index of cohesiveness for each group, the resulting array seems to support this hypothesis:

TABLE 12-4. Relation of Group Cohesiveness to Group Identification, 1956

Cohesiveness	Mean Identification Score[a]	Group
High	2.5	Southern Negro
	2.2	Non-Southern Negro
	2.2	Jewish
Low	1.8	Union member
	1.6	Catholic
	1.6	Member, union household

[a] The response to the two identification questions (see p. 307) are scored such that a maximum value on the index is 3.0, when the most positive response is made to both items. The corresponding minimum value is 0.0, when the most negative response is made to both items. About 61% of Southern Negroes responded positively toward the group on both items; the corresponding proportion among Catholics was 28%.

Key and Munger have linked the waxing and waning of group voting to changes in social differentiation of this sort.[10] Perhaps the reputed erosion of the "Catholic vote"—the latter days of which we may be capturing in Tables 12-1 and 12-2—is due to the social assimilation which that group has experienced in this country over the past few generations. In any case, we cannot predict directly from group cohesiveness to distinctiveness in voting patterns, without taking into account other elements of the general model.

[10] V. O. Key, and Frank Munger, "Social Determination and Electoral Decision: The Case of Indiana," *American Voting Behavior*, ed. Eugene Burdick and Arthur Brodbeck (The Free Press, Glencoe, Ill., 1959).

The Relationship of the Group to the World of Politics

If the relationship between individual and group is summarized by the concept of identification, attempts to deal with the relationship of the group to the world of politics focus upon a vaguer concept of *proximity*. All of our secondary membership groups except the political party have their basic existence outside of the political order. At this point it becomes important to specify this distance from the world of politics more precisely.

Proximity is not in itself an ideal concept, for the dimensions it subsumes are somewhat heterogeneous. It does, however, carry some intuitive meaning. Groups as perceived objects may be located according to their proximity to the world of politics. They are, as we say, more or less political. The political party lies at the center of politics; the American Bowling Congress, on the other hand, stands at some remove. In this rough sense we would have little trouble indicating "how political" any of a series of groups is to be considered.

If we analyze our intuitions concerning proximity, we find that they depend upon the frequency with which we have seen the group *qua* group associated intimately with objects that are clearly political—issues, candidates, and parties. We would think, for example, of lobbying activity, political pronouncements, and candidates who publicize the fact of membership in that group. We would consider what we know of the primary goals of the group, and their apparent relevance to politics. The perceived relationship between the group and the world of politics has substantial grounding in objective events, constituted largely by the actions of group leaders. But perceptions of this sort are never a perfect mirror of events in the external world, and we could not expect that all individuals, or even all group members, would perceive the relationship of the group to politics in precisely the same manner. Thus we shall think of proximity as a subjective dimension, a tendency to associate group and politics at a psychological level.

Where proximity has partisan significance we would hypothesize that: *as proximity between the group and the world of politics increases, the political distinctiveness of the group will increase.*

Or, at the individual level: *as perception of proximity between the group and the world of politics becomes clearer, the susceptibility of the individual member to group influence in political affairs increases.*

Now the concept of proximity will have to undergo further refinement before these hypotheses have full meaning. But we may first test the proposition in a general way. For two decades prior to the merger in 1955, there were visible differences between the leadership of the American Federation of Labor (AFL) and that of the Congress of Industrial Organizations (CIO) concerning the role of the labor union in politics. The CIO was more committed to the belief that the union movement depended upon political decisions for survival and pioneered in large-scale attempts to instruct the rank and file in preferred patterns of political behavior. The role of its Political Action Committee under Sidney Hillman in the 1944 presidential campaign was symbolic of this endeavor. Traditionally, the AFL had placed primary emphasis upon bettering the lot of the laborer within the immediate work context, and its more subdued political efforts had been self-consciously "non-partisan," in the spirit of Samuel Gompers. In our terms, then, there were differences in the proximity of the two largest labor groupings to politics.

By the time of the 1956 presidential election, the merger of the AFL and CIO had been completed, an event too recent for substantial change in the influence situation. If we make a simple division of our union members according to their one-time AFL or CIO affiliation, we find that our AFL respondents voted 51 per cent Democratic, whereas 60 per cent of the CIO members favored Stevenson. This is not a large difference, but differences of almost exactly the same magnitude have emerged in the voting patterns of the two groups in every presidential election covered by nationwide surveys since the time of the original schism in 1935. It has never been clear whether this difference stemmed from differences between the groups as agents of influence or from differences in the life situation of members. For example, the AFL is made up of craft unions with skilled workers who might be expected, on status grounds alone, to be less Democratic than the unskilled members of the CIO. But the difference between the two organizations in 1956 withstands all such tests. Furthermore, the distinctions in vote cannot be traced to variation in cohesiveness; AFL members are almost identical with CIO members in their aggregate strength of identification with the group. Finally, the necessary perceptual conditions are present. More CIO members saw their union leaders as intending to vote Democratic than was the case with AFL respondents.

Thus our general sense of differences in proximity between two groups has provided a simple test for the basic hypothesis. We are able to predict a heightening of group influence over and above the effects of group identification. But we must specify a good deal more precisely the dimensions that are involved in our general sense of proximity, and attempt to measure them more objectively.

We have suggested that perceptions of proximity between one's group and the world of politics rest upon associations that have been built up between the group and the political objects. How do these links become established? In some cases, the associations are directly given, as when the political candidate is a highly visible member of the group. The link is, so to speak, "built into" the object of orientation itself. We shall discuss phenomena of this sort under the general heading of *group salience* in politics. More often, however, the establishment of associations between the group and politics depends on conscious effort by elements within the group to propagate certain standards of member behavior. This *transmission of standards* is a communication process, and its effectiveness depends on the clarity with which the standard is transmitted and the insistence that accompanies it.

But the perceived proximity of the group to the world of politics depends on more than the perception of a group standard at a point in time. While the successful transmission of a group standard in a particular situation may increase the member's sense of proximity, we would propose that the effect of any particular standard, once received, will vary according to the individual's generalized, preexisting sense of proximity between group and politics. Thus proximity has an important time depth, based on the frequency with which the group has been seen to take a political position in the past. In part, then, proximity is dependent upon reception of past standards; in part, too, it is dependent on the individual's sense of the *fitness* of group activity in politics. Underlying values that deny the group a legitimate role in the political world act as barriers to reduce the sense of proximity, however clearly standards may be received.

What we have roughly labeled proximity, then, has a number of dimensions that demand independent treatment. We shall discuss several of these, illustrating their effects with case studies from various groups. Throughout, we encounter evidence that the perceived relationship of the group to politics, like the relationship of the individual to the group, bears directly upon the strength of group forces in the field at the time of political decision.

The transmission of group political standards. Whatever the process of communication that alerts the member to a partisan group standard, we can think of group norms as forces, having a given direction and varying degrees of strength. The standard prescribes support of one party, candidate, or issue position, and forbids support of the other. And these prescriptions are propagated with varying amounts of urgency or intensity.

There are two conditions in which group standards may lack sufficient clarity to permit influence. The end result of each is the same—a lack of distinctiveness in the aggregate group vote—but the differences are of considerable theoretical interest. In one case, the usual channel for communication of such norms is silent as to a particular standard, or emits it very weakly. In the other case, conflicting standards are conveyed to the membership.

When standards conflict, there are several possible outcomes. At one extreme, we might find that no single member became aware of the conflict in standards, but that various sets of members felt pressures in opposing directions. Here is the point at which analysis of influence at the individual level becomes more accurate than that at a group level. For in such a situation, even if every member responded to influence, the aggregate outcome might lead the observer to believe that no influence had occurred at all.

At the other extreme, all members may be aware of a conflict in standards. To some degree, the group force is cancelled out: even if the member is concerned with respectability in the eyes of the group, he can pick the standard that would best suit his desires independent of group considerations and act accordingly without feeling guilt. If, however, the situation is ripe for influence—if the individual is motivated to conform to the group—it is unlikely that events will work out in just this way. A conflict in group standards usually occurs as a result of decentralization of leadership. Few large and far-flung groups can long maintain a leadership with monolithic control over group standards. Among the secondary membership groups this is especially true. But if an unwieldy group tends to develop its subgroups with their conflicting standards, the general model still applies. Although awareness of different standards among other elements of the total group may relax group pressures to some degree, the individual is likely to feel most strongly the forces from the subgroup with which he is most strongly identified.

A case study: weakness of group standards. There is a good deal of variation within each of our secondary groups in the clarity of standards conveyed to the membership. In the labor union movement, although there is a centralized leadership structure, there are radically different approaches to the problem of politics from one international union to another. This variation, to some degree, cuts across the old AFL and CIO distinction, since some AFL unions expend much effort in political activity, whereas there are CIO internationals that attempt relatively little.

To capture this variation in 1956 we analyzed the political content of the pre-election editions of the official journals from several dozen of the large internationals whose members fell in our sample. The differences from journal to journal were sharp and therefore made classification quite simple. At one extreme, large portions of the journal were given over to the elections, with fervently partisan pro-Democratic materials in abundance. As the proportion of content devoted to the campaign decreased, the tone became less strident. Short factual accounts of the AFL-CIO endorsement of the Democratic ticket, with mild editorials indicating the importance of voting for "candidates favorable to labor" became typical. A number of other journals made no partisan comment at all, nor did they report endorsements by other related groups. Finally, the journal of one giant union, though making no endorsement, included a picture of the international president in a friendly moment with President Eisenhower.

We have no evidence that the union members involved drew their perceptions of standards from these particular journals. But we assumed that these journals were representative of the political efforts of the internationals. Whatever the actual channels of communication, members faithfully reflected differences in clarity of standard from international to international by their reports of how they thought leaders of their union would vote. Where standards were clear in the group publications, member perceptions of leader behavior were clear and unidirectional. Where no standards were communicated, a much smaller proportion felt they knew how leaders would vote, and their guesses were less unanimously in a Democratic direction.

Within internationals where standards were most clear according to the content analysis of journals, the vote division was 67 per cent Democratic. This fell to 55 per cent, then to 51 per cent, and finally to 44 per cent where standards were least clear. These differences occurred even though the proportion of high identifiers from category to category only varies over a range of 3 per cent. In other words, we cannot explain the variation in vote by differences in group cohesiveness.[11]

[11] The relative cohesiveness of union internationals, arrayed according to differences in clarity of standards, appears as follows: (footnote continued page 316).

As Table 12-5 indicates, however, group identification plays an interesting role. For among low identifiers, differences in clarity lead to no reliable variation in the vote; it is among high identifiers that clear standards appear to have effects. There is no reason to believe that the nature of the identification bond differs in unions without clear standards. It simply appears that in these cases the high identifier is provided with no clear direction for his behavior, so that his union loyalty receives no distinctive political expression.

TABLE 12-5. Variation in Union Vote as a Function of Differences in Clarity of Standards and Strength of Member Identification, 1956[a]

	Clarity			
	High		Low	
High identification	81%	66%	59%	43%
Low identification	50%	42%	41%	45%

[a] The entry in each cell represents the per cent Democratic of the two-party vote.

Conflicting standards: a case study. We have found the Negro community to be the most cohesive of the groups we have surveyed. Furthermore, Negroes, as we shall see, are almost unanimous in their belief that the group has a right to further its ends by political activity. Several of the necessary conditions for influence are fulfilled. In 1952, there was a good deal of solidarity among Negro leaders in their endorsement of the Democratic presidential ticket. And the Negro vote itself in 1952 was very distinctively Democratic.

In 1956, however, Negro leaders were much less enthusiastic about the Democratic Party, owing in part to the role of Southern Democratic legislators in blocking civil rights legislation and in part to Republican sympathy with Negro aspirations. The National Association for Ad-

	N	Mean Identification Score
High clarity (Democratic)	51	1.7
Medium clarity	136	1.6
Lowest clarity	89	1.7
Medium clarity (Republican)	36	1.5

This table may be readily compared with Table 12-4 on page 310, showing analogous differences across the secondary groups themselves.

vancement of Colored People adopted a posture of watchful waiting, with occasional executive threats of a Republican endorsement. The two senior United States Congressmen from the Negro community gave clear public support to opposing candidates for the Presidency: Adam Clayton Powell in New York City endorsed Eisenhower, whereas William L. Dawson of Chicago supported the Stevenson candidacy.

This conflict in standards was reflected in the perceptions of Negroes in our sample. When asked how they thought Negroes around the country would vote in the 1956 election, responses had shifted sharply away from the near Democratic unanimity that the same question elicited in 1952. Furthermore, the conflict was most clearly perceived at the level of the leadership. Almost as many Negroes saw the leadership voting Republican as Democratic in 1956. The distinctiveness of the Negro vote fell off sharply.

We hypothesized that when a secondary group fragments into subgroups propagating standards that conflict, much the same influence process goes on, with identification focused on the appropriate subgroup rather than the total group. In Chicago, where Dawson had stood firm for the Democrats, there was an over-all decline of 5 per cent in the Democratic presidential vote, by comparison with 1952. Within the city, three of the most clearly Negro wards declined 4 per cent, 4 per cent, and 9 per cent—close to the city average.[12] In New York City, the picture was different. In the heavily colored New York Assembly Districts 11 and 12, which included much of Powell's constituency, the Democratic presidential vote fell about 15 per cent. And this occurred despite a fraction of a per cent increase in the Stevenson vote in New York County as a whole. The effect of conflicting standards is to reduce the distinctiveness of the total group vote; but where we can isolate subgroups, we find evidence of influence.

The political salience of the group. In some situations, the need for active propagation of group standards is at a minimum, because the standard is self-evident. This is the case when important political objects of orientation embody group cues, so that the course of behavior characteristic of a "good" group member cannot be held in doubt. Fundamentally, this situation is no more than a special case of the transmission of clear and strong standards. But it deserves separate treatment because it implies a simpler and less fallible com-

12 "The Ethnic-Religious Factor in the 1956 Election" (unpublished manuscript, Library of Jewish Information, The American Jewish Committee, September 1957), p. 69.

munication process and because it involves a stratagem dear to the hearts of political tacticians.

Political salience, then, refers to any heightening of awareness of a particular group membership at the time when the individual is oriented to the political world. This dimension is one component of the model that is especially subject to short-term variation, since salience usually depends on the most transient objects of political orientation: the candidates and the issues.

Political salience of the group is high, for example, when a candidate for the election is recognized as a member of the group. Attracting the votes of members of a particular group by nominating a candidate who is a group member is, of course, a time-worn strategy in the art of political maneuver. Frequent executive appointment of group members to high posts is of the same order, although perhaps less potent in creating salience. There can be no doubt that group influence is exerted in this manner, not only in a positive way for identified group members, but in a negative direction when non-members take the group as a negative reference point. It is our thesis that the success of the maneuver among group members depends upon the values of other variables in the total model. High salience alone does not create a unanimous group response.

The political salience of the group can also be increased by a coincidence between group goals and current political issues. Most groups have goals beyond recruitment and self-perpetuation. Where there is formal organization, some of these goals may be stated in the charter or constitution. But groups with less formal organization have goals as well, which center in the first instance around the immediate welfare of members and in the second around whatever acts the group deems worthy of undertaking toward the external world. Among large-scale minority groups major goals have to do with rectifying the social restrictions that accompany group membership. We can imagine that groups accord various goals different levels of importance or priority. Similarly, in any political campaign, issues vary in importance. The degree of salience that accrues with regard to issues in any particular situation is some joint function of the importance of the issue in the campaign and the importance of the goal to the group. One of the central issues of the 1948 campaign was the Taft-Hartley Act, which union leadership felt threatened vital aspects of the movement. To the degree that these elements communicated to the rank and file, the labor union ought to have been particularly salient for members voting in the election. Since that time, civil rights controversies have tended to increase the political salience of Negro membership.[13]

Salience: a case study. At a presidential level political candidates are usually chosen who represent majority groupings, rather than any of the minorities under discussion in this chapter. Therefore, we do not frequently have an opportunity to observe the effects of salience created by candidate presentation. However, at lower levels of government such candidacies are frequent, and they occur on both party tickets. The behavior of Catholic voters toward Catholic candidates for the United States Congress allows us to examine the salience phenomenon.

We recall that in Table 12-2 the presidential vote among Catholics in 1956 was barely more Democratic than that among a Catholic control group (a margin of 3 per cent). We find a much more distinctive vote if we shift the scene to those congressional races in which a Catholic candidate was pitted against a non-Catholic (Table 12-6).

TABLE 12-6. Political Salience: The Vote of Catholics for Catholic Congressional Candidates in Races Involving Non-Catholics, 1956[a]

	Catholic Identification		
	High	Low	Total Group
Catholic voters	63% (43)	59% (51)	61% (94)
Catholic control	...	...	49% (76)

[a] The per cent entry refers to the proportion of the indicated group voting for the Catholic candidate in the split-religion congressional race. The figure in parentheses indicates the number of cases involved in each proportion.

Furthermore, Catholic voters are quite willing to cross party lines to support a candidate of the same creed. Thus if we decompose Table 12-6, we find that where the Catholic candidate is a Democrat, Catho-

[13] Perception that a party has supported the group position on a series of specific issues important to the group leads to a generalized sense that the party is solicitous of group welfare. The conduct of political campaigns is often hinged on attempts by party leadership to build such generalized beliefs. And it is the wealth of such beliefs abroad in the electorate that make it necessary to consider a "group" variable as one of the six partisan attitudes (Chapter 4).

lics vote over 10 per cent more Democratic than their control group; but where the Catholic candidate is Republican, Catholics vote over 10 per cent more *Republican* than their controls.

By sacrificing a large proportion of our cases, we can refine the data in a manner that sharpens these relationships further. Only about one third of our citizens who vote for a congressional candidate can think of his name shortly after the election. Obviously, the theory underlying the salience hypotheses demands that the voter recognize the candidate as a group member if salience effects are to emerge. The fact that the voter cannot recall his congressman's name after the election does not of itself mean that in the polling booth a Catholic name on the ballot may not have heightened the salience of the group and attracted a member vote. But there is a good deal of straight-ticket voting, in which names may not be read carefully; and the names themselves are not always unequivocal cues. If we restrict our attention to those voters who can refer to their congressional choices by name after the election, we should clear away some individuals for whom we could little expect salience to be operative.

Although the cases for analysis are few, Table 12-7 shows a group vote much more distinctive yet than that in Table 12-6. And the inadequate number of cases is offset somewhat by the fact that similar

TABLE 12-7. Group Salience: The Vote of Catholics for Catholic Candidates Whose Names Can Be Recalled, in Races Involving Non-Catholics, 1956[a]

	Catholic Identification		
	High	Low	Total Group
U. S. House of Representatives			
Catholic voters	85% (13)	69% (13)	77% (26)
Catholic control	...	...	51% (25)
U. S. Senate			
Catholic voters	86% (22)	57% (28)	70% (50)
Catholic control	...	...	49% (47)

[a] The per cent entry refers to the proportion of the indicated group who voted for the Catholic candidate in the split-religion congressional or senatorial race. The figure in each parenthesis indicates the number of cases involved in each proportion.

results are to be found when we look for the same patterns within the 1956 U. S. Senatorial races in which Catholics were involved. These similarities emerge even though the Catholic voters appearing in both segments of the table are few indeed.

There is, therefore, substantial evidence that the salience of a group membership, created by group cues in the political object, intensifies group forces in the member's psychological field at the time of the vote decision. On the other hand, we should note that the sharpening of findings from Table 12-6 to Table 12-7 indicates that lack of attention to candidates for House and Senate may make severe inroads upon the vote increment which the aspirant can reap from salience effects. Since knowledge of presidential candidates far exceeds that of congressional candidates, it would be dangerous to extrapolate from these data in predicting the effects—positive as well as negative—of a minority-group candidacy at the presidential level.

The legitimacy of group political activity. However strong the group identification, and however firm the association between group and political objects, the member may resist the intrusion of "non-political" groups upon the political scene. There are cultural values bound up with beliefs about democracy and the individual that inveigh against such activity. The sophisticated view of democracy as a competition between interest groups does not have great popular currency. Voting, whether at the mass or the legislative level, is morally a matter of individual judgment and conscience; recognition of group obligation and interests is thoroughly taboo to some Americans.

Because of various historical emphases, the taboos are strongest where religious groupings are involved. Pride in religious freedom in a nation heterogeneous in its creeds has lent strong support to the doctrine of the separation of church and state. For minorities whose European traditions were less stringent in this regard—the Catholics are a case in point—these values may be cultivated as proof of Americanism.

We asked members of various groups whether they felt it was "all right" for organizations representing the group to support legislative proposals and candidates for office. The responses to these questions showed a fairly strong relationship with the group identification variable. The more highly identified a group member, the more likely he was to grant the group a right to engage in political activity. Table 12-8 shows that the legitimacy responses bear a considerable relationship to presidential vote even after the effects of group identification are taken into account.

TABLE 12-8. Presidential Vote Across Four Secondary Membership Groups with Democratic Voting Standards, by Strength of Group Identification and Belief in Legitimacy of Group Political Activity, 1956[a]

Belief in Legitimacy of Group Political Activity	Group Identification			
	High	Medium	Low	Total
Strong	72%	64%	55%	65%
Medium	62%	55%	45%	53%
Weak	67%	45%	33%	41%
Total	69%	56%	43%	

[a] Each cell entry represents the per cent Democratic of the two-party vote for the appropriate combination of group identification and sense of legitimacy. The "Total" column shows the simple relationship between legitimacy and the vote, with no control on identification. The "Total" row shows the simple relationship between identification and the vote, without control on legitimacy.

Although we are confident that identification with the types of groups that we are discussing rarely results from prior agreement with the group political standards, we can be less sure of the status of the legitimacy variable. It would not be at all surprising if some group members, disagreeing with group standards, were not more likely to deny that the group should engage in political activity. A sense of legitimacy would be an effect, rather than a cause, of acceptance of the group position in politics. Nevertheless, there are indications that we are measuring some of the value elements called for by the model. For example, within each level of group identification, members of the two religious groups—Catholics and Jews—show much greater reluctance to accept the legitimacy statements than either of the two more secular groupings—Negroes and union members. Also, with identification controlled, there is somewhat less readiness to grant legitimacy among older people. This fact would conform with the impressions that popular values opposing frank interest-group politics represent an older America.

We have discussed several aspects of the relationship that the member perceives to exist between his group and the world of politics. The measurements appropriate for this portion of the model, when combined with the values that characterize the bond between the individual and the group, should help us to calculate the strength of group forces on the member at the point of political decision. By extension, a summation of values over the set of group members should lead to improved estimates of the distinctiveness of the group vote. And when we observe the values specified by the model shifting over time, we would expect group distinctiveness to increase or to fall off accordingly.

It should be clear that both the individual-group term and the term relating the group to politics are necessary components of this system of variables. Thus, if the labor union is one of our less cohesive groups, its Democratic vote is well maintained by the transmission of clear political standards from a relatively centralized leadership. And if the Negroes, extremely cohesive and almost unanimous in their belief in the legitimacy of group political activity, currently enjoy a potential for high vote distinctiveness, the conflict in leadership standards in 1956 served to cut away the group vote. In contrast, the Catholics are low on every variable in the scheme. Cohesiveness is not strong, and there is resistance to group intrusion in politics. Given little active transmission of group political standards as well, the absence of a distinctive Catholic presidential vote in 1956 was only to be expected.

The backgrounds of group identifications. The salience of the group and, to a lesser degree, the policies of leadership concerning the transmission of group standards are determined by situational factors. Short-term fluctuations in the distinctiveness of a group vote are likely to be traced to these components of the model. Factors like legitimacy and group identification are likely to remain more stable in the aggregate over a period of time. We have indicated some of the sources of feelings about legitimacy. It is natural to inquire as well concerning the roots of group identification. Why do some group members identify with the group whereas others fail to?

This is a difficult problem, and our evidence to date is fragmentary. But we can draw a few general conclusions about major determinants of identification. There are numerous groups, of course, that are created for the purpose of political and ideological persuasion, such as the National Economic Council or the American Civil Liberties Union. Members are recruited and come to identify with the group on the basis of pre-existing beliefs and sympathies. Here the case for influence is much less clear, except as group activity serves to reinforce and guide member efforts. But in most groups formed along occupational, ethnic, or religious lines membership is more likely to determine attitudes than are attitudes to determine membership.

There is little doubt of this fact in the groups we have watched most closely. Except in some semi-organized areas of the South, even membership in the labor union is effectively involuntary. If labor union members vote distinctively, we cannot say that only workers with certain attitudes join the union; rather, we must concede that influence exists. But if membership is involuntary, identification is not. How can we be sure that high union identification plays a formative role in the development of political attitudes?

There is a clear and substantial relationship between strength of union identification and length of membership in the union. The longer an individual has belonged to the union, the more likely he is to identify strongly with it, and we can find no other causative factors that begin to approach this relationship in strength. A relationship between age and union identification has been observed before, but it was never clear whether the relationship existed because of simple contact with the union over time, or because the unusual "barricades" generation of the 1930's would currently constitute the bulk of older union members. Our data show clearly that older men who have recently joined the union have weak identification with it, whereas younger men aged 25 and 30 who have belonged to the union for longer periods show stronger identifications with it. In fact, if we control length of union membership, we find that the relationship between age and union identification is somewhat negative.[14] The later in life a person joins a union, the less completely he will be identified with it given any particular length of membership. His identification will still increase with length of membership, but the level will not be quite as strong as it would be for a person who had joined when younger.

This cluster of findings is of considerable theoretical significance. In the first place, it makes it difficult to maintain that identification with the union results as a rule from existing political attitudes similar to those represented by the union. Instead, we get a sense of an acculturation process—slow and cumulative influence over a period of time, with identification as the key intervening factor. It appears that a potent force in the growth of group identifications is simple contact and familiarity, just as an immigrant comes to identify with the new

[14] The multiple correlation (Pearson) of age and length of membership with strength of identification is 0.36. The partial correlation between length of membership and identification with age controlled is 0.33. The partial correlation between age and union identification, with length of membership controlled, is −0.09. Since the function is not quite linear—identification appears to increase slightly more rapidly in the first five years of membership than it does later on—a logarithmic transformation was performed on the number of years involved in age and length of membership.

country and accept its customs as time passes. Furthermore, like the immigrant, identifications never become as strongly rooted if the initiate is no longer young.

These findings are important from another point of view as well. For the pattern of relationships between age, length of membership, and strength of identification is precisely the same as we found where the group involved is the political party. That is, party identification appears to grow stronger with age; but the critical variable, instead of being age, is length of psychological membership in the party. With length of membership controlled, age is negatively related to party identification, just as it is in the union case.[15]

There are further points of similarity. In the case of party identification, we find that over time individuals tend to desert the neutral middle ground of the party continuum in favor of the extremes. As far as the union is concerned, there is no analogous "anti-union" pole on the identification scale, in quite the same sense that strong Democratic identification is an anti-Republican pole. But we do find that those few persons who have been union members for long periods of time yet who have remained unidentified, are less likely to vote Democratic than any of the other union subgroups isolated (Table 12-9).

TABLE 12-9. Presidential Vote among Union Members in 1956, According to Identification and Length of Union Membership[a]

	Length of Membership		
	0–4 Years	5–14 Years	15 Years or More
High union identification	50% (26)	66% (74)	68% (71)
Low union identification	49% (47)	45% (77)	33% (39)

[a] The entry in each cell refers to the per cent Democratic of the two-party vote within the indicated group. Figures in parentheses indicate the number of cases involved in each proportion.

Not only are they much more Republican in their vote than union members generally; they are even more Republican than the control group matched with union members on aspects of life situation (33 per cent Democratic vote as opposed to 36 per cent for the control

[15] See Chapter 7, pp. 163–164.

group). Thus lack of identification among long-standing members of the union may have actively negative implications not present among new members who are not yet strongly identified.

We find no such clear relation between age and group identification among Catholics, Negroes, and Jews. Age, in these groups, logically coincides with "length of membership." There is some faint increase in identification among older Catholics, and an equally faint decrease in identification among older Negroes. We would expect these differences to appear if Catholic cohesiveness is waning and if the current civil rights ferment is beginning to sharpen cohesiveness among Negroes. But these tendencies are very weak, and there is no trend visible at all in the Jewish situation. We must conclude that no reliable relationship is present.

The contrast in the development of identification between these groups and the union or party is sharp. We are led to consider differences in the characteristics of the several groups that might account for such variation. It is obvious that the individual takes on serious membership in a union or in the psychological group represented by a political party later in life than is the case with the other groups. The individual grows up within the atmosphere of a religious or ethnic group in a much more inclusive sense than with either the party or the union. Of course, there are highly politicized families in which children may readily pick up parental allegiances. Transmission of these allegiances from generation to generation is doubtless high. But until the individual begins to vote with regularity, these values are likely to remain peripheral. Whereas in Europe political involvement may become serious in adolescence, there is considerable evidence that in the United States it is typically postponed until the individual is beyond his twenties.[16]

Thus, different patterns of identification may be traced to basic differences in types of groups. Nevertheless, it is possible to suggest a more general proposition to cover all cases. Instead of considering age or even the absolute length of time of group membership as the proper independent variable, let us employ the *proportion of the individual's life* spent as a member. Recast in this fashion, the presence of the strong positive relationship between length of membership and identification, the negative relationship between age and identification with length of membership constant, and the fact that certain ascribed groups show no variation with age would all be predicted by a single independent variable. If there is no relationship between "length of membership" and identification among Catholics,

[16] See Chapter 7, p. 164.

Jews, and Negroes, it is because members of these groups have held membership for 100 per cent of their lives, and variation in their identification must be explained with other factors. We arrive at the general proposition that one fundamental determinant of group identifications is the proportion of one's life spent in close (psychological) contact with the group.

Secondary Groups, the Political Party, and the Influence Process

If the political party, and psychological membership in it, fit a more general model for social memberships and political influence, it is equally clear that the party has a peculiar location in the space that the model encompasses. We have laid out with some care what seem to be the components of the relationship between any group and the world of politics. This effort was necessary because the secondary groups with which we dealt were not at base political, and this fact turns out to be a crucial limitation in the political influence they can wield. Now if we were to fill in the values that the scheme requires for prediction, we would find that in the case of the party, proximity is at an upper limit, for the party has a central position in the world of politics. In all major elections, its salience is absolutely high: one candidate is always a group member, the prime group goal is political victory, and all controversial issues represent subordinate goals that the group has assumed. The legitimacy of its activity in politics goes without question for the major parties at least, and the communication of their standards is perfect.

Therefore, we would expect that the political influence of psychological membership in a party would be extremely potent, relative to other secondary memberships. If we take distinctiveness of political attitudes and behavior as a criterion, this proposition cannot be questioned. We are most directly interested, at this point, in suggesting the processes by which non-political membership groups come to have a certain amount of political influence. Thus far we have paid little attention to the fact that these processes have duration over time. The political influence of secondary memberships, as witnessed in the distinctiveness of a group vote, is not necessarily a product of the immediate situation. The labor union need not indoctrinate its membership anew at each election. If the labor vote was distinctive in 1956, there is no need to presume that this distinctiveness represents only the political action of the union during the 1956 campaign. Influence, when successful, has enduring effects, and in this sense the distinctiveness of a group vote at any point in time represents cumulative influence. We hypothesize that the political party plays a crucial role in the durability of this influence.

When a political candidate is a member of one's group, or when the issues of politics bear directly upon goals important to the group, membership in that group becomes salient in the individual's orientation to politics. In these instances, the need for political translation, for communication of specific standards regarding proper group behavior, is slight. But under normal circumstances, when salience is not high, the group, if it is to have influence, must lend the observed world political meaning in terms relevant to the group.

Now issues and candidates are transient political objects; the entity that endures is the party. If group influence leads the identified member to take on identification with the party, then little renewal of influence is needed. The individual has, as it were, acceded to a self-steering mechanism, that will keep him politically "safe" from the point of view of group standards. He will respond to new stimuli as a party member and code them properly. As time passes, his identification with the party will increase of its own accord, because the individual will find that event after event demonstrates—in non-group matters as well as group matters now—the rectitude of his own party and the obnoxiousness of its opponent.

If there were no parties, but only a flux of candidates and issues, it does not follow that there would be no political influence exerted by other membership groups. The psychological economy of the individual demands parties as an organizing principle, and if bereft of this, there might be much more straightforward dependence on other groups for guidance. In situations of this sort, secondary groups with quite apolitical origins have in fact come to function as political parties.[17] But where parties exist, influence from non-political secondary groups is likely to have a good deal of continuity.

These speculations would lead us to expect that individuals strongly identified with a secondary group that maintains clear political standards would show a distinctive tendency not only to identify with the prescribed party, but also to identify *strongly*. This should be true whether we compare such individuals with other members less strongly identified, or with control groups, allowing identification with either

[17] As an example, see Key's treatment of factionalism in the South. Secondary groups constitute one type of nucleus for the factions that compete for political power in a one-party system. V. O. Key, *Southern Politics* (Alfred Knopf, New York, 1950), pp. 52–57.

party to be included for purposes of contrasting over-all strength of identification.

More crucially yet, if secondary groups with continuing political standards can bind identified members to a political party, we would expect that strong party identification would be most distinctive among *young* group members. In general, younger adults do not tend to identify strongly with a party. In fact, after a certain amount of observation of the total population, we come to have a set of norms about the mean strength of party identification that may be expected for a given age interval. If group forces do act to push the member toward a firm location in the party scheme, it seems reasonable to imagine that they speed up the establishment of strong party ties. The young member of such a secondary group should, then, show "prematurely" strong party identification.

TABLE 12-10. Strength of Party Identification among Younger Members (under 40) of Non-Political Secondary Groups, 1956[a]

	Group Identification			
	High	Low	Total Group	Control Group[b]
Union household	2.23	2.05	2.14	1.83
	(76)	(78)	(154)	(242)
Catholic	2.05	2.00	2.03	1.91
	(64)	(48)	(112)	(177)
Negro (Non-South)	2.16	2.00	2.07	1.80
	(13)	(16)	(29)	(31)
Jew	. . .	. . .	1.94	1.86
			(17)	(18)

[a] The entry in each cell represents a mean strength of party identification for the group indicated. The four steps of the identification continuum are scored 0, 1, 2, and 3 from "independent" to "strong" categories. For the control groups, all steps of the party continuum are used. For the test groups, only the Democratic half of the continuum is used. The figures in parentheses indicate the number of cases involved in each mean.

[b] The control groups, like the test groups, are restricted to those individuals under 40 years of age.

This hypothesis receives support from the data in Table 12-10. The patterns are sharpest in the union case, where comparisons drawn between high and low identifiers or between members and non-member controls are both statistically significant. Among Catholics, the contrasts are somewhat attenuated, as we might expect if Catholic political distinctiveness is in the process of eroding.[18] Cases are too few among Negroes and Jews for precise evaluation. Here as elsewhere, however, all absolute differences run in the predicted direction.[19]

These differences in strength of party identification between secondary group members and their controls tend to fade out in older age groupings. Apparently individuals floating relatively free of concentrated group pressures for political commitment move toward the extremes of the party continuum more gradually over the life span. Therefore, in the later age categories, they have nearly "caught up" to group members in this regard.

Given the flux of objects like candidates and issues, group influence is likely to be most effective when meaningful contact is established between the group and the party, for parties subsume candidates and issues and, more important, endure over time. However, this proposition is true only if we define influence in a very particular way, that is, as cumulative over time. That is, an individual led to a Democratic orientation by a group membership in 1930 is likely to register a manifestation of that influence in 1956.

But for the practical politician who wants to know how many votes a group leader can "deliver" to one party or the other in a specific election, influence may have a rather different meaning. Here we encounter a paradox. If party identification is a trustworthy bridge from group identification to "proper" political behavior, it is also a structure which, once laid down, is not readily moved. Thus the mechanisms that are best calculated to build a reliably distinctive group vote are at the same time mechanisms that tend to undermine the maneuverability of the group in politics.

When political events cause a group leadership to switch official support to the opposing party, the strong party loyalties that it has

[18] The difference in means between Catholics and non-Catholic controls is significant at the 0.15 level.

[19] Several possible artifacts that might lead to the patterns appearing in Table 12-10 have been checked and eliminated. For example, it might be suggested that young people, whether group members or not, tend to identify more strongly with the Democratic Party. Hence we would "build in" a relationship by using only the Democratic half of the party continuum in the test group, while using the total party range in the control case. However, it is readily shown that if control group scores are also restricted to the Democratic half of the continuum, the crucial contrasts become much more, rather than less, sharp (revised control group values, which may be inserted in Table 12-10, are Union, 1.70; Catholic, 1.83; Negro, 1.72; and Jews, 1.19). Similarly, findings are not substantially changed by including, halving, or excluding the middle or "independent" category in computing means.

helped to create and reinforce may be reversed only with great difficulty.[20] We can imagine that these loyalties, even when direct creations of group influence, gain some functional autonomy as they grow stronger. They come to have a force of their own, rather than remaining dependent on forces from the non-political secondary group. And, since the political party can exert unusually intense influence on political motives, this force may turn out to be stronger than any counter-force that the non-political group can bring to bear *in politics* at a later date. It would follow from the general outlines of our theory that when such reversals of group standards occur, the new influence will have most effect among the youngest group members.

The political party may be treated, then, as a special case of a more general group-influence phenomenon. The party may be located within our model, and values on appropriate dimensions may be calculated for the party member at any point in time. The nature of the group, so located, ensures the power of its influence within the world of politics. But of great significance also is the role of the party as a bridge between other social groupings and that political world. The influence of other secondary groups in politics comes to have more enduring effects as loyalties directed toward them may be transferred to abiding political loyalties.

Power and Limitations of the Model

We have taken our first step in exploring some of the deeper "social" reaches of the funnel by sketching a system of variables that will help explain the political effects of membership in secondary social groups. The model is inspired by observation of four such groups: labor unions, Negroes, Catholics, and Jews. These groups were chosen because of the significance commonly accorded them in recent American politics and the consequent discussion they have evoked as elements in the electoral process. Such a list does not exhaust the social memberships that might be shown to have "real effects" on political behavior. But we have tried to conceive working

[20] It is interesting to note that for large-scale, secondary groups at the national level, these switches are rare and tend to be limited to rebellious factions. Many aspects of political process seem to converge toward maintenance of these continuities. Factors such as the dependence of the party on group support and the loyalties and interpersonal commitments built up between group leaders and the party enhance the temptation to work for reform within the chosen party when things go awry. These facts make treatment of influence in its cumulative sense the more meaningful.

dimensions for the model that may be readily applied to a great variety of other social groups, on the community as well as the national level. And, when it became of interest to apply the scheme to a grouping that seems superficially to contrast greatly with the other groups considered, we encountered no difficulty in treating the political party as another special case of the group phenomenon.

Tentatively, then, we consider the model to be extremely general. It is designed to illuminate many concrete social phenomena. Yet it is crucial to recognize its limitations. It is not presumed to span all cases in which sociological divisions of the electorate coincide with differences in political behavior. The very dimensions required—the prominence of group identification, for example—suggest that distinctive behavior which appears within aggregates having no psychological reality to "members" as groups, must be accounted for by rather different mechanisms.

Distinctive behavior does often characterize aggregates that cannot be conceptualized as groups. Individuals in their twenties may behave in a manner distinct from individuals in their thirties; but we do not suppose that these distinctive features arise because the individuals involved are guided by cues from a reference group of "people twenty to twenty-nine" that has psychological reality. Instead, we assume that certain life experiences are common to individuals in the same age category, and that individual responses to the same stimuli turn out to show some similarity.

It is precisely these common aspects of life situation that we felt necessary to control in attempting to assess the strength of group forces on the member. We wished to remove from consideration those sources of similar behavior that might arise without group mediation. And it is this source of similarity that lies explicitly beyond the scope of the model.

Having come to grips with the problem of group influence, we shall presently consider these other sources of social similarity in politics. But if we distinguish sharply between parallel behavior of individuals and group-mediated behavior, we must recognize that we are using two ideal types that are not likely to be found in pure form. In fact, some social phenomena have interest because of the combination of these types of social behavior that they represent. It is to one of the most important of these, the social class, that we turn our attention.

The Role of Social Class ◇ 13

Of all the social groupings into which electorates may be divided, it is likely that the *social class* has drawn the most consistent attention from students of mass political behavior. In the first place, the notion of social class provides an inclusive analytic concept. When we focus upon some distinctive minority, our observations may be relevant for only a small fraction of the total population. But the concept of class embraces the entire electorate; all citizens may be seen to have some relative position in a status structure. A "lower" class comes to have meaning because there is an "upper" class that serves as its foil; hence, analyses of social class come to deal with the total social structure at once.

Likewise, the concept of class is sufficiently general to permit wide application. Every nation has its minorities, but it is not always clear how specific subgroups, differing in composition and goals, may be compared from nation to nation. As for the social class, however, current evidence in sociology indicates that all societies are stratified into "upper" and "lower" layers as a result of unequal distribution of values and honors. In various times and places the characteristics of these layers have varied superficially. There have been the landed gentry, the nobility, the shipper, or the merchant representing the upper stratum; and rising in challenge the tenant, the commoner, the artisan, or the trade unionist. Each group or, loosely speaking, "class," has had specific economic goals, and each has been expressed in the vocabulary of its period. But the concept of class reduces such historical diversity to a set of minimum common elements, a reduction that is indispensable if we aspire to more powerful theory.

Class phenomena attract broad interest, too, because they represent a junction between the social, the economic and the political order. The class, a social phenomenon, is yet defined in economic terms; and if class membership is conceived to have motivational significance, then the motives engaged are presumed to be economic. It is because of this economic aspect, furthermore, that the social class becomes linked with political strife. Political power signifies some potential for control of the economic system. If stratification arises from unequal distribution of rewards, then there is likely to be competition between the classes for control of the allocation process.

Theories of social class in politics have been strongly conditioned by the pages of history that deal with revolution. In the classical view there is a political *status quo* characterizing most societies in most epochs, in which the masses are governed by an elite that has long enjoyed a disproportionate share of social rewards. There are shared values, if implicit ones, concerning the bases of legitimate authority and the use of power to maintain the operative economic system. The unequal distribution of rewards, however, remains a potential source for discord between the more and the less privileged; large-scale economic misfortune, threatening the very survival of lower-status groups, activates their hostility toward the established order. As ferment increases, the upper ranks spring to its defense. Political and economic beliefs of lower groups develop in new and radical directions and become increasingly distinct from those of the elite. In some instances, when conflict is initiated, the *status quo* is altered, and previously deprived elements assume political control. The new elite rearranges the allocation system in its favor and comes to defend the institutions that have legitimized its position. In this manner the process comes full circle.

A schema of this sort, composed from the work of various European theorists, does not find ready illustration in the history of the United States. Nonetheless, competition between upper- and lower-status groups appears to have been an element of some importance in political matters since the birth of the American republic. The precise nature of this role is subject to scholarly debate, and our resources of data, particularly for the currents of mass behavior in the earlier elections, are meager or non-existent. But we know that at the time our political system was designed, influential minds found in the "different sentiments and views" of the various classes "the most common and durable source of faction."[1] We know furthermore that the emergence of Jacksonian democracy—whatever its popular base—frightened gentlemen of the upper strata as a triumph of "mobocracy." And

[1] *The Federalist, No. X.*

more recently, in the rise of trade unions and in the class-saturated political alignments formed in the wake of the Great Depression of the 1930's, the recurrent importance of social class in American politics is well documented.

We treat the social class apart from other social phenomena to some degree because of its popularity and its transitional position between the purely social and the purely economic. The most important consideration dictating separate treatment, however, lies in the nature of the social class itself. For whatever popularity the concept enjoys, its intellectual status has remained controversial, even among sociologists. Nobody wishes to deny the reality of differences in status and privilege within the large social unit; yet the meaning that can be attributed these distinctions by the investigator is constantly subject to dispute. A large portion of social theory seems to presume that the social class is a self-conscious group striving toward recognized goals. This assumption is challenged by theorists who feel it tends to reify what is usually no more than an analytic construct imposed on the situation by the investigator. Status differences exist, and these differences are related to differences in attitudes and behavior. They do not, however, assure us that the social class has reality as a group, or that class "members" come to behave distinctively because they take the class as a reference point in decisions about behavior.

Thus the argument comes to rest on the nature of the class as a group. It is our thesis that the "group" reality of the social class is variable. Under certain circumstances, it is not difficult to conceptualize the social class as a "group." Under other circumstances, it is hard to see it as more than a vague demographic aggregate, arbitrarily marked off for purposes of analysis. When and to the degree that the social class is a group, we shall find our theory of the preceding chapter quite applicable to it. But as the variable nature of the social class is one of its most intriguing characteristics, it requires separate discussion as a special and marginal case of the group phenomenon.

The Social Class as Political Group

Whether it is appropriate to consider the social class a "group" with "members" depends naturally upon one's definition of "group." Some definitions have proved more fruitful than others, and this fact will affect our approach to the problem of the social class in politics.

Formal organization: an "objective reality" of groups. The social class *per se* rarely becomes formalized as an organization. There is no official class leadership and no official class policy. A variety of organizations, such as the trade union or the manufacturers' association, may be stimulated into existence in the defense of interests that coincide to a substantial degree with class interests, although they are usually less inclusive.[2] Where such organizations exist, they are proper objects of study in themselves and should conform to some of the general propositions of the preceding chapter. But only a minority of the population belongs to such organizations. If we consider the social class as an inclusive entity, then we can anticipate some of the vagaries of class influence on voting behavior. In treating the Negro, for example, we discussed the implications of loose organization and diffuse leadership upon the propagation of clear group standards. In these terms, the social class is an even more extreme case.

The phenomenon of the social class warrants treatment apart from the specific organized groups that further various class interests, because it has group characteristics that the demographic category lacks. Despite an absence of formal organization, leadership, or even informally accredited spokesmen, the social class may have reality as a group in the minds of many people. When the citizen being interviewed tells the investigator that he favors the Democratic Party "because it is the party of the common man, not the party of the big shots," it seems clear that he sees the society as divided into at least two camps representing conflicting interests, and that he feels he shares the interests of one of these camps. It is in this sense that the social class may have psychological reality as a group.

Identification: a "subjective reality" of groups. We have already discussed the concept of group identification in several different contexts. The social class transcends the simple "demographic aggregate" to the degree that individuals in the population identify with a social class. When there is a "*we* feeling" directed toward other members of the class grouping as a whole, rather than purely toward other union

[2] The distinction drawn here is that which the German social theorist Weber discussed between "classes" and "parties." The class is a product of the economic order; the party operates in the political order. ". . . 'Parties' live in a house of 'power.' Their action is oriented toward the acquisition of social 'power,' that is to say, toward influencing a communal action no matter what its content may be. . . . For party actions are always directed toward a goal which is striven for in a planned manner. . . . In any individual case, parties may represent interests determined through 'class situation' or 'status situation,' and they may recruit their following respectively from one or the other. But they need be neither. . . ." From *Max Weber: Essays in Sociology,* trans. H. H. Gerth and C. Wright Mills (Oxford University Press, New York, 1946), p. 94.

members or other businessmen, then the class may influence behavior in the sense of our previous discussion of group influence.

It is clear that "identification with the class as a group" has much the same meaning as the Marxian concept of *class consciousness.* Other theorists of rather different persuasions have accepted the significance of the distinction between Marx's class *an sich* (a class not yet conscious of itself), and the class *für sich* (where consciousness of the social role of the group has developed). Max Weber also stressed the importance of the stage in class development in which the actors come to feel "that they belong together," and may hence engage in "communal action."[3] For both Marx and Weber, class differences arise inevitably from the facts of the economic order; yet for both, classes as such do not exist until a sense of class identification has spread among potential class members.

A number of modern class theorists have honored this distinction terminologically, and it is convenient for us to adopt this practice.[4] *Stratification* refers to the differentiation of the population as a result of the unequal distribution of social values and honors. The product of stratification is a set of *social strata.* The social class, on the other hand, refers to a grouping of people who feel a sense of identification and shared interest as a result of membership in a common stratum of the society. This psychological unity tokens a degree of functional cohesiveness that the term *stratum* does not connote. Thus at base the psychological circumstances of identification determine whether a class exists.

The distinction between the stratum and the class may be fruitfully applied to debate over the value and accuracy of the class concept. Whether we are correct in thinking of classes as distinct entities becomes an empirical matter. This view may be more or less correct, according to the conditions under which our observations are made. Social strata, the molds in which social classes may form, seem present in all societies. But the class itself emerges and disappears over a period of time. It is this sporadic quality in the social class as group phenomenon that has required our special attention. An adequate approach to the problem of social class in politics involves consideration of the conditions under which a sense of class identification develops in the social stratum.

[3] *Ibid.*, p. 183.

[4] Richard Centers, *The Psychology of Social Classes* (Princeton University Press, Princeton, N. J., 1949), p. 206.

Status Polarization

However helpful the distinction between "stratum" and "class," it should not mislead us into thinking that a society may properly be described in such "either-or" terms. Traditional accounts create this impression. The development of the social class is discussed as a two-stage affair, with class identification serving as a catalyst to permit the passage of a group from one stage to the other. The first stage or "steady state" of the society is characterized by mere social strata, the skeletal circumstances upon which class may develop; the second is the stage of association and communal action among class members.

Such clear stages, although undoubtedly useful as ideal types, are likely to be the empirical exceptions in history. This is certainly true if we mean by the second or "social class" stage an active and clearcut struggle of classes for political power. Rather, we may expect that in most societies at most times, accurate description would locate the situation somewhere between these extremes. There are individuals in the population who identify with their social class and who behave in ways that reflect these identifications. Yet these identifiers are only sprinkled through the population. There is likely to be a minimum of communication between class members about class interests, save in isolated or even insulated pockets of the society. Antagonisms are well below the pitch that catapults the individual into political action groups.

There is no good vocabulary in classic treatments to describe a situation of this sort. It is a mixed type: social classes do not exist in the full-blown sense; yet the feeling of class interest is, in a mild way, abroad in the land. Unfortunately, we cannot write such a situation off as a "transition" phase, as classic accounts seem to imply. If economic misfortune descends upon such a nation, we may suppose that there will be some movement toward more crystallized classes. But the rapidity of such movement, as well as the extremes to which the situation may carry, is likely to depend upon the degree to which some class perceptions existed in the preceding "steady state."

In other words, it is desirable to think of these different states of a society as differences in degree, rather than of kind, between ideal types or qualitative stages. We shall attempt to approach the problem quantitatively rather than qualitatively. We shall refer to the condition of active discord between social strata as *status polarization.* We shall think of this polarization entirely as a matter of degree; a society may be more or less polarized, at any point in time. We cannot specify a degree of polarization beyond which a stratum becomes a class; the simple dichotomy is inadequate to express differences along the underlying continuum of polarization which we posit. But when the status groups of a society are sharply polarized, we shall assume that the entities that past theorists have labeled "classes" are present; and when a society is "depolarized," we shall presume that the concept of social strata is more appropriate.

Status polarization, then refers to the degree to which upper and lower status groups in a society have taken up mutually antagonistic value positions. The nature of the concept is dictated by the class phenomenon itself. Theorists like Marx and Weber have recognized the critical role of an opposing social stratum in the development of a social class. A lower class grouping comes to have significance as an entity because there is an upper class grouping that is perceived as opposed to it. The solidification of a stratum into a class depends in a peculiar way upon parallel solidification and pressure from an antagonistic stratum.[5] It is this fact which makes the term "polarization" appropriate.

Class polarization is by definition a group-level concept. A single element cannot polarize; the term has meaning only as a description of concurrent motion of two or more elements—in our case, status groups. The parallel concept at the individual level we take to be class identification. Although a number of modifications remain to be discussed below, we can say in a rough way that *variation in the status polarization of a society reflects variation in the intensity and extent of class identification among its members.* When polarization is high, most of the citizenry must have perceived a conflict of interests between strata and have taken on class identifications with fair intensity. When polarization is low, either few people are identifying, or extant identifications are weak, or both.

Since polarization is bound up with divergences in values and interests, the concept is linked not only with status groups but with specific areas of conflict as well. If a society is on the brink of class war, we are likely to feel that it is more polarized in a completely general sense than one in which class interests are a matter of no concern. But we will find it useful to think of the degree of polarization as varying, not only over time, but from sphere to sphere within a social system as well. Under certain conditions, for example, there may be more status polarization visible in the economic sphere than in the political sphere. Generally speaking, we may hypothesize that polarization emerges first in connection with economic values, and that beyond a certain degree

[5] Marx and Engels, *Communist Manifesto.*

of intensity it will spread to other areas. As it becomes manifest in values less immediately bound up with economic interest, a more salient and generalized antagonism exists between class groups.

Finally, it is important to consider that the course of events depends not simply upon the intensity that polarization attains in sensitive spheres of the social system; it is also important to ascertain how constituent class identifications are distributed in the population. Polarization may become so intense within subgroups of a society that violence occurs, even when the vast bulk of the society is indifferent to the interests at stake. Therefore it matters whether intense identifications are clustered within groups enjoying internal communication, and hence the potential for pooled action, or are scattered more homogeneously through the mass population. Such considerations will form a part of our analysis. We feel, however, that the leaven of apathy toward class within any defined group as large as the total society is an important part of our understanding of the situation. Therefore a general measure of status polarization in one or another sphere carries meaning without reference to the distribution of identifications within the population. Where identifications are concentrated, there may be violent incidents even when polarization is not high in the total society; but in such a case we would expect little expansion of hostilities. For the purposes of understanding the broad flow of events, then, we shall consider first the degree of polarization within the bounds of the larger society. A theory of the social context of political behavior must undertake to specify (1) the conditions in the total society that serve to thrust status polarization into the political order; and (2) the conditions that act to increase or limit polarization within that order.

Determining Social Class

The ambiguous nature of the class as a group poses important problems. Who "really" belongs to which class? In the groups discussed in the preceding chapter we had little difficulty separating nominal members of the group from non-members. Similarly, in a caste society the location of an individual in the hierarchy of strata is quite clear. But in the United States and other modern democracies, the persistent or extreme formalization of social differences is absent. The distance that once separated serf from master has been filled in with a variety of roles and occupations that defy simple class assignment. Furthermore, there are strong American cultural values that inveigh against recognition of class differences. No other group that we have considered is begrudged the very reality of its existence in this manner.

These ambiguities have implications in two directions. First, if numerous individuals in the society are located in positions that are relatively indeterminate with respect to class lines, must we not expect a considerable attenuation of the role that class can play in political behavior? Secondly, if status is frequently ambiguous, how do we assign individuals to a social class for purposes of analysis? The first problem is an empirical matter, which we shall postpone for the moment. The second is methodological and must be considered immediately.

The two common solutions to the problem of assigning individuals to status groupings reflect some of the controversies over class phenomena that we have discussed. On the one hand, there are those whom Centers has called the "objectivists," who define class operationally according to some objective criterion like income, occupation, or education. This practice distinguishes what we have called social strata. Choice between objective criteria has been in some cases a matter of practical convenience and in others a matter of sharp theoretical dispute. Many observers feel that any accessible criterion catches enough of the differences between strata to serve as a worthwhile tool. Or a number of criteria may be statistically combined to make a compound measure of status. Other observers feel that class theory should dictate the choice. Marx's position that the relation of the individual to the means of production is the determinant from which all else flows has led to a preference for occupation as a measure.

The opposing "subjectivists" look for evidence of psychological identification with a particular class as a criterion of membership. While the objective approach can theoretically locate any individual at some rank in a hierarchy, the subjectivists are willing to assume that some people, at a psychological level, float free of a class structure and are hence unassignable.

Richard Centers, as an exponent of the subjectivist view, devised a relatively satisfactory method of getting individuals to locate their own position in class terms.[6] He asked a national sample in 1945: "If you were asked to use one of these four names for your social class, which would you say you belonged in: the middle class, lower class, working class, or upper class?" Analysis revealed that the responses gave meaningful insights into patterns of behavior. With regard to political variables, for example, people who chose to designate themselves as working class were more frequently Democratic in their voting

[6] See the account of early studies in Centers, *op. cit.*, Chapter IV.

and party affiliation and chose more "radical" alternatives on a number of issue questions dealing with the role of government in the economy. Middle class identifiers were more likely to be Republican and "conservative" in their politico-economic attitudes.

The study also showed that although occupation appeared to be the primary determinant of subjective class, identification of this sort was not always congruent with objective role in the social structure. For example, about one quarter of the people interviewed were either blue-collar workers who identified with the middle class, or white-collar people identifying with the working class. Nor was there any tendency for people who "misidentified" in this way to claim a higher status; in fact, members of the white-collar stratum designated themselves as "working class" more frequently than manual laborers chose the "middle class." People who thus placed themselves in a subjective class incongruent with their occupational stratum thought and behaved like hybrids; they were less conservative than white-collar, middle-class identifiers, yet more conservative than blue-collar, working-class identifiers.

Centers had set out to test the Marxist proposition that position in relation to the system of production leads the individual to "a consciousness of membership in some social class. . . ."[7] He provided a satisfactory method for the assessment of social class at a subjective or psychological level. But the simple fact of choice between alternative class names posed by an interviewer may be only a pale shadow of the concept of "class consciousness" important in Marxist theory, or of that "identification" that we have linked with status polarization and the development of a class group from the demographic aggregate distinguishable only as a stratum. Only 2 per cent of Centers' sample responded that they did not know what class they were in or said that they did not believe in social classes. It does not necessarily follow that 98 per cent of Americans are "class conscious," except in a restricted sense of the term.

Class consciousness, class identification and self-assignment. The subjectivist faces the problem of identifying and measuring the type of orientation toward class that he deems important. Marx was not particularly explicit in his treatment of the concept of class consciousness. It apparently involved for him not only a sense of solidarity but a coherent set of beliefs concerning the historic role of the class and its ultimate mission (an "ideology").

Centers, though sympathetic to the Marxist definition, did not capture its spirit with his simple question requiring self-classification. The interviewer posed a set of alternatives, and the respondent chose

[7] Centers, *op. cit.*, pp. 28–29.

from among them, thereby locating his position on a type of scale. We are given no indication of how important this sense of location was to the individual interviewed. Nor have we assurance that he had so located himself in the past under his own initiative. If the individual were asked to indicate the county in which he resides, he might do so accurately without warranting the inference that he feels a positive sense of belongingness to the county as a "functionally cohesive grouping." The case that Centers may build for the existence of class consciousness in the United States rests rather on his demonstration of the fact that a fair proportion of the people have concrete notions as to what comprises a class; that the same notions are shared among many in the population; and that members of these "classes" often hold attitudes appropriate to their apparent interests.

One demonstration of the weakness of the Centers question as a means of assessing class consciousness comes from our own data. In asking the Centers question in 1956 we preceded it with this query:

> There's quite a bit of talk these days about different social classes. Most people say they belong either to the middle class or to the working class. Do you ever think of yourself as being in one of these classes?

Respondents who replied affirmatively were then asked "Which one?," whereas those who responded negatively were asked which class they would choose if they had to make a choice. About four per cent of the sample indicated that they usually thought of themselves as belonging in some other class, like an upper or lower class, or that they did not know to which class they belonged. But one out of every three respondents indicated that he never thought of himself as being in one of the classes mentioned, yet was subsequently willing to choose one of the class names.

This in itself is no conclusive finding; we might simply be encountering evasiveness. But we find further that people confessing awareness of their social class actually think and behave differently on political matters than do those individuals who say initially that they are unaware. For example, within the "aware" group in 1956, working-class identifiers tended to divide their presidential vote 14 per cent more Democratic than did middle-class identifiers. Among the "unaware" group, however, this class-related difference nearly fades from sight: the unaware working class are only 2 per cent more Democratic than the unaware middle class. It is hard to consider that these unaware individuals participate in any "consciousness of class." Yet they comprise one third of the national population.

In asking people about their awareness of social class we were not explicitly attempting to find an operational definition for our concept of class identification. Rather, we wished simply to sort out a set of people for whom the notion of class was salient and self-allocation somewhat habitual. An attempt to measure class identification itself would have prompted a concern with *intensity* of feeling about class allegiance. The distinction involving awareness does not inform us of the intensity of identification in those cases where the individual is aware. Nonetheless, awareness is at the very least a precondition for class identification. We readily see that the distinction in voting behavior between the aware and the unaware gives results conceptually parallel to those in Chapter 12, where a full identification variable was present. That is, where we feel there can be no identification—among the unaware—there is no significant tendency to behave in group-relevant ways. Among the aware, such a tendency is present. Thus the class is another case of a social grouping that may be fitted to the model for group influence proposed in the preceding chapter.

Awareness of class, as measured, behaves as a variable of the *group identification* type. It is distinct from the traditional concept of class consciousness in that it includes a lower register of class feeling. We presume that anyone who is class conscious is automatically aware of class. But some of those who, according to our measure are aware of class, may lack the intensity of feeling about class interest implied in the Marxian concept. At the same time, awareness of class is something beyond simple self-location as studied by Centers. The behavior of our unaware individuals, which appears relatively free of class meaning, strongly suggests that class *feeling* is not adequately measured by the self-assignment procedure alone.

Our operational treatment of class. As tools for the ensuing discussion, we shall determine the class membership of the individual in part by his subjective location in the status hierarchy, as modified with the "awareness" distinction. We also have at our disposal a full battery of objective indicators of class, such as occupation, education, and income. Of the objective criteria, occupation tends to predict political attitudes and voting most efficiently, and we shall generally turn to it when we wish a measure of this type.[8] Although subjective class is less closely related to occupation status than are any of the other

[8] Dependent on our purposes, the gross occupational categories may be arrayed in descending order from large businessmen, the professions, small business and clerical or sales, to skilled, semi-skilled and unskilled laborers; or we may use a simpler division into "white collar" (clerical and above) and "blue collar" occupations. Often farm occupations are deleted, since their location in the hierarchy should depend to some degree upon factors like the scale of farming, the extent of land owned, etc. In the few cases where use of the complete sample has been desirable, people in farm occupations have been equated with skilled laborers.

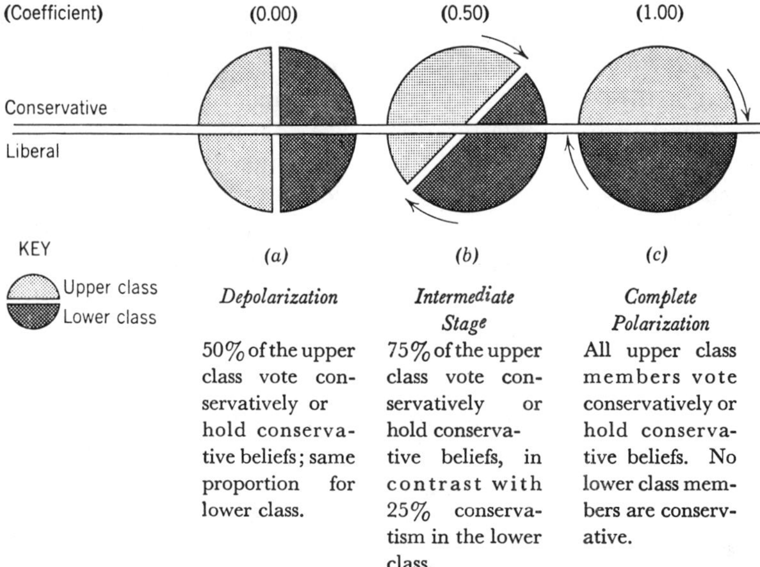

Fig. 13-1. Status polarization.

objective measures, it shows relationships with political attitudes and behavior that are of about the same magnitude as those that emerge when occupation alone is used. If our only concern were prediction, there would be little reason to choose between them. The addition of the "awareness" variant to the subjective measure, as shown previously, makes the predictive value of the subjective measure stronger than that of occupation.

In the first portion of our discussion of findings, the choice exercised among status measures is of little consequence: we would come to the same substantive conclusions regardless of our selection. Later, however, we shall consider a new level of information provided by examination of differences between the various status dimensions.

We shall also need a set of operations to measure the political manifestations of status polarization. For this purpose we shall employ coefficients of correlation that represent the *strength* of relationship between class indicators and political attitudes or behavior. The size of such coefficients will increase as lines of class cleavage swing more and more closely into alignment with broad divisions of political opinion. Figure 13-1 illustrates this variation schematically. In a state of complete political depolarization (Fig. 13-1*a*), we see that knowledge of a person's social status tells us nothing about his political attitudes or behavior. In other words, there is no relationship between status and the political variables. Whatever compound of past experience and current attitudes is leading to aggregate differences in political partisanship, it is likely to be independent of the concurrent fact of social stratification. The role of social class is at its lowest ebb. In the state of perfect polarization (Fig. 13-1*c*), to know a person's class is to know his political ideals and allegiances, automatically and without margin for error. The social classes have become solidary and mutually antagonistic. The correlation coefficient, reflecting such differences in the state of the group, provides us with a convenient metric for graphing trends.

Short-Term Fluctuation in Status Polarization

The extensive modern literature on social class and political behavior has shown persistently that individuals of higher status (subjectively or objectively) tend to give "conservative" responses on questions of economic policy and tend as well to vote Republican; individuals of lower status respond more "radically" and vote Democratic. This simple finding has assured us that social class has some bearing on the way in which the individual behaves politically. It has also served theorists as evidence of the importance of the economic motive in political behavior. But there is much that it does not tell us. In the first place, it is a static generalization. It does not allow us to anticipate variation in class voting from election to election. It casts no light upon the waxing and waning of class-based political discord. Secondly, the relationships on which the generalization is based are quite modest ones. If it is evidence of an economic motive in political behavior, we might wonder why it is so weak, rather than marvel that it appears at all.

We find marked short-term variation in the clarity of status voting in this country over the past score of years. If we take some measure of status—any of the common indicators will do—and examine the strength of relationship between this measure and the vote for president, using national survey data collected over the four past presidential elections, we find the trend represented in Fig. 13-2. We see first that the relationship has been positive over this time. That is, lower-status groups have continually favored the Democratic Party, and higher-status the Republican Party, but at some times this fact is quite prominent; at other times the association is almost trivial. Instead of a static disposition toward leftist or rightist voting, according

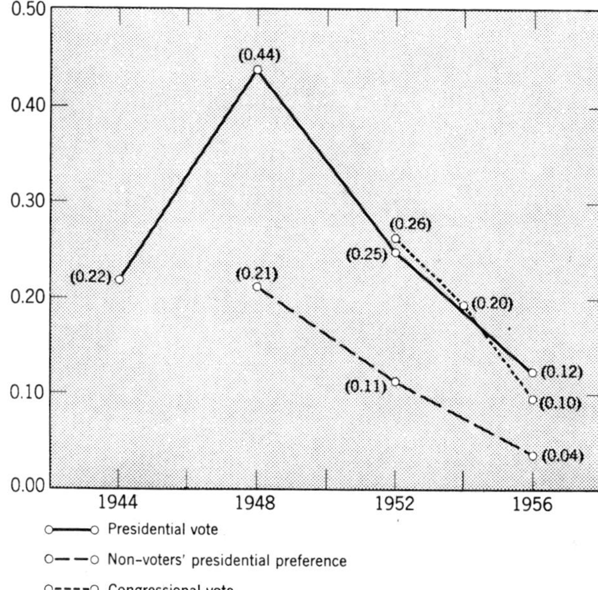

The points shown represent degree of relationship tau-beta between the occupation status of non-farm respondents and their partisan vote or preference. When subjective class is used, permitting assignment of farm respondents, the same pattern appears for the three elections for which data are available. Generally, the trend is the same when any of the standard measures of status are paired against any of a variety of political attitudes and behaviors.

The figure for 1944 is based on a national survey taken in October of that year by the National Opinion Research Center, as compiled in "psychological variables in the behavior of voters," Sheldon J. Korchin, unpublished doctoral dissertation, Harvard University, 1946. Virtually the same coefficient is computable from the 1945 survey utilized by Richard Centers, in which respondents were asked to recall their 1944 presidential vote. (Figures for the last three elections are based on national sample data from the Survey Research Center, University of Michigan.)

Fig. 13-2. Status polarization of presidential and congressional votes, 1944–1956.

to one's class, Fig. 13-2 suggests that the role of social class in political behavior is a dynamic one. It is this phenomenon we have chosen to conceptualize as status polarization; and our aim is to specify conditions under which it fluctuates.

Lipset, Lazarsfeld, Barton, and Linz (1954), in reviewing a large body of literature on voting, have made the only substantial approach to this problem. They undertook to explain the variation in solidarity of leftist voting among lower status groups in a variety of national settings. By shrewd inference concerning the crucial characteristics held in common by those groups that had turned out to be most uniformly radical, they set up a provocative series of general conditions that apparently facilitate class voting within the lower portions of the status hierarchy.[9]

Nevertheless, though they have endeavored to account for variation in frequency of class voting, the conditions specified are rooted in gross and enduring characteristics of social structure and the economic system. They are addressed to differences in voting tendencies between subgroups of any population at any point in time; they do not prepare us for short-term fluctuation in the magnitude of class influence on politics within a given society.[10] We are not indifferent to the basic properties of social structure that are likely to affect polarization phenomena, but we need explanatory devices that will illuminate as well the short-term variation.

The fact that status polarization of the vote has varied so widely in only a dozen years might suggest that it is unduly influenced by superficial aspects of the immediate political situation, such as the pairing of two competing personalities in a given presidential race or the

[9] Seymour Lipset *et al.*, "The Psychology of Voting: An Analysis of Voting Behavior," *Handbook of Social Psychology*, ed. Gardner Lindzey (Addison-Wesley Publishing Co., Cambridge, Mass., 1954), II, pp. 1134–1143. The approach of Lipset *et al.* is somewhat different than ours. It assumes at the outset that "class solidarity" in political behavior is more spotty in the lower ranges of the status hierarchy. Berelson, Lazarsfeld, and McPhee appear to have stated the parent generalization: "White-collar and business groups have greater political solidarity than workers, as indicated by party preference." [Bernard Berelson, Paul F. Lazarsfeld, and William N. McPhee, *Voting: A Study of Opinion Formation in a Presidential Campaign* (University of Chicago Press, Chicago, 1954), p. 333.] "Solidarity" in this case seems to depend on the degree to which lower or upper strata deviate from 50 per cent in their two-party vote proportion. (*Ibid.*, pp. 57, 75.) Though the hypothesis may well have underlying merit, it needs reformulation and a more convincing empirical base. It appears to be confirmed by two community studies. Some five national surveys in three countries between 1944 and 1954 showed the lower classes giving more solidary support to leftist parties than white-collar and business groups gave to rightist parties. Farm occupations excluded, blue-collar workers do not outnumber white-collar workers in most western democracies by as much as 2 to 1. As a logical matter, then, whenever a gross current is running to the left (that is, when somewhat more than 50 per cent of an electorate supports the left), it is quite unlikely that lower-status groups will split their vote closer to 50–50 than do higher-status groups. Similarly, the original finding is almost certain to be true in communities or periods in which the over-all vote divides in favor of the right.

[10] One possible exception is the effect of the "insecurity of income" as suffered by occupational groups like one-crop farmers and large-scale fishermen. Peculiarities of voting behavior associated with such groups will be examined in detail and related to questions of social class in Chapter 15 ("Agrarian Political Behavior").

campaign themes chosen for emphasis in a certain year by the parties. A variety of supporting data lend assurance that this is not the case. While the trend line in Fig. 13-2 covers a considerable range, it does not oscillate wildly. Instead, it declines in an orderly and almost linear fashion. The 1952 observation falls very close to the midpoint of the range defined by the 1948 and 1956 observations.

Moreover, comparable coefficients for the congressional vote in 1952, 1954, and 1956 (dotted line, Fig. 13-2) show precisely the same orderly downward trend. The 1954 observation is of particular interest here, in addition to the fact that it represents an independent sampling of the adult population. It might be argued that the 1952 or 1956 points fall as they do because of the candidacy of Eisenhower or Stevenson. Yet in 1954 neither name was on the ballot, and the observation for that election takes its proper place in the declining polarization trend. Furthermore, since congressional races involve a plethora of candidate pairings, it is hard to attribute this variation in polarization to peculiar candidate pairings.

Finally, we encounter evidence of precisely the same trend in status polarization over this period when we depart from matters of parties and elections entirely. For example, we may relate status not simply to one or another partisan choice, but to economic issue responses of the kind that contributed to the "social welfare" attitude scale in Chapter 9. Typically, lower-status persons tend to select "liberal" alternatives whereas those of higher status give "conservative" responses. But the clarity of such class differences varies over time also. Unfortunately, we do not have a standard battery of issue items applied to the population periodically since 1944. Nevertheless, highly comparable questions posed in 1945 and 1956 show a depolarization quite like that of the vote over the same period.[11] And although

[11] The questions used for 1945 were selected from the Richard Centers study (*op. cit.*) on the basis of their close content similarity with several of the issue questions asked in the 1956 SRC study. For example, Centers had asked, "Which one of these statements do you most agree with? (1) The most important job for the government is to make it certain that there are good opportunities for each person to get ahead on his own. (2) The most important job for the government is to guarantee every person a decent and steady job and standard of living." The 1956 SRC study asked as an agree-disagree item: "The government in Washington ought to see to it that everyone who wants to work can find a job." The polarization coefficient (calculated in both cases for White males, using occupation status) was 0.37 in 1945. In 1956 it was 0.17. Downward trends of very similar slope were found for three other questions having to do with government welfare activity and the role of government in areas traditionally restricted to private enterprise. See Philip E. Converse, "The Shifting Role of Class in Political Attitudes and Behavior," *Readings in Social Psychology*, ed., Eleanor Maccoby, Theodore Newcomb, and Eugene Hartley, 3rd edition (Henry Holt and Co., New York, 1958), pp. 388–399.

the domestic issue items used in 1948 were less comparable in content, they show more intense polarization than any of the domestic issue questions in either 1945 or 1956. Hence the trends in economic attitudes appear to follow those of political choice remarkably in this era.

Evidence of this order leads to the conclusion that the broad lines of change in vote polarization are rooted in events that transcend the immediate circumstances of any particular election. Even if such fluctuations depended entirely on events within the political order, they would be of interest. But the fact that they seem to reflect broader conditions in the society adds greatly to their fascination. At a minimum, we would suppose that change of this scope must depend on a configuration of social and economic events, with their psychological derivatives; and, where we observe signs of polarization in the electoral process, additional factors arising from the political system must condition the phenomenon as well.

The Conditions of Status Polarization: Key Psychological Terms

We have described elsewhere certain perceptual conditions and "orientations" that accompany the tendency to vote in accord with one's status location.[12] More broadly, however, we may distinguish two major dimensions of variability at a psychological level that provide crucial insight into the polarization phenomenon. Ultimately, we may trace these differences to broader social, economic, and political conditions; at the outset, however, they have interest as more than "intervening states."

Class awareness and identification. In our theoretical discussion we have suggested the importance of clear class identifications in the development of status polarization. We have also shown that the third of the population unaware of its class makes no contribution to the status polarization of the vote and hence, by default, serves to depress it. The same contrasts between the aware and the unaware seem to emerge wherever class differences are visible in partisanship or economic attitudes. Thus, for example, people who associate themselves with the "working class" and are aware of this location are 19 per cent more Democratic in their party identification than the aware "middle class"; the comparable difference among unaware people is

[12] Converse, *ibid.*

10 per cent. Similarly, on an issue attitude like the question of government guarantees of full employment, the aware working-class people give 22 per cent more frequent "liberal" responses than the middle-class aware; among the unaware this class difference fades to 14 per cent.

We presume the contrasts between the aware and unaware to be conceptual counterparts for the differences between high and low group identifiers (Table 12-3). We should remember that the observed discrepancies are present even in 1956, when status polarization was at low ebb. In times of higher polarization, these differences should become correspondingly magnified, as identifications become more intense among the aware individuals of both class groups. The fact that there is some residual class differentiation of attitudes and behavior among the unaware may be readily traced to social influence in primary groups, where attitudes "appropriate" to the individual's class may be taken on without recognition of their class relevance.[13]

It follows that signs of status polarization in a society are limited by the proportion of the population unaware of their social class. If we can determine the conditions under which persons come to think of themselves as class members, we should arrive at clues that will help us reconstruct some of the sources of variation in polarization over time. It is harder to specify these conditions than might be imagined. Awareness of class, like the various group identifications of Chapter 12, shows little tendency to vary systematically with common sociological divisions of the population. Men and women, the educated and the uneducated, the various occupational strata, and the major ethnic and racial subdivisions of the population all show about the same two thirds rate of "awareness" that characterizes the nation as a whole.

Nevertheless, there are two points at which class awareness does show revealing variation. One involves differences in awareness across age grades in the population, and the other involves the rural-urban continuum. The first leads to consideration of past economic history, whereas the second sheds light upon the role of broader social patterns in the polarization phenomenon. We shall consider the evidence for each later in the chapter.

Levels of conceptualization. We have observed that correlations between status and political behavior are normally rather low. Discussions in earlier chapters create the suspicion that this is not primarily because people are disinterested in their social class location

13 The process of influence in class directions that seems at the same time devoid of any class frame of reference on the part of the actor will be analyzed on page 372.

but because they fail to translate class interest into political terms. In some cases this may spring from confusion over relevant alternatives; more often it probably reflects ignorance of the fact that political alternatives are relevant at all, even among those "aware" of their social class.

If these surmises are correct we would expect that signs of class voting would be clearest among the most sophisticated and would tend to diminish as we proceed to those whose view of politics is simpler or more fragmentary. Figure 13-3, utilizing the "levels of conceptualization" developed in Chapter 10, shows this effect with great clarity.

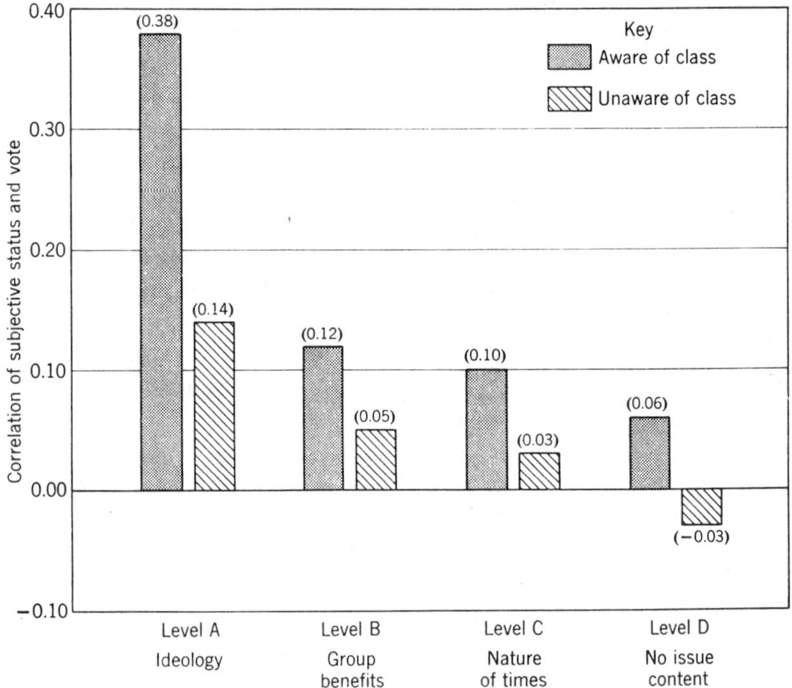

Fig. 13-3. Relation of levels of conceptualization to status voting, 1956. Individuals who rank as highly sophisticated about politics and who are at the same time aware of their social class contribute disproportionately to levels of status polarization as measured with the presidential vote, 1956. The "levels of conceptualization" are described in detail in Chapter 10. The tau-beta correlation expresses the extent to which self-identified middle-class people voted Republican and working-class people voted Democratic.

Indeed, persons assigned to Level A as ideologues or near-ideologues who were at the same time aware of their social class contributed very disproportionately to the slight degree of status polarization that characterized the 1956 election. At other levels class voting is barely visible save as we "purify" our groups by removing those persons unaware of their social class.

Once again we see that the people who organize their political behavior in the manner often assumed by sophisticated investigators are those who are most similar to such analysts in political concept formation. The familiar picture of the democratic process as a clearinghouse for conflict of class interest becomes increasingly inappropriate as we move to layers of the electorate more remote from the informed observer. If the role of social class in mass political behavior is less potent than we are frequently led to believe, these discrepancies in sophistication appear to be largely responsible. If we wish to deal with social class in its traditional garb in politics, we are dealing with a fairly restricted and sophisticated portion of the population.

We have found class awareness to be a useful intervening variable in explaining shifts in polarization because it may be seen to vary in response to a variety of broad external conditions. From this point of view, the levels of conceptualization have a rather anomalous status. Earlier we showed that this kind of sophistication was strongly dependent upon education and political involvement. The education component is fixed early in life and remains constant. Hence it does not seem helpful in accounting for fluctuations in polarization. Rather, the fact that there are poorly educated persons in all societies poses a fundamental limiting condition on status polarization in politics. But political involvement is more responsive to external conditions. Of course it can be doubted that isolated bursts of political enthusiasm on the part of the individual provide much real sophistication. Yet, we may imagine that some events external to the political order can drive persons to an enduring interest in politics.

The fixed nature of the education component does not render it uninteresting. It is difficult to examine the rates of status voting within categories of education as we have within levels of conceptualization, for education is itself a measure of status too highly correlated with other measures that might be used to assess polarization. But this analytic difficulty is of content significance. If upper-status levels tend to be more sophisticated in their approach to politics, the organization of political behavior in class terms will be more effective at these levels. This fact probably underlies the frequent assertion that upper-status groups are more "solidary" than lower, where class interests are involved in politics.[14]

[14] Berelson, Lazarsfeld, and McPhee, *op. cit.*, p. 333. See also Lipset *et al.*, *op. cit.*, p. 1134.

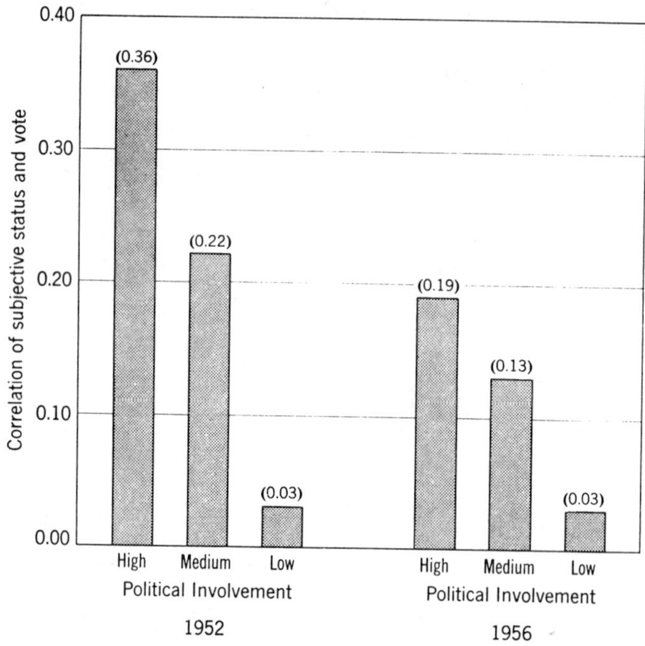

Fig. 13-4. Relation of political involvement to status voting, 1952 and 1956. The prevalence of status voting varies directly with political involvement. In 1952, when the level of status polarization in the total sample was higher, this relationship was sharp. As polarization declined between 1952 and 1956, it diminished in clarity. However, there remained no doubt of the association even in 1956 voting patterns.

It is feasible, however, to examine differences in class voting within degrees of political involvement. As involvement is a component in the levels of conceptualization, we are not surprised to find the orderly gradients of Fig. 13-4. The more involved the individual is in politics, the more likely he is to cast his vote according to class lines. In this case we have the benefit of a comparable figure for the 1952 election, which provides some insight as to what goes on when polarization varies over time. There are two opposing possibilities. In the first, gross levels of polarization would increase because some tendency to vote in class terms would be spreading to lower and lower levels. If this were the case, some of our interpretations might be untenable, as we have assumed that there are important psychological barriers that would make it difficult for the poorly involved to organize their behavior in class terms whatever the external circumstances.[15]

[15] This is not to say that no class-like economic protest can arise from the normally apathetic and unsophisticated. However, when it does it tends to take unexpected forms. We shall examine these phenomena in Chapter 15.

Or we might in the second instance assume that gross levels of polarization could increase because individuals already involved were voting more and more purely in class terms. Here, the differences in rates of class voting between the most involved and the least involved would grow sharper and sharper as gross levels of polarization increased. Although any conclusions based on as few as two observations in time must remain tentative, the data presented in Fig. 13-4 certainly appear to support this second alternative. Differences in the class behavior of the involved were much sharper relative to the uninvolved at the high levels of polarization in 1952 than we find them to be in 1956.

The suggestion is, then, that the decline in polarization between 1952 and 1956 sprang from changes in behavior among the more sophisticated. In a time of depolarization, the behavior of the involved voter becomes less and less distinct from that of the apathetic, *with respect to the class axis.* This statement does not mean that the sophisticated lose interest in politics when class interests are not clearly perceived. Other axes of political dispute may engage the attention of the politically alert. The relationship between involvement and class voting may simply be a special case of a more general phenomenon: whatever the current major dimensions of political conflict, they are reflected less clearly where involvement is lower.[16]

Up to this point we have stressed the permissive effects of high involvement and sophistication on the organization of political behavior in class terms. It is possible to turn the reasoning about and suggest that perception of a class stake in politics may lead the individual to higher involvement. We shall encounter evidence later which implies that such economic perceptions are indeed potent catalysts to increased political interest, particularly at lower-status levels. However, this does not seem the most feasible primary construction to place upon the data. This interpretation seems to imply a closer equation of political involvement with the tendency to vote in class terms than the evidence appears to support.

We have seen that individuals highly involved in 1956 had shifted their attention from the class dimension in some degree since 1952. We can imagine that elections may be sharply contested when status

[16] This proposition is of interest only as we conceive that the same involved individuals actually shift their interests to new dimensions of political dispute. It might be suggested instead that a change in the content of concern registered among the involved means that different people have become involved in politics. To some degree this may occur. However, current evidence suggests that turnover in the personnel of the highly involved is not great from election to election.

polarization is absent. Conversely, and for much the same reasons, elections may show high levels of status polarization in conjunction with low over-all levels of voter interest. The 1948 election, marking a low point in vote turnout for its era, is a case in point. An examination of aggregate statistics suggests that turnout dropped off most radically in those areas where we typically observe little or no status polarization: in the South the decrement in the vote was very marked, and it was disproportionate in rural areas of the North as well. Not all of the decline, however, can be accounted for in this manner; it remains visible even in the large Northern industrial states where polarization tends to focus. It is as though most of the forces that propelled citizens to the polls in 1944 and 1952—including dramatic personalities and the whole quadrant of foreign issues—had dropped from sight, leaving only one force, the increasing polarization of socio-economic attitudes, active in an opposing direction. Where these attitudes had some significance, the decline in turnout was not large; but where they enjoyed little leverage, the failure of the citizenry to participate became striking. If we were to ignore the dependence of involvement on other sources as well as socio-economic concern, these aspects of the 1948 election would remain incomprehensible.

In short, when external conditions warrant, status polarization occurs in politics primarily among those who are sophisticated and for whom class position is salient. We have introduced these two intervening psychological dimensions separately because as an empirical matter they are independent of one another. That is, knowledge of a respondent's level of conceptualization does not help us predict whether he will report awareness of his class location. At all levels of conceptualization the probability of class voting increases if there is some sensitivity to social class location, although these differences are not large save among the sophisticated. But political sophistication and class awareness vary independently.

With these facts in mind, we may turn to some of the broader external conditions that enhance and inhibit the development of status polarization in the political system. Both class awareness and the involvement component of sophistication will provide useful clues to the impact of these conditions as we proceed.

The Economic Background of Status Polarization

In view of the economic axis of class feeling we would readily assume that status polarization should increase in time of depression, and decrease in periods of prosperity. Figure 13-2 provides support for this proposition. The most striking feature of the polarization trend in the recent past has been the steady and rapid depolarization between 1948 and 1956. This decline occurred in a post-war period when the nation was enjoying a striking ascent to prosperity and a consequent release from the pressing economic concerns that had characterized the Depression. Therefore, the basic outlines of variation in polarization fit our preconceptions of changes in the economic state of the union.

We have indicated that although class awareness shows little variation across most sociological divisions of the electorate, there are differences in the proportion who express awareness as a function of age. These differences are far from striking in their magnitude but are nonetheless intriguing. Across a fair portion of the age continuum we find rising awareness with increasing years. But there are significant irregularities here that seem to betray the overlay of historical events (Fig. 13-5). The high proportion of people in their early fifties (1956) who are aware of class is particularly interesting. When we deal with age we cannot be sure that patterns that make historical sense are not due instead to the phenomena of the life cycle. Perhaps awareness builds up through the active working lives of people in a particular age grade, to fade out rapidly after retirement. However, the age group in which awareness is most prevalent includes those individuals who were in their twenties and thirties during the depths of the Great Depression, a generation long assumed to have been strongly affected by economic events. Although people who were over sixty in

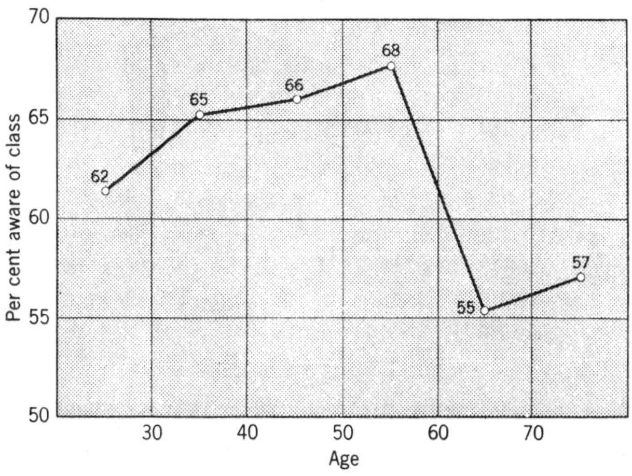

Fig. 13-5. Relation of age to differences in class awareness.

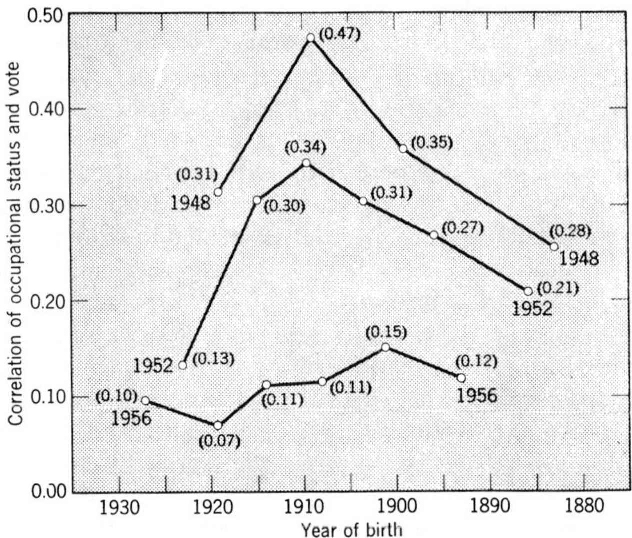

Fig. 13-6. Relation of age to status polarization, 1948, 1952, 1956. The points shown represent degree of relationship tau-beta between the occupation status of non-farm respondents and their presidential vote, by age category. The age groupings within each of the three election samples (1948, 1952, and 1956) are linked by lines. The data points are located on the time dimension according to the mean year of birth of the respondents included in each grouping.

1956 also experienced the Depression, they tended more often to be vocationally established, and may have resisted some of the new definitions of social reality in class terms that appealed to a younger age cohort.

This interpretation is bolstered by the fact that this "Depression generation" is also prominent in its status voting. People falling in this cohort contributed disproportionately to the high levels of vote polarization recorded in the 1948 and 1952 elections. Figure 13-6 provides a "natural history" of the class-related political behavior of various age categories over the period of polarization decline from 1948 to 1956. We see that in 1948 and, to a slightly lesser degree in 1952, this intermediate portion of the age continuum clearly contained more class-oriented voters than any other age group. But by 1956, these orientations had become scarcely visible.[17] We cannot say

[17] It might be noted that comparisons drawn in Fig. 13-6 are based on relatively raw data. For example, involvement is related to age as well as to status voting; with involvement controlled, the contrast in status voting between the middle-age group and older voters is considerably sharpened. Among 1952 voters, 39 citizens

that the decline in polarization between 1948 and 1956 depended entirely on changing patterns of behavior within this group. Status voting falls away within other age strata as well. But it is this portion of the electorate that showed the greatest relative depolarization and that best illustrates fading effects of the Depression.

We may also trace out the progressive obliteration of past disaster by surveying changes in the proximal attitudes of this "Depression generation" from election to election. We have pointed out elsewhere that a concern over issues of domestic policy is a striking accompaniment of status voting.[18] In 1952, respondents of the critical age category reacted to the election in terms of domestic issues with a frequency significantly greater than any other age cohort. By 1956, however, these persons were no more likely to bring up domestic issues in their spontaneous evaluations of the political scene than were people of other ages. There was a major decline in references to prosperity and depression between 1952 and 1956; it appears the rate of decline was highest within this critical group. It is in this sense that involved people who had contributed to high levels of polarization in 1948 and 1952 increasingly turned their attention to other axes of political dispute by 1956.

What we may be observing in Fig. 13-2 are the declining effects of the Great Depression of the 1930's rather than other economic perturbations that have occurred in the interim. When we have data covering a much larger span of time, we may be able to state precisely the magnitude of economic dislocation necessary to modify the role of social class in the political system. At the current time we can only make preliminary observations. But the postwar period surveyed here had its high prosperity marred by two economic troughs in 1949 and 1953–1954. Of course these recessions bore little resemblance to the appalling collapse of the economy after 1929. Yet they were highly visible national experiences, observed with apprehension in all quarters and acccompanied by grave unemployment.

The second of these two disturbances is more interesting from the point of view of our data, as it very nearly coincided with the 1954 Congressional election. Although recovery was apparent by the time voters went to the polls in November of that year, much of the campaign had been conducted under the threat of serious collapse, a

falling in the depression group who were at the same time highly involved, registered a polarization coefficient of 0.87, the highest we encounter in our analysis. Furthermore, with such refinements, we do find clearer vestiges of depression-born behavior in the crucial age stratum even in the 1956 sample.

[18] Converse, *op. cit.*

situation exploited by Democrats attempting to regain control of Congress. Yet the polarization coefficient referring to the Congressional vote in this election (Fig. 13-2) seems to suggest that polarization was declining steadily throughout this period. Pending the slow accumulation of further data, then, we conclude that although economic distress is a prime mover in enhancing the role of social class in politics, it must constitute a severe and prolonged trauma before its effects are felt.

If the postwar years had been ones of marginal economic security—without severe depression or full prosperity—the Depression generation might have remained distinctive in its manner of relating class to politics. By the same token, it would be psychologically sound to presume that this orientation has not disappeared, but has only become latent after 15 years of unnecessary apprehension.[19] The higher rate of class awareness in this group remains visible in 1956, as a symbol of this potential. If the nation were to suffer new economic distress of the magnitude undergone in the 1930's before these people fade from the population, we would expect them to return to their former class orientations. In such an event, polarization might rise higher than it did in the 1930's, since a leaven of older people, insensitive to class and bound to former party alignments, would no longer be present.

The role of war in status polarization. We have linked the decline of status polarization in politics between 1948 and 1956 to increasing prosperity and fading memories of the Great Depression of the 1930's. But the economic state of the nation cannot be seen to determine the level of polarization completely. If the progress of polarization after 1936 involved only the receding spectre of depression, we should expect it to show a constant decline within our recorded history. Between 1944 and 1948 the general trend of the economy was upward, and the Depression was more remote by four years. Yet the polarization of the presidential vote shows an increase between these elections. How may we account for this discrepancy?

A concern with domestic issues, largely economic in substance, characterizes the person who votes in accord with his class position. Yet there are other types of issues that may compete with such concern.

[19] The weathering of mild economic storms under Republican Administrations may have been particularly effective in reducing the economic apprehension that the Depression-molded voter brought to the polling booths through the 1952 election. The data cited in Chapter 3 concerning the change in partisan character of references to prosperity and depression reflect this interaction of the political and the economic extremely well.

The threat of war, for example, focuses attention in other directions. The impact of war—modern war in particular—is not distributed along class lines. Policies that will maintain or win peace have the same meaning for all. Hence war is a basic public concern that may eclipse those problems of domestic economics leading to cleavage among status interest groups. In general, the advent of war against external foes is said to focus the energies of the public upon a common task; threat from without unifies societal values and subdues internal faction.

If we compare the behavior of voters whose concern over domestic issues outweighs their interest in foreign policy with those for whom the reverse is true, it is clear that higher rates of status voting attach to the domestic issue group. Among voters concerned primarily with foreign issues, such tendencies are almost invisible.[20]

It appears plausible therefore that much of the variation in Fig. 13-2 could be understood in terms of an interplay between war and depression. Polarization tendencies carrying over from the Great Depression may have been dampened as a result of the national crisis posed by the Second World War, rebounding upward after that conflict was concluded. The temporary lull in foreign threat from 1945 to 1950, along with the outbreak of "postponed" strikes in major industries, the struggle in Congress to place legislative controls on the activities of labor unions, and the development of first anxieties over an "inevitable" postwar depression, all must have contributed to a rise in the relative salience of domestic issues that had lain dormant during the war. After the 1948 peak of polarization, however, the renewal of the threat of global war and the outbreak of hostilities in Korea may have acted, in concert with increasing prosperity, to depress the level of status polarization once again.

Political Manifestations of Status Polarization

Status polarization is a generic concept. The magnitude of polarization within different spheres of a society may show discrepant levels at any given time. For example, one may conceive of dispute existing between classes over the fundamentals of the economic system, in the absence of political alignments that will express this disagreement. In this case, economic polarization would outrun the manifestations of polarization in the political order. Conversely, we might imagine that events might bring a depolarization of economic attitudes, with

[20] Converse, *op. cit.*

political alignments being readjusted only after some lag. Under such circumstances, polarization in politics might temporarily appear higher than that within the economic realm.

Economic attitudes of class relevance were showing much the same increase and decline of polarization in the period from 1944 to 1956 that were registered in partisan choice at the presidential and congressional level in this period. Hence we contend that the primary lines of fluctuation in polarization in this era had to do with events in the economic rather than the political order. Nonetheless, it would be unwise to assume that the trend of status polarization in politics has remained unmodified by the context of parties and candidates within which voters have arrived at political decision. In fact, we can isolate a number of circumstances of these years that would appear, on theoretical grounds, to have facilitated the prevailing direction of polarization change.

The role of the candidates. Each of the four presidential elections represented in Fig. 13-2 paired candidates that seem intuitively to "fit" the polarization of the vote registered in their respective elections. Thus polarization reached its peak in 1948, when Harry Truman met Thomas E. Dewey in the presidential race. Truman displayed a pugnacious social consciousness, hotly defending the rights of the "common man" and the underprivileged. He was himself a "common man" with few of the graces of the middle class. His opponent, on the other hand, conveyed a sober and conservative image that had little to offend the middle classes and little to attract the less privileged. In such a setting, a class-flavored vote division might well be expected.

The other three elections were dominated by two men of tremendous popular appeal, Franklin Delano Roosevelt and Dwight D. Eisenhower. Roosevelt had in earlier elections shown no qualms about making direct appeals to the less-privileged of the society while freely criticizing the upper strata. These class themes, however, were not a part of the 1944 campaign, and his war leadership, the primary issue of the election, was not a subject for differential class appeal. Furthermore, his personal bearing was palatable to middle class groups who were to be offended by his successor. Dwight Eisenhower lacked the clear class background of Roosevelt, Truman, or Dewey; he was neither aristocrat nor full-blown "common man." In his campaigns he avoided any recognition of the political relevance of differences between such interest groupings as social classes. Neither his personal image nor the issue themes that he espoused were calculated to charm one class or repel another. In the elections that he dominated, polarization of the vote was relatively low.

We have presented data that suggest that the major lines of change in vote polarization from 1944 to 1956 were not dependent upon the personalities of the five presidential candidates in this era. Trends in polarization of economic attitudes must be conditioned by other events than the choice of candidates in presidential elections. Similarly, we have seen that polarization of the congressional vote in 1954, when none of the presidential candidates was on the ballot, registered the same declining trend found for presidential votes.

Nonetheless, two observations may be made concerning the role of candidates in the political polarization phenomenon. First, since the personalities associated with the past four elections have been types that, in a *post hoc* vein, lead us to expect in each instance the specific change in polarization that has actually been observed, we cannot disengage the candidates from the polarization phenomenon. It may be that each pairing of candidates during this period has facilitated the existing motion of polarization, so that the magnitude of variation was larger than otherwise might have occurred. That is, had Eisenhower run for the presidency in 1948, there might have been a crest of polarization, but one somewhat less marked than that which the Dewey-Truman contest evoked. Conversely, had Truman run in 1952, the decline in polarization of the presidential vote might have been less sharp.

Secondly, it is hard even conceptually to disassociate the man from the times. Each pairing of presidential candidates seemed to fit the tenor of its times. Yet to what degree are the salient features of these personalities a direct product of the times in which they operated? Roosevelt the wartime leader presented a different image from the Roosevelt who lashed out at "economic royalists." Clearly these changes depended less on the man than upon external events well beyond his control. Harry Truman was not responsible for the timing of the Taft-Hartley Act; if Eisenhower had run in 1948 could he have maintained the same class neutrality with this issue prominent? On the other hand, Truman was delighted to make the most of the Taft-Hartley furor, and another man might have kept it from becoming such a focal point for the campaign. In short, we cannot hope to determine here whether the times make the man, or the man the times. We suspect that a good deal of the aura of each election, and the connotations that have come to surround the protagonists of each race, have been determined by the context in which they were destined to operate. But we would not gainsay the capacity of these personalities to muffle or amplify the class divisions of the moment.

The role of the political parties. The role of the parties in modifying the level of status polarization in politics may be analyzed from a number of vantage points. But we may immediately propose that unless the parties differentiate themselves in matters of policy relevant to class interest, we have little reason to expect partisan preference to reflect whatever polarization exists in other spheres of the social system.

In reality, both a perceptual and an institutional condition must be fulfilled for partisan behavior to manifest status polarization. The class-oriented voter, to act in accord with his class position, must perceive that differences exist between the parties that are relevant to class interests. As Fig. 13-7 suggests, individuals who fail to arrive at such perceptions are much less likely to engage in class voting. However attentive the class-oriented voter may be, the differences that he *can* perceive are limited by the divergence that actually exists between the positions of competing parties. There are some important circumstances in which party differentiation on class matters is not likely to be clear.

Let us suppose that a society has remained in a state of depolarization for a considerable period. The primary axes of political dispute have been devoid of class implication, as in the case of the Civil War period in American history. Then the moratorium is ended as events in the economic sphere touch off a trend toward status polarization.

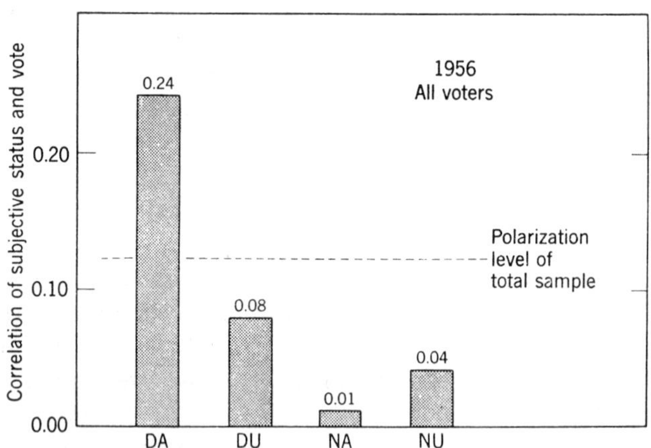

Fig. 13-7. Status voting: class awareness and perception of party differences on domestic issues. DA: Perceives that the two parties take different stands on at least one of four issues of domestic policy, *and* is aware of his subjective class position. DU: Perceives at least one party difference but is *not* aware of his subjective class position. NA: Perceives no party differences on any of four issues *but* is aware of subjective class position. NU: Perceives no differences *and* is unaware of subjective class position.

After some specifiable point, we would expect groups to be generated that would give focus and ideological content to the dissatisfaction of one class or the alarm of the other.[21] But we would have no assurance, at such a point, that class roles would be assumed by existing political parties, or that extrapolitical class groupings would be able to take over the functions of the political party. Where political systems and cultural values have permitted, both eventualities have occurred. But in many instances there is a considerable period during which intensified class feelings can find no political expression. Either the parties communicate no desire to become instruments of these interests, or they make ambiguous gestures of support to the same or to both strata.

In sum, then, circumstances may arise in which status polarization outside the political order is inadequately reflected in matters of political partisanship. This pattern of events is most likely to characterize a period of rising polarization in a political system bound to traditional parties. If status polarization continues to mount, we would expect either that (1) new parties will break through institutional barriers, or that (2) events will force the existing parties to a clearer class alignment.

It would be ill-advised, however, to dwell upon the lag in party policies without noting as well the lag that is evident in the public response to the parties. There is reason to believe that in a system of long-standing parties it is the rare exception that any large proportion of the public departs from the existing parties in search of new policy positions.[22] Usually calamity that is sufficient to make any broad segment of the public demand new answers is at the same time sufficient to stimulate change in the policies of even traditional "patronage" parties. And under such circumstances, enduring loyalties to the existing parties tend to maintain the traditional system.

The role of party identification. For the period of declining polarization that we have observed we can trace out the conserving influence of party identification. The individual's identification with his party comes to have a force autonomous of the events which established the initial loyalty. Thus a person drawn to the Democratic Party on economic grounds during the 1930's is likely to retain this allegiance after economic problems have become less salient. Alignments captured in a measurement of party identification should retain some flavor of past events. When status polarization is declining, its

21 Such a point would be specified in terms of a critical level of polarization, relative to a certain distribution of nascent class feelings.

22 We shall consider some of the circumstances under which new pressures do occasionally lead to successful "third" parties in Chapter 15.

manifestation in current voting behavior should be less marked than that witnessed by distributions of party identification between classes.

We have been measuring party identification only since 1952, a fact that leaves a limited time series for comparison. But numerous pieces of evidence support our deductions. For example, among non-Southern voters, polarization of the vote fell from 0.29 to 0.13 between 1952 and 1956; the polarization of party identification over the same period declined from 0.28 to 0.21.[23] Thus the relationship between status and party identification varied in the same direction as that between status and vote, but less sharply, supporting the hypothesis.

If we follow the same logic extrapolating backward in time, we must conclude that in 1948 the polarization of the vote rose well above that of party identification, since the two coefficients were almost equal in 1952. We would have reason to feel comfortable with this proposition, in view of the fact that 1948 appears to mark a crest for status polarization between 1944 and 1952. The hypothetical party identification coefficient for 1944, though undoubtedly above that manifested by the vote in that year, would not be expected to rise as rapidly or fall as sharply from 1944 through 1948 to 1952.

When forces act to change partisan alignments in the electorate the bonds of party allegiance constitute an inertia that is only slowly overcome. If this statement is true, then we would expect inertia to be marked among those who identify most strongly. In the face of pressure toward political change, Independents and weak identifiers will succumb most readily. Therefore, the marks of the past should be most visible among strong party identifiers. With regard to class, we have developed the thesis that status voting patterns established in the 1930's have been eroding since that time. Status voting should then be most prevalent among the strongly identified and least clear for people toward the "independent" end of the identification continuum.

This configuration of relationships emerges handsomely from our 1952 materials (Fig. 13-8) and appears substantially intact in 1956 as well. In this era, the probability of status voting was much higher among strong partisans than among weak or independent people. Findings of this nature do not, of course, guarantee that signs of polarization would emerge first among independent people and last among strong identifiers, over a period of rising polarization. The positive

[23] It should be pointed out that some portion of this change is accounted for not by individuals shifting their party allegiance but by normal turnover of personnel in the electorate due to mortality in the older cohorts and new voters of the younger generation.

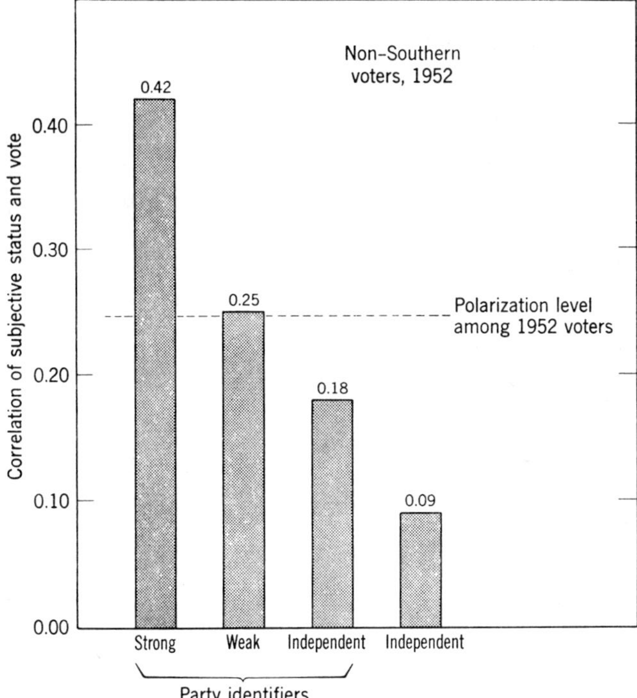

Fig. 13-8. Status voting: strength of party identification, 1952. In 1952, prevalence of status voting increased with strength of party identification. The height of each bar indicates the degree of relationship between subjective class location and the presidential vote within each category of identification.

relationship between strength of party identification and status voting might turn out, when full data were available, to be constant through both waxing and waning polarization. It seems reasonable to expect that status voting would be greater among weak identifiers than among strong as polarization changed direction.

One further datum is relevant at this point. The South, as so frequently happens in political analysis, presents class patterns that are often anomalies. Generally speaking, polarization is lower in the South than in other regions of the nation; many of the materials presented in this chapter for the entire nation show sharper patterns when the South is excluded from consideration. We lack the data that would permit us to reconstruct the course of polarization in the South during the 1940's. Between 1952 and 1956, however, when levels were declining elsewhere, there was an actual increase in polarization in the South, from a coefficient not much above zero to a point of clear significance in 1956.[24] Coupled with this rise, we find status voting more prevalent among *weak* party identifiers than among strong in the South in 1952, and a residual difference, no longer strong enough for statistical significance, in the same direction in 1956. In other words, patterns characterizing the regions outside the South in a period of rapid depolarization are reversed in the South, where there seems instead to be a mild increase in polarization.

This pattern of findings in the South is of particular interest as it lends weight to our interpretation of the association between status voting and strength of party identification. We have also found a strong association between political involvement and status voting, and we know that there is some correlation between involvement and strength of partisan commitment. Hence it would be possible to argue that Figs. 13-4 and 13-8 merely say the same thing in different terms. Although it is easy to demonstrate that both political involvement and identification strength, with the other held constant, continue to show strong gradients in status voting, the South provides a more convincing test. With polarization rising in the South, status voting within identification categories shows a gradient the reverse of that which we find where polarization is declining. This fact supports the "lag" interpretation. At the same time in the South there is no reversal of the relationship between involvement and status voting: in both 1952 and 1956 Southerners who voted most according to class lines were the most involved. Hence different interpretations of the type given for the two patterns seem warranted.

We feel confident, then, in viewing party identification as a conserving influence in mass political behavior. This influence is particularly clear when changes in polarization outside the political order create forces toward change within that order. When there is sudden economic dislocation and a rapid rise in polarization, as was probably the case after 1929, the lag it creates may be brief, especially among young citizens less firmly bound to the current parties. When polarization is receding, however, and no major conflicts of another nature arise to realign the parties on a different axis, the strength of party allegiances may maintain polarization in political partisanship above that which we would otherwise predict.

24 This trend may reflect growing industrialization and urbanization in the South, processes that are likely in the long run to blur traditional differences in political behavior generally.

Status Polarization and Social Structure

The role of social class in American politics is further illuminated if we compare current American social structure with that of other nations and other times. Within any society the progress of status polarization may depend, by and large, on economic events. The political expression it receives is conditioned in turn by current characteristics of the political system. But political process is embedded in a social system that has certain properties. As these properties vary from nation to nation, the levels that polarization is likely to attain under equal degrees of economic stress and political facilitation vary as well. Thus broad features of social structure have a bearing on the *potential* for status polarization. We can locate several properties of the American social system that appear to condition the polarization potential of the nation in this way.

Urbanization. Although class awareness shows little tendency to follow common sociological divisions of the population, one such correlate emerges with some clarity. Contact with modern urban life increases the likelihood of class awareness. The level of awareness is highest in the central cities of large metropolitan areas and declines steadily through smaller cities to a low among people living in sparsely settled areas. It is particularly low among people in farm occupations. Furthermore, the probability that an individual thinks of himself as a class member shows some variation according to the amount of his life that he has spent in urban areas where ideas of social class are abroad. Among people who reside in large metropolises, those who have lived in such urban concentrations all of their lives are more likely to be aware of class than metropolitan people who grew up on farms (Table 13-1).

Hence class awareness may well be determined in part by some "proportion of life in contact" formula of the type suggested for group identification in Chapter 12. These findings fit common assumptions that the migration of populations to urban areas tends to stimulate perceptions of social class, and it follows that urbanization is likely to increase the potential for status polarization in a society.

Class identification and the problem of status ambiguity. If vague class distinctions in a society create severe problems for the analyst who wishes to assign his subjects to a unique position in the status hierarchy, they can be expected to lead to confusion on the part of the actors themselves. If a class location is ambiguous, we would expect less clarity in class-relevant behavior and, as a consequence, a reduced potential of the social group for status polarization.

Up to this point our findings have not depended upon any particular mode of defining status; any of the various measures might be substituted to produce the same conclusions. As we focus upon peculiarities of the social system, however, we must pay closer attention to the interplay of various status dimensions. In discussing operational

TABLE 13-1. Class Awareness as a Function of Urban-Rural Residence and Background, 1956[a]

	Type of Place Where Respondent Grew Up		
Current Residence	Metropolis over 100,000 (1930)	City or Town	Farm
Metropolis over 100,000	72%	69%	63%
City 10,000–99,999	66%	65%	61%
Village and rural, non-farm	64%	59%	64%
Farm	...[b]	...[b]	50%

[a] The per cent entry in each cell indicates the proportion of the group falling in the cell which is classified as "aware" of its class position.

[b] Cases too few for stable estimates.

definitions of class and status we noted that some students use objective criteria whereas others depend upon the subject's self-assignment. Of the several objective indices of status, occupation tends to generate the strongest relationships with political variables. Subjective class shows relationships of about the same magnitude. Occupation is more highly related to subjective class than are any of the other objective criteria.

The relationship, however, *between subjective status and occupation* is not extremely high. In other words, a substantial proportion of individuals assign themselves to a class other than that to which they would be assigned by the sociologist employing occupation as a criterion. Blue-collar workers of varying skill can and do identify with the middle class, whereas white-collar persons frequently identify with the "working" class.[25] It is these people "misidentifying" across class

[25] We shall use occupation as our objective criterion of "misidentification." This choice is somewhat arbitrary, but the most defensible choice among alternatives. Other objective measures would pose problems of cutting points best fitted to the subjective distinction between "working" and "middle" class groups. In any event,

lines who are symptomatic of status ambiguity in the culture.[26] Therefore it is among this group we must look for evidence of political behavior that is, from a class point of view, indeterminate.

Such behavior is readily demonstrable, as data compiled by Richard Centers have shown. Figure 13-9 compares the prevalence of recognizable class voting among individuals whose subjective class matches their occupation with class voting found among misidentifiers. This

the logic of the ensuing analysis is such that results would be essentially the same even if one of the other common objective criteria were employed.

[26] We use the term "misidentification" only with some hesitation. We do not intend to imply that the misidentifier is either dishonest or suffers distorted perceptions. At the outset, the term need be no more than a denotation of an analytic category.

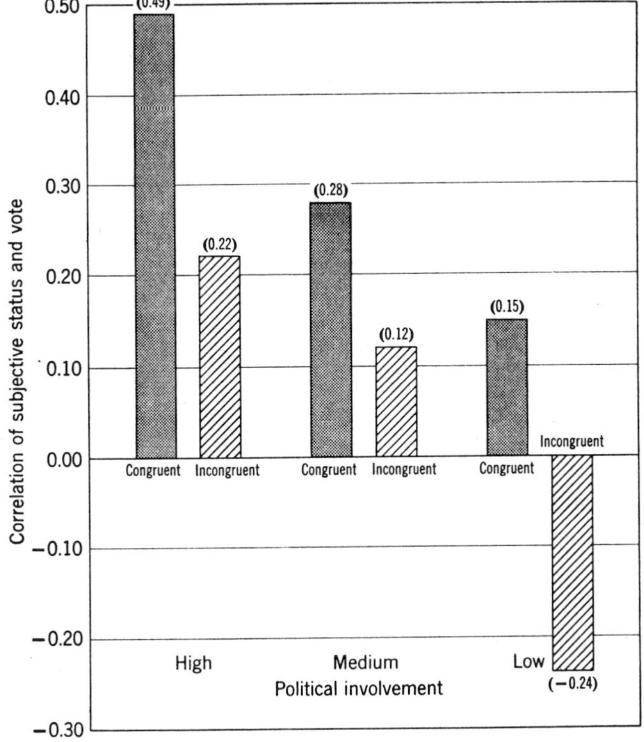

Fig. 13-9. Status voting: political involvement and types of class identification, 1952. This figure elaborates on Fig. 13-4, with persons of differing involvement further subdivided according to type of class identification. The solid bars include persons whose subjective class location is congruent with occupation, that is, blue-collar people choosing the "working class" and white-collar people of "middle-class" identification. The shaded bars include blue-collar workers identifying with the "middle class" and white-collar, "working-class" individuals.

comparison is drawn separately within the three levels of political involvement employed previously. In each case, it is clear that most of the evidence for class voting within each group is contributed by voters whose class identification is congruent with occupation. As expected, tendencies toward class voting are indistinct among misidentifiers. Blue-collar workers who say they are middle class do not vote in a manner that is very distinct from that of white-collar, working-class identifiers.

Our initial presumption is that class voting is blurred among misidentifiers because such persons behave under cross-pressures. In this case, the cross-pressures as operationally defined consist of a sociological variable (occupation) on the one hand and a psychological variable (perception of class location) on the other. The individual has reason to identify with one class, but the occupational milieu in which he operates from day to day consists primarily of members of the "opposing" class. The class with which he sympathizes has one set of political norms, but his active social group, to the degree it is class-oriented, has opposing norms. Under these cross-pressures, the aggregate of such marginal individuals behaves in a manner that does not clearly fit either set of norms.

The addition of the involvement distinction communicates further information. If misidentifiers behave under cross-pressures, then the pressure that tends to carry the day varies systematically according to degree of involvement in the political process (Fig. 13-9). A positive correlation between subjective class and vote means that working-class identifiers vote Democratic whereas middle-class identifiers tend to vote Republican. For the *congruent* identifiers a positive correlation also means that blue-collar people are voting more Democratic than are white-collar people. But among *misidentifiers* a positive correlation, although signifying a more Democratic vote among working-class identifiers, also implies *ipso facto* a *negative* correlation of equivalent magnitude between occupation and vote. Thus a bar above the line in Fig. 13-9 indicates that amid cross-pressures, misidentifiers are more likely to follow the norms of their class identification than they are to succumb to norms of their occupational milieu. A negative correlation (a bar falling below the line), on the other hand, means that influence from the social milieu overrides any hypothetical pressure that may be felt as a result of class identification.

We find therefore that while the involved misidentifier more often than not follows his class identification in preference to his occupational milieu, the situation is reversed among the most apathetic third of the population. Although there are no substantial differences in class awareness across the six groups analyzed in Fig. 13-9, differences in behavior lead us to suspect that either of two conditions obtains among the politically apathetic: (1) the choice of a class location is relatively meaningless in itself; or (2) this choice is not endowed with any of its traditional political meaning. In either case the behavioral result is the same: the pressure stemming from class identification is weak relative to that stemming from the actual social group, and partisan choice, to the degree that it shows traces of class influence at all, reflects occupation primarily.[27]

We have made several assumptions in interpreting Fig. 13-9 that bear further examination. Most critically, we have presumed that the indeterminate class behavior of misidentifiers results from a conflict of forces. The same findings might be generated if no individual among the misidentifiers actually was in conflict. The aggregate of misidentifiers might consist of two types, (1) individuals who would follow norms of their preferred class without concern about their actual status, either because the occupational milieu is predominantly of the opposing class or because no norms are perceived in the actual occupational milieu; and (2) individuals for whom the statement of class location has little political meaning and who will follow the norms of the occupational milieu with little sense of class interest. Such an amalgam of two types in the misidentifying group would produce the blurred class picture that we find in our data, yet individuals themselves would be behaving without conflict.

Earlier we introduced a method for determining whether or not the field of proximal attitudes is actually conflicted where sociological cross-pressures are suspected. We may apply this technique to test the hypothesis that behind the indeterminate class behavior of misidentifiers lies actual conflict in political attitudes. We would not expect to find conflict across all categories of involvement, however. We speculated that among the apathetic the incongruent class identification has little political meaning and hence cannot be seen to exert much counter-pressure to norms of the social or occupational milieu. If the measure of subjective class is ignored as politically meaningless for the least involved, then both congruent and incongruent identifiers in Fig. 13-9 show a weak *positive* relationship between occupation and presidential vote. In this case, we would expect to find misidentifiers

[27] Although the negative correlation among the misidentifying apathetic is not strong, a similar correlation of almost the same magnitude emerges when the same table is drawn from 1956 data. The 1956 graph duplicates the 1952 findings, although all coefficients are lower, reflecting the over-all decline in status polarization of the vote.

more conflicted in their political attitudes than congruent types, except among those least politically involved, where we have no reason to expect any signs of increased conflict.

Table 13-2 confirms this pattern of predictions in each detail.

TABLE 13-2. Consistency of Attitude as a Function of Appropriate Class Identification and Political Involvement, 1952[a]

	Political Involvement[b]		
	High	Medium	Low
Subjective class congruent with occupation status	318%	202%	123%
Subjective class incongruent with occupation status	206%	135%	145%

[a] The entry in each cell represents the per cent increase of individuals *observed* to have consistent attitudes over the number that would be expected by chance alone. This statistic is discussed in detail in connection with Table 6-5. The higher the value entered for a subgroup, the greater the proportion of the group that has a consistent attitudinal field, relative to chance expectations. The reversal occurring among the least involved falls far short of statistical significance at any reasonable level of confidence.

[b] Differences within horizontal rows have to do with the strong relationship between high involvement and attitudinal consistency discussed in Chapter 4. The table is constructed to examine differences which remain between groups arrayed vertically (that is, with involvement controlled).

Where there is some political involvement, class misidentification is associated with greater inconsistency of the field of proximal attitudes. If involvement is low there is no significant difference between congruent persons and those who misidentify in choice of social class location. Therefore, we seem warranted in assuming that among politically involved types the relatively indeterminate class behavior of misidentifiers is linked with actual psychological conflict.

Class misidentification leads to cross-pressures and thereby restrains the level of polarization in a society. It follows that the more frequent class misidentification is within a society, the lower the potential of that society for status polarization.[28] For a given degree of economic pressure structured along class lines, class-relevant behavior in the

[28] The "frequency of misidentification" is another expression for the degree of relationship between subjective and objective definitions of status.

group as a whole will remain more diffuse if there is a greater leaven of individuals who have no clearcut class interest to follow.

If the proportion of misidentifiers is an important datum in assessing the polarization potential of a society, then any characteristics of the social structure that promote misidentification serve at the same time to limit that potential. On the basis of current data it is possible to suggest a number of such characteristics.

First, it appears that the degree of misidentification in a society depends on the way in which its population is distributed along a status continuum. If we analyze the proportion of misidentifiers within successive groups along any of our objective status dimensions, we find that the rate of misidentification is low at the extremes (about 15 or 20 per cent) and rises symmetrically to a peak (approaching 50 per cent) at the center of the continuum. In other words, the closer an individual is located to a hypothetical dividing line between the two major classes by virtue of his objective situation, the more likely he is to locate himself psychologically on the other side of that line.[29]

The caste society, with its sharply delineated strata, would have relatively few if any marginal people of ambiguous status. As we move from the caste extreme toward societies without gulfs defining status layers, however, the proportion of the population that occupies marginal locations increases. We would presume that as a result, the rate of misidentification increases as well, and the potential of the society for status polarization is consequently reduced. The United States, with its relatively swollen ranks of intermediate statuses—highly skilled labor and clerical workers—falls toward the extreme of the continuum. It is unrealistic to think of its structure as a single class, for there are sharp differences in economic rewards garnered at the extremes. Yet a large portion of the population constitutes a mode in the center of the continuum. Other things equal—including the important elements of expectation and aspiration—it would seem that

[29] The same empirical result would emerge if we had made an increasing number of classification errors as to objective position, close to the hypothetical line. However, it is hard to discard the finding on these grounds. In the first place, the coding decision at stake involves a distinction between blue- and white-collar occupations. This distinction is more reliably made than many others further from the midline, such as that between semi-skilled and unskilled laborers. More persuasively yet, individuals who appear to misidentify *only* as a result of classification error would in reality have a subjective class congruent with their occupation, and hence should behave politically as other congruent individuals. They clearly do not. The increased confusion about class position for border-line persons has been demonstrated by several investigations of the Centers self-classification procedure. See Joseph A. Kahl and James A. Davis, "A Comparison of Indexes of Socio-Economic Status," *American Sociological Review,* XX (June, 1955), 325.

the United States has less potential for polarization than nations with other types of status structure.

We may also link the rate of social mobility in a society with the nature of its polarization potential. We find that when proximity to a hypothetical dividing line between classes is held constant, misidentification is more likely where the individual has, in times past, had some kind of contact with the opposing class milieu. For example, within each category of white-collar occupations, individuals of lower educational background are more likely to identify with the working class than are comparable people of high education. Similarly, blue-collar people of relatively high education are more likely to identify with the middle class. These situations are symptoms of mobility: a person's educational background, whatever his current status position, tends to reflect the status of his father's occupation. When education appears discrepant with current occupation, it is usually the case that the individual's current status differs from that of the family in which he was reared. When upward or downward mobility of this sort occurs, we tend to find what we classify as misidentification, and signs of conflict in political behavior where class is concerned. Even a relatively remote factor such as a wife's father's occupation status exerts a visible pull that, when discrepant with a man's current status, increases the probability of misidentification.[30]

Within societies in which movement of individuals upward or downward in the status hierarchy is rare, the possibility of misidentification arising from this source is minimized, and the potential of the society for status polarization is consequently increased. At the other extreme, the "open-class" society characterized by a high rate of social mobility maintains some ceiling on polarization potential by keeping its members' class identification as it were, "off balance."

Another aspect of social structure that affects the polarization potential of the society is worthy of special mention, although it is dependent in some degree on the characteristics already discussed. The more outnumbered individuals of upper or lower occupation statuses are within a particular residential milieu, the more likely they are to misidentify with the dominant class grouping. For example, the ratio of white- to blue-collar occupations is highest in the suburbs of America's metropolitan areas. Blue-collar workers who live in these suburbs are more likely to "misidentify" with the middle class than they are when they reside in more "working-class" neighborhoods.[31]

[30] Note for example Table 78 in Centers, *op. cit.*, p. 182.

[31] Once again, we must stress the conditional nature of the term "misidentify." The skilled worker who partakes of American suburbia has, from many points of

The reverse of this situation produces parallel results. The highest proportion of blue-collar workers (farm occupations aside) appear in rural areas. White-collar people of a given status residing in rural areas are more likely to consider themselves working class than are their counterparts in other, less homogeneous settings. We presume that physical proximity alone is not responsible for this "contamination" of identifications across class lines; rather, the heightened interaction that proximity permits, where psychological barriers to intercourse are few, is undoubtedly the intervening mechanism. Therefore the social system that does not exact residential segregation of the classes, and social norms which permit interaction, combine in the United States to blur lines of class identification still further. We may summarize the foregoing discussion as follows:

1. Increasing urbanization of a society increases its potential for status polarization.
2. A status structure with heavily populated occupation (or other status) categories ranked near the boundaries between socially defined classes has less potential for polarization than a structure in which intermediate statuses are thinly populated or do not exist.
3. An open-class society, in which social mobility across culturally-defined boundaries between classes is frequent, has less potential for polarization than a society in which avenues to such mobility are blocked.
4. A social structure that allows a high rate of informal interaction between members of different classes has less potential for status polarization than a society in which there are economic barriers to proximity or normative barriers to interaction.

These general formulations are not new for social theory, but it is interesting that they emerge so clearly from our empirical analysis of the role of class in politics. Furthermore, we find that we can trace out some of the intervening psychological conditions—such as inappropriate class identification—which mediate these phenomena. As we expand our observations over time and across cultures, we can hope for more precise formulations linking social structure and social class to events in the political system.

---

view, a perfect right to consider himself "middle class," whatever the color of his collar. What is critical from a theoretical point of view, however, is the fact that his political attitudes and behavior remain distinct from those of his white-collar neighbor where class considerations are involved.

Class Interests and Social Groupings

We have surveyed a number of conditions under which the individual is more likely to follow recognizable class criteria in his political decisions. The degree to which these conditions are fulfilled across a population at any point in time has substantial implications for the course of political events. When conditions are ripe, the social class mediates behavior more frequently and uniformly. It is then less a stratum and more nearly a social grouping in the sense we employed the term in the preceding chapter. The implementation of group-relevant behavior comes to hinge on group identifications.

When status polarization is less than extreme, the social class is likely to remain a rather amorphous reference point for behavior, even for those whose status is unambiguous. If a person sensitized to class interests interacts primarily with others who are relatively indifferent to such concerns, he is less likely to engage in the efforts that social groupings stimulate and direct. As far as class is concerned, nascent status polarization tends to foster more formal social groupings, which take class interests as group goals. However, a moderate level of polarization that characterizes the society as a whole may mask two rather different situations, according to whether such groupings have in fact developed. In either case, of course, some individuals are much more motivated than others to the expression of class interest. But in one case, interested individuals are no more likely to interact with others who share the same intensity of interest than they are to interact with more indifferent persons. In the second case, the distribution of class concern follows lines of communication and interaction, so that pockets of class activity develop within the society.

We shall maintain that the degree of status polarization that characterizes the society as a whole is the more significant datum. Nonetheless, if we are to understand the finer grain of political events, it becomes important to assess as well the *distribution* of class interest in the population, relative to such focuses for interaction as more formal social groupings. There may be only a small portion of the population infused with class feeling; yet if these few are organized into cohesive groups, their activity may become disproportionately significant.

We have treated the union as a cohesive interest group with certain mechanisms for member influence. We assume that influence is exerted through the business community in much the same way. We are interested here not in the mode of influence but in the content of that influence as it relates to social class and politics.

Class awareness is somewhat higher among union members than among non-union members of the same status level. Political involvement runs much stronger among union members than among comparable non-union people. As far as business is concerned we find no unusual report of class awareness. But businessmen at all levels of income are much more strongly involved in politics than their status or educational background would lead us to expect. This unusual heightening of involvement among union members in the lower half of the status hierarchy and the business community in the upper reaches is of a piece with our earlier findings concerning political involvement and class voting. For these groups show strong status polarization in their political behavior as well. This combination of circumstances lends support to our assumption that perception of an economic stake in politics leads to involvement, rather than the reverse. People do not as a rule come to choose business or unionized occupations in order to implement prior political involvement. Rather, the exceptional involvement seems to rise from the occupational situation and its intrinsic conflict of economic interest.

Another striking demonstration of the way in which the labor union contributes to maintenance of polarization is its apparent effect on the class identifications of its membership. Union members are in general more likely to maintain their identifications with the working class than are other people of similar occupation status. Furthermore, this tendency toward "proper" class identification increases as a function of identification with the union. And when union members are involved, "misidentification" fails to appear in some of the peculiar combinations of life situations where we have come to expect it. For example, all other data suggest that workers of lower status who receive unusually high wages should also show a higher rate of misidentification with the middle class than is true of low-income, low-occupation types. Instead, this group shows only a slight increase in misidentification. But we find at the same time that this group contains a surprising proportion of union members: the labor union clearly brings its membership financial rewards not available to others of the same occupational status. When we examine *non-union* people in this situation separately, we *do* find the expected large proportion of misidentifiers; but *union members* receiving wages normally associated with higher occupation strata *maintain their identification with the working class.* The labor union is dedicated to the promotion of such wage mobility; it must exert further influence on the membership to avoid dissolving its support in the process. Maintenance of appropriate class identification despite mobility is one challenge that the labor movement appears to meet.

Thus we find that groups somewhat more formal than the social class can, when class interests are incorporated as group goals, serve to heighten status polarization. Since the labor and management groupings are current points of heightened class sensitivity within the total society, they bear particularly close attention. At the same time we should not underestimate the significance of a polarization measure that encompasses the total society and thereby places such contestants in proper social perspective. The larger, more indifferent portion of the community serves to hold expression of tension within socially acceptable bounds in the manner ascribed by Truman to the "unorganized interest group."[32] Summary measures of polarization in the total society ignore pockets of ferment in the social structure. Further information as to the distribution of class concerns in the social structure is necessary in order to understand more localized events. Nonetheless, such summary measures do reflect as well the restraining forces constituted by the majority of peripherally involved. Thus yeast and leaven are represented in proportions that are dictated by the total social scene. It is likely that such an assessment best anticipates the direction of large-scale social and political events.

[32] David B. Truman, *The Governmental Process* (Alfred A. Knopf, New York, 1951), Chapter XVI. The author attributes the same moderating rôle to the fact of overlapping memberships that keep the individual's efforts from becoming too intensively devoted to goals of a single group. It is interesting to note in this regard that the segments of the population that tend to act as "unorganized interest groups" in the class case are extensively populated by individuals holding what are in effect overlapping memberships in opposing class camps—the types styled as "misidentifiers."

14 ◇ Economic Antecedents of Political Behavior

Economic interest has long been seen as a primary motive impelling political action. From the time of Shays' Rebellion through the Great Depression of the 1930's, the chronicle of American politics shows depressions and panics associated with ferment toward political change. The apparent tendency to "vote the pocketbook" has thus led observers to frequent discussions of the ebb and flow of political fortunes against the backdrop of business cycles and the economic state of the union.

We have already touched upon the role of economic factors in several contexts. We have noted, for example, that perceptions of a common economic fate underlie some portion of the cohesion and political effectiveness of secondary membership groups. Likewise, some element of economic interest is manifest in any treatment of the social classes, and we have dealt at some length with the part that economic dislocation plays in the rise of status polarization in politics.

However, even a treatment of social class in economic terms fails to exhaust facets of economic self-interest in politics that become clear when we focus directly upon the economic element itself. We have noted that class-oriented behavior in the current epoch was clear only among those voters of relatively high sophistication and involvement in politics. Yet this does not mean that the economic motive disappears in any sense below these levels. Quite to the contrary, at lower levels of sophistication there is a good deal of absorption with economic themes, whether phrased as global reactions to the "goodness" or "badness" of the times, or as narrow responses to concrete items of economic legislation such as social security. Therefore it seems important to consider more directly some of the economic antecedents of political behavior. In the following pages we shall continue to find signs of status polarization associated with economic pressure. However, we shall focus less upon these phenomena than upon the economic stimulus and its political impact.

We shall begin by observing the effects that economic pressure may have, not only in the status polarization of policy attitudes, but in the distribution of attitudes within occupational groupings and across status levels as well. We shall then consider the partisan implications that are imputed to economic dislocation, noting how strongly preexisting partisanship affects the political constructions placed upon the flow of economic events. Finally, we shall assess the utility for political analysis of measures of generalized *economic outlook* that have proved valuable for research in economic behavior.

Economic Pressure and Economic Concern

Although there has been no major economic catastrophe during the period of our studies, we have had an opportunity to observe some mild recessions that give insight into the character of public response to economic crisis, first in the simple expression of economic concern, and secondly in the contribution of such concern to political perceptions and behavior. Furthermore, at any point in time there are distinct economic pressure points across the nation; in 1956, for example, the industrial sector of the economy was enjoying boom times, but agricultural areas had been suffering a steady increase in economic pressure for several years. These facts permit contrasts that are not only of great intrinsic interest but which can also be presumed to cast light upon the effects of economic fluctuation over time.

The threat of unemployment. In the urban industrial economy, the threat of unemployment is one of the most concrete symptoms of economic pressure, and unemployment statistics provide one of the more prominent indices of economic strain. Maps based on these statistics illustrate the uneven geographic distribution of such pressure. Even for industrialized areas taken alone, the threat of unemployment always hangs more heavily over some parts of the nation than it does over others. There is, of course, a certain amount of short-term shifting in the identity of these "depressed areas." But unemployment tends to harass particular industries in particular epochs, and industries have stable geographic concentrations. As a result, there is some continuity to the economic topography of the nation over a longer term.

It is reasonable to hypothesize that individuals residing in areas currently undergoing high rates of unemployment or subject in a chronic way to such economic pressure would have different economic perspectives than persons living where these threats are less salient. A person need not himself be laid off work to feel economic apprehension when it happens around him; there can be a local economic climate just as there can be a community climate of partisan preference, and we can approach its analysis in much the same way.

Using census data on unemployment rates we can distinguish between respondents living in counties where the proportion of jobless has been in the recent past relatively high and those living where employment has been fairly full. We find immediately that attitudes toward governmental action in matters of employment vary according to community experience with unemployment. Where the unemployed had been numerous, respondents showed themselves, some seven years later, more willing to endorse the idea of federal intervention to ensure full employment.[1]

TABLE 14-1. Relation of Occupation and Unemployment in County to Attitudes toward Governmental Guarantees of Full Employment, 1956

	Per Cent Unemployed in County in 1949			
Occupation of Head of Household	Less than 3 Per Cent	4 or 5 Per Cent	6 or 7 Per Cent	Over 8 Per Cent
Professional or business	−8[a]	−2	+2	0
Clerical or sales	+5	+29	+27	+50
Skilled, semi-skilled or unskilled	+25	+36	+33	+48

[a] Entry is mean attitudinal position of all persons in the grouping. An entry of +100 would indicate that everyone agreed that the federal government "should see to it that anyone who wants to work can find a job." −100 would mean that everyone disagreed with the same statement of policy. These data pertain only to persons residing in the 33 non-Southern and non-Border states.

Further light is thrown upon this relationship when we distinguish individuals within each economic milieu according to their occupations (Table 14-1). Attitudes on the employment issue are polarized

[1] The unemployment data applied as a criterion reflect the economic situation in 1949, a "recession" year. We presume, however, that the county variation captured in this year has in some degree been duplicated in other recessions or depressions before and since.

along status lines in each category of county, with blue-collar occupations showing more interest in governmental protections against inability to find work. There is some indication here, moreover, that this polarization of attitudes between status groups is sharper where economic pressures have been more severe.

However, Table 14-1 also suggests that this form of economic pressure can have similar significance in the development of policy attitudes *across* class lines. That is, the increase of polarization in counties where unemployment has been greater is limited by the fact that the attitudes of business and professional people, like those at lower status levels, are also more "liberal" on the employment issue. The evidence of increased polarization occurs because blue-collar workers, undoubtedly threatened much more directly by job cutbacks, appear to react more sensitively. Where economic pressure has been slight, there is no impressive consensus among people of lower occupations on the issue; where there has been such pressure, intraclass agreement is much firmer. But the fact remains that the direction of attitude shift where there has been higher unemployment is the same, if reduced in magnitude, for higher-status occupations. In this sense, then, it appears that contact with the problem of unemployment has some common consequences across all three occupational groupings.

Economic worry. We find other striking illustrations of effects of current economic situations that are not to be comprehended simply in terms of status polarization or group membership. Let us shift our attention from unemployment and its implications in specific policy attitudes to factors associated with the expression of more generalized concern about personal economic problems. In the fall of 1956, about four out of every ten persons reported that they or their friends were worried about "how they would get along in the next year or so." In those counties outside of the South where most of the labor force was employed in *manufacturing* enterprises, something less than four out of ten persons reflected such economic tension; in northern areas comparably dependent upon *agriculture* for economic survival, more than six of every ten residents gave such a report. This was not unexpected, of course, in view of the continued crisis in the agricultural sector of our economy in the mid-1950's.

Within the northern agricultural areas the farmers themselves tended to be more worried than anyone else. However, other major occupation categories—professional people, businessmen, white-collar workers and skilled, semi-skilled or unskilled blue-collar workers—were only slightly less concerned. Moreover, economic worries cut directly across status lines, with six or seven out of ten in most of these occupation categories giving voice to their fears for the immediate future. On the other hand, in the manufacturing centers where over-all concern was very much less, lower-status persons were much more likely to report economic worries than were professional or business people. Where 45 per cent of blue-collar workers appeared worried, only about 25 per cent in high-status occupations were similarly troubled.

The reason for this contrast in the magnitude of class differences between the urban and rural setting is not completely obvious. However, it may spring in part from differences in rural and urban economic structure and social integration. Perceptions of shared economic difficulties may unite the members of the rural community. The "single industry" economic base in rural areas could well lead to such perceptions. The problem of the farm, in terms of both the social and economic structure of the community, is the problem of all. In the city, however, the workers' sense of economic threat is not necessarily shared by the occupants of higher-status positions, and a sharp differential in interpretations of the state of the local economy may result.

A second element in the economic situation of the electorate also pushes us to search for explanations of political behavior not implicit in the discussion of status polarization. Voting behavior in northern industrial counties in 1956 varied with the voters' economic worries; those who were more worried less often voted Republican. However, this pattern tended to cut across status lines rather than vary with status. As Table 14-2 (page 386) indicates, status polarization was not much accentuated by economic anxiety under the political and economic circumstances of 1956; but a loss in Republican electoral strength was evident among both white-collar and blue-collar citizens in that year.

Two general conclusions may be drawn from our consideration of issue attitudes on the employment question and of factors associated with individual economic worries. Both analyses illustrate the clear manner in which a person's economic situation can be reflected in his political and economic concerns. One's occupation, the economic base of one's community, the direct or indirect experience with economic crisis—all of these are unmistakable logical or temporal antecedents for one's political and economic interests. At the same time, both analyses suggest something of the complexity that surrounds these relationships. Although elements of status polarization may be observed, there are yet other political implications of these economic events that call for additional explanation. Some occupational groups are more united than others in reactions to a given politico-economic

TABLE 14-2. Relation of Concern about Economic Problems to Presidential Vote, by Occupational Groups, 1956[a]

	Worried about Economic Problems		Not Worried about Economic Problems	
Vote for President	White Collar	Blue Collar	White Collar	Blue Collar
Democratic	22%	40%	22%	37%
Republican	56	31	64	43
Other, including Non-Voters	22	29	14	20
	100%	100%	100%	100%
Number of cases	45	102	124	129

[a] This table is based on residents of northern industrial counties only. The question asked was "Do you think people around here have any worries about how they'll get along in the next year or so? I'm speaking of people like yourself and your friends."

issue; some groups are more sensitive than others to the connection between the local economic context and a relevant question of governmental policy; under other circumstances there is disagreement between status levels as to whether or not economic crisis exists, and yet there is apparently considerable agreement in the political response to the crisis that is felt.

Economic Pressures and Political Response

In the foregoing examples of economic stimulus and political response we have observed the linkage of factors widely separated in the funnel of causality. In the first instance, events located seven years back on the time axis were reflected in political attitudes only slightly removed from the contemporary matrix of partisan forces influencing the voter. Completion of the process of political translation doubtless contributed to the development of partisan attitudes and thence to individual vote decisions in 1956. In the second instance the time distance between stimulus and response was less, but the processes of communication and translation still necessarily intervened between the economic cause and the political result.

By this point it must be apparent that the process of political translation constitutes one of the ubiquitous problems of political analysis. In the search for an understanding of political behavior we repeatedly return to the task of *explaining* the linkage between the initiating stimulus and the political response. Just as it is not enough to note that businessmen vote Republican or that Negroes vote Democratic, so it is not fully satisfactory to do no more than observe that economic anxiety in 1956 was associated with a particular partisan behavior. In seeking out a fuller explanation for linkages such as those just observed, we can profitably turn again to the general argument, as well as some of the more specific guides, offered by the theoretical orientation first presented in Sections I and II.[2]

Party identification and attitude formation. As in many other areas of political analysis, an understanding of the role of party identification can provide the basis for organizing general explanations of political reaction to an economic stimulus. To illustrate, in a case of pervasive economic distress we may turn to data collected in the fall of 1958 just prior to the November elections of that year. In 1958, as in 1954, the congressional elections followed close on the heels of a recession in the national economy. Although the lowest point of the 1958 recession lasted only a very few months, the downturn was severe enough to be felt by a great many people. Almost four out of every ten families either experienced a reduction in income or employment during the period or else felt that their personal finances had in some way suffered under the impact of the recession.

In assessing the consequences of the recession for political attitudes, we take as our analytic first cause the *individual's perception* that the recession had some impact on his personal finances. This psychological impact of the recession was measured by responses to a question that asked specifically whether the recession of the past year made any difference to one's personal finances. The responses to this query were closely related to an independent report of the economic consequences of the recession. Such economic effects were measured, without explicit reference to the recession, by eliciting reports of reduced income or employment in the family or household unit experienced in the twelve months prior to November, 1958.[3]

[2] Because of special considerations pertinent to rural life, the economics of the farm vote will be discussed separately in the next chapter.

[3] The questions were: (1) "Has (anyone in the household) been unemployed or laid off at any time during the past twelve months? (1*a*.) Even though some people have not been unemployed, they may have less work. In some jobs overtime work has stopped or people are working shorter hours. Some people have also lost odd jobs they used to get some money from. Has anything like that happened to (anyone in the household) in the past twelve months? Could you tell me about it?"

Given the strong political overtones of a national recession, it is not surprising to note that in the North reactions to the recession of 1958 were also independently associated with the partisan affiliations of the people. As Table 14-3 shows, Republicans less often reported economic loss attributed to the recession, whereas Democrats were more likely to indicate personal economic deprivation as a result.[4]

To reflect the most immediate political consequence of the recession we turn to the public's evaluation of the way President Eisenhower's Administration handled the problem.[5] As we might expect, Republican identifiers were much more likely to think the Administration had done a good job than were Democrats. But for our present purposes, the important point is not only to establish this political antecedent of a political attitude, but also to document the role of economic antecedents in the development of partisan attitudes. In Figure 14-1 we may observe the interplay of the two factors: (1) party

---

(1*b*.) "About how much income did you people lose in the past 12 months because of being unemployed or working shorter hours? I mean, how much less than your regular wages did you (and other members of your family) earn altogether, counting unemployment compensation and the like as part of your earnings? Nobody can tell exactly, but can you give us an estimate?" (2) "As you know, we have had a recession in the past year. Would you say that this has affected your personal financial situation in any way? (If unfavorably affected) In what way? Could you tell me about it?"

A full explication of the data derived from these and other related questions will be provided by a forthcoming monograph on the impact of the 1953 recession upon unemployment, by William Haber, Wilbur Cohen, and Eva Mueller. In particular the distinctive uses made of subjective and objective measures of economic loss should be noted.

[4] At the same time there were, of course, striking variations in the incidence of reactions among the occupational groupings in the population. Although a negative reaction was reported in almost one of every two households headed by an unskilled worker, less than one in five of the families of professional and technical personnel gave a similar report. We may also note in passing the reverse side of the usual economic coin used to purchase the support of the widows and the retired in the fight against inflation. This fixed income segment of the economy gave least evidence of the recession in their reports of income and employment losses. Nevertheless, imposition of controls on occupational differences between Democratic and Republican partisans reduces only slightly the magnitude of the differences in their reaction to the recession. The remaining contrast between the groups of strong identifiers testifies to the important influence of political predispositions even on perceptions as intimate and as "reality bound" as those pertaining to personal experience with a recession.

[5] The question used to evoke these evaluations was: "Would you say that in the past year or so the federal government has done a good job or a poor job in dealing with the problem of recession and unemployment? What do you have in mind?"

identification and (2) personal reaction to the recession, with regard to appraisals of the Administration's handling of the recession.

All told, the role of party identification in the development of political attitudes related to the recession was threefold. In the first place, the partisanship of one's party affiliations apparently influenced one's likelihood of responding attitudinally to the events of the recession. Republicans, possibly sensing the likely assignment of political blame, less often admitted that the recession was important to their own financial situation; Democrats, probably equally anxious to establish Republican culpability, more often reported noxious effects of the recession. Beyond intruding such partisan interests into a reporting of economic "fact," party identifiers proceeded further to protect their own partisan investments through their estimates of the performance of the Republican national administration. Finally, at the same time in their eagerness to attack—or defend—the strongest partisans of both parties were apparently somewhat restricted in their freedom to adjust their assessments of the Eisenhower Administration so the assessments would reflect differences in their own personal financial plight. Partisanship drove both groups of Democrats (those not hurt as well as those hurt) to criticism and pushed both groups of Republicans (those hurt as well as those not hurt) into positions of support. Persons independent of party ties were not called upon to imagine—or deny—the harmful effects of the recession. Consequently, if they did not experience such effects they concluded quite reasonably

TABLE 14-3. Relation of Party Identification to Patterns of Personal Reaction to the Recession: North, 1958[a]

	Party Identification					
Personal Financial Reaction to Recession	Strong Dem.	Weak Dem.	Ind.	Weak Rep.	Strong Rep.	Total
No	61%	69%	69%	75%	74%	70%
Yes	39	31	31	25	26	30
	100%	100%	100%	100%	100%	100%
Number of cases	165	187	186	174	129	866

[a] From a national sample of adult citizens, interviewed in October, 1958. The total includes apolitical persons not classified in one of the five Party Identification groups.

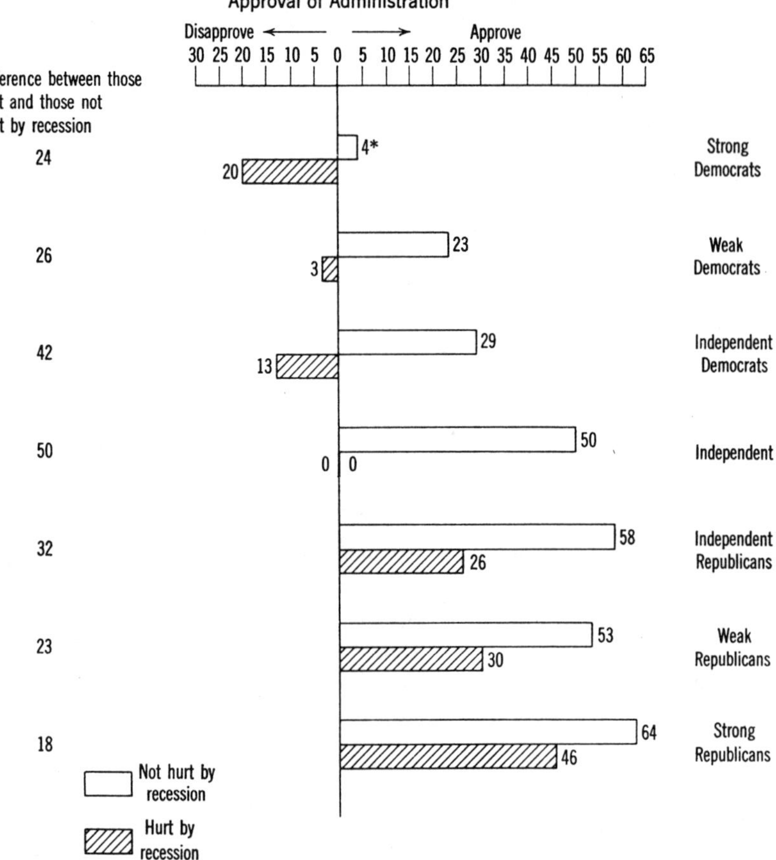

Fig. 14-1. Relation of evaluation of administration's handling of recession to party identification and personal reactions to the recession, 1958, North.

that Mr. Eisenhower and his cabinet must have done a good job. On the other hand, if they had cause to know that the recession had cut into the welfare of private individuals, they were equally free to reflect this personal knowledge in relatively frequent criticism of those responsible for national economic policy. In this third context party identification served to deaden the impact of economic events on partisan attitude formation.

Political consequences of politico-economic attitudes. The last link in the chain is added by drawing together the recession-inspired political attitudes and the vote intentions pertaining to the subsequent congressional elections. When the appropriate data are assembled, as in Table 14-4, below, two closely connected conclusions may be suggested. (1) The political attitudes expressed in evaluations of the Eisenhower Administration *are* related to the vote decision; and (2) there is *virtually no independent* association between the vote choice

TABLE 14-4. Relation of Personal Reaction to Recession and Evaluation of the Administration's Recession Policies to Intended Vote for Congress, 1958, by Party Identification (North)

Evaluation of Administration	Intended Vote	Did Not Recognize Impact of Recession			Recognized Impact of Recession		
		Dem.	Ind.	Rep.	Dem.	Ind.	Rep.
Good job	Dem. vote	60%	23%	2%	70%	31%	2%
	Rep. vote	6	23	70	6	19	73
	Non-vote	34	54	28	24	50	25
		100%	100%	100%	100%	100%	100%
Number of cases		82	65	142	63	36	55
Pro-con and poor job	Dem. vote	71%	32%	6%	69%	33%	14%
	Rep. vote	7	6	59	3	8	54
	Non-vote	22	62	35	28	59	32
		100%	100%	100%	100%	100%	100%
Number of cases		107	47	69	100	48	37

and the recognition of personal consequences of the recession. In short, the formation of relevant political attitudes provides *the* major connection between reaction to economic events and a subsequent decision at the polls.

We may also note an important contrast between the attitude-related behaviors of Democrats and those of the Independents and the Republican Party identifiers. The votes of the Democratic identifiers were least substantially related to variations in their evaluations of the Administration's recession policies. The Independents' allocation of support more clearly reflected their appraisals of the Administration. The Republicans, most of all, shifted their votes very sharply in accord with their assessments; the minority critical of their own Administration gave substantially less support to their own congressional candidates.[6]

These differences in the attitude-related behaviors of Democrats, Independents, and Republicans are explicable in the terms used in the discussion of differential reactions to the economic effects and the psychological impact of the recession. We implied that many Republicans were brought to criticize the Republican Administration primarily under the stress of economic deprivation. Their experiences with the recession presumably had added a new element to their cognitive and evaluative maps of the political world. They had come unwillingly to an awareness of, and a negative reaction to, their party's handling of a national problem. We now observe that the "forced" development of non-supportive attitudes apparently eventuated in a diminution of electoral support as well, both through increased defection to the Democratic candidate and an increase in non-voting.

The political position of the Democrats was crucially different throughout the recession period. As critics of the Administration, they used the recession as an opportunity to voice a general partisan disapproval. But many Democrats who reacted in this manner were undoubtedly already deeply committed to their own party and already convinced of the shortcomings of Republicanism. Consequently, the opportunity to criticize did not involve the addition of any fundamentally new weapons to their partisan armory; it merely provided an illustration of the iniquities of the enemy. And so the Democrats voted largely as they would have voted anyway—as good party members intent on a Democratic victory. Where a number of Republicans were dissuaded from giving support to their party, the same economic events did little more than sustain the partisan inclinations of the Democrats.

Thus, the distinction we observed between modes of personal reaction to economic crisis is not merely a party-related distinction concerning the origins of political attitudes. It is also a distinction that has important implications for the electoral expression of economic interest.

[6] Among Democrats, attitudes less than favorable to the Administration are associated with an apparent increase in the Democratic margin within the groups of only 10 and 2 per cent (an increased margin, per cent Democratic minus per cent Republican, of 10 per cent among those reporting no reaction and 2 per cent among those attributing personal loss to the recession). Among Independents, the same decrease in attitudinal support for the Republican Administration is associated with respective increases of 26 and 12 per cent in the Democratic vote margin. The comparable decrement in the Republican vote margin of Republican identifiers is a substantial 15 per cent in the first instance and an impressive 31 per cent in the second.

it is possible that had the recession become a full-fledged depression, even Democrats would have found new and additional cause to vote and vote down the Republicans. Independents' reactions might have become more exclusively anti-Administration reactions to economic deprivation; and Republicans in even larger numbers might have been driven to desert their party standards in mid-battle. On the other hand, a less severe recession with fewer real economic consequences for members of the electorate might have provoked a somewhat milder set of attitudinal reactions on the part of Independents and Republican identifiers, and virtually no electoral consequences. The political expression of economic interest can apparently take many different forms; and the meaning and consequence of the various forms can be explained only through understanding a rather complex network of factors, including both personal and situational, economic and political.

Economic Outlook and Political Behavior

Even if a case-by-case analysis of political behavior is in each instance relatively complete, leading to tentative conclusions or testable hypotheses, the net result may lack the sweep and the force of more clearly theoretical innovations. Our analysis of the non-group, non-class facets of the economic origins of political behavior has proceeded thus far without benefit of unifying concepts or techniques of comparative assessment. The concluding section of this chapter is devoted to an examination of a concept of sufficient generality as to allow us to locate it in the theoretical structure on which the book is based.

The concept is that of a person's *economic outlook.* As the name implies, this concept is a description of a set of rather general economic attitudes. The attitudes vary on a continuum that extends from confidence to lack of confidence, from optimism to pessimism. Economic outlook shares with other attitudes the basic components of perception and value. It is a compound of a person's perceptions of economic phenomena and of the values by which he judges that which he perceives.

Economic outlook differs from the other economic phenomena with which we have been concerned in at least one or two rather interesting ways. In the first place, it has no specific political referrent or content, or at least none that is very obviously important. Instead, it has relevance for a great variety of political decisions, ranging from partisan allegiance to questions of policy that do not deal at all directly with economic matters and on to the question of a preference between presidential candidates. A second and somewhat less unique characteristic of this economic entity is found in the uniformity of its political consequences for many segments of the population. It cuts across class lines, party lines, and through socio-economic groupings, usually showing in all settings the same relationships to a given political variable. It has been suggested elsewhere that a relatively high income may indicate a Republican vote in some contexts but not in others.[7] Such was not the case with economic outlook, at least in 1956. Wherever there was a variation in economic outlook among a group of people it had much the same meaning for merchants, carpenters, and day laborers, for Democrats, Independents, and Republicans, for ranchers and city dwellers alike.

As the concept of economic outlook has been developed for the following discussion, it is related to each of two quite different frames of reference that make up a person's economic world. These differing frames of reference, each contributing one major component to economic outlook, are (1) a person's view of his own economic situation and (2) his view of the business conditions that confront the nation.

Economic outlook, particularly as it has been employed in this analysis, includes a personal interpretation of economic affairs. At the same time, the manifest content of the concept certainly suggests that it must be conceptually and empirically related to a non-subjective definition of the economic facts of life. For example, in 1956 the individual's economic outlook was closely tied to the economic base of employment in the county where he lived. The resultant reflection of the farm crisis of the mid-1950's, permeating most social, economic, and political groupings in agricultural counties (without touching industrial centers), gives evidence that economic outlook does, through individual perceptions of the economic situation, reflect the "real" world. Moreover, it is clear from previous use that has been made of the particular economic attitudes involved in our measurement of economic outlook that there are significant changes in the national economy, particularly the consumer sector of the economy, which these attitudes foreshadow and reflect.[8] Economic events have an

[7] Warren E. Miller, "The Socio-Economic Analysis of Political Behavior," *Midwest Journal of Political Science*, II, August 1958, pp. 239–255.

[8] For a description of some of these uses, see George Katona and Eva Mueller, *Consumer Expectations, 1953–1956* (Institute for Social Research, The University of Michigan, Ann Arbor, Mich., 1956). A full explication of the theory underlying the interpretation of economic attitudes may be found in Katona's *Psychological Analysis of Economic Behavior* (McGraw-Hill, New York, 1951), and also in George Katona, *The Powerful Consumer* (McGraw-Hill, New York, 1960).

impact on both personal and national components of economic outlook.

In a similar manner both personal and national components of economic outlook are closely associated with a person's social and economic position in life. Such factors as education, income, and occupation are important antecedents of both sets of economic attitudes. As one might expect, the more education, the higher the income, or the more prestigeful the occupation one holds the more one is inclined to exhibit a confident outlook on economic matters. Inasmuch as this is true both for one's view of his personal financial situation and for one's view of the nation's business conditions, it seems that both of these components of economic outlook are associated with and stem from much the same set of experiences and conditions of life.

Despite a general sense of similarity in the origins of both components, there are a number of clear suggestions that we are not merely talking about two versions of the same set of attitudes. For one thing, the two components bear quite strikingly different relationships to the age of the individual. One's view of personal finances is very heavily colored by one's age, growing more and more pessimistic with the advancing years. One's impression of business conditions does not undergo any similar variation. The very old are neither more nor less pessimistic on this count than are the youngest members of the electorate.

A politically more pertinent difference between confidence in one's

---

The specific questions used to measure economic outlook were as follows: "We are interested in how people are getting along financially these days. Would you say that you and your family are better off or worse off financially than you were *a year ago?*"

"Now looking ahead—do you think that a year from now you people will be better off financially, or worse off, or just about the same as now?"

"Thinking of your income and expenses during the next year—would you say that it will be an average year for you, or better than average, or worse?"

"A *few years from now,* do you think you and your family will have a better income than you have now, or will you be in about the same situation, or in a less satisfactory situation?"

"Thinking about conditions in the country as a whole—Do you think that during the *next twelve months* we'll have good times financially, or bad times, or what?"

"Would you say that at present business conditions are better or worse than they were a year ago?"

"And how about a year from now, do you expect that in the country as a whole business conditions will be better or worse than they are at present, or just about the same?"

"Looking ahead, which would you say is more likely—that in the country as a whole we'll have continuous good times during the next five years or so, or that we will have periods of widespread unemployment or depression, or what?"

own affairs and confidence in the affairs of the nation lies in the different attitudes that are held by Democratic and Republican Party identifiers. When describing the state of their own pocketbooks, persons of opposite political affiliation do not differ in any systematic way. However, when it comes to describing business conditions there is a large and persistent difference between the attitudes of Democrats and Republicans. Comparing Democrats and Republicans of similar education, income or occupation, a Republican is, as we might expect, more likely than his Democratic counterpart to express satisfaction with the state of the nation's economy.

A third and perhaps more intriguing difference between these two major components of a person's economic outlook lies in yet another aspect of the individual's reaction to life. Perceptions and evaluations of *business conditions* are influenced by some very basic attitudes toward non-economic aspects of life. This is much less true of attitudes toward one's personal financial situation. The extremely general attitudes associated with confidence in the nation's business include one's sense of political efficacy, discussed earlier in Chapter 5. They include such social manifestations of general attitudes as are reflected in the feeling of personal competence and the tendency to resist the personal influence of others. To list the counterparts of these relationships we may say that persons with a relatively *pessimistic* outlook tend to be persons who feel *ineffective* in their own political activity, they experience a *lack of competence* in guiding their own lives, and they *attempt to avoid conflict* or disagreement in their relationships with other people.[9] From one point of view, the important fact is less the specific nature of these general, deep-seated attitudes and more the very fact that such basic personal characteristics are involved in perceptions and evaluations of economic phenomena.

Although the two dimensions of economic outlook with which we are concerned could be compared and contrasted at greater length, a simple empirical finding limits such a discussion. Despite a number of fascinating differences in the social, political, and personal correlates of the two dimensions, both dimensions have much the same implications for subsequent political predispositions and behaviors. Consequently, as we move to an examination of economic outlook we will cease to be concerned with the differences distinguishing these two

[9] These relationships stem primarily from those parts of economic outlook that emphasize long-range expectations rather than from the more situationally determined short-term expectations. Again it should be remembered that the indications of optimism and pessimism are relative indications and do not imply absolute postures toward economic events.

components. We will look, instead, at the political significance that can be attributed to the attitudes that make up our definition of the concept. Thus, as we define it, the public's economic outlook is one of the indicators of the rise and fall of the nation's economic fortunes. It is also a product for each individual, of a series of social, economic, and political circumstances. These circumstances, a person's life history, his personal traits and capacities, all play some part in defining his sense of optimism or pessimism, his confidence or lack of confidence in the past, present, and future of economic events.

Economic outlook and voting behavior. In describing the relationship between economic outlook (as measured by combining the two components) and political behavior we will follow the outline of Chapter 2 and take into account three different classes of factors or variables. First we will consider political behavior, the ultimate dependent political variable in our theoretical scheme. In this consideration the crucial questions are: (1) Is a person's economic outlook associated with his partisan choice between presidential candidates? (2) Is a person's economic outlook associated with his level of political participation? The answer to both of these important questions is substantially affirmative, at least for the one election that we can examine. In 1956, within each of the major categories of party identifiers, an optimistic view of economic affairs was associated with a larger margin of votes for Mr. Eisenhower.

The data in Table 14-5 suggest that optimists not only more often vote Republican but are also more often voters. Further investigation indicates that the latter finding is in part an artifactual product of regional differences. Northerners are more likely to be optimistic than are Southerners, and among Northerners there is virtually no difference in the voting rates of optimists and pessimists. Within the South, however, there is a clear tendency for the relatively less numerous optimists to vote at a higher rate. The outlook-political preference relationship is found among voters in both regions, but it is much sharper among Southern voters, particularly so for the strong party identifiers.

Economic outlook and partisan attitudes. The discovery that economic outlook is associated with political behavior is, by itself, not enough to satisfy us. We have noted (in Chapters 3–5) that the partisan attitudes reflected in the images of the parties and the candidates include a large allotment of concern with issues of personal and national economic significance. Isolation of that element of economic self-interest that is contained in a person's economic outlook may or may not be another way of describing attitudes that we have already

TABLE 14-5. Vote for President, as a Function of Economic Outlook, among Five Categories of Party Identifiers, 1956[a]

		Party Identification				
Economic Outlook	Vote for President	Strong Dem.	Weak Dem.	Ind.	Weak Rep.	Strong Rep.
Optimistic	Democratic	67%	42%	16%	5%	0%
	Republican	16	30	61	77	84
	Other, including non-voting	17	28	23	18	16
		100%	100%	100%	100%	100%
Number of cases		83	112	148	81	101
Pessimistic	Democratic	69%	40%	22%	5%	0%
	Republican	8	24	50	66	75
	Other, including non-voting	23	36	28	29	25
		100%	100%	100%	100%	100%
Number of cases		163	146	139	77	68

[a] The table includes both North and South.

explored at great length in our examination of the system of political motives. Consequently, we must next consider the relationship between economic outlook and a second class of variables—those included in our description of the political attitudes.

One response to this question may take the form of noting that in purely statistical terms economic outlook is correlated with all of the major partisan attitudes that we have examined. (This is certainly not unexpected, given the fact that the political attitudes and economic outlook are all related to a common third element, political behavior.) This is, however, a rather limited statement of the relationship of these variables. A more meaningful statement concerns the relationship of economic outlook to the partisan attitudes when all are considered as a set of attitudinal factors, all potentially independently related to political behavior. More particularly we may explore the possibility that economic outlook is an attitudinal factor *coordinate* with the other attitudinal factors but sufficiently different from them to make it conceptually distinct and empirically independent in its connection with voting behavior. When this possibility is tested, we see that this formulation is partially sustained. There is a statistically significant correlation between preference for presidential candidates and economic outlook even when the influence of other interrelated attitudes is statistically removed, but the magnitude of this correlation is not at all impressive. This, of course, is consonant with our earlier assumption that the six partisan attitudes embrace virtually the full spectrum of political evaluations.

If we conclude that economic outlook does not add greatly to our ability to predict, we do not conclude that economic outlook is not a meaningful political factor. To the contrary, given our interest in *understanding* political behavior, the identification of any factor that is related to political predispositions and behaviors but has no manifest political content is not easily dismissed. Instead, we must attempt to provide an interpretation that will locate that factor in our model of analysis.

Reviewing the pertinent information, it would seem that economic outlook must be placed, under our theoretical scheme, antecedent both to political behavior and partisan attitudes but between them and most of the more remote factors. The exact location will undoubtedly vary from person to person. To illustrate, let us consider the relationship between economic outlook and party identification. For some persons the causal chain may have started with the trauma of the Depression, led to the development of economic pessimism, attachment to the Democratic Party, and thence to a host of partisan attitudes toward domestic economic issues—attitudes that underlay their images of the parties and their candidates in 1956. For other persons, the chain may have started with party identification and led, in succession, to the adoption of the "party line" and the accretion of specific complaints or defenses as well as the development of an appropriate economic outlook. In other instances it may have been experiences with economic punishments or rewards that resulted in a given economic outlook; in conjunction with partisan perceptions of the activities of political parties, economic outlook may have been given a political translation and become a part of a person's political predispositions. Under these or other similar formulations we may conceive of economic outlook as a significant part of a network of causal relationships. It has no intrinsic political meaning of its own, hence we place it "behind" or otherwise separated from partisan attitudes. The activities of the political parties and candidates, the occurrence of political events that affect economic affairs—these and other happenings give political significance to it, hence we are able to make use of it to describe another of the ways in which economic factors play a role in political behavior.

The antecedents of economic outlook. Finally, we must consider economic outlook in relation to one additional class of variables, those which comprise the social and personal antecedents of one's economic outlook. In this instance our question may be: "Does the attitudinal offspring develop an independent life of its own, or does it remain no more than a reflection of its antecedents?" Examination of the relevant data discloses that even though one's economic outlook does reflect many facets of a person's life that we capture in our descriptions of personal, social, and economic characteristics, it still exerts an *independent* influence on the selected aspects of political involvement which we have examined. Although we must exercise considerable care in describing the full causal sequence, our final sketch discloses a coherent patterning of the many variables involved. It shows, in accord with the conceptual scheme described in Chapter 2, that factors such as party affiliation, education, income, or various personality characteristics are more or less independent variables—the starting point in the evolution of a particular political predisposition. Their causal role with regard to political behavior is in some small part funneled through the intervening variable, economic outlook, and in larger part directly related to such political phenomena as are reflected in the partisan attitudes. The intervening variable, economic outlook, is partially explained by these prior or antecedent factors. But when the economic outlook variable along with its antecedents is matched with the partisan attitudes, it independently explains a significant portion of their variance and leaves a part of the variance to be accounted for by other antecedent social and personal factors.

In sum, the variable labeled "economic outlook" is a politically significant economic attitudinal variable. Its utility lies not only in its ability to reflect summarily its antecedents but also in its ability to provide some small additional explanatory power for our investigation of partisan attitudes and political behavior. Our recognition of the political implications of economic outlook adds another dimension to our understanding of the economic antecedents of political behavior.

Prosperity and political change. One final comment on the political role of the individual's economic outlook is relevant. The association of expectations of economic prosperity with Republican voting preferences in 1956 immediately suggests an explanation for a time-honored query: does economic prosperity at election time give the incumbent an advantage at the polls? The successful candidate, the incumbent Republican President, Mr. Eisenhower, did apparently draw a disproportionately large part of his popular vote margin from the economic optimists in 1956. Unfortunately, we cannot speak with assurance for other elections. As we stated earlier in this discussion, we do not have directly comparable measures of economic outlook for any election year prior to 1956. Nevertheless, we do know something about a number of individual economic attitudes held by the persons to whom we talked in 1952. And the economic attitudes of Democrats who voted for Mr. Eisenhower in that year suggest a quite different interpretation of the relationship between economic optimism and political change.

On a number of highly specific measures of economic optimism and pessimism the rank and file Democrats-for-Eisenhower were, in 1952, not the most pessimistic but the most *optimistic* of major voting groups. As optimists, their decision to vote *for* a change in the national administration may, in a sense, have been made possible by their sanguine views of the domestic economy. Having no worries about the economic future they could turn their attention to other matters, and these other matters may have argued for a Republican vote. Instead of being an inhibiting, conserving mechanism, economic optimism may have been a facilitating, enabling mechanism related to political change in the 1952 election.

These two superficially contradictory findings may be reconciled by the thesis that economic optimism and pessimism derive their meaning for political choice from the immediate political context. In both 1952 and 1956, and presumably in the two preceding decades, optimism may have led to acceptance of the dominant Republican theme promising prosperity without governmental intervention, whereas pessimism may have created susceptibility to the Democratic themes decrying the "Hoover Depression" and promising dire economic consequences of a Republican victory. The crucial relationship, therefore, may have had nothing to do with the question of incumbency and the decision to change or not to change the party in control of the White House. It may have centered on the more strictly partisan question of the campaign themes emphasized by the parties. Our perspective concerning the political implications of economic outlook is too limited to provide grounds for unqualified acceptance of this thesis. Nevertheless, the rather substantial evidence of its empirical importance in 1956 (in the first situation in which it was systematically studied) and the less adequate data from 1952 underline the importance of continued attention to the concept.

Agrarian Political Behavior ◇ 15

Although the American farm population has formed a dwindling portion of the electorate over most of our nation's history, the peculiar problems of the farmer, his frequent dependence upon government, and his over-representation in most of our legislatures have maintained lively interest in his political responses. The "farm vote" is an entity that has meaning for the politician, journalist, and lay observer alike, and, among the reputed bloc votes, it holds fascination as one of the most unpredictable.

In the South, where alternatives to the Democratic Party are not given serious consideration, the rural vote is reliably Democratic. Outside the South, there is in most agricultural areas a traditional Republican leaning. But the magnitude of this rural Republican plurality is always in doubt until the votes are counted. Sometimes, as in 1956, a predicted "farm revolt" against the Republicans falls short of informed expectations. At other times, as in 1948, a shift toward the Democrats in rural Republican strongholds has caught observers unaware. In the national elections since 1948, the two-party vote division among farmers outside the South has fluctuated more sharply than it has within any of the other major occupation groupings or, for that matter, within any of the groups considered as voting blocs in Chapter 11.

The uncertainty shrouding the farm vote, however, is but one aspect of a larger syndrome of rural political behavior that has perplexed scholars. The term "farm revolt" itself reflects the long period in America's history in which massive and often violent protests were launched from rural areas against a system that brought economic hardship. With the Civil War aside, farm unrest was the primary source of political disturbance in America throughout the nineteenth century.

These facts of American history are familiar enough that we have come to take them for granted. The route from economic distress to political response is an obvious one. Yet for the farmer, this route is strewn with puzzling anomalies. Other groups in the society have undergone severe economic stress without comparable political results. No political party organized in the name of labor in this country has amassed the broad electoral support that has been captured almost overnight by a number of farm protest parties. On the other hand, the American labor movement, forced to work within the two-party structure, has achieved a much greater degree of continuity in its political efforts. For if farm protest throws up new third parties worthy of the name with relative ease, the mass support for these movements has in every instance vanished as quickly as it arose upon the easing of immediate economic pressures.[1] Once again, the labor movement provides a foil in its continuing accumulation of political influence after the Depression, in years of great industrial prosperity. In short, the farmer reacts to economic pressure with political protest; yet the response has an explosive quality—great force without duration—which is unique.

More singular yet is the issue content prominent in such rural movements. Like the movements themselves, it has lacked coherence and continuity: where it has been simple, it has been simplistic and crudely practical; where it has become complex, it is a jumble of panaceas that betray little understanding of either social structure or political process. The exceptions are equally telling, for upon the rare occasions in which something approaching a full-blown ideology has been employed, the substance has been borrowed wholesale from theories developed for the urban labor movement.

Finally, and perhaps most important, the common threads that seem to exist in the behaviors of rural populations have never been adequately understood within any familiar theory of social or political process. It is striking that the same "reasonable" expectations of

[1] Lipset, reviewing the course of agrarian ferment in this country, makes this peculiarity very clear. He writes of the first political parties generated by farm discontent: "The Independent parties were extremely short-lived. Most of them disappeared within two or three years . . ." and, of the rapid eclipse of the Greenback Party after culling a million votes in the off-year election of 1878: "This transitory character of organized rural protest was to prove characteristic of subsequent agrarian movements." Seymour Lipset, *Agrarian Socialism: The Cooperative Commonwealth Federation in Saskatchewan: A Study in Political Sociology.* The University of California Press, Berkeley, Calif., 1950), pp. 5–7.

analysts have been betrayed so many times by rural groupings in virtually the same way. This observation suggests a tactic: we will handicap ourselves if we become restricted either to theories of group influence or to theories of social class before we have plumbed the problem that the political behavior of the farmer poses. This is not to say that either is inappropriate. Elements of what may loosely be called "class struggle" are typically involved in agrarian protest. Yet to accept social class definitions facilely is to miss just those peculiar aspects of the farm problem that we have undertaken to explore. Similarly, at some levels of analysis the notions of group influence would be viable here also. But the units chosen as "groups" would in most cases have to be narrow, for the total farm community in the national population is severely fragmented into interests that are independent or even at times conflicting, based on traditional regional differences, special crop problems, and the like. Numerous investigations have documented the degree to which shifts in farm sentiment remain within boundaries defined by crop area.[2] Symptomatic of these divisions are the major farm organizations themselves, which have tended in recent years to range completely across the partisan spectrum.

Later we shall find it profitable to return to frames of reference suggested by both class and group influence conceptions. But let us first assess directly those prime peculiarities of rural political response, as we see them in our current samples, which evoke other times and settings.

Characteristics of Farm Political Behavior

Variability. We have indicated that one dominant feature of the political behavior of farmers is its variability. This variability is visible in aggregate statistics recording gross change in vote division within rural areas; it is visible as well in the vote division among farmers in our sequence of samples since 1948.

Any such net variability in an aggregate might logically be traced to irregular turnout as well as to shifts in partisan preference. When the partisan vote division is unstable in an area, we are likely to assume that inhabitants are crossing party lines with impunity from election to election. But the same effect may be produced if the area contains many irregular voters who drift into and out of the active ranks selec-

[2] Lipset, *op. cit.;* J. D. Hicks, *The Populist Revolt* (University of Minnesota Press, Minneapolis, Minn., 1931); V. O. Key, *Politics, Parties and Pressure Groups,* 4th edition (Thomas Y. Crowell Co., New York, 1958).

tively along party lines in various elections. It follows quite directly, of course, that where partisan choice is fluid *and* turnout is irregular at the same time, the potential variability becomes even more extreme.

These two sources of variability are hard to distinguish on the basis of net change alone. Nevertheless, cursory examination of recent aggregate statistics suggests that in addition to fluctuations in the rural partisan vote division, there appear to be shifts as well in rural turnout that are wider than is customarily found in more urban districts. Hence we suspect that variability in the rural vote is compounded of both turnout and partisan irregularity.

Recall data from our farm respondents concerning past political behavior permits us to analyze these sources of variability for individuals over time. We ask how frequently the individual has voted in past presidential elections. Some have voted in all; others though eligible have failed to participate in any. The residual group is the source of turnout variability, at least with regard to presidential elections, and the prevalence of these sporadic voters in a population grouping provides a measure of this source of variation. A parallel question concerning regularity of vote for a single party reveals variability in partisanship over time.[3]

Table 15-1 contrasts both types of variability for farmers and major occupation groupings within urban centers, outside the South. We see that the farmer shows greater variability in both senses than does the urban resident. We find also that within the urban sample, gradients of increasing variability tend to follow status lines. But of great significance is the fact that these gradients run in *opposing* directions. Variability in party voting increases among higher-status urban occupations; variability in turnout is greatest at lowest-status levels. Thus one source of variability characterizes each status extreme. The farmer, however, lies near the more variable pole on both dimensions; variability on one is not offset by stability on the other. The coming together of both types of variability defines rather dramatically the peculiar style of farm participation in the political process.[4]

[3] All analysis of these questions excludes, for obvious reasons, individuals too young to have acquired a voting history.

[4] In the data presented in this chapter we shall use the term "farmer" loosely to include any person living in a farm household. Since our immediate purpose is to assess the characteristics of the current "farm vote," the fact that farm housewives are included poses no conceptual problem. Inasmuch as we wish later to extrapolate from these materials to a time in which farm housewives were excluded from the vote, it is important to assure ourselves that the features of farm behavior portrayed are not in some way produced uniquely by the female contingent in the tables. Therefore comparable tables have been examined in which all women are

TABLE 15-1. Variability of Political Behavior for Farm and Urban Occupation Groupings[a]

			Urban					
	Farmer	Rural Non-Farm	Prof.	Bus.	Cler.	Skilled and Semi-Skilled	Un-skilled	Urban Total
Turnout variability	46%	43%	27%	28%	41%	43%	43%	39%
(Proportion who have voted in some past presidential elections, not in others.)	(205)	(382)	(121)	(226)	(174)	(488)	(87)	(1277)
Partisan variability	45%	38%	44%	40%	41%	36%	30%	37%
(Proportion who have voted for different parties for president in past elections.)	(190)	(346)	(118)	(220)	(171)	(444)	(81)	(1214)

[a] Data are restricted to individuals over 28 years of age who have grown up and currently reside outside the South. The number of cases involved in each proportion is entered in parentheses; results are accumulated for both the 1952 and 1956 samples. "Rural Non-Farm" includes respondents living in places of 2,500 or less who do not reside in farm households. "Urban" categories thus include all towns and cities over 2,500 population. The "Urban Total" figure is greater than the sum of cases in urban occupation categories because of additional cases left unclassified in these terms. The case numbers in the "Partisan Variability" row are less than those in the "Turnout Variability" row because respondents who have never voted are excluded from the base.

If the farmer fails to vote as a party regular from election to election, he also fails to vote as a party regular in marking any given ballot. As Table 15-2 demonstrates he is more likely to split his ticket between the parties than is his urban counterpart, or than other persons living in sparsely settled areas who are not engaged in farming.

What conditions underlie such variability? Numerous hypotheses spring to mind that have rather prosaic implications. For example, if

TABLE 15-2. Split-Ticket Voting by Non-Southern Farmers and Urban Occupation Grouping, 1956

			Urban					
Voted	Farmer	Rural Non-Farm	Prof.	Bus.	Cler.	Skilled	Semi-Skilled	Un-skilled
Straight-ticket	43%	51%	47%	55%	67%	64%	61%	60%
Split-ticket	57	49	53	45	33	36	39	40
	100%	100%	100%	100%	100%	100%	100%	100%
Number of cases	99	194	81	96	114	157	150	48

the farmer fails to vote in some presidential elections, need this reflect anything more significant than the fact that he lives in areas more remote from the polls and must depend on less reliable forms of transportation? Similarly, a phenomenon like split-ticket voting might symbolize a greater probability that the voter in the rural community has had some personal contact with one or another candidate on the slate, a fact that suffices to override party loyalty.

In the first case, it would be unreasonable to argue that distance from

excluded. While such a re-definition often shifts the absolute proportions in one direction or another, the urban-rural contrasts that are at issue remain of the same magnitude, or in some cases are actually sharper. Hence we feel confident that our later extrapolations are appropriate from this point of view. As a case in point, the reader might be interested in comparing the following table restricted to males, with the critical entries in Table 15-1:

	Farmer	Rural Non-Farm	Prof.	Bus.	Cler.	Skilled and Semi-Skilled	Un-skilled	Urban Total
Turnout variability	47%	40%	24%	31%	38%	42%	49%	38%
Partisan variability	52%	46%	51%	53%	45%	40%	29%	43%

the polls is not a factor in the irregularity of farm voting. Clearly it must be. Yet such a mechanical explanation does not cope with all known facts. It does not explain, for example, why more urban blue-collar eligibles than farmers have *never* voted in a presidential election, as we find. Nor does it explain why urban residents of early farm origin continue to turn out more irregularly than natives of urban centers.[5] Similarly, the hypothesis concerning candidate familiarity and ticket splitting may have some grain of truth, yet it is quite inadequate to account for all aspects of our data. For example, we find that the individual of farm origin who has moved to the city continues to split his ticket there, in contrast with his totally urban counterpart (Table 15-3). No theory of local familiarity that explains ticket-splitting in the rural setting appears to have much bearing on this evidence of continuity.

TABLE 15-3. Relation of Place of Origin and Current Residence to Split-Ticket Voting, Outside the South, 1956

Current Residence:	Farm		Rural Non-Farm		Urban White-Collar		Urban Blue-Collar	
Where Resident Grew Up:	Farm	Non-Farm	Farm	Non-Farm	Farm	Non-Farm	Farm	Non-Farm
Straight-ticket	40%	57%	40%	59%	45%	59%	56%	64%
Split-ticket	60	43	60	41	55	41	44	36
	100%	100%	100%	100%	100%	100%	100%	100%
Number of cases	78	21	80	114	42	249	89	266

In short, some relatively mechanical facts of the farmer's life situation may contribute to peculiarities observed in his political behavior. But a large part of this peculiarity must reside in a state of mind, a total posture toward the ongoing political process that survives changes in external aspects of his life situation. Thus the American farmer even in the 1950's shows himself to be sporadic in his voting and inconstant in his partisan attachments. The upshot of these characteristics for aggregate statistics from election to election is, of course, a peculiar fluidity in the partisan vote division. It is important to ascertain from our data what underlies these patterns of behavior.

[5] See R. Freedman and D. Freedman, "Farm-reared Elements in the Non-Farm Population," *Rural Sociology, 21* (1956), 50–61.

The Motivational Roots of Variable Political Behavior

We have seen that in the urban status hierarchy, variability in turnout and partisanship tended to shift in opposite directions along the status continuum. That is, lower-status people were more likely to flow in and out of the active electorate, but in so doing were more apt to abide by the same party preference over a period of time. The combination of high variability in both regards was unique for the farmer. Yet we know from material in preceding chapters that this combination *for individuals* is not particularly extraordinary. The syndrome is familiar and, in a motivational sense, quite comprehensible. Let us review its essentials.

Partisan variability. The partisan fluidity of farm behavior suggests immediately that the affective bond between the farmer and the

TABLE 15-4. Relation of Place of Origin and Current Occupation and Residence to Strength of Party Identification, Outside the South[a]

Current Residence:		Farm		Rural Non-Farm		Urban White-Collar		Urban Blue-Collar	
Where Resident Grew Up:		Farm	Non-Farm	Farm	Non-Farm	Farm	Non-Farm	Farm	Non-Farm
Strength of party identification	Strong	23%	26%	29%	33%	41%	38%	33%	38%
	Weak	47	45	41	37	33	34	38	38
	Independent	30	29	30	30	26	28	29	24
		100%	100%	100%	100%	100%	100%	100%	100%
Number of cases		173	55	181	263	88	504	150	575
Mean age		45	43	49	43	49	43	46	42

[a] Data are accumulated for both the 1952 and 1956 samples. In view of the strong relationship between age and strength of party identification, the mean age within each category is indicated. Where a farm group shows weaker identification than its non-farm counterpart, it does so *in spite of* its greater mean age. The table excludes respondents who had grown up in the South but had come to one of the regions outside the South.

political party of his choosing is unusually weak. And we do find that strength of party identification is lower among farmers outside the South than among either blue-collar or white-collar urban types. Furthermore, as Table 15-4 suggests, this difference between farm and city is a difference between poles of a continuum, in a temporal sense as well as a spatial sense. The semi-rural people—those living in villages and sparsely settled areas, but not on active farms—have identifications of an intermediate strength between the poles defined by the farm on one hand and the city on the other. Similarly, although the differences are not large, we get the sense again that people with life experience limited to the farm and those who have always lived in urban centers pose the sharpest contrasts: individuals of mixed experience fall between these poles.[6] These gradients were apparent in our assessment of comparative behavior; they are present again as we compare motivational differences.

We emphasize the evidence for gradients of this sort because it seems to be of basic conceptual significance. We have depended on these gradients to demonstrate that peculiarities of farm behavior reside not in mechanical peculiarities of farm life but in the motivations and dispositions of the farmer as actor himself. They attest, furthermore, to the proposition that however peculiar farm political behavior may appear, there is no reason to believe that it differs *qualitatively* from political behavior in other settings. The farmer represents no more than an extreme of a continuum. His peculiarities are those of degree, not kind. Urban individuals selected to represent extremes of the same characteristics might be expected, under conditions to be specified, to behave in the same way.

Political involvement. It has been hypothesized that since most farmers tend to be exposed to economic pressures that demand government action, they will show unusual involvement in political affairs.[7] At an elite level, the power and vigor of the "farm lobby" even in

[6] It is at this point that our data for Southern farmers diverge most radically from those characterizing areas outside the South. Southern farmers show a stronger sense of identification with their party (almost always Democratic) than do Southerners living in urban areas. Fifty-nine per cent of these farmers in 1956 professed strong party identification. Furthermore, the same gradients emerge as in Table 15-4, although all of them are reversed: urban residents of farm origin are more strongly identified than urban residents of urban background, etc. We take this situation to be rather unusual, a product of the long-standing one-party system. There is no evidence to suggest that some of the *behavioral* gradients are reversed as well, although the variability of Southern farm behavior, presuming it exists, is hard to document within the framework of national elections. If the South is making some progress toward a two-party system, and if this progress centers in the cities, then we might expect less automatic strong identification in the urban setting. In any event, we suspect that the reasons for the Southern reversal are irrelevant to the line of argument being developed here.

[7] Seymour Lipset *et al.*, "The Psychology of Voting: An Analysis of Political Behavior," *Handbook of Social Psychology*, ed. Gardner Lindzey (Addison-Wesley Publishing Co., Cambridge, Mass., 1954), II, p. 1129.

modern industrial democracies offers striking evidence for this contention. But if we think in terms of the farmer at the *mass* level, as is our aim, the expectation of high political involvement does not follow. Materials in earlier chapters have led us to associate variable political behavior and weak party ties with low levels of involvement.

Farmers are no exception to the rule: instead, they seem to epitomize it. Of course we would expect rural people in the South to be rather remote from national political wars, as our data on political involvement clearly show them to be. Outside the South as well, however, the farmer—and particularly the farmer who spends full time working his farm—professes remarkably little interest in the election campaign or concern over its outcome. In 1952, for example, when political interest was high but there were no strong economic pressures peculiar either to farm or city, the non-Southern farmer expressed much less active sense of political involvement than any urban occupation stratum save the small bottom layer of unskilled laborers (Table 15-5).

TABLE 15-5. Political Involvement for Farm and Urban Occupation Groupings Outside the South, 1952[a]

			Urban					
Involvement	Farm	Rural Non-Farm	Prof.	Bus.	Cler.	Skilled	Un-skilled	Urban Total
High	19%	31%	57%	53%	47%	36%	28%	42%
Medium	51	41	32	34	30	39	33	34
Low	30	28	11	13	23	25	39	24
	100%	100%	100%	100%	100%	100%	100%	100%
Number of cases	121	209	56	136	100	271	60	767[b]

[a] The table excludes respondents currently residing outside the South who had grown up in the South.

[b] The "Urban Total" category includes 134 cases not readily assignable to the five major urban occupation categories.

If rural vote turnout statistics are a satisfactory guide, this involvement had probably been lower still, although selective along party lines, in 1948. By 1956, however, the distribution of economic pressures had shifted between farm and city. The industrial sector of the economy was in good health; but the farmer had suffered five years of declining prices and rising costs, and the fall election was billed as another "farm revolt."

Data for 1956 show a mild decline in involvement of about the same magnitude within each of the major urban occupation strata. Rural non-farm people showed a decline in involvement between 1952 and 1956 as well, although somewhat less marked. The level of involvement among non-Southern farmers remained constant between the two years. This stability against a backdrop of declining interest elsewhere in the broader electorate betokens some source of motivation peculiar to the farm that arose in 1956: we presume this source to lie in the heightened economic pressures that had built up since the preceding election. We noted earlier that worry about the economic future was, at the time of the 1956 election, most severe in agricultural areas. But more striking than the fact of higher *relative* farm involvement in 1956 is the fact that even under this degree of pressure, the level that this involvement attains remains modest. For this "exercised" segment of the 1956 electorate *still failed to register political interest equivalent to that of the skilled worker in the urban status hierarchy.*

More generally, we know that there tends to be a gradient of declining political involvement as we move from urban concentrations to sparsely settled rural areas, whether we look within the South or outside it. Moreover, this indifference, like all the other peculiarities we have observed, has continuity for individuals over a period of time despite changes in life situation. If we array our involvement data after the fashion of Tables 15-3 and 15-4, we find very substantial decrements of involvement among urban residents of farm origin, when contrasted to lifetime urban residents.[8] Once again, then, an examination of political involvement places the farmer as no more than an extreme point on an urban-rural continuum. Whatever vigorous political activity marks the "farm lobby" at an elite level, we get the impression that its mass base is thin indeed.

We know enough about political involvement to push the matter back a step in the causal sequence. For matching the urban-rural gradient of political involvement is another having to do with amount of formal education. Educational attainment falls off as we move from urban to rural areas, and among rural people even outside the South, average education of farmers is lowest. There is ample evidence that these two characteristics—involvement and education—are functionally related.[9] Within any geographical grouping we may define, there is

[8] The 1956 data show migrants from the farm even less involved than the "parent" farm population. This appears to substantiate further the belief that temporary economic pressures on the farmer were responsible for the *relative* increase in involvement. Migrants to the city retained the motivational dispositions of the farm but escaped the immediate economic pressure.

[9] This relationship has been observed in Chapter 10 and will be discussed in greater detail in Chapter 17.

a substantial association between educational background and current sense of political involvement, and some relationship remains when other status dimensions are controlled. Here, too, the direction of causality seems unequivocal. Thus one source of rural indifference to politics may reasonably be located in the low levels of education that characterize these areas.

But education alone is not sufficient to account for observed differences in involvement between the farmer and people of urban background. For example, Table 15-5 suggested that the political involvement of non-Southern farmers under the "base-line" conditions of 1952 was a rough match for the narrow bottom stratum of urban unskilled workers. Yet if we isolate those unskilled workers from other urban types, we find an average education inferior even to that of the farmer. In other words, if we control education, farm political involvement for a year like 1952 does not even compare favorably with the most *déclassé* 10 per cent of the urban social structure.

Earlier we rejected physical remoteness as a simple "mechanical" explanation that would account *in toto* for farm irregularity in turnout. In a much less mechanical sense, this remoteness may be of considerable causal significance in understanding low farm political involvement. The full-time farmer has been much less firmly bound up with the flow of national events than any other group in the society. He has tended to work alone in an occupation which, save for the winter months, has left little leisure to attend to the world beyond the horizon. Interest grows from roots of information, and a continuing flow of information nourishes abiding interest. Even today the farmer may be less constantly exposed to political information than the urban resident; and certainly his exposure three or four decades ago can have borne no comparison to the flow of information available in urban areas. We know that interest in politics, like partisanship, is readily transmitted within the family from generation to generation. The current American farmer may bear the signs not only of some lingering remoteness from national politics, but apathy inherited from preceding eras in which the political communication system was much less developed.

However impressive the evidence of relative indifference to national politics on the part of the farmer, the picture is not one of unrelieved apathy, particularly outside the South. In fact, if we restrict our analyses to the farm community itself, we find differences in political involvement that tend to support a number of extant hypotheses concerning agrarian politics. Lipset *et al.* have suggested that if involvement increases due to exposure to economic pressures requiring government action, then farmers who "produce for national and world markets" should show unusual involvement.[10] *Within the farm community* this hypothesis finds support in our data. If we isolate a set of farmers whose primary products clearly flow into relatively local markets (vegetable, dairy, or poultry farmers) or whose produce is broadly diversified, we find a level of political involvement that was extremely low in 1956 relative to that of urban residents or other farmers. It must be noted that full-time farmers of this sort tend *also* to be less well educated than large-scale farmers producing for national and world markets, a fact that accounts for a portion of the involvement difference in a manner alien to the spirit of the hypothesis. But to the degree that our dwindling supply of cases permits control, there appear to be residual differences according to crop type even with education held constant.

Organizational membership and involvement. Somewhat more potent factors than market or crop emerge when we survey the role of farm organizations within the farm community. Members of farm organizations (among non-Southern farmers) tend to be more politically involved than non-members, and this difference is not well accounted for by discrepancies in education. Furthermore, within the set of farm organization members, political involvement increases very substantially as a function of identification with the farm organization.[11] Such a finding, however, must be immediately tempered by a glance at the scope of this influence across the farm community, which is remarkably narrow. A majority even of non-Southern farmers in our sample belong to no such farm organizations, and of those who do belong, the proportion willing to indicate "a great deal of interest" in the organization is small. In fact, members of farm organizations show almost exactly the same distribution of interest in those organizations as is reported by union members for their local union organization. Given the fact that union membership is notoriously involuntary, this similarity is in itself striking. We find further that the interested farm organization members are disproportionately constituted of part-time farmers who have an urban occupation as well, along with somewhat higher education. If we restrict our attention to the minority of full-time, non-Southern farmers who belong to farm organizations, only 26 per cent express great interest in their organization (base N of 34) as opposed to 44 per cent among union members (base N of 428).

[10] Lipset *et al., op. cit.*

[11] There is a rank-order correlation (tau-beta) of 0.27 between political involvement and degree of interest expressed in the farm organization to which the respondent belongs.

Such sparse membership, along with a lack of much strong interest even among the minority who belong to such organizations, is striking in view of the solid expression of loyalty to farmers as an occupation grouping revealed by our group identification questions. It is also striking that such a "flat" response to farm organizations was made at a point when the farmer was as hard pressed economically as he had been in a decade, and when the several farm organizations were serving as vociferous spokesmen for him. The vigor of a pressure group at an elite level may be a poor guide to the fervor of the mass base that it represents.

On the other hand, the farmer's lack of enthusiasm about the farm organization is reminiscent of his lack of commitment to the political organization. It is relatively easy to imagine the farmer feeling remote from the national political process and the group structures it entails; it is a little harder to understand his aloofness from group structures erected in the name of his interest, unless it be that for one reason or another he has difficulty committing his interest to any continuing group enterprise that transcends the local setting. In this event, aloofness from the political party would be but a special case of a broader phenomenon.

It is likewise intriguing that interest in a farm organization and political involvement, although both are rare, tend to coincide, and are most prominent among those farmers whose lives are not totally absorbed in farm work and who appear to have some functional relationship with urban life. Yet even here we should not lose sight of the fact that "high" political involvement is "high" only relative to the farm community itself and would not necessarily appear intense against a broader social backdrop. For example, if we take the tiny group of highly identified members of farm organizations in the "revolt" year of 1956 we still find an aggregate pitch of interest somewhere near levels registered in 1956 by white-collar clerical workers, or those that characterized skilled and semi-skilled workers in 1952. Although we are not disinterested in the internal workings of the farm community itself, it seems valid to keep our observations in the perspective provided by urban citizens, since our interest lies in the political role that has distinguished farmer from urbanite.

Against the backdrop of the total society, then, the American farmer is without question somewhat indifferent to national political affairs. Several of the underlying factors that we shall stress to explain the character of the farm response have been accorded passing mention by students of these matters. In the involvement dimension, however, we encounter a critical piece of the puzzle that has been generally missed or misunderstood. To be sure, our account matches the older assumptions concerning a remote and "inert" peasantry. But more recent scholars, fascinated by the explosions that have marked political life in rural areas, have assumed quite understandably that they are dealing with individuals whose relationship with the political process is intense. As a result they have directed their efforts toward hypotheses to explain this intensity of farm involvement.

In view of the record, one could hardly gainsay the fact that farmers do at times become intensely involved in the political process. But it is our contention that the peculiar behaviors displayed at such points take their shape from the fact that the rural person is not accustomed, in the normal run of events, to any great attentiveness toward politics. Such irregularity of involvement brings us full circle from motivational condition to variable behavior once again. The farmer's low sense of involvement under normal circumstances is a crucial datum. Yet it is equally crucial that the farmer can, under extraordinary conditions, become more intensely involved.

The Economic Sensitivity of the Farmer

If one dominant characteristic of farm political behavior is its variability, a second that has received much attention is its economic sensitivity. The farm vote is frequently described as a "pocketbook" vote. In fact, this description is often accorded the status of a motivational explanation for the variability of rural voting. It does not in itself provide complete satisfaction: it does not make clear precisely why this vote should be more an affair of the pocketbook than some other vote. Let us survey the evidence that may be brought to bear upon the contention of peculiar economic sensitivity in the same spirit with which we explored the political motivations that seemed relevant to the farm problem.

We have noted that between 1952 and 1956 the economic situation of the American farmer deteriorated rather rapidly. Prices of many farm products had fallen off, and yet the cost of farm materiel was on the rise. The farm prosperity of the 1940's had faded though boom times reigned elsewhere in the economy. The new Republican Administration, in an effort to discharge large farm surpluses, had challenged past Democratic farm policy.

This was, in brief, the setting that led to expectations of a farm revolt against the Republicans in the 1956 election. We have seen that economic concern was manifest in agricultural areas (Chapter 14), and that there was some, although perhaps more tenuous, translation of this economic concern into a political involvement that, relative to that in urban areas, was above its 1952 level among farmers. Let us assess first the partisan implication of this economic pressure.

One simple measure of degree of economic pressure from farmer to farmer may be based on a question asked in 1956 concerning the trend in prices that the farmer felt he had encountered in the four years since the previous presidential election. The experience of any farmer was dependent, of course, on factors such as his geographic location and the types of produce that he attempted to market. Few farm respondents, however, had felt any upward motion of prices during the 1952–1956 period. Some felt that the price picture had not changed much from their point of view; the remainder reported that their prices had gone down over the four-year period.

TABLE 15-6. Relation of Trend of Prices Received by the Farmer, 1952–1956, to His 1956 Vote[a]

	Reported Price Trend		
	Up a Little; Same; or Mixed Trends Balancing Out	Down a Little	Down a Lot
Proportion Voting Democratic	13%	39%	66%
Number of cases	27	36	29

[a] This table is based on non-Southern farmers only. In the South, the same pattern was present, although somewhat less distinctly. With prices for tobacco and fruit on the rise and cotton holding fairly well in the 1952–1956 interval, Southern farmers felt less beleaguered in general. Nevertheless, of 21 Southern farmers who saw prices slightly up or mixed, only 52 per cent voted Democratic. Of those 19 who saw prices declining, 84 per cent voted Democratic.

As Table 15-6 indicates, there was a very sharp relationship between price patterns that the farmer had experienced prior to 1956 and the partisan direction of his presidential vote in that year. We should not conclude uncritically that the direction of the farm vote was as thoroughly determined in the 1956 election by immediate experiences with prices as this table may suggest. On one hand, we have confidence that the perceptions of price trends depend on a solid reality base. That is, in the aggregate, the farmers' reports conform well with general trends shown by national statistics on farm income during this period. Furthermore, pairing of our knowledge of the farmer's major crop, in those cases where one crop was primary, with known price trends for the crop from 1952 to 1956, gives further evidence that these perceptions were not determined in any simple manner by pre-existing party loyalty. That is, it does not appear to be true that Democratic farmers, in order to carp at a Republican Administration, were complaining unrealistically about their financial fortunes.

It is plausible however that prices were in fact declining more sharply under farmers of Democratic leanings than under those of Republican predisposition, for political partisanship among farmers is related to various types of farm situations. Most clear is the link between the number of acres that the individual farms and his party preference in 1956 (Table 15-7). Undoubtedly the fact that the small farmer looks with relative favor upon the Democratic Party is itself bound up with reactions to economic pressures in time past and the farm legislation of the New Deal period. But to the degree that the small farmer already held pro-Democratic views in 1952, and to the degree that the small farmer suffered more severe economic pressures between 1952 and 1956, some portion of the relationship in Table 15-6 would exist even if the current economic situation had no relevance in immediate political decisions.

TABLE 15-7. Relation of Size of Farm to 1956 Presidential Vote

	Non-South		South	
	Small Farm (0–139 Acres)	Large Farm (140 and Above)	Small Farm (0–44 Acres)	Large Farm (45 and Above)
Proportion voting Democratic	53%	29%	73%	60%
Number of cases	36	55	22	20

Short-term economic pressures reflected in recent price trends continue to show, however, a substantial relationship with the 1956 vote even when farm size is controlled. Although it is not our custom to present data involving as few cases as the cells of Table 15-8, the great clarity with which the patterns match *a priori* expectations and the congruence between regional findings have led us to preserve all analytic distinctions here. We may evaluate these patterns over the

TABLE 15-8. Relation of Farm Price Trends and Farm Size to 1956 Presidential Vote of Farmers

	Southern Small Farm		Southern Large Farm		Non-Southern Small Farm		Non-Southern Large Farm	
Prices are . . .	Down	Up or Same	Down	Up or Same	Down	Up or Same	Down	Up or Same
Proportion voting Democratic	100%	55%	70%	50%	62%	33%	41%	6%
Number of cases	9	11	10	10	26	9	37	17

table as a whole, without overemphasizing the absolute size of any single entry. In a general way, the table is striking in the degree that the farm vote appears accounted for by three factors of differing "time depth": (1) the long-standing traditions of rural northern Republicanism and Democratic voting in the South; (2) more recent trends presumed to be of New Deal–Fair Deal vintage, which have won support for the Democrats from the small farmer and Republican support from larger farmers; and (3) current, short-term economic pressures. Yet for our immediate purposes the table is most relevant as it demonstrates the strength of these current economic forces in affecting the farm vote.

Other aspects of the data also lead to the conclusion that the relationship between prices and vote in 1956 represents in no small measure a simple and direct reaction on the part of farmers to economic events since the preceding election. Our independent knowledge of the partisan fluidity of the farm vote makes this degree of rapid partisan change seem plausible. Moreover, we find in our data that the association between price trends and party identification is somewhat less strong than that between price trends and current vote (1956). In other words, farm people who voted counter to their normal party affiliation in the 1956 election appear to have done so as a function of their immediate economic situation. With the addition to this fact of the weaker party ties of the farmer, which may signify that some Democratic preferences appearing here are backed by a Democratic party identification that is relatively new, the economic element in the farmer's partisan choice seems reliably documented.

The status polarization of the farm community as a function of both stable and short-term differences in economic fortune (Tables 15-6, 15-7, and 15-8) illustrates with great clarity the folly of treating the farm vote as unitary, in the group sense, even to the modest extent with which we earlier subscribed to this notion for labor unions, Negroes, and Jews. The farmer appears to respond to his own economic situation, with little reference to the manner in which others in the same occupational category are faring. Since prices and hence economic situations are tied to specific crops, economic winds frequently blow in several directions at once across rural America, leading to a variegated response. The "farm revolt," if represented by any gross unidirectional shift in farm partisanship, is likely to come about only when economic difficulty faces a large proportion of farmers at once.

The role of the economic in determining farm responses to political affairs, as well as its role in fragmenting the farm community as a political group, is convincingly demonstrated by attitudes of farmers toward key issues of governmental farm policy. In 1956 we asked all farm respondents to react to the following proposition, which seemed to strike at a major controversy extant with regard to the "farm problem": "If a farmer can't sell things he raises at a profit, the government should buy them and limit the amount the farmer can produce."

Reactions to this issue betray broad cleavages within the farm community. It is, from one point of view, two issues rather than one, since it couples the possibility of price supports with the possibility of production controls. Yet this was the practical dilemma that seemed to face the American farmer in 1956. Differences in response tend to follow lines of difference in economic situation, and the broad divergence of opinion reflects the heterogeneity of farm needs across the nation.

At the grossest level, in the South, where both large and small farmer have tended to benefit from price supports of such commodities on the "basic" list as tobacco, corn, and cotton, there was a much wider margin of support for the proposal (75 per cent) than elsewhere in the nation (40 per cent). Within both regions, however, there are visible battle lines that follow differences in farm size. Smaller farmers are more frequently hostile toward a support program than are the large farmers. Apparently this is in part due to the fact that small farmers, particularly outside the South, are less likely to produce crops that fall within the support program; at the same time, the smaller farmer has greater difficulty limiting his acreage and reacts negatively to that portion of the program.

This interpretation is bolstered by the fact that within the sets of large and small farmers, there is a clear relationship between the perception that government policies affect crop prices received and warmth toward the price support question.[12] The majority of small farmers see no effect of government policy on their prices, and this majority is almost unanimous in its antagonism to the combination of price support and acreage control. But among those small farmers who do see some effect, the support program is more likely to be welcomed. Precisely the same pattern appears among large farmers, with those few large farmers who feel no effects of government policies tending to oppose supports and with the remainder favoring them.

The cleavages are compounded when these conflicting policy demands are laid against a partisan political backdrop. Responses to the support issue are related to party identification. Democratic farmers tended to accept supports, and Republican farmers to oppose them, undoubtedly reflecting the national posture of the two major parties during this period. But this alignment is a confused one, since the smaller farmer is at the same time partial toward the Democrats yet hostile toward the Democratic position on the price support problem. Table 15-9 (page 422) summarizes this conflict, as reflected in partisan voting patterns. If the smaller farmer seems drawn to the Democrats yet doubtful about their price support position, the larger farmer is caught in the same cross currents, exactly reversed. This conflict of forces sums up the difficulties to be encountered in treating the American farmer as a voting bloc. And the clear economic roots of these cleavages lend weight once again to the contention of particular economic sensitivity among farmers.

Economic motivation and turnout. We have already introduced evidence which implies that as economic pressure on the farm increases, the political involvement of the farmer, relative to an urban backdrop, increases as well. The suggestion is obvious that short-term economic pressures lie behind the spurts in vote turnout that mark the farm vote. Now that we have located focuses of economic pressure within the total farm community in 1956, we can attempt to document this proposition at a finer level of analysis.

[12] By and large it is likely that farmers reporting an effect of government policies on their prices are those who were eligible for benefits under the existing crop program. Given the variety in crop production that characterizes a large portion of the nation's farms, it is difficult, with nothing more than our knowledge of the respondent's major crop, to know precisely who has been affected and in what degree. We can isolate a set of farmers whose single major crop falls on the "basic" list of the Commodity Credit Corporation and hence has enjoyed price supports. Within this pure group outside the South, 61 per cent favored the support-control proposal, whereas it was acceptable to only 34 per cent of the residual category. And this small pure group was also much more likely to report that government policy had had an effect on the prices received for crops.

TABLE 15-9. Relation of Views on Price Supports and Farm Size to 1956 Presidential Vote of Farmers[a]

	Small Farm		Large Farm	
	Reactions to Support Program		Reactions to Support Program	
	Pro	*Anti*	*Pro*	*Anti*
Proportion Voting Democratic	72%	50%	44%	23%
Number of cases	25	30	41	31

[a] This table is based on the total sample of farmers. The pattern is sharper still, taking the non-South alone, where the Democratic vote proportions across the four categories are, from left to right, 73 per cent, 42 per cent, 36 per cent, and 18 per cent.

As we have seen, the small rather than the large farmer was in most direct revolt against the Republican Administration in 1956. More specifically, the small farmer *who had perceived his prices to have declined* during the 1952–1956 period was most severely concerned. Now under normal circumstances we would expect that the *large* farmer, in view of his higher education and political involvement, would show a vote turnout higher than that of the small farmer. But if it is true that economic pressure leads to a surge in political involvement, we might expect some visible reversal of this normal expectation in 1956.

Table 15-10 supports this prediction of an unusual pattern in political involvement in 1956. Although small Southern farmers whose prices have fallen show a level of political involvement higher than any of the other Southern categories, this motivation is not reflected in a higher turnout rate in the South, and one is led to suspect that other barriers are intervening to prevent expression at the polls among these rural Southerners.[13] Though cases are again fewer than we would like, the turnout rates across types of farm size and economic pressure outside the South also support the prediction (Table 15-11).

Thus the data suggest that it was the small farmer suffering declining prices who was most motivated in his political response during

[13] Even with Negroes removed, the vote turnout in this category remains low.

TABLE 15-10. Relation of Price Trends and Farm Size to 1956 Political Involvement[a]

Political Involvement	Small Farm: Prices Down	Small Farm: Prices Up, Mixed	Large Farm: Prices Down	Large Farm: Prices Up, Mixed
High	34%	29%	23%	21%
Medium	48	32	43	35
Low	18	39	34	44
	100%	100%	100%	100%
Number of cases	44	28	56	34

[a] The involvement measure is based on a combination of responses having to do with the individual's interest in the campaign and his concern over its outcome. To avoid strong extraneous factors entering from the Southern portion of the sample, all Negroes are excluded from the table.

TABLE 15-11. Relation of Price Trends and Farm Size to 1956 Presidential Vote Turnout (Non-South)

	Small Farm: Prices Down	Small Farm: Prices Up, Mixed	Large Farm: Prices Down	Large Farm: Prices Up, Mixed
Proportion voting	93%	(75%)	86%	82%
Number of cases	28	(12)[a]	43	22

[a] Figures are shown in parentheses because of the limited number of cases.

the 1956 election. Without information on the same farmers over a period of time we cannot be entirely sure that the heightened motivation within this group is a *temporary* heightening. Yet the entire structure of our materials strains toward the conclusion that save for economic pressure, this group would not have pulled out of line in this fashion. The special economic pressure within this subset, defined by farm size and production of crops that were hit by price declines, was not present in 1952. It is present in 1956, and the group shows unexpected political involvement. We assume, then, that we witness here a spurt of involvement as a very simple reaction to economic pressure.

Economic motivation and farm political behavior. It is phenomena of the type demonstrated previously that have led to the perception that the farm vote is a "pocketbook vote." The economic current in farm political motivation is clear even in modern America, and the fact that older agrarian political unrest sprang up in times of severe economic hardship needs no documentation here. Yet the fact that farmers react politically to economic pressure in no sense answers the problem posed by the peculiarities that surround such protest. Other groupings have pocketbooks, and other groupings experience economic hardship. Why does rural economic protest appear peculiar?

We are forced to maintain either (1) that farmers suffer economic pressures that differ in their intensity or quality from those suffered by other groups in the society; or (2) that farmers have, for whatever reason, a different political style of coping with pressures of the same generic type as those encountered elsewhere in the society.

Lipset *et al.* recognizing that response to economic pressure is not in itself a solution of the farm puzzle, appear to pursue the first line of thought. It is argued that the farmer—and the one-crop farmer in particular—has a position in the social structure that is unique from an economic point of view. He suffers extraordinary insecurity of income, owing to the vagaries of weather on one hand and world or national commodity markets on the other; he is peculiarly dependent upon governmental action for regulation and maintenance of the markets that are his economic life-lines.[14]

Many of these observations have merit and undoubtedly have important bearing on the situation. Yet we are not convinced that this approach moves to the heart of the problem. We are not convinced, for example, that economic pressure as it bears upon the one-crop farmer differs in a critical way from economic pressure that has borne upon the urban laborer. Nor are we convinced that this approach copes with the most tell-tale peculiarities of rural political behavior. The explanation, as it stands, suggests that groups like one-crop farmers may turn out to be perennial troublemakers in the political system; but key facts, such as the transience of this troublemaking and its ideological fickleness or incoherence, are noted but are left unassimilated.

Let us, then, take the opposing fork of the argument. Let us assume that although economic pressures on the farmer and on the laborer exhibit many interesting qualitative differences, we shall be safe in conceptualizing economic pressure in very simple terms. We shall presume that such pressure has but one dimension of variability that

[14] *Op. cit.*, pp. 1128 ff.

requires attention, and that is its intensity. If this intensity is the same upon farmer and laborer and the nature of the response varies, then we are called upon to explain this variation in terms of differences between farmer and laborer as political actors.

Farmer and Laborer: Reflections on the Mass Base of Protest Movements

We have already indicated some of the more notable similarities and differences between the political dispositions of the farmer and the urban laborer. Both are poorly educated, and one consequence of this fact is a lowered capacity to organize a steady input of political information. With restricted information goes a reduced sense of involvement in the outcome of political events. This psychological remoteness leads in turn to sporadic political participation.

Though there are broad similarities between farmer and laborer in these terms, the farmer if anything suffers by comparison. He shares the laborer's primary handicaps, but these have been compounded by the circumscribed provincialism of his rural life. In a simple physical way, he lies outside the flow of major political events. We find vestiges of this difference even in our current American data, where "normal" farm involvement, once education is controlled, does not compare favorably with the lowest reaches of the urban status hierarchy. If our views on sources of these lingering contrasts in involvement are valid, the discrepancies must have been a good deal sharper a century ago. We would suppose, for example, that education in the agrarian West was more often abbreviated, of poor quality, or absent altogether than it was even at lower status levels in the Eastern cities.

We presume that it is this physical remoteness that has led to the point of sharpest contrast between the farmer and urban laborer. For despite gross similarities in the involvement dimension, there are marked differences in the way the two occupation types are bound into existing group structures in the society. That is, the farmer has a lower incidence of membership in social groupings than the urban laborer and, where membership exists, is more apathetic toward the group. This appeared to be true in terms of occupational organizations, and in terms of political memberships we have noted major contrasts between farmer and laborer in sense of allegiance to a political party and, as a consequence, in regularity of support for the party at the polls.

Our view of these critical differences can be expanded in a number of directions. Impressionistically, we might compare the daily round of an urban laborer, like "Sam Hodder" of Chapter 10, with that of the farmer, in terms of informal social communication, group contacts, and flow of political information. Sam confessed that he read little and gained most of his knowledge of politics through informal conversation. In general, we can imagine that his life revolved around a number of informal primary groups. He spent his time either within a work group, or a group of male companions with whom he passed leisure time in drinking or other recreational forms, or within his family itself. His wife probably did not know much about politics or pay much attention to it; but in the work group and peer group we can imagine Sam would encounter, along with persons less interested or knowledgeable about politics than he, other "opinion leaders" who did have more political involvement. The union itself was one focus for such involvement. Though Sam was not an extremely active member himself, his immediate associates must have included a number who participated more earnestly.

What are the group counterparts for the farmer? The nature of the work round would vary according to the character of the farming, an important fact in itself. But if we take as a prototype the small family farm, there is no regular work group. Activities are carried on within the family, and the farmer himself works largely in solitude. Although access to other informal groupings for leisure activities has increased with advances in transportation, such contacts undoubtedly remain more sporadic than in Sam Hodder's case, and the disparity forty years ago must have been great indeed. In short, the small farmer's life has revolved very largely around his own family circle, and here, for better or for worse, he has been the only possible "political opinion leader." This is not to say, of course, that the farmer has had no group contact outside the family. He is likely to have held a church membership, although once again our stereotypes of rural Protestant churches do not lead us to expect much political content. And he has had contacts as well at points of market, as he buys his supplies and sells his produce; here, in times of economic hardship, he is likely to encounter a fair amount of political discussion. But in normal times such information is not likely to be extensive, and the contact is the exception rather than the rule in his daily life, as it is with Sam Hodder.

We can trace out some of these differences in a more formal way with our data from 1952 and 1956. There is good reason to question how much organizational "reach" the traditional parties have into the hinterlands. In the revolt year of 1956, when excitement about the election was off from its 1952 pitch in urban areas, there is evidence that party organization did extend its efforts into rural areas where there was believed to be heightened political ferment. In general only about one person in ten, in the adult population, reports having been personally contacted by a party worker in connection with the election, although this figure is somewhat higher outside the South, approaching a ratio of one person in five. In 1956, 23 per cent of our non-Southern farmers reported such contact, and 17 per cent of rural non-farm persons had the same experience.

There was a good deal of focus upon the farm problem in connection with the 1956 election, and of course physical access to rural areas had been improving steadily for a century. In 1952, the principal campaign efforts were not directed toward any particular urban or rural segment of the electorate, as there were no notable economic lines of stress between city and country to prompt such attention. In this more normal setting, though patterns of urban contact were much as they were to be in 1956, party contact in rural areas was very slight indeed. Only 7 per cent of non-Southern farmers reported being contacted, and the comparable figure for non-farm rural persons was 9 per cent. Thus the likelihood of experiencing direct contact with a party worker seems to have been twice as great for the *unskilled* urban laborer in 1952 as it was for the farmer, and of course the probability was larger still for the semi-skilled or skilled laborer.

When we turn to other forms of partisan participation in the campaign, we find the type of differences between farmer and laborer that would follow from facts already introduced. In terms of active party work, the adoption of official party membership, or attendance at political rallies and meetings, the farmer, whether Southern or non-Southern, was less likely to have participated than the urban blue-collar worker. In an examination of most of these tables, the only live question is whether or not farm participation will exceed that of the urban unskilled. At times this is the case, although at other points the farmer is simply the most inactive of all isolated occupation categories. In every instance his participation is substantially less than that of urban blue-collar workers taken as a whole.

Furthermore, a comparison of 1952 and 1956 data gives little reason to believe that when the farmer is more exercised about politics this involvement will receive expression in partisan group participation. In 1956 he was more likely to have been contacted by a party worker seeking his vote; but there is no sign of any increase in his voluntary participation in partisan activity. Even in terms of informal communication we get no sense of heightened activity. The farmer in 1956 was less likely to have attempted to influence the partisan intention of some other person than was the urban blue-collar worker (such attempts reported by 21 per cent of non-Southern farmers, as opposed to 29 per cent of urban laborers).

Data cited earlier in connection with membership in farm organizations raise the possibility that lack of firm bonds between the farmer and traditional political group structures is but a special case of a broader insulation of the farmer from group activity. In 1952 we explored the types of group participation in which a subsample of our respondents was involved, including both formal organizations and informal groupings such as poker clubs and sewing circles. Participation in informal group activity is less among farm people than it is among urban blue-collar workers and, if church memberships are excepted, the same observation may be extended to more formal groupings as well.[15]

It is in this sense, then, that although both farmer and laborer are poorly educated and relatively uninvolved in the political process, the farmer is distinct in the degree to which he floats free of the group life of the larger society. Hence we need no unique explanation to cover the farmer's lack of commitment to either of the political parties; he appears to stand on the periphery of social process more generally speaking, and his low sense of commitment to a party is simply a case in point.

The urban laborer is little more absorbed in politics than the farmer. But he does find himself imbedded in a network of group contacts, and experiences a flow of informal communication on political matters that can fill some of the gap left by his lack of attention to published news. Of course his relative indifference tends to weaken his sense of partisan commitment, as well as his regular attendance at the polls. Thus he is, if anything, slightly less strongly identified with a party than his higher-status urban counterpart and votes much less regularly. But when he does vote he is more likely to support the same party (Table 15-1), and if status differences in involvement are controlled, the urban laborer actually expresses stronger partisan loyalty than the urbanite of higher status. Furthermore, where there is membership in some secondary group having political norms, a rare occurrence in rural areas but common in the city, we have seen the urban worker drawn even more tightly into the traditional party

[15] Ronald Freedman, unpublished data, 1952 Election Study, Survey Research Center, The University of Michigan, Ann Arbor, Mich.

structure.[16] Beyond the one-party South, the greatest differences in strength of party identification emerge between the full-time farmer, apathetic toward farm organizations, and the urbanite, highly identified with a secondary grouping that transmits political standards in the name of group welfare.

Therefore the farmer and the laborer share some crucial characteristics but stand in sharp contrast on others. What happens politically when heavy economic pressures are brought to bear upon these different political actors? In both cases we would expect an upsurge in political involvement and greater turnout at the polls. But the partisan character of the response should differ substantially.

Earlier we examined the results of industrial recession upon the economic and political attitudes of the urban population affected. We saw that pre-existing party loyalties turned out to be the primary determinant of the political meaning attributed to the recession. That is, the partisan felt indignation about the economic state of affairs in the degree to which he could believe that the opposing party was responsible. If this was not possible, he tended to belittle the fact of the recession or to dissociate it from the realm of politically significant facts. Thus economic disorder in the urban setting had a minimal effect upon patterns of partisan choice. This partisan determination of the reaction was, of course, least apparent where party loyalties were weakest: among the small group of Independents in the center of the party continuum.

Here we have examined the effects of rural economic hardship upon the economic and political attitudes of the *farm* population affected, and the results were strikingly different. When a simple index of economic pressure was coupled with accounts of partisan behavior among farmers, we carried away a vivid impression of the potency of such forces in determining the partisan direction of behavior. In fact, no tables in this volume demonstrate a tighter link between immediate economic pressure and partisan response than those which spring from an analysis of the farm vote.

The directness and simplicity of this link is, of course, what we have taken as a witness of the peculiar economic sensitivity of the farmer. Yet we must be cautious in assuming that there is anything truly peculiar to the farmer here. It seems psychologically unsound to believe that the farmer, when subjected to a given degree of economic pressure, suffers more intensely or is more motivated to act than the urban laborer. What is peculiar is not the sensitivity itself;

16 See Chapter 12.

rather, it is the manner in which *partisan meaning* is ascribed to economic pressure. For the urban laborer, be he Republican or Democrat, economic pressure prompts attitude formation and behavior within channels that are group-defined and of long standing. Where such loyalties to a party are lacking, as they tend to be among farmers, these channels are faint or simply do not exist. The farmer is psychologically free to march to the polls and "vote the rascals out," whether or not he himself may have helped establish them in power in the first place. The result is political behavior that fluctuates sharply in its partisan character and, for the analyst, data that show spectacular links between simple economic pressure and partisan choice.

The farmer does not thereby behave as a man apart but simply as the political independent of low involvement behaves in any setting. Urban populations certainly contain individuals who, in the normal course of events, are apathetic toward political participation, yet who flow into the active electorate under sufficiently extreme provocation. These persons tend to style themselves as "Independents" and feel little allegiance to the traditional parties.[17] The critical point is that in the urban setting they are greatly outnumbered by committed partisans, most of whom vote with regularity. Thus their behavior is largely concealed, as it is not in rural areas. If urban populations were divided into "wards" on the basis of long-term political involvement, we would predict that the vote totals for the uninvolved over time would show the same variability in turnout and in partisan vote division as that registered in rural areas. We would suggest furthermore that such persons, under sufficient stress and proper cultivation by radical third parties of the left or right, would massively desert the traditional party structure in a manner that could never be expected of the more modal urban voter.

Farm and labor movements in American political history. These observations have rather clear implications when we examine past behavior of the farmer and laborer in this country. We propose that it would take long unrelieved economic disaster before the urban

[17] Although the interpretation is a popular one, there is no reason to believe that such people, rural or urban, stay away from the polls under ordinary circumstances because they are "alienated" from the system in any affective sense. If there is an alienation, it appears to be cognitive: such persons tend to be poorly educated or, if educated, interested in other things than politics. They are little aware of any effect which a remote government has upon their lives, except as events may suddenly go awry in a manner completely beyond their control. The fact that in crisis they turn to the polls itself seems an indication that they do not customarily fail to participate out of disgust at "the system." When events arouse affect, they participate; when things are going well, there is an absence of motivation.

laborer would begin to depart from the existing structure of traditional parties on any large scale. Yet, at the onset of economic difficulty in rural areas in times past, new parties have had nearly the same chance to capture farm indignation as the old, for the farmer has had little psychological anchor in the "normal" elements of the ongoing political process.

It might be argued that we have begged the question by confusing effect for cause. If the urban laborer is, in 1956, tightly bound into the traditional party structure, does this not merely reflect the direction in which the laborer has been led by his elites in times past? If the farmer floats free of this party structure, is it not because his leaders have more frequently drawn him toward third-party solutions for his economic problems?

We do not believe that such an interpretation adequately covers several historical facts. In the first place, it seems reasonable to assume that any new elite with a clear-cut ideology will welcome the third-party alternative as a rapid and pure assault on the control of power. The existing party controls an attractive base of mass support. To capture this support by capturing the party name or symbol means, however, a slow process of infiltration of the existing party elite, with the threat of compromise in principle at every step. The third party, constructed *de novo* as an instrument of elite ideology, avoids these uncertainties, although it does indeed cast the question of success back upon the adroitness of the new elite in drawing together a base of mass support.

In these terms, it would be striking if early American labor elites had not, at propitious times, attempted to secure mass support for third-party solutions. We know that they did, as did comparable elites in European industrial democracies as well. The major thrust of the modern American laboring movement did not come to rest within the traditional party structure because this was the initial reflex of radical labor leadership but because all attempts to draw the urban laborer into third-party ventures were dismal failures.[18]

[18] We are well aware that third-party movements in the name of labor have succeeded in establishing themselves in numerous European industrial democracies. However, several of these have gained broad footing only when the existing fabric of political groups and institutions has been rent by war and occupation. These seem to pose no problem for our theory; instead, the fact that such moments in national histories have been *more* propitious for the successful establishment of labor parties than moments of grave economic disorder in the industrial sector is virtually a case in point. The remaining labor parties that have gained *entrée* under less disruptive conditions have grown very slowly and painfully. None of them has careened into prominence on the basis of an electoral explosion in which

The success of third parties in the agrarian setting, on the other hand, was remarkable. As we have noted, the American West of the nineteenth century spawned third party after third party, not of the sort of fringe labor party that quadrennially in our day attracts a minute portion of the national vote; but vigorous social movements that, in their brief ascendance, captured astonishing popular support almost overnight in rural areas.[19] It is an irony of almost epic proportions that political programs generated in the city on behalf of urban labor and tailored to its policy concerns often won warmer reception on the remote prairies in times of economic stress. The most successful attempt to build a third party for labor in the United States, represented by the Socialist Party just after the turn of the century, appears to have attained the modest electoral pinnacle which it achieved not on the basis of urban labor support but largely from agrarian areas.[20] Thus when agrarian leaders attempted to move toward third-party solutions, the rural mass electorate flowed without hesitation into the new party vessels. But when urban labor leaders attempted the same stratagem under parallel conditions, the outcome was failure. It was only as the efforts of the labor movement came to be directed within the traditional party structure that some political leverage was achieved.

Our interpretation of rural rebellion provides effortless explanations of a number of other peculiarities associated with these events. For example, it follows that as education among farmers comes to approximate that of persons in the urban setting, and as advances in transportation and communication bring him into closer contact with the traditional groups and forms of the society, the distinctive character of the farmer's political response should fade as well. For better or for worse, he becomes a more "socialized" political actor. We would profess to see such an evolution in the quality of rural political protest over the period since colonial times. Rural protest has become increasingly channeled within the guidelines set by the existing parties.

---

their claim to mass support multiplied eightfold, as did that of the Nazi Party in Germany between 1928 and 1930. It is this explosion that links the Nazi Party with events in Russia in 1917 and the prairie outbursts in our own country in the late nineteenth century.

[19] Since 1860 only one "urban" state in one presidential election (Pennsylvania, 1912, for Theodore Roosevelt) has cast its electoral vote for a third party, and in this case the candidate was closely associable with the existing party structure. Yet during this time about two dozen agrarian states have, at one point or another, contributed third party electors in a presidential vote.

[20] Lipset, *Agrarian Socialism,* p. 12.

Any such reading, of course, presumes that the critical catalyst—economic pressure—has remained essentially constant over this period. If it could be shown that economic deprivation in the "troughs" of the farm price cycle has been less and less intense, then it would be a moot point as to which factor best accounted for behavior change. It is certainly not our contention in this regard that the 1952–1956 period constituted one of the major farm catastrophes, any more than the 1958 industrial recession lends itself to comparison with the Great Depression. The sharpest drop in price index between 1951 and 1956 for a major category of agricultural product (livestock) was on the order of 30 per cent. This figure may understate the degree of pressure involved, for the costs of farm supply items were rising in counterpoint. But the American farmer of the 1950's had a relatively comfortable margin built up against the level of barest subsistence that he undoubtedly lacked in frontier days.

But it would seem that the period of the 1920's and early 1930's did involve economic torment within many sectors of the farm community that would form a reasonable parallel to some of the situations arising in the late nineteenth century. Although there was limited third-party activity in rural areas during this epoch, these efforts never achieved the sudden blossoming of large-scale electoral support so characteristic of earlier farm revolts.[21] And, although it is undoubtedly true that pressures were less severe in the 1950's, we take it as significant also that there was much less sign of any nascent rural third-party movements in 1956 than there had been even in time of distress two and three decades before.

Our causal interpretation for this slow evolution of rural behavior toward the urban norm is in no way attached to the stability of the political system as it may be conceived to "mature" automatically over a period of time. In this country, the "binding in" of rural populations has coincided with the lengthening shadow of political tradition. This situation need not have occurred. We would propose, for example, that in underdeveloped areas where the peasant continues to exist uneducated and remote from the mainstream of urban life, his potential for the behaviors manifested by the American

21 That some of the political pressure generated in rural areas was drained off in New Deal support after 1932 strikes us as a perfectly cogent argument to fit facts gleaned from election statistics in these areas. Our hypothesis clearly does not imply that, other things equal, the farmer *avoids* political solution within the traditional party structure; indeed, any such position imputes to the farmer a grasp of the total political situation that we shall contend that he lacks. Normally, however, the traditional "patronage" parties do not attempt to develop concrete and vivid programs of farm aid such as those proposed under the New Deal aegis.

farmer in an earlier epoch will remain intact, however "ancient" and apparently mature the political system of the country may be.

Our account sheds equal light upon one of the most perplexing features of rural protest at a mass level, its unique transience. This characteristic has often been obscured by scholarly preoccupation with the rise of totalitarian movements. Usually in these latter cases the guiding elite that has benefited from rural revolt has succeeded in acquiring full power. This has meant the suspension of further democratic process and hence the obliteration of clues as to subsequent rural reactions. Yet if we look at those cases in which democratic process has been sustained—and the farm revolts of the nineteenth century provide the most striking examples—it is consistently true that the mass base, *upon relief from the most immediate economic grievances,* has disappeared as rapidly and unexpectedly as it coalesced.

Although few investigators have examined these revolts without becoming intrigued by this peculiarity, we know of no case in which it has been subjected to explanation. We would certainly have reason to be dissatisfied with the view that since such movements rise when pressure is exerted, they should fall when grievances are redressed. This is the action-reaction formula which, though it resounds with truth, sidesteps the fact that this pattern is peculiar to farm behavior, a matter which has been the sum and substance of our puzzle. Other economically insecure groups have, under pressure of repeated economic crises in the urban setting, slowly forged links with the political process. Such movements have come thereby to enjoy continuing loyalty from a mass base that extends into periods of high prosperity. Continuing loyalty provides a mechanism for protection at any time that prosperity is once again undermined. None of the American farm outbursts has acquired such continuity.

We feel that our interpretation not only can accommodate this aspect of rural behavior, but in an obvious way would demand it. The rural mass base collapses as economic pressure is relieved for precisely the same motivational reasons that permitted its implausible formation. Its clientele is overburdened with individuals whose ties with political parties are extremely weak; and the proof of the matter is nowhere more clear than in the fact that they were lured away from the traditional party structure in such haste. The psychological function that party identification plays seems such that the first response of the party faithful to economic storm is not the third-party solution but some attempt to affix responsibility and look for succor in a manner best calculated to preserve existing party loyalty. If pressure continues and none of the traditional parties can effectively relieve it, then we might expect a growing willingness to consider third-party alternatives. But this would be a slow process even at the individual level; over the aggregate of party faithful it would indeed be hard to imagine sudden inroads of these massive proportions.

By the same token, the mass base that forms with great rapidity will wither away quickly because it is saturated with individuals who do not frequently participate in politics when "times are good." Such persons, upon solution of the immediate problem, will resume their normal posture of sporadic attention to politics, or will drift on small pretext to some other party that catches their attention.

This is not to say of course that the mass base is made up only of individuals who are usually apathetic. There are bound to be some genuine converts who are accustomed to continuous political participation even among the early adherents. And, too, the success of an electoral explosion of this sort will draw in political opportunists of many stripes to add to the sophisticated hard core of the movement. But the crucial question is one of proportions, and we submit that the type of political actor necessary to lend any movement a germ of continuity *at the mass level* cannot be rapidly won, and hence must remain in the extreme minority in any broad-gauge electoral support that emerges under one or another label in the brief span between two elections.

Such continuity of political behavior depends, at a rarefied level of education and involvement, upon commitment to an ideology or, at a less rarefied level, upon some "ideology by proxy" that hinges upon trust in group leadership—of the party or semi-political group—based on tangible past rewards. Such ideology and such group bonds we assume cannot be overthrown in a day and replaced by new ones that have the same motivational significance for behavior, even under extraordinary social or economic pressure. Hence it follows that any large mass base that coalesces very suddenly under stress must be made up largely of (1) those persons who, if capable of developing ideology or group bonds, are too new to political or social process to have already become committed, that is, the young; or (2) persons who have shown little propensity for developing either type of commitment, despite "presence" for some time as a system member. It is in the latter group, of course, that the farmer is prominent. And although the young represent some potential for continuity, the farmer and his unsophisticated, apathetic urban counterpart do not.

Ideology and the mass base of protest movements. It is the matter of ideology that constitutes the final puzzle surrounding rural protest movements. Though investigators have frequently left the transience of rural protest unexplained, a great deal of effort and ingenuity has been devoted to the search for plausible links between the pattern of reforms proposed by the elite of the movement and needs imputed to the rank and file.

Most discussions of this problem share an underlying assumption that there need be some basic congruence between the ideology proposed by the elite and the motivations of the mass base in flocking to its electoral support. Certainly such movements must have points of strong attraction. But to presume that the mass base is endorsing the ideology as the analyst conceives it is to presume that such programs—that usually call for change in the pattern of political and economic relationships—are in some real sense comprehended by more than a handful within the mass base. The argument developed in Chapters 9 and 10 tended to call this assumption into question even for the moderately educated and moderately involved voter. It should be clear that no commonly recognized political actor would be less likely to fulfill this assumption than the farmer.

If we are willing to part with such preconceptions, then some of the most resistant problems surrounding rural behavior appear spurious. To be sure, new riddles arise in place of the old. We are not satisfied that we can predict what manner of ideology may be developing at elite levels at the proper time and the proper place to capture a given surge of rural protest. But the verb "capture" is deliberately chosen. Rare is the ideology so pristine that it does not permit campaign promises shaped to the immediate needs of an oppressed grouping, promises that are concrete and meaningful within the limits of the individual's daily experience. If such a message is successfully communicated, the remote and abstract superstructure of ideas that defines the movement in the eyes of the sophisticated may matter little. And this statement is true not because sufficient pressure can force a man to accept strange bedfellows. Ingrained in such a formulation is the same assumption that the actor understands the ideology sufficiently to be discomfited by its implications. Rather, it is true because the concrete promises are self-contained and the implications of larger means and ends need not be cognized or comprehended at all.

We get some sense of the nature of the appeals that may attract farm support from our free-answer materials. In analyzing levels of conceptualization (Chapter 10) we paid special attention to farm respondents. In part, this attention sprang from the fact that although many mentions of farm interest were made warranting inclusion in the "single-group interest" category, most of these interviews seemed of a visibly lower calibre than those in which some other interest group was involved. Hence these farm responses were assigned to a distinct category that could bear separate analysis. It should be stated that some farmers did give comments that merited classification at higher levels. Yet, as one might expect, the bulk of farm interviews fell in the special farm category. Two interviews drawn randomly from this group after the manner of Chapter 10 capture rather eloquently the modal farmer's view of the political situation.

The first of these interviews came from a small Mississippi farmer whose prices had been declining. There is the familiar profession of great ignorance about politics, with virtually no other content. However, Stevenson's name elicited the remark: "Now wait a minute—ain't he the one gonna give money to the farmers? My boys an' me needs that."

Much the same flavor comes through in the second interview, taken with the wife of a New Jersey farmer. She launched her comments about politics with references to the "good pay we used to get for our crops during the War, even when some went bad," and went on to talk about politicians as "slick." When questioned about Stevenson's good points, she indicated: "I haven't read about him. My husband and I don't care to watch the speeches on TV." But when asked if there was anything about Stevenson that might make her want to vote against him, she said, "Well, no. Maybe I should vote for him if he is going to help the farmers get more money."

It does not seem difficult to imagine the perception getting abroad that a candidate or party is going to "get the farmers more money" with little accompanying notion as to the changes in law or governmental relationships that such aid might entail. Not only are these people largely oblivious of the way in which their own aid might be implemented, they tend as well to hold an extremely narrow perspective on political process. They evince little awareness as to what is going on in other sectors of the society; their criteria for political decision are totally wrapped up in the tangible benefits that may flow to the farmer.

This paucity of anything resembling ideological comprehension in rural areas is vividly illustrated in another manner. If we assume that the elite that is thrust up by economic stress is itself rural, with at best a moderate background of political involvement or contact with sophisticated political views, then we are not surprised by those numerous traces of ideological incoherence among rural elites found in the historical record. Lipset describes the difficulties encountered by American agrarian leaders in fashioning a far-sighted program, even after several agrarian explosions had occurred:

> The lack of a long-term program for social change accounted, in part, for the failure of Populism to become a permanent radical protest movement. The farmers struck out at random at the most visible economic evils that affected them. They opposed the banks, the railroads, the wheat-elevator companies, and the shortage of money, but they saw each evil as an evil in itself, not as part of a total economic system. They accepted without question the support of any group that would join them. By focussing on specific transitory evils, the agrarian leaders failed to lay the education base for a new radical movement.[22]

As might be expected, the leadership of earlier revolts had been even less coherent. Their groping to shore up indignant protest with a constructive program makes clear why urban labor ideology has frequently been transplanted almost without change to the rural setting as a program for the farmer. We must note that as protest against economic exploitation, these philosophies are not necessarily inappropriate. But the fit is, at points, awkward, and the history of ideas does contain ideologies more purely rural in bent.[23]

Once we assume that a rural elite generated by economic disaster is not apt to have the capacity to develop its own program or philosophy, the question whether or not any ideology becomes attached to the electoral outburst at an elite level depends on factors of cultural diffusion or, more simply put, upon what may be within sight at the moment. In the Saskatchewan case examined by Lipset, the farm population included an unusual proportion of recent migrants from industrial areas abroad. There was a large contingent of trade union members and erstwhile Fabian Socialists. It is not surprising, then, that this movement found an ideology quickly and that its elite was prominently populated by the sophisticated new arrivals.[24] In the American West, however, there apparently was little knowledge of urban ideas, and there were years of floundering before the rural elites who had been activated by economic stress even found that plausible bodies of ideas were available which might be borrowed. The confusion thereby caused when power was actually attained is reflected in a passage by Hicks:

> Generally speaking, the experiments with Populism in the West had done little to engender confidence in the ability of the new party to rule.

[22] Lipset, *op. cit.*, p. 9.

[23] These have tended to spring from the minds of sophisticated, urbanized persons. Jefferson, though a planter's son, spent his early life at law. Quesnay was a French court physician. It is likely that most ideational structures indigenous to rural people have been mystic or pietistic, with little reference to the political, social, or economic systems.

[24] Lipset, *op. cit.*, p. 25. This seems an inverse case of the "binding in" of rural populations.

> Some legislation favored by the Populists had reached the statute books, but usually such of this as stood the test of the courts was as much the work of other parties as of the Populists. Purely Populist legislation was all too frequently found defective and unconstitutional. In administrative matters the Populists were even less successful. Evidently their genius lay in protest rather than in performance.[25]

Of course as we return from these descriptions of elites to a consideration of the mass base that supported them, we must water down our expectations accordingly. The development or even grafting on of an ideological program is a slow and painful process for those relatively capable individuals who have been drawn most passionately into the cause of protest. Therefore our assumption that an ideology *per se* is not likely, in the short span of a year or two, to have permeated a mass base that is less involved and less sophisticated than the elite seems sound indeed. Hence the question as to why this or that ideology was so irresistible that large numbers flocked to its support seems calculated to lead to blind alleys and contradictions.

It should be strongly emphasized that our argument is focused entirely on the nature of continuities between elite and mass base. We are not questioning the value of efforts to understand the transmission and diffusion of ideologies. Obviously, the nature of the ideology that captures such a surge of protest is of tremendous consequence for the history of nations. But we say that the character of the ideological superstructure, as the analyst conceives it, is normally irrelevant to the motivations behind any sudden mass base that it may achieve.

The Agrarian Movement as a Class Phenomenon

It is, in our estimation, no mere happenstance that sophisticated urban observers have felt more at home in analyzing the class currents of urban politics than in predicting "comparable" events in rural areas. In addition to the heightened role of historical accident in the latter case, there is as well a greater hiatus between urban preconceptions about political decision making and the types of perceptions and motives that guide political behavior among farmers. This is not to say that the urban laborer is entirely understood. It is our impression that accounts of his "ideology" are frequently overdrawn. To the degree that he is bound into group structures with more sophisticated elites, however, the broad currents of his behavior are found to move as anticipated.

[25] Hicks, *op. cit.*, p. 299.

We saw in our discussion of social class (Chapter 13) that class expression was clearest in the voting of those most strongly involved in the political process. Even in urban areas, apathetic people who do vote show little or no tendency to vote according to "appropriate" class lines. For the more involved, we were unable to judge in any final way whether perception of class interest led to involvement or involvement led to a more orderly expression of self-interest in class terms. But the contrasts with the behaviors of the farmers and the uninvolved more generally are clear.

This contrast is haunting, because it may certainly be argued that rural protest, when it occurs, is equally a class expression. That is, it is a demand for more tangible benefits on the part of a segment of the population suffering economic distress. Yet it is important to locate these outbursts relative to "normal" class assumptions. In terms of an electoral system they are powerful forces, because they attain such partisan unity. Nevertheless the partisan unity is not, from the viewpoint of the class analyst, an effective unity. For one thing, it is entirely sporadic. More important, when it does arise it may achieve short-run goals; but there is at best one chance in two that it will carry in directions that the observer would deem appropriate or "rational" in the long run.

If we wish to consider agrarian protest a class phenomenon, we must recognize that it is class expression at the opposing end of the continuum of involvement, political sophistication, and capacity for group identification. With these facts firmly in mind, class analysis may be useful. But failure to recognize these basic characteristics will lead to a continuing failure of "reasonable" expectations.

Population Movement ◇ 16

The movement of peoples is a fascinating theme in American history. The commonplace fact of large scale migration to the West was transformed by Frederick Jackson Turner into a provocative thesis on the development of our modern culture.[1] The persuasive argument of Turner, as well as the more recent rebuttals, are of passing interest to us because they stand as landmarks of scholarly analytic concern with the consequences of population movement.[2] More recently, and somewhat more narrowly, professional students of politics have turned to basic social and economic characteristics of the population for explanation of new developments in national politics. Arthur Holcombe made evident the extent to which urbanization replaced regional politics with the now familiar phenomena of the rural-urban conflict.[3] Of still more recent vintage are the arguments advanced by such observers as Louis Harris and Samuel Lubell.[4] Their understanding of political cleavage in mid-twentieth century rested in part on the perceptive realization that movement away from the central city and into the burgeoning suburbs had serious political implications beyond the mere redistribution of political partisans.

[1] Frederick J. Turner, *The Frontier in American History* (Henry Holt and Co., New York, 1921).

[2] Harold J. Laski, *The American Democracy* (Viking Press, Inc., New York, 1948).

[3] Arthur N. Holcombe, *The New Party Politics* (W. W. Norton and Co., New York, 1933).

[4] Louis Harris, *Is There a Republican Majority?* (Harper and Brothers, New York, 1954). Samuel Lubell, *The Future of American Politics* (Harper and Brothers, New York, 1952), and particularly *The Revolt of the Moderates* (Harper and Brothers, New York, 1956).

The winning of the West, the growth of the city, and the rise of suburbia have contemporary as well as historical interest for us in our present analysis. More than half of the present residents of our large cities grew up in other and smaller cities. Almost 40 per cent of the people who grew up in large cities have now moved to smaller cities, into the suburbs, or to a home in the country. At least one of every two members of the electorate of the 1950's had moved far enough from the home in which he grew up to be living in a place of different population size.[5] Looking at population movement in terms of the crossing of state boundaries, four out of ten native White Americans have moved from one state to another since growing up, and three out of every twenty have moved from one of four major geographic regions to another. As of the 1950's almost half the voters in the Far West had grown up in the South or in the East and had moved west in their adult years.[6]

These gross views of population movement do not capture any change of residence within the same town or city, nor do they reflect intrastate movement, which does not also involve a shift in population size of place of residence. Even without including such less dramatic movement in a description of change in residence, almost 60 per cent of the adult population can still be described as "movers."

At least three kinds of political effects may be identified as possible concomitants of population movement. The first is the aggregate change in political composition of areas that "movers" leave and into which they move. Of course, if each area were perfectly homogeneous, and if there were no differences between the areas, no amount of shuffling and exchanging of personnel would produce any immediate alteration in their composition. Barring the existence of these conditions, however, movement of people in and out of politically different counties or congressional districts or states redistributes partisans and participants. The total impact of such movement and redistribution depends on a number of factors, some of which we shall examine shortly.

[5] Here and later in the chapter we mean to distinguish three categories for the size of place of residence: (1) metropolitan centers; (2) suburbs, smaller cities, and large towns; and (3) rural villages, open country residences, and farms. The categories are so defined that a change in the population size of one's place of residence cannot be the result of national changes in urbanization but occurs only by a personal change in residence as a result of geographical movement *and* the crossing of a boundary between places of different population size.

[6] U. S. Bureau of the Census, Series P-25, #198 (1959). In this chapter as well as elsewhere throughout the book we utilize the Bureau of the Census definitions of regional boundaries separating Northeast, South, Midwest, and Far West.

Another kind of political effect associated with change of residence occurs when the individuals who move undergo political change. Such changes may be categorized under two distinct headings. In one situation a common factor or set of factors puts into motion both the residential change and the political change. For example, a person's financial success may lead to changes in a wide range of behaviors and values. Some of these may be associated with a style of life and may result in a new house or a new car or new kinds of entertainment and recreation. Others may be associated with the individual's view of the efficiency of government and the level of taxation, or with the role of government in providing social welfare services. Moving from one income bracket to another may be accompanied by related changes in political values, perceptions, and behaviors. Many observers of American politics profess to have witnessed such a system of change in American social and political life after World War II. The details supposedly involved were changes *away from* economic insecurity and Democratic affiliation *to* prosperity and identification with the Republican Party.

In some instances, the switch from Democratic to Republican politics is thought to have been the result of a second way in which individual change is related to a change in residence. Instead of a common prior factor that produces both social and political change, it is hypothesized that political change is the later result of moving and of the social changes that moving implies. A change of residence, for whatever reason, places a person in a new environment and in responding to the new environment he undergoes political change. Thus in the classic contemporary example, the working man moves to the suburbs as a Democrat, but there associates with Republicans and with greater or lesser speed takes on Republican characteristics.

All three kinds of political change that can be associated with population movements and changes in residence are potentially important, in part because of the local base on which American politics rests. If we elected a President on the basis of the total popular vote—rather than on the base of the unit rule disposition of a state's electoral votes—the sheer redistribution of political partisans would not be important in the study of the presidential electorate. There have been, however, major redistributions of members of the electorate that are important because they result in a shift in the balance of power both among and within political units. Changes in personal political predispositions are also in evidence in the national electorate. In our discussion we shall not always be able to distinguish empirically between political effects that are concomitants of change in residence and those political effects that are caused by the act of moving. Whatever their respective importance, their combined importance may be considerable and we shall review something of the net result.

Our discussion of population movement centers on two aspects of individual moving: (1) interstate movement, which will be analyzed largely in terms of regional population movements, and (2) movement from place to place which results in a change in the population size of one's place of residence. The time dimension embraced by our definition of a change in residence includes two points in each person's life history, the period in which "he was growing up" and "now" (1952 or 1956). The occurrence of moving is further pinpointed by some analyses of how long each person has lived in the community of present residence.[7]

Interregional Migration

The broadest class of political change—redistribution of the population with or without accompanying individual changes—will be discussed in terms of regional populations. The end result of all the moving to and fro that has gone on in the past half century or more finds about one out of every seven persons living in a region other than

TABLE 16-1. Regional Distribution of "Native Born"

	Present Residence				
	North-east	South	Mid-west	Far West	Total
Grew up in region	92%	92%	89%	52%	86%
Grew up in another region	8	8	11	48	14
	100%	100%	100%	100%	100%

[7] We will distinguish people who may have moved to their present home in the postwar period (having lived in the community ten years or less) from those who must have moved in earlier (because they have lived there for more than ten years). Between the time a person "was growing up" and "now" he may have lived in a dozen other states and in places of a dozen different sizes. This we do not know. We do know (1) where he grew up—by city size and by state, (2) where he now lives, and (3) how long he has lived there.

that in which he grew up. The proportion of native born in regional populations varies as shown in Table 16-1.[8]

Who are the movers? As a single gross category they are men who tend to be somewhat better educated and who have considerably better jobs and higher incomes than the natives of the regions they leave. As this syndrome of characteristics strongly suggests, for some of these people, geographical mobility is associated with upward social mobility —professional and business men on the make and on the move, leaving home territory for greener pastures. To go beyond such generalities we must examine some of the larger categories of movers.[9]

All told, there are probably as many patterns of regional movement as there are highways to carry the transients to their new homes. For our purposes, however, we shall be satisfied to examine three major groups: (1) people who have moved to the Far West, (2) those who have moved to the South, and (3) the remainder, those who have moved from the South or from a northern region into either the Midwest or the Northeast.

The necessary first consideration of our investigation must be an attempt to determine how different the *natives* of each region are—one group from another. By describing the native residents we can develop some idea of the extent to which movers are unique or atypical persons in terms of their region of origin; and we may learn something of the extent to which their movement reshapes the political outlines of their newly adopted regional homes. To the first query the simple answer is that in two regions, the Northeast and Midwest, the native-born-and-bred residents are amazingly similar to each other and are markedly different from their counterparts in the South and the Far West. The following summary indicates some of those characteristics that distinguish the four regional core groups:

Native *Westerners* are slightly younger and somewhat better educated but with nationally "average" incomes and occupation status. They are

[8] The only difference as large as one percentage point between these data from the 1952 and 1956 Survey Research Center national samples and the 1950 Census data on region of present residence and birth lies in the fact that the more recent survey data reflect the continued influx into the Far West. They show only 52 per cent native born instead of the 57 per cent reported by the 1950 Census.

[9] Even though almost 30 per cent of all Negroes have moved to a new home in a new region, they are too few in absolute numbers in our sample data to analyze within these categories. Consequently, Negroes have been excluded from the general investigation of regional movement and will be considered separately at the end of the discussion. Unless specifically noted, the following discussion pertains only to native born Whites.

more Democratic in affiliation and vote than are other people living outside the South, even though considerably less so than Southerners.

Southerners are the least well-educated and have considerably lower incomes than any other regional group. They vote less but are, of course, the most heavily pro-Democratic in both party identification and vote. Moreover, the South contains fewer Independents, and where the other groups report a small but uniform change in party identification away from the Democratic Party, Southerners (in 1952 and 1956) reported less gross change and (along with native Westerners) almost no net gain for the Republican Party.

The residents of the Northeast and Midwest are very much alike, but *Northeasterners* have higher family incomes and are slightly more pro-Republican in their party identification and in their traditional voting habits.

The West and how it grew. Half of all the people who have moved to a region other than that in which they grew up have moved to the Far West. There, in turn, they constitute almost half of the total population of that region. They constitute a prime example of a massive redistribution of the population, and they provide us with a considerable potential for observing important political implications in population movements.[10]

Our analysis allows us to identify two streams of westward migration, one from the South and the other from the North. Working within these broad classifications we are tempted to conclude that persons who have moved West have the characteristics of their region of nativity—only more so. A summary view of the contribution of population movement to the formation of the Western electorate is provided by Table 16-2.

Northerners who have moved West are relatively well educated (28 per cent have attended college) and they tend to hold white-collar jobs. They show a Democratic majority in their party affiliations and they vote with about the same diligence as their former neighbors in the Midwest and Northeast. There are at least two interesting points of political difference, however, between the movers and those they left behind. The movers' affinity for the Republicans nearly equals that of the other Northerners, but it does not depend on any pro-Republican advantage resulting from changes of party identification. This stands in contrast to the quite visible pro-Republican change reported by the natives of their home regions. The implication is, of course, that at sometime past these movers were markedly *more* pro-Republican than their former associates, who have since caught up

[10] For a brief historical review of this movement see V. O. Key, Jr., *American State Politics* (Alfred A. Knopf and Co., New York, 1956), Chapter 8, especially p. 219.

TABLE 16-2. Political and Social Characteristics of Three Components of the Western Electorate, 1952–1956

	Native Westerners	Northern Migrants	Southern Migrants	Total Western Population
Per cent Democratic of two-party presidential vote, 1952 and 1956	40	27	60	38
Per cent who voted in 1952 and 1956	81	78	69	79
Party identification				
Per cent Democratic	45	39	57	45
Per cent Republican	26	34	20	28
Per cent party identifiers who have never changed parties	82	80	79	81
Per cent who always vote				
Democratic	39	28	53	33
Republican	18	26	12	21
Age				
Per cent 21–35	31	20	17	26
Per cent over 65	11	21	15	15
Education				
Per cent grade school only	26	30	36	29
Per cent college	22	28	14	22
Income				
Per cent under $4000	43	47	46	44
Per cent over $6000	21	18	14	19
Occupation				
Per cent manual-blue collar	43	33	46	40
Per cent professional and business	25	28	18	24
Number of cases	(307)	(202)	(79)	(588)
Proportion of Western Population	52%	34	14	100%

with them. The second difference lies in their presidential votes of 1952 and 1956. The movers gave Mr. Eisenhower almost 75 per cent of their votes in these two elections—significantly more than the Republican proportion cast by those they left behind.

It is evident that this Northern migration to the West has meant the introduction of a relatively heavily Republican population into a region dominated by sentiments that were much more pro-Democratic. There is little evidence, however, that the incoming Republicans have been converted or softened in their Republicanism. Instead, their contribution to Western politics would seem to be more that of minimizing political differences between the Far West and the other Northern regions. They constitute a third of the Western population, and without them the Democrats hypothetically would outnumber the Republicans by more than 2 to 1 in the eleven Western States.

The second stream of Western migration, that from the South, constitutes about 14 per cent of the total Western population. (Northern migrants contribute 34 per cent of the total.) Both groups of western immigrants are considerably older than any other group of movers or non-movers we shall examine.[11] Despite the age of the Southern migrants, their educational attainments are about the same as those of the Southern non-mover. However, they are somewhat lower than the average for the North, and markedly below the educational background of other migrants to the West. Although the income level of the Southern migrants is equivalent to that of the Northern migrants (and above that of the native South), their average occupational status is very low—lower than that of the South generally and much lower than that of their fellow migrants.

If these former Southerners now differ somewhat in socio-economic terms from the people still living in the South, they have retained a major part of the Southern pattern of political behavior. Their voting rate is low, only two-thirds voted in 1952 and 1956, and the vote that is cast is very strongly Democratic. Where native Southerners reported an average vote of some 56 per cent for Mr. Stevenson in 1952 and 1956, the Southerners in the West reported that 60 per cent of their votes had been cast for him—a truly remarkable record in those years of Mr. Eisenhower's dominance. Although they followed the national pattern in reporting a diminution of Democratic Party identification over the years, they still ranked only slightly behind the South in their continuing Democratic allegiances.

Thus, in their political behavior the former Southerners provide a marked contrast to the other newcomers to the West in the extremity of their Democratic predispositions. Moreover, as with the Northern migrants to the West, four out of five party identifiers among the Southern migrants report no change in party identification, and their

[11] Limitations of sample size prevent an intensive study of those who moved West at different points in time. Such data as are available indicate that the relatively advanced age of Southern migrants to the West is *not* a direct function of the time of moving. Those who moved before or during World War II appear to be slightly older than the native Western population, but younger than the more recent Western immigrants from the South.

reported Democratic partisanship does not depart substantially from that of the Southerners who had not ventured from home. Finally, although their report of prior regularity in party support at the polls did indicate a somewhat lower level of Democratic devotion than reported by the native Southerner, the presidential vote of the Southerners in the West both in 1952 and 1956 more than reflected the Democratic sentiments of their region of origin.[12]

In short, the movement of an extremely Democratic group into a *relatively* more Republican environment appears to have resulted in virtually no individual change or dilution of Democratic allegiances. The North-to-West movement brought a relatively Republican group into a relatively more pro-Democratic region where they remained as Republicans and, in like manner, showed little sign of political acculturation. Both movements contribute a significant portion of the political complexion of the Far West. Both must be described primarily as a redistribution of partisans and participants. The absence of the Northern emigrant would leave Western politics nearly as strongly Democratic as the politics of the Solid South. Their presence, however, gives the West an electorate that is to some extent an amalgam of North and South. With party identification as the vehicle for transmission of hereditary loyalties, it is not surprising to find transplanted partisans confounding some of the traditions of non-partisanship once so strong in the coastal states.

Movement to the South. Northerners moving to the South are the second major category we shall discuss. Though a relatively small group, less than 2 per cent of the total White population and slightly less than 10 per cent of the Southern Whites, they are worth describing because of their possible strategic contribution to American politics. These migrants are also of interest because they are, in fact, quite different from the usual description of the Yankee who has gone South. In the first place they are not merely Northerners who have retired and moved to the sunny climes. They boast a very high current average income—certainly not merely the annuities of pensioners from the North—and two of every five are presently engaged in a professional or business career. A third have attended college and nine out of ten have at least some high school education.

As one might expect, their political predispositions do not strongly

[12] Insofar as the data reflect an enduring Republican partisanship for some few Southern migrants to the West, we are probably observing the consequence of including Border states in our regional definition of the South. The absence of a pro-Republican change in their party identifications may, however, be the result of the strong pro-Democratic climate into which they presumably moved.

favor the Democratic Party—they divide about equally between Democratic and Republican allegiance—and their reports of changing party identification do not indicate they are succumbing to the appeals of Southern Democracy. In 1952 and 1956 they resembled Northern migrants to the Far West as they cast over two thirds of their votes for Mr. Eisenhower. However, their contribution to the Republican effort in the South was limited not only by their restricted numbers but also by a modest rate of voting—only 68 per cent voted despite socioeconomic characteristics that would suggest a much higher rate.

The long-term significance of this movement of Northerners into the South is not readily assessed. There are many imponderables that will eventually determine that significance—the development of effective Republican organizations, the active participation of these Northerners in Southern politics, and the national ebb and flow of partisan fortunes, among others. These migrants would seem to possess considerable potential to influence Southern politics. Above all other groups in our population analysis they feel themselves to be politically effective. They also appear to possess an unusually well organized set of political attitudes, showing more partisan consistency in their appraisal of national political objects than does any other group. Finally, they show little sign of being changed themselves by the environment around them. They report a change in party identification no more frequently than does the rest of the nation, and the changes they do report follow the national mode *away from the Democratic Party,* not to it.

The invasion of the North. The third and last stream of regional population movement which we shall consider is composed of persons moving into the Midwest or Northeast. As with the case of the Far West, this immigration has two distinct parts, one from the South and the other consisting of movement within the North itself. The two parts are polar opposites on almost every social, economic, and political dimension we have considered. The Southern White migrants, a minuscule 4 per cent of the Northern population, are young (40 per cent under 35), poorly educated (40 per cent have not gone beyond grade school), and tend to hold low status jobs (60 per cent are blue collar). Nevertheless, their sense of personal political effectiveness compares favorably with all but one or two of our groups, and their level of participation apparently reflects their Northern environment. Their turnout rate is well above that of the other Southerners we have examined—72 per cent voted in 1952 and 1956. They predictably reflect their Southern origin in the Democratic nature of their party identifications and in their vote for President.

On the other hand, the Northerners who have moved from one northern region to another are not particularly young. This group, constituting slightly more than two per cent of the northern population, is well educated; over half of them are business and professional people and they report an extremely high average family income. As fits the stereotype of people with such social and economic characteristics they are heavily pro-Republican in their political sentiments. Only 25 per cent call themselves Democrats while 52 per cent identify themselves with the Republican Party. A share of this Republican predominance is apparently of relatively recent origin in that some 18 per cent describe themselves as *former* Democrats, whereas only 7 per cent report they have left the Republican ranks. The members of this category of movers are highly motivated as citizens and manifest their sense of great political effectiveness as 89 per cent voted for President in 1952 and 1956. They voted three to one for Eisenhower.

The two groups that compose the Northern immigration are of interest because of the extreme differences between them. They do not, however, give us any new insights into the impact of moving on the politics of the movers. And, contrary to the situation in the Far West, these migrants comprise such a small portion of the electorates they join as to accomplish little in the way of an immediate reshaping of the regional politics in their new homes.

Negro migration from the South. A quite different impact on local, regional, and national politics has resulted from the migration of Southern Negroes. We may first note that the attention given to the growing Negro vote in the North reflects the visibility and strategic location of that vote rather than its size alone. Even though the proportion of Negroes who have moved from one region to another is double the proportion of Whites who have changed regions (29 per cent of all Negroes against 13 per cent of all Whites), Negroes still constitute but one fifth of all such movement. In absolute numbers the Negroes who have moved North are almost equalled by the Northern Whites who have moved South.

The social and economic characteristics of the migrant Negro provide an insightful commentary on the contemporary nature of the American dilemma. Compared to Southern Negroes who *have not* left the region, the immigrants now in the North are of about the same age, but they have received more years of formal education. They do not on the average hold higher status jobs, but their average income is much higher. Some 35 per cent report a family income of over $4000, whereas only 6 per cent of the Southern Negroes give a similar report. In both the North and the South the non-farming Negro is a blue-collar worker in more than seven out of ten cases; he is a white-collar man in only one out of ten. The better education of the Northern Negro is thus likely to be associated with a much higher income—but not necessarily with a substantially higher occupational status.

Historically the Southern Negro has been described as Republican, and since the days of the New Deal, at least, the Northern Negro has been thought to be staunchly Democratic. In comparison to White Southerners, the native Negro is more often a Republican and less often a Democrat. This does not mean that the typical Southern Negro described himself as a Republican in the middle of the twentieth century. Far from it. In 1952 and 1956 three out of every four Southern Negroes who claimed a partisan allegiance described themselves as Democrats rather than as Republicans. And those who did vote, voted just as heavily for the Democratic candidate as did the Southern White. Moreover, the *ratio* of Democratic to Republican Party identification was *just* as high among Southern Negroes as among Negro migrants to the North. Nevertheless, some contrast with the Negro who had moved North was still evident. If half the Southern Negroes voted Democratic, over three fourths of the Northern migrants did so. And where three out of ten Southern Negro voters reported a traditional Republican vote, less than one in ten in the North gave a similar report. The sharpest contrast was provided, of course, in the extent of participation. Only one in six Southern Negroes reported a vote in 1952 and 1956 whereas four in six immigrants in the North reported voting. The greater political involvement of Northern Negroes was also evident on a number of attitudinal dimensions such as sense of personal political effectiveness and range of attention to national political events and objects.

The contrasts and similarities between movers and non-movers among southern-born Negroes become quite understandable when viewed in relation to the characteristics of Negroes who have lived all of their lives in the North. When the three groups of Negroes are compared, it is apparent that the natives of the two regions represent social, economic, and political extremes. The emigrants to the North occupy a position suggestive of partial but not complete transition from one subculture to the other. For example, native Northerners and immigrant Northerners voted at the same rate; but the immigrants supported their vote with less confidence in their own political effectiveness than did the natives. They had come a long way from the political fatalism of the native Southern Negro, exhibiting differences too large to be explained by their somewhat better education. As Table 16-3 indicates, in some respects their political partisanship stands at mid-passage between the extreme homogeneity of the native Northerner and the visibly less uniform commitments in the South.

TABLE 16-3. Relation of Regional Movement of Negroes to their Political Characteristics, 1952–1956

	Southern-Born Southern Residents	Southern-Born Northern Residents	Northern-Born Northern Residents
Party identification			
Per cent Democratic	46	61	49
Per cent Republican	14	19	12
Vote			
Per cent Democratic of two-party vote in 1952 and 1956	55	77	82
Usual vote			
Per cent Democratic	17	55	55
Per cent Republican	7	5	3
Political efficacy			
Per cent high	8	17	34
Per cent low	71	47	26
Motivational level			
Per cent high	4	17	14
Per cent low	16	16	9
Per cent voted in 1952 and 1956	16	64	66
Number of cases	(186)	(77)	(47)

Our inspection of four categories of travelers has provided evidence relating population movement to individual political change. Three of the four categories contain very few individuals who have changed to conform to their new environment. Northerners moving west and south and White Southerners moving west have retained or accentuated the distinctions that set them apart from their new neighbors. Only Southern Negroes moving north have showed any tendency to shed some of their traditional attitudes and thereby become more like their new associates and less like those who remained behind.

Urbanization, Suburbanization and Political Change

In this era of urbanization it may come as something of a surprise to note that some 21 per cent of the total population has moved away from the city or away from larger towns and cities to smaller ones than those in which the movers grew up.[13] At the same time, as indicated in

TABLE 16-4. Relation of Place of Residence "When Growing Up" to Present Place of Residence, 1956

	Place Where Grew Up		
Present Residence, 1956	Metropolitan Center	City or Town	Rural Area or Farm
Metropolitan center	13[a]	9	7
City or town	6	19	14
Rural area or farm	4	11	17

[a] Entry is proportion of total population.

Table 16-4, three out of five persons who have moved to a residence in a different population density category have moved into more densely populated centers.

[13] A full and systematic analysis of rural-to-urban and urban-to-rural population movement would necessitate consideration of at least as many types of movement as confronted us in our review of regional movement. As in that situation, however, the availability of data limits our exploration to those categories of the population large enough to constitute a substantial element in a national sample. One further and important simplification comes from our inspection of the data; we shall not treat suburban areas as a special population category.

There are several reasons for this omission of special treatment of the suburbs. First, when we proceed with a comparison of persons who were brought up in metropolitan central city areas but have now moved to less densely populated places, we cannot discern any substantial empirical differences between the subgroupings that are identified in our data. Persons who have moved from the central city to the suburbs look just like persons who have moved to non-suburban cities or to small hamlets and places of residence in the open country. Empirically, we have no evidence to indicate that major social or economic or political differences exist among these various kinds of movers from the metropolitan centers; and a discussion of them would, at best, be compelled to point out a lengthy series of similarities. Second, the nature of our data does not allow us to investigate the many smaller categories subsumed under the single heading, "suburb." Undoubtedly part of our failure to note unique characteristics of suburban political behavior must be traced to the fact that we are not able to distinguish the residents of a Levittown-type suburb from those in a Park Forest or a Redwood City from a Marin County. We can only describe as one group the residents of the heterogeneous category of places that share the general character of being suburban areas. This means, of course, that we cannot accommodate in our analysis the crucially important qualitative differences among types of suburban communities. Finally, much of our interest in the movement of peoples is directed at the broad implications which that movement

Some aspects of the rural-urban movement are closely tied to the interregional movement that we examined earlier. We find, for example, that a large fraction of the urban-to-rural movement has taken place among people who are life-long residents of the Northeast. In that area twice as many, 26 per cent to 13 per cent, have moved to places less urban as have moved to places more urban. Similar percentages apply to the North-to-South migrants. Almost half of these regional movers have moved to places of residence less urban, and only a fourth have moved into areas more densely populated than those where they lived when growing up. On the other hand we have the South-to-North movers. Some 56 per cent of them have moved into places of residence more urban whereas only 17 per cent have moved into communities that are less urban. A similar pattern may be noted among lifelong residents of the Midwest, where a third of the people now live in more highly urbanized communities and only a sixth have moved to places less urban. Among the other groups of regional movers and non-movers, a 4–3 ratio of more urban to less urban movement is generally maintained.

The difference between these major patterns of movement is also related to the point in recent history in which the moves took place. Over half of the people who moved into more highly urban areas moved there before the Second World War, and over half of those who moved to communities less urban moved there *after* the war.

Social mobility and political change. The voters who have deserted the metropolitan centers in favor of suburbia have drawn much comment from the political commentators and analysts. One favorite theme has held that this change in residence is an indicator of upward social mobility and has been accompanied by a change in politics that has seen Democrats turned into Republicans. We shall not attempt to verify or deny this thesis as it applies to particular suburbs or even to the categories of suburbs in which this phenomenon has been reported. We will, however, move directly to a confrontation of the hypothesis that upward social mobility, outward geographical mobility away from the metropolitan center, and a turn away from Democracy

has for political change. In this chapter, as elsewhere in the book, we are primarily interested in the delineation of the more general relationships that tied the world of politics to the other elements of social life. Of course, we strive wherever possible to discover how pervasive these generalizations may be—do they apply to all segments of the electorate or are they present some places but absent in others? Nevertheless, our failure to make such tests of all possible contingencies does not jeopardize the basic validity of the conclusions drawn, and the generalizations do provide an important base line and perspective for the eventual application and testing of the general conclusion in the more particularized situations of interest.

to Republicanism are interrelated. It may be noted in passing that this analysis is a story with a more general moral as its conclusion. It illustrates how more appropriate data may affirm the accuracy of observations based on less appropriate data while at the same time disclosing a basic fallacy in the conclusions drawn from those observations.[14]

In line with other studies, we shall indicate that many of the emigrants from big city living occupy the top rung of the social and economic ladder. They tend to be well-educated members of well-to-do families of professional people and businessmen. They are more often than not Republicans, and they reflected this in their voting in 1956.

A full analysis of the problem, however, does not support the simple thesis that upward social mobility has led to a Republican surge among these ex-city dwellers. The first data to indicate a flaw in the theory concern the widespread occurrence of social mobility. Whether defined by occupational status or subjective social class affiliation, and whether described in terms of intergenerational movement or by the intragenerational mobility of the individual, upward social mobility is shared in identical measure among all of the relevant population groupings. Table 16-5, utilizing one important aspect of mobility—intergenerational change in social class—illustrates how mobility cuts uniformly across all population categories except for those involving persons who grew up on farms. The upward social mobility of the former urbanites is fully matched by that of the folk they left behind, as well as by all other groups of non-rural origin.

The data in Table 16-5 are based on the citizen's classification of himself as a member of one of the major social classes and on his judgment concerning the social class of his parents. A quite independent measure of the same phenomenon may be constructed from relevant information about occupations of the two generations. When detailed data on the occupational status of the citizen's present family head and that of the citizen's father are compared we observe exactly the same thing noted concerning subjective class identification. There are virtually no differences in intergenerational occupational mobility among persons raised in towns or metropolitan centers.

The same general conclusion may also be derived from data pertaining to intragenerational occupational changes. As Table 16-6 indi-

[14] All of the following data and the discussion they support refer only to native-born Northern Whites. Non-Whites and Southern residents deserve similar attention, but the available data are not adequate to do more than indicate the necessity for dealing separately with the three groups.

TABLE 16-5. Intergenerational Change in Subjective Social Class, 1956

<table>
<tr><th></th><th colspan="3">Place Where Grew Up</th></tr>
<tr><th>Present Residence</th><th>Metropolitan Center</th><th>City or Town</th><th>Rural Area or Farm</th></tr>
<tr><td>Metropolitan center</td><td>+8[a]</td><td>+8</td><td>+3</td></tr>
<tr><td>City or town</td><td rowspan="2">+8</td><td>+9</td><td>−1</td></tr>
<tr><td>Rural area or farm</td><td>+9</td><td>+1</td></tr>
</table>

[a] Entry is per cent who classify themselves as Middle Class minus per cent who classify their parents as Middle Class. +Indicates upward mobility.

cates, again with the exception of people of rural origins who now live in the metropolis, the extent of individual upward mobility is virtually identical among all groupings. Thus, even before turning our attention to questions of stability and change in political partisanship, it is apparent that any *differences* among the population groups in their movements away from the Democrats or to the Republican fold cannot be explained by differences in the incidence of upward social mobility.

TABLE 16-6. Intragenerational Occupational Mobility, 1956

<table>
<tr><th></th><th colspan="3">Place Where Grew Up</th></tr>
<tr><th>Present Residence</th><th>Metropolitan Center</th><th>City or Town</th><th>Rural Area or Farm</th></tr>
<tr><td>Metropolitan center</td><td>4.5[a]</td><td>4.7</td><td>3.8</td></tr>
<tr><td>City or town</td><td rowspan="2">4.7</td><td>4.8</td><td>4.5</td></tr>
<tr><td>Rural area or farm</td><td>4.9</td><td>4.8</td></tr>
</table>

[a] Entry is mean for the group. A mean of 4.0 would indicate no net movement upward or downward for the group; a score of 4.0+ indicates a preponderance of upward mobility, a score of less than 4.0 suggests net downward mobility. Inasmuch as the status ranking of farmers is most difficult to ascertain, the scores in the right-hand column should be treated with some reservations.

The second relevant datum in this analysis concerns change in political partisanship. Our most direct indicator of this is the citizen's report of change in his own sense of partisan identification. Although the picture of change in party identification is not as uniform across all groups as was the pattern of intragenerational occupational mobility, it is so uniform as to undercut decisively the hypothesis that we are testing. Table 16-7 shows that former metropolitan residents have indeed moved away from the Democrats and toward the Republicans in their party loyalties. A total net shift of 16 percentage points in their partisan division has been recorded in this group (inferentially from a possible earlier division of something like 40 Democratic–30 Independent–30 Republican to the present 32 Democratic–30 Independent–38 Republican, from a 10-point Democratic margin to the present 6-point Republican margin). The table discloses, too, a 12-point shift in the same direction on the part of lifelong metropolitan residents. A Democratic to Republican switch by 2 per cent of the former metropolitan dwellers, or an Independent to Republican movement by 4 per cent, would account for all of the difference we observe between the two groups. This scarcely can be taken as evidence that the trend toward Republicanism is significantly greater on the part of the émigrés from the big city.

TABLE 16-7. Changes in Party Identification, 1956

	Place Where Grew Up		
Present Residence	Metropolitan Center	City or Town	Rural Area or Farm
Metropolitan center	−12[a]	−5	−9
City or town	−16	−3	−8
Rural area or farm	(−16, bracketed with city or town)	−10	+1

[a] Entry is per cent who classify themselves as former Republicans minus per cent who classify themselves as former Democrats. The minus sign indicates that changes away from Democratic identification were more frequent than changes away from Republican identification.

The further implication that upward social mobility is, in general, *not* associated with changes in party identification away from the Democratic Party may be tested directly. As Table 16-8 indicates, even among the people who report both a change in partisanship and a change in their own occupational status there is no suggestion of a relationship between the two kinds of change.[15]

[15] Similarly, when we compare the occupational status of our respondents with that of their parents we find very little evidence that upward or downward changes in

If the validity of these data is granted, the logic of the argument follows quite readily. The hypothesis is that upward social mobility among émigrés from the metropolis has been accompanied by conversion to Republicanism. The implication has been that movement

TABLE 16-8. Relation of Reported Changes in Own Occupational Status to Changes in Self-Identification with Parties, 1956

	Occupational Mobility	
	Down	Up
Changes in party identification		
From Republican to Democratic	28%	24%
From Republican to Independent	8	12
From Democratic to Independent	32	29
From Democratic to Republican	32	35
	100%	100%
Number of cases	47	121

out from the city is associated with upward social mobility, whereas retention of a central city address means either downward mobility or at least an absence of change in social status. It appears, to the contrary, that upward social mobility has been experienced every bit as often by the non-movers as by those who have traded convenience for space, and it is associated equally in both groups with pro-Republican changes in political partisanship. Moreover, the absence of a really unique change in political allegiance among ex-urbanites further indicates that movement out of the metropolitan centers cannot stand as the factor responsible for change in partisan loyalties that cut across non-movers as well.

We may speculate that the visibility of suburban politics has been responsible for explanations of political behavior that now must be qualified. The mushrooming colonies of former big city dwellers are

status from one generation to the next are associated with shifts toward the Republican or Democratic Party. Upward mobile people are slightly more likely to have shifted from Democratic to Republican identification than those people whose status has moved downward, but both types of status-changers are much more likely to have moved toward the Republican Party than away from it. Their changes in status appear to have very little relationship to their changes in partisanship.

indeed properly described as containing a great many Republicans, many former Democrats, and many upwardly mobile residents. What has been missed are the similar movements away from the Democratic Party and upward on the social scale that have gone on, quite independently, in the less visible homes of the old central city areas as well. Moreover, without actual knowledge about the political histories of the former urbanites, the extent of their traditional Republicanism could not be determined. With our reports of their own past behavior at the polls, we can now establish that much of their Republican sentiment is of extremely long duration, if not a matter of family heritage. The combination of a tradition of Republican sympathy and an "average" rate of defection on the part of the minority Democrats adds up, of course, to the formidable Republican strength that many of these communities brought to the political wars in the 1950's.

The metropolitan electorate—past and present. It would be possible to devote considerable time to the scrutiny of each of the population categories identified in Table 16-1. One result of such an examination is the conclusion that the most interesting groups are those that either now or at some earlier time composed the metropolitan electorate. Two groupings in particular stand out: one comprised of persons who grew up in a major city but have since moved to smaller cities or towns or to homes in the country; the other consisting of persons who were raised in rural hamlets or on farms and who have now become central city residents of a major metropolis. These two groups stand at the polar extremes among the array of population groupings with regard to almost every social and economic characteristic. We may note in Table 16-9 that the urban emigrants enjoy the highest occupational status, boast the most substantial family incomes, and are individually the most likely to have received a college education. At the other extreme the immigrants from the country are not well equipped in terms of formal education (only one out of two has gone beyond grade school), and a generally low occupational status is reflected in the low proportion whose families had incomes in excess of $6000 in 1956.

On each count, the native of the metropolis stands roughly midway between the extremes, sharing his position with former residents of towns and cities. But when we turn to a study of the clearly political variables, this order among sometime metropolitan residents changes rather drastically.

Emigrants from the metropolis and migrants to it are arrayed in almost identical fashions on the party identification continuum (Table 16-10 II, page 463). Despite great differences in their social origins, the

TABLE 16-9. Social and Economic Characteristics of Population Groups, 1956

I. Occupational Status

	Place Where Grew Up		
Present Residence	Metropolitan Center	City or Town	Rural Area or Farm
Metropolitan center	4.7[a]	4.6	3.7
City or town	5.5	4.7	4.4
Rural area or farm		4.9	4.9

[a] Entry is the mean for the group, based on a status ranking of the occupations of the head of the household. The following graph shows the status distribution for the two extreme groups, former metropolitan residents and present metropolitan residents who grew up in rural areas.

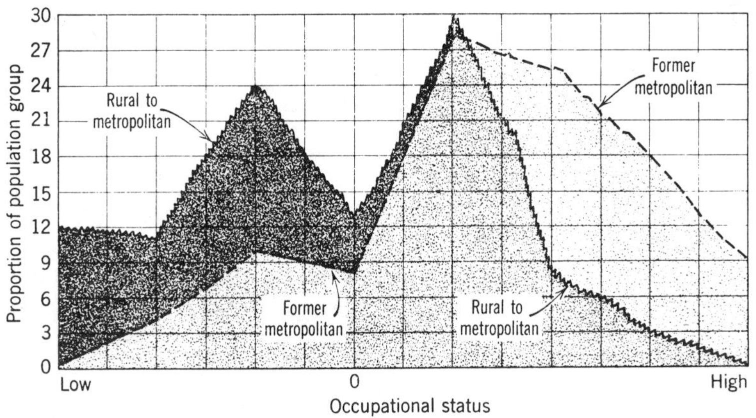

(*Table 16-9 continued next page*)

former big city dwellers and the onetime country folk are remarkably similar in the nature of their underlying partisan allegiances. Furthermore, members of both groups present a remembered history of almost unalloyed support for Republican presidential candidates. And their behavior in 1956 proved no exception. Only two groupings gave Mr. Eisenhower more support than did the former metropolitan dwellers, and one of those was the immigrants from the rural areas. The latter group—although socially and economically the most disadvantaged of the three components of the metropolitan electorate—gave Mr. Eisenhower almost four out of every five votes they cast.

TABLE 16-9 (*continued*)

II. *a.* Proportion with College Education

	Place Where Grew Up		
Present Residence	Metropolitan Center	City or Town	Rural Area or Farm
Metropolitan center	15	24	9
City or town	36	28	12
Rural area or farm		17	9

II. *b.* Proportion with Grade School Education Only

	Place Where Grew Up		
Present Residence	Metropolitan Center	City or Town	Rural Area or Farm
Metropolitan center	23	22	50
City or town	12	19	40
Rural area or farm		23	41

III. *a.* Proportion with Family Income Over $6000

	Place Where Grew Up		
Present Residence	Metropolitan Center	City or Town	Rural Area or Farm
Metropolitan center	46	38	14
City or town	54	34	19
Rural area or farm		42	20

III. *b.* Proportion with Family Income Under $4000

	Place Where Grew Up		
Present Residence	Metropolitan Center	City or Town	Rural Area or Farm
Metropolitan center	22	32	57
City or town	18	26	48
Rural area or farm		23	44

On the other hand, the lifelong inhabitants of the metropolitan centers constitute a sturdy core of Northern Democratic support. In 1956 they provided the strongest resistance to the Eisenhower sweep of the North. And even this was not commensurate with their predominant partisan loyalties. They are, as part II of Table 16-10 indicates, even more heavily Democratic in their division of party allegiances than the other two groups are Republican in theirs.

TABLE 16-10. Political Characteristics of Population Groups, 1956

I. 1956 Republican Vote for President

	Place Where Grew Up		
Present Residence	Metropolitan Center	City or Town	Rural Area or Farm
Metropolitan center	54[a]	61	78
City or town	67	67	66
Rural area or farm		76	57

[a] Entry is Republican proportion of the two-party vote among native-born Northern White voters.

II. *a*. Proportion Identified with Democratic Party

	Place Where Grew Up		
Present Residence	Metropolitan Center	City or Town	Rural Area or Farm
Metropolitan center	55	44	30
City or town	32	27	35
Rural area or farm		28	35

II. *b*. Proportion Identified with Republican Party

	Place Where Grew Up		
Present Residence	Metropolitan Center	City or Town	Rural Area or Farm
Metropolitan center	23	29	40
City or town	38	43	37
Rural area or farm		37	32

TABLE 16-10 (*continued*)

II. *c*. Voter Turnout in 1956 Presidential Election

Present Residence	Place Where Grew Up: Metropolitan Center	City or Town	Rural Area or Farm
Metropolitan center	88[a]	79	73
City or town	88	86	81
Rural area or farm		77	85

[a] Entry is proportion of group reporting a vote cast for president by native-born Northern White voters.

There are, nevertheless, some expected political manifestations of the social and economic characteristics of the three groups. These appear in the area of political participation. As the last part of Table 16-10 indicates, the onetime rural residents had the poorest record of turnout in 1956. The former members of the metropolitan electorate shared honors with the neighbors they left behind in demonstrating their civic virtue. The low turnout of former farmers reflects the agrarian political heritage described earlier. It is also consistent with their presently relatively low sense of political efficacy. At the same time, the migrant from metropolitan living was supported in his participation by a sense of efficacy commensurate with his objectively demonstrated ability to attain the higher goals among those valued by our society.

Residential mobility among Democrats and Republicans. Probably because they are *less* visible, people who have moved *into* the metropolitan centers have not been the object of extended scrutiny or comment. Nevertheless they are in some ways as unique as the urban-to-rural mover—and in their greater numbers (60 per cent greater than the number of outward movers) they constitute a category of considerable political importance. Before turning to a closer examination of these new members of the metropolitan electorate, we may draw attention to an interesting consequence of their Republican affiliation that we have already observed. When viewed in conjunction with the staunch Republicanism of the big city émigré, they complete a picture of a preponderantly Republican circulation through the metropolitan center.

One corollary of the exodus of Republicans from the metropolitan centers lies in the heavy Democratic preponderance among the metropolitan residents who do not move. If a third of the emigrants are Democrats, over half of the metropolitan-bred non-movers are Democrats. The striking extent of partisan differential in this movement out from the metropolitan center is highlighted by the discovery that 71 per cent of the Democrats raised in a metropolitan center still live there or in another similar central city area, whereas only 46 per cent of the metropolitan-bred Republicans have resisted the movement away from these central cities.

The influx of Republicans from rural areas has also produced a partisan differential, this time related to the origins of the present metropolitan electorate. Whereas 58 per cent of the present metropolitan Democrats grew up in a metropolitan center, only 41 per cent of the metropolitan Republicans have a similar point of origin.

The net result of the two streams of movement, in and out of the major metropolitan centers, apparently has been to leave the partisan balance within the metropolitan center almost unchanged. The Republican dominated in-migration has almost exactly offset the out-migration. Among all persons who grew up in the metropolis, the division in party identification is 47 per cent Democrats, 25 per cent Independents and 28 per cent Republicans; among the present residents of the same cities the division is 49 per cent Democrats, 24 per cent Independents and 27 per cent Republicans. But here the balancing out ends. Among Democrats who are sometime residents of a metropolitan center, 47 per cent are life-long residents (Table 16-11 I); among sometime metropolitan Republicans, only 28 per cent have spent their lives in a metropolitan home.

The definitive explanation of the greater residential stability of Democrats or the greater mobility of Republicans is not at hand. There are, however, two lines of speculation that may be suggested. In the first place, the Republican character of the movement into the metropolis seems quite reasonable. After all, the in-migrants come from farms, villages, towns, and smaller cities. The preponderance of Republican sentiment in these places is well documented in voting statistics as well as in Table 16-10. Only if some further confounding set of factors made non-metropolitan *Democrats,* rather than Republicans, *more* likely to move to the metropolis would we find Democrats heavily represented among the newcomers to the metropolitan electorate. As it is, knowing the immigrants to be predominantly Republican and knowing their places of origin to be populated largely by Republicans, we can satisfactorily conclude that there is nothing very extraordinary in the partisan division of the newcomers.

TABLE 16-11. Present Residence and Origin of Sometime Metropolitan Residents, by Party, 1956

I. Democrats

	Place Where Grew Up	
	Metropolitan	Elsewhere
Now live in metropolitan center	47% (109)	34% (78)
Now live elsewhere	19% (45)	

II. Independents

	Place Where Grew Up	
	Metropolitan	Elsewhere
Now live in metropolitan center	32% (52)	38% (50)
Now live elsewhere	30% (40)	

III. Republicans

	Place Where Grew Up	
	Metropolitan	Elsewhere
Now live in metropolitan center	28% (43)	40% (61)
Now live elsewhere	32% (50)	

To the extent that this argument is persuasive, the explanation of party differences among big city emigrants is made more difficult. Despite a sometime Democratic-Republican division of 47–28 in the metropolitan electorate, the emigrants divide 33–37 in favor of Republican identifications. This situation occurs because, as we have noted, 53 per cent of the sometime metropolitan Republicans have moved out, whereas only 29 per cent of their Democratic counterparts have left for less crowded surroundings. But why the difference between 53 per cent and 29 per cent?[16]

The data pertaining to intergenerational occupational mobility suggest a promising line of speculation and future inquiry. Among persons whose occupational status is lower than that of their father's there are no party differences in the frequency of movement away from the big city. But among persons who have achieved upward mobility and have exceeded their father's occupational status, the differences are striking indeed. Among Democrats the proportion of non-movers is 76 per cent (N = 62); among Republicans the same proportion is only 37 per cent (N = 40). Moreover, comparing the upward mobile with the downward, upward mobility *increases* the proportion of non-moving Democrats, from 66 per cent to 76 per cent. Upward mobility among Republicans decreases non-moving or, stated positively, increases the frequency of movement out. Where only 37 per cent of the downward mobile Republicans move out, a full 63 per cent of the upward mobile follow the trail to suburbia, exurbia and beyond.[17]

In the absence of needed data we can only speculate about the meaning of these discrepancies in partisan response to intergenerational mobility. It seems likely that fairly basic differences in social values are involved. It may be that the Republicans, despite their own metropolitan origins, are more often linked through enduring family ties to ancestral beginnings in small cities, towns, and on farms. Although at least one generation removed, they may reflect the consequences of an earlier era of urbanization and central city growth. With a heritage of values and traditions congenial to non-metropolitan life they may seize the opportunity created by occupational success and escape from the metropolis. The urban Democrat, on the other hand, may be the child of a thoroughly urban culture. Whether the metropolis of his family line once was Warsaw or Rome or Dublin, or Boston, Baltimore, or New York, he may accept more often the way of life of the metropolitan center. For him occupational success may provide the means to exploit and enjoy the treasures of the city, not freedom to leave the familiar for the unknown.

[16] The difference does not appear to be a function of financial ability to move. Indeed, there is a tendency for the difference to be accentuated among higher income families where freedom to move is least limited by such factors.

[17] Intragenerational mobility does not appear to be at all related to change of residence for Republicans, although it is related to Democratic movement. Among Independents, both intergenerational and intragenerational mobility are sharply related to changes in residence. In all instances upward mobility is associated with movement away from the metropolitan center.

Changing electorates. The greater residential mobility of Republicans, in the setting of metropolitan politics, is in itself of considerable interest. But the implications are even more intriguing when we recall the greatly different social and economic characteristics of people who move into and out of the metropolitan centers. In aggregate group characteristics these two groups are similar politically but dissimilar on other dimensions. It remains for us to discover the extent to which the dissimilarities are particularly true of the Republicans (or the Democrats) in each group or the extent to which they cut across all political comparisons that we might make.

We are, of course, interested in the social and economic comparisons because they will indicate the extent to which the "circulation" of partisans out of and into the city changes the clientele to which each party must appeal. Toward this end we will present three sets of data for each social or economic characteristic. We will use the life-long metropolitan residents as a basis for evaluating the character of movement in each direction; this evaluation will be the object of the first two sets of data. The third set will show the net result accruing because of the movement within each category of party identification; that is, between Democrats who have moved out compared to Democrats who have moved in. Let us consider education as the first social characteristic of interest and let us first compare movers with non-movers. People who have moved *out* of the central city are better educated than those who stayed behind. The extent to which this is true is reflected by the following measure of *differences in education level* within each partisan group:

Emigrants compared to non-movers among:

Democrats	+18 ⟶	(18% more with college education among emigrants, or 18% more with grade school education among life-long residents)
Independents	+28	
Republicans	+32	

People who have moved *into* the central city also differ from those already there, but they do so by virtue of being *less* well educated. The differences within each of these groups of partisans are:

Immigrants compared to non-movers among:

Democrats	−5
Independents	−11
Republicans	−30

If outgoing Democrats were *better* educated than non-movers by a mean difference of +18, and if incoming Democrats were *less well* educated than non-movers to the extent of a difference of −5, the net difference between those moving in contrasted with those moving out is −23. For Independents, the difference in educational level is somewhat greater, expressed by a difference score of −39. For Republicans, the difference amounts to −62. The comparable data pertaining to income are as follows:

Emigrants compared to non-movers on family income:

Democrats	+6	⟶ (6% more with income over $6000
Independents	+31	*or* 6% fewer with incomes under $4000)
Republicans	+9	

Immigrants compared to non-movers:

Democrats	−28
Independents	−20
Republicans	−58

Net difference between movers, immigrants compared to emigrants:

Democrats	−34
Independents	−51
Republicans	−67

As far as the background variables of education and income are concerned, the differences between incoming and outgoing citizens are greatest among Republicans and least among Democrats. The same is true with regard to the occupation of those citizens in the labor force. The following data refer to differences in proportions of white-collar jobs in each pair of groups:

Emigrants compared to non-movers:

Democrats	−5	⟶ (5% fewer in white-collar jobs among
Independents	+30	emigrants than among non-movers)
Republicans	+25	

Immigrants compared to non-movers:

Democrats	−15
Independents	+10
Republicans	−10

Net difference between movers, immigrants compared to emigrants:

Democrats	−10
Independents	−20
Republicans	−35

Much the same picture is presented by data pertaining to the citizen's subjective social class position. There is virtually no difference between incoming and outgoing Democrats, the former include only 5 per cent fewer middle class people. Incoming Independents include 26 per cent fewer middle class persons than do Independents who have moved from the metropolis; the comparable difference among Republicans is 23 per cent fewer among immigrants than among emigrants.

Some of the consequences of the parade into and out of the metropolis are by now apparent. The movement involves Republicans more often than Democrats, and the social and economic differences between the pairs of Republicans are far more extreme than are those for comparable Democratic groups. It is fair to conclude that the nature of metropolitan Republicanism has changed rather dramatically during the recent decades. For example, instead of a one-time Republican metropolitan electorate composed of 35 per cent with some college education and only 18 per cent with no more than grade school behind them, metropolitan Republicans now have only 19 per cent with some college and a full 37 per cent with no more than grade school education. For Democrats the change has been from 11 per cent college and 20 per cent grade school to 11 per cent college and 27 per cent grade school. Among Republicans the change in occupational composition has been from 48 per cent white-collar to 29 per cent white-collar; among Democrats the change has been a much smaller decline, from 36 per cent to 32 per cent.[18]

For politician and analyst alike the influx of relatively low status Republicans in metropolitan politics suggests fascinating potentials for political change. Although we cannot further elaborate our investigation by a study of those movers who came into the city most recently, the data do indicate that the Republicans who have moved

[18] Some small part of the presumed one-time white-collar, metropolitan Republicans may in fact have become white-collar *after* leaving the city, but the differential rates of intragenerational occupational change are not great enough to explain all of the "old vs. new" difference on that basis. Moreover, the incoming Republicans are not younger than those who have left, and it seems unlikely that they will grow into the social and economic positions vacated by the emigrants. Finally, inasmuch as we are dealing with people over 21 years of age, it seems unlikely that the marked differences in education (which underlie much of occupational selection) were created by high status movers going to college *after* they left the city, and it is equally unlikely that the 50 per cent of the Republican immigrants who have no more than grade school education will raise their formal educational attainments in the future. In other words, although this argument is based on a partial reconstruction of former Republican and Democratic followers (ignoring losses due to death), it does not appear to rest on past or future changes in individuals' social and economic position so much as on the movement of very different groups of people into and out of the major party ranks in the big city.

into the metropolis from other areas are heavily concentrated among the recent movers. More specifically, most Democrats who have moved into the metropolitan center from elsewhere have been living in their present homes since before World War II.[19] Most of the incoming Republicans moved to their present residences after the War. Even assuming that these Republican newcomers may be unable to achieve complete insulation from the politics of their new neighbors, social integration (and the subsequent acceptance of community norms) appears to be a very slow process. It is a matter of critical significance for metropolitan politics, however, whether these Democratic influences may in time make themselves felt.

Our data, of course, record in 1956 only the expected manifestations of a Republican heritage supported by Republican Party identification. There were virtually no signs of an impending shift by the new metropolitan Republicans. However, we cannot overlook our other evidence of the way in which one's economic or social situation influences one's political outlook. Given the kinds of self-interest suggested by their position in the social structure and given the durable strength of the northern urban Democratic leadership and organizations, it would seem we have discovered in these new members of metropolitan Republicanism an acid test for the durability of party identification.

The last point to be made concerns the phenomenon of status polarization in politics. In preceding chapters we have analyzed in some detail the conditions that facilitate and inhibit polarization. Now, through our study of rural-metropolitan population movement, we have identified yet another facet of the problem. Viewed in terms of status polarization, the newcomers to metropolitan politics constitute a major unpolarized segment of the electorate. The Republican newcomers are not of sufficiently low status to reverse the direction of status polarization when placed next to the new Democrats. They are, instead, merely similar—so similar as to contribute a depressing effect on the level of polarization within the total metropolitan electorate. Moreover, the changing of polarization within the metropolitan centers has been furthered by the nature of the movement *away* from the cities. Among the former metropolitan residents polarization is considerably more pronounced than among the nonmovers, and, of course, much more accentuated than among the unpolarized newcomers. The three groups of sometime metropolitan dwellers thus display three distinctly different levels of polarization, ranging from high polarization among emigrants to no polarization among immigrants. And another consequence of population

19 The reader is reminded that this analysis excludes Negroes.

flow around the metropolitan center is thus observed in the reduction of polarization within the metropolitan electorate. The reduction has taken place, however, without necessary reference to class ideology, economic stress or any of the other elements that were identified earlier in the analytic delineation of the components of polarization. The redistribution of political partisans has again been of major importance, even in the absence of individual political change.

The Electoral Effects of Other Social Characteristics ◇ 17

In addition to the historical imprint of a region or the pressures of group interest that the voter reflects, other attributes he possesses as a member of the society contribute to an understanding of his political behavior. Most of the characteristics that we shall encounter in this chapter refer to sociological categories in the population rather than to self-conscious groups. They represent the elements of "life situation" that we took pains to cancel out of our calculation of group effects in Chapter 12. Being a Catholic or a labor union member locates the individual as part of a group conscious of itself as a group. We usually reserve the term "membership" for such location. Membership in this sense presumes shared orientations, group identifications, and some sense of common interest.

Simple location in a social category does not involve these characteristics. Persons fifty years old may differ in attitudes and behavior from those thirty years old. But we do not think of groups of fifty-year-olds or thirty-year-olds, which in some sense mediate these differences. Though an individual of a certain age is likely to associate intimately with people of the same age and be influenced by these associations, common age is not the focus of the relationship. It is not considered the reason for association, nor is there a sense of unity with unknown individuals of the same age in other parts of the country.

Of course, differences between the group and the category are relative. Just as social class at some times tends to form conscious membership groups and at other times represents no more than a location in the social structure, so may groups form around other social characteristics that ordinarily represent no more than categories. Some minor organizations, for example, are based self-consciously on age, and occasionally these groups become involved in political activity. The Townsend movement, centering in California during the Depression, had a program tailored largely to the economic problems of the retired and thereby created the essentials of a group from raw materials of a demographic category.

To the degree that a social attribute becomes the focus for a self-conscious group, the model for group influence set forth in Chapter 12 should be applicable. But the characteristics to be discussed here rarely constitute "real" groups for more than a minute fraction of the population. Therefore, the concept of group identification is largely irrelevant. Nevertheless, individuals who are located in a given category are likely to behave differently from those who fall in another category. We must consider the further types of intervening mechanisms that might lead to these differences. In most instances, such differences arise in one of two broad ways:

1. *As results of differential exposure to politically relevant experiences.* Social attributes tend to define certain unique experiences that people of given categories have undergone or are undergoing. To the degree that like experiences elicit like reactions, individuals with the same attributes may come to behave in the same fashion without any conscious reference to one another. People do not become alert to problems of pensions and fixed incomes until a certain age. But there are common elements to the pressures that people of this age bring to politics. The fact of similar pressures does not in itself guarantee similar partisan choice among older people; indeed, the guidance of dissatisfaction into a common partisan channel is one of the distinctive functions of the social group as political agent. But when cues available to the old are free of ambiguity—when it is clear that one party is a "hard money" party—distinctive behavior may appear in the aggregate without group mediation. Similarly, we have seen that certain biases in the responses of older people seem to flow from the fact that they all experienced the Depression at a critical period in their life history.

2. *Those differences based on socially defined roles.* In some cases cultural values exist that prescribe interests or behaviors for individuals belonging to specific social categories. These prescriptions may be more or less like group standards; they are distinguished by their diffuseness, their "assumed" quality. A woman need not take an interest in politics. Of course she does not need to conceal it if she is

politically informed. And yet, wives in our samples are quick to respond, on discovering that the subject of the interview is political, "Oh, you better wait and talk to my husband. He's the one who keeps track of those things." In sharp contrast, most husbands would feel chagrined to bow before the political knowledge and judgment of their wives in this manner, although they would do so without embarrassment in some other areas. A man is supposed to know something about politics; a woman need not.

In the first case, like stimuli bring like responses. Various social categories are differentiated in their behaviors because they receive different stimuli. In the second, the same stimuli presented to members of different categories bring different responses, as a function of social prescriptions regarding appropriate behavior for the members of each category.

We shall attempt to spell out the political implications of a series of social attributes, seeking in each instance the intervening states that shed light on the reasons for the existence of the relationship. Our major emphasis will be upon variation in political participation. In general, social characteristics that do not tend to become bases for group action in a certain partisan direction show much more significant relationships with vote turnout and other aspects of political participation.

Education

We have noted several ways in which people with varying formal education differ in their political behavior. Though education is itself one measure of status differences, it may strike us as somewhat derivative as a tool for analysis of political partisanship in a status context. People of higher education tend to come from higher-status backgrounds and subsequently fill higher-status occupational niches in the society. If we go directly to a status dimension, such as occupation, we can predict partisan behavior with greater accuracy than if we employ education alone. And with the occupation factor held constant, the residual relationship between education and partisanship tends to be trivial or non-existent.

Formal education, nevertheless, has many striking consequences for political behavior that are independent of status implications and that undoubtedly remain constant in strength even in times when class differences lose most of their partisan importance. Some of these differences are matters of sheer information. The greater an individual's education, the more likely he is to attend to sources of political information and hence to know "what is going on." His view of political objects and events will be more specific and more highly differentiated. We saw in Chapter 8, for example, that there are substantial differences in familiarity with current issues of public policy according to differences in educational background (Table 8-2).

The educated person is distinct from the less educated not only in the number of facts about politics at his command, but also in the sophistication of the concepts he employs to maintain a sense of order and meaning amid the flood of information. In fact, it is psychologically sound to presume that the two phenomena go hand in hand. Without some rather abstract modes of "coding" incoming information, little of the volume of specific stimuli will be retained. The individual will develop an effective shell against the bombardment of information, on the despairing note that "politics is so complicated that a person like me can't really understand what is going on."

As we have indicated in Chapter 10, the frames of reference that help to make complexity comprehensible are dependent in part upon the background about the political process communicated in the educational system and in part upon differences in cognitive capacity that are highly related as well to extent of education. Just as there are wide differences in cognitive structure as a consequence of differences in education, there are differences as well in motivation to participate in the political process that are of profound significance. Higher-status people tend to take a more active role in politics, and, although education is secondary to occupation as a focus for partisan differences, it is the dimension of status that seems most central in matters of political participation. Since occupation is a better measure of current status than is education, increased participation at upper levels of the society probably results less from motivation to protect status position than from the fact that people at upper-status levels are better educated and better equipped cognitively to maintain political interest.

Only a small fraction of the adult population engages in much political activity beyond the act of voting itself. But in the various other types of participation that we record, there is some visible upper-status bias within this fraction. On occasion, some other measure of status than education may predict a specific type of participation equally well. Thus, for example, income serves as well as or better than the education dimension to discriminate those who made some kind of financial contribution to the parties or candidates during the campaign. Generally, however, education serves as the best predictor of these forms of participation among status dimensions. Perhaps the strongest relationship with education appears in the tendency to talk informally with others with a view toward influencing their vote decision. Table 17-1 summarizes this relationship. The "opinion leader"

TABLE 17-1. Relation of Education to Attempts to Influence Others, by Region, 1956

"Did you talk to any people and try to show them why they should vote for one of the parties or candidates?"	Non-South			South		
	Grade School	High School	College	Grade School	High School	College
Yes	20%	29%	45%	19%	27%	34%
No	80	71	55	81	73	66
	100%	100%	100%	100%	100%	100%
Number of cases	362	654	232	178	232	99

role in political choice is not widely sought, but it is more likely to be sought by the more highly educated. Educational differences are less marked in some of the other forms of participation: membership in political organizations and campaign work are less clearly dependent on status lines.

The strongest evidence of status difference comes, however, in the ultimate casting of a ballot, as Table 17-2 shows. Aside from geographical differences between the South and other regions of the country, no other social characteristic commonly employed in our research bears such a strong relationship to turnout in presidential elections.

Our data provide a fairly clear picture of the types of motivation to participate that distinguish the more highly educated people and hence may be presumed to intervene between education and higher turnout at the polls. We have indicated that interest and involvement in the outcome of the current election vary strongly as a function of education (Table 17-3). We have assumed extensive interplay between these motivational correlates of education and the cognitive differences mentioned previously. The more meaning an individual can find in the flow of political events, the more likely it is that these events will maintain his interest. The person who makes little sense of politics will not be motivated to pay much attention to it. And, of course, the more interested the individual, the richer the cognitive background which he accumulates for subsequent political evaluations.

TABLE 17-2. Relation of Amount of Formal Education to Differences in Presidential Vote Participation, by Region[a]

	No Education; Some Grade School	Completed Grade School	Some High School	Completed High School	Some College	Completed College
Non-South: per cent voting	70%	68%	77%	87%	92%	93%
Number of cases	334	365	455	720	230	179
South: per cent voting	32%	50%	50%	63%	80%	85%
Number of cases	301	113	193	185	92	68

[a] Figures in this table are based on a combination of data from the 1952 and 1956 election samples.

TABLE 17-3. Relation of Amount of Formal Education to Differences in Political Involvement, by Region[a]

	Non-South			South		
	Grade School	High School	College	Grade School	High School	College
Involvement						
High	23%	32%	48%	21%	28%	47%
Medium	35	46	43	33	40	42
Low	42	22	9	46	32	11
	100%	100%	100%	100%	100%	100%
Number of cases	786	1213	405	404	378	160

[a] Figures in this table are based on a combination of data from the 1952 and 1956 election samples.

There is no significant relationship between strength of party identification and formal education, but the educated stand out with great clarity on the motivational dimensions we call "sense of political efficacy" and "sense of citizen duty." These highly generalized attitudes show strong relationships with education on the one hand (Tables 17-4 and 17-5) and with vote turnout on the other. With

TABLE 17-4. Relation of Education to Sense of Political Efficacy, by Region, 1956

	Non-South			South		
	Grade School	High School	College	Grade School	High School	College
Sense of political efficacy						
High	21%	43%	75%	10%	33%	71%
Medium	25	32	19	16	33	16
Low	54	25	6	74	34	13
	100%	100%	100%	100%	100%	100%
Number of cases	348	649	226	179	229	98

more formal schooling an individual is more likely to feel that he has influence on political events. And he is more likely to feel a sense of civic responsibility about voting, however hopeless the cause and however small his vote against the total number cast.

It is not surprising, of course, that a well-educated person should feel greater confidence in his effect on the political process. He has only one vote, but in many other ways his education is likely to ensure him greater community influence. In part, this is a status matter. But the fact that political efficacy is more strongly related to education than to other dimensions of status that may symbolize equal strength in the power structure suggests that education contributes to the attitude in a more direct way. Undoubtedly we capture here some basic beliefs concerning the way in which democratic process works, beliefs traceable to the educational experience.

TABLE 17-5. Relation of Education to Sense of Citizen Duty, by Region, 1956

	Non-South			South		
	Grade School	High School	College	Grade School	High School	College
Sense of citizen duty						
High	33%	54%	63%	14%	45%	55%
Medium	38	36	33	32	40	40
Low	29	10	4	54	15	5
	100%	100%	100%	100%	100%	100%
Number of cases	359	649	226	180	230	98

Although feelings of involvement in the current election, sense of political efficacy, and sense of citizen duty appear to depend substantially on education and in turn help to predict which persons in the electorate will vote, this causal sequence alone does not exhaust our understanding of the motivational complex behind vote participation. The broad motivational attitudes lead to considerable differences in behavior even within narrowly defined educational categories. As Table 17-6 suggests, however, this additional predictive capacity itself varies systematically with education. Within categories of education, further knowledge of motivational attitudes improves our prediction of turnout substantially at the lower levels of education; but this increment wanes very notably at higher levels. People of college background tend to go to the polls however indifferent they may be to the election outcome and however cynical they may be about the importance of their participation.

This lack of symmetry between educational groups may reflect increased social pressure to vote, among higher educational milieus. At the lowest-status levels involvement in politics is not widespread and voting is somewhat sporadic. There is a minimum of external forces on the individual to vote: any interpersonal expectations that would induce him to the polls despite lack of interest are attenuated. Whether such a person votes depends far more heavily, then, upon his internal value structure. In higher milieus, however, most people

TABLE 17-6. Relation of Involvement, Efficacy, and Education to Vote Turnout, Outside the South, 1956

	Grade School	High School	College
High efficacy, high involvement			
Proportion voting	96%	89%	96%
Number of cases	48	197	137
High efficacy, low involvement: or low efficacy, high involvement			
Proportion voting	81%	83%	87%
Number of cases	158	287	59
Low efficacy, low involvement			
Proportion voting	53%	68%	92%
Number of cases	156	173	36

have some interest in politics, and voting is "the thing to do." Those few who do not share this interest are out of step. Their apathy is not a socially useful excuse for failure to vote. Hence the minority of well educated who lack interest go to the polls anyway.

Thus differences in education have a variety of consequences for political behavior. The development of mass suffrage not only has potential effects in changing the balance of partisan electoral power between class groupings. It greatly increases the proportion of the electorate that operates with a rather impoverished understanding of political process and a minimal background of information. It probably increases the partisan fluidity of the vote from election to election by raising the proportion of people who float into and out of the active electorate; it may contribute fluidity as well in more changeable partisan attitudes among the less educated voters. On the other hand, the effects of a relaxation of status requirements for the suffrage is tempered by the failure of many of the citizens thereby enfranchised to vote.

Occupation

A person's occupation can affect his partisan preference independently of simple status considerations. An occupation defines the group of people with whom the individual works and thereby delimits spheres of primary-group influence. Jobs that entail working with people rather than things add another dimension of experience according to the nature of the clientele. A criminal lawyer or a doctor in a welfare clinic may have a different perspective on social and political problems than the corporation lawyer or the exclusive medical specialist. In some cases the occupation imposes peculiar interests and values that may be of political relevance. Status considerations aside, a businessman is likely to assume that well-run government means primarily the balanced budget of the sound non-profit institution, whereas the social worker is likely to put first priority on necessary governmental services. Finally, some occupations are drawn into an unusually direct relationship with government at one or more levels, and this fact must influence political responses.

Industry. Occupations may be arrayed not only in terms of the standard status hierarchy, but also according to the sectors of the economy represented, close to what the Census Bureau calls "industries." There are administrators and clerical workers, for example, across a wide range of occupational milieus: government service, retail sales, manufacturing, transportation and communication, and professional services. Therefore "industry" may be thought of as a dimension fairly independent of the occupation status ladder.

The most distinctive industrial grouping in terms of 1956 partisan vote division is constituted by those private services that cater to financial or business enterprise. Included here are occupations in advertising, accounting, various forms of industrial consultation, banking, real estate, and insurance. Individuals in this general category voted over 75 per cent Republican in 1956, by contrast with the national vote division of 57 per cent. No other industrial grouping deviates as sharply. Of course, a portion of this Republican dominance may be simply attributed to the fact that occupations included in this category tend to lie at the higher status levels. But even after controlling the status factor, this grouping remains sharply Republican. The business and professional people classified here (N = 31) voted 78 per cent Republican, whereas all other people of business occupation related to other industrial sectors, weighted to match the status distribution in the business-service category, show a vote of 70 per cent Republican (unweighted N = 153). Similarly, among occupations in which parallel professional services are dispensed, but with the general public rather than private business as the basic clientele, the vote is less Republican still (62 per cent) despite status levels equivalent to those in the business-service group. Thus the "businessman's businessman" is more Republican than the typical businessman himself. It is likely that exclusive occupational contact with a business clientele builds particularly firm values concerning the proper role of government and private enterprise, sound fiscal policy, and the problem of government welfare activity.

Other important mechanisms operate within industrial classifications as well. A person's work situation may put him in closer contact with people at status levels different from his own than he is likely to experience otherwise in his day-to-day living. Leisure time will tend to be spent with others of the same income and education level. But within a job experience there may be a good deal of cross-status contact, and it would not be surprising for such contact to influence political attitudes across status levels. Within industrial groupings where lower-status workers predominate, higher-status people are less likely to vote Republican than they are at similar status levels in other industries. Likewise, clerical personnel in the sphere of services to private business are more likely to vote Republican than are clerical personnel in industries where over-all status levels are lower. In short, occupation, although a central index of status, can also provide a social medium in which status differences in political attitudes may become blurred.

Sex

The possibility of sex differences in political behavior remains a subject of interest in part because female suffrage is still disputed in some modern Western democracies and in part because our own acceptance of female activity in politics is of rather recent vintage. Women's right to vote did not become universal in the United States until 1920, yet sufficient time has passed to invite evaluation of its consequences.

We may ask at the outset what changes female suffrage has wrought in the actual voting public. It is hard to estimate how rapidly women took up their new privileges after passage of the Nineteenth Amendment. The popular vote for President in 1916 was somewhat over 18 million, and in 1920, after the Constitution was amended, it surpassed 26 million, a figure about 45 per cent greater than the previous total. However, these figures taken alone are inadequate. A large number of states, primarily the new western additions to the union, had given women full suffrage prior to the election of 1916. Almost one third of the 1916 popular presidential vote came from states where women voted.

If we attempt to proceed state by state, comparing increments in the aggregate vote after women were first given a chance to vote, the fact of continual population growth and the presence of non-citizen immigrant groups remain unknown quantities. With rough corrections for these factors, however, we get the impression that women voters added to previous presidential vote totals by a factor of about two thirds in their first sallies to the polls. Currently, after forty intervening years, women double the vote that would result if men voted alone. Therefore, it is apparent that there has been some slow increase in vote participation by women in the first decades of their franchise.

The fact that the female vote approximates that of males in absolute size does not mean, however, that women are as apt to vote as men. Women outnumber men by more than a 52–48 ratio in the adult population.[1] If they voted at a rate equal to that for males, the absolute size of their vote would of course be larger. Actually, the vote participation rate among women in our samples is consistently 10 per cent below that of men, as an over-all estimate.

The basic differences that mark the political participation of men and women we take to lie in vestigial sex roles. A "role" here is a cluster of expectations about behavior considered "appropriate" for the occupant of a social position or category. A sex role for political behavior includes, then, that portion of expectations about behavior proper for a male or female that involves political responses. A century ago political sex roles were clear-cut. A man was supposed to be the political agent for the family unit. A woman not only had no need to concern herself with politics; to one degree or another, political activity was unseemly for her.

The Nineteenth Amendment and the entry of women into high political office represent some of the clearer bench marks of changing sex roles in politics. Yet social roles are deeply ingrained in day-to-day assumptions about behavior in any culture, and these assumptions are not rapidly uprooted. Decades after the first successes of the

[1] Bureau of the Census data for April, 1956. Within our samples, the proportion of women tends to be slightly higher still, as the fragment of the adult population excluded from consideration—those adults residing in military establishments, logging and mining camps, penal institutions and the like—are disproportionately male in composition.

suffragettes many wives wish to refer our interviewers to their husbands as being the person in the family who pays attention to politics. Or the woman may say in so many words: "I don't know anything about politics—I thought *that* business was for men, anyway."

The 10 per cent difference in the turnout rate of men and women is a gross summary at a point in a process of social change. Such change obviously does not occur at an even pace within all segments of a society. The gross differential in vote turnout conceals a good deal of variation among social groupings. It is in this variation that we may view the dynamics of social change; and imbedded here are the clues that help us to judge whether change is still proceeding or has run its course.

We would presume that a shift of role definition of this sort would have its genesis within the most educated strata of the society. Subsequently it would ramify slowly downward through the status hierarchy and outward geographically from the more cosmopolitan centers to increasingly remote areas of the nation.[2] And, too, we would expect that in some degree, the progress of change would depend upon actual turnover of members of the society. It would be consummated as senior generations, schooled in older points of view, slowly faded from the population, their places taken by younger people for whom new arrangements are merely the "normal."

Table 17-7 permits us to examine the distinctiveness of political sex roles across region, education, and age levels. Sex differences in turnout are generally sharper in the South than at equivalent age and education ranges elsewhere in the country. This differential probably reflects a lag in sex-role change in this area, relatively sheltered as it seems to be from many modern cultural innovations. Though there are irregularities in the remainder of the table, there are substantial indications that sex differences in turnout are least at higher levels of education. This point is clearest in the South (note row labeled "Average Differences") but is visible at lower levels outside the South as well. These differences emerge independently of the strong background correlation, present for both sexes, between education and turnout. The increase in participation with education is steeper for women than for men. Although turnout rates are higher for both sexes at each succeeding level of education, the poorly educated woman

[2] The fact that the more remote western states formally accepted female suffrage before the eastern sector of the country is not a contradiction of this proposition. An elite engaged in building a system of institutions *de novo,* as was generally the case in the West, is unusually open to the incorporation of new ideas that might make little headway against long-standing institutional arrangements.

TABLE 17-7. Relation of Region, Education, and Age to Sex Differences in Presidential Vote Turnout[a]

Age	Non-South				South (White)[b]			
	Grade School	High School	College	Average Differences	Grade School	High School	College	Average Differences
Under 35	+16% (107)	+5% (460)	−2% (151)	+6%	+5%[c] (44)	+15% (152)	+1% (52)	+7%
35–54	+9% (326)	+2% (534)	+5% (188)	+5%	+53% (122)	+14% (106)	−8% (50)	+20%
55 or over	+16% (352)	+2% (222)	+7% (61)	+8%	+23% (103)	+28% (70)	+11% (47)	+21%
Average Differences	+14%	+3%	+3%		+27%	+19%	+1%	

[a] Figures in this table are based on a combination of data from the 1952 and 1956 election samples. The primary per cent entries in each cell represent a simple subtraction of the proportion of women within the category voting for President from the same proportion among men. Positive percentages indicate that men turned out at a higher rate than women; negative percentages indicate higher female vote proportion. The entry in parentheses refers to the number of cases involved in the comparison.

[b] In view of legal and extralegal restrictions on Negro voting in the South, along with the distinctive age and education characteristics of the Southern Negro, this portion of the table is restricted to Southern Whites.

[c] There is an unusually low ceiling on this entry, as only 28 per cent of Southern White males of grade school education under 35 voted for President in these elections.

is less likely to vote than her male counterpart; but the behavior of college women is very little different from that of college men. Vestiges of older political sex roles are most apparent, then, at lowest social levels.

To the degree that the South is a relatively rural area, Table 17-7 supports the prediction of sharper sex differences at greater distances from metropolitan areas. But there is further evidence favorable to the proposition within the non-South alone. If we subdivide each cell of Table 17-7 according to residence in (1) large metropolitan areas, (2) cities and towns, and (3) villages and rural places, some categories are left with too few cases for reasonable comparison. The Southern portion of the sample is generally too small to bear such subdivision; and differences in proportions among college people outside the South grow too unstable also. But sex differences averaged across three categories of age and the two lower education groupings within type of residence outside the South reveal the following differences:

		Average Differences in Turnout Proportions of the Sexes
Non-South	Metropolitan	+5%
	City and town	+20%
	Village and rural	+28%

The evidence for differences in sex roles as a function of age are much less clear in Table 17-7 (note "Average Difference" columns). Hypothetically, most of the women over 55 at the time the data were gathered had "come of age" politically before female suffrage had been generally accepted. We would expect larger differences between the sexes in the bottom row of primary cells. In an absolute sense, the differences are largest for this row, but not significantly so. The hypothesis, however, may have some merit not apparent on the basis of this table alone. For there are additional barriers to vote turnout among younger women that are present neither for younger men or older women.

A large proportion of women under 55 are occupied with problems of child rearing. In our 1956 sample we may subdivide respondents as to the presence or absence of children in the family unit. Among younger people who are single or married without children, we find little or no "average difference" in turnout between men and women across categories of education and age outside the South.[3] Actually,

[3] Once again, numbers of cases are too few in the South to support this analysis.

childless women of grade school education appear to vote at a lower rate than childless males of the same education, but at the college level such women actually vote *more* frequently than parallel males, with no difference in the intermediate high school level.

Mothers of young children, however, are consistently less likely to vote than are fathers of young children across all levels of education within both the 21–34 and 35–54 age groups. As usual, the differences are sharpest where education is least, and diminish to a small increment of 5–6 per cent in turnout rate of college fathers over college mothers. But the average difference of 11 per cent is substantially clearer than the same comparison among the childless. Furthermore, this dip in participation among mothers of small children does not appear to be matched by a slackened political involvement within this grouping. We pointed earlier to situations in which turnout rate may be surprisingly high among people with limited interest in the political situation. Here we seem to see an inverse case, in which voting is less frequent than the aggregate level of involvement would lead us to expect. The presence of young children requiring constant attention serves as a barrier to the voting act.

This barrier is not present for older women, yet sex differences in vote turnout do not diminish accordingly. We could account for this combination of circumstances by assuming that women who grew up before formal acceptance of female participation in politics have continued to act under some constraint not felt in younger generations. This is not to gainsay the fact that any age effect to be found in the current era is at best weak. If there once were strong age differentials among women in acceptance of new sex role definitions, it is likely that the resistant age cohorts have by and large passed from the population.

Our analysis may be brought to bear on expectations for future female vote participation. If primary responsibility for young children leads to some small reduction in turnout potential, this effect is likely to leave a permanent discrepancy in participation between the sexes. On the other hand, evidences for lag in the diffusion of new sex role definitions in rural areas and in the least educated strata suggest that the trend toward higher female participation has not run its course. It is possible that there are factors in these milieus that lend strength to clearer sex role differentiation and that these factors are highly resistant to change. Heavy labor required for economic subsistence in the rural setting and at the lowest educational levels may act to maintain the sex lines of an earlier society. However, to the degree that simple diffusion of role definitions is at stake, we may expect that sex differentials in vote turnout may diminish further.

Education plays a double role in the causal nexus surrounding these sex differences. By controlling education in Table 17-7, we underscore contrasts between the sexes independent of differences in schooling. But we conceal the fact that women tend to show different levels of education than men, and that these differences, strongly related to turnout, are themselves undergoing change. The proportion of women receiving some college education has increased much more rapidly in recent decades than has the comparable proportion for men. But if newer political sex roles gain increasing acceptance at lower educational levels, and if the average education of women rises more rapidly than that of men, two forces will be acting to erode sex differences in turnout.

The extension of the franchise to women, then, though not immediately accepted by all those affected, still constituted a sweeping change in the size and composition of the electorate. Facts concerning the degree to which women have accepted the franchise do not, however, inform us as to the consequences of such change in the definition of the electorate. Some consequences are felt on the side of the candidates and the parties.

Sex differences in the approach to politics. If we consider the motivational patterns underlying vote turnout, we find in the first instance that differences in current involvement between men and women are congruent with the turnout differentials already explored. That is, women are somewhat less likely to express a sense of involvement in the current situation. And this discrepancy is clearest at the lowest levels of education, being fairly well obliterated or even reversed among college-educated men and women (Table 17-8).[4]

But there is substantial variety in the pattern of sex differences on other dimensions of motivational significance. There is no evidence, for example, that differences in intensity of party loyalty between the sexes help to account for sex differences in turnout. Women are about as likely to feel strong identification with a political party as men. Nor is there more than a marginal difference between men and women in the sense of citizen duty. Within cells representing the lowest levels of education, men do rank higher than women here; but among high school and college people divided by age and region, women are frequently more apt to endorse the common "oughts" of good citizenship than are men. Thus neither party loyalty nor sense of civic responsibility looms large in motivational differences between the sexes.

[4] Rank-order correlations between education and political involvement within gross age groupings run consistently over 0.3 for women, while remaining close to 0.1 for men.

TABLE 17-8. Relation of Sex, Education, and Region to Political Involvement[a]

	Men			Women		
	Grade School	High School	College	Grade School	High School	College
Non-South						
High involvement	27%	36%	49%	19%	30%	46%
Medium involvement	36	45	41	34	46	46
Low involvement	37	19	10	47	24	8
	100%	100%	100%	100%	100%	100%
Number of cases	387	494	219	399	719	186
South						
High involvement	29%	33%	38%	14%	25%	57%
Medium involvement	32	39	49	33	41	35
Low involvement	39	28	13	53	34	8
	100%	100%	100%	100%	100%	100%
Number of cases	187	146	77	217	232	83

[a] Figures in this table are based on a combination of data from the 1952 and 1956 election samples.

It is the sense of political efficacy that, with factors like education, age, and region controlled, differs most sharply and consistently between men and women. Men are more likely than women to feel that they can cope with the complexities of politics and to believe that their participation carries some weight in the political process (Table 17-9). We conclude, then, that moralistic values about citizen participation in democratic government have been bred in women as in men; what has been less adequately transmitted to the woman is a sense of some personal competence vis-à-vis the political world.

Belief in personal efficacy is one of the more prominent attitudes mediating turnout. Its weakness among women returns us directly to the question of sex roles. For this dimension of political motivation, more than any other, is relevant to role beliefs that presume the woman to be a submissive partner. The man is expected to be dominant in action directed toward the world outside the family; the woman is to accept his leadership passively. She is not expected, therefore, to see herself as an effective agent in politics.

It is our belief that sex differences in turnout rate fail to capture the full significance of sex role differentiation for the nature of the political response. Many women who manifest a clear sense of politi-

TABLE 17-9. Relation of Sex, Education, and Region to Sense of Political Efficacy, 1956

	Men			Women		
	Grade School	High School	College	Grade School	High School	College
Non-South						
High efficacy	32%	47%	83%	13%	40%	68%
Medium efficacy	31	29	12	20	34	25
Low efficacy	37	24	5	67	26	7
	100%	100%	100%	100%	100%	100%
Number of cases	150	267	116	198	382	110
South						
High efficacy	16%	37%	78%	3%	31%	56%
Medium efficacy	12	28	15	20	36	22
Low efficacy	72	35	7	77	33	22
	100%	100%	100%	100%	100%	100%
Number of cases	89	82	55	90	147	27

cal sex roles by indicating personal indifference and dependence upon the husband's judgment, *do* respond nevertheless to civic expectations about vote participation. It is for this reason that a 10 per cent sex differential in turnout is misleading.

This pervasive influence of role definitions is best captured in the sophistication with which men and women approach their political evaluations. In Chapter 10 we developed a classification of types of concept formation that respondents manifested in free-answer invitations to evaluate political objects. Table 17-10 indicates the degree

TABLE 17-10. Relation of Sex and Education to Level of Conceptualization, 1956

	Grade School		High School		College	
	Male	Female	Male	Female	Male	Female
Level of conceptualization						
A. Ideology	8%	1%	17%	5%	34%	27%
B. Group benefit	43	33	52	44	36	34
C. Nature of times	30	26	19	26	19	21
D. No issue content	19	40	12	25	11	18
	100%	100%	100%	100%	100%	100%
Number of cases	251	291	354	537	175	155

to which men tend to cluster at the more sophisticated levels, and women tend to dominate the lower ranks. Although the familiar tendency is visible here for sex differences to appear larger the lower the amount of formal education, some contrast remains even among the college educated. Women who tend to "leave politics to the menfolks" even though they are willing to go to the polls register here as having a more impoverished level of political concept formation.[5]

What is the significance of these sex differences for the electoral process? We have suggested earlier that a disproportionate amount of the partisan fluidity that is shown by voters from election to election may come from the politically unsophisticated. If this is so, it would follow that the addition of women to the electorate might have as a consequence greater variability in the partisan division of the vote over time. However, in the case of women, there is an added consideration. The wife who votes but otherwise pays little attention to politics tends to leave not only the sifting of information up to her husband but abides by his ultimate decision about the direction of the vote as well. The information that she brings to bear on "her" choice is indeed fragmentary, because it is second hand. Since the partisan decision is anchored not in these fragments but in the fuller political understanding of the husband, it may have greater stability over a period of time than we would otherwise suspect.

Of course some wives, as well as some women without husbands, do strike out on their own politically. This is not to say that they are any more insulated from primary-group influence than men. But at least they have no single and immediate source of political cues that they are satisfied to accept without question, as wives often have. It is doubtful that such "liberated" women contribute much to the sex bias in levels of conceptualization. We believe this bias arises largely because of female willingness to leave political matters to men. The ultimate behavior of the dependent wife springs from the more sophisticated concepts of her husband. On the other hand, the independent woman may well fill in a set of political concepts more parallel in quality to those employed by men. Hence the actual political consequences of sex contrasts in Table 17-10 may be rather small.

[5] In Chapter 10 we subdivided the lowest level of respondents (Level D) into those who were (*a*) party oriented; (*b*) candidate oriented; and (*c*) unable to venture any political content at all. Though women predominate in Level D, they do not cluster within the candidate-oriented type, as might be hypothesized. Actually, the proportion of women is highest in the third group and lowest in the candidate category.

The dependence of a wife's vote upon her husband's partisan predispositions appears to be one reason why the entrance of women into the electorate has tended to make little visible difference in the partisan distribution of the national vote. Issues may arise from time to time to polarize the sexes: the Prohibition issue of the 1920's may have had some such consequence. In the current era, there is no reason to believe that women *as women* are differentially attracted to one of the political parties.

Women in our samples consistently show slight differences in vote partisanship by comparison with men, being 3–5 per cent more Republican. However, much of this discrepancy is traceable not to something unique in female political assessments, but to aggregate differences in other social characteristics between the sexes. For example, greater life expectancy among women means that their inclusion in the electorate increases the average age of the voter slightly. One of the current partisan consequences is a minor increase in the proportion of eligible voters of Republican disposition. Women are less likely to vote in the solidly Democratic South. Vote turnout for women slopes off more rapidly at lower levels of education than it does for men, and there is a mild tendency for voters at these levels, male or female, to be more Democratic. In general, if we take a large variety of other social characteristics into account, there are no residual differences in partisanship between men and women.

Age

In treating the origins of party identification, we analyzed earlier the relationships between age and political partisanship. But differences in age have other consequences for the political process as well. Generally, older citizens are more likely to cast a presidential vote than are members of the younger generation.

As Fig. 17-1 indicates, turnout does not increase steadily as we move up the age scale. In fact, among the aged it actually declines again, undoubtedly due to infirmities that make trips to the polling place more difficult. Furthermore, among active adults, the sharpest differences in participation occur in the earliest years after eligibility is attained. Under the conditions of motivation that existed in 1952 and 1956, for example, only about half of the quadrennial crop of newly eligible actually voted in their first presidential elections. Nonetheless, there remains a visible increase in vote participation as a function of age throughout the period of active life.

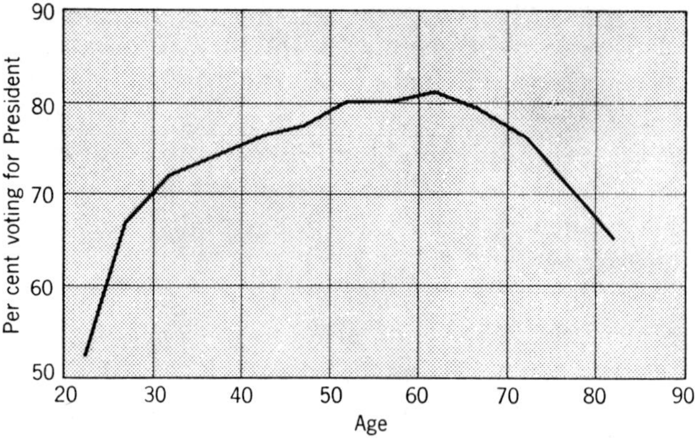

This table is based on a combination of data from the 1952 and 1956 samples. The absolute proportions associated with each age could be expected to vary according to motivational conditions attending the specific election. The fact that over-all participation remained at approximately the same level between 1952 and 1956 made combination feasible in this case. Likewise, absolute proportions are certain to vary between presidential and other off-year elections. Our current assumption is that the form of the curve remains general, however.

Fig. 17-1. Relation of age to voting participation.

This relationship between age and vote turnout is of more than normal interest for the increase in turnout among older citizens is totally independent of education. In fact, it runs at cross grain to the education factor, for the older generation of the adult population has had considerably less formal education than the younger. When we add income to education as a second explanatory factor for turnout, we do not gain much additional accuracy; when we add age to education, however, the increase is substantial. This fact is dramatically underscored in Table 17-11, where we summarize the relationship between a number of the social characteristics treated in this chapter and vote turnout. The oldest group of high school and college males in the South shows a decline in participation by comparison with the middle-aged cohort. Otherwise, there is a steady and at times spectacular increase of vote participation as a function of age.

Not only is age independent of education as a correlate of participation; it appears that the motivational differences that arise as a result of education are not the same as the processes that draw disproportionate numbers of older people to the polls. The final behavior—increased participation—is the same for older citizens and better-educated citizens alike. But the motivational picture is quite different in the two instances.

TABLE 17-11. Relation of Age, Education, Sex, and Region to Presidential Vote Turnout[a]

	Age: 34 or Less			Age: 35–54			Age: 55 or Over		
	Grade School	High School	College	Grade School	High School	College	Grade School	High School	College
Non-South									
Male	60% (52)	78% (175)	88% (81)	80% (156)	87% (222)	96% (103)	87% (179)	93% (96)	100% (31)
Female	44% (55)	73% (285)	90% (70)	71% (170)	85% (312)	91% (85)	71% (173)	91% (126)	93% (30)
South									
Male	19% (32)	55% (69)	81% (32)	55% (87)	80% (54)	88% (33)	63% (72)	71% (21)	82% (11)
Female	13% (47)	41% (111)	74% (23)	22% (97)	56% (86)	82% (38)	31% (75)	58% (33)	86% (22)

[a] The primary entry in each cell indicates the proportion voting for president within the category. The number of cases involved in each proportion is indicated in parentheses. Figures in this table are based on a combination of data from the 1952 and 1956 election samples.

None of the major motivational terms intervening between increased education and higher vote turnout vary systematically by age in a manner that would convince us that they are intervening terms here as well. There is some evidence that expressions of current involvement are least intense among people in their early twenties and rise thereafter; but this upturn in interest along the age continuum is slight and occurs so early that as soon as we compare an age cohort as large as that from 21–35 with the cohort covering the middle two decades of the adult range (35–54) differences are trivial, despite the fact that turnout increases steadily and rather sharply between the two groups. Similarly, if there is any pattern at all to changes in involvement after age 55, it is in the direction of reduced interest, despite the continuing increase in turnout shown in Table 17-11. The sense of political efficacy and the sense of citizen duty, both of which show significant variation with education, fail to show any systematic pattern of age differences whatever.

What motivational processes, then, can account for increases in vote turnout as a function of age? One cluster of motivational elements shows steady development with age. These elements have to do with the relationship of the individual to the political party. Fundamental differences in the nature of the primary political objects—parties, issues, and candidates—influence the character of the perceptions they generate in the electorate. Candidates and issues are fairly transient parts of the political landscape, and images which grow up around them have relatively little time depth. But the parties, which have endured for a century, have accumulated an array of perceived characteristics referring not only to 1955 but to aspects of party behavior of importance in 1945 and 1935 as well. In Chapter 13 this property of party perceptions was underscored again. The data at that point gave evidence of a marked historical element unique in the behaviors of strong party identifiers. Thus the class-bound political alignments of the 1930's and 1940's were preserved most clearly in the class voting of the most intensely identified.

These findings take on further significance as we consider the increase of turnout as a function of age. For the only elements that distinguish the motivational system of the older voter from that of the younger have to do with perceptions of and affect toward the parties. In the first place, although the more elderly citizen directs about the same volume of comment toward the candidates and the issues as the younger person, he communicates a significantly fuller image of the parties. The current *dramatis personae* of the political world and the issues over which they strive are not visibly more familiar to the older generation than to the younger. But the older person has observed the parties over a longer period of time and appears to have built a richer set of connotations concerning them. For the young voter the Democratic Party is, for better or for worse, the party of Stevenson and Truman. For the older voter the Democrats represent not only this but Roosevelt's leadership through the Second World War and the Depression as well.

An apparent corollary of this fact has been examined in detail earlier.[6] Individuals become increasingly identified with their political party the longer they have remained committed to it psychologically. If something causes a shift in party allegiance, the pattern is broken and identifications start again at a weak and hesitant level. Since most individuals hew to a single party throughout their lives, strength of party identification increases with age. Strong commitment to a party increases the probability that a person will vote. Therefore, we may presume that one reason why older people are more likely to vote lies in their stronger sense of party allegiance.

The political party is the focus for the individual's accumulation of political understanding over extended periods of time. We can imagine the generalization process that occurs as the citizen increasingly organizes the flux of specific issues and candidates into a set of attributes characterizing the parties themselves in a much broader sense. At the same time, through the self-reinforcing mechanisms discussed in Chapter 7, party loyalties intensify. If we find traces of past political alignments in the behavior of strong party identifiers, it is in part because these people are older and have a much more direct link with the past.

Young people not only vote less, then, but appear less securely bound to the existing party system as well. They are less likely to evaluate political objects in party terms and show less affective involvement in the fortunes of any particular party *qua* party. A political party signifies little more to them than its current leaders, be they attractive or unattractive. Like farm people, they are rather free psychologically to shift their vote from party to party and to move into and out of the electorate as well. In time of crisis they may suddenly flock to the polls in proportions that create great surges in the electoral support of a party promising salvation. And they may in crisis depart from the traditional party structure entirely. They have little base for the suspicion with which older voters may view the lineage of the *parvenus* among political parties. They have little feeling for the lineage of any of the contestants.

[6] See Chapter 7.

These observations have significance for political practice. It is probable that movements to reduce the voting age in effect imply a more fluid electorate.[7] Whether such fluidity is a matter for concern or a desirable source of "flexibility" in the political system depends upon our various normative persuasions. Likewise, any system of compulsory voting, which would drive an unusual proportion of very young people into the active electorate, would have similar consequences.

[7] We hesitate to make the statement more categoric, because it is conceivable that some of the observed age effects are functionally linked to the minimum age of eligibility. That is, if citizens did not receive the franchise until age 50, they might show the same behavior patterns in their fifties as people in their twenties under existing voting regulations. In fact, we would predict such an outcome if there were reason to believe that under these conditions adults under 50 would pay as little serious attention to political events as American adolescents do in the current era. However, we suspect that the adult would feel the weight of political events in a manner that would contrast with the adolescent whether or not he was yet eligible to vote.

Personality Factors in Voting Behavior ◇ 18

The part "personality" plays in the mass political process has been the subject of much controversy. Harold Lasswell, who fostered an interest in personality as a tool in political analysis, once wrote: "The significance of political opinions is not to be grasped apart from the private motives which they symbolize."[1] From this viewpoint personality differences so color the processes of perception and the development of attitudes that any account of behavior—political as well as social or economic—must lean heavily on personality theory. On the other hand, much competent analysis in the area of voting behavior has proceeded without reference to personality concepts.

Such discrepancies in viewpoint arise in part because investigators become wedded to limited categories of explanatory variables. It would be unusual for a student of personality to design a study of political behavior employing both personality and economic variables. This is an entirely reasonable outcome of focused interest and disciplinary competence. But it is through such restriction that the student loses perspective on the full range of antecedents that may fruitfully be brought to bear on behavior of this complexity. Particularly after experiencing empirical success in prediction with one or another aspect of personality, it is easy for him to feel that if all the dimensions of personality might be captured at once, political behavior could be adequately accounted for in these terms alone.

Throughout this volume we have drawn conceptual tools from a variety of domains. This eclecticism poses its own problems. For example, a shift of conceptual domain sometimes merely means that

[1] H. D. Lasswell, *Psychopathology and Politics* (University of Chicago Press, Chicago, 1930), p. 172.

we are cutting into the same process in another way or at another point in time. It has been important to keep such facts in mind as we have proceeded. But the use of a variety of tools at once serves to maintain perspective on the utility of each in the analysis of political behavior. We may approach the problem of personality in this light.

We would like to suggest some of the conditions under which personality factors may be expected to intrude most clearly in the electoral process. First, however, we must recognize that the role assigned to personality varies according to one's viewpoint on what the term "personality" embraces. There is room here for a range of opinion, and one of the gulfs separating proponents of personality analysis from those who find it less helpful is a product of the definitional problem itself. If our view of personality is relatively inclusive, then we are more likely to consider it all important in any form of behavior; as we limit it progressively, its apparent value shrinks. Inasmuch as we have covered a wide variety of antecedents to the political response, it is important at the outset to distinguish those antecedents that we shall consider as "personality factors."

What Is Personality?

Behavior is commonly seen as a product of interaction between the person and his environment. Logically, then, differences in behavior may spring from variation in either element. On the one hand, we may think of the same person responding to different stimulus situations. We would then expect behavior to vary, and this variation could be linked directly with variation in the immediate environment. At an opposite extreme, we may imagine two persons confronted by precisely the same stimulus situation. If differences in behavior emerge, we may presume that variation is due not to discrepancies in environment but to differences in the response disposition of each person.

Although the student of personality may be profoundly interested in the prior stimulus situations that have built these different response dispositions, it is clear that personality analysis of current responses has to do exclusively with variation on the "person" side of the equation. We have attributed some of the variation in voting behavior over a period of time to changes in the immediate events serving as stimulus objects from election to election. We can comfortably exclude from analysis of personality factors at the mass level the response differences that arise simply because stimulus events vary.

But once personality has been located within the response dispositions that the person brings to the situation, the process of definition is more difficult. Some theorists describe personality in a fashion to include any response tendency that emerges consistently in the behavior of the individual. If we were to accept a definition of this breadth, then much of this volume has already been given over to a discussion of "personality." From this viewpoint a variable similar to party identification would be a prime personality factor, as it represents a potent response tendency that, under certain circumstances, pervades individual processes of perception, cognition, and decision making to a marked degree and appears as well to have great stability over extended periods of time.

Party identification may be shaped by "deeper" personality factors, but we resist the suggestion that a sense of party loyalty is in itself fruitfully classified as such a factor. Some observers have spoken of variables of this sort as aspects of the individual's "political personality." This usage is not the colloquial one in which any social attitude or response is loosely styled as an expression of personality. The qualification *"political"* personality seems to warn us that what is intended is an analogy: we are invited to think of political dispositions as organized in the same fashion as "deeper" personality dimensions. In these terms, the location of party identification as part of "political personality" is hardly offensive. Given the durability of such identification and its pervasive effects in political decision processes, such an analogy is most apt. But it seems more useful in the long run to seek clarification of the basic differences between an antecedent of this sort and true personality factors than to blur them by analogy. Basic insights provided by personality theory can be potent tools in understanding many aspects of behavior; but to make the study of personality all inclusive is to waste its unique strengths.

The personality theorist seeks to isolate a limited set of concepts that will permit him to characterize successfully the underlying flavor of a wide range of behaviors in which the individual engages. Hence he is interested in terms that are, for any person, stable and highly generalized. In an earlier chapter we conceived of attitudes as ordered in a hierarchy, according to the specificity or generality of the attitude-object involved. If attitudes are used at all as primary terms in personality theories, they are attitudes at a very generalized level, such as attitudes toward "authority," rather than attitudes toward oranges or presidential candidates.

Personality theory, however, has tended to seek even greater parsimony by gravitating toward concepts in which the object of action or affect is left undefined. Thus a school known as "trait psychology" placed stress not on the predicate object, but on the adverb, the *how* word of the action sentence, investigating qualities such as pessimism, gregariousness, timidity, and the like.

A more promising departure of this sort traces its ancestry to Freud and psychoanalytic theory. On the basis of much clinical observation it came to be felt that distinctive patterns of behavior in extremely varied situations reflected constellations of underlying needs and a characteristic means of adapting these needs to the environment. The multitude of specific objects that the individual might pursue or avoid were pursued because they satisfied a need or were avoided because they increased a sense of need. Personality theory, in these terms, became a matter of understanding (1) the way in which certain classes of objects (or "goals") became attached to certain needs as means of satisfaction; and (2) what behavior could be expected to occur in the course of goal seeking, in cases such as frustration of pursuit of these goals or conflict between mutually exclusive goals.

The use of goals as a concept brought back into systematic thought the notion of the object toward which behavior was directed. Economy was preserved through primary emphasis on the basic need that prompted reactions to specific objects. Some simplicity can be achieved when objects of orientation can be generalized into broader and broader classes. Within an approach in which underlying needs are stressed, the way in which objects are to be grouped is not defined by the investigator as a logical matter but by the acting subject, according to his need. A particular object may help to gratify one need for a certain individual and another quite different need for someone else. Conversely, behavior of the same individual toward vastly different classes of objects—kicking the cat and advocating an aggressive foreign policy—may share the same need as a source. A personality analysis of more superficial reactions to specific objects, then, is highly functional and dynamic in tone: we ask at each point what deeper needs are satisfied by surface behavior.[2]

The conception of personality as referring to certain characteristic lines of organization from deeper dynamics to surface behavior is often useful. But it becomes misleading when it is taken to mean that behavior or the dispositions that prompt behavior can only be under-

[2] An extended discussion and application of this approach *vis-à-vis* surface attitudes of a political nature is presented in M. Brewster Smith, Jerome S. Bruner, and Robert W. White, *Opinions and Personality* (John Wiley and Sons, New York, 1956).

stood in terms of personality factors. For personality factors do not totally shape response dispositions; they only contribute to these dispositions under certain circumstances. There are other important factors affecting response dispositions that few observers would wish to recognize as aspects of basic personality. These other determinants are important in political behavior.

Other factors governing response dispositions. To specify the nature of some of these other determinants casts further light on what a "personality factor" is and permits us at the same time to organize a number of the antecedents of behavior which we have employed in this volume.

We may suggest two broad classes of behavior determinants that seem to require conceptualization as independent of the individual's personality system: (1) differences in past or present access to information and in capacity for cognitive processing of such information, where we include the formation of associations and generalizations linking concrete events; and (2) differences due to acceptance of different social expectations, social definitions, and culture content. We do not, of course, contend that there is no interaction between these elements and the personality system. In fact, it may be argued that variation in these elements early in life contributes to the establishment of much that is distinctive in personality. Yet after the basic dynamic patterns of deeper personality are integrated, differences in these "non-personality" determinants can affect behavior in a relatively direct fashion with little engagement or influence from the personality system *per se*.

Variations in behavior traceable to simple cognitive differences may be readily illustrated. Let us present two individuals of differing personality systems with a puzzle to be solved. One of these persons has encountered puzzles of this sort before and hence solves it easily. The other, for whom the puzzle is unfamiliar, does not. We would suspect in this circumstance that standardization of initial information would go a long way toward making responses the same. Yet the presence or absence of a certain piece of information accessible to memory does not reflect in any integral way upon the dynamics of the personality system. Several observations need be drawn. First, the fact that differences in information may govern who solves the puzzle does not mean that such a puzzle situation can reveal nothing about personality. Motivation to persevere in search of a solution, reaction to the frustration of failure, and the like may indeed cast light on personality differences between our subjects. It is when some affective or motivational term comes to loom large that the student of personality has greatest interest in the outcome, for most of his analytic concepts rest on affective processes. Quite generally we may say that most complex and non-routine behavior sequences tend at some point to reflect motivation and affect, although the visibility of these elements may vary a great deal.

The proposition that motivational elements enter most behavior sequences is different from the contention that all aspects of such sequences not stimulus-determined are determined by personality factors. The student of personality may say that he has no interest in who solves the puzzle, as this depends on information; his variables are perseverance, reactions to frustration, and so on. This position is perfectly innocuous, since it is a statement of taste. Problems arise when it is forgotten that other factors help to determine some aspects of response dispositions as well, or when the implication is drawn that who solves the puzzle is of no scientific import. In some analytic situations it may be the crucial datum we would like to predict. In short, then, personality may account for all aspects of behavior that intrigue the student of personality. But there is conceptual room here for other important aspects of behavior outcomes that are not to be understood in terms of personality concepts at all.

We have had frequent occasion to stress the tremendous range of differences in information to be found in a cross section of a national population. In Chapter 10 we pushed the matter a step further by suggesting that there are equally broad differences in the manner in which incoming information becomes conceptualized. Personality variables contribute little to an understanding of these purely cognitive differences, despite the fact that, as we have tried to show, such differences are responsible for marked variation in political attitudes and behavior of great social significance.

Social expectations concerning behavior form a second broad class of behavior determinants that deserve to be distinguished from personality factors. Once again, personality differences may affect whether the person succumbs to any given social expectation, particularly when affect has become focused in a specific behavior area.

Nonetheless, when social expectations are not questioned but rather are assimilated automatically as guides to behavior, the resulting *content* of behavior thereby socially transmitted cannot be seen as determined by personality. Once again, the student of personality may deny interest in the actual culture content transmitted. This remains entirely legitimate. But if the transmission is "Republican" instead of "Democratic" this fact is not a matter of indifference to the student of political behavior.

A tremendous portion of normal behavior—language and other use of symbols, as well as participation in the many social roles pertaining to occupation, age, sex, and other categories—is socially stereotyped in this manner. When an individual deviates from a role prescription and, in a sense, "innovates," we may have some clue to his personality system, both in the fact that he has deviated and in the direction in which his deviation is carried. But the content of behavior that follows social expectations and definitions in direct fashion betrays little about the personality of the actor. If an individual believes in racial superiority in certain areas of the South, we have much less insight into his personality dynamics than we would feel in observing the same attitudes in a person from another more tolerant milieu.

Just as there is some degree of interaction between the personality system and the cognitive system, so there is interaction between the personality system and the content of social expectations. The study of "culture and personality" is directly concerned with this interstitial area, and concepts such as that of "national character" rest on the assumption that patterns of social expectation distinctive to a society can bear on the development of personality *per se*. It is claimed that child training affects adult personality, and we know that child training practices differ from social group to social group. This is true not only between cultures and nations, but between subcultures within the same nation, such as class, ethnic, and racial groupings. Similarly, social role expectations can affect in systematic ways the developing structure of personality. The woman who has been schooled in appropriate female behavior within a culture that expects her to faint whenever difficulties loom in the environment could not be expected to have a strong sense of mastery over that environment, although the latter term carries us deep into concerns of personality dynamics.

Therefore if we find some clear personality factor that varies systematically by social category, this is in itself no evidence that there is anything "spurious" about its conceptual status as an element of basic personality. There are undoubtedly many concepts useful in the analysis of complex behavior that would defy rigid classification as either social expectation or basic personality factor. We can recognize these indeterminate cases as evidence of articulation between basic personality and social expectations without losing a grip on the conceptual distinction. In many cases, the distinction is clear, and the entire direction of inquiry may depend on the proper recognition of the distinction.

Personality factors and partisan choice. It is particularly appropriate at this point to consider the nature of the articulation that we might expect between deeper elements of personality and the partisan direction of political choice. Some students of political behavior, intrigued by personality theory, have presumed that proper understanding of personality dynamics would show some personality types turning up heavily as adherents of the Democratic Party, whereas other types would be differentially attracted to the Republican Party. To the best of our knowledge, studies designed toward this end that have used subjects at all representative of a normal population have consistently showed negative results. It has apparently not been easy to demonstrate that personality factors discriminate between Democrats and Republicans.

Once again, much of what we have said about the apparent recruitment mechanisms whereby the normal citizen comes to support a traditional party leads us to suspect that personality considerations would play a minor role indeed in determining such partisan choice. In Chapter 7 we described the transmission of party affiliation from parents to children. There seems little doubt but that this is one of the most prominent single mechanisms whereby an individual takes on a partisan inclination. Families, between generations as well as within generations, tend to show fair homogeneity in their responses to social definitions and expectations. The transmission of a religious creed, for example, is usually successful, and we know that the religious creed bears marked conceptual resemblance to party allegiance.

On the other hand, the family often shows considerable heterogeneity in its personality types. Personality theory is one of the more effective bodies of knowledge that may be brought to bear on behavior differentiation within the family not clearly rooted in role expectations. Not only are there innate differences in children born into the same family; these differences often become emphasized within the family system, so that complementary or even opposing personality trends are developed. To the degree that there is family transmission of entities like religious or political allegiances, we can imagine that parties and creeds become peopled with a wide range of personality types, save where the creed itself leads to biases in behavior. The ideologies of politics are so remote from the cognitions of most citizens that it is hard to imagine this happening with any great incidence in the political case.

The family is not the only social agent transmitting political norms. Other social groupings may be less heterogeneous in terms of personality and more heterogeneous politically than the family. But throughout we see the operation of mechanisms not highly selective in terms of personality types. In sum, there is little evidence to make us expect much continuity between deeper personality factors and partisan choice.

Under certain exceptional conditions the mechanisms of social transmission are disrupted in a manner of interest in terms of personality theory. Some individuals may be disposed to deviate from the norms and expectations of their social milieus. Adolescent rebellions against parental dictates come readily to mind. The incidence of such rebellion within the area of political preference is not large. Although some form of rebellion, covert if not overt, is likely to mark the development of the individual in the family, it seems theoretically reasonable to suppose that it will focus in behaviors where affect is high for the child and is perceived as being high for the parent.[3] The position of politics is so peripheral in the lives of most people that we would expect politics to become involved in conflict as an emotionally charged area only rarely. Instead, conflict within the family is likely to center on more emotionally focal problems such as courtship, jobs, school, and disposition of family possessions.

Similarly, the failure of larger social groupings to develop a perfectly homogeneous vote is often presumed to depend on "willful" deviation following personality lines. Once again the evidence for such deviation is weak. A substantial portion of the failure of the membership to attain such homogeneity may be due to concurrent membership in other groups to which felt loyalties are stronger, including here the family and the political party itself. Another substantial portion seems traceable to simple ignorance of what the group political standards are supposed to be, a matter that is once again far more cognitive than motivational or affective.[4]

However this may be, knowledge that a person is disposed to deviate from a political expectation in his social environment helps little in predicting the partisan direction of the deviation. Firm though the links may be between personality and a conformity-deviation dimension, we cannot relate personality to partisanship unless we know the social context that the individual is accepting or rejecting. If that context is Republican and the individual has no need to deviate from

[3] Maccoby *et al.* report data from a study of developing partisan choices among youth, which give indications in this direction. See Eleanor E. Maccoby, Richard E. Matthews, and Alton S. Morton, "Youth and Political Change," *Public Opinion Quarterly*, XVIII (Spring, 1954), 23–39.

[4] Some aspects of the data presented in Chapter 12 have this flavor. Clearer evidence in the union case is presented in Philip E. Converse and Angus Campbell, "Political Standards in Secondary Groupings," *Group Dynamics*, ed. Dorwin Cartwright and Alvin Zander (2d edition; Row, Peterson and Co., Evanston, Ill., 1960).

these expectations, he may proceed in a Republican direction. But if the group is Democratic, conformity means support of the Democrats instead. Naturally, we are intensely interested in the conformity-deviation dimension within any specified partisan milieu. But without this initial frame of reference, there is little theoretical ground on which to predict that conformity or deviation will produce more Republicans or Democrats.[5]

If deeper personality factors play an extremely limited role in partisan choice, we should still be able to spell out some of the conditions under which its role would be maximized. In the first place, we would expect little articulation between personality and partisanship for individuals whose voting reflects an established family pattern or one undertaken by the individual early in life. Our reasoning here is precisely that employed in Chapter 9 in connection with the analysis of "resistance to change." This latter variable is a quasi-personality factor itself, and McClosky has shown convincing relationships between it and other measures of personality dimensions.[6] If we restrict our attention to people who have changed their party identification after their early adult years, there is some trace of a relationship in the expected direction between the response to change and the newly selected party (Table 9-3). Of course this finding emerges only with a handful of the electorate; in the total sample there is no significant relationship between this disposition and partisanship.

Such analysis has to do with individuals who have more or less definitively reversed their party allegiances. We might also suppose that short-term deviation from party identification could arise as deeper personality needs became engaged by some transient element of the election. One aspect of the 1952 election suggested a plausible relationship between a personality measure and partisan choice. The nation was engaged in a small but frustrating overseas conflict, and stood in the shadow of a more massive and frightening "cold war." The Republican candidate was a national hero, the triumphant military figure of the Second World War. The Republican campaign made effective use of this combination of circumstances to stress this candidate potential for strong leadership and effective military policies. Therefore, it seemed reasonable to hypothesize that voters particularly attracted in a Republican direction on the basis of Eisenhower's

[5] See Franz Alexander, "Emotional Factors in Voting Behavior," *American Voting Behavior,* ed. Eugene Burdick and Arthur Brodbeck (The Free Press, Glencoe, Ill.; 1959), Chapter 16, p. 300.

[6] McClosky, *op. cit.*

promise of strong leadership would tend to show higher scores on a measure of "authoritarianism."[7]

This hypothesis found no support in our national cross-section survey data. A parallel analysis that isolated a set of respondents particularly engrossed in the image of Eisenhower as a strong leader tended to be slightly distinct from a control group in a number of attitudes and behaviors. These differences, however, had no clear interpretation in terms of standard personality theory; more instructive was the fact that less than 2 per cent of the sample could be classified in the critical group.[8]

The intrusion of deeper personality factors in partisan decisions probably is dependent upon intense political involvement. From this point of view, the 1952 election seemed a useful testing ground, as turnout figures suggested that this campaign motivated voters more strongly than most. There is serious question whether politics is ever sufficiently important for enough persons that deeper needs of the strict personality type would become engaged in any very visible way across the electorate. When we speak of high public involvement in an election, we must remember that the term is entirely relative. The fact that additional numbers of fringe voters are drawn over the motivation threshold to turn out and vote need not mean any intense absorption in the political situation. Even in high-tension campaigns that draw a large vote, the arena of politics remains remote for most of the electorate, and political behavior is peripheral by comparison to the day-to-day concerns—what Franz Alexander calls "the private life"—that truly absorb the individual's affective energies. Yet there are individuals scattered here and there in the society for whom political behavior is consuming activity. These people include political elites quite generally; they also include persons drawn in an active way to extreme political causes.[9]

[7] The measure of authoritarianism was that which arose from the California studies of ethnocentrism reported in T. W. Adorno, Else Frenkel-Brunswik, Daniel J. Levinson, and R. Nevitt Sanford, *The Authoritarian Personality* (Harper and Brothers, New York; 1950). Part of the authoritarian syndrome investigated clinically was a strong need for dependence on authority and a general tendency to idealize authority.

[8] James C. Davies, "Charisma in the 1952 Campaign," *American Political Science Review,* XLVIII (December, 1954), 1083–1102.

[9] Such persons are of a type almost diametrically opposed to that of much of the mass base of protest movements in Chapter 15. These people presumably are attracted by aspects of the extreme ideology that gear into their own personality needs and are likely to be vocal activists.

Some of the clearest links between personality dynamics and partisanship have turned up in studies of such specialized subgroups in the population. Thus, for example, McClosky found that a sample of McCarthy supporters, culled from a much larger parent population, was distinctive from that parent population on a number of personality measures.[10] Similarly, Eysenck appears to have generated some of his findings with a sample that, from a political as well as a social point of view, was rather unusual.[11] Almond, examining the lines of recruitment into Communist parties, felt that personality factors played a visible role in determining the middle-class activists drawn to the movement, but he was more impressed by the social mechanisms operative in giving the party its working-class rank and file.[12] Newcomb also traced out continuities between personality factors and attitude development in his Bennington Study. Here the social setting was an exceptional one in which "being right" in terms of national politics became an important condition for social acceptance and prominence in campus life. Hence politics became a matter of day-to-day concern with great emotional impact.[13]

Under unusual circumstances such as these, then, personality factors may come to play a more decisive role in partisan choice. But in the broad electorate, devoted in an habitual way to a pair of traditional parties, there is little reason to expect much visible instruction of personality dynamics in the determination of who is a Republican and who is a Democrat.

Personality and Issue Perceptions

If there are good theoretical grounds for believing that the role of underlying personality is marginal in the *direction* of partisanship, there are equally good grounds for supposing that personality may play a larger part in reactions to policy questions of the sort we posed to our respondents. Despite the fact that the policy controversies

[10] H. McClosky, unpublished paper presented at the American Psychological Association meetings, September, 1957.

[11] H. J. Eysenck, *The Psychology of Politics* (Routledge and Kegan Paul, London; 1954). For comment on sampling and other methodological problems see R. Christie, "Eysenck's Treatment of the Personality of Communists," and "Some Abuses of Psychology," both in *Psychological Bulletin,* LIII (November, 1956).

[12] Gabriel A. Almond, *The Appeals of Communism* (Princeton University Press, New York; 1943).

[13] Theodore M. Newcomb, *Personality and Social Change* (The Dryden Press, New York; 1943).

raised are, like political matters generally, quite remote from the daily lives of most of the electorate, other factors enter to permit a response more colored by personality, First, the items are asked in such a way that the primary structuring agent in the formation of political perceptions—the party itself—is absent from the stimulus. Since much of the electorate is unclear about the positions of the parties on the various issue items, party determination of issue responses is minimal, and there is greater room for intrusion of personality factors.

Furthermore, the issues presented for evaluation lack the historical depth of the traditional party structure. A person's parents may have been Democratic or Republican, and he may take these preferences as social transmissions without their becoming visibly affected by his own personality dynamics. However, if the parents had been exercised over issues of public policy, these controversies are likely to have become obsolete. New issues have arisen within his own generation for which the simpler, traditional cues are lacking. The degree to which this is true depends of course upon the substance of the issue itself.[14]

Finally, issues tend to pose alternatives that gear into personality dynamics in a much clearer way than is true of partisan choice. For example, persons typed as "authoritarians" have shown themselves to be suspicious of evil and dangerous forces that they perceived to be active in the world beyond their familiar social milieu.[15] Trends of this sort might find ready expression in responses to many matters of public policy. On the domestic front, for example, the authoritarian should be less sympathetic with the civil rights of minority groups and should resist the notion that the federal government might be concerned with their welfare. On foreign issues, it might be predicted as well that the authoritarian would be unlikely to grant foreign nations much "benefit of doubt" and would favor a "tough-minded" approach to diplomacy.

It is in this sense that issue alternatives may mesh directly and clearly with underlying needs, where party choice does not. If an individual were less bound to a party by his social past and if the parties were to become clearly differentiated on an axis having to do

[14] The failure to conceive of issue positions in broad ideological terms as discussed in Chapter 10 is one barrier to a sense of continuity in the issue landscape over time. A person who relates domestic problems to questions of "laissez faire" or who relates foreign issues to an isolationist dimension can shift many specific new issues that may arise into place on such a broader frame of reference. Where policy perceptions are concrete and fragmented, the constant threads of controversy over time are much less apparent.

[15] T. W. Adorno *et al., op. cit.*

with aggressiveness and chauvinism there might be some redistribution of citizens between the parties in a manner revealing personality selection. In the current period the public does not appear at all well informed concerning party differences in these matters. There is frequent judgment and fair consensus as to the capacity each party has demonstrated for avoiding war; but there is less comment and no consensus as to the respective means toward peace that the parties advocate.

"Authoritarianism" and aggressive issue responses. Hypotheses linking aggression to policy positions on governmental response to outgroups have been so frequent that we have used interview items devoted to authoritarianism to test for some of these relationships. However, the current measures of authoritarianism based on the California studies (the "F" scale) are subject to methodological frailties that require prior comment.

The usual authoritarian items are of a simple agree-disagree variety, in which the "agree" position is the authoritarian response. Christie, believing that responses to these items were powerfully influenced by a tendency within some segments of the population to agree to any flat proposition, reversed some of the F-scale items so that it was necessary to *disagree* to be considered "authoritarian." In our 1956 study, we employed a battery of ten authoritarian items, five of which were in the traditional "agree" form and five of which were reversed in their direction.

A comparison of responses to the two halves of the battery is disturbing, because people who look like "high authoritarians" where agreement means an authoritarian response tend to look like "low authoritarians" on the reversed items. In other words, there is a *negative* correlation between the two halves of the battery rather than the strong *positive* correlation that should emerge if people were responding to the content of the questions rather than their form. A simple "response set" seems to underlie a great many answers to the items of the usual authoritarianism scale.

This fact in turn casts strange light upon a number of the findings that have emerged where this type of measure has been used. For example, analysts of political behavior have been concerned to discover in a variety of studies that people of lower educational levels in this country appear to have marked "authoritarian" tendencies. With the reversed half of the scale alone one would conclude that it is the upper educational groups who are threats to democratic institutions, for here they register as significantly more "authoritarian" than people at lower levels (Table 18-1).

The tendency to acquiesce to broad statements is highly correlated

TABLE 18-1. Relation of Education Status to "Authoritarianism," as Measured by Reversed Items, 1956

Authoritarianism	Grade School	High School	College
Low	37%	21%	19%
Low-med.	27	28	26
High-med.	25	36	32
High	11	15	23
	100%	100%	100%
Number of cases	176	298	103

with education. It might be argued that such an uncritical approach to items posed by an interviewer (who, *vis-à-vis* lower class people is more often than not a status superior) is itself a sign of submission to authority. However, the tendency for poorly educated people to be uncritical of sweeping statements and to be "suggestible" where inadequate frames of reference are available has long been recognized. It is our impression, based in part on materials presented in Chapter 10, that fuller verbal responses that are less routine than a simple indication of agreement show precisely the same qualities. It is hard to conceive that these modes of thinking are brought on entirely by the presence of an "authority figure." It is interesting to note in this regard that sophisticated respondents with more differentiated perceptions find it difficult to accept such categoric statements whether formulated in an "authoritarian" direction or reversed. Thus there is a clear tendency to "disagree" at higher levels of education which approaches that of the "acquiescence" effect demonstrable among the less educated. These differences in response sets are of great interest because of the underlying differences in cognitive processes they betray.[16] But it is certainly not clear that all of the personality dynamics implied by the "authoritarian syndrome" are documented by the response set alone.

Hence it has seemed important to see what kind of explanatory tool the authoritarian items represent with the response set removed.

[16] These have been discussed in other terms than those of the authoritarian studies. See Cantril's discussion of impoverished frames of reference in *The Psychology of Social Movements* (John Wiley and Sons, New York; 1941), or Rokeach on dogmatic thinking [Milton Rokeach, "Political and Religious Dogmatism: An Alternative to the Authoritarian Personality" (*Psychological Monographs,* Vol. 70, No. 18; Washington, D. C.: The American Psychological Association, Inc., 1956)].

It is possible to treat the scales in such a manner that individuals are ranked as "high" or "low" authoritarians only if they are so classifiable on both halves of the scale. The resulting array of respondents shows only a slight residual correlation with the acquiescence factor as measured independently with another battery of agree-disagree items.

Treated in this manner, "authoritarianism" loses many of its familiar social correlates. Some residual relationship with education remains, the more poorly educated being once again the more authoritarian. For a number of reasons, we have seen fit to control education in our use of the measure. For example, it has often been suggested that many of the "personality" differences reported in *The Authoritarian Personality* smack strongly of differences in education, and the emergence of the response set is certainly not calculated to still these fears.[17] In any event, the theory as stated should not be embarrassed by such controls; there is no reason why different personality dynamics should not continue to be revealed along lines of aggression disposition or response to authority within even narrow classes of education.

With these controls exercised, the measure performs poorly in a number of hypotheses suggested by the theory that could be confirmed by the untreated scale. Of the fifteen tests provided by three categories of education and five issue positions, only three were strong enough in the proper direction to be clearly significant, although appropriate trends of borderline significance appeared in about three or four other comparisons. The remaining half or more of the tests showed, if anything, more negative than positive trends. Its most successful performance of the measures came when it was paired with issue perceptions which appeared to involve some elements of hostility toward minorities or other out-groups.

Nevertheless, this erratic performance may in itself be instructive. Although the same people are involved in each of the various tests, it seems striking that all three of the clear confirmations appear in the five tests involving college people; at least one of the more marginal confirmations is found here as well. Within the remaining four fifths

[17] See the discussions by Hyman, Sheatsley, and Christie in *Studies in the Scope and Method of "The Authoritarian Personality,"* ed. R. Christie and Marie Jahoda (The Free Press, Glencoe, Ill.; 1954). It is undoubtedly important to distinguish between the personality dynamics explored clinically in the California studies within groups of limited education differences and the faults of measures inspired by these studies when applied to a more heterogeneous population. That is, one can find the syndrome entirely credible in itself while suspending belief as to the meaning of responses from poorly educated individuals that look like those of more sophisticated people shown to have such personality trends. Data presented below increase our sense of the importance of this distinction.

of the population, positive and negative trends appear in nearly equal number. This may be a consequence of the fact that educated persons respond more to the *content* of the authoritarian items in the manner presumed by the investigator and less to the sheer *form* in which the items are cast. That is, although the positive and reversed halves of the measure still intercorrelate far too poorly among college respondents to assure us of reliable assessment, there is at least a positive correlation between halves approaching significance when college people are isolated. This is not the case within other education categories.

This observation is particularly significant in view of the fact that much of the California clinical work was completed with relatively well-educated subjects. Apparently the dynamics posited can be picked up with some clarity at a college level. That is, our initial hypothesis was that "authoritarianism" includes at least some component of hostility toward the out-group that should register in attitudes of public policy of the type we have employed. This finds confirmation where college-educated people are involved. For the remaining 80 per cent of the population, however, results stand at a dubious trace level. In short, as we move down the education ladder we find an increasing tendency to respond to normal F-scale items in the manner characteristic of those few college people who show personal dynamics of hostility. That the same responses mean the same dynamics for the less well educated cannot be satisfactorily demonstrated with our data.

Personality and Vote Participation

Other aspects of political behavior as well as reactions to policy controversies may reflect personality dynamics. The sheer fact of participation in the political process—whether it be in the form of voting or in further actions—tokens some inner motivational state much more clearly than the case of simple professions of partisanship. To be sure, some people seem to go to the polls through direct social pressure, despite little personal interest. By and large, however, the conceptual characteristics of political action are quite different from those involved in expressions of partisan preference. A person may accept a party rather automatically from his social milieu and remain within its clientele for long periods of time. But direct political participation cannot be accomplished for the individual by others. There must be some sources of energy that are entirely personal and that must be activated afresh with each ensuing election.

Hence it seems reasonable to look for some influence of personality organization on the inclination to participate politically. In Chapter 5 we discussed the role of factors like political efficacy and citizen duty in promoting vote participation. Variables of this sort, in contrast to measures of involvement in the current election, may be conceived as lying at a relatively "deep" level in any hierarchy of dispositions. That is, they represent highly generalized orientations toward the world of politics and could be expected to remain rather stable over a period of time. In this sense, they are approaching "personality" status. If we wished to think in terms of "political personality," they would warrant prominent attention. However, it may be worthwhile to conceive of them as dependent in part on aspects of underlying personality in a more general sense and to seek their roots in full-blown personality terms.

The measure of political efficacy is designed to capture differences between individuals in a basic sense of control over the workings of the political system. The politically efficacious individual feels that his vote counts in the operation of government and feels furthermore that there are other reasonable ways in which he can influence the progress of the system beyond going to the polls. What underlies the sense of political efficacy? To some degree, we would suppose that simple past experience with political matters would play an important role in its determination. That is, an individual who finds himself on the losing side in election after election is likely to feel less politically potent than the individual who contributes regularly to the tide of victory. Similarly, the person who finds himself constantly tormented by decisions of local government without perceived redress of grievances may come to feel that his capacity for political control is weak indeed.

At the same time, a belief in political efficacy may be determined in part by broader personality trends than those which reflect immediate political experience. The sense of control or mastery over the environment is an important component in modern personality theory. A term like "the ego" is often used as a shorthand for the many adaptive mechanisms that the individual develops as a means of reconciling his basic needs with the limitations of the physical and social environment. The ego functions that may be posited are extremely various. One of the more summary dimensions that may be abstracted to reflect individual differences at this level has to do with "ego strength," or the integration and efficiency of the individual's characteristic adaptive patterns. Although the individual is not presumed to be entirely aware of the dynamics of his ego functioning, he is aware in a general way as to how successful he is in transactions with his environment. We may speak, then, of a "sense of personal effectiveness," representing feelings of mastery over the self and the environment. The person lacking such a sense of mastery may either be tense and anxious about the course of his personal life, or may be resigned in a fatalistic way to a succession of events with which he does not feel that he can cope adequately.

It seems reasonable to suppose that, political experiences aside, differences in ego strength should influence beliefs in personal efficacy *vis-à-vis* the political process. Therefore we have attempted to measure this general sense of personal effectiveness with a set of eight items, none of which has any manifest political content. As they are "agree-disagree" items, they suffer the same problems of response set encountered with the authoritarian measure and must be treated in the same way to produce an array of respondents that is minimally correlated with the acquiescence factor.

TABLE 18-2. Relation of Sense of Personal Effectiveness to Sense of Political Efficacy, 1956

	Sense of Personal Effectiveness				
Political Efficacy	Low	Med. Low	Medium	Med. High	High
Low	33%	29%	23%	16%	4%
Medium	26	24	18	19	27
High	41	47	59	65	69
	100%	100%	100%	100%	100%
Number of cases	92	112	151	159	68

Table 18-2 summarizes the expected relationship between the generalized sense of effectiveness of ego strength and the belief in personal political efficacy. We have already seen that political efficacy is strongly related to education (Chapter 17), and we have discussed the role of the education process in strengthening this sense of efficacy. Since ego strength is also related to education, it is important to indicate the conceptual status that we accord to these three terms.

The evidence suggests rather clearly that the sense of political efficacy is a product of an interplay between education and ego strength. We have already argued that education fulfills one of its primary functions in providing tools with which the individual can cope more effectively with the environment. Hence, education appears to lead to increased ego strength. On the other hand, it has been shown that adolescents with a stronger sense of personal competence are more likely to have higher social aspirations and, undoubtedly, are likely to pursue their education farther as a result.[18] Thus education and ego strength show a substantial statistical relationship and may be considered as interacting factors in a causal nexus.

At the same time, the intercorrelation of these two factors is lower in magnitude than the correlation of either with political efficacy, a fact that suggests that both education and ego strength make independent contributions to the development of a sense of political efficacy. Among individuals with a similar sense of competence, the better educated are significantly more likely to rate high in political efficacy. And within levels of education, higher ego strength leads to higher efficacy. Therefore, neither component is superfluous in our understanding of the manner in which a sense of political efficacy develops.

As we would expect from our knowledge of political efficacy, differences in the sense of personal effectiveness are related to expressions of political involvement and to vote turnout, even within categories of education (Table 18-3). In this instance, the control exercised on education is in many senses an "overcontrol," since we see education as part of the sequence leading through ego strength to political efficacy and on to increased political participation.[19] With such a control, we see that relationships are least distinct among the college educated, in contrast to the pattern of findings where authoritarianism was involved. There appears to be more social pressure toward voting and involvement in higher-status milieus. At lower levels, the individual is more dependent on personal motivations, and hence personality becomes a more visible discriminant.

The fact that aspects of personality organization affect political participation is congruent with theory underlying the ego functions. Political affairs are, for most people, peripheral to their day-to-day lives. The efficiency of ego functioning bears directly on the way in

[18] Elizabeth Douvan and Joseph Adelson, "The Psychodynamics of Social Mobility in Adolescent Boys," *Journal of Abnormal and Social Psychology,* LVI (January 1958).

[19] This was not the case in dealing with the authoritarian measure. The California investigators were quite concerned about maintaining a conceptual disengagement between education and the personality dynamics central to their interest. Hence it is hard to feel that controls on education here are in any sense excessive, given the theory.

TABLE 18-3. The Relation of Sense of Personal Effectiveness to Political Involvement and Vote Turnout, by Education

	Sense of Personal Effectiveness			
Education	Low	Low Med.	High Med.	High
Grade school				
Per cent voting	43%	47%	72%	82%
Per cent involved	32%	34%	48%	41%
Number of cases	47	47	60	22
High school				
Per cent voting	67%	79%	80%	82%
Per cent involved	48%	45%	62%	57%
Number of cases	67	61	136	34
College				
Per cent voting	...	90%	90%	88%
Per cent involved	...	76%	73%	86%
Number of cases	[a]	29	52	22

[a] Nine cases involved in this column have been merged with the next adjacent column to give a sufficient number of cases.

which the individual can or must allocate his energies in dealing with the environment. Where such functioning is chaotic, more energy is drained off in the maintenance of the psychological economy and less remains to initiate and create beyond the immediate emotional necessities. Where the ego is strong, however, the individual can maintain a higher level of involvement in these secondary areas of behavior.

THE ELECTORAL DECISION AND THE POLITICAL SYSTEM ◇ SECTION V

This book has sought primarily to show the influences on individual voting behavior. Taking the individual's voting act as a starting point, we have moved backward in time and outward from political influences to trace the intricate pattern of causality leading to behavior at the polls. If the discussion has dealt at times with historical or economic conditions, social structure, or other large factors, these have been treated as parts of a total configuration underlying the behavior of individual people. The vote of the individual elector has been the datum we have sought finally to explain.

Keeping to this task has limited our view in two respects. In the first place, fixing attention on the individual voter has kept us from accounting for the decision of the electorate as a whole. Certainly voting is an individual act; yet it is the collectivity of voters that makes the electoral decision, and we should use what we know of individual motivation to describe the forces on the decision of the total electorate. In the second place, confining our view to the *antecedents* of voting has kept us from assessing the place of the electoral process in the full political system. Voting by the American electorate occurs within a broader political order, and we should add what we know of electoral behavior to theories of the more general system in which it is set.

In two final chapters we extend our view in each of these directions. Chapter 19 shifts the terms of reference from the voter to the full electorate and from individual choice to the collective decision. In doing so it remains within the framework of motivational concepts set forth in earlier chapters and utilizes these concepts to probe the national vote decision. The discussion deals first with the elections of 1952 and 1956, reorganizing the data of Chapter 4 to show the attitudinal components of the electorate's decision. It then moves to a somewhat broader consideration of American presidential elections, proposing a system of classification within which they may be understood.

Chapter 20 returns to a question asked in the opening chapter of this book: what aspects of the wider political order can be traced to the character of voting behavior as we find it in the American electorate? The manner in which the public reaches the judgments it must periodically give is of substantial importance in determining what is done in other decision processes of the political system and, indeed, in determining the structure of the system itself. Our final chapter argues this view by examining three such effects: the impact of electoral behavior on political leadership; its influence on party strategy; and its effect on the nature of the party system.

The Electoral Decision ◇ 19

The difficulty of knowing what motivates the electorate has not lessened popular interest in diagnosing the factors causing the outcome of a national election. The day after a presidential election a national inquest opens into the causes of the result. In political circles, in the mass media, and among the general public a host of explanatory factors is examined and the responsibility of each for the outcome is assessed. With the passage of time this body of popular comment is delivered into the hands of the political historian, who also seeks to interpret the result and establish its place in the broader eras defined by the ebb and flow of party strength.

Despite the universal interest in what has influenced our elections, interpretation has scarcely risen above the simplest impressionism. The explanations offered for an electoral result are astonishingly varied, they depend typically on the slenderest evidence, and disagreements are commonplace even among knowledgeable observers. The plain fact is that there has not been an explicit means of assessing the relative importance of several influences on an election and of assessing its character in a wider set of elections.

Yet a way of assessing these things ought to be within reach. We are able to account for the behavior of the individual voter, at least within tolerable limits. If we understand the forces on the individual citizen, we should be able to sum their effects and resolve the winning majority into its component elements. Our understanding of an election may be carried still further if we compare the partisan direction of the forces acting on the decision with the direction of the nation's predominant partisan loyalties. In some elections the attitudinal forces on the decision are consistent with the party identifications of a majority of the public. But in other elections they are not. Indeed, in some contests the conflict is sufficiently marked that strong attitudes toward the current elements of national politics will *alter* the distribution of partisan loyalties held by the population. In the final pages of this chapter we will exploit this fact in devising a classification of presidential elections that can be used to interpret the decisions of any electoral era.

Components of the Decision

We have seen in Chapter 4 that the individual's voting act is profoundly influenced by his feeling toward the objects to which this act relates. Indeed, we have seen that if we measure the partisan direction and intensity of his attitude toward six discernible elements of the world of politics we are able to predict quite well his behavior at the polls. To say whether any given person will vote Republican or Democratic we need to know where he falls on these dimensions of partisan feeling, that is, whether his attitude toward each political object is pro-Republican or pro-Democratic and with what strength.

Knowing the direction and intensity of the attitude forces on the individual we would have little difficulty telling which of these forces had pulled him more strongly in a given partisan direction. If we knew, for example, that a Republican voter in 1956 was moderately favorable to the Democrats on domestic issues and to the Republicans on foreign issues, that he was neutral toward the parties as managers of government and on questions of group interest, and that he was slightly unfavorable to Stevenson but very strongly favorable to Eisenhower we could readily order these forces according to how much they tended to move him in the Republican direction. It would seem intuitively clear that his attitude toward Eisenhower had drawn him most strongly toward the Republicans, followed, in order, by his attitude toward foreign issues and toward Stevenson; that his attitude related to groups and to the performance of the parties had not had an effect in either direction; and that his attitude toward domestic issues had tended to draw him in the Democratic direction.

Just as the votes of individual people are added together to reach a collective decision,[1] so we may sum the attitude forces on persons in a

[1] For simplicity we assume here that a popular majority elects a President. The rule by which a collective decision is formed out of individual choices is of course more complicated than this, and the overweighting of votes in states of small population, the unit rule in casting a state's votes in the Electoral College, and the constitutional freedom of Electors can be of great practical importance.

sample of the electorate to assess the impact of these forces on the national vote decision. Although the manner in which this is done will not be reviewed here,[2] the method permits us to say whether a given dimension of attitude has moved the electorate more in the Republican or Democratic direction and to what degree. As a result, we are able to decompose an election outcome into a set of attitudinal components.

When the vote of the Eisenhower years is resolved into its components, these methods lead to findings of considerable interest, which are summarized in Fig. 19-1. In the design of this figure the direction in which a bar goes out from the mid-line indicates which party the corresponding dimension of attitude has helped more. If the bar extends to the left, the factor has been generally pro-Democratic. If it extends to the right, the factor has been pro-Republican. The length of the bar indicates the relative magnitude of a factor's influence on the two-party division of the vote. The greater the bar's length, the greater the importance of the dimension of attitude in enlarging or lessening the winning majority. It is readily apparent that in both these years the sum of the lengths in the Republican direction is greater than the sum in the Democratic direction.

An inspection of this figure suggests that the Eisenhower victory of 1952 resulted from the combined effects of three factors. The Republican majority in that year appears to have been formed, first of all, out of the strongly anti-Democratic attitude toward the performance of the parties. The second Truman term was characterized by a growing criticism of the President and his Administration on the question of honesty in government. Revelations of irregularities, ranging from minor peccadilloes of patronage and favoritism to serious malfeasance in the Bureau of Internal Revenue, raised doubts as to the moral fibre of the Federal Administration. Although none of the accusations involved such high crimes as those with which the Harding Administration was entangled in the Teapot Dome scandal, they appear to have had a much greater political impact. Partly because they came at the end of a long period of one-party rule and partly because of the insistent publicity they were given by the press, the moral lapses of the Truman Administration, real and fancied, had a strong influence on the electorate.

The second factor that appears to have moved the electorate in the Republican direction was the favorable response to Eisenhower as a

[2] A description of the methods used appears in Donald E. Stokes, Angus Campbell, and Warren E. Miller, "Components of Electoral Decision," *American Political Science Review*, LII (June 1958), 367–387.

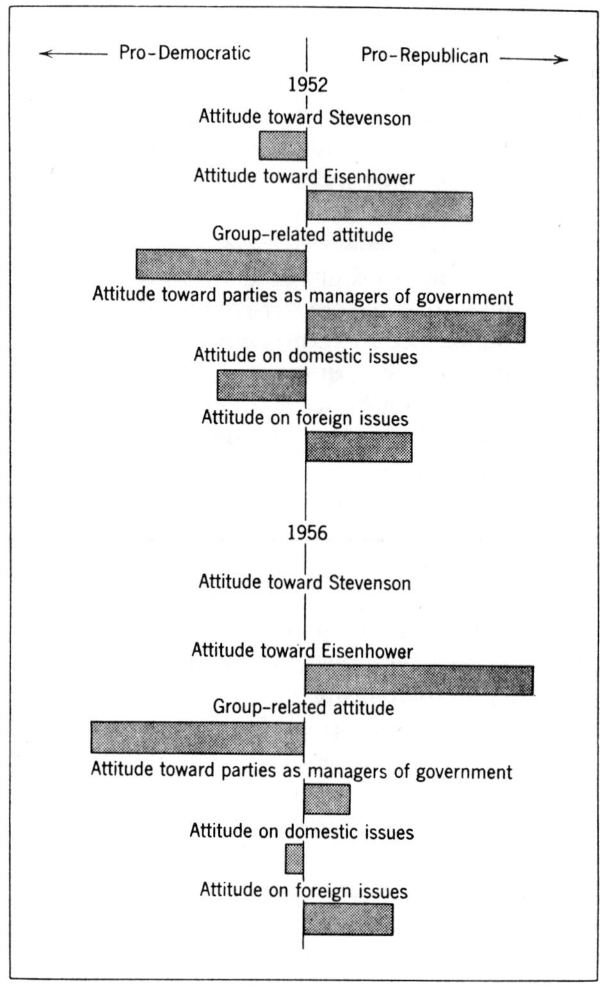

Fig. 19-1. Attitudinal forces on the presidential vote.

person. General Eisenhower's record as a military hero had developed a strongly positive feeling toward him in all elements of the population before he had become associated in any way with partisan politics. Moreover, the Eisenhower candidacy seemed extraordinarily well suited to the demands of the time. Eisenhower's unparalleled reputation as a successful military leader gave promise of an answer to the desperate question of Korea. And his freedom from association with the seamier aspects of party politics and his widely acknowledged personal integrity carried a special appeal to many people who were disturbed at the level of political morality in Washington.

The third factor that contributed to the Republican majority of 1952 was the public's response to issues of foreign policy. The Korean conflict and other aspects of America's role in the cold war had generated attitudes that were decidedly favorable to the Republicans. Frustration and resentment over the stalemated Korean War, which had never been well understood by the American people, were widespread and intense. There probably have been few times in American history when the people have been asked to maintain a posture of determination in the face of such provocation. As the action in Korea dragged into its third year, it became an increasingly partisan issue, with the Republican leadership arguing either that this country should never have been involved in Korea in the first place or that the Democratic Administration should have brought our involvement there to a successful conclusion. It was an argument of great popular appeal that the Democrats apparently did not effectively answer.

This combination of factors appears to have overwhelmed the effects of several factors that tended to reduce the size of the Republican majority in 1952. The most important of these was the feeling that the Democrats were more favorable than the Republicans to the welfare of certain groupings within the population. But the magnitude of the Republican victory seems also to have been diminished by the pro-Democratic response of the public to issues of domestic policy and by the public's response to the new Democratic candidate, although the net effect of popular attitudes toward the personal qualities of Mr. Stevenson was relatively slight.

Although the election of 1956 seemed in many ways a rematch of the contest four years earlier, Fig. 19-1 shows how different were the components of the Republican victory in the two elections. In the latter year the popular appeal of Eisenhower was unquestionably of paramount importance. The public's approval of Mr. Eisenhower as a person was even greater in the second of these elections, and it seems to have contributed more to the Republican majority than did two other pro-Republican factors together. In 1956 the Republican margin was increased once more, though to a lesser extent than in 1952, by popular feeling about foreign affairs, particularly the overriding issues of war and peace. And it was increased, too, by the public's estimate of party performance in managing the federal government, although with the corruption issue largely spent, this dimension of feeling contributed far less than it did to the Republican cause in the earlier election. Four years out of office seemed to have cleared the image of the Democratic Party of much of the shadow which had fallen over it at the end of its long tenure in Washington.

Among the components of the 1956 vote, the strongly pro-Democratic sense of group interest appears to have been virtually the sole force reducing the size of Eisenhower's victory. The image of the Democratic Party as the friend of the common man, the Negro, the farmer, and the laborer still shone as brightly as before. However, the prosperity of Eisenhower's first term and the moderately progressive approach of the Republican Administration to social welfare policy appear to have weakened considerably the advantage of the Democrats in domestic affairs. And public attitude toward the personal attributes of Mr. Stevenson appears to have been no more an asset than a liability to his cause in his second quest of the presidency.

The paramount importance of Eisenhower's personality in the Republican victory of 1956 makes quite clear why it was that the Republicans, in winning the presidency, were unable to win control of Congress. Eisenhower's personal appeal was not completely without force on the congressional vote, since the practice of straight-ticket voting carried the choice that many people made between presidential candidates over to their choice between congressional candidates. Yet the influence of his appeal undoubtedly was much less on the vote for the House and Senate than it was on the vote for the presidency, whereas the other components of the Eisenhower victory probably had very much the same influence on the congressional vote as they had on the presidential vote.[3] The result of this difference was that Eisenhower captured 57 per cent of the two-party vote for President; yet the Democrats won both houses of Congress. It was the first time since 1848 that a split of this kind had occurred, and in that earlier year Zachary Taylor had won with less than an actual majority of the total vote. It is evident that an election is likely to reach the outcome of 1956 only if the victory of the winning candidate for President depends to an unusual degree on his own personal appeal.

Electoral Components and Party Identification

When the individual acts toward the world of politics, as he does in casting a vote, his behavior is guided immediately by evaluations of the things he sees in that world. By measuring these evaluations we are

[3] An exception to this statement would of course be attitude toward Stevenson. We need not consider this factor since it did not move the electorate more in one partisan direction than the other, as is shown by Fig. 19-1.

able to account for the individual's partisan choice, and by summing their effects across the electorate we are able to resolve an electoral decision into its attitudinal components. Yet evaluations of politics are not formed wholly anew in each presidential campaign. Some evaluations persist through time, and so do certain *dispositions* to evaluate the elements of politics in a given partisan way. Most Americans have an enduring partisan orientation, a sense of party identification, which has wide effects on their attitudes toward the things that are visible in the political world.

Were party identification the sole determinant of the psychological forces on behavior, the attitudinal components of the vote would agree in their partisan direction with the party loyalties of a majority of the electorate. In such a case the public's evaluation of each element of politics it sees in the presidential campaign would be "biased" in the direction of the majority's party allegiance, and the vote would be biased in the same direction. Undoubtedly in many of our national elections the forces on the vote have very largely been reflections of long-term party loyalties. But we know that party identification is not the sole influence on how the voter appraises the things he is acting toward. In some elections the public's evaluations of the current elements of politics may not agree with its predominant partisan allegiances, and when they do not, in a system where the standing balance of party identification is not too uneven, the difference between evaluations of current political objects and long-term partisan loyalties may be wide enough to elect the candidate of the minority party. Indeed, one of the most telling characteristics of any election is how much other influences have caused the components of the decision to depart from those we would expect to find if party identification were the only determinant of the forces immediately governing behavior.

The reality of such a departure can be shown by an example within the span of our studies. Let us consider the election of 1952. The distribution of party identification in that year favored the Democrats by about three to two, although the Democratic advantage in the loyalties of those who voted was not quite so marked. Therefore, if party identification had been the sole determinant of popular attitudes toward the two candidates, the issues of domestic and of foreign policy, and other elements of politics, the distribution of popular feeling on each of these dimensions would have been pro-Democratic and a majority of the electorate would have voted for the Democratic candidate. Yet we know from Fig. 19-1 that the actual components of the 1952 vote were more pro-Republican than pro-Democratic. Other influences had deflected the forces on the vote from what we would have expected on the basis of party identification alone. The nature of this departure is seen more clearly if we re-draw the components for the election of 1952 in Fig. 19-1 in order to show the relative force of each dimension of attitude in moving the electorate not from an even division of the vote but from the division we would have expected if the electorate's predominantly Democratic Party loyalties had been the sole influence on its appraisal of the elements of politics. The components of the 1952 vote, redrawn to "take out" the influence of party identification, are shown in Fig. 19-2. The bars of the reconstructed figure make clear how strongly other influences in 1952 were moving the electorate in the Republican direction.

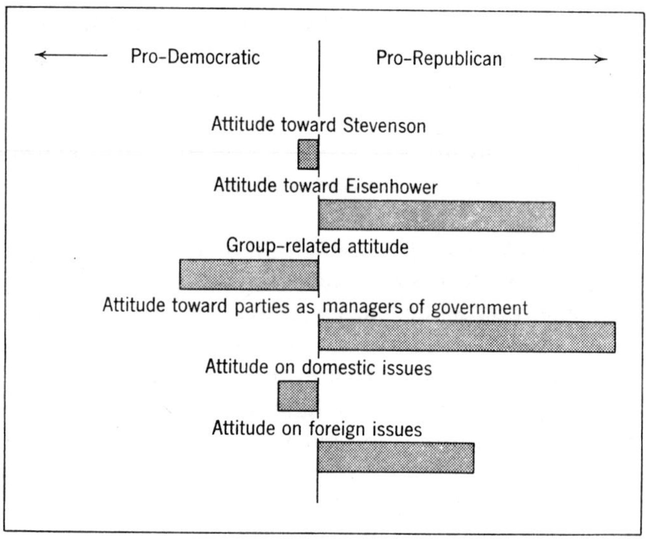

Fig. 19-2. Attitudinal components of the vote with effect of party identification removed, 1952.

At some moments of electoral history the attitude forces on the vote may depart so widely from standing party loyalties that these partisan identifications are altered. If the attitudes surrounding the issues of politics, its great personalities, and the current style and performance of the parties are intense enough and conflict strongly enough with long-term partisan allegiances, these allegiances may change. We have cited in Chapter 7 the impact that great national crises may have on existing party loyalties. The crisis leading to the Civil War acted so strongly on prior partisan allegiances that the popular base of one of the existing parties was shattered and the popular support of the other radically transformed while a wholly new party catapulted itself into control of the national government.

A Classification of Presidential Elections

When we look to other campaigns beyond the two elections with which this book has been primarily concerned, we find a long succession of presidential contests resembling each other closely in the institutional framework within which they are conducted, but differing substantially from year to year as the new candidates, the contemporary issues, and the minority parties that spring to life have given them individuality. As we have just seen, it is possible to describe the disordered confusion of acts and events that make up an election in terms of the basic partisan attitudes that we have conceived as directly underlying the individual voting act. And a good deal of the meaning of an election for future years can be indicated by comparing the force of these attitudes with the electorate's long-term partisan loyalties. We propose now to reach beyond these recent elections and apply our theory of political motivation more broadly, using it to develop a more generalized system of classification of presidential elections.

We propose to classify American presidential elections into three basic types, which we may call maintaining, deviating, and realigning.[4] A *maintaining* election is one in which the pattern of partisan attachments prevailing in the preceding period persists and is the primary influence on forces governing the vote. In this sense many, if not most, presidential elections during the past hundred years have been maintaining elections. If we assume that during the period immediately following the Civil War the majority of the electorate were Republican in their partisan sympathies and that this majority declined to something near an even balance during the 1876–1892 period and was revitalized in 1896, we may conclude that the numerous Republican victories down through the 1920's fall largely in this category.

Among more recent elections we would describe the contest of 1948 as a maintaining election. The events surrounding the campaign of that year seemed signally devoid of circumstances that could generate forces running counter to existing partisan loyalties. In 1948 the total popular vote was 48.4 million, the lowest turnout in relation to the

[4] The reader will recognize that this classification is an extension of V. O. Key's theory of critical elections. See V. O. Key, Jr., "A Theory of Critical Elections," *Journal of Politics, 17* (February 1955), 3–18. See also V. O. Key, Jr., "Secular Realignment and the Party System," *Journal of Politics, 21* (May 1959), 198–210.

size of the total adult population since 1928. No compelling political issue stirred intense reaction throughout the electorate. Although the Taft-Hartley Act and the elimination of certain wartime economic controls were offensive to some groups of voters, the nation was prosperous, employment was high, and the threat of economic stress was slight. Similarly, international issues had receded in the mind of a public that appeared to concern itself with world affairs only under the greatest compulsion. The attempt of the short-lived Progressive Party to arouse public interest in issues of foreign policy proved a failure. It was, in other words, an election in which no overriding issue intruded to deflect the electorate from voting with its standing partisan allegiances.

Neither was it an election in which significant numbers of voters were activated by the personalities or accomplishments of the presidential candidates. Neither President Truman nor Governor Dewey stirred the enthusiasm of the general electorate. On the contrary, they were both criticized for presumed inadequacies and were undoubtedly seen in highly partisan terms. The Democratic victory in 1948 is sometimes referred to as a personal triumph for Mr. Truman, but the evidence does not support this interpretation. A presidential nominee who runs behind his party in the election returns, as Truman did in well over half the states in which there was a Democratic candidate for Governor or Senator, can hardly be said to be leading his party to victory. In the election to which we refer, Truman and Dewey both drew their support primarily from the most highly committed followers of their parties. Neither was able to swing the independent vote in any significant way, attract any sizable number of defectors from the opposition party, or stimulate any important fraction of the in-and-out vote to go to the polls in his behalf. These are the marks of strong candidate appeal, and they were not present in the 1948 election.

It is likely, then, that in 1948 the electorate responded to current elements of politics very much in terms of its existing partisan loyalties. Apparently very little of the political landscape attracted strong feeling in that year. But what feeling there was seemed to be governed largely by antecedent attachments to one of the two major parties. On election day the Democrats turned out to support Truman and the Republicans to support Dewey. Neither party marshalled its forces at full strength. But Mr. Truman was fortunate in representing a party whose followers considerably outnumbered the opposition, and the electoral decision maintained his party in power.

In a *deviating* election the basic division of partisan loyalties is not seriously disturbed, but the attitude forces on the vote are such as to bring about the defeat of the majority party. After the personalities or events that deflected these forces from what we would expect on the basis of party have disappeared from the scene, the political balance returns to a level that more closely reflects the underlying division of partisan attachments. A deviating election is thus a temporary reversal that occurs during a period when one or the other party holds a clear advantage in the long-term preferences of the electorate.

In the previous pages we have described characteristics of the Eisenhower victory of 1952 that establish this election as a deviating one. The election of Woodrow Wilson in 1916 suggests itself as an additional example. There seems little doubt that during the period of the Wilson elections the electorate was predominantly Republican. Wilson attained the White House in 1912 with a minority (42 per cent) of the total vote, as Roosevelt and Taft split the Republican Party; his incumbency and the public emotion aroused by the shadow of the First World War apparently provided the additional votes he needed in 1916 to reach the narrow plurality that he achieved over his Republican opponent. According to Key, the Democratic gains of 1916 were due principally to "a short-term desertion of the Republican Party by classes of British origin and orientation."[5] The temporary character of the Democratic victory began to become apparent in the 1918 elections when the Republican Party won control of the Congress. In 1920 and the two elections following, the minority status of the Democratic Party was again convincingly demonstrated.

The definition we have given of a deviating election implies that in such an election more people than usual will cross party lines in casting their votes. As a result, the events of a deviating election can easily suggest that traditional party loyalties have become less important. To be sure, they have—in an immediate sense. But if our view of the motivational basis of voting is correct, a deviating election should not be taken as evidence of a secular decline in the importance of party identification. In Chapter 6 we have examined the profound impact of party allegiance even in elections in which a great many people voted against their traditional loyalties. What is more, the interrelations of education, political involvement, and strength of partisanship suggest that as the electorate becomes more sophisticated and involved psychologically in politics, it may well become more, rather than less, fixed in its partisan commitments. In any event, demonstrating a lasting decline in the role of party identification needs more evidence than that which one or two deviating elections can supply.

[5] V. O. Key, Jr., "A Theory of Critical Elections," *op. cit.*, 11.

Key has pointed out that there is a third type of election, characterized by the appearance of "a more or less durable realignment" of party loyalties. In such a *realigning* election, popular feeling associated with politics is sufficiently intense that the basic partisan commitments of a portion of the electorate change. Such shifts are infrequent. As Key observes, every election has the effect of creating lasting party loyalties in some individual voters, but it is "not often that the number so affected is so great as to create a sharp realignment."

We have said that changes in long-term party allegiances tend to be associated with great national crises. The emergence of the Republican Party and its subsequent domination of national politics were the direct outgrowth of the great debate over slavery and the ultimate issue of the Civil War. The election of 1896, following the panic of 1893, is regarded by Key as a "critical" election since "the Democratic defeat was so demoralizing and so thorough that the party made little headway in regrouping its forces until 1916." It may be argued that the Democratic Party did not in fact hold the loyalties of a clear majority of the electorate at the time of the Cleveland elections, but the election statistics make it appear that whatever hold it did have on the voters was greatly weakened after 1893.

The most dramatic reversal of party alignments in this century was associated with the Great Depression of the 1930's. The economic disaster that befell the nation during the Hoover Administration so discredited the Republican Party that it fell from its impressive majorities of the 1920's to a series of defeats, which in 1936 reached overwhelming dimensions. These defeats were more than temporary departures from a continuing division of underlying party strength. There is little doubt that large numbers of voters, especially among the younger age groups and those social and economic classes hardest hit by the Depression, were converted to the Democratic Party during this period. The program of welfare legislation of the New Deal and the extraordinary personality of its major exponent, Franklin D. Roosevelt, brought about a profound realignment of party strength, which has endured in large part up to the present time.

Key has pointed out that the shift toward the Democratic Party that occurred in the early 1930's was anticipated in the New England area in the 1928 election. It is difficult to determine whether the changes in these successive election years were actually part of the same movement. Since the shifts in New England were highly correlated with the proportions of Catholic voters in the communities studied, it would not be unreasonable to attribute them to the presence of Governor Alfred E. Smith at the head of the Democratic ticket in 1928. Had the depression not intervened, the New England vote might have returned to its pre-1928 levels in the 1932 election. It may be recalled, however, that the Smith candidacy had not only a religious aspect but a class quality as well. The resemblance of the class contrast between Smith and Hoover in 1928 and that between Truman and Dewey in 1948 is more than casual. It may well be that New England voters, having moved into the Democratic ranks in 1928 for reasons having to do with both religious and economic considerations, found it easy to remain there in 1932 when economic questions became compellingly important.

The ambiguity of the relation between the Hoover-Smith contest of 1928 and the Roosevelt elections of the 1930's, at least in New England, emphasizes the importance of having adequate measures of the attitude forces on the vote and of the distribution of party identification if we are to interpret the character of an election. This ambiguity also cautions us against too easily associating with a single election a major realignment of party strength. In order to describe with confidence the movement of part of the electorate from the Republican to the Democratic Party a generation ago, we would need to know when it was that these people formed a stable emotional attachment to the Democratic Party. If we had this information we might well find that an attachment of this kind appeared in some of the changers as early as 1928, whereas it appeared in others only in the late 1930's or early 1940's, after they had voted Democratic several times. It is worth noting that the Democratic harvest of votes continued through the mid-thirties. Although Roosevelt's margin of victory in 1932 was large (59 per cent of the two-party vote), it was not until 1936 that the Democratic wave reached its peak. The long-entrenched Republican sympathies of the electorate may not have given way easily in the early years of the Depression. Had not Roosevelt and his New Deal won the confidence of many of these people during his first term—or even his second—there might well have been a return to earlier party lines similar to that which occurred in 1920. From this point of view we might speak not of a realigning *election* but of a realigning *electoral era.*

What is more, it is clear that the changes of such an era arise not alone from changes in the party loyalties of those who are past the age of socialization to politics. It comes as well from the relative advantage of the party that dominates the era in recruiting new identifiers from among those who are first developing their political values. The past histories of persons we have interviewed in the 1950's indicate that the New Deal–Fair Deal era produced a lasting change in party strength primarily by attracting to the Democratic Party most of the age cohort entering the electorate during the 1930's and 1940's.

One other aspect of change has been evident in most periods of lasting displacements of party strength. We have said that the distinguishing characteristic of a realigning era is a shift in the distribution of party identification. By this we mean that a *net* shift occurs, benefiting one party rather than the other. But it is clear that a net shift in the party balance does not imply that individual changes have been in one direction only. Such a shift may result from partially compensating changes of party loyalties in several population groups.[6] For example, one party may gain strength over-all from a greater polarization of politics along class lines. We know that this is part of what happened in the 1930's, as the Depression and New Deal prompted working-class people to identify more closely with the Democratic Party and middle-class people with the Republican Party. Which party gains more from a reshuffling of this sort depends on which class grouping is the larger and how strongly each grouping moves toward complete homogeneity of opinion. Lasting changes in the party balance may also accompany political realignments along regional lines. This was what happened in the elections after the Civil War. And, as Key has made clear, the realignment accompanying the election of 1896 moved the industrial East toward the Republican Party and the West toward the Democrats, giving our presidential politics a regional cast that persisted through subsequent elections. If the Republicans gained from this dual sectional movement, it was largely because the East was by far the more populous region.

We do not mean to say that changes in the political loyalties of groups are an indispensable part of long-term displacements of party strength. We may think of factors, such as a protracted foreign war, which would benefit one party or the other in virtually all groups. Yet there are two reasons why a change in the group basis of politics is likely to presage a lasting shift in the party balance. First, changes in the political loyalties of groups tend to be associated with issues that persist through time. We may suppose, for example, that issues which sharpen class differences will prove to be more durable than the impact of a magnetic political figure who has drawn strength to his party from a great many groups. Second, changes in party loyalty occurring on a group basis tend to be reinforced by group opinion processes. Attitudes rooted in social groups are likely to be more stable than are attitudes that are denied the status of group norms.

[6] Indeed, the concept of realignment as it is used by Key includes the idea of change in the group basis of party strength.

In view of all that we have said, how are we to characterize the two elections for which we have adequate survey data? The Eisenhower elections were clearly not maintaining elections. Neither were they realigning elections in the sense of a profound shift of the nation's party identifications having occurred in this period. Yet the question might well be raised of whether they were not the early elections of a realigning electoral era. We believe they were not, for reasons that a brief review of our findings may serve to make clear.

The most immediately relevant information that we can draw out of these studies is the fact that in both 1952 and 1956 the number of people who called themselves Democrats outnumbered those who identified themselves as Republicans, and this ratio showed no tendency to move in the Republican direction between the two years. What is more, the Republican Party did not recruit a heavy majority of young voters who were coming into the electorate, although these years did see the Democratic proportion of new voters reduced to something like half.

A second important item is the evidence that for the most part those Democrats and Independents who voted for Eisenhower at the time of his two elections preferred the man but not the party. This is dramatically demonstrated by the high proportion of ticket-splitting reported by these people. Three out of five in 1952 and three out of four in 1956 were not willing to support the Republican slate even though they voted for its presidential candidate. It is especially significant that this separation of the candidate from his party was greater in the second Eisenhower election than in the first. If we compare 1952 to 1932 it seems probable that the potential for shift created by the Democratic victory in 1932 was realized in 1936, whereas whatever readiness for shift was present in the electorate in 1952 seems to have largely faded out by 1956.

That the Republican Party did not prepare the ground in the Eisenhower years for a basic shift of party loyalties is attested by the congressional vote in 1954 and 1956. Without Eisenhower's name at the top of their ticket in 1954 the Republicans could not hold either house of Congress. And even with Eisenhower again heading the ticket in 1956 the Republican congressional candidates ran several percentage points *further* behind their pace setter than they had in 1952, and in doing so they once again lost both houses of Congress. There is evidence from our 1956 survey that Eisenhower's coattails were not without influence and that without them the Republican candidates for Congress would have fared even more poorly than they did.

We may observe, finally, that political change in the Eisenhower years was not accompanied by a marked realignment of the loyalties of groups within the electorate. The factors in these years that deflected the vote from what we would have expected on the basis of party identification alone, acted quite generally across the electorate and were all of a relatively brief duration. The Far Eastern War, which had influenced popular opinion so powerfully in 1952, was settled within a year of Eisenhower's first victory. What corruption there was in the prior Democratic Administration ended perforce when the party was turned out of power. And, above all, the Eisenhower personality could not continue to be a prime influence on the behavior of the electorate with the coming of new candidates.

These considerations lead us to the conclusion that the Eisenhower elections did not presage a critical realignment of partisan attachments. They did not seriously threaten the prevailing Democratic majority, and the factors that made them possible seem not to have been of a long-term character. One may ask how long a party can hope to hold the White House if it does not have a majority of the party-identified electorate. There would not appear to be any certain answer to this question. The unfolding of national and international events and the appearance of new political figures to take the place of the old hold the potential for unforeseeable political consequences. We should expect, however, that the circumstances that keep a minority in power would tend over time to increase the proportion of the electorate whose loyalty it commanded. If this increase does not occur, the minority party cannot hope to continue its tenure in office over a very extended period.

Electoral Behavior and the Political System ◇ 20

When studies of voting have moved beyond a purely descriptive level, they have searched for the causes rather than the effects of electoral behavior. In virtually every case these studies have sought to discover what has influenced the vote and have given slight attention to the question of what the vote has influenced. The voting act has served as the datum to be explained, and electoral research has been absorbed in finding the antecedent factors, immediate and remote, that help account for voting turnout and partisan choice.

This book may suggest what the rewards of this orientation of research can be. Yet studies that look only to the *determinants* of voting fail to consider a number of problems for which systematic knowledge of electoral behavior is of great importance. We have said that popular elections are one of several means of decision making in the political system, that this system coheres largely because its decision processes are bound together by relations of mutual influence, and that, as a result, decisions of the electorate are of interest for their influence on what occurs elsewhere in the system. Our quest of understanding should not end with the discovery of the causes of electoral decisions; it should extend to their consequences as well.

To be sure, this point of view is not totally foreign to electoral research.[1] Yet the effects of electoral behavior are treated much more

[1] For example, Berelson *et al.* conclude their volume on *Voting* with a chapter laying the characteristics of electoral behavior against the requirements of a political system. See also the earlier discussion by Berelson, "Democratic Theory and Public Opinion," *Public Opinion Quarterly,* XVI (Fall, 1952), 313–330, and the essay by Talcott Parsons, "'Voting' and the Equilibrium of the American Party System," in *American Voting Behavior,* ed. Eugene Burdick and Arthur J. Brodbeck (The Free Press, Glencoe, Illinois; 1959), pp. 80–120.

in the literature of decision making in other arenas of government. For what we know of the electorate's impact we must look not to research on voting but to studies of legislative assemblies, of executive and administrative agencies, and of the political parties. Almost no research has had as its primary objective the description of influence relations connecting the electoral process with other decision processes of American government.

This is in part due to the variety of the disciplines contributing to voting research. But the more important reasons are methodological. Attempting to connect the behavior of mass electorates with the behavior of other, more specialized sets of political actors raises formidable problems of data collection. Anyone who wants, for example, to describe systematically the mutual perceptions of constituents and their representatives, faces novel and imposing problems of method, which are quite enough to explain why students of legislative behavior have not extended their view to encompass the behavior of constituent electorates as well.

It seems apparent that tracing the influence relations between the electorate and those who play other roles in the political system is a task for research that fixes its attention explicitly on these relations. But the absence of such studies ought not to prevent our saying what we can on the basis of research that is oriented primarily toward behavior within a single decision process. A great deal of value has been learned about the impact of electoral decisions by those who have studied legislative or administrative bodies. In the same spirit—but from a very different perspective—we offer here some comments on the relation of the electoral process to other elements of the political system.

In describing this relation, voting research can make a unique contribution by suggesting the significance for politics of *psychological* aspects of the electorate's behavior. The significance of broad social variables or other influences that we conceive as causally antecedent to psychological factors is generally easier to see. For example, it is often noted that the severity of group conflict in politics is lessened by the fact that individuals may belong to several groups—religious and class groups, for example—whose memberships do not fully coincide. Voting research can play a useful role in showing that the political effects of the cross-cutting of sociological groups is transmitted partly through the electoral process. But detailed studies are hardly needed to see the connection between this aspect of American society and the nature of group conflict. The situation may be quite different, however, in showing the significance of psychological elements of voting for the political system. The presence of these factors is established only by research directly focused on them, and this research can enlarge a good deal our understanding of their implications for the larger political order.

What psychological dimensions of voting are of greatest importance for the political system? Our discussion will focus on several closely related aspects of the electorate's response to politics, of which we have spoken again and again in preceding chapters—the low emotional involvement of the electorate in politics; its slight awareness of public affairs; its failure to think in structured, ideological terms; and its pervasive sense of attachment to one or the other of the two major parties. These properties of the electorate's cognitive and affective orientation to politics can be shown to have profound consequences for other elements of the political system. Three consequences of this sort will concern us here. The first of these has to do with the situation of elected leadership in American politics. The nature of the electorate's behavior is a basic determinant of the pressures experienced by those elected to office. The second effect has to do with the problem of party strategy. The structure of political opinion influences the type of strategy that can maximize a party's electoral appeal. The third effect has to do with the structure of the party system itself. The electorate's response to politics tends in several ways to sustain the competition of two major parties. These problems are of considerable importance; indeed, each touches a fundamental aspect of American politics. Although our comments will be far from exhaustive, the psychological dimensions we treat can throw important light on problems of wide political significance.

Electoral Behavior and the Pressures on Leadership

The popular election is a device of control. It is much else, too, but in the practice and normative theory of democracy elections are important largely as a means by which the acts of government can be brought under the control of the governed. And yet, as a formal matter, the electorate does not vote on what government shall do. Referenda on public laws, either statutory or constitutional, have not been more than ancillary features of popular elections. The public's explicit task is to decide not what government shall do but rather *who shall decide* what government shall do. If the two decisions are bound together, as they are in the practice of every democratic state, it is because candidates for office are judged partly for the position they take on public policies, while policies are judged partly for the impact they have on the electorate's choice between candidates.

The fact that public policy is tied to public opinion by the perceptions policy-forming elites and the electorate have of each other deserves the fullest appreciation. It means at the very least that the relation between governors and governed depends on the intellective processes by which the electorate reviews and expresses its judgment of public affairs. Commentaries on democracy often assume two basic facts about the electoral decision: first, that the public is generally in possession of sufficient information regarding the various policy alternatives of the moment to make a rational choice among them (that is, that it has clear goals and is able to assess what the actions of government mean for these goals), and, second, that the election in fact presents the electorate with recognizable partisan alternatives through which it can express its policy preferences. Let us review the evidence as to the policy awareness of the electorate. To what extent does the public have policy goals, either discrete or structured as general ideological dimensions? Does it relate these goals to current policy issues? And does it perceive the position of the parties on current policy issues? The answers to these questions have a good deal to say about the guidance that policy-forming elites receive from the mass electorate.

Our detailed inquiry into public attitudes regarding what we took to be the most prominent political issues of the time revealed a substantial lack of familiarity with these policy questions. Some individuals are sensitive to the full range of contemporary political events; they know what they want their government to do and they use their vote in a very purposive manner to achieve within their power the policy alternatives that they prefer. Such people do not make up a very large proportion of the electorate. The typical voter has only a modest understanding of the specific issues and may be quite ignorant of matters of public policy that more sophisticated individuals might regard as very pressing. Our measures have shown the public's understanding of policy issues to be poorly developed even though these measures usually have referred to a general problem which might be the subject of legislation or (in the area of foreign affairs) executive action, rather than to particular bills or acts.

Neither do we find much evidence of the kind of structured political thinking that we might expect to characterize a well-informed electorate. We have been able to identify a pattern of attitudes regarding certain questions of welfare legislation and a similar cluster of attitudes toward internationalist foreign policies. These express rather gross dimensions of opinion, however; they do not relate to each other or to other political attitudes with which one might expect to find them associated in a larger attitudinal structure. When we examine the attitudes and beliefs of the electorate as a whole over a broad range of policy questions—welfare legislation, foreign policy, federal economic programs, minority rights, civil liberties—we do not find coherent patterns of belief. The common tendency to characterize large blocs of the electorate in such terms as "liberal" or "conservative" greatly exaggerates the actual amount of consistent patterning one finds. Our failure to locate more than a trace of "ideological" thinking in the protocols of our surveys emphasizes the general impoverishment of political thought in a large proportion of the electorate.

It is also apparent from these protocols that there is a great deal of uncertainty and confusion in the public mind as to what specific policies the election of one party over the other would imply. Very few of our respondents have shown a sensitive understanding of the positions of the parties on current policy issues. Even among those people who are relatively familiar with the issues presented in our surveys—and our test of familiarity has been an easy one—there is little agreement as to where the two parties stand. This fact reflects the similarity of party positions on many issues, as well as the range of opinion within parties. But it also reflects how little attention even the relatively informed part of the electorate gives the specifics of public policy formation.

We have, then, the portrait of an electorate almost wholly without detailed information about decision making in government. A substantial portion of the public is able to respond in a discrete manner to issues that *might* be the subject of legislative or administrative action. Yet it knows little about what government has done on these issues or what the parties propose to do. It is almost completely unable to judge the rationality of government actions; knowing little of particular policies and what has led to them, the mass electorate is not able to appraise either its goals or the appropriateness of the means chosen to serve these goals.

It is not altogether surprising that this statement is true. For a large part of the public, political affairs are probably too difficult to comprehend in detail. For example, we may suppose that the people we have described as feeling "politically ineffective" are virtually beyond the reach of political stimulation. An additional part of the electorate is no doubt capable of informing itself about political matters but is unwilling to pay the cost that such information-getting would entail. Very few people seem motivated strongly enough to obtain the information needed to develop a sensitive understanding of decision making in government. It is a rather unusual individual whose deeper personality needs are engaged by politics, and in terms of rational self-interest, the stakes do not seem to be great enough for the ordinary citizen to justify his expending the effort necessary to make himself well informed politically.

The quality of the electorate's review of public policy formation has two closely related consequences for those who must frame the actions of government. First, it implies that the electoral decision typically will be ambiguous as to the specific acts government should take. As we shall note presently, the electorate's behavior is not totally without cues to those who hold legislative or executive authority. But these are not generally centered about specific acts or policies. The thinness of the electorate's understanding of concrete policy alternatives—its inability to respond to government and politics at this level—helps explain why it is that efforts to interpret a national election in terms of a policy mandate are speculative, contradictory, and inconclusive.

The second consequence of the quality of the public's review of policy formation is that the electoral decision gives great freedom to those who must frame the policies of government. If the election returns offer little guidance on specific policies, neither do they generate pressures that restrict the scope of President and Congress in developing public policy. Of course, those involved in policy formation *do* experience intense "public" pressures for and against particular policy alternatives. But these emanate almost entirely from limited, special publics, often speaking through organizations, and not from the electorate as a whole. To be sure, the fact that the wider public has so little to say on specific policies strengthens the position of special publics and particular "interests" in making their demands on government. Yet in important respects the latitude of government decision makers in framing public policies is enlarged by the fact that the details of these policies will be very largely unknown to the general electorate.

Of course, if it is *thought* to be directed to specific policies, the electoral decision can be a source both of guidance and pressure as to these policies. This occurrence is especially likely when concrete policy alternatives are prominent in the election campaign; having been the focus of debate before the public, they appear to be endorsed or rejected by the public's decision, even though they may really be little understood. Yet the notorious gap between the policy implications of an electoral result that are advertised in advance and what actually happens suggests how well the decision makers of American government appreciate the diffuse character of the electorate's judgment. For example, we might suppose that the Democratic victory of 1948 would have been read as a mandate to repeal the Taft-Hartley Act, which Truman had castigated in his campaign. The fact that the law subsequently escaped even amendment may be traced to several factors, but almost certainly a prime cause was the sense in the Congress of how little an appraisal of the particular provisions of this act had influenced the electorate's choice.

However great the potential ability of the public to enforce a set of concrete policy demands at the polls, it is clear that this power is seldom used in American politics. Yet it would be altogether wrong to suppose that the electoral process does not profoundly influence the course of government. Unquestionably it does. The decisions of the electorate play a role primarily in defining broad goals of governmental action or very generalized means of achieving such goals. Because these tend over time to become matters on which there is consensus in American society, this function of the electoral process may go largely undetected. But even a rough comparison of our system with one in which a regularized expression of popular opinion is not possible suggests how important is electoral behavior for stating broad objectives of government.

Perhaps the classic example of this in our time has to do with the responsibility of the federal government for the national economy. There is no doubt that the degree of this responsibility has undergone revolutionary change over the past thirty years because the public has demanded it. The ideas of Franklin Roosevelt have prevailed over those of Herbert Hoover because a judgment in Roosevelt's favor was rendered by the public in the elections of the 1930's and 1940's. The judgment was hardly based on a detailed review of policies: it is clear both that the Hoover Administration took constructive steps to deal with the economic collapse and that the program of the Roosevelt Administration, while containing the seeds of an adequate countercyclical economic policy, was not sufficient to promote recovery prior to the onset of the Second World War. What the public endorsed was the New Deal's belief that the federal government should assume responsibility for the nation's economic welfare. The electoral history of the era established beyond challenge the place of economic prosperity as a goal of public policy.

The importance of the public's concern with certain broad objectives of government is quite clear in our studies. We have seen in the preceding chapter that the electoral decision results from a comparison of the total image of one of the candidate-party alternatives with the image of the other. A good deal of the public response to these political actors simply expresses feeling or affect. Many people see this party or that candidate as "honest," "dependable," "capable," or, more generally, as just "good." In a similar way, a large proportion of the electorate sees the parties or candidates as good or bad for this or that segment of the public, often referring to the group with which they themselves identify. But our examination of public attitude shows that certain generalized goals of government action enter the image of the parties and candidates and that these goals play a major role in electoral change.

Earlier chapters have shown how much the goal of economic prosperity colored the image of the parties in the years of our studies. The reservation the electorate had about the ability of the Republicans to serve this goal was the largest obstacle to their victory in the election of 1952. The remarkable decline in the widespread association of the Republican Party with economic depression during the prosperous years of the first Eisenhower term clearly did not have to do with specific acts or policies; it seemed to spring almost entirely from the fact that a high level of economic activity had been sustained even with someone of Herbert Hoover's party in the White House.

A second general goal about which the public communicated its profound concern in the Eisenhower years was the preservation of peace. In 1952 the public unquestionably was searching for a solution to an irregular war that had become oppressive, and its vote appears to have been in large part an expression of lack of confidence in the capacity of the Democratic Party to deal with the problem. Here again, the public's concern was not focused on specific remedial policies. It is very doubtful indeed if the voters who elected Mr. Eisenhower to the presidency had any clear idea of exactly what he and the Republican Party proposed to do about the Korean War, except that Eisenhower would make a personal inspection. Their mandate to the president-elect was to produce a solution and, far from prescribing specific policies he should follow, they gave him virtually unlimited freedom of action. When the Korean War was settled on terms far short of complete victory, the end of the fighting won broad public approval. In 1956, with the country at peace, the vote expressed the confidence which the electorate felt in Eisenhower's ability to serve this goal.

Our conclusion that the major shifts of electoral strength reflect the changing association of parties and candidates with general societal goals rather than the detail of legislative or administrative action is affirmed by what we know of the voters most susceptible to change.

The segment of the electorate most likely to alter its image of these political actors is not the part that is best informed about government but the part that is least involved in politics, psychologically speaking, and whose information about details of policy is most impoverished. Change is not limited entirely to people of low information and involvement, but they are more likely than others to respond to the wars or economic recessions or other gross changes in the political environment that may generate substantial shifts at the polls. The extraordinary fact that these people supply much of the dynamic of politics makes it clearer why the behavior of the electorate imparts a concern for broad goals of policy or generalized means of achieving these goals more than for the specific content of public policy. To be sure, changes in the party balance between elections may reflect changes in the voting patterns of social groups that are especially affected by particular policy issues. In this case, the better informed and more highly involved members of a group may be the more likely to change. A shift of Negroes away from the Democratic Party may occur first among those who are aware of the deep division within the party over civil rights. But the broadest movements of party strength between elections, usually cutting across a great many social groups, are fed disproportionately by shifts among the less involved and poorly informed members of the electorate.

If government is influenced by the broad policy concerns that enter the electorate's decision, it is influenced too by public attitudes that have little immediate relationship to specific candidates or parties. Political leaders respond to many elements of public opinion that *could* affect an electoral decision, even though these opinions may not have influenced the public's choice in any actual election. In gaging popular attitudes, political leaders develop a strong sense of what the permissible bounds of policy are. Large areas of public policy do not enter into political discussion because there is broad consensus that they lie outside the range of tolerance. These largely unspoken but widely accepted injunctions may have far greater significance in the electoral mandate than such issues as may become the subject of partisan controversy. They set the limits within which the parties offer policy alternatives.

Of course, parties and candidates also are inhibited from offering "extreme" policy proposals by the fact that political leaders share many of the value beliefs of the electors to whom they appeal. Because these beliefs are shared, the stands on issues of those seeking office are kept within acceptable limits not by their reading of public attitude but by their own internal values. Yet the significance of their readings of public opinion should not be discounted. The fact that political leaders are sensitive to how the electorate would react to policies that are not now—and may never be—issues between candidates in any actual election establishes an important additional link between public opinion and government.

The limits of what is acceptable differ in different parts of the electorate and at different points in time. For many years public officials in the South have adopted the doctrine of White supremacy as a political and social imperative. Representatives in strong labor union districts do not offend the sensitivities of organized labor. Local circumstances in various segments of the electorate create different prescriptions; people who seek office in those areas know which political questions may become subjects of discussion and which may not. There are also broad national issues that lie outside the range of tolerable discourse. The nationalization of industry, governmental control of the press, the compromising of national sovereignty in world federations—such proposals are not discussed in political campaigns because it is generally agreed that they go beyond public tolerance.

The range of opinion that is seen to fall within tolerable limits is not altogether rigid; the pressure of ongoing events can force very considerable changes. The orthodox philosophy of private enterprise, which was largely unquestioned in American politics during the 1920's, became the subject of very heated controversy during the 1930's. The range of opinions offered in public discussion of economic problems broadened greatly under the stimulus of the Depression, with many proposals that would have been unthinkable during the earlier decade being seriously advocated. During the subsequent twenty years a new set of assumptions developed, largely abandoning conservative laissez-faire doctrines and accepting a substantial commitment to economic welfare programs. The limits of discussion of governmental economic policies were thus defined at a level very different from that of the pre-Depression period. There is reason to believe that a similar although less pronounced shift has taken place in the area of foreign policy with the traditional antagonism to "foreign entanglements" giving way in the face of inexorable pressures toward greater concern with international affairs. There is still considerable difference of opinion as to the proper character of the nation's foreign relations, but the advocacy of full-blown isolationism, which was not uncommon during the 1920's, now to all intents and purposes lies outside the range of controversy.

Electoral Behavior and Party Strategy

One way of describing a party's strategic problem in securing an electoral majority is to say that it must assume positions of greater acceptance than its opposition on the dimensions of political controversy that influence electoral choice.[2] What is meant by this can be suggested by an idealized example, which will provide a starting point in talking about the competition of parties in American national politics. Let us suppose that all political controversy is focused on a single dimension, the "left-right" or "liberal-conservative" continuum so prominent in popular discussion. We may place each party on this continuum in terms of how "liberal" its policies are; and we may also place each voter in terms of how "liberal" he wants the policies of government to be. It is reasonable to assume that when the electorate chooses between parties at the polls an individual voter will support the party that is closer to his own position, though he may fail to vote at all if no party is markedly closer than the others.

If we regard the position of the parties as fixed, the question of which party of a two-party system will secure a majority depends on how the electorate is distributed across this dimension of political con-

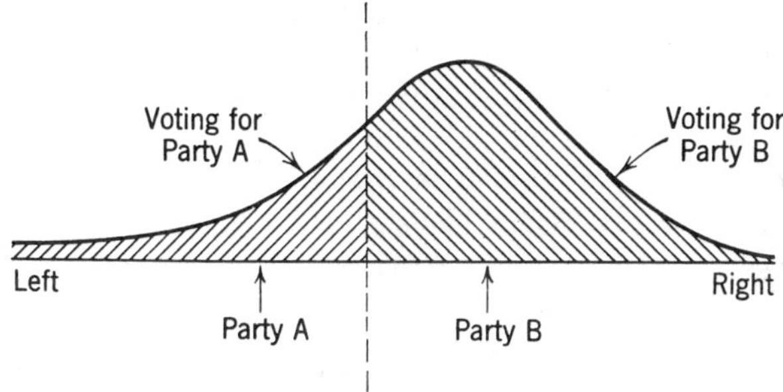

troversy. If the distribution of voters is of the foregoing form, for example, the majority of votes goes to Party B. In reality, the position of the parties is not fixed but may be changed to enhance their elec-

[2] For a more extended discussion of the concepts treated here see Anthony Downs, *An Economic Theory of Democracy* (Harper and Brothers, New York; 1957), Chapter 8, and Duncan MacRae, Jr., *Dimensions of Congressional Voting* (University of California Press, Berkeley and Los Angeles; 1958), Appendix C. Our discussion differs from that of Downs in treating as a variable the *structure* of the space in which parties and electors are located.

toral appeal. In the example given, Party A could increase its proportion of the vote by moving to the right, Party B by moving to the left. Indeed, with a single mode in the distribution of popular opinion and with perfect information about the nature of that distribution, the two parties would tend to gravitate toward adjacent positions on the scale. Something of this sort helps explain the similarity of the stands frequently adopted by parties in the real world.

Of course, political controversy need not be centered on a single dimension or even on relatively few stable dimensions. We would suppose rather that the extent to which it *is* is one of the most important *variables* characterizing the politics of a democratic community. If an electorate responds to public affairs in terms of one or a few well-defined and stable ideological dimensions on which there is little movement of opinion, political controversy will be relatively tightly bounded and the possibilities of party maneuver—and alternation in office—relatively circumscribed. But if an electorate responds to public affairs in a less structured fashion, politics will be more fluid, party strategy will include or may consist primarily of exploiting new dimensions of opinion, and the likelihood of party alternation in power will be greater.

All this suggests important consequences of the lack of ideological structure in the political thought of the American electorate. We have seen that the stable qualities of the public's response to political affairs have to do primarily with long-term loyalties to the parties rather than ideological commitments against which current acts or policies of the parties could be evaluated. The forces not based on party loyalty that influence the decisions of the American electorate appear almost wholly free of ideological coloration. As a result, their impact on the party balance is much more variable than would otherwise be the case. This may perhaps be seen most clearly in the importance for the vote of popular reactions to the personalities of the changing figures nominated for President. The major role played by candidate appeal suggests the absence of overriding public concern to judge the policies of the candidates and their parties against the standards received from well-elaborated political ideologies.

An awareness of this situation is reflected in the strategies of American political parties. Despite the common tendency to impute more structure to popular thought than it actually has, American party leaders show by their willingness to exploit new and relatively temporary dimensions of popular feeling that they know the public's response to politics is not dominated by fixed ideological dimensions.

Especially is this evident in the tendency of the party out of power to conceive its problem not as one of winning adherents on an established dimension of political controversy but rather as one of developing new dimensions of opinion, on which it can overcome its competitive disadvantage. The difference in these strategic outlooks expresses much of the difference in what the Taft and Eisenhower forces urged the Republican Party to do in the convention of 1952. The Taft view was that the party should take a plainly conservative position on the left-right dimension that had emerged out of the struggle over the New Deal by nominating a candidate whose conservative stand was unquestioned. The belief that such a course would lead to majority support at the polls was based on the assumptions that the electorate was moving to the right and that the party had previously failed to attract its full potential vote because of non-voting among those who felt it was aping the Democrats. The strategic view that implicitly was endorsed by a majority of the Republican convention was that the party should exploit quite different dimensions of opinion, especially by nominating a war hero of enormous popular appeal. The slogan "Corruption, Korea, and Communism," with which the Republican Party went into the campaign, suggests nicely the free-wheeling character of this strategy. Each of the elements of the slogan referred to a subject of public concern, real or imagined, that was relatively new and transitory; and none of the three bore much relation to the others, except for an alliterative one.

It may well be that no mass democratic electorate has evidenced as much structure in its political thought as is found in the intellective processes of those who hold public office. Yet there must be times and places where this structure is more developed than we have found it in the American electorate of our studies. One is tempted to cite contemporary British politics as a case in which a good deal of political controversy has been focused on an ideological dimension that is much more clearly defined than any in American politics of the 1950's. The strategic problem of the Labor Party has been that it enjoys only minority support on this dimension and has been blocked from enlarging its support by the fact that the Conservative Party in the postwar era has moved very nearly into an adjacent position. We may suspect that the way out for the Labor Party—and perhaps typically for the opposition party in a two-party system—will come not through a change in the shape of public opinion on the *established* dimension but through the emergence of *new* dimensions of political controversy on which it enjoys a more favorable position.

Electoral Behavior and the Party System

Few aspects of a political system are of greater importance than the number of parties having a realistic chance to control government. Certainly the number of parties competing effectively in the electoral process is a tremendously significant aspect of the context in which the electorate must reach a decision; the influence of a two-party system on American electoral behavior has been implicit in every chapter of this book. Yet this influence does not move in one direction only. The electorate's response to politics is part of the context in which political parties operate, and the behavior of the electorate can have important effects on the party system itself. We feel that this is specifically true of American politics. Our studies lead us to believe that the persistence of a national two-party system in the United States depends in some measure on the way in which the American electorate reaches its decision.

In probing the influences on the structure of the party system we will consider only the problem of the *persistence* of two parties. Given the nature of the system and of mass behavior as we find them in contemporary politics, we will identify forces tending to continue two parties as major competitors for public office, and particularly, for the presidency. Important as it is, the problem of identifying the historical forces that have led to the present condition of American politics will not concern us. It should be clear, too, that we do not suppose the entire explanation for the persistence of two parties lies in the attitudes and behavior of the electorate. Obviously legal and institutional arrangements of American government are of great importance; for example, the fact that control of the executive branch depends on control of a single office has played a fundamental role in bringing those who would control the national executive within two great coalitions. If our studies of the electorate can help explain an important yet perplexing attribute of American government, the explanation we give will at best be a partial one.

To account for the persistence of a two-party system we must be able to say, first, why there are not *more* than two parties and, second, why there are not *less* than two. An important answer to both these questions lies in the electorate's profound loyalty to the existing parties. Our studies regularly have shown that three quarters of the adult population grants outright its allegiance to the Republican or Democratic Party and that most of those who call themselves Independents acknowledge some degree of attachment to one of the parties. These partisan identifications typically extend far into an individual's past—if not into the past of his forebears as well—and appear highly resistant to change. The individual's partisan choice at the polls does not invariably follow his sense of party loyalty; we are able to specify the conditions under which he will vote against that loyalty. Yet the effects of party identification are so pervasive that the decision of the electorate to a great extent expresses its attachment to the two established parties.

The conserving influence of party identification makes it extremely difficult for a third party to rise suddenly and with enough popular support to challenge the existing parties. If the forces on the vote were formed wholly anew in each campaign, new or minor parties would be able to establish themselves fairly easily as serious contenders for power. But these forces are not made anew; they are formed in large measure by the political past, in which a third party has not had a place. The fact that the great prize of American politics—control of the presidency and, with it, control of the executive branch of the national government—is indivisible means that a new party must fairly rapidly attract sufficient electoral strength to contend seriously for this prize. If it cannot, it will quickly lose the support it has gained. Yet it is exactly this rapid accretion of electoral strength that popular commitments to the established parties tend to preclude. These commitments are not immutable; a crisis of politics could generate forces of sufficient strength to pry the electorate loose from its fixed loyalties. But the depressing effect of party identification on the opportunity of new parties can scarcely be doubted.

If party identification tends to limit the number of parties to two, it tends also to strengthen the second party by stabilizing the electoral competition of the parties. The substantial effect of long-term partisan loyalties on the vote reduces the amplitude of the swings from one major party to the other. We are accustomed to accepting as a great victory the outcome of a national election in which the winning party attracts not 20, 30, or 40 per cent more than an equal division of the vote but a mere 10 per cent more. Since the strength of the two parties is not uniformly distributed geographically, the moderate extent of fluctuations in the vote means that the minority party is never deprived altogether of office in our federal system of government. Even in the face of a "landslide" the party out of power nationally will hold many seats in the Congress, and it will also retain control of a number of state governments. But if the damping effect of party identification were removed and the electoral tides were to run at full strength, the second party might well be forced into a minority position everywhere at once and be deprived of the forum and leadership it requires to return to power in national government at a later time.

The action of party identification in moderating electoral movements explains why a minority party is not destroyed overnight. Yet it cannot explain why a second party is not shut out of power indefinitely. For this, additional factors need to be found. Party identification moderates the electoral cycle, but other influences must account for the cycle itself—for the tendency of the division of the vote, having favored one party, to swing back to the advantage of the other party. Alternation in office seems so natural in a two-party system that the need for explanation may not be very clear. But why is it that the party vote oscillates about an equal division over time rather than developing a persistent, and perhaps increasing, margin for a majority party? The answer to this question is really far from obvious.

Undoubtedly a number of factors are at work. Yet our studies suggest a hypothesis about the public's response to politics that may supply a key to understanding: the party division of the vote is most likely to be *changed* by a negative public reaction to the record of the party in power. If true, the hypothesis accounts simply enough for the attribute of party competition we seek to explain. A majority party, once it is in office, will not continue to accrue electoral strength; it may preserve for a time its electoral majority, but the next marked *change* in the party vote will issue from a negative response of the electorate to some aspect of the party's conduct in office, a response that tends to return the minority party to power. The greater the majority party's share of the underlying identifications of the electorate, the greater is the probability of its winning elections and holding office. But the greater also is the probability of its losing strength by being in office when a calamity occurs that arouses the public's ire against those in power. Hence, the greater the majority party's strength, the greater the likelihood of its strength being reduced.

One aspect of this hypothesis needs to be specified very clearly. The crux of our theory is that changes in the party balance are induced primarily by negative rather than positive attitudes toward the party controlling the executive branch of federal government. Yet unfavorable feeling toward a party that is being turned out of power may well be coupled with favorable feeling toward the party that follows it in office if the latter copes successfully with problems the public feels were mishandled by the preceding administration. This sort of positive attitude may well play an important role in fixing or augmenting a change in party strength resulting from the public's negative reaction to the record of the other party. But *new* positive attitudes, unrelated to the issues that brought a turnover of party control, are not likely to initiate a shift in the party balance.

The historical evidence on these questions is not as plentiful as we should like, but what there is seems to support the hypothesis, and so do certain of the data of our studies. We would cite, first of all, the importance of public reaction to economic distress. If our reading of electoral history is correct, there have been two fundamental shifts in party strength since the Reconstruction Era, each of them undoubtedly yielding a change in the long-term party identifications of a substantial portion of the electorate. The first of these occurred in the election of 1896 under the impact of the panic of 1893. The second occurred in the elections of the 1930's under the impact of the Great Depression. In each of these cases economic collapse directed strong negative feeling toward the party in power and greatly reduced its electoral strength. In each case the party succeeding to office won broad public favor by its apparent success—or at least its energy—in dealing with the problem that had aroused intense popular feeling. Compare the change wrought in party fortunes in either of these cases with the change occurring when a party already in office witnesses a surge of economic prosperity. This prosperity clearly benefits the administration party, but it has nothing like the magnitude of the effect that would result from economic distress. A party already in power is rewarded much less for good times than it is punished for bad times.

We would cite, secondly, the influence of war on the party balance. Our surveys clearly have shown the consequences to the Democratic Party of having incurred the public's displeasure over Korea. If the personal appeal of Mr. Eisenhower is ignored for the moment, we may say that a Democrat was kept out of the White House after 1952 as much by negative attitudes provoked during the Korean action as by any other factor. It is instructive to compare this effect with the political effect of the Second World War. By any reasonable standards the Korean War was of lesser importance for our national interests and its impact on the common citizen relatively slight. Yet the extraordinary fact is that the negative feeling it generated influenced the electoral balance much more than did any positive feeling arising out of the winning of the Second World War. Indeed, if the supreme fact of victory in the First or Second World Wars benefited the party in power, this advantage appears from the election returns to have succumbed to the negative feeling aroused by the disruptions and grievances of war. Roosevelt's losses in the election of 1944 were not sufficient to cost him his office; yet neither were the allied victories in Europe and the Pacific sufficient to prevent an erosion of his strength. And the Democratic Party lost the congressional election two years later, just as the party of Wilson had lost the congressional election of 1918.

Why should the electorate be more likely to punish an incumbent party for its mistakes than to reward it for its successes? Part of the answer almost certainly lies in the low salience politics has for the general public. Because of the slight political involvement of the electorate, very little crosses the threshold of public awareness and becomes associated with the image of the party holding office. (Of course, even less becomes associated with the image of the minority party when it is out of office.) As long as public affairs go well, there is little to motivate the electorate to connect events of the wider environment with the actors of politics, and the successes of an administration are likely to go virtually unnoticed by the mass public. But when events of the wider environment arouse strong public concern the electorate is motivated to connect them with the actors of politics, typically, with the incumbent party. An economic or military or other form of calamity can force events across the threshold of political awareness, to the detriment of the administration party. And because these matters have gained broad public awareness, the party coming to power may attract considerable positive feeling by coping successfully with the problems that have driven its predecessor from office, whereas the new Administration's later successes in other areas of policy may evoke little public response. Caught by the fact that the electorate is more likely to be moved by their mistakes in office, the two parties continue to alternate in power, with neither developing such a commanding edge that its opponent is excluded permanently from winning the presidency.

What of the states? If the nature of electoral response makes it probable that the national party division of the vote will tend to oscillate about an even division, why is it that year in and year out many of our states are firmly in the hands of one party? Of course, even in strongly one-party states the division of the vote often reflects the shifts of party strength that bring a turnover of control in national government. But it is clear that the dominant party in many states does *not* suffer a continuing, secular decline in strength until effective two-party competition is restored. How is this fact to be reconciled with the argument of the preceding pages?

The answer depends on the fact that the nation as a whole is a self-contained political system in a sense that a state is not. The forces generating, maintaining, and altering the party identifications that keep one party in power in many states have primarily a national focus. Our most deeply one-party area—the South—was delivered into the hands of the Democratic Party by the Civil War and Reconstruction Era, as many northern areas were delivered at the same time into the hands of the Republican Party. And the forces that have prevented a serious erosion of the Democratic Party's hold on the South have had to do chiefly with struggles over national policy, particularly affecting racial questions. Indeed, in many ways the southern states are one-party states *only* in national politics, with intraparty factions serving more or less adequately as political parties at the state level.[3] Paradoxically, the fact that we have one-party as well as two-party states, which has often been cited to show that the states are distinct political systems, is evidence that in vital respects we have a *national* politics. If a southern state—or the South as a region—were to become truly a self-contained political system, the whole meaning of its one-party character would be lost.

Since the forces that are most important in fixing and changing long-term party loyalties are primarily national in character, the fact that a party may remain in power in state government over a great many years does not undermine our hypothesis. In certain respects the electorate's response to national politics *is* carried over to state politics. Even if control of state government by the dominant party of a one-party state is not seriously threatened, it will tend to win office by a smaller margin when the "same" party is being turned out of power in national government. But subsequent turnover of control at the national level removes the basis for a continued decline of the party's strength in the state, and the growth of the minority party is shut off at a point that may be far short of what it would need to compete seriously for office. Of course, the mechanisms that induce repeated changes of party control in national government are not wholly absent from state politics. In states that have a fairly even division of basic party strength, negative reactions to a state administration can be quite important in returning the opposition party to power, particularly if the state election does not coincide with a presidential election. And in one-party states dissatisfactions with a state administration can be of great importance in transferring power from

[3] The classic statement of this view is given in V. O. Key, Jr., *Southern Politics in State and Nation* (Alfred Knopf, New York; 1950).

one intraparty faction to another. But these local considerations are by no means enough to guarantee effective competition between the Republican and Democratic Parties in each of the states.

From all this it should be clear that the response of the electorate to politics is a major determinant of the structure of the party system—as it is a determinant of the strategies of the parties and of the behavior of policy-forming elites. To be sure, electoral behavior offers no simple or sovereign theories of politics, and we do not arrogate to voting a primary role in the political system. Even to establish the effects of voting behavior treated here we have had to accommodate institutional factors such as the nature of the executive, the separation of powers in national government, and the federal character of our political system. And if we were to write comprehensively of the political order we would have to consider a great many things lying outside the electoral process.

Yet an understanding of electoral behavior throws a good deal of light on the political system. By vesting in a mass public the power to make a critical type of decision, our form of government implies that the public's orientations to politics will have wide influence throughout the political order. We have explored here some effects of the electorate's slight involvement in politics and limited awareness of public affairs; of the non-ideological quality of its thinking; and of the pervasive character of its partisan commitments. If our argument runs true, these qualities of the prevailing response to politics account for important elements of American government. Indeed, their power to do so suggests that important additional connections are to be found by a closer mapping of the influence relations binding the electoral process to the other means of decision in the political system.

Index